John Exshaw

The Plays and Poems of William Shakspeare Vol.3

John Exshaw

The Plays and Poems of William Shakspeare Vol.3

ISBN/EAN: 9783742839473

Manufactured in Europe, USA, Canada, Australia, Japa

Cover: Foto ©Andreas Hilbeck / pixelio.de

Manufactured and distributed by brebook publishing software (www.brebook.com)

John Exshaw

The Plays and Poems of William Shakspeare Vol.3

THE
PLAYS AND POEMS

OF

WILLIAM SHAKSPEARE.

VOLUME THE THIRD.

CONTAINING

TEMPEST.
TWO GENTLEMEN OF VERONA.
MERRY WIVES OF WINDSOR.
MEASURE FOR MEASURE.

DUBLIN:

PRINTED BY JOHN EXSHAW, No. 98, GRAFTON-STREET.

1794.

TEMPEST.

PERSONS REPRESENTED.

Alonso, *king of Naples.*
Sebastian, *his brother.*
Prospero, *the rightful duke of Milan.*
Anthonio, *his brother, the usurping duke of Milan.*
Ferdinand, *son to the king of Naples.*
Gonzalo, *an honest old counsellor of Naples.*
Adrian, } *lords.*
Francisco,
Caliban, *a savage and deformed slave.*
Trinculo, *a jester.*
Stephano, *a drunken butler.*
Master of a ship, Boatswain, and Mariners.

Miranda, *daughter to* Prospero.

Ariel, *an airy spirit.*
Iris,
Ceres,
Juno, } *spirits.*
Nymphs,
Reapers,

Other spirits attending on Prospero.

SCENE, *the sea, with a ship; afterwards an uninhabited island.*

This enumeration of persons is taken from the folio, 1623.
STEEVENS.

TEMPEST.

ACT I. SCENE I.

On a ship at sea.

A storm with thunder and lightning.

Enter a Ship-master and a Boatswain[2].

Master. Boatswain,—

Boats. Here, master: What cheer?

Mast.

---

[1] *The Tempest* and *The Midsummer's Night's Dream* are the noblest efforts of that sublime and amazing imagination peculiar to Shakspeare, which soars above the bounds of nature without forsaking sense; or, more properly, carries nature along with him beyond her established limits. Fletcher seems particularly to have admired these two plays, and hath wrote two in imitation of them, *The Sea Voyage* and *The Faithful Shepherdess*. But when he presumes to break a lance with Shakspeare, and write in emulation of him, as he does in *The False One*, which is the rival of *Antony and Cleopatra*, he is not so successful. After him, Sir John Suckling and Milton catched the brightest fire of their imagination from these two plays; which shines fantastically indeed in *The Goblins*, but much more nobly and serenely in *The Mask at Ludlow-Castle*. WARBURTON.

No one has been hitherto lucky enough to discover the romance on which Shakspeare may be supposed to have founded this play, the beauties of which could not secure it from the criticism of Ben Jonson, whose malignity appears to have been more than equal to his wit. In the induction to *Bartholomew Fair*, he says: "If there be never a " *servant monster* in the fair, who can help it, nor a nest of *antiques*? " He is loth to make nature afraid in his plays, like those that beget " *Tales*, *Tempests*, and such like drolleries." STEEVENS.

I was informed by the late Mr. Collins of Chichester, that Shakspeare's TEMPEST, for which no origin is yet assigned, was formed on a romance called AURELIO AND ISABELLA, printed in Italian, Spanish, French, and English, in 1588. But though this information has not proved true on examination, an useful conclusion may be drawn from it, that Shakspeare's story is somewhere to be found in an Italian novel, at least that the story preceded Shakspeare. Mr. Collins had searched this subject with no less fidelity than judgment and industry;

Mast. Good: Speak to the mariners: fall to't yarely³, or we run ourselves aground: bestir, bestir. [*Exit.*

Enter Mariners.

Boats. Heigh, my hearts; cheerly, cheerly, my hearts; yare, yare: Take in the top-sail: Tend to the Master's

but his memory failing in his last calamitous indisposition, he probably gave me the name of one novel for another. I remember he added a circumstance, which may lead to a discovery,—that the principal character of the romance, answering to Shakspeare's Prospero, was a chemical necromancer, who had bound a spirit like Ariel to obey his call, and perform his services. It was a common pretence of dealers in the occult sciences to have a demon at command. At least Aurelio, or Orelio, was probably one of the names of this romance, the production and multiplicity of gold being the grand object of alchemy. Taken at large, the magical part of the TEMPEST is founded on that sort of philosophy which was practised by John Dee and his associates, and has been called the Rosicrucian. The name Ariel came from the Talmudistic mysteries with which the learned Jews had infected this Science. T. WARTON.

Mr. Theobald tells us, that the *Tempest* must have been written after 1609, because the Bermuda islands, which are mentioned in it, were unknown to the English until that year; but this is a mistake. He might have seen in Hackluyt, 1600, folio, a description of Bermuda, by Henry May, who was shipwrecked there in 1593.

It was however one of our author's last works. In 1598 he played a part in the original *Every Man in his Humour.* Two of the characters are *Prospero* and *Stephano.* Here Ben Jonson taught him the pronunciation of the latter word, which is always *right* in the *Tempest:*
" Is not this *Stephano,* my drunken butler ?"
And always *wrong* in his earlier play, the *Merchant of Venice,* which had been on the stage at least two or three years before its publication in 1600:
" My friend *Stephano,* signify, I pray you," &c.
— So little did a late editor know of his author, when he idly supposed his *school literature* might perhaps have been lost by the *dissipation of youth,* or the *busy scenes* of public life! FARMER.

This play must have been written after 1609, when Bermudas was discovered, and before 1614, when Jonson sneers at it in his *Bartholomew Fair.* In the latter plays of Shakspeare, he has less of pun and quibble than in his early ones. In *The Merchant of Venice* he expressly declares against them. This perhaps might be one criterion to discover the dates of his plays. BLACKSTONE.

See a note on *The cloud-capt Towers,* &c. act iv. STEEVENS.

See also *An Attempt to ascertain the order of Shakspeare's Plays,* ante. MALONE.

³ In this naval dialogue, perhaps the first example of sailor's language exhibited on the stage, there are, as I have been told by a skilful navigator, some inaccuracies and contradictory orders. JOHNSON. Dr.

TEMPEST. 5

ter's whistle:—Blow, till thou burst thy wind, if room enough [4]!

Enter ALONSO, SEBASTIAN, ANTHONIO, FERDINAND, GONZALO, *and others.*

Alon. Good boatswain, have care. Where's the master? Play the men [5].

Boats. I pray now, keep below.

Ant. Where is the master, boatswain?

Boats. Do you not hear him? You mar our labour; Keep your cabins: you do assist the storm.

Gon. Nay, good, be patient.

Boats. When the sea is. Hence! What care these roarers for the name of king? To cabin: silence: trouble us not.

Gon. Good; yet remember whom thou hast aboard.

Boats. None that I more love than myself. You are a counsellor; if you can command these elements to silence, and work the peace for the present [6], we will not hand a rope more; use your authority. If you cannot, give thanks you have liv'd so long, and make yourself ready in your cabin for the mischance of the hour, if it so hap.—Cheerly, good hearts. —Out of the way, I say. [*Exit.*

Gon. [7] I have great comfort from this fellow: methinks, he hath no drowning mark upon him; his complexion is perfect

---

Dr. Johnson has observed, that in the naval dialogue in the first scene of this play there are some inaccuracies and contradictory orders; but the observation, which he says, was made by a skilful seaman, is founded on a mistake. These orders should be considered as given, not at once, but successively, as the emergency required. One attempt to save the ship failing, another is tried. MALONE.

[3] —*fall to't yarely,*] i. e. readily, nimbly. Our author is frequent in his use of this word. STEEVENS.

[4] —*room enough.*] We might read——*blow till thou burst thee, wind! if room enough.* And yet, desiring the *winds* to blow till they burst their *winds*, is not unlike many other conceits of Shakspeare.
STEEVENS.

[5] *Play the men.*] i. e. act with spirit, behave like men. Ἄνηρ ἔστε, φίλοι. So in *K. Henry IV.* P. I. sc. vi.

" When they shall hear how we have play'd the men."

Again, in Marlowe's *Tamburlaine,* 1590, P. II.

" Viceroys and peers of Turkey, *play the men.*" STEEVENS.

Again, in Scripture, 2 Samuel, x. 12.

" Be of good courage, and let us *play the men* for our people."
MALONE.

[6] —*of the present*] It may mean of the present *instant.* STEEVENS.

B 3 [7] *Gon.*

fect gallows. Stand fast, good fate, to his hanging; make the rope of his destiny our cable, for our own doth little advantage: If he be not born to be hang'd, our case is miserable. [*Exeunt.*

Re-enter BOATSWAIN.

Boats. Down with the topmast; yare, lower, lower; bring her to try with main-course [8]. [*A cry within.*] A plague upon this howling! they are louder than the weather, or our office.—

Re-enter SEBASTIAN, ANTHONIO, *and* GONZALO.

Yet again? What do you here? Shall we give o'er, and drown? Have you a mind to sink?

Seb. A pox o' your throat! you bawling, blasphemous, incharitable dog!

Boats. Work you, then.

Ant. Hang, cur, hang! you whoreson, insolent noisemaker, we are less afraid to be drown'd than thou art.

Gon. I'll warrant him from drowning; though the ship were no stronger than a nut-shell, and as leaky as an unstanch'd wench [9].

Boats. Lay her a-hold, a-hold [1]; set her two courses [2]; off to sea again, lay her off.

Enter MARINERS *wet*.

Mar. All lost! to prayers, to prayers! all lost! [*Exeunt.*

Boats. What must our mouths be cold?

---

[7] *Gon.*] It may be observed of Gonzalo, that, being the only good man that appears with the king, he is the only man that preserves his cheerfulness in the wreck, and his hope on the island. JOHNSON.

[8] —*bring her to try with main-course.*] Probably from Hackluyt's *Voyages*, 1598: "And when the bark had way, we cut the hauser, and so gate the sea to our friend, and *tried out* all that day *with our maine course*." MALONE.

[9] —*an unstanch'd wench.*] *Unstanch'd*, I believe, means incontinent. STEEVENS.

[1] *Lay her a-hold, a-hold;*] *To lay a ship a-hold*, is to bring her to lie as near the wind as she can, in order to keep clear of the land, and get her out to sea. STEEVENS.

[2] —*set her two* courses;] The courses are the main-sail and fore-sail. JOHNSON.

Gon.

Gon. The king and prince at prayers! let us assist them,
For our case is as theirs.
  Seb. I am out of patience.
  Ant. We are merely [3] cheated of our lives by drunkards.—
This wide-chopp'd rascal;—Would thou might'st lie drowning,
The washing of ten tides!
  Gon. He'll be hang'd yet;
Though every drop of water swear against it,
And gape at wid'st to glut him [4].
  [*A confused noise within.*] Mercy on us!—We split!
  we split!—Farewell, my wife and children!—Farewell,
  brother!—We split, we split, we split [5].
  Ant. Let's all sink with the king.   [*Exit.*
  Seb. Let's take leave of him.   [*Exit.*
  Gon. Now would I give a thousand furlongs of sea for
an acre of barren ground; long heath [6], brown furze, any
thing: The wills above be done, but I would fain die a dry
death!   [*Exit.*

SCENE II.

The inchanted island: before the cell of Prospero.

Enter PROSPERO *and* MIRANDA.

Mira. If by your art, my dearest father, you have
Put the wild waters in this roar, allay them:
The sky, it seems, would pour down stinking pitch,

---

3 ———*merely*———] in this place signifies *absolutely*. STEEVENS.
4 *to glut him.*] i. e. to *englut* or swallow him. MALONE.
5 *Mercy on us! we split, we split! Farewell my wife and children,* &c.]
These lines (as Dr. Johnson has observed) should be considered as spoken
not by any determinate characters of the present play, but by various
sailors on board the vessel. MALONE.
  In the old copy these words were absurdly printed as spoken by one
person. Dr. Johnson's arrangement is proved to be right, not only by
the reason of the thing, but by a similar passage in *Coriolanus*, Act V.
sc. ult. " He kill'd my son;—my daughter," &c. where the words, *all
people* are prefixed to the speech. MALONE.
6 ——— *long heath.*] Sir T. Hanmer reads *ling*, heath, *broom*, furze.—
Perhaps rightly, though he has been charged with tautology. I find
in Harrison's Description of Britain, prefixed to our author's good
friend Holinshed, p. 91: " *Brome, beth, firze, brakes, whinnes, ling,*"
&c. FARMER.

B 4   But

But that the sea [7], mounting to the welkin's cheek,
Dashes the fire out. O, I have suffer'd
With those that I saw suffer! a brave vessel,
Who had no doubt some noble creature in her,
Dash'd all to pieces. O, the cry did knock
Against my very heart! Poor souls! they perish'd.
Had I been any god of power, I would
Have sunk the sea within the earth, or ere [8]
It should the good ship so have swallow'd, and
The freighting souls within her.

 Pro. Be collected;
No more amazement: tell your piteous heart,
There's no harm done.

 Mira. O, woe the day!

 Pro. No harm [9].
I have done nothing but in care of thee,
(Of thee, my dear one! thee, my daughter!) who
Art ignorant of what thou art, nought knowing
Of whence I am; nor that I am more better [1]
Than Prospero, master of a full poor cell [2],
And thy no greater father.

 Mira. More to know
Did never meddle with my thoughts [3].

            Pro.

---

[7] *But that the sea,* &c.] So, in *King Lear:*
 "The sea in such a storm as his bare head
 "In hell-black night endur'd, would have buoy'd up,
 "And quench'd the stelled fires." MALONE.

[8] *Or ere,* is *before.* STEEVENS.

[9] *Pro. No harm.*] I know not whether Shakspeare did not make Miranda speak thus: *O, woe the day! no harm?* To which Prospero properly answers:
    I have done nothing but in care of thee.
Miranda, when she speaks the words, *O, woe the day!* supposes, not that the crew had escaped, but that her father thought differently from her, and counted their destruction *no harm.* JOHNSON.

[1] ——*more better*——] This ungrammatical expression is very frequent among our oldest writers. STEEVENS.

[2] ——full poor *cell,*] i. e. a cell in a great degree of poverty. So, in *Antony and Cleopatra:* "I am *full sorry.*" STEEVENS.

[3] *Did never* meddle *with my thoughts.*] To *meddle,* in this instance, seems to signify to *mingle.* Hence the substantive *medley.* STEEVENS.
 See Howell's DICT. 1660, in v. to *meddle;* "se mêler de." So, in Spenser's *Shepheard's Calender,* (April):
 "The red rose *medled* with the white y-fere,
 "In either cheeke depeincten lively cheere."

               Again,

Pro. 'Tis time
I should inform thee further. Lend thy hand,
And pluck my magic garment from me.—So;
[*Lays down his mantle.*
Lie there my art [4].—Wipe thou thine eyes; have comfort.
The direful spectacle of the wreck, which touch'd
The very virtue of compassion [5] in thee,
I have with such provision in mine art
So safely order'd, that there is no soul [6]—
No, not so much perdition as an hair,
Betid to any creature in the vessel
Which thou heard'st cry, which thou saw'st sink. Sit down;
For thou must now know further.

Mira. You have often
Begun to tell me what I am; but stopp'd,
And left me to a bootless inquisition;
Concluding, *Stay, not yet.*—

Pro. The hour's now come;
The very minute bids thee ope thine ear;
Obey, and be attentive. Canst thou remember

Again, in Lewknor's translation of Contareno's *Commonwealth and Government of Venice*, 1598: "—which scrolles being first all well *medled* together are put into the pott." MALONE.

[4] *Lie there my art.*] Sir W. Cecil, lord Burleigh, lord high treasurer, &c. in the reign of queen Elizabeth, when he put off his gown at night, used to say, *Lie there, lord treasurer.* Fuller's *Holy State*, p. 257. STEEVENS.

[5] —— virtue *of compassion*—] Virtue, the most efficacious part, the energetic quality; in a like sense we say, *The virtue of a plant is in the extract.* JOHNSON.

[6] —— *no soul*—] Such interruptions as the present are not uncommon to Shakspeare. He sometimes begins a sentence, and before he concludes it, entirely changes the construction, because another, more forcible, occurs. As this change frequently happens in conversation, it may be suffered to pass uncensured in the language of the stage.
STEEVENS.

So, in the *Winter's Tale*:
" —— Beseech you
" Of your own state take care; *this dream of mine*,—
" Being now awake, I'll queen it no inch farther,
" But milk my ewes and weep."
Again, in *Cymbeline*:
" He liv'd in the court—
" —— to the grave
" A child that guided dotards; *to his mistress*,
" For whom he now is banish'd,—her own price
" Proclaims how she esteem'd him and his virtue." MALONE.

B 5   A time

A time before we came unto this cell?
I do not think thou canst; for then thou wast not
Out three years old [7].

Mira. Certainly, sir, I can.

Pro. By what? by any other house, or person?
Of any thing the image tell me, that
Hath kept with thy remembrance.

Mira. 'Tis far off;
And rather like a dream, than an assurance
That my remembrance warrants: Had I not
Four or five women once, that tended me?

Pro. Thou hadst, and more, Miranda: But how is it,
That this lives in thy mind? What seest thou else
In the dark backward and abysm of time [8]?
If thou remember'st aught, ere thou cam'st here,
How thou cam'st here, thou may'st.

Mira. But that I do not.

Pro. Twelve years since, Miranda, twelve years since,
Thy father was the duke of Milan, and
A prince of power.

Mira. Sir, are not you my father?

Pro. Thy mother was a piece of virtue, and
She said—thou wast my daughter! and thy father
Was duke of Milan; and his only heir
A princess;—no worse issued [9].

Mira. O the heavens!
What foul play had we, that we came from thence?
Or blessed was't, we did?

Pro. Both, both, my girl:
By foul play, as thou say'st, were we heav'd thence;
But blessedly holp hither.

Mira. O, my heart bleeds
To think o' the teen [1] that I have turn'd you to,
Which is from my remembrance! Please you, further.

Pro. My brother, and thy uncle, called Anthonio,—
I pray thee, mark me,—that a brother should
Be so perfidious!—he whom, next thyself,

---

[7] *Out three years old.*] i. e. quite three years old, three years old full-out, complete. STEEVENS.

[8] —— *abysm of time?*] i. e. abyss. MALONE.

[9] *A princess;—no worse issued*] The old copy reads—*And princess—.* The emendation was proposed by Mr. Steevens. *Issued* is (as he observes) *descended.* MALONE.

[1] —*teen*—] is sorrow, grief, trouble. STEEVENS.

Of all the world I lov'd, and to him put
The manage of my state; as, at that time,
Through all the signiories it was the first,
And Prospero the prime duke; being so reputed
In dignity, and, for the liberal arts,
Without a parallel; those being all my study,
The government I cast upon my brother,
And to my state grew stranger, being transported,
And rapt in secret studies. Thy false uncle—
Dost thou attend me?
    Mira. Sir, most heedfully.
    Pro. Being once perfected how to grant suits,
How to deny them; whom to advance, and whom [2]
To trash for over-topping [3]; new created
The creatures that were mine; I say, or chang'd them,
Or else new form'd them: having both the key [4]
Of officer and office, set all hearts i' the state
To what tune pleas'd his ear; that now he was
The ivy, which had hid my princely trunk,
And suck'd my verdure out on't.—Thou attend'st not.
    Mira. O good Sir, I do.
    Pro. I pray thee, mark me.

[2] — *whom to advance, and* whom] The old copy has *who* in both places. Corrected by the editor of the second folio. MALONE.

[3] *To trash for over-topping;*] *To trash,* as Dr. Warburton observes, is to cut away the superfluities. This word I have met with in books containing directions for gardeners, published in the time of queen Elizabeth.

Mr. Warton's note, however, on — "*trash* for his quick hunting," in the second act of *Othello,* leaves my interpretation of this passage exceedingly disputable. STEEVENS.

To trash for over-topping may either mean to lop them because they did over-top, or in order to prevent them from over-topping. So Lucetta, in the second scene of *The Two Gentlemen of Verona,* says,

"— I was taken up for laying them down:
"Yet here they shall not lie *for catching* cold."

This mode of expression is not frequent in Shakspeare, but occurs in every play of Beaumont and Fletcher:

"We'll have a bib *for* spoiling of your *doublet.*"
                                               The Captain.

"Stir my horse *for* catching cold. *Love's Pilgrimage.*
"—all her face patch'd *for* discovery. *The Pilgrim.*
That is, to prevent discovery. MASON.

[4] — *both the key*] Key in this place seems to signify the key of a musical instrument, by which he set *hearts to tune.* JOHNSON.

This doubtless is meant of a key for tuning the harpsichord, spinnet, or virginal; we call it now a tuning hammer. Sir J. HAWKINS.

I thus

I thus neglecting worldly ends, all dedicated
To closeness, and the bettering of my mind
With that, which, but by being so retir'd,
O'er-priz'd all popular rate, in my false brother
Awak'd an evil nature: and my trust,
Like a good parent [5], did beget of him
A falsehood, in its contrary as great
As my trust was; which had, indeed, no limit,
A confidence sans bound. He being thus lorded,
Not only with what my revenue yielded,
But what my power might else exact,—like one,
Who having, unto truth, by telling of it,
Made such a sinner of his memory,
To credit his own lie [6], he did believe
He was, indeed, the duke; out of the substitution,
And executing the outward face of royalty,
With all prerogative:—Hence his ambition growing,—
Dost thou hear?

Mira. Your tale, sir, would cure deafness.

Pro. To have no screen between this part he play'd
And him he play'd it for, he needs will be
Absolute Milan: Me, poor man!—my library
Was dukedom large enough; of temporal royalties
He thinks me now incapable: confederates,
So dry he was for sway [7], with the king of Naples,

---

[5] *Like a good parent,*] Alluding to the observation, that a father above the common rate of men has commonly a son below it. *Heroum filii noxa.* JOHNSON.

[6] ——————— *like one,*
Who having, unto truth, by telling of it,
Made such a sinner of his memory,
To credit his own lie.] There is perhaps no correlative, to which the word *it* can with grammatical propriety belong. *Lie*, however, seems to have been the correlative to which the poet meant to refer, however ungrammatically. STEEVENS.

There is a very singular coincidence between this passage and one in Bacon's *History of King Henry VII.* (Perkin Warbeck) "did in all things notably acquit himself; insomuch as it was generally believed—that he was indeed *Duke Richard*. Nay, *himself, with long and continual counterfeiting, and with oft telling a lie, was turned by habit almost into the thing he seemed to be; and from a liar to be a believer.*" MALONE.

Ibid.—*Me, poor man! my library*
Was large enough;] i. e. was large enough *for.* Of this kind of ellipsis see various examples in a note on *Cymbeline.*

The old copy has —*into truth.* Corrected by Dr. Warburton.
MALONE.

[7] *So dry he was for sway,*——] i. e. So *thirsty.* The expression, I am told, is not uncommon in the midland counties. STEEVENS.

To give him annual tribute, do him homage;
Subject his coronet to his crown, and bend
The dukedom, yet unbow'd (alas, poor Milan!)
To moſt ignoble ſtooping.

Mira. O the heavens!

Pro. Mark his condition, and the event; then tell me,
If this might be a brother.

Mira. I ſhould ſin
To think but nobly [8] of my grandmother:
Good wombs have borne bad ſons.

Pro. Now the condition,
The king of Naples, being an enemy
To me inveterate, hearkens my brother's ſuit;
Which was, that he in lieu of the premiſes,—
Of homage, and I know not how much tribute,—
Should preſently extirpate me and mine
Out of the dukedom; and confer fair Milan,
With all the honours, on my brother: Whereon,
A treacherous army levy'd, one midnight
Fated to the purpoſe, did Anthonio open
The gates of Milan; and, i'the dead of darkneſs,
The miniſters for the purpoſe hurried thence
Me, and thy crying ſelf.

Mira. Alack, for pity!
I, not rememb'ring how I cried out then [9],
Will cry it o'er again; it is a hint [1],
That wrings my eyes to't.

Pro. Hear a little further,
And then I'll bring thee to the preſent buſineſs
Which now's upon us; without the which, this ſtory
Were moſt impertinent.

Mira. Wherefore did they not
That hour deſtroy us?

Pro. Well demanded, wench;
My tale provokes that queſtion. Dear, they durſt not;
(So dear the love my people bore me) nor ſet
A mark ſo bloody on the buſineſs; but

[8] *To think but nobly*] *But* in this place ſignifies *otherwiſe than.*
STEEVENS.

[9] — *cried* out] Perhaps we ſhould read—cried *on't.* STEEVENS.

[1] — *a hint.*] Hint is *ſuggeſtion.* So, in the beginning ſpeech of the
ſecond act: ———our *hint* of woe
Is common—. STEEVENS.

With

With colours fairer painted their foul ends.
In few, they hurried us aboard a bark;
Bore us some leagues to sea; where they prepar'd
A rotten carcass of a boat [2], not rigg'd,
Nor tackle, sail, nor mast; the very rats
Instinctively had quit it [3]: there they hoist us,
To cry to the sea that roar'd to us; to sigh
To the winds, whose pity, sighing back again,
Did us but loving wrong.

 Mira. Alack! what trouble
Was I then to you!

 Pro. O! a cherubin [*]
Thou wast, that did preserve me! Thou didst smile,
Infused with a fortitude from heaven,
When I have deck'd the sea [4] with drops full salt;
Under my burden groan'd; which rais'd in me
An undergoing stomach [5], to bear up
Against what would ensue.

[2] — *of a boat,*] The old copy reads — of a *butt.* HENLEY.
It was corrected by Mr. Rowe. MALONE.

[3] — had *quit it:*] Old copy—*have* quit it. Corrected by Mr. Rowe. MALONE.

[*] *O! a cherubin,* &c.] The modern editions read *cherubim,* but *cherubin* is the reading of the old copy, and, though inaccurate, was the constant language of Shakspeare's time. In Bullokar's *English Expositor,* 8vo. 1616 we find " CHERUBIN, *one* of the highest order of angels." So, in Sir Thomas Overbury's characters, 1616: [*A Precisian*] " He thinks every organist is in the state of damnation, and had rather hear one of Robert Wisdome's Psalms than the best hymn *a cherubin* can sing." Again, in *The Spanish Tragedy,* 1605:
" Back'd with a troop of fiery *cherubins.*" MALONE.

[4] — deck'd *the sea*—] *To deck the sea,* if explained, to honour, adorn, or dignify, is indeed ridiculous, but the original import of the verb *deck* is, to *cover;* so in some parts they yet say *deck the table.* This sense may be borne; but perhaps the poet wrote *fleck'd,* which I think is still used, in rustic language, of drops falling upon water. JOHNSON

The following passage in *Antony and Cleopatra* may countenance the verb *deck* in its common acceptation:
" —— do not please sharp fate
" To *grace* it with your sorrows."
What is this but *decking* it with *tears?* STEEVENS.

To *deck,* I am told, signifies in the North, to *sprinkle.* See Ray's DICT. *of North Country words,* in verb. to *deg,* and to *leck;* and his DICT. *of South Country words,* in verb. *dag.* The latter signifies *dew* upon the grass;—hence *daggle-tailed.* In Cole's Latin Dictionary, 1679, we find——" *To* dag, *collutulo, irroro.*" MALONE.

[5] *An undergoing* stomach,] *Stomach* is *pride, stubborn resolution.* So Horace, "——gravem Pelidæ *stomachum.*" STEEVENS.

              Mira.

Mira. How came we ashore;
Pro. By Providence divine.
Some food we had, and some fresh water, that
A noble Neapolitan, Gonzalo,
Out of his charity, who being then appointed [6]
Master of this design, did give us †; with
Rich garments, linens, stuffs, and necessaries,
Which since have steaded much: so, of his gentleness,
Knowing I lov'd my books, he furnish'd me,
From my own library, with volumes that
I prize above my dukedom.
Mira. Would I might
But ever see that man!
Pro. Now, I arise [7] :—

Sit

[6] ——who *being then appointed*, &c.] Such is the old reading. We might better read,——he *being*, &c. STEEVENS.

† Some food we had, and some fresh water, that
A noble Neapolitan, Gonzalo,
Out of his charity, (*who being then appointed*
Master of this design;) *did give us;*] Mr. Steevens has suggested, that we might better read—*he* being then appointed; and so we should certainly now write: but the reading of the old copy is the true one, that mode of phraseology being the idiom of Shakspeare's time. So, in *The Winter's Tale:*
"——'This your son-in-law,
"And son unto the king (*whom* heavens directing,)
"Is troth-plight to your daughter."
Again, in *Coriolanus:*
"—— waving thy hand,
"*Which* often, thus, *correcting thy stout heart,*
"Now humble as the ripest mulberry,
"That will not hold the handling; or, say to them," &c.
MALONE.

[7] *Pro. Now I arise:*] Why does Prospero *arise?* Or, if he does it to ease himself by change of posture, why need he interrupt his narrative to tell his daughter of it? Perhaps these words belong to Miranda, and we should read:
Mira. Would I might
But ever see that man!—Now, I arise.
Pro. Sit still, and hear the last of our sea-sorrow.
Prospero in page 9 had directed his daughter to *sit down*, and learn the whole of this history; having previously by some magical charm disposed her to fall asleep. He is watching the progress of this charm; and in the mean time tells her a long story, often asking her whether her attention be still awake. The story being ended (as Miranda supposes) with their coming on shore, and partaking of the conveniences provided for them by the loyal humanity of Gonzalo, she therefore first expresses

Sit still, and hear the last of our sea-sorrow,
Here in this island we arrived; and here
Have I, thy school master, made thee more profit
Than other princes[8] can, that have more time
For vainer hours, and tutors not so careful.

Mira. Heavens thank you for't! And now, I pray you, sir,
(For still 'tis beating in my mind,) your reason
For raising this sea-storm?

Pro. Know thus far forth.—
By accident most strange, bountiful fortune,
Now my dear lady[9], hath mine enemies
Brought to this shore: and by my prescience
I find my zenith doth depend upon
A most auspicious star, whose influence
If now I court not, but omit[1], my fortunes
Will ever after droop.—Here cease more questions;
Thou art inclin'd to sleep; 'tis a good dullness[2],
And give it way;—I know thou canst not choose.—

[*Miranda sleeps.*

Come away, servant, come: I am ready now;
Approach, my Ariel, come.

Enter ARIEL.

Ari. All hail, great master! grave sir, hail! I come

expresses a wish to see the good old man, and then observes that she may *now arise*, as the story is done. Prospero, surprised that his charm does not yet work, bids her *sit still*; and then enters on fresh matter to amuse the time, telling her (what she knew before) that he had been her tutor, &c. But soon perceiving her drowsiness coming on; he breaks off abruptly, and leaves her *still sitting* to her slumbers.
BLACKSTONE.

[8] *Than other princes*—] The first folio reads—*princesse*. HENLEY. Corrected by Mr. Rowe. MALONE.

[9] *Now my dear lady*, is, *now my auspicious mistress*. STEEVENS.

[1] —*I find my zenith doth depend upon*
A most auspicious star; whose influence
If now I court not, but omit, &c.] So, in *Julius Cæsar:*
" There is a tide in the affairs of man,
" Which taken at the flood, leads on to *fortune;*
" *Omitted*, all the voyage of their life
" Is bound in shallows and in miseries. MALONE.

[2] —— *'tis a good dulness.*] Dr. Warburton rightly observes, that this sleepiness, which Prospero by his art had brought upon Miranda, and of which he knew not how soon the effect would begin, makes him question her so often whether she is attentive to his story. JOHNSON.

To answer thy best pleasure; be't to fly,
To swim, to dive into the fire, to ride
On the curl'd clouds; * to thy strong bidding, task
Ariel, and all his quality ³.
  Pro. Hast thou, spirit,
Perform'd to point ⁴ the tempest that I bad thee?
  Ari. To every article.
I boarded the king's ship; now on the beak ⁵,
Now in the waste ⁶, the deck, in every cabin,
I flam'd amazement: Sometimes, I'd divide,
And burn in many places ⁷; on the top-mast,
The yards and boltsprit would I flame distinctly,
Then meet, and join. Jove's lightnings ⁸, the precursors
O' the dreadful thunder-claps ⁹, more momentary

* So in Isaiah, xix. i. " The Lord *rideth* on the swift cloud."
                                        MALONE.
³ —*quality.*] i. e. all of his *fellowship*; " the crew of meaner spirits." See *Hamlet*, A. II. Sc. 2. " Will they pursue the *quality*" &c.
                                            MALONE.
⁴ *Perform'd to point*—] i e. to the minutest article. STEEVENS.
⁵ —*beak,*] The beak was a strong pointed body at the head of the ancient gallies; it is used here for the forecastle, or the bolt-sprit.
                                            JOHNS.
⁶ —*waste,*] The part between the quarter-deck and the forecastle.
                                            JOHNS.
⁷ ——— *Sometimes I'd divide,*
And burn in many places; &c.] Perhaps our author, when he wrote these lines, remembered the following passage in Hackluyt's *Voyages*, 1598: " I do remember that in the great and boysterous storme of this foule weather, in the night there came upon the toppe of our maine yarde and maine maste a certaine little light; much like unto the light of a little candle, which the Spaniards call the *Suerpo Santo.*———*This light continued aboord our ship about three houres, flying from maste to maste, and from top to top, and sometimes it would be in two or three places at once.*"
  So also De Loier, speaking of strange sights happening in the seas," *Treatise of Spectres*, 4to. 1605, p. 67, b. " Sometimes they shall see the fire which the saylors call *Saint Hermes*, to fly uppon their shippe, and *to alight upon the toppe of the mast*; and sometimes they shall perceive a wind that sheweth such stormes as will run round about their shippe and play about it in such sort, as by the hurling and beating of the clouds will raise uppe *a fire that will burne uppe the yardes, the sayles, and the tacklings of the shippe.* MALONE.
⁸ *Jove's* lightnings,—] The old copy reads—*lightning.* Corrected by Mr. Theobald. MALONE.
⁹ ——— *precursors*
  O' the dreadful thunder-claps,] So, in *K. Lear:*
" 'Vant couriers of oak-cleaving thunderbolts." STEEVENS.

And

And fight-out-running were not: The fire, and cracks
Of sulphurous roaring, the most mighty Neptune
Seem'd to besiege, and make his bold waves tremble,
Yea, his dread trident shake.

Pro. My brave spirit!
Who was so firm, so constant, that this coil
Would not infect his reason?

Ari. Not a soul
But felt a fever of the mad [1], and play'd
Some tricks of desperation: All, but mariners,
Plung'd in the foaming brine, and quit the vessel [*],
Then all a-fire with me: the king's son, Ferdinand,
With hair up-staring, (then like reeds, not hair,)
Was the first man that leap'd; cried, *Hell is empty,
And all the devils are here.*

Pro. Why, that's my spirit!
But was not this nigh shore?

Ari. Close by, my master.

Pro. But are they, Ariel, safe?

Ari. Not a hair perish'd;
On their sustaining garments [²] not a blemish,
But fresher than before: and as thou bad'st me,

---

[1] *But felt a fever of the mad,*] Not a soul but felt such a fever as madmen feel, when the frantic fit is upon them. STEEVENS.

[*] — *and quit the vessel,*] Quit is, I think, here used for *quitted.* So, in *K. Lear:*
"——— 'Twas he inform'd against him,
"And *quit* the house on purpose, that their punishment
"Might have the freer course."
So, in *King Henry VI. P. I. lift,* for *lifted:*
"He ne'er *lift* up his hand, but conquered." MALONE.

Ibidem. On *their* sustaining *garments,* &c.] The word *sustaining* in this place does not mean *supporting,* but *enduring;* and by their *sustaining garments* Ariel means, their garments which bore, without being injured, the drenching of the sea. MASON.

Perhaps *sustaining* is here used for *sustained.* So, in *Antony and Cleopatra, all-obeying,* for *all-obeyed.* Mr. Mason's interpretation, however, may be the true one; and the word *sustaining* may also have been used for *suffering,* in the passage quoted from *King Lear.* Their garments could not be called *sustaining,* in the sense which Mr. Steevens attributes to the word, for it is well known that the clothes of a person who has fallen into the sea, when they become thoroughly wet, instead of sustaining him, render him less able to keep himself from sinking.
MALONE.

[²] — sustaining *garments—*] i. e. their garments that bore them up, and supported them. So, *K. Lear,* Act IV. sc. iv.
"In our *sustaining* corn." STEEVENS.

In

In troops I have difpers'd them 'bout the ifle:
The king's fon have I landed by himfelf;
Whom I left cooling of the air with fighs,
In an odd angle of the ifle, and fitting,
His arms in this fad knot.

   Pro. Of the king's fhip,
The mariners, fay, how haft thou difpos'd,
And all the reft o' the fleet?

   Ari. Safely in harbour
Is the king's fhip; in the deep nook, where once
Thou call'dft me up at midnight to fetch dew
From the ftill-vex'd Bermoothes [3], there fhe's hid:
The mariners all under hatches ftow'd;
Whom, with a charm join'd to their fuffer'd labour,
I have left afleep: and for the reft o' the fleet,
Which I difpers'd, they all have met again;
And are upon the Mediterranean flote [4],
Bound fadly home for Naples;
Suppofing that they faw the king's fhip wreck'd,
And his great perfon perifh.

   Pro. Ariel, thy charge
Exactly is perform'd; but there's more work:
What is the time o' the day [5]?

---

[3] *From the ftill-vex'd Bermoothes,*] Thus the iflands now known by the name of *Bermudas* were frequently, though not always, called in our author's time.—Hackluyt, in his *Voyages*, 1598, calls "the fea about the *Bermudas* a hellifh place, for thunder, lightning, and ftormes." So alfo the Continuator of Stowe's Annals, 1615, defcribing the arrival of the Englifh at thefe iflands in 1609: "Sir George Somers fitting at the fterne, feeing the fhip defperate of relief, looking every minute when it would finke, he efpied land, which, according to his and Captain Newport's opinion, they judged fhould be that dreadful coaft of the *Bermudes*, which iflands were of all nations faid and fuppofed to be *inchanted, and inhabited with witches and devils*; which grew by reafon of accuftomed monftrous thunder, ftorme, and tempeft, neere unto thofe iflands, alfo for that the whole coaft is fo wonderous dangerous of rockes, that few can approach them but with unfpeakable hazard of fhipwreck."
                                                       MALONE.

[4] — *the Mediterranean flote,*] Flote is *wave.* Flot. Fr. STEEVENS.

[5] *What is the time o' the day?*] This paffage needs not to be difturbed, it being common to afk a queftion, which the next moment enables us to anfwer; he that thinks it faulty may eafily adjuft it thus:
   Pro. *What is the time o' the day? Paft the mid feafon?*
   Ari. *At leaft two glaffes.*
   Pro. *The time 'twixt fix and now*——. JOHNSON.
   Mr. Upton propofes to regulate this paffage differently:
   Ari. *Paft the mid feafon, at leaft two glaffes.*
   Pro. *The time,* &c. MALONE.

Ari. Past the mid season.

Pro. At least two glasses: The time 'twixt six and now
Must by us both be spent most preciously.

Ari. Is there more toil? Since thou dost give me pains,
Let me remember thee what thou hast promis'd,
Which is not yet perform'd me.

Pro. How now? moody?
What is't thou can'st demand?

Ari. My liberty.

Pro. Before the time be out? no more.

Ari. I pray thee,
Remember, I have done thee worthy service;
Told thee no lies, made thee no mistakings, serv'd
Without or grudge, or grumblings: thou didst promise
To bate me a full year.

Pro. Dost thou forget [6]
From what a torment I did free thee?

Ari.

---

[6] *Dost thou forget*] That the character and conduct of Prospero may be understood, something must be known of the system of enchantment, which supplied all the marvellous found in the romances of the middle ages. This system seems to be founded on the opinion that the fallen spirits, having different degrees of guilt, had different habitations allotted them at their expulsion, some being confined in hell, *some* (as Hooker, who delivers the opinion of our poet's age, expresses it,) *dispersed in air, some on earth, some in water, others in caves, dens, or minerals under the earth*. Of these, some were more malignant and mischievous than others. The earthy spirits seem to have been thought the most depraved, and the aerial the least vitiated. Thus Prospero observes of Ariel:

———*Thou wast a spirit too delicate
To act her earthy and abhorr'd commands.*

Over these spirits a power might be obtained by certain rites performed or charms learned. This power was called *The Black Art*, or *Knowledge of Enchantment*. The enchanter being (as king James observes in his *Demonology*) one *who commands the devil, whereas the witch serves him*. Those who thought best of this art, the existence of which was, I am afraid, believed very seriously, held, that certain sounds and characters had a physical power over spirits, and compelled their agency; others, who condemned the practice, which in reality was surely never practised, were of opinion, with more reason, that the power of charms arose *only* from compact, and was no more than the spirits voluntarily allowed them for the seduction of man. The art was held by all, though not equally criminal, yet unlawful, and therefore Casaubon, speaking of one who had commerce with spirits, blames him, though he imagines him *one of the best kind who dealt with them by way of command*. Thus Prospero repents of his art in the last scene. The spirits were always considered as in some measure enslaved to the enchanter, at least for a time, and as serving with unwillingness; therefore Ariel so often

bega

Ari. No.

Pro. Thou doſt; and think'ſt it much, to tread the ooze
Of the ſalt deep *;
To run upon the ſharp wind of the north;
To do me buſineſs in the veins o' the earth,
When it is bak'd with froſt.

Ari. I do not, ſir.

Pro. Thou lieſt, malignant thing! haſt thou forgot
The foul witch Sycorax, who, with age, and envy,
Was grown into a hoop? haſt thou forgot her?

Ari. No, ſir.

Pro. Thou haſt: Where was ſhe born? ſpeak? tell me.

Ari. Sir, in Argier [7].

Pro. Oh, was ſhe ſo? I muſt,
Once in a month, recount what thou haſt been,
Which thou forget'ſt. This damn'd witch, Sycorax,
For miſchiefs manifold, and ſorceries terrible
To enter human hearing, from Argier,
Thou know'ſt, was baniſh'd; for one thing ſhe did,
They would not take her life: Is not this true?

Ari. Ay, ſir.

Pro. This blue-ey'd hag was hither brought with child,
And here was left by the ſailors: Thou, my ſlave,
As thou report'ſt thyſelf, waſt then her ſervant:
And, for thou waſt a ſpirit too delicate
To act her earthy and abhorr'd commands,
Refuſing her grand heſts, ſhe did confine thee,
By help of her more potent miniſters,
And in her moſt unmitigable rage,
Into a cloven pine; within which rift
Impriſon'd, thou didſt painfully remain
A dozen years; within which ſpace ſhe died,
And left thee there; where thou didſt vent thy groans,
As faſt as mill-wheels ſtrike: Then was this iſland,

begs for liberty; and Caliban obſerves, that the ſpirits ſerve Proſpero with no good will, but *hate him rootedly.*—Of theſe trifles enough.
                                                                   JOHNSON.

* ——— *to tread the ooze*
Of the ſalt deep; ———
To do me buſineſs in the veins of the earth.] So Milton,
Par. Loſt.
    " Or do his errands in the gloomy deep."

7 — *in* Argier.] *Argier* is the ancient Engliſh name for *Algiers.*
                                                                   STEEVENS.

(Save

(Save for the son that she did litter here,
A freckled whelp, hag-born,) not honour'd with
A human shape.

Ari. Yes; Caliban her son.

Pro. Dull thing, I say so; he, that Caliban,
Whom now I keep in service. Thou best know'st
What torment I did find thee in: thy groans
Did make wolves howl, and penetrate the breasts
Of ever-angry bears; it was a torment
To lay upon the damn'd, which Sycorax
Could not again undo; it was mine art,
When I arriv'd, and heard thee, that made gape
The pine, and let thee out.

Ari. I thank thee, master.

Pro. If thou more murmur'st, I will rend an oak,
And peg thee in his knotty entrails, till
Thou hast howl'd away twelve winters.

Ari. Pardon, master:
I will be correspondent to command,
And do my spriting gently.

Pro. Do so; and after two days
I will discharge thee.

Ari. That's my noble master!
What shall I do? say what? what shall I do?

Pro. Go make thyself like a nymph o'the sea; be subject
To no sight but thine and mine; invisible [8]
To every eye-ball else. Go, take this shape,
And hither come in it: go, hence, with diligence.

[*Exit* ARIEL.

Awake, dear heart, awake! thou hast slept well;
Awake!

Mira. The strangeness [9] of your story put
Heaviness in me.

Pro.

---

[8] *Go make thyself like a nymph o' the sea: be subject
To no sight but thine and mine; invisible,* &c.] The words—" be
" subject"—having been transferred in the first copy of this play to the
latter of these lines, by the carelessness of the transcriber or printer, the
editor of the second folio, to supply the metre of the former, introduced
the word *to*;—reading,, " like *to* a nymph o' the sea." The regulation
that I have made shews that the addition, like many others made by
that editor, was unnecessary. MALONE.

— *a nymph o' the sea;*] There does not appear to be sufficient cause
why *Ariel* should assume this new shape, as he was to be invisible to all
eyes but those of Prospero. STEEVENS.

[9] *The*

Pro. Shake it off: Come on:
We'll visit Caliban, my slave, who never
Yields us kind answer.
    Mira. 'Tis a villain, sir,
I do not love to look on.
    Pro. But, as 'tis,
We cannot miss him : * he does make our fire,
Fetch in our wood; and serves in offices
That profit us. What, ho! slave! Caliban!
Thou earth, thou! speak.
    Cal. [*within.*] There's wood enough within.
    Pro. Come forth, I say; there's other business for thee:
Come, thou tortoise! when? †

    Re-enter ARIEL, *like a water-nymph.*

Fine apparition! My quaint Ariel,
Hark in thine ear.
    Ari. My lord, it shall be done.   [*Exit.*
    Pro. Thou poisonous slave, got by the devil himself
Upon thy wicked dam, come forth!

    Enter CALIBAN.

    Cal. As wicked dew as e'er my mother brush'd
With raven's feather from unwholesome fen,
Drop on you both ¹ ! a south-west blow on ye,
And blister you all o'er!
                                           Pro.

---

⁹ *The strangeness—*] Why should a wonderful story produce sleep? I believe experience will prove, that any violent agitation of the mind easily subsides in slumber, especially when, as in Prospero's relation, the last images are pleasing. JOHNSON.

The poet seems to have been apprehensive that the audience, as well as Miranda, would sleep over this long but necessary tale, and therefore strives to break it. First, by making Prospero divest himself of his magic robe and wand; then by waking her attention no less than six times by verbal interruption; then by varying the action when he rises and bids her continue sitting; and lastly, by carrying on the business of the fable while Miranda sleeps, by which she is continued on the stage till the poet has occasion for her again. WARNER.

* *We cannot* miss him.] That is, as Mr. Mason has observed, *We cannot do without him.* This provincial expression is still used in the midland counties. MALONE.

† *When?*] This expression of impatience occurs often in our old dramas. MALONE.

¹ Cal. *As wicked dew as e'er my mother brush'd
    With raven's feather from unwholesome fen,
    Drop on you both!*] It was a tradition, it seems that Lord
                                                 Falkland,

Pro. For this, be sure, to-night thou shalt have cramps, Side-stitches that shall pen thy breath up; urchins [2] Shall for that vast of night that they may work [3], All exercise on thee: thou shalt be pinch'd

Falkland, Lord C. J. Vaughan, and Mr. Selden concurred in observing, that Shakspeare had not only found out a new character in his Caliban, but had also devised and adapted a *new manner of language* for that character. WARBURTON.

Whence these critics derived the notion of a new language appropriated to Caliban, I cannot find: they certainly mistook brutality of sentiment for uncouthness of words. Caliban had learned to speak of Prospero, and his daughter; he had no names for the sun and moon before their arrival, and could not have invented a language of his own without more understanding than Shakspeare has thought it proper to bestow upon him. His diction is indeed somewhat clouded by the gloominess of his temper, and the malignity of his purposes; but let any other being entertain the same thoughts, and he will find them easily issue in the same expressions. JOHNSON.

As wicked dew,—] *Wicked*; having baneful qualities. So Spenser says, *wicked weed*; so, in opposition, we say herbs or medicines have *virtues*. Bacon mentions *virtuous bezoar*, and Dryden *virtuous herbs*.
JOHNSON.

[2] —*urchins*] i. e. *hedge-hogs*. *Urchins* are enumerated by R. Scott among other terrific beings. They are perhaps here put for *fairies*. Milton in his *Masque* speaks of " urchin blasts," and we still call any little dwarfish child, an *urchin*. The word occurs again in the next act.
STEEVENS.

In the *M. W. of Windsor* we have " *urchins*, ouphes, and fairies;" and the passage to which Mr. Steevens alludes, proves, I think, that *urchins* here signifies beings of the fairy kind:

" His *spirits* hear me,
" And yet I needs must curse; but they'll nor *pinch*,
" Fright me with *urchin-shews*, pitch me i'the mire, &c.
MALONE.

[3] — *for that vast of night that they may work*,] The *vast of night* means the night which is naturally empty and deserted, without action; or when all things lying in sleep and silence, makes the world appear one great uninhabited *waste*. So in *Hamlet*:

" In the dead *waste* and middle of the night."
It has a meaning like that of *nox vasta*.

It should be remembered, that, in the pneumatology of former ages, these particulars were settled with the most minute exactness, and the different kinds of visionary beings had different allotments of time suitable to the variety or consequence of their employments. During these spaces, they were at liberty to act, but were always obliged to leave off at a certain hour, that they might not interfere in that portion of night which belonged to others. Among these we may suppose *urchins* to have had a part subjected to their dominion. To this limitation of time Shakspeare alludes again in *K. Lear*: *He begins at curfew, and walks till the second cock.* STEEVENS.

As thick as honey-combs, each pinch more ſtinging
Than bees that made them.

 Cal. I muſt eat my dinner.
This iſland's mine, by Sycorax my mother,
Which thou tak'ſt from me. When thou cameſt firſt,
Thou ſtroak'dſt me, and mad'ſt much of me; would'ſt give me
Water with berries in't; and teach me how
To name the bigger light, and how the leſs,
That burn by day and night: and then I lov'd thee,
And ſhew'd thee all the qualities o' the iſle,
The freſh ſprings, brine pits, barren place, and fertile;
Curs'd be I, that did ſo!—All the charms [4]
Of Sycorax, toads, beetles, bats, light on you!
For I am all the ſubjects that you have,
Which firſt was mine own king: and here you ſty me
In this hard rock, whiles you do keep from me
The reſt of the iſland.

 Pro. Thou moſt lying ſlave,
Whom ſtripes may move, not kindneſs: I have us'd thee,
Filth as thou art, with human care; and lodg'd thee
In mine own cell, till thou did ſeek to violate
The honour of my child.

 Cal. Oh ho, oh ho!—'would it had been done!
Thou didſt prevent me; I had peopled elſe
This iſle with Calibans.

 Pro. Abhorred ſlave [5];
Which any print of goodneſs will not take,
Being capable of all ill! * I pitied thee,
Took pains to make thee ſpeak, taught thee each hour
One thing or other: when thou didſt not, ſavage [6],

             Know

---

[4] *— All the charms*] The latter word, like many others of the ſame kind, is here uſed as a diſſyllable. MALONE.

[5] *Abhorred ſlave*;] This ſpeech, which the old copy gives to Miranda, is very judiciouſly beſtowed by Theobald on Proſpero. JOHNSON.

 Mr Theobald found, or might have found, this ſpeech transferred to Proſpero in the alteration of this play by Dryden and D'Avenant.
                MALONE.

* *Which any print of goodneſs will not take,*
 Being capable of all ill!] So, in Harrington's tranſlation of *Orlando Furioſ.*, 1591:

  "The cruel Eſſelyno, that was thought
  "To have been gotten by ſome wicked devil,
  "That never any goodneſs had been taught,
  "But ſold his ſoule to ſin and doing evil." MALONE.

Know thine own meaning, but would'st gabble like
A thing most brutish, I endow'd thy purposes
With words that made them known: But thy vile race [7],
Though thou didst learn, had that in't which good natures
Could not abide to be with; therefore wast thou
Deservedly confin'd into this rock,
Who hadst deserv'd more than a prison.

Cal. You taught me language; and my profit on't
Is, I know how to curse: The red plague rid you [8],
For learning me your language!

Pro. Hag-seed hence!
Fetch us in fewel; and be quick, thou wert best,
To answer other business. Shrug'st thou, malice?
If thou neglect'st, or dost unwillingly
What I command, I'll rack thee with old cramps;
Fill all thy bones with aches; make thee roar,
That beasts shall tremble at thy din.

Cal. No, 'pray thee!—
I must obey: his art is of such power,   [*Aside.*
It would control my dam's god, Setebos [9],
And make a vassal of him.

                                Pro.

---

[6] *——— when thou didst not, savage,*
Know thy own meaning.] By this expression, however defective, the poet seems to have meant—*when thou didst utter sounds, to which thou hadst no determinate meaning:* but the following expression of Mr. Addison, in his 389th Spectator, concerning the Hottentots, may prove the best comment on this passage; "———having no language among them but a confused gabble, which is *neither well understood by themselves, or others.*" STEEVENS.

[7] *But thy vile race,*] *Race,* in this place, seems to signify original disposition, inborn qualities. In this sense we still say—*The race of wine;* and Sir W. Temple has some where applied it to works of literature.
                                                 STEEVENS.

[8] *The red plague—*] I suppose from the redness of the body, universally inflamed. JOHNSON.

The *erysipelas* was anciently called the *red plague*. STEEVENS.
So again, in *Coriolanus:*
    "Now the *red pestilence* strike all trades in Rome!"
The word *rid,* which has not been explained, means to *destroy.* So, in *K. Henry* IV. p. ii.
    "——— If you ever chance to have a child,
    "Look, in his youth, to have him so cut off,
    "As deathsmen! you have *rid* this sweet young prince."
                                                   MALONE.

[9] *— my dam's god, Setebos.*] A gentleman of great merit, Mr. *Warner,* has observed on the authority of *John Barbot,* that "the *Patagons* are

Pro. So, slave; hence! [*Exit* CALIBAN.

Re-enter ARIEL, *invisible, playing and singing;* FERDINAND *following him.*

Ariel's Song.

Come unto these yellow sands,
  And then take hands:
Court'sied when you have, and kiss'd[1],
  (The wild waves whist)
Foot it featly here and there;
And, sweet sprites, the burden bear[2].
  Hark, hark!
bur. Bowgh, wowgh.   [*dispersedly.*
  The watch-dogs bark:
bur. Bowgh, wowgh.   [*dispersedly.*
  Hark, hark! I hear
The strain of strutting chanticlere
Cry, Cock-a-doodle-doo.

Fer. Where should this music be? i' the air, or the earth *?
It sounds no more:—and sure, it waits upon

---

are reported to dread a great horned devil, called *Setebos*."—It may be asked, however, how *Shakspeare* knew any thing of this, as *Barbot* was a voyager of the present century?——Perhaps he had read *Eden's* History of Travayle, 1577, who tells us, p. 434, that the *giantes*, when they found themselves fettered, roared like bulls, and cried upon *Setebos* to help them."—The *metathesis* in *Caliban* from *Canibal* is evident.
                                                                    FARMER.

We learn from Magellan's voyage, that *Setebos* was the supreme god of the Patagons, and Cheleule was an inferior one. TOLLET.

Setebos is also mentioned in Hackluyt's *Voyages*, 1598. MALONE.

[1] *Court'sied when you have, and kiss'd*,] As was anciently done at the beginning of some dances.
          The wild waves whist;
i. e. the wild waves being silent (or whist) STEEVENS.
'The lady's hand only was kiss'd, as it should seem, previous to the dance. See Winwood's *Memorials*, vol. ii. p. 44: "—— at this he was taken out to dance, and footed it like a lusty old gallant with his country-woman. He took out the queen, and forgot not to *kiss her hand*." MALONE.

[2] — *the burden bear*.] Old copy—bear the burden. Corrected by Mr. Theobald. MALONE.

* *Where should this music be? i' the air, or the earth?* So, Milton, in his *Il Penseroso:*
    " And, as I walk, sweet music, breathe,
    " Above, about, or underneath!" MALONE.

C 2   Some

Some god of the island. Sitting on a bank,
Weeping again the king my father's wreck [3],
This musick crept by me upon the waters;
Allaying both their fury, and my passion,
With its sweet air: thence I have follow'd it,
Or it hath drawn me rather:—But 'tis gone.
No, it begins again.

Ariel sings. *Full fathom five thy father lies* [4];
  Of his bones are coral made;
  Those are pearls, that were his eyes:
  Nothing of him that doth fade,
  But doth suffer a sea-change,
  Into something rich and strange.
  Sea-nymphs hourly ring his knell:
  Hark, now I hear them,—ding-dong-bell.

[*Burden*, ding-dong.

[3] *Weeping* again *the king my father's wreck,*] Thus the old copy; but in the books of Shakspeare's age *again* is sometimes printed instead of *against* [i. e. opposite to] which I am persuaded was our author's word, agen, A. S. signifies both *adversus* and *iterum*. In *Julius Cæsar* we find *against* used in the first of these senses:
  " Against the capitol I met a lion——."
Lydgate, in his *Troiebeke*, describing Priam's palace, uses *again* in the sense of *against:*
  " And even *agayne* this kynges royal see,
  " In the partye that was thereto contrayre,
  " Yrayfed was by many crafty stayre
  " In brede and length a full rich aultere." MALONE.

The placing Ferdinand in such a situation that he could still gaze upon the wrecked vessel, is one of Shakspeare's touches of nature. *Again* is inadmissible; for this would import that Ferdinand's tears had ceased for a time; whereas he himself tells us, afterwards, that from the hour of his father's wreck they had *never* ceased to flow:
  "——— Myself am Naples,
  " Who with mine eyes, *ne'er since at ebb*, beheld
  " The king my father wreck'd."
However, as our author sometimes forgot to compare the different parts of his play, I have made no change. MALONE.

[4] *Full fathom five thy father lies,* &c.] Ariel's lays, [which have been condemned by Gildon as trifling, and defended not very successfully by Dr. Warburton,] however seasonable and efficacious, must be allowed to be of no supernatural dignity or elegance; they express nothing great, nor reveal any thing above mortal discovery.
The reason for which Ariel is introduced thus trifling is, that he and his companions are evidently of the fairy kind, an order of beings to which tradition has always ascribed a sort of diminutive agency, powerful but ludicrous, a humorous and frolick contentment of nature, well expressed by the songs of Ariel. JOHNSON.

Fer.

Fer. The ditty does remember my drown'd father:—
This is no mortal bufinefs, nor no found
That the earth owes⁵:—I hear it now above me.
  Pro. The fringed curtains of thine eye advance,
And fay, what thou 'feeft yond'.
  Mira. What is't? a fpirit?
Lord, how it looks about :—Believe me, fir,
It carries a brave form :—But 'tis a fpirit.
  Pro. No, wench; it eats and fleeps, and hath fuch fenfes
As we have, fuch : This gallant, which thou feeft,
Was in the wreck; and but he's fomething ftain'd
With grief, that's beauty's canker, thou might'ft call him
A goodly perfon: he hath loft his fellows,
And ftrays about to find them.
  Mira. I might call him
A thing divine; for nothing natural
I ever faw fo noble.
  Pro. It goes on, I fee,   [*Afide.*
As my foul prompts it :—Spirit, fine fpirit, I'll free thee
Within three days for this.
  Fer. Moft fure, the goddefs
On whom thefe airs attend!—Vouchfafe, my prayer
May know, if you remain upon this ifland;
And that you will fome good inftruction give,
How I may bear me here : My prime requeft,
Which I do laft pronounce, is, o you wonder!
If you be made, or no⁶?
                                           Mira.

⁵ *That the earth owes:*] *To owe,* in this place, as well as many others, fignifies *to own.* STEEVENS.
⁶ ——— *My prime requeft*
Which I do laft pronounce, is, o you wonder!
If you be made, or no?] A paffage in *Lilly's Galathea* feems to countenance the text of the firft folio; " The queftion among men is common, *are you a maide?*"—yet I cannot but think, that Dr. Warburton reads very rightly, " If you be *made*, or no." When we meet with an harfh expreffion in *Shakfpeare,* we are ufually to look for a *play upon words. Fletcher* clofely imitates the *Tempeft* in his *Sea-Voyage:* and he introduces *Albert* in the fame manner to the ladies of *his* Defert Ifland:
  " Be not offended, goddeffes, that I fall
  " Thus proftrate," &c.
Shakfpeare himfelf had certainly read, and had probably now in his mind, a paffage in the third book of the *Fairy Queen,* between *Timias* and *Belphebe:*
  " *Angel* or *Goddefs!* do I call thee *right?*
  " There-at fhe blufhing, faid, ah! gentle fquire,

Mira. No wonder, sir;
But, certainly a maid.
    Fer. My language! heavens!—
I am the best of them that speak this speech,
Were I but where 'tis spoken.

                                            Pro.
    " Nor *goddess* I, nor *angel*, but the *maid*
    " And *daughter* of a woody nymph," &c. FARMER.

The first copy reads—if you be *maid*, or no. *Made* was not suggested by Dr. Warburton, being an emendation introduced by the editor of the fourth folio. It was, I am persuaded, the author's word: There being no article prefixed adds strength to this supposition. Nothing is more common in his plays than a word being used in reply, in a sense different from that in which it was employed by the first speaker. Ferdinand had the moment before called Miranda a goddess; and the words immediately subjoined,—" Vouchsafe my prayer,"—show, that he looked up to her as a person of a superior order, and sought her protection, and instruction for his conduct, not her love. At *this* period, therefore, he must have felt too much awe to have flattered himself with the hope of possessing a being that appeared to him celestial; though afterwards, emboldened by what Miranda says, he exclaims, " O, if a virgin, &c." Words that appear inconsistent with the supposition that he had already asked her whether she was one or not. She had indeed told him, she was; but in his astonishment at hearing her speak his own language, he may well be supposed to have forgotten what she said; which, if he had himself made the inquiry, would not be very reasonable to suppose.

It appears from the alteration of this play by Dryden and Sir W. D'Avenant, that they considered the present passage in this light:

                    —— " Fair excellence,
    " If, as your form declares, you are divine,
    " Be pleas'd to instruct me, how you will be worship'd;
    " So bright a beauty cannot sure belong
    " To human kind."

In a subsequent scene we have again the same inquiry:

    Alon. Is she the *goddess* that hath sever'd us,
        And brought us thus together?
    Fer. Sir, she's *mortal*.

Our author might have remembered Lodge's description of Fawnia, the Perdita of his *Winter's Tale:* " Yet he scarce knew her, for she " had attired herself in rich apparel, which so increased her beauty, " that she resembled rather an *angel* than a *creature.*" *Dorastus and Fawnia,* 1592.

Again, in Lily's *Mayde's Metamorphoses,* 1600:

    " Well met, fair *nymph*, or *goddesse* if ye be."

So also, (as Dr. Farmer has observed) in Stanyhurst's translation of Virgil, 1583:

    " O to thee, faire virgin, what terme may rightly be fitted?
    " Thy tongue, thy visage, no *mortal* frayltie resembleth.
    " —— No doubt, a *goddesse!*" MALONE.

I have said " that nothing is more common in these plays than a word being used in reply in a sense different from that in which it was
                                                    employed

Pro. How! the best?
What wert thou, if the king of Naples heard thee?
Fer. A single thing, as I am now, that wonders
To hear thee speak of Naples: He does hear me;
And, that he does, I weep: myself am Naples;
Who with mine eyes, ne'er since at ebb, beheld
The king my father wreck'd.
Mira. Alack, for mercy!
Fer. Yes, faith, and all his lords; the duke of Milan,
And his brave son, being twain [7].
Pro. The duke of Milan,
And his more braver daughter, could control thee [8],
If now 'twere fit to do't:—At the first sight   [*Aside.*
They have chang'd eyes:—Delicate Ariel,
I'll set thee free for this.—A word, good sir;
I fear, you have done yourself some wrong [9]: a word.
Mira. Why speaks my father so ungently? This
Is the third man that I saw e'er; the first,
That e'er I sigh'd for: pity move my father,
To be inclin'd my way!
Fer. O, if a virgin,
And your affection not gone forth, I'll make you
The queen of Naples.

employed by the first speaker." Here follow my proofs. In *As you like it,* Orlando, being asked by his brother, " Now, sir, what *make* you here?" [i. e. What do you do here?] replies, " Nothing; I am not taught to *make* any thing." So in *K. Henry VI.* p. iii.

 "———— Henceforward will I bear
 " Upon my target three fair shining *suns.*
 " *Rich.* Nay, bear three *daughters.*"
Again, in *K. Henry IV.* p. ii.
 " *Ch. Just.* Your means are very slender, and your *waste great.*
 " *Fal.* I would it were otherwise, I would my means were greater, and my *waist* slenderer."
Again, in *K. Richard III.*
 " With this, my lord, myself hath *nought* to do.
 " *Glo. Naught* to do with mistress Shore?" &c. MALONE.

[7] *And his brave son, being twain.*] This is a slight forgetfulness. Nobody was lost in the wreck, yet we find no such character introduced in the fable as the son of the duke of Milan. THEOBALD.

[8] ———— *control thee,*] Confute thee, unanswerably contradict thee.
JOHNSON.

[9] *I fear, you have done yourself some wrong:*] i. e. I fear that in asserting yourself to be *king of Naples,* you have uttered a falsehood, which is below your character, and consequently injurious to your honour. So, in the *Merry Wives of Windsor:* " This is not well, master Ford, this *wrongs you.*" STEEVENS.

Pro. Soft, sir; one word more.—
They are both in either's powers: but this swift business
I must uneasy make, lest too light winning   [*Aside.*
Make the prize light.—One word more; I charge thee,
That thou attend me: thou doft here usurp
The name thou ow'st not; and hast put thyself
Upon this island, as a spy, to win it
From me, the lord on't.

Fer. No, as I am a man.

Mira. There's nothing ill can dwell in such a temple:
If the ill spirit have so fair an house,
Good things will strive to dwell with't.

Pro. Follow me.—   [*to* FERD.
Speak not you for him; he's a traitor.—Come.
I'll manacle thy neck and feet together:
Sea-water shalt thou drink, thy food shall be
The fresh-brook muscles, wither'd roots, and husks
Wherein the acorn cradled: Follow.

Fer. No;
I will resist such entertainment, till
Mine enemy has more power.   [*He draws.*

Mira. O dear father,
Make not too rash a trial of him, for
He's gentle, and not fearful [1].

Pro. What, I say,
My foot my tutor [2]! Put thy sword up, traitor;
Who mak'st a shew, but dar'st not strike, thy conscience
Is so possess'd with guilt: come from thy ward [3];
For I can here disarm thee with this stick,
And make thy weapon drop.

Mira. Beseech you, father!

Pro. Hence hang not on my garments.

---

[1] *He's gentle, and not fearful.*] i. e. terrible; producing fear. In our author's age *fearful* was much more frequently used in the sense of *formidable* than that of *timorous*.
  We have the same thought in Lily's *Euphues*, 1580: "Then how vain is it, that the *foot* should neglect his office, to correct the face!"
                                                            MALONE.

[2] *My foot my tutor!*] So, in the *Mirrour for Magistrates*, 1587, p. 163:
    "What honest heart would not conceive difdayne,
    "To see the *foot* surmount above the *head*?"   HENDERSON.

[3] *— come from thy ward;*] Desist from any hope of awing me by that posture of defence. JOHNSON.

Mira.

Mira. Sir, have pity;
I'll be his surety.
   Pro. Silence: one word more
Shall make me chide thee, if not hate thee. What,
An advocate for an impostor? hush!
Thou think'st, there are no more such shapes as he,
Having seen but him and Caliban; Foolish wench!
To the most of men this is a Caliban,
And they to him are angels.
   Mira. My affections
Are then most humble; I have no ambition
To see a goodlier man.
   Pro. Come on; obey: [*to* FERDINAND.
Thy nerves are in their infancy again [4],
And have no vigour in them.
   Fer. So they are:
My spirits, as in a dream, are all bound up [5].
My father's loss, the weakness which I feel,
The wreck of all my friends, or this man's threats,
To whom I am subdued, are but light to me [6],
Might I but through my prison once a day
Behold this maid: all corners else o' the earth
Let liberty make use of; space enough
Have I, in such a prison.
   Pro. It works:—Come on.—
Thou hast done well, fine Ariel!—Follow me.—
              [*to* FERD. *and* MIR.
Hark, what thou else shalt do me.   [*to* ARIEL.
   Mira. Be of comfort;
My father's of a better nature, Sir,
Than he appears by speech; this is unwonted,
Which now came from him.
   Pro. Thou shalt be as free

---

[4] *Thy nerves are in their infancy again,*] So Milton in his *Masque at Ludlow Castle*:
  " Thy nerves are all bound up in alabaster." STEEVENS.

[5] *My spirits, as in a dream, are all bound up,*] Alluding to a common sensation in dreams; when we struggle, but with a total impuissance in our endeavours, to run, strike, &c. WARBURTON.

[6] *— are but light to me,*] This passage, as it stands at present, with all allowances for poetical licence, cannot be reconciled to grammar. I suspect that our author wrote — " *were* but light to me," in the sense of —*would be.*—In the preceding line the old copy reads—*nor* this man's threats. The emendation was made by Mr. Steevens. MALONE.

C 5   A

As mountain winds: but then exactly do
All points of my command.
 Ari. To the syllable.
 Pro. Come, follow: speak not for him.   [*Exeunt.*

ACT II. SCENE I.

Another part of the island.

Enter ALONSO, SEBASTIAN, ANTHONIO, GONZALO, ADRIAN, FRANCISCO, *and Others.*

 Gon. Beseech you, Sir, be merry: you have cause
(So have we all) of joy; for our escape
Is much beyond our loss; Our hint of woe [7]
Is common; every day, some sailor's wife,
The masters of some merchant, and the merchant,
Have just our theme of woe: but for the miracle,
I mean our preservation, few in millions
Can speak like us: then wisely, good Sir, weigh
Ou sorrow with our comfort.
 Alon. Pr'ythee, peace.
 Seb. He receives comfort like cold porridge.
 Ant. The visitor [8] will not give him o'er so.
 Seb. Look, he's winding up the watch of his wit; by and by it will strike.
 Gon. Sir—
 Seb. One:—Tell.
 Gon. When every grief is entertain'd, that's offer'd, Comes to the entertainer—
 Seb. A dollar.

---

[7] *Our hint of woe*—] *Hint* is that which recalls to the memory. The cause that fills our minds with grief is common. JOHNSON

[8] *The visitor*—] Gonzalo gives not only advice, but comfort, and is therefore properly called *The visitor*, like others who visit the sick or distressed to give them consolation. In some of the Protestant churches there is a kind of officers termed Consolators for the sick. JOHNSON

                   Gon.

Gon. Dolour comes to him, indeed [9]; you have spoken truer than you purpos'd.
Seb. You have taken it wiselier than I meant you should.
Gon. Therefore, my lord—
Ant. Fie, what a spend-thrift is he of his tongue!
Alon. I pr'ythee, spare.
Gon. Well, I have done: But yet—
Seb. He will be talking.
Ant. Which of them, he, or Adrian, for a good wager, first begins to crow?
Seb. The old cock.
Ant. The cockrel.
Seb. Done: The wager?
Ant. A laughter.
Seb. A match.
Adr. Though this island seem to be desert—
Seb. Ha, ha, ha!
Ant. So, you've pay'd [1].
Adr. Uninhabitable, and almost inaccessible.
Seb. Yet,
Adr. Yet—
Ant. He could not miss it.
Adr. It must needs be of subtle, tender, and delicate temperance [2].
Ant. Temperance was a delicate wench [3].
Seb. Ay, and a subtle; as he most learnedly deliver'd.
Adr. The air breathes upon us here most sweetly.
Seb. As if it had lungs, and rotten ones.
Ant. Or, as 'twere perfum'd by a fen.
Gon. Here is every thing advantageous to life.
Ant. True; save means to live.
Seb. Of that there's none, or little.
Gon. How lush [4] and lusty the grass looks? how green?
Ant.

---

[9] Dolour *comes to him, indeed;*] The same quibble occurs in *the Tragedy of Hoffman,* 1637:
 " And his reward be thirteen hundred *dollars,*
 " For he hath driven *dolour* from our heart." STEEVENS.

[1] *— y—e pay'd.*] Old Copy—*you'r* paid. Corrected by Mr. Steevens. To *pay* sometimes signified—*to beat,* but I have never met with it in a metaphorical sense; otherwise I should have thought the reading of the folio right: you are *beaten;* you have *left.* MALONE.

[2] *temperance.*] *Temperance* here means *temperature.* STEEVENS.

[3] *Temperance was a delicate wench.*] In the puritanical times it was usual to christen children from the titles of religious and moral virtues.
 STEEVENS.

Ant. The ground, indeed, is tawny.
Seb. With an eye of green in't [5].
Ant. He misses not much.
Seb. No; he doth but mistake the truth totally.
Gon. But the rarity of it is, (which is indeed almost beyond credit)—
Seb. As many vouch'd rarities are.
Gon. That our garments, being, as they were, drench'd in the sea, hold notwithstanding their freshness, and glosses; being rather new dy'd, than stain'd with salt water.
Ant. If but one of his pockets could speak, would it not say, he lies?
Seb. Ay, or very falsely pocket up his report.
Gon. Methinks, our garments are now as fresh as when we put them on first in Africk, at the marriage of the king's fair daughter Claribel [*] to the king of Tunis.

Seb.

[4] *How* lush, &c.] *Lush*, i. e. of a *dark full* colour, the opposite to *pale* and *faint*. Sir T. HANMER.
The word is still used in the midland counties in this sense. Mr. Henley, however, is of opinion that *lush* here signifies—*rank*. So, in *A Midsummer Night's Dream*:
"Quite overcanopied with *luscious* woodbine."
I think Sir T. Hanmer's interpretation is right. MALONE.
The word *lush* has not yet been rightly interpreted. It appears from the following passage in Golding's translation of Ovid, 1587, to have signified *juicy*, *succulent*:

"What? seest thou not, how that the year, as representing plaine
"The age of man, departes himself in quarters foure: first, baine
"And tender in the spring it is, even like a sucking babe,
"Then greene and void of strength, and *lush* and *foggy* is the blade;
"And cheers the husbandman with hope."

Ovid's lines (M. t. xv) are these:
Quid? non in species succedere quattuor annum
Aspicis, ætatis peragentem imitamina nostræ?
Nam tener et lactens, puerique simillimus ævo,
Vere novo est. Tunc herba recens, et roboris expers,
Turget, et insolita est, et spe delectat agrestem.

Spenser, in his *Shepheard's Calender*, (Feb.) applies the epithet *lusty* to *green*:
"With leaves engrain'd in *lustie greene*." MALONE.

[5] *With an eye of green in't.*] An *eye* is a small shade of colour. STEEVENS.

[*] *Claribel*] Shakspeare might have found this name in the bl. l. *History of George Lord Faukenbridge*, a pamphlet that he probably read when he was writing *King John*. CLARIBEL is there the concubine of King Richard I. and the mother of Lord Falconbridge. MALONE.

Claribel

Seb. 'Twas a sweet marriage, and we prosper well in our return.

Adr. Tunis was never grac'd before with such a paragon to their queen.

Gon. Not since widow Dido's time.

Ant. Widow? a pox o' that! How came that widow in? Widow Dido [6]!

Seb What if he had said, widower Æneas too? good lord, how you take it!

Adr. Widow Dido, said you? you make me study of that: She was of Carthage, not of Tunis.

Gon. This Tunis, Sir, was Carthage.

Adr. Carthage?

Gon. I assure you, Carthage.

Ant. His word is more than the miraculous harp [7].

Seb. He hath rais'd the wall, and houses too.

Ant. What impossible matter will he make easy next?

Seb. I think, he will carry this island home in his pocket, and give it his son for an apple.

Ant. And, sowing the kernels of it in the sea, bring forth more islands.

Gon. Ay?

Ant. Why, in good time.

Gon. Sir, we were talking, that our garments seem now as fresh, as when we were at Tunis at the marriage of your daughter, who is now queen.

Claribel is also the mistress of Phaon in Spenser's *Faery Queen*, b. ii. c. iv. MALONE.

[6] —*Widow Dido!*] The name of a widow brings to their minds their own shipwreck, which they consider as having made many widows in Naples. JOHNSON.

Perhaps our author remembered " An inscription for the statue of Dido," copied from Ausonius, and inserted in *Davison's* Poems:

" O most unhappy *Dido*,
" Unhappy wife, and more unhappy *widow!*
" Unhappy in thy mate,
" And in thy lover more unfortunate! &c."

The edition from whence I have transcribed these lines was printed in 1621, but there was a former in 1608, and another some years before, as I collect from the following passage in a letter from Mr. John Chamberlain to Mr. Carlton, July 8, 1602: " It seems young Davison means to take another course, and turn poet, for he hath lately set out certain sonnets and epigrams." Chamberlain's Letters, vol. i. among Dr. Birch's Mss. in the British Museum. MALONE

[7] —*the miraculous harp.*] Alluding to the wonders of Amphion's music. STEEVENS.

Ant.

Ant. And the rareft that e'er came there.
Seb. Bate, I befeech you, widow Dido.
Ant. O, widow Dido; ay, widow Dido.
Gon. Is not, Sir, my doublet as frefh as the firft day I wore it? I mean, in a fort.
Ant. That fort was well fifh'd for.
Gon. When I wore it at your daughter's marriage?
Alon. You cram thefe words into mine ears, againft The ftomach of my fenfe [8] : 'Would I had never Marry'd my daughter there! for, coming thence, My fon is loft; and, in my rate, fhe too, Who is fo far from Italy remov'd, I ne'er again fhall fee her. O thou mine heir Of Naples and of Milan, what ftrange fifh Hath made his meal on thee!
Fran. Sir, he may live;
I faw him beat the furges under him,
And ride upon their backs; he trod the water,
Whofe enmity he flung afide, and breafted
The furge moft fwoln that met him: his bold head
'Bove the contentious wave he kept, and oar'd
Himfelf with his good arms in lufty ftroke
To the fhore, that o'er his wave-worn bafis bow'd,
As ftooping to relieve him: I not doubt,
He came alive to land.
Alon. No, no, he's gone.
Seb. Sir, you may thank yourfelf for this great lofs;
That would not blefs our Europe with your daughter,
But rather lofe her to an African;
Where fhe, at leaft, is banifh'd from your eye,
Who hath caufe to wet the grief on't.
Alon. Pr'ythee, peace.
Seb. You were kneel'd to, and importun'd otherwife
By all of us; and the fair foul herfelf
Weigh'd, between lothnefs and obedience, at
Which end o' the beam fhe'd bow [9]. We have loft your fon,

I fear,

---

[8] *The ftomach of my* fenfe: By *fenfe*, I believe is meant both *reafon* and *natural affection*. So, in *Meafure for Meafure*:

" Againft all *fenfe* do you importune her. STEEVENS.

[9] Weigh'd, *between lothnefs and obedience, at Which end o' the beam fhe'd bow.*] *Weigh'd* means *deliberated*. It is ufed in nearly the fame fenfe in *Love's Labour's Loft* and in *Hamlet*. The old copy reads—*fhould* bow. *Should* was probably an abbreviation
of

I fear, for ever: Milan and Naples have
More widows in them of this business' making,
Than we bring men to comfort them [1] : the fault's
Your own.

   Alon. So is the dearest o' the loss.

   Gon. My lord Sebastian,
The truth you speak doth lack some gentleness,
And time to speak it in: you rub the sore,
When you should bring the plaister.

   Seb. Very well.

   Ant. And most chirurgeonly.

   Gon. It is foul weather in us all, good Sir,
When you are cloudy.

   Seb. Foul weather?

   Ant. Very foul.

   Gon. Had I plantation of this isle, my lord,—

   Ant. He'd sow it with nettle-seed.

   Seb. Or docks, or mallows.

   Gon. And were the king of it, What would I do?

   Seb. 'Scape being drunk, for want of wine.

   Gon. I' the commonwealth I would by contraries
Execute all things: for no kind of traffick
Would I admit; no name of magistrate [2];
                                      Letters

of *she would*, the mark of elision being inadvertently omitted [*sh'ould*]. Thus *he has* is frequently exhibited in the first folio—*h'as*. Mr. Pope corrected the passage thus: "at which end the beam should bow." But omission of any word in the old copy, without substituting another in its place, is seldom safe, except in those instances where the repeated word appears to have been caught by the compositor's eye glancing on the line above, or below, or where a word is printed twice in the same line. MALONE.

[1] *Than we bring men to comfort them:*] It does not clearly appear whether the king and these lords thought the ship lost. This passage seems to imply, that they were themselves confident of returning, but imagined part of the fleet destroyed. Why, indeed, should Sebastian plot against his brother in the following scene, unless he knew how to find the kingdom which he was to inherit? JOHNSON.

[2] ——————— *for* no kind of traffic

Would I admit; no name of magistrate, &c.] Our author has here closely followed a passage in Montaigne's ESSAIES, translated by John Florio, folio, 1603: "It is a nation, (would I answer Plato,) that "hath *no kind of trafficke, no knowledge of letters*, no intelligence of num-
"bers, *no name of magistrate*, nor of *politick superioritie; no use of service*, "*of riches*, or of *povertie; no contracts, no successions, no partitions; no occu-*
"*pation, but idle;* no respect of kindred, but common; no apparel but "natural; *no use of wine, corn, or metal.* The very words that import
                                                   "lying,

Letters should not be known; riches, poverty,
And use of service, none; contract, succession,
Bourn, bound of land [3], tilth, vineyard, none [4]:
No use of metal, corn, or wine, or oil:

" lying, falsehood, *treason*, dissimulations, covetousness, envie, detrac-
" tion and pardon, were never heard amongst them." This passage
was pointed out by Mr. Capell, who knew so little of his author as to
suppose that Shakspeare had the original French before him, though he
has almost literally followed Florio's translation.

Montaigne is here speaking of a *newly discovered country* which he
calls " Antartick France." In the page preceding that already quoted
are these words: " The other testimonie of antiquitie to which some
" will refer the *discoverie* is in Aristotle, (if at least that little book of
" unheard-of wonders be his,) where he reporteth that certain Cartha-
" ginians having sailed athwart the Atlantick sea, without the strait of
" Gibraltar, discovered a great fertile ISLAND, all replenished with
" goodly woods, and deep rivers, farre distant from any land."

Whoever shall take the trouble to turn to the old translation here
quoted, will, I think, be of opinion that, in whatsoever novel our author might have found the *fable* of *the Tempest*, he was led by the perusal of this book to make the *scene* of it an unfrequented island. The title
of the chapter, which is—" *Of the Conniballes*," evidently furnished
him with the name of one of his characters. In his time almost every
proper name was twisted into an anagram. Thus, " *I moyl in law*,"
was the anagram of the laborious William Noy, Attorney General to
Charles I. By inverting this process, and transposing the letters of the
word *Canibal*, Shakspeare (as Dr. Farmer long since observed) formed
the name of *Caliban*. MALONE.

[3] Bourn, *bound of land*, &c.] A *bourn*, in this place, signifies a *limit*,
a *meer*, a *land-mark*. STEEVENS.

[4] *And use of service, none; contract, succession,*
Bourn, bound of land, tilth, vineyard, none:] The defective metre of
the second of these lines affords a ground for believing that some word
was omitted at the press. Many of the defects however in our author's
metre have arisen from the words of one line being transferred to another. In the present instance the preceding line is redundant. Perhaps the words here, as in many other passages, have been shuffled out
of their places. We might read—

And use of service, none; succession,
Contract, bourn, bound of land, tilth, vineyard, none.

Succession being often used by Shakspeare as a quadrisyllable. It must
however be owned, that in the passage in Montaigne's Essays the words
contract and *succession* are arranged in the same manner as in the first
folio.

If the error did not happen in this way, *bourn* might have been used
as a dissyllable, and the word omitted at the press might have been
none:

—————contract, succession,
None; bourn, bound of land, tilth, vineyard, none. MALONE.

No occupation ; all men idle, all ;
And women too ; but innocent and pure :
No sovereignty :—
  Seb. And yet he would be king on't.
  Ant. The latter end of his commonwealth forgets the beginning.
  Gon. All things in common nature should produce
Without sweat or endeavour : treason, felony,
Sword, pike, knife, gun, or need of any engine [5],
Would I not have ; but nature should bring forth,
Of its own kind, all foizon [6], all abundance,
To feed my innocent people [7].
  Seb. No marrying 'mong his subjects?
  Ant. None, man : all idle ; whores, and knaves.
  Gon. I would with such perfection govern, Sir,
To excell the golden age [8].
  Seb. 'Save his majesty !
  Ant. Long live Gonzalo !
  Gon. And, do you mark me, Sir ?—
  Alon. Pr'ythee, no more ; thou dost talk nothing to me.
  Gon. I do well believe your highness ; and did it to minister occasion to these gentlemen, who are of such sensible and nimble lungs, that they always use to laugh at nothing.
  Ant. 'Twas you we laugh'd at.

[5] —*any* engine,] An *engine* is the *rack*. So, in *K. Lear :*
" —like an *engine*, wrench'd my frame of nature
" From the fix'd place."
It may, however, be used here in its common signification of instrument of war, or military machine. STEEVENS.
[6] —*all foizon*,] *Foison* or *Foizon* signifies plenty, *ubertas*. EDWARDS.
[7] ————————nature *should bring forth*,
Of its own kind, all foison, all abundance,
To feed my innocent people.] " And if notwithstanding, in divers
" fruits of those countries that were never tilled, we shall find that in
" respect of our's they are most excellent, and as delicate unto our taste,
" there is no reason Art should gain the point of our great and puissant
" mother, *Nature*." Montaigne's *Essaies*, ubi sup. MALONE.
[8] *I would with such perfection govern, Sir,*
To excell the golden age.] So Montaigne, ubi supra : " Me
" seemeth that what in those [newly discovered] nations we see by ex-
" perience, doth not only EXCEED *all the pictures wherewith licentious*
" *poesie hath proudly imbellished the* GOLDEN AGE, and all her quaint inven-
" tions to fain a happy condition of man, but also the conception and
" desire of philosophy." MALONE.

Gon.

Gon. Who, in this kind of merry fooling, am nothing to you: so you may continue, and laugh at nothing still.

Ant. What a blow was there given?

Seb. An it had not fallen flat-long.

Gon. You are gentlemen of brave mettle [9]; you would lift the moon out of her sphere, if she would continue in it five weeks without changing.

Enter ARIEL *invisible, playing solemn music.*

Seb. We would so, and then go a bat-fowling.

Ant. Nay, good my lord, be not angry.

Gon. No, I warrant you; I will not adventure my discretion so weakly. Will you laugh me asleep, for I am very heavy?

Ant. Go sleep, and hear us.

[*All sleep but* ALON. SEB. *and* ANT.

Al n. What, all so soon asleep! I wish mine eyes
Would, with themselves, shut up my thoughts: I find,
They are inclin'd to do so.

Seb. Please you, sir,
Do not omit the heavy offer of it:
It seldom visits sorrow; when it doth,
It is a comforter.

Ant. We two, my lord,
Will guard your person, while you take your rest,
And watch your safety.

Alon. Thank you: Wond'rous heavy.—

[ALONSO *sleeps.* Exit ARIEL.

Seb. What a strange drowsiness possesses them?

Ant. It is the quality o' the climate.

Seb. Why
Doth it not then our eye-lids sink? I find not
Myself dispos'd to sleep.

Ant. Nor I; my spirits are nimble.
They fell together all, as by consent;
They dropp'd, as by a thunder-stroke. What might,
Worthy Sebastian?—o. what might?—No more:—
And yet, methinks, I see it in thy face,
What thou should'st be: the occasion speaks thee; and

[9] —*of brave* mettle;] The old copy has—*metal.* The two words are frequently confounded in the first folio. The epithet, *brave,* shews clearly, that the word now placed in the text was intended by our author. MALONE.

My

My strong imagination sees a crown
Dropping upon thy head.
  Seb. What, art thou waking?
  Ant. Do you not hear me speak?
  Seb. I do; and, surely,
It is a sleepy language; and thou speak'st
Out of thy sleep: What is it thou did'st say?
This is a strange repose, to be asleep
With eyes wide open; standing, speaking, moving,
And yet so fast asleep.
  Ant. Noble Sebastian,
Thou let'st thy fortune sleep, die rather; wink'st
Whiles thou art waking.
  Seb. Thou dost snore distinctly;
There's meaning in thy snores.
  Ant. I am more serious than my custom: you
Must be so too, if heed me; which to do,
Trebles thee o'er [1].
  Seb. Well; I am standing water.
  Ant. I'll teach you how to flow.
  Seb. Do so: to ebb,
Hereditary sloth instructs me.
  Ant. O,
If you but knew, how you the purpose cherish,
Whilst thus you mock it! how, in stripping it,
You more invest it! Ebbing men, indeed,
Most often do so near the bottom run,
By their own fear, or sloth.
  Seb. Pr'ythee, say on,
The setting of thine eye, and cheek, proclaim
A matter from thee; and a birth, indeed,
Which throes thee much to yield.

---

[1] *I am more serious than my custom; you Must be so too, if heed me; which to do Trebles thee o'er.*] You must put on more than your usual seriousness, if you are disposed to pay a proper attention to my proposal; which attention if you bestow, it will in the end make you *thrice w' at* you are Sebastian is already brother to the throne; but being made a king by Anthonio's contrivance, would be (according to our author's idea of greatness) *thrice* the man he was before. In this sense he would be *trebled* o'er. So, in *Pericles,* 1609:
"——— the master calls,
"And *trebles* the confusion." STEEVENS.
Again, in the *Merchant of Venice:*
"——— Yet, for you,
"I would be *trebled* twenty times myself." MALONE.

  Ant.

Ant. Thus, Sir,
Although this lord of weak remembrance [2], this,
(Who shall be of as little memory,
When he is earth'd,) hath here almost perfuaded
(For he's a spirit of perfuasion, only
Profeffes to perfuade [3],) the king, his son's alive;
'Tis as impoffible that he's undrown'd,
As he, that fleeps here, swims.

Seb. I have no hope
That he's undrown'd.

Ant. O, out of that no hope,
What great hope have you! no hope, that way, is
Another way fo high an hope, that even
Ambition cannot pierce a wink beyond [4],
But doubts difcovery there. Will you grant, with me,
That Ferdinand is drown'd?

Seb. He's gone.

Ant. Then, tell me,
Who's the next heir of Naples?

Seb. Claribel.

Ant. She that is queen of Tunis; she that dwells
Ten leagues beyond man's life; she that from Naples
Can have no note [5], unlefs the fun were poft,

---

[2] — *this lord of weak remembrance,*] This lord, who, being now in his dotage, has outlived his faculty of remembering; and who, once laid in the ground, shall be as little remembered himfelf, as he can now remember other things. JOHNSON.

[3] *(For he's a fpirit of perfuafion, only*
Profeffes to perfuade,)] He is one who profeffes the art of perfuafion, and profeffes nothing elfe. STEEVENS.
So in *Troilus and Creffida:* " —— why he'll anfwer nobody, he *profeffes* not anfwering. MALONE.

[4] — *a wink beyond,*] That this is the utmoft extent of the profpect of ambition, the point where the eye can pafs no farther, and where objects lofe their diftinctnefs, fo that what is there difcovered is faint, obfcure, and doubtful. JOHNSON.

[5] —— *she that from Naples*
Can have no note, *&c.*] *Note* is notice, or information. MALONE.
Shakfpeare's great ignorance of geography is not more confpicuous in any inftance than in this, where he fuppofes Tunis and Naples to have been at fuch an immeafurable diftance from each other. He may however be countenanced by *Apollonius Rhodius,* who fays, that both the *Rhone* and *Po* meet in one, and difcharge themfelves into the gulph of *Venice;* and by *Æfchylus,* who has placed the river *Eridanus* in *Spain.*
STEEVENS.

(The

(The man i' the moon's too flow,) till new-born chins
Be rough and razorable; she, from whom [6]
We all were sea-swallow'd, though some cast again [7];
And, by that destiny [8], to perform an act,
Whereof what's past is prologue; what to come,
In yours, and my discharge [9].
  Seb. What stuff is this?—How say you?
'Tis true, my brother's daughter's queen of Tunis;
So is she heir of Naples; 'twixt which regions
There is some space.
  Ant. A space whose every cubit
Seems to cry out, *How shall that Claribel
Measure us back to Naples?*—Keep in Tunis [1],
And let Sebastian wake!—Say, this were death
That now hath seiz'd them; why, they were no worse
Than now they are: There be, that can rule Naples,
As well as he that sleeps; lords, that can prate
As amply, and unnecessarily,
As this Gonzalo; I myself could make
A chough [2] of as deep chat. O, that you bore
The mind that I do! what a sleep were this
For your advancement? Do you understand me?
  Seb. Methinks, I do.
  Ant. And how does your content
Tender your own good fortune?
  Seb. I remember,
You did supplant your brother Prospero.
  Ant. True:
And, look, how well my garments fit upon me;

---

[6] *—she, from whom*] i. e. in coming from whom. The old copy has—*she that* from, &c.; which cannot be right. The compositor's eye probably glanced on a preceding line, "*she that* from Naples—." The emendation was made by Mr. Rowe. MALONE

[7] *— though some* cast *again;*] *Cast* is here used in the same sense as in *Macbeth*, act. ii. sc. 3 —" though he took my legs from me, I made a shift to *cast* him." STEEVENS.

[8] *And, by that* destiny,] It is a common plea of wickedness to call temptation destiny. JOHNSON.

[9] *In yours, and my discharge.*] i. e. Depends on what you and I are to perform. STEEVENS.

[1] *—Keep in Tunis,*] Claribel, (says he) *keep where thou art, and allow Sebastian time to awaken those senses, by the help of which he may perceive the advantage which now presents itself.* STEEVENS.

[2] A *chough* is a bird of the jack-daw kind. STEEVENS.

TEMPEST.

Much feater than before: My brother's servants
Were then my fellows, now they are my men.

Seb. But, for your conscience—

Ant. Ay, Sir; where lies that? if it were a kybe,
'Twould put me to my slipper; but I feel not
This deity in my bosom: twenty consciences,
That stand 'twixt me and Milan, candy'd be they,
And melt, ere they molest [3]! Here lies your brother,
No better than the earth he lies upon,
If he were that which now he's like, that's, dead [4];
Whom I with this obedient steel, three inches of it,
Can lay to bed for ever: whiles you, doing thus,
To the perpetual wink for aye [5] might put
This ancient morsel [6], this Sir Prudence, who
Should not upbraid our course. For all the rest,
They'll take suggestion [7], as a cat laps milk;
They'll tell the clock to any business that
We say befits the hour.

Seb. Thy case, dear friend,
Shall be my precedent; as thou got'st Milan,
I'll come by Naples. Draw thy sword: one stroke
Shall free thee from the tribute which thou pay'st;
And I the king shall love thee.

Ant. Draw together:
And when I rear my hand, do you the like,
To fall it on Gonzalo.

Seb. O, but one word.   [*They converse apart.*

Music. Re-enter ARIEL *invisible.*

Ari. My master through his art foresees the danger

---

[3] *———candy'd be they,*
And melt, ere they molest!] i. e. Let twenty consciences be first
congealed, and then dissolved, ere they molest me, or prevent me from
executing my purposes. MALONE.

[4] *— that's, dead;*] *That's* is not here used for *who is*, but (as Mr.
Steevens has observed) for "*id est.*" *If he were that which now he's
like*, that is to say, *dead.* MALONE.

[5] — *for aye*]— i. e. for ever. STEEVENS.

[6] *This ancient morsel,*] So we say a *piece of a man.* JOHNSON.
So, in *Measure for Measure:*
"How doth my dear *morsel*, thy mistress?" STEEVENS.
So, in *Antony and Cleopatra:*
"———— I found thee as a *morsel* cold.
"Upon dead Cæsar's trencher." MALONE.

[7] —*take suggestion,*] i. e. receive any hint of villainy. JOHNSON.

That

That you, his friend, are in; and sends me forth,
For else his project dies, to keep them living⁸.

[*Sings in* Gonzalo's *ear.*

    While you here do snoring lie,
    Open-ey'd conspiracy
       His time doth take:
    If of life you keep a care,
    Shake off slumber, and beware:
       Awake! awake!

Ant. Then let us both be sudden.
Gon. Now, good angels, preserve the king! [*They wake.*
Alon. Why, how now, ho! awake! Why are you drawn⁹?
Wherefore this ghastly looking?
Gon. What's the matter?

---

⁸ —*to keep* them *living.*] By *them*, as the text now stands, Gonzalo and Alonzo must be understood. Dr. Johnson objects very justly to this passage. "As it stands, says he, at present, the sense is this. He sees *your* danger, and will therefore save *them*." He therefore would read —"That *these* his friends are in."
    The confusion has, I think, arisen from the omission of a single letter. Our author, I believe, wrote
        ———— and sends me forth,
For else his projects dies, to keep them living.
i. e. he has sent me forth, to keep his projects alive, which else would be destroyed by the murder of his friend Gonzalo.—The opposition between the life and death of a project appears to me much in Shakspeare's manner. So, in *Much ado about nothing*; What *life* is in that, to be the *death* of this marriage?"—the plural noun joined to a verb in the singular number is to be met with in almost every page of the first folio. So, to confine myself to the play before us, edit. 1623:
    "My old *bones akes.*"
Again, *ibid:*
    ———"At this hour
"*Lies* at my mercy all my *enemies.*"
Again, *ibid:*
    "His *tears runs* down his beard—."
Again: "What *cares* these *roarers* for the name of king?"
It was the common language of the time; and ought to be corrected, as indeed it generally has been in the modern editions of our author, by changing the number of the verb. Thus, in the present instance we should read—For else his projects *die*, &c. MALONE.

⁹ —*drawn?*] Having your swords drawn. So, in *Romeo and Juliet:*
    "What, art thou *drawn* among these heartless hinds!"
                                     JOHNSON.

Seb.

Seb. Whiles we stood here securing your repose,
Even now, we heard a hollow burst of bellowing
Like bulls, or rather lions; did it not wake you?
It struck mine ear most terribly.

Alon. I heard nothing.

Ant. O, 'twas a din to fright a monster's ear;
To make an earthquake! sure, it was the roar
Of a whole herd of lions.

Alon. Heard you this, Gonzalo?

Gon. Upon mine honour, Sir, I heard a humming,
And that a strange one too, which did awake me:
I shak'd you, Sir, and cry'd; as mine eyes open'd,
I saw their weapons drawn:—there was a noise,
That's verity[1]: 'Tis best we stand upon our guard:
Or that we quit this place: let's draw our weapons.

Alon. Lead off this ground: And let's make further search
For my poor son.

Gon. Heavens keep him from these beasts!
For he is, sure, i' the island.

Alon. Lead away.

Ari. Prospero my lord shall know what I have done:
[*Aside.*
So, king, go safely on to seek thy son. [*Exeunt.*

SCENE II.

Another part of the island.

Enter CALIBAN *with a burden of wood.*

A noise of thunder heard.

Cal. All the infections that the sun sucks up
From bogs, fens, flats, on Prosper fall, and make him
By inch-meal a disease! His spirits hear me,
And yet I needs must curse. But they'll nor pinch,
Fright me with urchin shows, pitch me i' the mire,
Nor lead me, like a fire-brand, in the dark
Out of my way, unless he bid 'em; but
For every trifle are they set upon me;
Sometime like apes, that moe[2] and chatter at me,
And after, bite me; then like hedge-hogs, which

---

[1] *That's verity:*] The old copy reads, that's *verily.* STEEVENS.
The emendation was made by Mr. Pope. MALONE.

[2] *that moe*] i. e. Make mouths STEEVENS.

Lie tumbling in my bare-foot way, and mount
Their pricks at my foot-fall; sometime am I
All wound with adders [3], who, with cloven tongues,
Do hiss me into madness;—Lo! now! lo!

Enter TRINCULO.

Here comes a spirit of his; and to torment me,
For bringing wood in slowly: I'll fall flat;
Perchance, he will not mind me.

Trin. Here's neither bush nor shrub, to bear off any weather at all, and another storm brewing; I hear it sing i' the wind: yond' same black cloud, yond' huge one, looks like a foul bumbard [4] that would shed his liquor. If it should thunder, as it did before, I know not where to hide my head: yond' same cloud cannot choose but fall by pailfuls.—What have we here? a man or a fish? Dead or alive? A fish: he smells like a fish; a very antient and fish-like smell; a kind of, not of the newest, Poor-John. A strange fish! Were I in England now, (as once I was,) and had but this fish painted [5], not a holiday fool there but would give a piece of silver: there would this monster make a man [6]; any strange beast there makes a man: when they will not give a doit to relieve a lame beggar, they will lay out ten to see a dead Indian [7]. Legg'd like a man! and his fins like arms! Warm, o' my troth! I do now let loose my opinion, hold it no longer; this is no fish, but an islander, that hath lately suffer'd by a thunder-bolt. [*Thunder.*] Alas! the storm is come again: my best way is to creep under his gaberdine [8];

there

---

[3] — *wound* with adders,] Enwrapped by adders *wound* or twisted about me. JOHNSON.

[4] — *a foul* bumbard—] A large vessel for holding drink. THEOBALD.
Mr. Upton would read— a *full* bumbard. See a note on—" I thank the Gods, I am *foul*;" *As you like it*, act. iii sc. iii. MALONE.

[5] —*this fish painted*,] To exhibit fishes, either real or imaginary, was very common about the time of our author. STEEVENS.

[6] —*make a man*;] That is, make a man's fortune. So, in *Midsummer Night's Dream*;—" we are all *made men*." JOHNSON.

[7] —*a dead Indian*.] And afterwards—*Men of Inde*. Probably some allusion to a particular occurrence, now obscured by time. In *Henry VIII*. the *porter* asks the mob, if they think—*some strange Indian*, &c. *is come to court*—In the year 1577 was entered on the books of the Stationers' Company, " A description of the purtrayture and shape of " those strange kinde of people whiche the wurthie Mr. Martin Four- " bosier brought into England in A°. 1576. STEEVENS.

[8] —*his gaberdine*;] A *gaberdine* is properly the coarse frock or outward

there is no other shelter hereabout: Misery acquaints a man with strange bedfellows: I will here shroud, till the dregs of the storm be past.

Enter STEPHANO, *singing; a bottle in his hand.*

Ste. *I shall no more to sea, to sea,*
  Here shall I die a-shore;—

This is a very scurvy tune to sing at a man's funeral: Well, here's my comfort. [*drinks.*

The master, the swabber, the boatswain, and I,
  The gunner, and his mate,
Lov'd Mall, Meg, and Marian, and Margery,
  But none of us car'd for Kate:

For she had a tongue with a tang,
Would cry to a sailor, Go hang:
She lov'd not the savour of tar nor of pitch,
Yet a tailor might scratch her where-e'er she did itch:
Then to sea, boys, and let her go hang.

This is a scurvy tune too: But here's my comfort. [*drinks.*
Cal. Do not torment me: Oh!
Ste. What's the matter? Have we devils here? Do you put tricks upon us with savages, and men of Inde? Ha! I have not 'scap'd drowning, to be afeard now of your four legs; for it hath been said, As proper a man as ever went upon four legs cannot make him give ground: and it shall be said so again, while Stephano breathes at nostrils.
Cal. The spirit torments me: Oh!
Ste. This is some monster of the isle, with four legs; who hath got, as I take it, an ague: Where the devil should he learn our language? I will give him some relief, if it be but for that: If I can recover him, and keep him tame, and get to Naples with him, he's a present for any emperor that ever trod on neats-leather.

---

ward garment of a peasant. *Gaberdina,* Spanish. The *gaberdine* is still worn by the peasants in Sussex. STEEVENS.

It here however means, I believe, a loose felt cloak. Minsheu in his DICT. 1617, calls it " a rough Irish mantle, or horseman's coat. *Gaban,* Span. and Fr.—*Læna, i. e.* vestis quæ super cætera vestimenta imponebatur." See also Cotgrave's DICT. in v. *gaban,* and *galleverdine.* MALONE.

Cal.

Cal. Do not torment me, pr'ythee; I'll bring my wood home faster.

Ste. He's in his fit now; and does not talk after the wisest: He shall taste of my bottle: if he have never drunk wine afore, it will go near to remove his fit: if I can recover him, and keep him tame, I will not take too much [9] for him; he shall pay for him that hath him, and that soundly.

Cal. Thou dost me yet but little hurt; thou wilt anon, I know it by thy trembling [1]: Now Prosper works upon thee.

Ste. Come on your ways; open your mouth; here is that which will give language to you, cat [2]; open your mouth: this will shake your shaking, I can tell you, and that soundly: you cannot tell who's your friend; open your chaps again.

Trin. I should know that voice: It should be—But he is drown'd; and these are devils: O! defend me!

Ste. Four legs, and two voices; a most delicate monster! His forward voice [3] now is to speak well of his friend; his backward voice is to utter foul speeches, and to detract. If all the wine in my bottle will recover him, I will help his ague: Come,—Amen [4]! I will pour some in thy other mouth.

Trin. Stephano,—

Ste. Doth thy other mouth call me? Mercy! mercy!

---

[9] —*too much*—] *Too much* means *any sum, ever so much*. It has, however been observed to me that when the vulgar mean to ask an extravagant price for any thing, they say with a laugh, I won't make him pay twice for it. This sense sufficiently accommodates itself to Trinculo's expression. STEEVENS.

I think the meaning is, Let me take what sum I will, however great, *I shall not take too much for him*: it is impossible for me to sell him too dear. These words, however, may mean (as Mr. Mason has observed) " I will not take for him even more than he is worth."
MALONE.

[1] —*I know it by thy trembling:*] This *tremor* is always represented as the effect of being possess'd by the devil. So, in the *Comedy of Errors:*
" Mark how he *trembles* in his ecstacy!" STEEVENS.

[2] ——*cat;*] Alluding to an old proverb, that *good liquor will make a cat speak.* STEEVENS.

[3] *His forward voice,* &c.] The person of Fame was anciently described in this manner. STEEVENS.

[4] —*Amen!*] Means, stop your draught; come to a conclusion. *I will pour some,* &c. STEEVENS.

This is a devil, and no monster: I will leave him ; I have no long spoon [5].

Trin. Stephano!—if thou beest Stephano, touch me, and speak to me ; for I am Trinculo ;—be not afeard,—thy good friend Trinculo.

Ste. If thou beest Trinculo, come forth, I'll pull thee by the lesser legs : if any be Trinculo's legs, these are they. Thou art very Trinculo, indeed : How cam'st thou to be the siege of this moon-calf [6] ? Can he vent Trinculos?

Trin. I took him to be kill'd with a thunder-stroke :— But art thou not drown'd, Stephano? I hope now, thou art not drown'd. Is the storm over-blown? I hid me under the dead moon-calf's gaberdine, for fear of the storm : And art thou living, Stephano? O Stephano, two Neapolitans 'scap'd!

Ste. Pry'thee, do not turn me about; my stomach is not constant.

Cal. These be fine things, an if they be not sprights. That's a brave god, and bears celestial liquor :
I will kneel to him.

Ste. How did'st thou 'scape? How cam'st thou hither? swear by this bottle, how thou cam'st hither. I escap'd upon a butt of sack, which the sailors heav'd over-board, by this bottle! which I made of the bark of a tree, with mine own hands, since I was cast a-shore.

Cal. I'll swear, upon that bottle, to be thy true-subject ; for the liquor is not earthly.

Ste. Here ; swear then how thou escap'dst.

Trin. Swam a-shore, man, like a duck ; I can swim [7] like a duck, I'll be sworn.

Ste. Here, kiss the book : Though thou can'st swim like a duck, thou art made like a goose.

---

[5] *I have no long spoon.*] Alluding to the proverb, *A long spoon to eat with the devil.* STEEVENS.

See *Com. of Errors*, act iv. sc. iii. and Chaucer's *Squier's Tale*, ver. 10916 of the late edit.

" Therefore behoveth him a ful long spone,
" That shall ete with a fend." TYRWHITT.

[6] *—to be the siege of this moon-calf?*] *Siege* signifies *stool* in every sense of the word, and is here used in the dirtiest. A *moon-calf* is an inanimate shapeless mass, supposed by Pliny to be engendered of woman only. See his Nat. Hist. b. x. ch. 64. STEEVENS.

[7] *I can swim—*] I believe Trinculo is speaking of Caliban, and that we should read—" 'a can swim" &c. See the next speech. MALONE.

Trin.

Trin. O Stephano, hast any more of this?

Ste. The whole butt, man; my cellar is in a rock by the sea-side, where my wine is hid. How now, moon-calf? how does thine ague?

Cal. Hast thou not dropp'd from Heaven [8]?

Ste. Out o' the moon, I do assure thee: I was the man in the moon, when time was.

Cal. I have seen thee in her, and I do adore thee: my mistress shew'd me thee, and thy dog, and thy bush.

Ste. Come, swear to that; kiss the book: I will furnish it anon with new contents: swear.

Trin. By this good light this is a very shallow monster:—I afeard of him?—a very weak monster [9]:—The man i' the moon?—a most poor credulous monster:—Well drawn, monster, in good sooth.

Cal. I'll shew thee every fertile inch o' the island; And I will kiss thy foot [1]: I pr'ythee, be my god.

Trin. By this light, a most perfidious and drunken monster; when his god's asleep, he'll rob his bottle.

Cal. I'll kiss thy foot: I'll swear myself thy subject.

Ste. Come on then; down, and swear.

Trin. I shall laugh myself to death at this puppy-headed monster: A most scurvy monster! I could find in my heart to beat him,—

Ste. Come, kiss.

Trin. —but that the poor monster's in drink: An abominable monster!

Cal. I'll shew thee the best springs; I'll pluck thee berries; I'll fish for thee, and get thee wood enough.

---

[8] *Hast thou not dropp'd from heaven?*] The new-discovered Indians of the Island of St. Salvador asked, by signs, whether Columbus and his companions *were not come down from heaven*. TOLLET.

[9] *I afeard of him?—a very weak monster:*] It is to be observed, that Trinculo the speaker is not charged with being afraid; but it was his consciousness that drew this brag from him. This is nature.

WARBURTON.

[1] —*kiss thy foot:*] This is a common expression, to denote profound obeisance. So, in *Timon of Athens:*

"Follow his strides, his lobbies fill with tendance,—
"Make sacred even his *stirrop*, and through him
"Drink the free air."

Again, in *Titus Andronicus:* "— When you come to him, [the emperor,] at the first approach, you must kneel, *then kiss his foot*, then deliver your pigeons." MALONE.

A plague upon the tyrant that I serve!
I'll bear him no more sticks, but follow thee,
Thou wond'rous man.

Trin. A most ridiculous monster; to make a wonder of a poor drunkard.

Cal. I pr'ythee, let me bring thee where crabs grow;
And I with my long nails will dig thee pig-nuts;
Shew thee a jay's nest, and instruct thee how
To snare the nimble marmozet; I'll bring thee
To clust'ring filberds, and sometimes I'll get thee
Young sea-mels [2] from the rock: Wilt thou go with me?

Ste. I pr'ythee now, lead the way, without any more talking.—Trinculo, the king and all our company else being drown'd, we will inherit here.—Here; bear my bottle! Fellow Trinculo, we'll fill him by and by again.

Cal. *Farewell master; farewell, farewell.*

[*Sings drunkenly.*]

Trin. A howling monster; a drunken monster.

---

[2] *Young sea-mels—*] The old copy reads—*scamels*. Mr. Holt asserted that *limpets* are in some places called *scams*. But not having found the word *scamel* in any ancient English book, I have adopted the emendation proposed by Mr. Theobald. Mr. Steevens's observation on the epithet "*young*" appears to me decisive. In Lincolnshire, as I learn from Sir Joseph Banks, the name *sea-mall* is applied to all the smaller species of gulls. Plott, the same gentleman adds, in his *History of Staffordshire,* p. 231, gives an account of the mode of taking a species of gull, called in that country Pewits, (the black-capped gull of Lincolnshire) with a plate annexed, at the end of which he writes—" they being accounted a good dish at the most plentiful tables."
With respect to the place from which Caliban says he will fetch these young sea-mels, or sea-mews, Shakspeare might have learned from Pliny's *Natural History,* 1600, (a book that he is known to have looked into,) " As touching the gulls or *sea-cobs,* they build in *rockes.*" p. 287.
MALONE.

Theobald very reasonably proposed to read *sea-malls,* or *sea-mells.* An *e* by these careless printers was easily changed into a *c,* and from this accident, I believe, all the difficulty arises, the word having been spelt by the transcriber *sea-mels.* Willoughby mentions the bird, as Theobald informs us [*larus cinereus minor*].—Had Mr. Holt told us in what part of England limpets are called *scams,* more attention would have been paid to his assertion.

I should suppose, at all events, a *bird* to have been design'd, as *young* and *old fish* are taken with equal facility; but *young birds* are more easily surprised than *old ones.* Besides, Caliban had already proffered to *fish* for Trinculo. In Cavendish's second voyage, the sailors eat *young gulls* at the isle of Penguins. STEEVENS.

Cal.

Cal. *No more dams I'll make for fish ;*
    Nor fetch in firing
    At requiring,
  Nor scrape trenchering [3], *nor wash dish ;*
  *'Ban, 'Ban, Ca—Caliban,**
  Has a new master—Get a new man.

Freedom, hey-day! hey-day, freedom! freedom, hey-day, freedom!

Ste. O brave monster! lead the way.   [*Exeunt.*

ACT III. SCENE I.

Before Prospero's *Cell.*

Enter FERDINAND, *bearing a log.*

Fer. There be some sports are painful [4] ; and their labour
Delight in them sets off [5]: some kinds of baseness

                                      Are

---

[3] *Nor scrape* trenchering,] In our author's time trenchers were in general use; and male domestics were sometimes employed in cleansing them. " I have helped (says Lily, in his *History of his life and times,* ad an. 1620,) to carry eighteen tubs of water in one morning;—all manner of drudgery I willingly performed; *scrape trenchers,* &c."
                                                  MALONE.

* *'Ban, 'Ban, Ca—Caliban.*] Perhaps our author remembered a song of Sir P. Sidney's:
    " Da, da, da —Daridan."
      Astrophel and Stella, fol. 1627. MALONE.

[4] *There be some sports are* painful; *and their* labour
  Delight *in them sets off:*]
      Molliter austerum studio fallente laborem.
                       Hor. sat. 2. lib. ii. STEEVENS.
We have again the same thought in *Macbeth* :
  " The *labour we delight* in physicks *pain.*"
After " and," *at the same time* must be understood. Mr. Pope, unnecessarily, reads—" *But* their labour—," which has been followed by the subsequent editors.
  In like manner, in *Coriolanus,* act iv. the same change was made by him. " I am a Roman, *and* (i. e. and *yet*) my services are, as you are, against them." Mr. Pope reads——" I am a Roman, *but* my services, &c. MALONE.

Are nobly undergone; and moſt poor matters
Point to rich ends. This my mean taſk would be [5]
As heavy to me, as odious; but
The miſtreſs, which I ſerve, quickens what's dead,
And makes my labours pleaſures: O, ſhe is
Ten times more gentle, than her father's crabbed;
And he's compoſed of harſhneſs. I muſt remove
Some thouſands of theſe logs, and pile them up,
Upon a ſore injunction: My ſweet miſtreſs
Weeps when ſhe ſees me work; and ſays, ſuch baſeneſs
Had ne'er like executor. I forget [6]:
But theſe ſweet thoughts do even refreſh my labours;
Moſt buſy-leſs, when I do it [7].

Enter MIRANDA; *and* PROSPERO *at a diſtance.*

Mira. Alas, now! pray you,
Work not ſo hard: I would, the lightning had
Burnt up thoſe logs, that you are enjoin'd to pile!
Pray ſet it down, and reſt you: when this burns,
'Twill weep for having weary'd you: My father
Is hard at ſtudy; pray now, reſt yourſelf;
He's ſafe for theſe three hours.

Fer. O moſt dear miſtreſs,
The ſun will ſet before I ſhall diſcharge
What I muſt ſtrive to do.

Mira. If you'll ſit down,
I'll bear your logs the while: Pray, give me that;
I'll carry it to the pile.

Fer. No, precious creature:
I had rather crack my ſinews, break my back,
Than you ſhould ſuch diſhonour undergo,
While I ſit lazy by.

---

[5] *This my mean taſk would be*] The metre of this line is defective in the old copy, by the words *would be* being transferred to the next line. Our author and his contemporaries generally uſe *odious* as a triſyllable. MALONE.

[6] *I forget:*] Perhaps Ferdinand means to ſay—I forget *my taſk*; but *that is not ſurpriſing, for I am thinking on Miranda, and* theſe ſweet thoughts, &c. He may however mean, that he *forgets or thinks little of the baſeneſs of his employment.* Whichſoever be the ſenſe, *And,* or *For,* ſhould ſeem more proper in the next line, than *But.* MALONE.

[7] *Moſt buſy-leſs, when I do it.*] The old copy has—*buſy leſt.* Corrected by Mr. Theobald. MALONE.

Mira.

Mira. It would become me
As well as it does you: and I should do it
With much more ease; for my good will is to it,
And yours it is against [8].
 Pro. Poor worm! thou art infected;
This visitation shews it.
 Mira. You look wearily.
 Fer. No, noble mistress; 'tis fresh morning with me,
When you are by at night [9]. I do beseech you,
(Chiefly, that I might set it in my prayers,)
What is your name?
 Mira. Miranda:—O my father,
I have broke your hest [1] to say so!
 Fer. Admir'd Miranda!
Indeed, the top of admiration; worth
What's dearest to the world! Full many a lady
I have ey'd with best regard; and many a time
The harmony of their tongues hath into bondage
Brought my too diligent ear: for several virtues
Have I lik'd several women; never any
With so full soul, but some defect in her
Did quarrel with the noblest grace she ow'd,
And put it to the foil: But you, O you,
So perfect, and so peerless, are created
Of every creature's best [2].
 Mira. I do not know
One of my sex; no woman's face remember,
Save, from my glass, mine own; nor have I seen
More that I may call men, than you, good friend,
And my dear father: how features are abroad,
I am skill-less of; but, by my modesty,
(The jewel in my dower,) I would not wish
Any companion in the world but you;
Nor can imagination form a shape,

[8] *And yours it is against.*] Perhaps we should read, *And yours is it against.* STEEVENS.

[9] ——'*tis fresh morning with me,*
When you are by at night.]
 Tu mihi curarum requies, tu nocte vel atra
   Lumen——.
              Tibul. Lib. iv. El. xiii. MALONE.

[1] —*hest*] For *behest*; i. e. command. STEEVENS.

[2] *Of every creature's best.*] Alluding to the picture of Venus by Apelles. JOHNSON.

D 5   Besides

Besides yourself, to like of: But I prattle
Something too wildly, and my father's precepts
I therein do forget.

   Fer. I am, in my condition,
A prince, Miranda; I do think, a king;
(I would, not so!) and would no more endure
This wooden slavery, than I would suffer [3]
The flesh-fly blow my mouth*:—Hear my soul speak;—
The very instant that I saw you, did
My heart fly to your service; there resides,
To make me slave to it; and, for your sake,
Am I this patient log-man.

   Mira. Do you love me?

   Fer. O heaven, O earth, bear witness to this sound,
And crown what I profess with kind event,
If I speak true; if hollowly, invert
What best is boded me, to mischief! I,
Beyond all limit of what else i' the world [4],
Do love, prize, honour you.

   Mira. I am a fool [5],
To weep at what I am glad of.

                                                                          Pro.

---

[3] *—than I would suffer, &c.*] The old copy reads—Than to suffer. The emendation is Mr. Pope's. STEEVENS.

I have here, with all the modern editors, incautiously adopted an emendation made by Mr. Pope. But the reading of the old copy—than to suffer—is right, however ungrammatical. So, in *All's well that ends well:* "No more of this, Helena, go to, no more; lest it be rather thought you affect a sorrow, *than to have.*" MALONE.

* *The flesh-fly blow my mouth:*] i. e. swell and inflame my mouth. So in *Antony and Cleopatra:*
   "Here is a vent of blood, and something *blown.*"
Again, *ibidem:*
   "———— and let the water-flies
   "*Blow* me into abhorring." MALONE.

[4] *—of what else i' the world,*] i. e. of aught else; of whatsoever else there is in the world. I once thought that we should read—*aught* else. But the old copy is right. So, in *King Henry VI.* P. iii:
   "With promise of his sister, and *what else,*
   "To strengthen and support king Edward's place." MALONE.

[5] *I am a fool,*
To weep at what I am glad of.] This is one of those touches of nature that distinguish Shakspeare from all other writers. It was necessary, in support of the character of Miranda, to make her appear unconscious that excess of sorrow and excess of joy find alike their relief from tears; and as this is the first time that consummate pleasure had made any near approaches to her heart, she calls such a seeming contradictory expression of it, *folly.*

                                                                          The

Pro. Fair encounter
Of two moſt rare affections! Heavens rain grace
On that which breeds between them!
 Fer. Wherefore weep you?
 Mira. At mine unworthineſs, that dare not offer
What I deſire to give; and much leſs take
What I ſhall die to want: But this is trifling;
And all the more it ſeeks[6] to hide itſelf,
The bigger bulk it ſhews. Hence baſhful cunning!
And prompt me, plain and holy innocence!
I am your wife, if you will marry me[7];
If not, I'll die your maid: to be your fellow[8]
You may deny me; but I'll be your ſervant,
Whether you will or no.
 Fer. My miſtreſs, deareſt,
And I thus humble ever.
 Mira. My huſband then?
 Fer. Ay, with a heart as willing
As bondage e'er of freedom: here's my hand.
 Mira. And mine, with my heart in't[9]: And now fare
   well,

The ſame thought occurs in *Romeo and Juliet:*
 " Back, fooliſh tears, back to your native ſpring!
 " Your tributary drops belong to woe,
 " Which you, miſtaking, offer up to joy." STEEVENS.
[5] —it ſeeks—] i. e. my affection ſeeks. MALONE.
[7] *I am your wife, if you will marry me,* &c.]
  Si tibi non cordi fuerant connubia noſtra,
  Attamen in veſtras potuiſti ducere ſedes,
  Quæ tibi jucundo famularer ſerva labore;
  Candida permulcens liquidis veſtigia lymphis,
  Purpureave tuum conſternens veſte cubile.
         Catul. 62. MALONE.
[8] —*your fellow,*] i. e. companion. STEEVENS.
[9] Ferd. ——— *here's my hand.*
  Mira. *And mine, with my heart in't.*] It is ſtill cuſtomary in the
weſt of England, when the conditions of a bargain are agreed upon,
for the parties to ratify it by joining their hands, and at the ſame time
for the purchaſer to give an earneſt. To this practice the poet alludes.
So, in *the Winter's Tale:*
 " Ere I could make thee open thy white hand,
 " And clap thyſelf my love; then didſt thou utter
 " *I am your's for ever.*"
Again, in *the Two Gent. of Verona:*
 " *Pro.* Why then we'll make exchange; here, take you this.
 " *Jul.* And ſeal the bargain with a holy kiſs.
 " *Pro.* Here is my hand for my true conſtancy." HENLEY.

Till half an hour hence.

Fer. A thousand, thousand! [*Exeunt* FER. *and* MIR.

Pro. So glad of this as they, I cannot be, Who are surpriz'd with all; but my rejoicing At nothing can be more. I'll to my book; For yet, ere supper-time, must I perform Much business appertaining. [*Exit.*

SCENE II.

Another part of the island.

Enter STEPHANO *and* TRINCULO; CALIBAN *following with a bottle.*

Ste. Tell not me;—when the butt is out, we will drink water; not a drop before: therefore bear up, and board 'em¹: Servant-monster, drink to me.

Trin. Servant-monster? the folly of this island! They say, there's but five upon this isle: we are three of them; if the other two be brain'd like us, the state totters.

Ste. Drink, servant-monster, when I bid thee; thy eyes are almost set in thy head.

Trin. Where should they be set else; he were a brave monster indeed, if they were set in his tail².

Ste. My man-monster hath drown'd his tongue in sack: for my part, the sea cannot drown me: I swam³, ere I could recover the shore, five-and-thirty leagues, off and on,

---

¹ *Bear up, and board 'em:*] A metaphor alluding to a chace at sea.
                                                                  SIR J. HAWKINS.

² *He were a brave monster indeed, if they were set in his tail.*] I believe this to be an allusion to a story that is met with in *Stowe*, and other writers of the time. It seems, in the year 1574, a whale was thrown ashore near *Ramsgate.* "A monstrous fish (says the chronicle) "but not so monstrous as some reported,—for his eyes were in his head, "and not in his back." *Summary*, 1575, p. 562. FARMER.

³ *I swam,* &c.] This play was not published till 1623. *Albumazar* made its appearance in 1614, and has a passage relative to the escape of a sailor yet more incredible. Perhaps, in both instances, a sneer was meant at the *Voyages of Ferdinando Mendez Pinto*, or the exaggerated accounts of other lying travellers:

"—five days I was under water; and at length
"Got up and spread myself upon a chest,
"Rowing with arms, and steering with my feet,
"And thus in five days more got land." Act iii. sc. v.
                                                              STEEVENS.

by

by this light.—Thou shalt be my lieutenant, monster, or my standard.

Trin. Your lieutenant, if you list; he's no standard [4].

Ste. We'll not run, monsieur monster.

Trin. Nor go neither: but you'll lie, like dogs; and yet say nothing neither.

Ste. Moon-calf, speak once in thy life, if thou beest a good moon-calf.

Cal. How does thy honour? Let me lick thy shoe; I'll not serve him, he is not valiant.

Trin. Thou liest, most ignorant monster; I am in case to justle a constable: Why, thou debosh'd [5] fish, thou, was there ever man a coward, that hath drunk so much sack as I to-day? Wilt thou tell a monstrous lie, being but half a fish, and half a monster?

Cal. Lo, how he mocks me; wilt thou let him, my lord?

Trin. Lord, quoth he!—that a monster should be such a natural!

Cal. Lo, lo, again: bite him to death, I pr'ythee.

Ste. Trinculo, keep a good tongue in your head; if you prove a mutineer, the next tree—The poor monster's my subject, and he shall not suffer indignity.

Cal. I thank my noble lord. Wilt thou be pleas'd to hearken once again to the suit I made to thee?

Ste. Marry will I: kneel, and repeat it; I will stand, and so shall Trinculo.

Enter ARIEL, *invisible.*

Cal. As I told thee before, I am subject to a tyrant; a sorcerer, that by his cunning has cheated me of the island.

Ari. Thou liest.

Cal. Thou liest, thou jesting monkey, thou:
I would, my valiant master would destroy thee:
I do not lie.

Ste. Trinculo, if you trouble him any more in his tale, by this hand, I will supplant some of your teeth.

Trin. Why, I said nothing.

---

[4] *Your lieutenant, if you list; he's no standard.*] Meaning, he is so much intoxicated, as not to be able to stand. The quibble between *standard,* an ensign, and *standard,* a fruit tree, that grows without support, is evident. STEEVENS.

[5] —*thou debosh'd*—] i. e. *debauched.* See Cotgrave's DICT. in v.
MALONE.

Ste.

Ste. Mum then, and no more;—proceed.

Cal. I say, by sorcery he got this isle; from me he got it. If thy greatness will revenge it on him,—for, I know, thou dar'st; but this thing dare not—

Ste. That's most certain.

Cal. Thou shalt be lord of it, and I'll serve thee.

Ste. How now shall this be compass'd? Can'st thou bring me to the party?

Cal. Yea, yea, my lord; I'll yield him thee asleep, where thou may'st knock a nail into his head.

Ari. Thou liest, thou canst not.

Cal. What a py'd ninny's this[6]? Thou scurvy patch!—I do beseech thy greatness, give him blows, and take his bottle from him: when that's gone, he shall drink nought but brine; for I'll not shew him where the quick freshes are.

Ste. Trinculo, run into no further danger: interrupt the monster one word further, and, by this hand, I'll turn my mercy out of doors, and make a stock-fish of thee.

Trin. Why, what did I? I did nothing: I'll go further off.

Ste. Didst thou not say, he lied?

Ari. Thou liest.

Ste. Do I so? take thou that. [*strikes him.*] As you like this, give me the lie another time.

Trin. I did not give the lie:—Out o' your wits, and hearing too?—A pox o' your bottle! this can sack, and drinking do.—A murrain on your monster, and the devil take your fingers!

Cal. Ha, ha, ha!

Ste. Now, forward with your tale.—Pr'ythee stand further off.

[a] *What a py'd ninny's this?*] It should be remember'd that *Trinculo* is no *sailor*, but a *jester*, and is so called in the ancient *dramatis personæ*; he therefore wears the party-colour'd dress of one of these characters.
STEEVENS.

Dr. Johnson observes, that Caliban could have no knowledge of the striped coat usually worn by fools; and would therefore transfer this speech to Stephano. But though *Caliban* might not know this circumstance, *Shakspeare* did. Surely he who has given to all countries and all ages the manners of his own, might forget himself here, as well as in other places. MALONE.

Cal.

Cal. Beat him enough: after a little time,
I'll beat him too.
Ste. Stand further.—Come, proceed.
Cal. Why, as I told thee, 'tis a custom with him
I' the afternoon to sleep: there thou may'st brain him,
Having first seiz'd his books; or with a log
Batter his skull, or paunch him with a stake,
Or cut his wezand with thy knife: Remember,
First to possess his books, for without them
He's but a sot, as I am, nor hath not
One spirit to command[7]: They all do hate him,
As rootedly as I: Burn but his books;
He has brave utensils, (for so he calls them,)
Which, when he has a house, he'll deck withal.
And that most deeply to consider, is
The beauty of his daughter; he himself
Calls her a non-pareil: I never saw a woman,
But only Sycorax my dam, and she;

[7] ——————— *Rememer*
First to possess his books, for without them
He's but a sot, as I am, nor hath not
One spirit to command:] In a former scene Prospero says—
——————— " I'll to my *book*;
" For yet, ere supper time, must I perform
" Much business appertaining."
Again, in Act v:
" And deeper than did ever plummet sound,
" I'll drown my *book*."
In the old romances the sorcerer is always furnished with a *book*, by reading certain parts of which he is enabled to summon to his aid whatever dæmons or spirits he has occasion to employ. When he is deprived of his book, his power ceases. Our author might have observed this circumstance much insisted on in the *Orlando Inamorato* of Boyardo, (of which, as the Rev. Mr. Bowle informs me, the first three Cantos were translated and published in 1598,) and also in Harrington's Translation of the *Orlando Furioso*, 1591.
A few lines from the former of these works may prove the best illustration of the passage before us.
Angelica, by the aid of Argalia, having bound the enchanter Malagigi,
" The damsel searcheth forthwith in his breast,
" And there the damned *boote* she straightway founde,
" Which circles strange and shapes of fiendes exprest;
" No sooner she some wordes therein did sound,
" And opened had some damned leaves unblest,
" But *spirits* of th' ayre, earth, sea, came out of hand,
" Crying alowde, what is't you us *command*?" MALONE.

But

But she as far surpasseth Sycorax,
As greatest does least.

Ste. Is it so brave a lass?

Cal. Ay, lord; she will become thy bed, I warrant,
And bring thee forth brave brood.

Ste. Monster, I will kill this man: his daughter and I will be king and queen; (save our graces!) and Trinculo and thyself shall be vice-roys:—Dost thou like the plot, Trinculo?

Trin. Excellent.

Ste. Give me thy hand; I am sorry I beat thee: but, while thou liv'st, keep a good tongue in thy head.

Cal. Within this half hour will he be asleep;
Wilt thou destroy him then?

Ste. Ay, on mine honour.

Ari. This will I tell my master.

Cal. Thou mak'st me merry: I am full of pleasure
Let us be jocund: Will you troul the catch [8]
You taught me but while-ere?

Ste. At thy request, monster, I will do reason, any reason: Come on, Trinculo, let us sing. [*Sings.*

   Flout 'em, and skout 'em; and skout 'em, and flout 'em;
     Thought is free.

Cal. That's not the tune.

        [*Ariel plays the tune on a tabor and pipe.*

Ste. What is this same?

Trin. This is the tune of our catch, play'd by the picture of No-body [9].

Ste. If thou beest a man, shew thyself in thy likeness: if thou beest a devil, take't as thou list.

Trin. O, forgive me my sins!

Ste. He that dies, pays all debts: I defy thee:—Mercy upon us!

Cal. Art thou afeard [1]?

Ste. No, monster, not I.

---

[8] — *Will you* troul *the catch*,] To *troul* a catch, I suppose, is to dismiss it *trippingly from the tongue.* STEEVENS.

[9] *This is the tune of our catch, play'd by the* picture *of* No-body.] A ridiculous figure, sometimes represented on signs. *Westward for Smelts,* a book which our author appears to have read, was printed for John Trundle in Barbican, at the *sign* of the *No-body.* MALONE.

[1] — *afeard?*] Thus the old copy. To *affear,* is an obsolete verb with the same meaning as to *affray.* STEEVENS.

Cal.

Cal. Be not afeard; the isle is full of noises,
Sounds, and sweet airs, that give delight and hurt not.
Sometimes a thousand twangling instruments
Will hum about mine ears; and sometime voices,
That, if I then had wak'd after long sleep,
Will make me sleep again: and then, in dreaming,
The clouds, methought, would open, and shew riches
Ready to drop upon me; that when I wak'd,
I cry'd to dream again.

Ste. This will prove a brave kingdom to me, where I shall have my music for nothing.

Cal. When Prospero is destroy'd.

Ste. That shall be by and by: I remember the story.

Trin. The sound is going away: let's follow it,
And after do our work.

Ste. Lead, monster; we'll follow,—I wou'd I could see this taborer: he lays it on.

Trin. Wilt come? I'll follow, Stephano².   [*Exeunt.*

SCENE III.

Another part of the island.

Enter ALONSO, SEBASTIAN, ANTHONIO, GONZALO, ADRIAN, FRANCISCO, *and others.*

Gon. By'r lakin³, I can go no further, Sir;
My old bones ache: here's a maze trod, indeed,
Through forth-rights, and meanders! by your patience,
I needs must rest me.

Alon. Old lord, I cannot blame thee,
Who am myself attach'd with weariness,
To the dulling of my spirits: sit down, and rest.
Even here I will put off my hope, and keep it
No longer for my flatterer: he is drown'd,
Whom thus we stray to find; and the sea mocks
Our frustrate search on land: Well, let him go.

---

² *Wilt come? I'll follow, Stephano.*] The words *Wilt come* are, I believe, addressed to Stephano, who, from a desire to see the " taborer," lingers behind. *Will you come,* or not (says Trinculo)? If you will not, *I'll follow* Caliban without you. MALONE.

³ *By'r lakin,*—] i. e. The diminutive only of our lady, i. e. ladykin. STEEVENS.

Ant.

Ant. I am right glad that he's so out of hope.

[*Aside to* Sebastian.

Do not, for one repulse, forego the purpose
That you resolv'd to effect.

Seb. The next advantage
Will we take throughly.

Ant. Let it be to-night;
For, now they are oppress'd with travail, they
Will not, nor cannot, use such vigilance
As when they are fresh.

Seb. I say, to-night: no more.

Solemn and strange music; and Prospero *above, invisible. Enter several strange Shapes, bringing in a banquet; they dance about it with gentle actions of salutation; and, inviting the king,* &c. *to eat, they depart.*

Alon. What harmony is this? my good friends, hark!
Gon. Marvellous sweet music!
Alon. Give us kind keepers, heavens! What were these?
Seb. A living drollery [4]: Now I will believe,
That there are unicorns; that, in Arabia
There is one tree, the phœnix' throne [5]; one phœnix
At this hour reigning there.

---

[4] *A living drollery:*—] i. e. A drollery not represented by wooden machines, but by personages who are alive. MALONE.

Shows, called *drolleries,* were in Shakspeare's time performed by puppets only. From these our modern *drolls,* exhibited at fairs, &c. took their name. STEEVENS.

[5] — *one tree, the phænix' throne;*] So again, in one of our author's Poems, p. 734, edit. 1778:
"Let the bird of loudest lay,
"On the *sole* Arabian tree, &c."

Our poet had probably Lily's *Euphues,* and his *England,* particularly in his thoughts: signat. Q. 3. — "As there is but one phœnix in the world, so is there but *one tree* in Arabia wherein she buildeth." See also Florio's Italian Dictionary, 1598: "*Rasin,* a tree in Arabia, whereof there is but *one* found, and upon it the phœnix sits."

MALONE.

For this idea our author might have been indebted to Phil. Holland's Translation of Pliny, b. xiii. chap. 4. "I myself verily have heard
"strange things of this kind of tree; and namely in regard of the
"bird *Phœnix,* which is supposed to have taken that name of this
"date tree (called in Greek φοῖνιξ); for it was assured unto me, that
"the said bird died with that tree, and revived of itselfe as the tree
"sprung again." STEEVENS.

Ant.

Ant. I'll believe both;
And what does else want credit, come to me,
And I'll be sworn 'tis true: Travellers ne'er did lie,
Though fools at home condemn them.
   Gon. If in Naples
I should report this now, would they believe me?
If I should say, I saw such islanders [6],
(For, certes [7], these are people of the island,)
Who, though they are of monstrous shape, yet, note,
Their manners are more gentle, kind, than of
Our human generation you shall find
Many, nay, almost any.
   Pro. Honest lord,
Thou hast said well; for some of you there present
Are worse than devils.   [*Aside.*
   Alon. I cannot too much muse [8],
Such shapes, such gesture, and such sound, expressing
(Although they want the use of tongue) a kind
Of excellent dumb discourse.
   Pro. Praise in departing [9].   [*Aside.*
   Fran. They vanish'd strangely.
   Seb. No matter, since
They have left their viands behind; for we have stomachs.—
Will't please you taste of what is here?
   Alon. Not I.
   Gon. Faith, Sir, you need not fear: When we were boys,
Who would believe that there were mountaineers [1],
Dew-lapp'd like bulls, whose throats had hanging at 'em
Wallets of flesh? or that there were such men,

---

  [6] —*such* islanders,] The old copy has *islands*. The emendation was made by the editor of the second folio. MALONE.

  [7] *For* certes,] *Certes* is an obsolete word, signifying *certainly.*
                                                        STEEVENS.

  [8] —*muse*,] To *muse*, in ancient language, is to admire. STEEVENS.

  [9] *Praise in departing.*] i. e. Do not praise your entertainment too soon, lest you should have reason to retract your commendation. It is a proverbial saying. STEEVENS.

  [1] —*that there were mountaineers*, &c.] Whoever is curious to know the particulars relating to these *mountaineers* may consult *Maundeville's Travels*, printed in 1503, by Wynken de Worde; but it is yet a known truth that the inhabitants of the Alps have been long accustom'd to such excrescences or tumours.

        Quis tumidum guttur miratur in Alpibus? STEEVENS.

Whose heads stood in their breasts[2]? which now we find,
Each putter-out on five for one[3], will bring us
Good warrant of.

Alon. I will stand to, and feed,
Although my last:—no matter since I feel
The best is past:—Brother, my lord the duke,
Stand to, and do as we.

Thunder and lightning. Enter ARIEL, *like a harpy*[4]; *claps his wings upon the table, and, with a quaint device, the banquet vanishes.*

Ari.

---

[2] —— *men,*
Whose heads stood in their breasts?] Our author might have had this intelligence likewise from the translation of Pliny, B. v. chap. 8: "The Blemmyi, by report, have no heads, but mouth and eies both in their breasts." STEEVENS.
Or he might have had it from Hackluyt's *Voyages,* 1598: "On that branch which is called *Caora* are a nation of people, whose heads appear not above their shoulders. They are reported to have their eyes in their shoulders, and their mouths in the middle of their breasts." MALONE.

[3] *Each putter-out* on *five for one,* &c.] The old copy reads—*of five for one.* The emendation was made by Mr. Theobald. Perhaps it ought rather to be corrected by only transposing the words: "Each putter out of *one for five*—." So, in the *Scourge of Folly,* by John Davies, of Hereford, printed about 1611:
"Sir Solus straight will travel, as they say,
"And gives out *one for three,* when home comes he."
MALONE.

The ancient custom here alluded to was this. In this age of travelling, it was customary for those who engaged in long expeditions to place out a sum of money, on condition of receiving great interest for it at their return home. So Puntarvolo (it is Theobald's quotation) in Ben Jonson's *Every Man out of his Humour:* "I do intend, this year of jubilee coming on, to travel; and (because I will not altogether go upon expence) I am determined to put forth some *five* thousand pound, to be paid me *five* for *one,* upon the return of my wife, myself, and my dog, from the Turk's court in Constantinople."
STEEVENS.
It appears from Moryson's ITINERARY, 1617, Part i. p. 198, that "this custom of giving out money upon these adventures was first used in court, and among noblemen;" and that some years before his book was published, "bankerouts, stage-players, and men of base condition, had drawn it into contempt," by undertaking journeys merely for gain upon their return. MALONE.

[4] *Enter Ariel, like a harpy,* &c.] Milton's *Par. Reg.* B. ii.
———"with that
"Both table and provisions vanish'd quite,
"With sound of harpies' wings, and talons heard."

Ari. You are three men of sin, whom destiny
(That hath to instrument this lower world [5],
And what is in't,) the never-surfeited sea
Hath caused to belch up [6]; and on this island
Where man doth not inhabit; you 'mongst men
Being most unfit to live. I have made you mad;
      [*seeing Alonso, Sebastian, &c. draw their swords.*
And even with such like valour men hang and drown
Their proper selves. You fools! I and my fellows
Are ministers of fate; the elements
Of whom your swords are temper'd, may as well
Wound the loud winds, or with bemock'd-at stabs
Kill the still-closing waters, as diminish
One dowle that's in my plume [7]; my fellow-ministers
Are like invulnerable: if you could hurt,
Your swords are now too massy for your strengths,
And will not be uplifted: But, remember,
(For that's my business to you,) that you three
From Milan did supplant good Prospero;
Expos'd unto the sea, which hath requit it,
Him, and his innocent child: for which foul deed
The powers, delaying, not forgetting, have
Incens'd the seas and shores, yea, all the creatures,
Against your peace: Thee, of thy son, Alonso,
They have bereft; and do pronounce by me,
Lingering perdition (worse than any death
Can be at once,) shall step by step attend
You, and your ways; whose wraths to guard you from
(Which here, in this most desolate isle, else falls

    At subitæ horrifico lapsu de montibus adsunt
    Harpyiæ, & magnis quatiunt clangoribus alas,
    Diripiuntque dapes. Virg. Æn. iii.   STEEVENS.

[5] *That hath to instrument this lower world,* &c.] i. e. that makes use of this world, and every thing in it, as its *instruments*, to bring about its ends. STEEVENS.

[6] *Hath caused to belch up;*] The old copy reads—to belch up *you*. Corrected by Mr. Theobald. MALONE.

[7] *One* dowle *that's in my* plume;] Bailey, in his Dictionary, says that *dowle* is a feather, or rather the single particles of the down.
                                          STEEVENS.
Cole, in his Latin Dict. 1679, interprets "young *dowle*" by "*lanugo*." The old copy reads—in my *plume*. Corrected by Mr. Rowe.
                                          MALONE.

Upon your heads,) is nothing, but heart's sorrow,
And a clear life ensuing [8].

He vanishes in thunder: then to soft music, enter the Shapes again, and dance with mops and mowes [9], *and carry out the table.*

 Pro. [*Aside.*] Bravely the figure of this harpy hast thou
Perform'd, my Ariel; a grace it had, devouring;
Of my instruction hast thou nothing 'bated,
In what thou hadst to say: so, with good life [1],
And observation strange, my meaner ministers
Their several kinds have done: my high charms work,
And these, mine enemies, are all knit up
In their distractions: they now are in my power;
And in these fits I leave them, whilst I visit
Young Ferdinand, (whom they suppose is drown'd,)
And his and my lov'd darling. [*Exit* Pro. *from above.*

 Gon. I' the name of something holy, Sir, why stand you
In this strange stare?

 Alon. O, it is monstrous! monstrous!
Methought, the billows spoke, and told me of it;
The winds did sing it to me; and the thunder,
That deep and dreadful organ-pipe, pronounc'd
The name of Prosper; it did bass my trespass [2].
Therefore my son i'th the ooze is bedded; and

---

 [8] —————— *is nothing, but heart's sorrow,*
And a clear life ensuing.] The meaning, which is somewhat obscured by the expression, is—*a miserable fate, which nothing but contrition and amendment of life can avert.* MALONE.
 —*clear life*—] Pure, blameless, innocent. JOHNSON.
 So in *Timon:* " —roots, you *clear* heavens" STEEVENS.

 [9] —*with mops and mowes.*] So, in *K. Lear:* "—and Hibbertigibbet of *mopping* and *mowing*" To *mop* and to *mowe* seems to have the same meaning, i. e. to make mouths or wry faces. STEEVENS.
 The old copy, by a manifest error of the press, reads—with *mocks.* See p. 73. Penult.—" Will be here with *mop* and mowe." MALONE.

 [1] —*with good life,*] *With good life* may mean, with *exact presentation of their several characters, with observation strange* of their particular and distinct parts. So we say, he acted to the *life.* JOHNSON.
 Life seems to be used in the chorus to the fifth act of *K. Henry V.* with some meaning like that wanted to explain the approbation of Prospero:
  " Which cannot in their huge and proper *life*
  " Be here presented." STEEVENS.

 [2] —bass *my trespass.*] The deep pipe told it me in a rough bass sound. JOHNSON.

I'll seek him deeper than e'er plummet sounded,
And with him there lie mudded. [*Exit.*
　Seb. But one fiend at a time,
I'll fight their legions o'er.
　Ant. I'll be thy second. [*Exeunt* SEB. *and* ANT.
　Gon. All three of them are desperate; their great guilt,
Like poison given to work a great time after [3],
Now 'gins to bite the spirits:—I do beseech you
That are of suppler joints, follow them swiftly,
And hinder them from what this ecstasy [4]
May now provoke them to.
　Adri. Follow, I pray you. [*Exeunt.*

ACT IV.

Before Prospero's *Cell.*

Enter PROSPERO, FERDINAND, *and* MIRANDA.

　Pro. If I have too austerely punish'd you,
Your compensation makes amends; for I
Have given you here a third of mine own life [5],
　　　　　　　　　　　　　　　　　　　Or

---

[3] *Like poison given,* &c.] The natives of Africa have been supposed to be possessed of the secret how to temper poisons with such art as not to operate till several years after they were administered, and were then as certain in their effect, as they were subtle in their preparation. So in the celebrated libel called *Leicester's Commonwealth*: "I heard him once myselfe in publique act at Oxford, and that in presence of my lord of Leicester, maintain that poyson might be so tempered and given, as it should not appear presently, and yet should kill the party afterwards at what time should be appointed." STEEVENS.

[4] —*this* ecstasy] *Ecstasy* meant not anciently, as at present, *rapturous pleasure,* but alienation of mind. Mr. Locke has not inelegantly stiled it *dreaming with our eyes open.* STEEVENS.

[5] —*a* third *of mine own life,*] The word *thread* was formerly spelt *third,* as appears from the following passage:

　"Long maist thou live, and when the sisters shall decree
　"To cut in twaine the twisted *third* of life,
　"Then let him die, &c."

See comedy of *Mucedorus,* 1619. signat. e. 3. HAWKINS.

　The late Mr. *Hawkins* has properly observed that the word *thread* was anciently spelt *third.* The following quotation should seem to
　　　　　　　　　　　　　　　　　　　　　　place

Or that for which I live; whom once again
I tender to thy hand: all thy vexations
Were but my trials of thy love, and thou
Hast strangely stood the test⁶: here afore Heaven,
I ratify this my rich gift: O Ferdinand,
Do not smile at me, that I boast her off,
For thou shalt find she will outstrip all praise,
And make it halt behind her.

   Fer. I do believe it,
Against an oracle.

   Pro. Then, as my gift⁷, and thine own acquisition
Worthily purchas'd, take my daughter: But
If thou dost break her virgin knot before
All sanctimonious ceremonies⁸ may

---

place the meaning beyond all dispute. In *Acolastus*, a comedy, 1540, is this passage: " —one of worldly shame's *children*, of his countenance, and " THRIDE of his body." STEEVENS.

   Again, in *Tancred and Gismund*, a tragedy, 1592, Tancred, speaking of his intention to kill his *daughter*, says,

" Against all law of kinde, to shed in twaine
" The golden *threede that doth us both maintain*."

Mr. Tollet was of opinion that " a *third* of my own life" here signifies a *fibre* or *part* of my own life: " Prospero (he adds) considers himself as the stock or parent tree, and his daughter a *fibre* or *portion* of himself, and for whose benefit he himself lives. In this sense the word is used in Markham's *English Husbandman*, edit. 1635, p 146."
                                        MALONE.

⁶ —*strangely stood the test:*] Strangely is used by way of commendation, *merveilleusement, to a wonder*; the sense is the same in the foregoing scene, with *observation strange*. JOHNSON.

⁷ —*my gift,*] My guest, *first folio.* JOHNSON.
The emendation is Mr. Rowe's. *Guesle* and *Guifte*, as they were anciently written, were easily confounded. MALONE.

⁸ *If thou dost break her* virgin knot *before*
All sanctimonious ceremonies, &c.] This, and the passage in *Pericles, Prince of Tyre,*

" Untide I still my *virgin knot* will keepe,"
are manifest allusions to the zones of the ancients, which were worn as guardians of chastity by marriageable young women. Puellæ, contra, nondum viripotentes, hujusmodi zonis non utebantur: quod videlicet immaturis virgunculis nullum, aut certe minimum, a corruptoribus periculum imminerct: quas propterea vocabant αμιτρες, nempe *discinctas*. There is a passage in NONNUS, which will sufficiently illustrate Prospero's expression.

Κύρες δ' ἐγγὺς ἴκανε καὶ ἀτρέμας ἄκρον ἐρύσσας
Δεσμὸν ἀσιλήτοιο φυλάκτορα λυσατο μίτρης
Φειδομένη παλάμῃ, μὴ παρθένον ἱπιδείσετε.
                                        HENLEY.

With

With full and holy rite be minister'd,
No sweet aspersion [9] shall the Heavens let fall
To make this contract grow, but barren hate,
Sour-ey'd disdain, and discord, shall bestrew
The union of your bed with weeds so loathly,
That you shall hate it both: therefore, take heed,
As Hymen's lamps shall light you.

  Fer. As I hope
For quiet days, fair issue, and long life,
With such love as 'tis now; the murkiest den,
The most opportune place, the strong'st suggestion
Our worser Genius can, shall never melt
Mine honour into lust; to take away
The edge of that day's celebration,
When I shall think, or Phœbus' steeds are founder'd,
Or night kept chain'd below.

  Pro. Fairly spoken:
Sit then, and talk with her, she is thine own.—
What, Ariel; my industrious servant Ariel!

Enter ARIEL.

  Ari. What would my potent master? here I am.
  Pro. Thou and thy meaner fellows your last service
Did worthily perform; and I must use you
In such another trick: go, bring the rabble [1],
O'er whom I give thee power, here, to this place:
Incite them to quick motion; for I must
Bestow upon the eyes of this young couple
Some vanity of mine art; it is my promise,
And they expect it from me.
  Ari. Presently?
  Pro. Ay, with a twink.
  Ari. Before you can say, *Come,* and *go,*
And breathe twice; and cry, *so, so;*
Each one, tripping on his toe [2],

---

[9] *No sweet aspersion—*] *Aspersion* is here used in its primitive sense of *sprinkling.* At present it is expressive only of calumny and detraction. STEEVENS.

[1] *—the rabble,*] The crew of meaner spirits. JOHNSON.

[2] ——— *Come, and go,—*
  Each one, tripping on his toe,] So Milton:
  " Come, and trip it as you go
  " On the light fantastic toe." STEEVENS.

VOL. III.   E   Will

Will be here with mop and mowe:
Do you love me, master? no.
 Pro. Dearly, my delicate Ariel: Do not approach,
Till thou dost hear me call.
 Ari. Well, I conceive.   [*Exit.*
 Pro. Look, thou be true; do not give dalliance
Too much the rein; the strongest oaths are straw
To the fire i'the blood: be more abstemious,
Or else, good night, your vow!
 Fer. I warrant you, Sir;
The white cold virgin snow upon my heart
Abates the ardour of my liver.
 Pro. Well.—
Now come, my Ariel; bring a corollary [3],
Rather than want a spirit; appear, and pertly.—
No tongue [4]; all eyes; be silent.   [*Soft music.*

A Masque. Enter IRIS.

 Iris. Ceres, most bounteous lady, thy rich leas
Of wheat, rye, barley, vetches, oats, and pease;
Thy turfy mountains, where live nibbling sheep,
And flat meads thatch'd with stover [5], them to keep;
Thy banks with pionied and twilled brims [6],

            Which

---

 [3] —*bring a corollary,*] That is, bring more than are sufficient, rather than fail for want of numbers. *Corollary* means *surplus*. *Corolaire,* Fr. See Cotgrave's Dictionary. STEEVENS.

 [4] *No tongue;*] Those who are present at incantations are obliged to be strictly silent; "else," as we are afterwards told, "the spell is marred." JOHNSON.

 [5] —*thatch'd with stover,*] *Stover* is generally used by law writers for an allowance of wood to be taken off another man's estate. In this sense Sir William Blackstone supposes it to be derived from the French word *estoffer,* to furnish. But it likewise sometimes signifies nourishment, or maintenance, in which sense Cowel derives it from *estouver,* *sovere.*—From Cole's English Dictionary 8vo. 1717, it appears that the word *stover* was then used in Essex, and signified "fodder for cattle;" the precise sense wanted here, being equally applicable to the preceding word "thatch'd," and to the subsequent part of the line. It probably has the same signification in Warwickshire. MALONE.

 [6] *Thy banks with* pionied, *and* twilled brims.] The old edition reads *pioned* and *twilled brims,* which gave rise to Mr. Holt's conjecture, that the poet originally wrote,
    —— with *pioned* and tilled *brims.*
Spenser and the author of *Mulcasses the Turk,* a tragedy, 1610, use *pioning* for digging. It is not, therefore, difficult to find a meaning for the word as it stands in the old copy; and remove a letter from *twilled,*
             and

Which spungy April at thy hest betrims,
To make cold nymphs chaste crowns; and thy broom groves [7],
Whose shadow the dismissed bachelor loves,
Being lass-lorn [8]; thy pole-clipt vineyard [9];
And thy sea-marge, steril, and rocky-hard,
Where thou thyself dost air: The queen o' the sky,
Whose watery arch, and messenger, am I,
Bids thee leave these; and with her sovereign grace,
Here on this grass-plot, in this very place,
To come and sport: her peacocks fly amain;
Approach, rich Ceres, her to entertain.

Enter CERES.

Cer. Hail, many-colour'd messenger, that ne'er
Dost disobey the wife of Jupiter;
Who, with thy saffron wings, upon my flowers
Diffusest honey drops, refreshing showers;
And with each end of thy blue bow dost crown
My bosky acres [1], and my unshrubb'd down,

and it leaves us *filled*. I am yet, however, in doubt whether we ought not to read *lilied* brims; for *Pliny*, B XXVI. ch. x. mentions the *water-lilly* as a preserver of chastity.

In the 20th song of Drayton's *Polyolbion*, the Naiades are represented as making chaplets with all the tribe of aquatic flowers; and Mr. Tollet informs me that Lyte's *Herbal* says, " one kind of *peonie* is called by " some, *maiden or virgin peonie*."

In *Ovid's Banquet of Sense*, by Chapman, 1595, *twill-pants* are enumerated among flowers.

If *twill* be the ancient name of any flower, the present reading, *pionied* and *twilled* may uncontrovertibly stand. STEEVENS.

Pionied is the emendation of Sir Thomas Hanmer. MALONE.

[7] —*and thy broom groves*,] A grove of *broom*, I believe, was never heard of, as it is a low shrub, and not a tree. Hanmer reads *brown* groves. STEEVENS.

Disappointed lovers are still said to wear the *willow*, and in these lines *broom groves* are assigned to that unfortunate tribe for a retreat. This may allude to some old custom. We still say that a husband *hangs out the broom* when his wife goes from home for a short time; and on such occasions a *broom* besom has been exhibited, as a signal that the house was freed from uxorial restraint, and where the master might be considered as a temporary bachelor. *Broom grove* may signify *broom bushes*. See *Genesta*, in Cowel's Law Dict. TOLLET.

[8] *Being lass-lorn*;] i. e. Forsaken of his mistress. STEEVENS.

[9] —*thy pole-clipt vineyard*,] To *clip* is to *twine round* or *embrace*. The poles are *clipt* or embraced by the vines. STEEVENS.

[1] *My bosky acres*,] *Bosky* is woody. *Bosquet*, Fr. STEEVENS.

E 2   Rich

Rich scarf to my proud earth; Why hath thy queen
Summon'd me hither, to this short-grass'd green²?

Iris. A contract of true love to celebrate;
And some donation freely to estate
On the bless'd lovers.

Cer. Tell me, heavenly bow,
If Venus, or her son, as thou dost know,
Do now attend the queen? since they did plot
The means, that dusky Dis my daughter got,
Her and her blind boy's scandal'd company
I have forsworn.

Iris. Of her society
Be not afraid: I met her deity
Cutting the clouds towards Paphos; and her son
Dove-drawn with her: here thought they to have done
Some wanton charm upon this man and maid,
Whose vows are, that no bed-rite shall be paid
Till Hymen's torch be lighted: but in vain;
Marses hot minion is return'd again;
Her waspish-headed son has broke his arrows,
Swears he will shoot no more, but play with sparrows,
And be a boy right out.

Cer. Highest queen of state,
Great Juno comes; I know her by her gait³.

Enter JUNO.

Jun. How does my bounteous sister? Go with me,
To bless this twain, that they may prosperous be,
And honour'd in their issue.

---

² *short-grass'd green?*] The old copy has—short-gras'd. The omission of the second *s* was probably owing to the carelessness of the transcriber. MALONE.

³ *Highest queen of state,*
Great Juno comes; I know her by her gait.] So, in *the Arraignment of Paris:*
"First statelie *Juno,* with her porte and grace." STEEVENS.

Highest *queen of state,*] Sir John Harrington has likewise used this word as one syllable:
"Thus said the *hy'st,* and then there did ensew—."
Orlando Fur. B. 29. St. 32. MALONE.

SONG.

Jun. Honour, riches, marriage-bleſſing,
Long continuance, and increaſing,
Hourly joys be ſtill upon you!
Juno ſings her bleſſings on you.

Cer. Earth's increaſe, and foiſon plenty [4];
Barns, and garners, never empty;
Vines, with cluſt'ring bunches growing;
Plants, with goodly burden bowing;
Spring come to you, at the fartheſt,
In the very end of harveſt!
Scarcity, and want, ſhall ſhun you;
Ceres' bleſſing ſo is on you.

Fer. This is a moſt majeſtic viſion, and
Harmonious charmingly [5]: May I be bold
To think theſe ſpirits?

Pro. Spirits, which by mine art
I have from their confines call'd to enact
My preſent fancies.

Fer. Let me live here ever;
So rare a wonder'd father, and a wife,
Make this place paradiſe.

Juno and Ceres *whiſper, and ſend* Iris *on employment.*

Pro. Sweet now, ſilence:
Juno and Ceres whiſper ſeriouſly;
There's ſomething elſe to do: huſh, and be mute,
Or elſe our ſpell is marr'd.

Iris. You nymphs, call'd Naiads, of the wand'ring
brooks [6],

---

[4] *Earth's increaſe, and foiſon plenty*, &c.] Theſe, as well as the foregoing lines, are in the old copy given to Juno. Mr. Theobald made the alteration. *And* is not in that copy. It was added by the editor of the ſecond folio. Earth's *increaſe*, is the *produce* of the earth. The expreſſion is ſcriptural: "Then ſhall the *earth* bring forth her *increaſe*, and God, even our God, ſhall give us his bleſſing." PSALM 67.
MALONE.

Foiſon plenty is plenty to the utmoſt abundance. See p. 41. n. 6.
STEEVENS.

[5] *Harmonious charmingly:*] i. e. charmingly harmonious. A ſimilar inverſion occurs in *A Midſummer Night's Dream*:
"But *miſerable moſt* to live unlov'd." MALONE.

[6] —*wand'ring brooks,*] The old copy reads—*windring.* Corrected by Mr. Steevens. MALONE.

With your sedg'd crowns, and ever-harmless looks,*
Leave your crisp channels 7, and on this green land
Answer your summons; Juno does command:
Come, temperate nymphs, and help to celebrate
A contract of true love; be not too late.

Enter certain Nymphs.

You sun-burn'd sicklemen, of August weary,
Come hither from the furrow, and be merry;
Make holy-day: your rye straw hats put on,
And these fresh nymphs encounter every one
In country footing.

Enter certain Reapers, properly habited: they join with the nymphs in a graceful dance; towards the end whereof Prospero starts suddenly, and speaks; after which, to a strange, hollow, and confused noise, they heavily vanish.

Pro. I had forgot that foul conspiracy   [*Aside.*
Of the beast Caliban, and his confederates,
Against my life; the minute of their plot
Is almost come. [*to the spirits.*] Well done; avoid; no more.

Fer. This is strange: your father's in some passion,
That works him strongly.

Mira. Never till this day,
Saw I him touch'd with anger so distemper'd.

Pro. You do look, my son, in a mov'd sort,
As if you were dismay'd: be chearful, Sir:
Our revels now are ended: these our actors,
As I foretold you, were all spirits, and
Are melted into air, into thin air:

---

* *With your sedg'd crowns, and ever-harmless looks,*] So, in Colding's translation of Ovid's *Metamorph.* B. IX. 1587:

"The noble stream of Calydon made answer, who did weare
"A *garland* made of reedes and flagges upon his sedgy heare."

MALONE.

7 *Leave your crisp channels,*] *Crisp,* i. e. *curling, winding.* Lat. *crispus.* So in *Hen. IV.* Part I. act i. sc. iv. Hotspur, speaking of the river Severn:

"And hid his *crisped* head in the hollow bank."

Crisp, however, may allude to the little wave or *curl* (as it is commonly called) that the gentlest wind occasions on the surface of waters.

STEEVENS.

And,

And, like the baseless fabric of this vision [8],
The cloud-capt towers, the gorgeous palaces,
The solemn temples, the great globe itself,
Yea, all which it inherit [9], shall dissolve,
And like this insubstantial pageant faded [1],

             Leave

[8] *And, like the baseless fabric of this vision, &c.*] The exact period at which this play was produced is unknown: It was not, however, published before 1623. In the year 1603, the *Tragedy of Darius*, by Lord Sterline, made its appearance, and there I find the following passage:

 " Let greatness of her glassy scepters vaunt,
 " Not scepters, no, but reeds, soon bruis'd, soon broken;
 " And let this worldly pomp our wits enchant,
 " All fades, and scarcely leaves behind a token.
 " Those golden palaces, those gorgeous halls,
 " With furniture superfluously fair,
 " Those stately courts, those sky-encount'ring walls,
 " Evanish all like vapours in the air."

Lord Sterline's play must have been written before the death of Queen *Elizabeth*, (which happen'd on the 24th of March, 1603) as it is dedicated to *James VI. King of Scots*.

Whoever should seek for this passage (as here quoted from the 4to, 1603) in the folio edition, 1637, will be disappointed, as Lord Sterline made considerable changes in all his plays, after their first publication.
              STEEVENS.

[9] — *all which it inherit*,] i. e. all who possess, who dwell upon it. So, in the *Two Gentlemen of Verona*:

 " This, or else nothing, will *inherit* her." MALONE.

[1] *And, like this insubstantial* pageant *faded*,] *Faded* means here—having vanished; from the Latin, *vado*. So, in *Hamlet*:

 " It *fad'd* on the crowing of the cock."

To feel the justice of this comparison, and the propriety of the epithet, the nature of these exhibitions should be remembered. The ancient English *pageants* were shows exhibited on the reception of a prince, or any other solemnity of a similar kind. They were presented on occasional stages erected in the streets. Originally they appear to have been nothing more than dumb shows; but before the time of our author, they had been enlivened by the introduction of speaking personages, who were characteristically habited. The speeches were sometimes in verse; and as the procession moved forward, the speakers, who constantly bore some allusion to the ceremony, either conversed together in the form of a dialogue, or addressed the noble person whose presence occasioned the celebrity. On these allegorical spectacles very costly ornaments were bestowed. See Fabian, II. 382. Warton's *Hist. of Poet.* II. 199. 202.

Perhaps our poet also remembered Spenser's *Ruines of Time*, 1591:

 " High *towers*, fair *temples*, goodly theatres,
 " Strong walls, rich porches, princelie pallaces,
 " Large streets, brave houses, sacred sepulchres,
 " Sure gates, sweet gardens, stately galleries,

Leave not a rack behind³: We are such stuff
As dreams are made on³, and our little life
Is rounded with a sleep.—Sir, I am vex'd;

Bear

"Wrought with faire pillours, and fine imageries,
"All these, (O pitie!) now are turn'd to dust,
"And overgrown with black oblivions rust." MALONE.

The well-known lines before us may receive some illustration from Stowe's account of the pageants exhibited in the year 1604, (not very long before this play was written,) on King James, his Queen, &c. passing triumphantly from the Tower to Westminster; on which occasion seven Gates or Arches were erected in different places through which the procession passed.—Over the first gate " was represented the " true likeness of all the notable houses, TOWERS and steeples, within " the citie of London."—— " The sixt arche or gate of triumph was " erected above the Conduit in Fleete-Streete, whereon the GLOBE " of the world was seen to move, &c. At Temple-bar a seaventh " arche or gate was erected, the forefront whereof was proportioned " in every respect like a TEMPLE, being dedicated to Janus, &c.— " The citie of Westminster, and dutchy of Lancaster, at the Strand " had erected the invention of a Rainbow, the moene, sunne, and " starres, advanced between two Pyramides, &c." ANNALS, p. 1429, edit. 1605. MALONE.

² *Leave not a* rack *behind*:] *Rack* is generally used by our ancient writers for a *body of clouds* sailing along; or rather for the *course of the clouds when in motion*. So, in *Antony and Cleopatra*:
"That which is now a horse, even with a thought
"The rack dislimns."
But no instance has yet been produced, where it is used to signify a *single small fleeting cloud*, in which sense only it can be figuratively applied here. I incline, therefore, to sir Thomas Hanmer's emendation, though I have not disturbed the text. MALONE.

I am now inclined to think that *rack* is a mis-spelling for *wreck*, i. e. *wreck*, which Fletcher likewise has used for a minute broken fragment. See his *Wife for a Month*, where we find the word mis-spelt as it is in the *Tempest*:
"He will bulge so subtilly and suddenly,
"You may snatch him up by parcels, like a *sea-rack*."
It has been urged, that " objects which have only a visionary and insubstantial existence, car, when the vision is faded, leave nothing *real*, and consequently no *wreck* behind them." But the objection is founded on misapprehension. The words—" Leave not a rack (or wreck) behind," relate not to " the baseless fabric of this vision," but to the final destruction of the world, of which the towers, temples, and palaces, shall (*like* a vision, or a pageant,) be dissolved, and leave no vestige behind. MALONE.

Sir T. H. instead of *rack*, reads *track*, which may be supported by the following passage in the first scene of *Timon of Athens*:
"But flies an eagle flight, bold, and forth on,
" *Leaving no* tract *behind*." STEEVENS.

³—*We are such stuff*
As dreams *are* made on,] I would willingly persuade myself, that
this

Bear with my weakness; my old brain is troubled.
Be not disturb'd with my infirmity:
If thou be pleas'd, retire into my cell,
And there repose; a turn or two I'll walk,
To still my beating mind.

   Fer. Mir. We wish your peace.   [*Exeunt.*
   Pro. Come with a thought:—I thank thee:—Ariel, come.

Enter ARIEL.

   Ari. Thy thoughts I cleave to [4]: What's thy pleasure?
   Pro. Spirit,
We must prepare to meet with Caliban [5].
   Ari. Ay, my commander: when I presented Ceres,
I thought to have told thee of it; but I fear'd
Lest I might anger thee.
   Pro. Say again, where didst thou leave these varlets?
   Ari. I told you, Sir, they were red-hot with drinking;
So full of valour, that they smote the air
For breathing in their faces; beat the ground
For kissing of their feet: yet always bending
Towards their project: Then I beat my tabor,
At which, like unback'd colts, they prick'd their ears,
Advanc'd their eye-lids, lifted up their noses
As they smelt music; so I charm'd their ears,
That, calf-like, they my lowing follow'd, through
Tooth'd briers, sharp furzes, pricking goss [6], and thorns,
Which

---

this vulgarism was introduced by the transcriber, and that Shakspeare wrote—*made of.* But I fear other instances are to be found in these plays of this unjustifiable phraseology, and therefore have not disturbed the text.

The stanza which immediately precedes the lines quoted by Mr. Steevens from Lord Sterline's *Darius,* may serve still further to confirm the conjecture that one of these poets imitated the other. Our author was, I believe, the imitator:

    " And when the eclipse comes of our glory's light,
      " Then what avails the adoring of a name?
    " A meer *illusion made to mock the sight,*
      " Whose belt was but the shadow of a *dream.*" MALONE.

  [4] *Thy thoughts I cleave to:*] To *cleave to* is *to unite with closely.* So, in *Macbeth:*
    " Like our strange garments, *cleave* not *to* their mould."
Again: " If you shall *cleave to* my consent." STEEVENS.
  [5] *—to* meet with *Caliban.*] *To meet with* is to *counteract;* to play stratagem against stratagem. JOHNSON.

  [6] —*pricking*

Which enter'd their frail shins: at last I left them
I' the filthy mantled pool beyond your cell,
There dancing up to the chins, that the foul lake
O'er stunk their feet.

Pro. This was well done, my bird:
Thy shape invisible retain thou still:
The trumpery in my house, go, bring it hither,
For stale to catch these thieves [7].

Ari. I go, I go. [*Exit.*

Pro. A devil, a born devil, on whose nature
Nurture can never stick [8]; on whom my pains,
Humanely taken, all, all lost [9], quite lost;
And as, with age, his body uglier grows,
So his mind cankers [1]: I will plague them all,

Re-enter ARIEL, *loaden with glistering apparel*, &c.

Even to roaring:—Come, hang them on this line [2].

PROSPERO *and* ARIEL *remain invisible. Enter* CALIBAN,
STEPHANO, *and* TRINCULO, *all wet.*

Cal. Pray you, tread softly, that the blind mole may not

---

[6] —*pricking gofs*,] I know not how Shakspeare distinguished *gofs* from *furze;* for what he calls *furze,* is called *gofs* or *gorse* in the midland counties. STEEVENS.

By the latter, Shakspeare means the low sort of *gorse* that only grows upon wet ground, and which is well described by the name of *whins* in Markham's *Farewell to Husbandry.* It has prickles like those on a rose-tree or a gooseberry. TOLLET.

[7] For stale *to catch these thieves.*] Stale is a word in *fowling,* and is used to mean a *bait* or *decoy* to catch birds. STEEVENS.

[8] Nurture *can never stick;*] Nurture is *education.* STEEVENS.

[9] —all, *all lost*,] The first of these words was probably introduced by the carelessness of the transcriber or compositor. We might safely read,—*are* all lost. MALONE.

[1] *And as, with age, his body uglier grows,*
So his mind cankers:] Shakspeare, when he wrote this description, perhaps recollected what his patron's most intimate friend, the great lord Essex, in an hour of discontent, said of queen Elizabeth; " *that she grew old and canker'd, and that her mind was become as crooked as her carcase:*"—a speech, which, according to Sir Walter Raleigh, cost him his head, and which, we may therefore suppose, was at that time much talked of. This play being written in the time of King James, these obnoxious words might be safely repeated. MALONE.

[2] —hang *them on* this line.] The old copy reads—hang *on* them. Corrected by Mr. Rowe. MALONE.

Hear

Hear a foot fall[3]: we now are near his cell.

Ste. Monster, your fairy, which, you say, is a harmless fairy, has done little better than play'd the Jack with us[4].

Trin. Monster, I do smell all horse-piss; at which my nose is in great indignation.

Ste. So is mine. Do you hear, monster? If I should take a displeasure against you; look you,—

Trin. Thou wert but a lost monster.

Cal. Good, my lord, give me thy favour still:
Be patient, for the prize I'll bring thee to
Shall hood-wink this mischance: therefore, speak softly;
All's hush'd as midnight yet.

Trin. Ay, but to lose our bottles in the pool—

Ste. There is not only disgrace and dishonour in that, monster, but an infinite loss.

Trin. That's more to me than my wetting: yet this is your harmless fairy, monster.

Ste. I will fetch off my bottle, though I be o'er ears for my labour.

Cal. Pr'ythee, my king, be quiet: See'st thou here,
This is the mouth o' the cell: no noise, and enter:
Do that good mischief, which may make this island
Thine own for ever, and I, thy Caliban,
For aye thy foot-licker.

Ste. Give me thy hand: I do begin to have bloody thoughts.

Trin. O king Stephano! O peer! O worthy Stephano! look, what a wardrobe here is for thee[5]!

---

[3] —*that the blind mole may not*
Hear a foot fall:] This quality of hearing, which the mole is supposed to possess in so high a degree, is mentioned in *Euphues*, quarto, 1581, p. 64. REED.

[4] —*has done little better than play'd the Jack with us.*] i. e. He has played *Jack with a lantern;* has led us about like an *ignis fatuus,* by which travellers are decoyed into the mire. JOHNSON.

[5] *O king Stephano! O peer! O worthy Stephano! look, what a wardrobe here is for thee!*] The humour of these lines consists in their being an allusion to an old celebrated ballad, which begins thus: *King Stephen was a worthy peer*—and celebrates that king's parsimony with regard to his wardrobe.—There are two stanzas of this ballad in *Othello*.
WARBURTON.

The old ballad is printed at large in *The Reliques of Ancient Poetry,* vol. i. PERCY.

Cal.

Cal. Let it alone, thou fool; it is but trash.

Trin. Oh, ho, monster; we know what belongs to a frippery⁶:—O king Stephano!

Ste. Put off that gown, Trinculo; by this hand, I'll have that gown.

Trin. Thy grace shall have it.

Cal. The dropsy drown this fool! what do you mean, To doat thus on such luggage? Let it alone⁷, And do the murther first: if he awake, From toe to crown he'll fill our skins with pinches; Make us strange stuff.

Ste. Be you quiet, monster.—Mistress line, is not this my jerkin? Now is the jerkin under the line⁸: now, jerkin, you are like to lose your hair⁹, and prove a bald jerkin.

Trin. Do, do: We steal by line and level, and't like your grace.

Ste. I thank thee for that jest; here's a garment for't: wit shall not go unrewarded, while I am king of this country: *Steal by line and level* is an excellent pass of pate; there's another garment for't.

Trin. Monster, come, put some lime¹ upon your fingers, and away with the rest.

Cal. I will have none on't: we shall lose our time, And all be turn'd to barnacles, or to apes²

With

---

⁶ —*we know what belongs to a* frippery:] A *frippery* was a shop where old cloaths were sold. *Fripperie*, Fr. The person who kept one of these shops was called a *fripper*. Strype, in the life of Stowe, says, that these *frippers* lived in Birchin-lane and Cornhill. STEEVENS.

⁷ Let *it alone*,] The old copy reads—Let's alone. For the emendation the present editor is answerable. Caliban had used the same expression before.—Mr. Theobald reads—Let's along. MALONE.

⁸ —*under the line,* &c.] An allusion to what often happens to people who pass the line. The violent fevers, which they contract in that hot climate, make them lose their hair. EDWARDS' MSS.

Perhaps the allusion is to a more indelicate disease than any peculiar to the equinoxial. Shakspeare seems to design an equivoque between the equinoxial and the girdle of a woman. STEEVENS.

⁹ *Now,* jerkin, *you are like to lose your* hair] Jerkins made of goat-skins seem to have been part of the wardrobe of the theatres in our author's time. [See a note on *The Winter's Tale*, Act iv. sc. iii.] However, as the apparel brought in by Ariel is described as splendid and glistering, the garments here spoken of were probably ornamented with tinsel, or gilt leather, and hung upon a *hair*-line MALONE.

¹ —*put some lime,* &c.] That is, *birdlime.* JOHNSON.

² —*to barnacles, or to apes,*] Skinner says *barnacle* is *Anser Scoticus*. The *barnacle* is a kind of shell-fish growing on the bottoms of ships, and

With foreheads villainous low [3].

Ste. Monster, lay-to your fingers; help to bear this away, where my hogshead of wine is, or I'll turn you out of my kingdom: go to, carry this.

Trin. And this.

Ste. Ay, and this.

A noise of hunters heard [4]. *Enter divers Spirits, in shape of hounds, and hunt them about;* Prospero *and* Ariel *setting them on.*

Pro. Hey, *Mountain*, hey!

Ari. *Silver!* there it goes, *Silver!*

Pro. Fury, Fury! there, *Tyrant*, there! hark, hark!

[CAL. STE. *and* TRIN. *are driven out.*

Go, charge my goblins that they grind their joints
With dry convulsions; shorten up their sinews
With aged cramps; * and more pinch-spotted make them,
Than pard, or cat o' mountain.

Ari. Hark, they roar.

Pro. Let them be hunted soundly: At this hour
Lie at my mercy all mine enemies:
Shortly shall all my labours end, and thou
Shalt have the air at freedom: for a little,
Follow, and do me service.   [*Exeunt.*

which was anciently supposed, when broken off, to become one of these geese. COLLINS.

[3] *With foreheads villainous low.*] Low foreheads were anciently reckoned among deformities. STEEVENS.

This opinion was perhaps peculiar to the age of Queen Elizabeth, and to England, whose customs and fashions Shakspeare gave to every country, and to all times. In his *Antony* and *Cleopatra* he makes a messenger assure the Egyptian Queen, that the forehead of her rival Octavia was " as low as she could wish it." MALONE.

[4] *A noise of hunters heard.*] Shakspeare might have had in view " *Arthur's Chace*, which many believe to be in France, saying that it is a kennel of black dogs, followed by unknown huntsmen, with an exceeding great sound of horns, as if it were a very hunting of some wild beast." See a *Treatise of Spectres* translated from the French of Peter de Loier, and published in quarto, 1605; p. 11. GREY.

" HECATE, (says the same writer, *ibid.*) as the Greeks affirmed, did use to send *doggs* unto men, to feare and terrifie them." MALONE.

* *Go, charge thy goblins, that they grind their joints*
With dry convulsions; shorten up their sinews
With aged cramps;] So Milton, in his Masque:
" He with his bare wand can unthread thy *joints,*
" And crumble all thy *sinews.*" MALONE.

ACT

ACT V.

SCENE, the same.

Enter PROSPERO *in his magic robes, and* ARIEL.

Pro. Now does my project gather to a head:
My charms crack not; my spirits obey; and time
Goes upright with his carriage [5]. How's the day?

Ari. On the sixth hour; at which time, my lord,
You said our work should cease.

Pro. I did say so,
When first I rais'd the tempest. Say, my spirit,
How fares the king and his followers?

Ari. Confin'd together
In the same fashion as you gave in charge;
Just as you left them; all prisoners, Sir,
In the lime-grove which weather-fends your cell;
They cannot budge, till you release [6]. The king,
His brother, and yours, abide all three distracted;
And the remainder mourning over them,
Brim-full of sorrow and dismay; but chiefly him,
That you term'd, Sir, *The good old lord, Gonzalo;*
His tears run down his beard, like winter's drops *
From eaves of reeds: your charm so strongly works 'em,
That if you now beheld them, your affections
Would become tender.

Pro. Dost thou think so, spirit?

Ari. Mine would, Sir, were I human.

---

[5] ———— *and time*
Goes upright with his carriage.] Alluding to one carrying a burthen. This critical period of my life proceeds as I could wish. Time brings forward all the expected events, without faultering under his burthen.
STEEVENS.

[6] *till your release.*] i. e. till you release them. MALONE.

* *His tears run down his beard,* like winter's drops
From eaves of reeds:] Milton probably remembered these lines, when he wrote
" Or usher'd with a shewer still,
" When the gust hath blown his fill,
" Ending on the rustling leaves,
" *With minute drops from off the eaves.*" MALONE.

Pro.

Pro. And mine shall.
Hast thou, which art but air, a touch⁷, a feeling
Of their afflictions? and shall not myself,
One of their kind, that relish all as sharply,
Passion as they⁸, be kindlier mov'd than thou art?
Though with their high wrongs I am struck to the quick,
Yet, with my nobler reason, 'gainst my fury
Do I take part: the rarer action is
In virtue than in vengeance: they being penitent,
The sole drift of my purpose doth extend
Not a frown farther: Go, release them, Ariel;
My charms I'll break, their senses I'll restore,
And they shall be themselves.
   Ari. I'll fetch them, Sir.   [*Exit.*
   Pro. Ye elves of hills, brooks, standing lakes, and groves⁹;
                                                      And

---

⁷ — *a* touch,] A *touch* is a *sensation.* So, in *Cymbeline:*
     " ———— a *touch* more rare
     " Subdues all pangs, all fears." STEEVENS.

⁸ ———— *that relish all as sharply,*
     Passion as they,] *Passion* is a verb in Shakspeare. I feel every thing with the same quick sensibility, and am moved by the same passions as they are. So, in his *Venus and Adonis:*
     " Dumbly she *passions,* frantickly she doateth." STEEVENS.

⁹ *Ye elves of hills, brooks, standing lakes, and groves;*] This speech Dr. Warburton rightly observes to be borrowed from Medea's in *Ovid:* and " it proves, says Mr. Holt, beyond contradiction, that Shakspeare was perfectly acquainted with the sentiments of the ancients on the subject of inchantments." The original lines are these:
     " Auræque, & venti, montesque, amnesque, lacusque,
     " Diique omnes nemorum, diique omnes noctis adeste."
The translation of which, by Golding, is by no means literal, and Shakspeare hath closely followed it. FARMER.

Whoever will take the trouble of comparing this whole passage with Medea's speech, as translated by Golding, quarto, 1576, will see evidently that Shakspeare copied the translation, and not the original. The particular expressions that seem to have made an impression on his mind are printed in Italics:
 " Ye ayres and windes, ye *elves of hills,* of *brookes,* of *woodes* alone,
 " Of *standing lakes,* and of the night, approche ye everych one.
 " *Through help of whom* (the crooked bankes much wondering at the
      thing)
 " I have compelled streames to run clean backward to their spring.
 " By charms I make the calm sea rough, and make the rough seas
      playne,
 " And cover all the sky with clouds, and *chase* them *thence* again.
 " *By charmes I raise and lay the windes,* and burst the viper's jaw,
 " And from the bowels of the earth both stones and trees do draw.
                                                                " Whole

And ye, that on the sands with printless foot
Do chase the ebbing Neptune [1], and do fly him,
When he comes back; you demy-puppets, that
By moon-shine do the green sour ringlets make,
Whereof the ewe not bites; and you, whose pastime
Is to make midnight mushrooms; that rejoice
To hear the solemn curfew; by whose aid
(Weak masters though ye be) [2] I have be-dimm'd
The noon-tide sun, call'd forth the mutinous winds,
And 'twixt the green sea and the azur'd vault
Set roaring war: to the dread rattling thunder
Have I given fire, and rifted Jove's stout oak
With his own bolt: the strong-bas'd promontory
Have I made shake; and by the spurs pluck'd up

" Whole woods and forests I remove, *I make the mountains shake*,
" And even the earth itself to groan, and fearfully to quake.
" *I call up dead men from their graves*, and thee, O lightsome moone,
" I darken oft, though beaten brass abate thy peril soone.
" Our sorcerie *dimmes* the morning faire, and darks *the sun at noone*.
" The flaming breath of fierce bulles ye quenched for my sake,
" And caused their unwieldy neckes the bended yoke to take.
" Among the earth-bred brothers you a *mortal warre did set*,
" And brought asleep the dragon fell, whose eyes were never shet."

MALONE.

Ye elves of hills, &c.] *Fairies* and *elves* are frequently in the poets mentioned together, without any distinction of character that I can recollect. Keysler says that *alp* and *elf*, which is *elf* with the *Swedes* and *English*, equally signified a mountain, or a dæmon of the mountains. This seems to have been its original meaning; but Somner's Dict. mentions elves or fairies of the mountains, of the woods, of the sea and fountains, without any distinction between elves and fairies.

TOLLET.

[1] ———— *with printless foot*
Do chase the ebbing Neptune,] So Milton, in his *Masque*:
" Whilst from off the waters fleet,
" Thus I set my *printless* feet." STEEVENS.

[2] (*Weak masters though ye be*)] The meaning of this passage may be; *Though you are but inferior masters of those supernatural powers,—though you possess them but in a low degree.* STEEVENS.

———— *by whose aid*
(*Weak masters though ye be*)
That is; ye are powerful auxiliaries, but weak if left to yourselves;—your employment is then to make green ringlets, and midnight mushrooms, and to play the idle pranks mentioned by Ariel in his next song;—yet by your aid I have been enabled to invert the course of nature. We say proverbially, " Fire is a good *servant*, but a bad *master*."

BLACKSTONE.

The pine, and cedar: graves, at my command,
Have wak'd their sleepers; oped, and let them forth
By my so potent art: But this rough magic
I here abjure: and, when I have requir'd
Some heavenly music, (which even now I do,)
To work mine end upon their senses, that
This airy charm is for, I'll break my staff,
Bury it certain fathoms in the earth,
And, deeper than did ever plummet sound,
I'll drown my book. [*Solemn music.*

Re-enter ARIEL: *after him,* ALONSO, *with a frantic gesture, attended by* GONZALO; SEBASTIAN *and* ANTHONIO *in like manner, attended by* ADRIAN *and* FRANCISCO: *They all enter the circle which* Prospero *had made, and there stand charmed; which* Prospero *observing, speaks.*

A solemn air, and the best comforter,
To an unsettled fancy's cure! ³—Thy brains,
Now useless, boil within thy skull: ⁴ there stand,
For you are spell-stopp'd.—
Holy Gonzalo, honourable man,
Mine eyes, even sociable to the shew of thine,
Fall fellowly drops.—The charm dissolves apace;
And as the morning steals upon the night,
Melting the darkness, so their rising senses
Begin to chase the ignorant fumes ⁵ that mantle

---

³ *To an unsettled* fancy's *cure!*] The old copy reads—*fancy.* For this emendation the present editor is answerable. So, in *King John*:

My widow's comfort, and my *sorrow's* cure.

Again, in *Romeo and Juliet*:

―――― *Confusion's cure*
Lives not in these confusions.

Prospero begins by observing, that the air which had been played was admirably adapted to compose unsettled minds. He then addresses Gonzalo and the rest, who had just before gone into the circle: "Thy brains, now useless, boil within thy skull, &c." [the soothing strain not having yet begun to operate]. Afterwards, perceiving that the music begins to have the effect intended, he adds, "The charm dissolves apace." Mr. Pope and the subsequent editors read—*boil'd.*
MALONE.

⁴ —boil *within thy skull:*] So, in the *Midsummer Night's Dream*:
"Lovers and madmen have such *seething* brains, &c."
STEEVENS.

Again, in the *Winter's Tale*: "Would any but these *boil'd brains* of nineteen and two-and-twenty hunt this weather?" MALONE.

⁵ —*the ignorant fumes*] i. e. the fumes of ignorance. HEATH.

Their

Their clearer reason.—O good Gonzalo,
My true preserver, and a loyal sir
To him thou follow'st; I will pay thy graces
Home, both in word and deed.— Most cruelly
Didst thou, Alonso, use me and my daughter:
Thy brother was a furtherer in the act;—
Thou'rt pinch'd for't now, Sebastian.—Flesh and blood [6],
You brother mine, that entertain'd ambition [7],
Expell'd remorse, and nature [8]; who, with Sebastian,
(Whose inward pinches therefore are most strong,)
Would here have kill'd your king; I do forgive thee,
Unnatural though thou art!—Their understanding
Begins to swell; and the approaching tide
Will shortly fill the reasonable shores,
That now lie foul and muddy. Not one of them,
That yet looks on me, or would know me:—Ariel,
Fetch me the hat and rapier in my cell;— [*Exit* ARIEL.
I will dis-case me, and myself present,
As I was sometime Milan:—quickly, spirit;
Thou shalt ere long be free.

ARIEL *re-enters, singing, and helps to attire* PROSPERO.

   Ari. Where the bee sucks, there suck I;
     In a cowslip's bell I lie [9]*:*

[6] *Thou'rt pinch'd for't now, Sebastian.—Flesh and blood,*] Thus the old copy: Theobald points the passage in a different manner, and perhaps rightly:
"Thou'rt pinch'd for't now, Sebastian, flesh and blood."
                                    STEEVENS.

[7] *That* entertain'd *ambition,*] Old copy—*entertain*. Corrected by the editor of the second folio. MALONE.

[8] — remorse *and* nature;] *Remorse* is by our author and the contemporary writers generally used for *pity*, or *tenderness of heart*. *Nature* is natural affection. MALONE.

[9] *In a* cowslip's *bell I lie:*] So, in Drayton's *Nymphidia*;
  "At midnight, the appointed hour;
  "And for the queen a fitting *bower*;
  "Quoth he, is that fair *cowslip* flower
  "On Hipcut hill that bloweth"

The date of this poem not being ascertained, we know not whether our author was indebted to it, or was himself copied by Drayton. I believe, the latter was the imitator. *Nymphidia* was not written, I imagine, till after the English Don Quixote had appeared in 1612.
                                      MALONE.

There I couch, when owls do cry [1].
On the bat's back I do fly
After summer, merrily [2]*:*
Merrily, merrily, shall I live now,
Under the blossom that hangs on the bough [3]*.*

Pro. Why, that's my dainty Ariel: I shall miss thee;
But yet thou shalt have freedom: So, so, so.—
To the king's ship, invisible as thou art:

' There

[1] *—when owls do cry.*] i. e. at night. Dr. Warburton thought that these words denoted the time of Ariel's flight to be *winter;* but owls, as Mr. Steevens has observed, are as clamorous in summer as in winter. As this passage is now printed, Ariel says that he reposes in a cowslip's bell during the night. Perhaps, however, a full point ought to be placed after the word *couch*, and a comma at the end of the line. If the passage should be thus regulated, Ariel will then take his departure by night, the proper season for the bat to set out upon the expedition. That the crying of owls was introduced as descriptive of night, and not to mark the season of the year, is proved by Shakspeare's frequent mention of the same bird in various places, in all of which the owl is introduced as an attendant upon night. So, in *Macbeth:*
" It was the owl that cry'd, the fatal bellman,
" That gives the stern'st good-night."
Again, in *K. Henry VI.* P. ii.
" Deep night, dread night, the silent of the night,
" When screitch-owls cry —."
Again, in his *Venus and Adonis:*
" The owl, night's herald, shrieks; 'tis very late," &c.
Again, in *Cymbeline:*
" The night to the owl, and morn to the lark, less welcome."
MALONE.

[2] *After summer merrily:*] Mr. Theobald reads—after *sunset*, " because the bat is not visible by day, but appears first about twilight." Dr. Warburton thinks *summer* is right, " the roughness of winter being represented by Shakspeare as disagreeable to fairies and such like delicate spirits, who on this account constantly follow *summer*."—Mr. Steevens thinks that, " the bat being no bird of passage, this expression is probably used to signify, not that Ariel *pursues summer*, but that *after summer is past*, he rides upon the soft down of a bat's back, which suits not improperly with the delicacy of his airy being."—I see, however, no reason why Ariel should bestride his bat with more ardour *after* summer than *before*, or *during* that season; unless we understand, with Dr. Warburton, that he goes in *pursuit* of summer, in whatever part of the globe it could be found (in which sense the word *after* is frequently used in the midland counties). So in a kindred sense, in *K. Lear:*
" —— while I to this hard house, ——
" (Which even but now, demanding *after* you,
" Deny'd me to come in) return," &c. MALONE.

Our

There shalt thou find the mariners asleep
Under the hatches; the master, and the boatswain,
Being awake, enforce them to this place;
And presently, I pr'ythee.
 Ari. I drink the air⁴ before me, and return
Or e'er your pulse twice beat.   [*Exit* ARIEL.
 Gon. All torment, trouble, wonder, and amazement
Inhabits here; Some heavenly power guide us
Out of this fearful country!
 Pro. Behold, sir king,
The wronged duke of Milan, Prospero;
For more assurance that a living prince
Does now speak to thee, I embrace thy body;
And to thee, and thy company, I bid
A hearty welcome.
 Alon. Whe'r thou be'st he, or no,
Or some inchanted trifle to abuse me,
As late I have been, I not know: thy pulse

Our author is seldom solicitous that every part of his imagery should correspond. I, therefore, think, that though the bat is "no bird of passage," Shakspeare probably meant to express what Dr. Warburton supposes. A short account, however, of this winged animal may perhaps prove the best illustration of the passage before us:

"The bat (says Dr. Goldsmith, in his entertaining and instructive
"*Natural History*,) makes its appearance in *summer*, and begins its flight
"in the dusk of the evening. It appears only in the *most pleasant*
"evenings; at other times it continues in its retreat, the chink of a
"ruined building, or the hollow of a tree. Thus the little animal even
"in summer sleeps the greatest part of his time, never venturing out by
"day-light, nor in *rainy* weather. But its short life is still more
"abridged by continuing in a torpid state during the *winter*. At the
"approach of the cold season, the bat prepares for its state of lifeless
"inactivity, and seems rather to choose a place where it may continue
"safe from interruption, than where it may be warmly or commodi-
"ously lodged."

When Shakspeare had determined to send Ariel in pursuit of summer, wherever it could be found, as most congenial to such an airy being, is it then surprising that he should have made the *bat*, rather than "the wind, his post-horse;" an animal thus delighting in that season, and reduced by winter to a state of lifeless inactivity? MALONE.

 ³ *Under the blossom that hangs on the bough.*] So, in *Godfrey of Bulloigne*, translated by Fairfax, 1600:
  "The goblins, fairies ————
  "Ranged in *flowerie dales*, and mountaines hore,
  "And under every trembling leaf they sit." ANONYMOUS.

 ⁴ *I drink the air.*—] *To drink the air*—is an expression of swiftness of the same kind as *to devour the way* in *Henry IV*. JOHNSON.

              Beats,

Beats, as of flesh and blood; and, since I saw thee,
The affliction of my mind amends, with which,
I fear, a madness held me: this must crave
(An if this be at all,) a most strange story.
Thy dukedom I resign [5]; and do intreat,
Thou pardon me my wrongs:—But how should Prospero
Be living, and be here?

Pro. First, noble friend,
Let me embrace thine age; whose honour cannot
Be measur'd, or confin'd.

Gon. Whether this be,
Or be not, I'll not swear.

Pro. You do yet taste
Some subtilties o' the isle, that will not let you
Believe things certain:—Welcome, my friends all:—
But you, my brace of lords, were I so minded,
 [*Aside to* SEB. *and* ANT.
I here could pluck his highness' frown upon you,
And justify you traitors; at this time
I'll tell no tales.

Seb. The devil speaks in him. [*Aside.*

Pro. No:—
For you, most wicked Sir, whom to call brother
Would even infect my mouth, I do forgive
Thy rankest fault; all of them; and require
My dukedom of thee, which, perforce, I know,
Thou must restore.

Alon. If thou be'st Prospero,
Give us particulars of thy preservation:
How thou hast met us here, who three hours since [6]

Were

---

[5] *Thy dukedom I resign;* —] The duchy of Milan being through the treachery of Anthonio made feudatory to the crown of Naples, Alonso promises to resign his claim of sovereignty for the future. STEEVENS.

[6] —*who three hours since*] The unity of time is most rigidly observed in this piece. The fable scarcely takes up a greater number of hours than are employed in the representation; and from the very particular care which our author takes to point out this circumstance in so many other passages, as well as here, it should seem as if it were not accidental, but purposely designed to shew the admirers of Ben Jonson's art, and the cavillers of the time, that he too could write a play within all the strictest laws of regularity, when he chose to load himself with the critic's fetters.

The *Boatswain* marks the progress of the day again—*which but three glasses since*, &c. and at the beginning of this act the duration of the time employed on the stage is particularly ascertained; and it refers to a

passage

Were wreck'd upon this shore; where I have lost,
How sharp the point of this remembrance is!
My dear son Ferdinand.

Pro. I am woe for't, Sir⁷.

Alon. Irreparable is the loss; and patience
Says, it is past her cure.

Pro. I rather think,
You have not sought her help; of whose soft grace,
For the like loss, I have her sovereign aid,
And rest myself content.

Alon. You the like loss?

Pro. As great to me, as late⁸; and, supportable
To make the dear loss, have I means much weaker
Than you may call to comfort you; for I
Have lost my daughter.

Alon. A daughter?
O heavens! that they were living both in Naples,
The king and queen there! that they were, I wish
Myself were mudded in that oozy bed,
Where my son lies. When did you lose your daughter?

Pro. In this last tempest. I perceive, these lords
At this encounter do so much admire,
That they devour their reason; and scarce think,
Their eyes do offices of truth, their words
Are natural breath⁹: but, howsoe'er you have
Been jostled from your senses, know for certain,

---

passage in the first act, of the same tendency. The storm was raised at least two glasses after mid-day, and Ariel was promised that the work should cease at the *sixth hour*. STEEVENS.

⁷ *I am woe for't, Sir.*] i. e. *I am sorry for it*. STEEVENS.
To be *woe* is often used by old writers to signify *to be sorry*. So, in the play of *The Four P's*, 1569:
"But be ye sure, I would be woe,
"That you should chance to beguile me so."

⁸ *As great to me, as late;*] My loss is as great as yours, and has as lately happened to me. JOHNSON.

⁹ ——— their words
Are natural breath.] An anonymous correspondent thinks that *their* is a corruption, and that we should read—*these* words. His conjecture appears not improbable. The lords had no doubt concerning *themselves*. Their doubts related only to *Prospero*, whom they at first apprehended to be some "inchanted trifle to abuse them." They doubt, says he, whether what they see and hear is a mere illusion; whether the person they behold is a living mortal, whether the words they hear are spoken by a human creature. MALONE.

That

'That I am Prospero, and that very duke
Which was thrust forth of Milan; who most strangely
Upon this shore, where you were wreck'd, was landed,
To be the lord on't. No more yet of this;
For 'tis a chronicle of day by day,
Not a relation for a breakfast, nor
Befitting this first meeting. Welcome, Sir;
This cell's my court: here have I few attendants,
And subjects none abroad: pray you, look in,
My dukedom since you have given me again,
I will requite you with as good a thing;
At least, bring forth a wonder, to content ye,
As much as me my dukedom.

The entrance of the cell opens, and discovers FERDINAND *and* MIRANDA *playing at chess.*

Mira. Sweet lord, you play me false.
Fer. No, my dearest love,
I would not for the world.
Mira. Yes, for a score of kingdoms [1], you should wrangle,
And I would call it fair play.
Alon. If this prove
A vision of the island, one dear son
Shall I twice lose.
Seb. A most high miracle!
Fer. Though the seas threaten, they are merciful:
I have curs'd them without cause. [*Fer. kneels to* Alon.
Alon. Now all the blessings
Of a glad father compass thee about!
Arise, and say how thou cam'st here.
Mira. O wonder!
How many goodly creatures are there here!
How beauteous mankind is! O brave new world,
That has such people in't!

---

[1] *Yes, for a score of kingdoms, &c.*] I take the sense to be only this: Ferdinand would not, he says, play her false for the *world*: yes, answers she, I would allow you to do it for something less than the world, for *twenty kingdoms*, and I wish you well enough to allow you, after a little *wrangle*, that your play was fair. So likewise Dr. Grey.
                                                    JOHNSON.

I would recommend another punctuation, and then the sense would be as follows:

    Yes, for a score of kingdoms you should wrangle,
    And I would call it fair play;

because such a contest would be worthy of you. STEEVENS.

Pro.

Pro. 'Tis new to thee.
Alon. What is this maid, with whom thou waſt at play?
Your eld'ſt acquaintance cannot be three hours:
Is ſhe the goddeſs that hath ſever'd us,
And brought us thus together?
Fer. Sir, ſhe's mortal;
But, by immortal providence, ſhe's mine;
I choſe her, when I could not aſk my father
For his advice; nor thought I had one: ſhe
Is daughter to this famous duke of Milan,
Of whom ſo often I have heard renown,
But never ſaw before; of whom I have
Receiv'd a ſecond life, and ſecond father
This lady makes him to me.
Alon. I am her's:
But O, how oddly will it ſound, that I
Muſt aſk my child forgiveneſs!
Pro. There, Sir, ſtop;
Let us not burthen our remembrances²
With a heavineſs that's gone.
Gon. I've inly wept,
Or ſhould have ſpoke ere this. Look down, you gods,
And on this couple drop a bleſſed crown;
For it is you, that have chalk'd forth the way
Which brought us hither!
Alon. I ſay, Amen, Gonzalo!
Gon. Was Milan thruſt from Milan, that his iſſue
Should become kings of Naples? O, rejoice
Beyond a common joy; and ſet it down
With gold on laſting pillars: In one voyage
Did Claribel her huſband find at Tunis;
And Ferdinand, her brother, found a wife,
Where he himſelf was loſt; Proſpero his dukedom,
In a poor iſle; and all of us, ourſelves,
When no man was his own³.

Alon.

---

² *Our* remembrances —] By the miſtake of the tranſcriber the word *with* being placed at the end of this line, Mr. Pope and the ſubſequent editors, for the ſake of the metre, read —*remembrance*. The regulation now made renders change unneceſſary.

We have the ſame phraſeology in *Coriolanus:*
"One thus deſcended, ———
"To be ſet high in place, we did commend
"To your *remembrances.*" MALONE.

³ *When no man was his own.*] i. e. *at a time when* no one was in his

Alon. Give me your hands: [*To* Fer. *and* Mir.
Let grief and sorrow still embrace his heart,
That doth not wish you joy!
  Gon. Be't so! Amen!

Re-enter ARIEL, *with the* MASTER *and* BOATSWAIN *amazedly following.*

O look, Sir, look, Sir, here are more of us!
I prophesy'd, if a gallows were on land,
This fellow could not drown :—Now, blasphemy,
That swear'st grace o'erboard, not an oath on shore?
Hast thou no mouth by land? What is the news?
  Boats. The best news is, that we have safely found
Our king, and company: the next, our ship,
Which, but three glasses since, we gave out split,
Is tight, and yare, and bravely rigg'd, as when
We first put out to sea.
  Ari. Sir, all this service
Have I done since I went.   } *Aside.*
  Pro. My trickly spirit⁴!
  Alon. These are not natural events; they strengthen,
From strange to stranger:—Say, how came you hither?
  Boats. If I did think, Sir, I were well awake,
I'd strive to tell you. We were dead on sleep⁵,
And (how, we know not,) all clapp'd under hatches,
Where, but even now, with strange and several noises

his senses. It is still said, in colloquial language, that a madman *is not his own man,* i. e. is not master of himself. STEEVENS.

⁴ *My* trickly spirit!]. is, I believe, my clever, adroit spirit. Shakspeare uses the same word elsewhere:

"——that for a *trickly* word

"Defy the matter." STEEVENS.

Trickly also signifies neat, elegantly adorned. See Florio's Dictionary, 1598: " *Nimfarsi,* to trim, to smug, to *trixie,* to deck or spruce himself up as a nymphe." The same writer interprets *Pargoletta,* " quaint, pretty, nimble, *trixie,* tender, small." See also Minsheu's Dict in v. to *trick.* MALONE.

⁵ — *dead* on sleep,] The old copy reads—*of* sleep. STEEVENS.

Mr. Pope has — dead *asleep,* but on sleep was the ancient English phraseology. So, in Gascoigne's *Supposes:* " —— knock again; I think they be *on* sleep." Again, in a song, said to have been written by Anna Boleyn:

" O death, rock me *on* slepe."

Again, in Campion's *History of Ireland* 1633: " One officer in the house of great men is a tale-teller, who bringeth his lord *on* sleep with tales vaine and frivolous." MALONE.

VOL. III.   F

Of roaring, shrieking, howling, gingling chains,
And more diversity of sounds, all horrible,
We were awak'd; straitway, at liberty:
Where we, in all her trim⁶, freshly beheld
Our royal, good, and gallant ship; our master
Capering to eye her: On a trice, so please you,
Even in a dream, were we divided from them,
And were brought moping hither.

   Ari. Was't well done?
   Pro. Bravely, my diligence. Thou shalt be } *Aside.*
       free.
   Alon. This is as strange a maze as e'er men trod;
And there is in this business more than nature
Was ever conduct of⁷: some oracle
Must rectify our knowledge.
   Pro. Sir, my liege,
Do not infest your mind with beating on
The strangeness of this business⁸; at pick'd leisure,
Which shall be shortly, single I'll resolve you
(Which to you shall seem probable) of every
These happen'd accidents⁹: till when, be chearful,
And think of each thing well.—Come hither, spirit; [*Aside.*

---

⁶ *— in all her trim,*] The old copy has—*our* trim. Corrected by Dr Thirlby. MALONE.

⁷ *— conduct of:*] Conduct *for* conductor. STEEVENS.

So, in *Romeo and Juliet:* " Come bitter *conduct,*" &c. MALONE.

Conduct is yet used in the same sense: the person at Cambridge who reads prayers in King's and Trinity College Chapels is still so styled. HESLEY.

⁸ *———wit¹ beating on*
   The strangeness, &c.] A similar expression occurs in one of the parts of *King Henry VI:*
   " ———your thoughts
   " *Beat* on a crown "

Beating may mean *hammering,* working in the mind, dwelling long upon. Miranda, in the second scene of this play, tells her father that the storm is still *beating* in her mind. STEEVENS.

A kindred expression occurs in *Hamlet:* " *Cudgel* thy brains no more about it." MALONE.

⁹ *——— I'll resolve you*
   (Which to you shall seem probable) of every
   These happen'd accidents:] I will inform you how all these wonderful accidents have happened; which, though they now appear to you strange, will then seem probable.

An anonymous writer pointed out the true construction of this passage, but his explanation is, I think, incorrect. MALONE.

Set

TEMPEST.

Set Caliban and his companions free:
Untie the spell. [*Exit* Ariel.] How fares my gracious Sir,
There are yet missing of your company
Some few odd lads, that you remember not.

Re-enter ARIEL, *driving in* CALIBAN, STEPHANO, *and*
TRINCULO, *in their stolen apparel.*

Ste. Every man shift for all the rest, and let no man take care for himself; for all is but fortune:—Coragio, bully-monster, Coragio!

Trin. If these be true spies which I wear in my head, here's a goodly sight.

Cal. O Setebos, these be brave spirits, indeed!
How fine my master is! I am afraid
He will chastise me.

Seb. Ha, ha;
What things are these, my lord Anthonio!
Will money buy them?

Ant. Very like; one of them
Is a plain fish, and, no doubt, marketable.

Pro. Mark but the badges of these men, my lords,
Then say, if they be true[1]:—This mis-shapen knave,—
His mother was a witch; and one so strong
That could control the moon[2], make flows and ebbs,
And deal in her command without her power:
These three have robb'd me; and this demi-devil
(For he's a bastard one,) had plotted with them
To take my life; two of these fellows you
Must know, and own; this thing of darkness I
Acknowledge mine.

Cal. I shall be pinch'd to death.

Alon. Is not this Stephano, my drunken butler?

Seb. He's drunk now: Where had he wine?

---

[1] —*true:*] That is, *honest.* A *true man* is, in the language of that time, opposed to a *thief.* The sense is, *Mark what these men wear, and say if they are honest.* JOHNSON.

[2] ———*and one so strong*
that could control the moon,] From Medea's speech in Ovid (as translated by Golding) our author might have learned, that this was one of the pretended powers of witchcraft:
"—— And thee, O lightsome *moon,*
" I darken oft, though beaten brass abate thy peril soon."
MALONE.

Alon. And Trinculo is reeling ripe; Where should they
Find this grand liquor that hath gilded them ³?—
How cam'st thou in this pickle?

Trin. I have been in such a pickle, since I saw you last, that, I fear me, will never out of my bones: I shall not fear fly-blowing ⁴.

Seb. Why, how now, Stephano?

Ste. O, touch me not; I am not Stephano, but a cramp ⁵.

Pro. You'd be king of the isle, Sirrah?

Ste. I should have been a sore one then.

Alon. This is a strange thing as e'er I look'd on.
[*Pointing to* CALIBAN.

Pro. He is as disproportion'd in his manners,
As in his shape:—Go, Sirrah, to my cell;
Take with you your companions; as you look
To have my pardon, trim it handsomely.

Cal. Ay, that I will; and I'll be wise hereafter,
And seek for grace: What a thrice-double ass
Was I, to take this drunkard for a god,
And worship this dull fool?

Pro. Go to; away!

Alon. Hence, and bestow your luggage where you found it.

Seb. Or stole it, rather. [*Exeunt* CAL. STE. *and* TRIN.

Pro. Sir, I invite your highness, and your train,
To my poor cell: where you shall take your rest
For this one night; which (part of it) I'll waste
With such discourse, as, I not doubt, shall make it
Go quick away; the story of my life,
And the particular accidents, gone by,

---

³ — *this grand* liquor *that hath* gilded *them?*] Shakspeare, to be sure, wrote—grand 'lixir, alluding to the *grand* Elixir of the alchymists, which they pretend would restore youth, and confer immortality. This, as they said, being a preparation of gold, they called *Aurum potabile.* The phrase of being *gilded* was a trite one on this occasion. Thus Fletcher, in his *Chances:*—" Duke. *Is she not drunk too!* Whore. *A little gilded o'er, sir; old sack, old sack, boys!"* WARBURTON.

As the alchymist's *Elixir* was supposed to be a liquor, the old reading may stand, and the allusion holds good without alteration.
STEEVENS.

⁴ — *fly-blowing*] This pickle alludes to their plunge into the stinking pool; and *pickling* preserves meat from *fly-blowing*. STEEVENS.

⁵ — *but a* cramp.] i. e. I am all over a *cramp.* Prospero had ordered Ariel to *soften up their sinews with aged cramps. Touch me not,* alludes to the *soreness* occasioned by them. In the next line the speaker confirms this meaning by a quibble on the word *sore.* STEEVENS.

Since

Since I came to this ifle: And in the morn,
I'll bring you to your fhip, and fo to Naples,
Where I have hope to fee the nuptial
Of thefe our dear-beloved folemniz'd;
And thence retire me to my Milan, where
Every third thought fhall be my grave.
   Alon. I long
To hear the ftory of your life, which muft
Take the ear ftrangely.
   Pro. I'll deliver all;
And promife you calm feas, aufpicious gales,
And fail fo expeditious, that fhall catch
Your royal fleet far off.—My Ariel;—chick—
That is thy charge; then to the elements   } *Afide.*
Be free, and fare thou well!—Pleafe you, draw near. [*Exeunt.*

EPILOGUE,

SPOKEN BY PROSPERO.

NOW my charms are all o'erthrown,
And what strength I have's mine own;
Which is most faint: now, 'tis true,
I must be here confin'd by you,
Or sent to Naples: Let me not,
Since I have my dukedom got,
And pardon'd the deceiver, dwell
In this bare island, by your spell;
But release me from my bands,
With the help of your good hands [6].
Gentle breath of yours my sails
Must fill, or else my project fails,
Which was to please: Now I want
Spirits to enforce, art to enchant;
And my ending is despair,
Unless I be reliev'd by prayer [7];
Which pierces so, that it assaults
Mercy itself, and frees all faults.
  As you from crimes would pardon'd be,
Let your indulgence set me free [8].

---

[6] *With the help, &c.*] By your applause, by clapping hands. JOHNS. Noise was supposed to dissolve a spell. So twice before in this play:
  "No tongue; all eyes; be silent."
Again: "———— hush! be mute;
  "Or else our *spell is marr'd*. STEEVENS.

[7] *And my ending is despair,*
  Unless I be reliev'd by prayer;] This alludes to the old stories told of the despair of necromancers in their last moments, and of the efficacy of the prayers of their friends for them. WARBURTON.

[8] It is observed of *The Tempest*, that its plan is regular; this the author of *The Revisal* thinks, what I think too, an accidental effect of the story, not intended or regarded by our author. But, whatever might be Shakspeare's intention in forming or adopting the plot, he has made it instrumental to the production of many characters, diversified with boundless invention, and preserved with profound skill in nature, extensive knowledge of opinions, and accurate observation of life. In a single drama are here exhibited princes, courtiers, and sailors, all speaking in their real characters. There is the agency of airy spirits, and of an earthly goblin. The operations of magic, the tumults of a storm, the adventures of a desert island, the native effusion of untaught affection, the punishment of guilt, and the final happiness of the pair for whom our passions and reason are equally interested.
JOHNSON.

TWO GENTLEMEN OF VERONA.

PERSONS REPRESENTED.

Duke of Milan, *father to* Silvia.
Valentine, } *Gentlemen of* Verona.
Protheus,
Anthonio, *father to* Protheus.
Thurio, *a foolish rival to* Valentine.
Eglamour, *agent for* Silvia *in her escape*.
Speed, *a clownish servant to* Valentine.
Launce, *servant to* Protheus.
Panthino*, *servant to* Anthonio.
Host, *where* Julia *lodges in* Milan.
Out-laws.

Julia, *a lady of* Verona, *beloved by* Protheus.
Silvia, *the duke's daughter, beloved by* Valentine.
Lucetta, *waiting-woman to* Julia.

Servants, Musicians.

SCENE, *sometimes in* Verona; *sometimes in* Milan; *and on the frontiers of* Mantua.

* *Panthino.*] In the enumeration of characters in the old copy, this attendant on Anthonio is called *Panthion*, but in the play, always *Panthino*. STEEVENS.

TWO GENTLEMEN OF VERONA.[1]

ACT I. SCENE I.

An open place in Verona.

Enter VALENTINE *and* PROTHEUS.

Val. Cease to persuade, my loving Protheus;
Home-keeping youth have ever homely wits:

Wer't

---

[1] Some of the incidents in this play may be supposed to have been taken from *The Arcadia*, book i. chap. 6. where Pyrocles consents to head the Helots. (The *Arcadia* was entered on the books of the Stationers' Company, Aug. 23d, 1588, and printed in 1590.) The love-adventure of Julia resembles that of Viola in *Twelfth Night*, and is indeed common to many of the ancient novels. STEEVENS.

Mrs. *Lenox* observes, and I think not improbably, that the story of *Protheus* and *Julia* might be taken from a similar one in the *Diana* of *George* of *Montemayor*.—" This pastoral romance," says she, " was translated from the *Spanish* in *Shakspeare's* time." I have seen no earlier translation than that of *Bartholomew Yong*, who dates his dedication in *November* 1598; and *Meres*, in his *Wit's Treasury*, printed the same year, expressly mentions the *Two Gentlemen of Verona*. Indeed *Montemayor* was translated two or three years before by one *Thomas Wilson*; but this work, I am persuaded, was never published *entirely*; perhaps some parts of it were, or the tale might have been translated by others. However, Mr. Steevens says, very truly, that this kind of love adventure is frequent in the old *novelists*. FARMER.

There is no earlier translation of the *Diana* entered on the books of the Stationers' Company, than that of B. Younge, September 1598. Many translations, however, after they were licensed, were capriciously suppressed. Among others, " The Decameron of Mr. John Boccace, Florentine," was " recalled by my lord of Canterbury's commands." STEEVENS.

This comedy, I believe, was written in 1595. See *An Attempt to ascertain the order of Shakspeare's plays*, ante. MALONE.

It is observable, (I know not for what cause,) that the style of this comedy is less figurative, and more natural and unaffected than the greater part of this author's, though supposed to be one of the first he

Wer't not, affection chains thy tender days,
To the sweet glances of thy honour'd love,
I rather would entreat thy company,
To see the wonders of the world abroad,
Than, living dully sluggardiz'd at home,

It may very well be doubted whether Shakspeare had any other hand in this play than the enlivening it with some speeches and lines thrown in here and there, which are easily distinguished, as being of a different stamp from the rest. HANMER.

To this observation of Mr. Pope, which is very just, Mr. Theobald has added, that this is one of Shakspeare's *worst plays, and is less corrupted than any other.* Mr. Upton peremptorily determines, *that if any proof can be drawn from manner and style, this play must be sent packing, and seek for its parent elsewhere. How otherwise,* says he, *do painters distinguish copies from originals? and have not authors their peculiar style and manner, from which a true critic can form as unerring judgment as a painter?* I am afraid this illustration of a critic's science will not prove what is desired. A painter knows a copy from an original by rules somewhat resembling those by which critics know a translation, which if it be literal, and literal it must be to resemble the copy of a picture, will be easily distinguished. Copies are known from originals, even when the painter copies his own picture; so, if an author should literally translate his work, he would lose the manner of an original.

Mr. Upton confounds the copy of a picture with the imitation of a painter's manner. Copies are easily known, but good imitations are not detected with equal certainty, and are, by the best judges, often mistaken. Nor is it true that the writer has always peculiarities equally distinguishable with those of the painter. The peculiar manner of each arises from the desire, natural to every performer, of facilitating his subsequent works by recurrence to his former ideas; this recurrence produces that repetition which is called habit. The painter, whose work is partly intellectual and partly manual, has habits of the mind, the eye, and the hand; the writer has only habits of the mind. Yet, some painters have differed as much from themselves as from any other; and I have been told, that there is little resemblance between the first works of Raphael and the last. The same variation may be expected in writers; and if it be true, as it seems, that they are less subject to habit, the difference between their works may be yet greater.

But by the internal marks of a composition we may discover the author with probability, though seldom with certainty. When I read this play, I cannot but think that I find, both in the serious and ludicrous scenes, the language and sentiments of Shakspeare. It is not indeed one of his most powerful effusions; it has neither many diversities of character, nor striking delineations of life, but it abounds in γνωμαι beyond most of his plays, and few have more lines or passages, which, singly considered, are eminently beautiful. I am yet inclined to believe that it was not very successful, and suspect that it has escaped corruption, only because, being seldom played, it was less exposed to the hazards of transcription. JOHNSON.

Wear

Wear out thy youth with shapeless idleness [2].
But, since thou lov'st, love still, and thrive therein,
Even as I would, when I to love begin.

Pro. Wilt thou be gone? Sweet Valentine, adieu!
Think on thy Protheus, when thou, haply, seest
Some rare note-worthy object in thy travel:
Wish me partaker in thy happiness,
When thou dost meet good hap; and, in thy danger,
If ever danger do environ thee,
Commend thy grievance to my holy prayers,
For I will be thy bead's-man, Valentine.

Val. And on a love-book pray for my success.
Pro. Upon some book I love, I'll pray for thee.
Val. That's on some shallow story of deep love,
How young Leander cross'd the Hellespont [3].
Pro. That's a deep story of a deeper love;
For he was more than over shoes in love.
Val. 'Tis true; for you are over boots in love,
And yet you never swom the Hellespont.
Pro. Over the boots? nay, give me not the boots [4].
Val.

---

[2] —*shapeless idleness.*] The expression is fine, as implying that *idleness* prevents the giving any form or character to the manners.
WARBURTON.

[3] ———— *some shallow story of deep love,*
How young Leander cross'd the Hellespont.] The poem of Musæus, entitled HERO AND LEANDER, is meant. Marlowe's translation of this piece was entered on the Stationers' books, Sept. 18, 1593, and the first two Sestiads of it, with a small part of the third, (which was all that he had finished,) were printed, I imagine, in that, or the following year. See Blount's dedication to the edition of 1637, by which it appears that it was originally published in an imperfect state. It was extremely popular, and deservedly, so, many of *Marlowe's* lines being as smooth as those of Dryden. Our author has quoted one of them in *As you like it.* He had probably read this poem recently before he wrote the present play; for he again alludes to it in the third act:
"Why then a ladder, quaintly made of cords,
"Would serve to scale another *Hero's* tower,
"So bold *Leander* would adventure it." MALONE.
Since this note was written, I have seen the edition of Marlowe's *Hero and Leander*, printed in 1598. It contains the first two *Sestiads* only. The remainder was added by Chapman. MALONE.

[4] —*nay, give me not the boots.*] A proverbial expression, though now disused, signifying, Don't make a laughing stock of me; don't play upon me. The French have a phrase, *Bailler foin en corne;* which Cotgrave thus interprets, *To give one the boots;* to sell him a bargain.
THEOBALD.

Perhaps

Val. No, I will not, for it boots thee not.
Pro. What?
Val. To be in love, where scorn is bought with groans;
Coy looks, with heart sore sighs; one fading moment's mirth,
With twenty watchful, weary, tedious nights:
If haply won, perhaps, a hapless gain;
If lost, why then a grievous labour won;
However, but a folly bought with wit,
Or else a wit by folly vanquished [5].
Pro. So, by your circumstance, you call me fool.
Val. So, by your circumstance, I fear you'll prove.
Pro. 'Tis love you cavil at; I am not love.
Val. Love is your master, for he masters you;
And he that is so yoked by a fool,
Methinks should not be chronicled for wise.
Pro. Yet writers say, As in the sweetest bud
The eating canker dwells [6], so eating love
Inhabits in the finest wits of all.
Val. And writers say, As the most forward bud
Is eaten by the canker ere it blow,
Even so by love the young and tender wit
Is turn'd to folly; blasting in the bud,
Losing his verdure even in the prime,
And all the fair effects of future hopes.
But wherefore waste I time to counsel thee,
That art a votary to fond desire?
Once more adieu: my father at the road
Expects my coming, there to see me shipp'd.
Pro. And thither will I bring thee, Valentine.
Val. Sweet Protheus, no; now let us take our leave.

Perhaps this expression took its origin from a sport the country people in Warwickshire use at their harvest-home, where one sits as judge, to try misdemeanours committed in harvest, and the punishment for the men is to be laid on a bench, and slapped on the breech with a pair of *boots*. This they call *giving them the boots*. The *boots*, however, were anciently an engine of torture. See MS. Harl. 6999—48. STEEVENS.

[5] *However, but a folly*, &c.] This love will end in a *foolish action*, to produce which you are long to spend your *wit*, or it will end in the loss of your *wit*, which will be overpowered by the folly of love.
JOHNSON.

[6] ——— *As in the sweetest bud*
The eating canker dwells,] So, in our author's 70th Sonnet,
" For canker vice the sweetest buds doth love." MALONE.

At

At Milan [7], let me hear from thee by letters,
Of thy success in love, and what news else
Betideth here in absence of thy friend;
And I likewise will visit thee with mine.

Pro. All happiness bechance to thee in Milan!

Val. As much to you at home! and so, farewell!

[*Exit* VALENTINE.

Pro. He after honour hunts, I after love:
He leaves his friends, to dignify them more;
I leave myself [*], my friends, and all for love.
Thou, Julia, thou hast metamorphos'd me;
Made me neglect my studies, lose my time,
War with good counsel, set the world at nought;
Made wit [8] with musing weak, heart sick with thought.

Enter SPEED.

Speed. Sir Protheus, save you: Saw you my master?

Pro. But now he parted hence, to embark for Milan.

Speed. Twenty to one then, he is shipp'd already;
And I have play'd the sheep, in losing him.

Pro. Indeed a sheep doth very often stray,
An if the shepherd be awhile away.

Speed. You conclude, that my master is a shepherd then, and I a sheep [9]?

Pro. I do.

Speed. Why then my horns are his horns, whether I wake or sleep.

Pro. A silly answer, fitting well a sheep.

Speed. This proves me still a sheep.

Pro. True; and thy master a shepherd.

Speed. Nay, that I can deny by a circumstance.

Pro. It shall go hard, but I'll prove it by another.

Speed. The shepherd seeks the sheep, and not the sheep

---

[7] At *Milan,*—] The old copy has—*To* Milan. The emendation was made by the editor of the second folio. The first copy however may be right. " *To Milan*"—may here be intended as an imperfect sentence. I am now bound for Milan. Or the construction intended may have been—Let me hear from thee by letters to Milan, i. e. addressed to me there. MALONE.

[*] *I leave, &c.*] Old copy—*I love*—. Corrected by Mr. Pope. MALONE.

[8] Made *wit*—] i. e. thou hast made, &c. MALONE.

[9] — a *sheep?*] The article, which is wanting in the original copy, was supplied by the editor of the second folio. MALONE.

the shepherd; but I seek my master, and my master seeks not me: therefore, I am no sheep.

Pro. The sheep for fodder follow the shepherd, the shepherd for food follows not the sheep; thou for wages followest thy master, thy master for wages follows not thee: therefore, thou art a sheep.

Speed. Such another proof will make me cry baa.

Pro. But dost thou hear? gav'st thou my letter to Julia?

Speed. Ay, Sir: I, a lost mutton, gave your letter to her, a laced mutton¹; and she, a laced mutton, gave me, a lost mutton, nothing for my labour.

Pro. Here's too small a pasture for such a store of muttons.

Speed. If the ground be overcharg'd, you were best stick her.

Pro. Nay, in that you are astray²; 'twere best pound you.

Speed. Nay, Sir, less than a pound shall serve me for carrying your letter.

Pro. You mistake; I mean the pound, a pinfold.

Speed. From a pound to a pin? fold it over and over, 'Tis threefold too little for carrying a letter to your lover.

Pro. But what said she? did she nod³?

Speed.

---

¹ *I, a lost mutton, gave your letter to her, a laced mutton;*] Speed calls himself a *lost mutton*, because he had lost his master, and because Protheus had been proving him a sheep. But why does he call the lady a laced mutton? Wenchers are to this day called *mutton-mongers*, and consequently the object of their passion must be the *mutton*.
THEOBALD.

A *laced mutton* was in our author's time so established a term for a courtezan, that a street in Clerkenwell, which was much frequented by women of the town, was then called *Mutton-lane*. It seems to have been a phrase of the same kind as the French expression—*caille coiffée*, and might be rendered in that language, *mouton en corset*. This appellation appears to have been as old as the time of king Henry III. "Item sequitur gravis pœna corporalis, sed sine amissione vitæ vel membrorum, si raptus sit de *concubina* legitima, vel *aliâ quæstum faciente*, sine delectu personarum: has quidem *oves* debet rex tueri pro pace suâ." Bracton *de Legibus*; lib. ii. MALONE.

² *Nay, in that you are* astray, &c.] From the word *astray* here, and *lost mutton* above, it is obvious that the double reference was to the first sentence of the general confession in the Prayer-Book. HENLEY.

³ —*did she nod?*] These words have been supplied by some of the editors, to introduce what follows. STEEVENS.

They were supplied by Mr. Theobald. In Speed's answer the old
spelling

Speed. I. [*Speed nods.*
Pro. Nod, I? why that's noddy [3].
Speed. You mistook, Sir; I say she did nod: and you ask me, if she did nod; and I say, I.
Pro. And that set together, is noddy.
Speed. Now you have taken the pains to set it together, take it for your pains.
Pro. No, no, you shall have it for bearing the letter.
Speed. Well, I perceive, I must be fain to bear with you.
Pro. Why, Sir, how do you bear with me?
Speed. Marry, Sir, the letter very orderly; having nothing but the word, noddy, for my pains.
Pro. Beshrew me, but you have a quick wit.
Speed. And yet it cannot overtake your slow purse.
Pro. Come, come, open the matter in brief: What said she?
Speed. Open your purse, that the money, and the matter, may be both at once deliver'd.
Pro. Well, Sir, here is for your pains: What said she?
Speed. Truly, Sir, I think you'll hardly win her.
Pro. Why? Couldst thou perceive so much from her?
Speed. Sir, I could perceive nothing at all from her; no, not so much as a ducat for delivering your letter: And being so hard to me that brought your mind, I fear she'll prove as hard to you in telling your mind [4]. Give her no token but stones; for she's as hard as steel.
Pro. What, said she nothing?
Speed. No, not so much as—*take this for thy pains.* To testify your bounty, I thank you, you have testern'd me [5];

spelling of the affirmative particle has been retained; otherwise the conceit of Protheus (such as it is) would be unintelligible. MALONE.

[3] —*that's noddy.*] *Noddy* was a game at cards. STEEVENS.
This play upon syllables is hardly worth explaining. The speakers intend to fix the name of *noddy*, that is, *fool*, on each other. REED.

[4] —*in telling* your *mind.*] The editor of the second folio, not understanding this, altered *your* to *her,* which has been followed in all the subsequent editions. The old copy is certainly right. The meaning is,—*She being so hard to me who was the bearer of your mind, I fear she will prove no less so to you, when you address her in person.* The opposition is between *brought* and *telling.* MALONE.

[5] —*you have* testern'd *me;*] You have gratified me with a *tester, testern,* or *testen,* that is, with a sixpence. JOHNSON.
The old reading is—*cestern'd.* STEEVENS.
This typographical error was corrected by the editor of the second folio. MALONE.

in requital whereof, henceforth carry your letters yourself: and so, Sir, I'll commend you to my master.

Pro. Go, go, be gone, to save your ship from wreck;
Which cannot perish, having thee aboard [6],
Being destined to a drier death on shore:—
I must go send some better messenger;
I fear, my Julia would not deign my lines,
Receiving them from such a worthless post. [*Exeunt.*

SCENE II.

The same. Garden of Julia's *house.*

Enter JULIA *and* LUCETTA.

Jul. But say, Lucetta, now we are alone,
Would'st thou then counsel me to fall in love?
Luc. Ay, Madam; so you stumble not unheedfully.
Jul. Of all the fair resort of gentlemen,
That every day with parle encounter me,
In thy opinion, which is worthiest love?
Luc. Please you, repeat their names, I'll shew my mind
According to my shallow simple skill.
Jul. What think'st thou of the fair Sir Eglamour [7]?
Luc. As of a knight well-spoken, neat and fine;
But, were I you, he never should be mine.
Jul. What think'st thou of the rich Mercatio?
Luc. Well, of his wealth; but of himself, so, so.
Jul. What think'st thou of the gentle Protheus?
Luc. Lord, lord! to see what folly reigns in us!
Jul. How now, what means this passion at his name?
Luc. Pardon, dear madam; 'tis a passing shame,
That I, unworthy body as I am,
Should censure thus [8] on lovely gentlemen.
Jul. Why not on Protheus, as of all the rest?
Luc. Then thus,— of many good I think him best.
Jul. Your reason?
Luc. I have no other but a woman's reason;
I think him so, because I think him so.

---

[6] *Which cannot perish,* &c.] The same proverb has been already alluded to. See p. 6. REED.

[7] —*fair* Sir Eglamour?] Sir Eglamour of Artoys is the hero of an ancient metrical romance. STEEVENS.

[8] *Should censure thus*—] To *censure*, in our author's time, generally signified to give one's judgment or opinion. MALONE.

Jul.

Jul. And would'st thou have me cast my love on him?
Luc. Ay, if you thought your love not cast away.
Jul. Why, he of all the rest hath never mov'd me.
Luc. Yet he of all the rest, I think, best loves ye.
Jul. His little speaking shows his love but small.
Luc. Fire, that is closest kept, burns most of all.
Jul. They do not love, that do not show their love.
Luc. O, they love least, that let men know their love.
Jul. I would, I knew his mind.
Luc. Peruse this paper, madam.
Jul. *To Julia,*—Say, from whom?
Luc. That the contents will show.
Jul. Say, say; who gave it thee?
Luc. Sir Valentine's page; and sent, I think, from Protheus:

He would have given it you, but I, being in the way,
Did in your name receive it; pardon the fault, I pray.
 Jul. Now, by my modesty, a goodly broker⁹!
Dare you presume to harbour wanton lines?
To whisper and conspire against my youth?
Now, trust me, 'tis an office of great worth,
And you an officer fit for the place.
There, take the paper, see it be return'd;
Or else return no more into my sight.
 Luc. To plead for love deserves more fee than hate.
 Jul. Will you be gone?
 Luc. That you may ruminate.   [*Exit.*
 Jul. And yet, I would I had o'erlook'd the letter.
It were a shame, to call her back again,
And pray her to a fault for which I chid her.
What fool is she, that knows I am a maid,
And would not force the letter to my view?
Since maids, in modesty, say *No,* to that ¹
Which they would have the profferer construe, *Ay.*
Fie, fie! how wayward is this foolish love,
That, like a testy babe, will scratch the nurse,
And presently, all humbled, kiss the rod!
How churlishly I chid Lucetta hence,
When willingly I would have had her here!

  ⁹ *— a goodly broker!*] A *broker* was used for matchmaker, sometimes or a procuress. JOHNSON.
  ¹ *—say* No, *to that,* &c.] A paraphrase on the old proverb, "Maids say nay, and take it." STEEVENS.

How angrily I taught my brow to frown,
When inward joy enforc'd my heart to smile!
My penance is, to call Lucetta back,
And aſk remiſſion for my folly paſt;—
What ho! Lucetta!

Re-enter LUCETTA.

Luc. What would your ladyſhip?
Jul. Is it near dinner-time?
Luc. I would, it were;
That you might kill your ſtomach [2] on your meat,
And not upon your maid.
Jul. What is't that you
Took up ſo gingerly?
Luc. Nothing.
Jul. Why didſt thou ſtoop then?
Luc. To take a paper up that I let fall.
Jul. And is that paper nothing?
Luc. Nothing concerning me.
Jul. Then let it lie for thoſe that it concerns.
Luc. Madam, it will not lie where it concerns,
Unleſs it have a falſe interpreter.
Jul. Some love of yours hath writ to you in rhime.
Luc. That I might ſing it, Madam, to a tune:
Give me a note: your ladyſhip can ſet.
Jul. As little by ſuch toys as may be poſſible:
Beſt ſing it to the tune of *Light o' love*.
Luc. It is too heavy for ſo light a tune.
Jul. Heavy? belike, it hath ſome burden then.
Luc. Ay; and melodious were it, would you ſing it.
Jul. And why not you?
Luc. I cannot reach ſo high.
Jul. Let's ſee your ſong:—How now, minion?
Luc. Keep tune there ſtill, ſo you will ſing it out:
And yet, methinks, I do not like this tune.
Jul. You do not?
Luc. No, Madam; it is too ſharp.
Jul. You, minion, are too ſaucy.
Luc. Nay, now you are too flat,
And mar the concord with too harſh a deſcant [3]:

---

[2] —*ſtomach*] was uſed for *paſſion* or *obſtinacy*. JOHNSON.
[3] —*too harſh a* deſcant:] *Deſcant* is a term in muſic. See Sir John Hawkins's note on the firſt ſpeech in *K. Richard III*. STEEVENS.

There.

There wanteth but a mean [4] to fill your song.

Jul. The mean is drown'd with your unruly base.

Luc. Indeed, I bid the base for Protheus [5].

Jul. This babble shall not henceforth trouble me.
Here is a coil with protestation!— [*Tears the letter.*
Go, get you gone; and let the papers lie:
You would be fingering them, to anger me.

Luc. She makes it strange; but she would be best pleas'd
To be so anger'd with another letter. [*Exit.*

Jul. Nay, would I were so anger'd with the same!
O hateful hands, to tear such loving words!
Injurious wasps; to feed on such sweet honey,
And kill the bees, that yield it, with your stings!
I'll kiss each several paper for amends.
Look, here is writ—*kind Julia;*—unkind Julia!
As in revenge of thy ingratitude,
I throw thy name against the bruising stones,
Trampling contemptuously on thy disdain.
And here is writ—*love-wounded Protheus:*—
Poor wounded name! my bosom, as a bed,
Shall lodge thee, till thy wound be throughly heal'd;
And thus I search it with a sovereign kiss.
But twice, or thrice, was Protheus written down:
Be calm, good wind, blow not a word away,
Till I have found each letter in the letter,
Except mine own name; that some whirlwind bear
Unto a ragged, fearful, hanging rock,
And throw it thence into the raging sea!
Lo, here in one line is his name twice writ,—
Poor forlorn Protheus, passionate Protheus,

[4] *— but a mean, &c.*] The *mean* is the *tenor* in music. STEEVENS.

[5] *Indeed, I bid the base for Protheus.*] The speaker here turns the allusion (which her mistress employed) from the *base in music* to a country exercise, *Bid the base:* in which some pursue, and others are made prisoners. So that Lucetta would intend, by this, to say, Indeed I take pains to make you a captive to Protheus's passion. WARBURTON.

Dr. Warburton is not quite accurate. The game was not called *Bid the Base,* but *the Base.* To *bid the base* means here, I believe, *to challenge to a contest.* So, in our author's *Venus and Adonis:*

"To *bid* the wind a *base* he now prepares,
"And wh'er he run, or fly, they knew not whether."

Again, in Hall's *Chronicle,* fol. 98. b. "The Queen marched from York to Wakefield, and *bade base* to the duke even before his castle." MALONE.

To the sweet Julia;—that I'll tear away;
And yet I will not, sith so prettily
He couples it to his complaining names:
Thus will I fold them one upon another;
Now kiss, embrace, contend, do what you will.

Re-enter LUCETTA.

Luc. Madam, dinner's ready, and your father stays.
Jul. Well, let us go.
Luc. What, shall these papers lie like tell-tales here?
Jul. If you respect them, best to take them up.
Luc. Nay, I was taken up for laying them down:
Yet here they shall not lie, for catching cold. *
Jul. I see, you have a month's mind to them. ⁶
Luc. Ay, Madam, you may say what sights you see;
I see things too, although you judge I wink.
Jul. Come, come, will't please you go? [*Exeunt.*

SCENE III.

The same. A Room in Anthonio's House.

Enter ANTHONIO *and* PANTHINO.

Ant. Tell me, Panthino, what sad talk ⁷ was that,
Wherewith my brother held you in the cloister?

---

* *Yet here they shall not lie* for *catching cold.*] i. e. lest they should catch cold.

So, in an ancient *Dialogue both pleasaunte and profitable,* by Willyam Bulleyn, 1564:

" My horse starteth, and had like to have unsaddled me; let me sit faster, *for falling.*"

Again, in Plutarch's Life of Antony, translated by Sir Thomas North: " So he was let in, and brought to her muffled as he was, *for being known.*" i. e. for fear of being known. See Mr. Mason's note on *The Tempest,* p. 18. n. *.

⁶ *I see, you have a* month's mind *to them.*] A *month's mind* was an *anniversary* in times of popery; or, as Mr. Ray calls it, a less solemnity directed by the will of the deceased. There was also *a year's mind,* and *a week's mind.* See *Proverbial Phrases.* GREY.

A *month's mind,* in the ritual sense, signifies not desire or inclination, but remembrance; yet I suppose this is the true original of the expression. JOHNSON.

In Hampshire, and other western counties, for " I can't *remember* it," they say, " I can't *mind* it." BLACKSTONE.

If this line was designed for a verse, we should read—*monthes* mind. So, in the *Midsummer Night's Dream:*

" Swifter than the moon*es* sphere."

Both these are the Saxon genitive case. STEEVENS.

⁷ — *what sad talk*] Sad is the same as *grave* or *serious.* JOHNSON.

Pant.

Pant. 'Twas of his nephew Protheus, your son.
Ant. Why, what of him?
Pant. He wonder'd, that your lordship
Would suffer him to spend his youth at home;
While other men, of slender reputation,
Put forth their sons to seek preferment out:
Some to the wars, to try their fortune there;
Some, to discover islands far away [8];
Some, to the studious universities.
For any, or for all these exercises,
He said, that Protheus, your son, was meet;
And did request me, to impórtune you,
To let him spend his time no more at home,
Which would be great impeachment to his age [9],
In having known no travel in his youth.
Ant. Nor need'st thou much impórtune me to that
Whereon this month I have been hammering.
I have consider'd well his loss of time;
And how he cannot be a perfect man,
Not being try'd, and tutor'd in the world:
Experience is by industry atchiev'd,
And perfected by the swift course of time:
Then, tell me, whither were I best to send him?
Pant. I think, your lordship is not ignorant,
How his companion, youthful Valentine,
Attends the emperor in his royal court [1].

Ant.

---

[8] *Some, to discover islands far away;*] In Shakspeare's time, voyages for the discovery of the islands of America were much in vogue. And we find, in the journals of the travellers of that time, that the sons of noblemen, and of others of the best families in England, went very frequently on these adventures. Such as the Fortescues, Collitons, Thornhills, Farmers, Pickerings, Littletons, Willoughbys, Chesters, Hawleys, Bromleys, and others. To this prevailing fashion our poet frequently alludes, and not without high commendations of it.

WARBURTON.

[9] —— *great impeachment to his age,*] *Impeachment* is *hindrance.*

STEEVENS.

Impeachment, in this passage, means reproach or imputation. So Demetrius says to *Helena* in *A Midsummer-Night's Dream:*
"You do *impeach* your modesty too much,
"To leave the city, and commit yourself
"Into the hands of one who loves you not." MASON.

[1] *Attends the emperor in his royal court.*] Shakspeare has been guilty of no mistake in placing the emperor's court at Milan in this play. Several of the first German emperors held their courts there occasionally, it being,

Ant. I know it well.

Pant. 'Twere good, I think, your lordship sent him thither:
There shall he practise tilts and tournaments,
Hear sweet discourse, converse with noblemen;
And be in eye of every exercise,
Worthy his youth and nobleness of birth.

Ant I like thy counsel; well hast thou advis'd:
And, that thou may'st perceive how well I like it,
The execution of it shall make known;
Even with the speediest expedition
I will dispatch him to the emperor's court.

Pant. To-morrow, may it please you, Don Alphonso,
With other gentlemen of good esteem,
Are journeying to salute the emperor,
And to commend their service to his will.

Ant. Good company; with them shall Protheus go:
And, in good time [2],—now will we break with him. [*]

Enter PROTHEUS.

Pro. Sweet love! sweet lines! sweet life!
Here is her hand, the agent of her heart;
Here is her oath for love, her honour's pawn:
O, that our fathers would applaud our loves,
To seal our happiness with their consents!
O heavenly Julia!

Ant. How now? what letter are you reading there?

Pro. May't please your lordship, 'tis a word or two
Of commendation sent from Valentine,
Deliver'd by a friend that came from him.

Ant. Lend me the letter; let me see what news.

being, at that time, their immediate property, and the chief town of their Italian dominions. Some of them were crowned kings of Italy at Milan, before they received the imperial crown at Rome. Nor has the poet fallen into any contradiction, by giving a duke to Milan at the same time that the emperor held his court there. The first dukes of that, and all the great cities in Italy, were not sovereign princes, as they afterwards became; but were merely governors, or viceroys, under the emperors, and removeable at their pleasure. Such was the *Duke of Milan* mentioned in this play. STEEVENS.

[2] *— in good time,*] *In good time* was the old expression when something happened which suited the thing in hand, as the French say, *à propos.* JOHNSON.

[*] *— now will we break with him.*] i. e. break the matter to him.
MASON.

Pro.

Pro. There is no news, my lord; but that he writes
How happily he lives, how well belov'd,
And daily graced by the emperor;
Wishing me with him, partner of his fortune.
 Ant. And how stand you affected to his wish?
 Pro. As one relying on your lordship's will,
And not depending on his friendly wish.
 Ant. My will is something sorted with his wish:
Muse not that I thus suddenly proceed;
For what I will, I will, and there an end.
I am resolv'd, that thou shalt spend some time
With Valentinus in the emperor's court;
What maintenance he from his friends receives,
Like exhibition [3] thou shalt have from me.
To-morrow be in readiness to go:
Excuse it not, for I am peremptory.
 Pro. My lord, I cannot be so soon provided;
Please you, deliberate a day or two.
 Ant. Look, what thou want'st, shall be sent after thee:
No more of stay; to-morrow thou must go.—
Come on, Panthino; you shall be employ'd
To hasten on his expedition.

      [*Exeunt* ANTHONIO *and* PANTHINO.

 Pro. Thus have I shunn'd the fire, for fear of burning;
And drench'd me in the sea, where I am drown'd:
I fear'd to shew my father Julia's letter,
Lest he should take exceptions to my love;
And with the vantage of mine own excuse
Hath he excepted most against my love.
O, how this spring of love resembleth [4]
 The uncertain glory of an April day;
Which now shews all the beauty of the sun,
 And by and by a cloud takes all away!

           Re-enter

---

[3] *—exhibition*] i. e. allowance. STEEVENS.

[4] *O, how this spring of love resembleth.*] It was not always the custom among our early writers to make the first and third lines rhime to each other; and when a word was not long enough to complete the measure, they occasionally extended it. Thus Spenser, in his *Faery Queen*, B. ii. s. 12:

  "Formerly grounded, and fast *sitteled.*"

Again, B. ii. c. 12:

  "The while sweet Zephirus loud *whisteled,*" &c.

From this practice, I suppose our author wrote *resembleth,* which, though it affords no jingle, completes the verse. Many poems have
              been

Re-enter PANTHINO.

Pant. Sir Protheus, your father calls for you;
He is in haste, therefore, I pray you, go.

Pro.

been written in this measure, where the second and fourth lines only rhime. STEEVENS.

Resembleth is here used as a quadrisyllable, as if it was written *resembeleth*. See *Com. of Errors*, Act V. sc. the last:

"And these two Dromios, one in *semblance*."

As you like it, Act ii. sc. ii.

"The parts and graces of the *wrestler*."

And it should be observed, that Shakspeare takes the same liberty with many other words, in which *l*, or *r*, is subjoined to another consonant. See *Com. of Errors*, next verse but one to that cited above:

"These are the parents to these *children*."

where some editors, being unnecessarily alarmed for the metre, have endeavoured to help it by a word of their own:

"These *plainly* are the parents to these children." TYRWHITT.

Thus much I had thought sufficient to say upon this point, in the edition of these plays published by Mr. Steevens in 1778. Since which the Author of *Remarks*, &c. on that edition has been pleased to assert, p. 7. "that Shakspeare does not appear, from the above instances at least, to have taken the smallest liberty in extending his words: neither has the incident of *l*, or *r*, being subjoined to another consonant any thing to do in the matter."—"The truth is," he goes on to say, "that *every* verb in the English language gains an *additional syllable* by its termination in *est, eth, ed, ing*, or, (when formed into a substantive) in *er*; and the above words, *when rightly printed*, are not only unexceptionable, but most just. Thus *resemble* makes *resemble-eth*; *wrestle*, *wrestle-er*; and *settle, whistle, tickle*, make *settle-ed, whistle-ed, tickle-ed*."

As to this *supposed* Canon of the English language, it would be easy to shew that it is quite fanciful and unfounded; and what he calls *the right method of printing the above words* is such as, I believe, was never adopted before by any mortal in writing them, nor can be followed in the pronunciation of them without the help of an entirely new system of spelling. But any further discussion of this matter is unnecessary; because the hypothesis, though allowed in its utmost extent, will not prove either of the points to which it is applied. It will neither prove that Shakspeare has not taken a liberty in extending certain words, nor that he has not taken that liberty chiefly with words in which *l*, or *r*, is subjoined to another consonant. The following are all instances of nouns, substantive or adjective, which can receive no support from the supposed Canon. That Shakspeare has taken a liberty in extending these words is evident, from the consideration, that the same words are more frequently used, by his contemporaries and by himself, without the additional syllable. Why he has taken this liberty chiefly with words in which *l*, or *r*, is subjoined to another consonant, must be obvious to any one who can pronounce the language.

Country, trisyllable.

T. N.

Pro. Why, this it is! my heart accords thereto;
And yet a thousand times it answers, no. [*Exeunt.*

ACT II. SCENE I.

Milan. A Room in the Duke's *Palace.*

Enter VALENTINE *and* SPEED.

Speed. Sir, your glove.
Val. Not mine; my gloves are on.
Speed. Why then this may be yours, for this is but one [5].

T. N. Act I. sc. ii. The like of him. Know'st thou this *country?*
Coriol. Act I. sc. iii. Die nobly for their *country*, than one.
 Remembrance, quadrisyllable.
T. N. Act I. sc. i. And lasting in her sad *remembrance.*
W. T. Act IV. sc. iv. Grace and *remembrance* be to you both.
 Angry, trisyllable.
Timon. Act III. sc. v. But who is man, that is not *angry.*
 Henry, trisyllable.
Rich. III. Act II. sc. iii. So stood the state, when *Henry* the Sixth—.
2 H. VI. Act II. sc. ii. Crown'd by the name of *Henry* the Fourth.
And so in many other passages.
 Monstrous, trisyllable.
Macb. Act IV. sc. vi. Who cannot want the thought how *monstrous.*
Othello. Act II. sc. iii. 'Tis *monstrous.* Iago, who began it?
 Assembly, quadrisyllable.
M. A. N. Act V. sc. last. Good morrow to this fair *assembly.*
 Douglas, trisyllable.
1 H. IV. Act V. sc. ii. Lord *Douglas* go you and tell him so.
 England, trisyllable.
Rich. II. Act IV. sc. i. Than Bolingbroke return to *England.*
 Humbler, trisyllable.
1 H. VI. Act III. sc. i. Methinks his lordship should be *humbler.*
 Nobler, trisyllable.
Coriol. Act. III. sc. ii. You do the *nobler.* *Cor.* I muse my mother—.
           TYRWHITT.

[5] Val. *Not mine, my gloves are on.*
Speed. *Why then, this may be yours; for this is but* one.] It should seem from this passage, that the word *one* was anciently pronounced as if it were written *on.* The quibble here is lost by the change of pronunciation; a loss, however, which may be very patiently endured.
           MALONE.

Val. Ha! let me see: ay, give it me, it's mine:—
Sweet ornament that decks a thing divine!
Ah Silvia! Silvia!

Speed. Madam Silvia! Madam Silvia!
Val. How now, sirrah?
Speed. She is not within hearing, Sir.
Val. Why, Sir, who bad you call her?
Speed. Your worship, Sir; or else I mistook.
Val. Well, you'll still be too forward.
Speed. And yet I was last chidden for being too slow.
Val. Go to, Sir; tell me, do you know madam Silvia?
Speed. She that your worship loves?
Val. Why, how know you that I am in love?
Speed. Marry, by these special marks: First, you have learn'd, like Sir Protheus, to wreath your arms like a malecontent; to relish a love-song, like a Robin-red-breast; to walk alone, like one that had the pestilence; to sigh, like a school-boy that had lost his A B C; to weep, like a young wench that had buried her grandam; to fast, like one that takes diet [6]; to watch, like one that fears robbing; to speak puling, like a beggar at Hallowmas [7]. You were wont, when you laugh'd, to crow like a cock; when you walk'd, to walk like one of the lions; when you fasted, it was presently after dinner; when you look'd sadly, it was for want of money: and now you are metamorphos'd with a mistress, that, when I look on you, I can hardly think you my master.

Val. Are all these things perceived in me?
Speed. They are all perceived without ye.

[6] — *takes diet*;] To *take diet* was the phrase for being under a regimen for a disease mentioned in *Timon*:
"— bring down the rose cheek'd youth
"To the tub-fast and *the diet.*" STEEVENS.

[7] — *Hallowmas.*] That is, about the feast of All Saints, when winter begins, and the life of a vagrant becomes less comfortable.
JOHNSON.

Is it worth remarking, that on *All-Saints-Day* the poor people in *Staffordshire*, and perhaps in other country places, go from parish to parish *a souling* as they call it; i. e. begging and *puling* (or singing small, as Bailey's Dict. explains *puling*) for *soul-cakes*, or any good thing to make them merry? This custom is mentioned by *Peck*, and seems a remnant of Popish superstition to pray for departed souls, particularly those of friends. The *souler's* song, in *Staffordshire*, is different from that which Mr. *Peck* mentions, and is by no means worthy publication.
TOLLET.

Val.

Val. Without me? they cannot.

Speed. Without you? nay, that's certain; for, without you were so simple, none else would [8]: but you are so without these follies, that these follies are within you, and shine through you like the water in an urinal; that not an eye, that sees you, but is a physician to comment on your malady.

Val. But, tell me, dost thou know my lady Silvia?

Speed. She, that you gaze on so, as she sits at supper?

Val. Hast thou observed that? even she I mean.

Speed. Why, Sir, I know her not.

Val. Dost thou know her by my gazing on her, and yet know'st her not?

Speed. Is she not hard-favour'd, Sir?

Val. Not so fair, boy, as well-favour'd.

Speed. Sir, I know that well enough.

Val. What dost thou know?

Speed. That she is not so fair, as (of you) well-favour'd.

Val. I mean, that her beauty is exquisite, but her favour infinite.

Speed. That's because the one is painted, and the other out of all count.

Val. How painted? and how out of count?

Speed. Marry, Sir, so painted, to make her fair, that no man 'counts of her beauty.

Val. How esteem'st thou me? I account of her beauty.

Speed. You never saw her since she was deform'd.

Val. How long hath she been deform'd?

Speed. Ever since you loved her.

Val. I have loved her ever since I saw her; and still I see her beautiful.

Speed. If you love her, you cannot see her.

Val. Why?

Speed. Because love is blind. O, that you had mine eyes; or your own eyes had the lights they were wont to have, when you chid at Sir Protheus for going ungartered [9]!

Val. What should I see then?

---

[8] *— none else would:*] None else would *be so simple.* JOHNSON.

[9] *— for going* ungartered!] This is enumerated by Rosalind in *As You Like It*, Act III. sc. ii. as one of the undoubted marks of love: " Then your hose should be *ungartered,* your bonnet unbanded, &c." MALONE.

Speed. Your own present folly, and her passing deformity: for he, being in love, could not see to garter his hose; and you, being in love, cannot see to put on your hose.

Val. Belike, boy, then you are in love; for last morning you could not see to wipe my shoes.

Speed. True, Sir; I was in love with my bed: I thank you, you swinged me for my love, which makes me the bolder to chide you for yours.

Val. In conclusion, I stand affected to her.

Speed. I would you were set; so, your affection would cease.

Val. Last night she enjoin'd me to write some lines to one she loves.

Speed. And have you?

Val. I have.

Speed. Are they not lamely writ?

Val. No, boy, but as well as I can do them:— Peace, here she comes.

Enter SILVIA.

Speed. O excellent motion [1]! O exceeding puppet! Now will he interpret to her.

Val. Madam and mistress, a thousand good morrows.

Speed. O, 'give ye good even! here's a million of manners. [*Aside.*

Sil. Sir Valentine and servant [2], to you two thousand.

Speed. He should give her interest; and she gives it him.

Val. As you enjoin'd me, I have writ your letter,
Unto the secret nameless friend of yours;
Which I was much unwilling to proceed in,
But for my duty to your ladyship.

Sil. I thank you, gentle servant: 'tis very clerkly done [3].

Val. Now trust me, madam, it came hardly off [4];

---

[1] *O excellent motion! &c.*] *Motion*, in Shakspeare's time, signified *puppet*, and sometimes a *puppet-show*. Speed means to say, that Silvia is a *puppet*, and that Valentine is to interpret *to*, or rather *for* her.
SIR J. HAWKINS.

[2] —*servant*,] Here Silvia calls her lover *servant*, and again, below, her *gentle servant*. This was the language of ladies to their lovers at the time when Shakspeare wrote. SIR J. HAWKINS.

[3] —*'tis very* clerkly *done*.] i. e. like a scholar STEEVENS.

[4] —*it came hardly off*;] A similar phrase occurs in *Timon*, Act. I. sc. i:
  " This *comes off* well and excellent." STEEVENS.

For,

For, being ignorant to whom it goes,
I writ at random, very doubtfully.

Sil. Perchance you think too much of so much pains?

Val. No, madam; so it stead you, I will write,
Please you command, a thousand times as much:
And yet,—

Sil. A pretty period! Well, I guess the sequel;
And yet I will not name it:—and yet I care not;—
And yet take this again;—and yet I thank you;
Meaning henceforth to trouble you no more.

Speed. And yet you will; and yet another yet. [*Aside.*

Val. What means your ladyship? do you not like it?

Sil. Yes, yes! the lines are very quaintly writ:
But since unwillingly, take them again;
Nay, take them.

Val. Madam, they are for you.

Sil. Ay, ay; you writ them, Sir, at my request;
But I will none of them; they are for you:
I would have had them writ more movingly.

Val. Please you, I'll write your ladyship another.

Sil. And, when it's writ, for my sake read it over:
And, if it please you, so; if not, why, so.

Val. If it please me, madam; what then?

Sil. Why, if it please you, take it for your labour;
And so good-morrow, servant. [*Exit* SILVIA.

Speed. O jest unseen, inscrutable, invisible,
As a nose on a man's face, or a weathercock on a steeple!
My master sues to her; and she hath taught her suitor,
He being her pupil, to become her tutor.
O excellent device! was there ever heard a better?
That my master, being scribe, to himself should write the letter?

Val. How now, Sir? what are you reasoning with yourself⁵?

Speed. Nay, I was rhiming; 'tis you that have the reason.

Val. To do what?

Speed. To be a spokesman from madam Silvia.

Val. To whom?

Speed. To yourself: why, she wooes you by a figure.

Val. What figure?

Speed. By a letter, I should say.

---

⁵ — *reasoning with yourself?*] That is, *discoursing, talking.* An Italianism. JOHNSON.

Val.

Val. Why, she hath not writ to me?

Speed. What need she, when she hath made you write to yourself? Why, do you not perceive the jest?

Val. No, believe me.

Speed. No believing you indeed, Sir: But did you perceive her earnest?

Val. She gave me none, except an angry word.

Speed. Why, she hath given you a letter.

Val. That's the letter I writ to her friend.

Speed. And that letter hath she deliver'd, and there an end [6].

Val. I would, it were no worse.

Speed. I'll warrant you, 'tis as well:
For often have you writ to her; and she, in modesty,
Or else for want of idle time, could not again reply;
Or fearing else some messenger, that might her mind discover,
Herself hath taught her love himself to write unto her lover.—
All this I speak in print [7]; for in print I found it.—
Why muse you, Sir? 'tis dinner time.

Val. I have dined.

Speed. Ay, but hearken, Sir: though the cameleon love can feed on the air, I am one that am nourish'd by my victuals, and would fain have meat: O, be not like your mistress; be moved, be moved. [*Exeunt.*

SCENE II.

Verona. *A Room in* Julia's *House.*

Enter PROTHEUS *and* JULIA.

Pro. Have patience, gentle Julia.

Jul. I must, where is no remedy.

Pro. When possibly I can, I will rturn.

Jul. If you turn not, you will return the sooner:
Keep this remembrance for thy Julia's sake.

[*giving a ring.*

Pro. Why then we'll make exchange; here, take you this.

Jul. And seal the bargain with a holy kiss.

Pro. Here is my hand for my true constancy;
And when that hour o'er-slips me in the day,

---

6 *— and there an end.*] i. e. there's the conclusion of the matter.
STEEVENS.

7 *— in* print;] Means *with exactness.* STEEVENS.

Wherein

Wherein I sigh not, Julia, for thy sake,
The next ensuing hour some foul mischance
Torment me for my love's forgetfulness!
My father stays my coming; answer not;
The tide is now: nay, not thy tide of tears;
That tide will stay me longer than I should;
Julia, farewell.—What! gone without a word? [*Exit* Jul.
Ay, so true love should do: it cannot speak;
For truth hath better deeds, than words, to grace it.

Enter Panthino.

Pant. Sir Protheus, you are staid for.
Pro. Go; I come, I come:—
Alas! this parting strikes poor lovers dumb. [*Exeunt.*

SCENE III.

The same. A Street.

Enter Launce, *leading a dog.*

Launce. Nay, 'twill be this hour ere I have done weeping; all the kind of the Launces have this very fault: I have received my proportion, like the prodigious son, and am going with Sir Protheus to the imperial's court. I think, Crab my dog be the sourest-natured dog that lives: my mother weeping, my father wailing, my sister crying, our maid howling, our cat wringing her hands, and all our house in a great perplexity, yet did not this cruel-hearted cur shed one tear: he is a stone, a very pebble-stone, and has no more pity in him than a dog: a Jew would have wept to have seen our parting; why, my grandam having no eyes, look you, wept herself blind at my parting. Nay, I'll show you the manner of it: This shoe is my father;—no, this left shoe is my father;—no, no, this left shoe is my mother;—nay, that cannot be so neither;—yes, it is so, it is so; it hath the worser sole: This shoe, with the hole in it, is my mother, and this my father; A vengeance on't! there 'tis: now, Sir, this staff is my sister; for, look you, she is as white as a lilly, and as small as a wand: this hat is Nan, our maid; I am the dog *:—no, the dog is himself, and I am the dog,—oh, the dog is me, and I am myself; ay, so, so.

---

* —*I am the dog:*—&c.] This passage is much confused, and of confusion the present reading makes no end. Sir T. Hanmer reads, *I*

so. Now come I to my father; *Father, your blessing;* now should not the shoe speak a word for weeping; now should I kiss my father; well, he weeps on: now come I to my mother, (O, that she could speak now!) like a wood woman⁸;—well, I kiss her;—why there 'tis; here's my mother's breath up and down: now come I to my sister; mark the moan she makes: now the dog all this while sheds not a tear, nor speaks a word; but see how I lay the dust with my tears.

Enter PANTHINO.

Pant. Launce, away, away, aboard; thy master is shipped, and thou art to post after with oars. What's the matter? why weep'st thou, man? Away, ass; you will lose the tide, if you tarry any longer.

Launce. It is no matter if the ty'd were lost⁹; for it is the unkindest ty'd that ever any man ty'd.

Pant. What's the unkindest tide?

---

am the dog, no, the dog is himself, and I am me, the dog is the dog, *and I am myself.* This certainly is more reasonable, but I know not how much reason the author intended to bestow on Launce's soliloquy.
JOHNSON.

⁸ —*like a wood woman!*] i. e. a frantic woman. The old copy reads—*would* woman. The emendation is Mr. Theobald's. MALONE.

There could be no doubt about the sense of this passage, had Launce said, "O, that *it* could speak like a good woman!" but he uses the feminine pronoun in speaking of the shoe, because it is supposed to represent a woman. MASON.

Oh! that she could speak now like a wood-woman!] I am not certain that I understand this passage. *Wood,* or crazy women, were anciently supposed to tell fortunes. *Launce* may therefore mean, that as her gestures are those of frantic persons, so he wishes she was possessed of their other powers, and could predict his fate. Or should we point the line as interrupted? Oh that she could speak now!—like a wood woman! meaning, I wish she could speak—but she behaves as if she were out of her senses! STEEVENS.

Print thus: Now come I to my mother (oh that she could speak now!) like a wood woman. Perhaps the humour would be heightened by reading (oh that the *shoe* could speak now!) BLACKSTONE.

I have followed the punctuation recommended by Sir W. Blackstone. The emendation proposed by him was made, I find, by Sir. T. Hanmer. MALONE.

⁹ —*if the* ty'd *were lost;*] This quibble, wretched as it is, might have been borrowed by *Shakspeare* from Lylly's *Endymion,* 1591: " *Epi.* You know it is said, the *tide* tarrieth for no man.—*Sam.* True. —*Epi.* A monstrous lye: for I was *ty'd* two hours, and tarried for one to unlose me." STEEVENS.

Launce.

Launce. Why, he that's ty'd here; Crab, my dog.

Pant. Tut, man, I mean thou'lt lose the flood; and, in losing the flood, lose thy voyage; and, in losing thy voyage, lose thy master; and, in losing thy master, lose thy service; and, in losing thy service,—Why dost thou stop my mouth?

Launce. For fear thou should'st lose thy tongue.

Pant. Where should I lose my tongue?

Launce. In thy tale.

Pant. In thy tail?

Launce. Lose the tide, and the voyage, and the master, and the service, and the tide¹? Why, man, if the river were dry, I am able to fill it with my tears; if the wind were down, I could drive the boat with my sighs.

Pant. Come, come away, man; I was sent to call thee.

Launce. Sir, call me what thou darest.

Pant. Wilt thou go?

Launce. Well, I will go. [*Exeunt.*

SCENE IV.

Milan. *A Room in the* Duke's *Palace.*

Enter VALENTINE, SILVIA, THURIO, *and* SPEED.

Sil. Servant,—

Val. Mistress?

Speed. Master, Sir Thurio frowns on you.

Val. Ay, boy, it's for love.

Speed. Not of you.

Val. Of my mistress then.

Speed. 'Twere good, you knock'd him.

Sil. Servant, you are sad.

Val. Indeed, madam, I seem so.

Thu. Seem you that you are not?

Val. Haply, I do.

Thu. So do counterfeits.

Val. So do you.

Thu. What seem I, that I am not?

Val. Wise.

Thu. What instance of the contrary?

Val. Your folly.

¹ *—and the* tide?] I should suppose these three words to be repeated through some error of the printer. STEEVENS.

Thu. And how quote you my folly [a]?
Val. I quote it in your jerkin.
Thu. My jerkin is a doublet.
Val. Well, then, I'll double your folly.
Thu. How?
Sil. What, angry, Sir Thurio? do you change colour?
Val. Give him leave, madam; he is a kind of cameleon.
Thu. That hath more mind to feed on your blood, than live in your air.
Val. You have said, Sir.
Thu. Ay, Sir, and done too, for this time.
Val. I know it well, Sir; you always end ere you begin.
Sil. A fine volley of words, gentlemen, and quickly shot off.
Val. 'Tis indeed, madam; we thank the giver.
Sil. Who is that, servant?
Val. Yourself, sweet lady; for you gave the fire: Sir Thurio borrows his wit from your ladyship's looks, and spends what he borrows, kindly in your company.
Thu. Sir, if you spend word for word with me, I shall make your wit bankrupt.
Val. I know it well, Sir: you have an exchequer of words, and, I think, no other treasure to give your followers; for it appears by their bare liveries, that they live by your bare words.
Sil. No more, gentlemen, no more; here comes my father.

Enter DUKE.

Duke. Now, daughter Silvia, you are hard beset.
Sir Valentine, your father's in good health:
What say you to a letter from your friends
Of much good news?

---

[a] *— how quote you my folly?*] To *quote* is to *observe*. STEEVENS.
Valentine in his answer plays upon the word, which was pronounced as if written *coat*.
So, in *The Rape of Lucrece*, 1594:
  " ———'the illiterate, that know not how
  " To cipher what is writ in learned books,
  " Will *cote* my loathsome trespass in my looks."
In our poet's time words were thus frequently spelt by the ear.
           MALONE.

Val.

Val. My lord, I will be thankful
To any happy meſſenger from thence.
　Duke. Know you Don Anthonio, your countryman?
　Val. Ay, my good lord, I know the gentleman
To be of worth, and worthy eſtimation,
And not without deſert ſo well reputed [3].
　Duke. Hath he not a ſon?
　Val. Ay, my good lord; a ſon, that well deſerves
The honour and regard of ſuch a father.
　Duke. You know him well?
　Val. I know him, as myſelf; for from our infancy
We have convers'd, and ſpent our hours together:
And though myſelf have been an idle truant,
Omitting the ſweet benefit of time,
To cloath mine age with angel-like perfection;
Yet hath Sir Protheus, for that's his name,
Made uſe and fair advantage of his days;
His years but young, but his experience old;
His head unmellow'd, but his judgment ripe;
And, in a word, (for far behind his worth
Come all the praiſes that I now beſtow,)
He is complete in feature, and in mind,
With all good grace to grace a gentleman.
　Duke. Beſhrew me, Sir, but, if he make this good;
He is as worthy for an empreſs' love,
As meet to be an emperor's counſellor.
Well, Sir; this gentleman is come to me,
With commendation from great potentates;
And here he means to ſpend his time a-while:
I think, 'tis no unwelcome news to you.
　Val. Should I have wiſh'd a thing, it had been he.
　Duke. Welcome him then according to his worth;
Silvia, I ſpeak to you; and you, Sir Thurio:—
For Valentine, I need not 'cite him to it [4]:
I'll ſend him hither to you preſently.　　　[*Exit* Duke.
　Val. This is the gentleman, I told your ladyſhip,
Had come along with me, but that his miſtreſs
Did hold his eyes lock'd in her cryſtal looks.
　Sil. Belike, that now ſhe hath enfranchis'd them
Upon ſome other pawn for fealty.

---

　[3] *And not without deſert,* &c] And not dignified with ſo much reputation without proportionate merit. JOHNSON.
　[4] *I need not 'cite him to it*: i. e. *incite* him to it. MALONE.

Val.

Val. Nay, sure, I think, she holds them prisoners still.
Sil. Nay, then he should be blind; and, being blind,
How could he see his way to seek out you?
Val. Why, lady, love hath twenty pair of eyes.
Thu. They say, that love hath not an eye at all.
Val. To see such lovers, Thurio, as yourself;
Upon a homely object love can wink.

Enter PROTHEUS.

Sil. Have done, have done; here comes the gentleman.
Val. Welcome, dear Protheus!—Mistress, I beseech you,
Confirm his welcome with some special favour.
Sil. His worth is warrant for his welcome hither,
If this be he you oft have wish'd to hear from.
Val. Mistress, it is: sweet lady, entertain him
To be my fellow-servant to your ladyship.
Sil. Too low a mistress for so high a servant.
Pro. Not so, sweet lady; but too mean a servant
To have a look of such a worthy mistress.
Val. Leave off discourse of disability:—
Sweet lady, entertain him for your servant.
Pro. My duty will I boast of, nothing else.
Sil. And duty never yet did want his meed:
Servant, you are welcome to a worthless mistress.
Pro. I'll die on him that says so, but yourself.
Sil. That you are welcome?
Pro. That you are worthless [5].

Enter SERVANT.

Ser. Madam [6], my lord your father would speak with you.
Sil. I'll wait upon his pleasure. [*Exit* Servant.] Come, Sir Thurio,
Go with me:—Once more, new servant, welcome:
I'll leave you to confer of home-affairs;
When you have done, we look to hear from you.
Pro. We'll both attend upon your ladyship.
[*Exeunt* SILVIA, THURIO, *and* SPEED.

---

[5] *That you are worthless.*] Dr. Johnson reads—*No, that you are worthless.* But perhaps the particle which he has supplied is unnecessary. *Worthless* was, I believe, used as a trisyllable. See Mr. Tyrwhitt's note, p. 121. MALONE.

[6] *Ser. Madam,—*] This speech, which was given in the old copies to Thurio, was properly transferred to the Servant by Mr. Theobald. MALONE.

Val. Now, tell me, how do all from whence you came?

Pro. Your friends are well, and have them much commended.

Val. And how do yours?

Pro. I left them all in health.

Val. How does your lady? and how thrives your love?

Pro. My tales of love were wont to weary you;
I know, you joy not in a love-discourse.

Val. Ay, Protheus, but that life is alter'd now:
I have done penance for contemning love;
Whose high imperious thoughts [7] have punish'd me
With bitter fasts, with penitential groans,
With nightly tears, and daily heart-sore sighs;
For, in revenge of my contempt of love,
Love hath chac'd sleep from my enthralled eyes,
And made them watchers of mine own heart's sorrow.
O, gentle Protheus, love's a mighty lord;
And hath so humbled me, as, I confess,
There is no woe to his correction [8],
Nor, to his service, no such joy on earth!
Now, no discourse, except it be of love;
Now can I break my fast, dine, sup, and sleep,
Upon the very naked name of love.

Pro. Enough; I read your fortune in your eye:
Was this the idol that you worship so?

Val. Even she; and is she not a heavenly saint?

Pro. No; but she is an earthly paragon.

Val. Call her divine.

Pro. I will not flatter her.

Val. O flatter me; for love delights in praises.

Pro. When I was sick, you gave me bitter pills;

---

[7] Whose *high imperious thoughts*—] For *these* I read *those*. I have contemned love and am punished. *These* high thoughts, by which I exalted myself above human passions or frailties, have brought upon me fasts and groans. JOHNSON.

I believe the old copy is right. *Imperious* is an epithet very frequently applied to *love* by Shakspeare and his contemporaries. So in *The Famous Historie of George Lord Faukonbridge*, 4to. 1616, p 15: "Such an *imperious* God is love, and so commanding. A few lines lower Valentine observes, that "love's a *mighty lord*." MALONE.

[8] — *no woe to his correction;*] No misery that *can be compared to* the punishment inflicted by love. Herbert called for the prayers of the Liturgy a little before his death, saying, *None to them, none to them.*

JOHNSON.

And I must minister the like to you.

   Val. Then speak the truth by her; if not divine,
Yet let her be a principality [1],
Sovereign to all the creatures on the earth.

   Pro. Except my mistress.

   Val. Sweet, except not any;
Except thou wilt except against my love.

   Pro. Have I not reason to prefer mine own?

   Val. And I will help thee to prefer her too:
She shall be dignified with this high honour,—
To bear my lady's train; lest the base earth
Should from her vesture chance to steal a kiss,
And, of so great a favour growing proud,
Disdain to root the summer-swelling flower [2],
And make rough winter everlastingly.

   Pro. Why, Valentine, what braggardism is this?

   Val. Pardon me, Protheus: all I can, is nothing
To her, whose worth makes other worthies nothing;
She is alone [3].

   Pro. Then let her alone.

   Val. Not for the world: why, man, she is mine own;
And I as rich in having such a jewel,
As twenty seas, if all their sand were pearl,
The water nectar, and the rocks pure gold.
Forgive me, that I do not dream on thee,
Because thou see'st me dote upon my love.
My foolish rival, that her father likes,
Only for his possessions are so huge,
Is gone with her along; and I must after,
For love, thou know'st, is full of jealousy.

   Pro. But she loves you?

   Val. Ay, and we are betroth'd; nay, more, our marriage hour,
With all the cunning manner of our flight,
Determin'd of: how I must climb her window;

---

[1] *— a principality,*] The first or *principal* of women. So the old writers use *state.* " *She is a lady, a great* state." Latymer. JOHNSON.
   There is a similar sense of this word in St. Paul's Epistle to the Romans, viii. 38 —" nor angels, nor *principalities.*" STEEVENS.
[2] *— summer-swelling flower*] The *summer-swelling* flower is the flower which swells in summer, till it expands itself into bloom. STEEVENS.
[3] *She is alone:*] She stands by herself. There is none to be compared to her. JOHNSON.

The ladder made of cords; and all the means
Plotted, and 'greed on, for my happineſs.
Good Protheus, go with me to my chamber,
In theſe affairs to aid me with thy counſel.

 Pro. Go on before; I ſhall enquire you forth:
I muſt unto the road [4], to diſembark
Some neceſſaries that I needs muſt uſe;
And then I'll preſently attend you.

 Val. Will you make haſte?
 Pro. I will.—   [*Exit* VALENTINE.
Even as one heat another heat expels,
Or as one nail by ſtrength drives out another,
So the remembrance of my former love
Is by a newer object quite forgotten [5].
Is it mine eye, or Valentinus' praiſe [6],
Her true perfection, or my falſe tranſgreſſion,
That makes me, reaſonleſs, to reaſon thus?
She's fair; and ſo is Julia, that I love;—
That I did love, for now my love is thaw'd;
Which, like a waxen image 'gainſt a fire [7],
Bears no impreſſion of the thing it was.

---

[4] — *the* road] The haven; where ſhips *ride* at anchor. MALONE.

[5] *Even as one heat another heat expels,*
 Or as one nail by ſtrength drives out another,
 So the remembrance of my former love
 Is by a newer object quite forgotten.] Our author ſeems here to have remembered *The Tragicall Hyſtory of Romeus and Juliet*, 1562:
 " And as out of a planke *a nayle a nayle doth drive,*
 " *So novel love out of the minde the auncient love doth rive.*"
So alſo, in *Coriolanus:*
   " One fire drives out one fire; *one nail one nail.*" MALONE.

[6] *Is it mine* eye, *or Valentinus' praiſe.*] The word *eye,* which is not in the firſt folio, was ſupplied by Dr. Warburton. The editor of the ſecond folio, finding the line defective, abſurdly filled it up thus:
  Is it mine *then,* or Valentinean's praiſe.
The old copy has—*Valentines,* and perhaps the Saxon genitive caſe was intended. The reading, however, that I have placed in the text, is juſtified by a former line. See page 119. MALONE.

[7] — *a* waxen image *'gainſt a fire,*] Alluding to the figures made by witches, as repreſentatives of thoſe whom they deſigned to torment or deſtroy. STEEVENS.

King James aſcribes theſe images to the devil, in his *Treatiſe of Dæmonologie:* — " to ſome others at theſe times he teacheth to make pictures of waxe or claye, that by the roaſting thereof, the perſons that they bear the name of may be continually ſicked, and dried away by continual ſickneſſe." See Servius on the 8th Eclogue of Virgil; Theoc. Idyl. ii. 22; Hudibras, p. 2 l. 2. v. 331. S. W.

Methinks,

Methinks, my zeal to Valentine is cold;
And that I love him not, as I was wont:
O! but I love his lady too, too much;
And that's the reason I love him so little.
How shall I dote on her with more advice⁸,
That thus without advice begin to love her?
'Tis but her picture I have yet beheld⁹,
And that hath dazzled my reason's light;
But when I look on her perfections,
There is no reason but I shall be blind¹.
If I can check my erring love, I will;
If not, to compass her I'll use my skill.

[*Exit.*

SCENE V.

A Street.

Enter SPEED *and* LAUNCE.

Speed. Launce! by mine honesty, welcome to Milan².

Launce. Forswear not thyself, sweet youth; for I am not welcome. I reckon this always—that a man is never undone, till he be hang'd; nor never welcome to a place, till some certain shot be paid, and the hostess say, welcome.

Speed. Come on, you mad-cap, I'll to the ale-house with you presently; where, for one shot of five pence, thou shalt have five thousand welcomes. But, Sirrah, how did thy master part with Madam Julia?

---

⁸ — *with more* advice,] *Is, on further knowledge, on better consideration.* STEEVENS.

The word is still current among mercantile people, whose constant language is "we are *advised* by letters from abroad;" meaning—*informed.* So, in bills of exchange, the conclusion always is, " without further *advice*—." MALONE.

⁹ *'Tis but her picture,* &c.] Protheus means, that, as yet, he had seen only her outward form, without having known her long enough to have any acquaintance with her mind. So, in *Cymbeline:*
" All of her, that is *out of door,* most rich!
" If she be furnish'd with a mind so rare, &c." STEEVENS.

¹ *And that hath dazzled my reason's light;*

But when I look, &c.] Our author uses *dazzled* as a trisyllable. The editor of the second folio not perceiving this, introduced *so,* (" And that hath dazzled *so,*" &c.) a word as hurtful to the sense as unnecessary to the metre. The plain meaning is, *Her mere outside has dazzled me;—when I am acquainted with the perfections of her mind, I shall be struck blind.* MALONE.

² — *to Milan.*] 'It is *Padua* in the former editions. See the note on Act iii. p. 146. POPE.

Launce.

Launce. Marry, after they closed in earnest, they parted very fairly in jest.

Speed. But shall she marry him?

Launce. No.

Speed. How then? Shall he marry her?

Launce. No, neither.

Speed. What, are they broken?

Launce. No, they are both as whole as a fish.

Speed. Why then, how stands the matter with them?

Launce. Marry, thus; when it stands well with him, it stands well with her.

Speed. What an ass art thou? I understand thee not.

Launce. What a block art thou, that thou canst not? My staff understands me [3].

Speed. What thou say'st?

Launce. Ay, and what I do too: look thee, I'll but lean, and my staff understands me.

Speed. It stands under thee, indeed.

Launce. Why, stand-under and understand is all one.

Speed. But tell me true, will't be a match?

Launce. Ask my dog: if he say, ay, it will; if he say, no, it will; if he shake his tail, and say nothing, it will.

Speed. The conclusion is then, that it will.

Launce. Thou shalt never get such a secret from me but by a parable.

Speed. 'Tis well that I get it so. But, Launce, how say'st thou, that my master is become a notable lover? *

Launce. I never knew him otherwise.

Speed. Than how?

Launce. A notable lubber, as thou reportest him to be.

Speed. Why, thou whoreson ass, thou mistakest me.

Launce. Why, fool, I meant not thee; I meant thy master.

---

[3] *My staff understands me.*] This equivocation, miserable as it is, has been admitted by Milton in his great poem, B. vi:

"—— The terms we sent were terms of weight,
"Such as we may perceive, amaz'd them all,
"And stagger'd many; who receives them right,
"Had need from head to foot well *understand*;
"Not *understood*, this gift they have besides,
"To shew us when our foes stand not upright." JOHNSON.

* —*how say'st thou, that my master is become a notable lover?*] i. e. (as Mr. Mason has elsewhere observed) What say'st thou to this circumstance,—namely, that my master is become a notable lover? MALONE.

Speed.

Speed. I tell thee, my master is become a hot lover.

Launce. Why, I tell thee, I care not though he burn himself in love. If thou wilt go with me to the ale-house, so [4]; if not, thou art an Hebrew, a Jew, and not worth the name of a Christian.

Speed. Why?

Launce. Because thou hast not so much charity in thee, as to go to the ale [5] with a Christian: Wilt thou go?

Speed. At thy service. [*Exeunt.*

SCENE VI.

The same. A Room in the Palace.

Enter PROTHEUS.

Pro. To leave my Julia, shall I be forsworn;
To love fair Silvia, shall I be forsworn;
To wrong my friend, I shall be much forsworn;
And even that power, which gave me first my oath,
Provokes me to this threefold perjury.
Love bad me swear, and love bids me forswear:
O sweet-suggesting love [6], if thou hast sinn'd,
Teach me, thy tempted subject, to excuse it!
At first I did adore a twinkling star,
But now I worship a celestial sun.
Unheedful vows may heedfully be broken;
And he wants wit, that wants resolved will
To learn his wit to exchange the bad for better.—
Fie, fie, unreverend tongue! to call her bad,
Whose sovereignty so oft thou hast preferr'd
With twenty thousand soul-confirming oaths.
I cannot leave to love, and yet I do;
But there I leave to love, where I should love.
Julia I lose, and Valentine I lose:
If I keep them, I needs must lose myself;

---

[4] *If thou wilt go with me to the ale-house,* so;] So, which is wanting in the first folio, was supplied by the editor of the second.
MALONE.

[5] — *the ale*] *Ales* were merry-meetings instituted in country places. STEEVENS.

[6] *O sweet-suggesting love,*] To *suggest* is to *tempt* in our author's language. So again:
"Knowing that tender youth is soon *suggested.*"
The sense is. *O tempting love, if thou hast* influenced me to sin, *teach me to excuse it.* JOHNSON.

If

If I lose them, thus find I by their loss,
For Valentine, myself; for Julia, Silvia.
I to myself am dearer than a friend:
For love is still more precious in itself:
And Silvia, witness heaven, that made her fair!
Shows Julia but a swarthy Ethiope.
I will forget that Julia is alive,
Remember'ring that my love to her is dead;
And Valentine I'll hold an enemy,
Aiming at Silvia as a sweeter friend.
I cannot now prove constant to myself,
Without some treachery used to Valentine: —
This night, he meaneth with a corded ladder
To climb celestial Silvia's chamber-window;
Myself in counsel, his competitor [7]:
Now presently I'll give her father notice
Of their disguising, and pretended flight [8];
Who, all enrag'd, will banish Valentine;
For Thurio, he intends, shall wed his daughter:
But, Valentine being gone, I'll quickly cross,
By some sly trick, blunt Thurio's dull proceeding.
Love, lend me wings to make my purpose swift,
As thou hast lent me wit to plot this drift [9]! [*Exit.*

SCENE

---

[7] *— in counsel, his competitor:*] *Myself, who am his* competitor *or rival, being admitted to his counsel.* JOHNSON.

Competitor *is confederate, assistant, partner.* So, in *Antony and Cleopatra:*
"It is not Cæsar's natural vice, to hate
"One great *competitor.*"
And he is speaking of Lepidus, one of the triumvirate. STEEVENS.

Perhaps Dr. Johnson's explanation of *competitor* is the true one, and "in counsel" here signifies, *in secret;* myself being secretly his rival. See a note on the *Merry Wives of Windsor,* Act I. sc. i. "It were better for you, if't were known in *counsel.*" I offer this rather as a possible, than a probable, interpretation. MALONE.

Mr. Steevens is right in asserting that competitor in this place means *confederate* or *partner.* The word is used in the same sense in *Twelfth Night,* where the clown, seeing Maria and Sir Toby approach, who were joined in the plot against Malvolio, says,
"The *competitors* enter."

[8] *— pretended flight;*] Pretended flight is *proposed* or *intended* flight. So, in *Macbeth:*
"— What good could they *pretend?*" STEEVENS.
Again, in *K. Richard III.*
"———— The Guildfords are in arms,
"And every hour more *competitors*
"Flock to the rebels." MASON.

[9] I suspect

SCENE VII.

Verona. *A Room in Julia's House.*

Enter JULIA *and* LUCETTA.

Jul. Counsel, Lucetta: gentle girl, assist me!
And, even in kind love, I do conjure thee,—
Who art the table wherein all my thoughts
Are visibly character'd and engrav'd,—
To lesson me; and tell me some good mean,
How, with my honour, I may undertake
A journey to my loving Protheus.

Luc. Alas! the way is wearisome and long.

Jul. A true-devoted pilgrim is not weary
To measure kingdoms with his feeble steps;
Much less shall she, that hath love's wings to fly;
And when the flight is made to one so dear,
Of such divine perfection, as Sir Protheus.

Luc. Better forbear, till Protheus make return.

Jul. O, know'st thou not, his looks are my soul's food?
Pity the dearth that I have pined in,
By longing for that food so long a time.
Didst thou but know the inly touch of love,
Thou would'st as soon go kindle fire with snow,
As seek to quench the fire of love with words.

Luc. I do not seek to quench your love's hot fire;
But qualify the fire's extreme rage,
Lest it should burn above the bounds of reason.

Jul. The more thou dam'st it up, the more it burns:
The current, that with gentle murmur glides,
Thou know'st, being stopp'd, impatiently doth rage;
But, when his fair course is not hindered,
He makes sweet music with the enamel'd stones,
Giving a gentle kiss to every sedge
He overtaketh in his pilgrimage;
And so by many winding nooks he strays,
With willing sport, to the wild ocean.
Then let me go, and hinder not my course:
I'll be as patient as a gentle stream,

---

⁹ I suspect that the author concluded the act with this couplet, and that the next scene should begin the third act; but the change, as it will add nothing to the probability of the action, is of no great importance.
  JOHNSON.

And

And make a paſtime of each weary ſtep,
Till the laſt ſtep have brought me to my love;
And there I'll reſt, as, after much turmoil,
A bleſſed ſoul doth in Elyſium.

   Luc. But in what habit will you go along?

   Jul. Not like a woman; for I would prevent
The looſe encounters of laſcivious men:
Gentle Lucetta, fit me with ſuch weeds
As may beſeem ſome well-reputed page.

   Luc. Why then your ladyſhip muſt cut your hair.

   Jul. No, girl; I'll knit it up in ſilken ſtrings,
With twenty odd-conceited true-love knots:
To be fantaſtic, may become a youth
Of greater time than I ſhall ſhow to be.

   Luc. What faſhion, madam, ſhall I make your breeches?

   Jul. That ſits as well, as—" tell me, good my lord,
" What compaſs will you wear your farthingale?"
Why, even that faſhion thou beſt lik'ſt, Lucetta.

   Luc. You muſt needs have them with a cod-piece [1], madam.

   Jul. Out, out Lucetta [2]! that will be ill-favour'd.

   Luc. A round hoſe, madam, now's not worth a pin,
Unleſs you have a cod-piece to ſtick pins on.

   Jul. Lucetta, as thou lov'ſt me, let me have
What thou think'ſt meet, and is moſt mannerly:
But tell me, wench, how will the world repute me,
For undertaking ſo unſtaid a journey?
I fear me, it will make me ſcandaliz'd.

   Luc. If you think ſo, then ſtay at home, and go not.

   Jul. Nay, that I will not.

   Luc. Then never dream on infamy, but go.
If Protheus like your journey, when you come,
No matter who's diſpleas'd, when you are gone:
I fear me, he will ſcarce be pleas'd withal.

---

[1] *— with a cod-piece,* &c.] Whoever wiſhes to be acquainted with this particular, relative to dreſs, may conſult Bulwer's *Artificial Changeling,* in which ſuch matters are very amply diſcuſſed. Ocular inſtruction may be had from the armour ſhewn as John of Gaunt's in the Tower of London. The ſame faſhion appears to have been no leſs offenſive in France. See Montaigne, chap. xxii. The cuſtom of ſticking pins in this oſtentatious piece of indecency was continued by the illiberal warders of the Tower, till forbidden by authority. STEEVENS.

[2] *Out, out, Lucetta!* &c.] Dr. Percy obſerves, that this interjection is ſtill uſed in the North. It ſeems to have the ſame meaning as *apage,* Lat. STEEVENS.

Jul. That is the least, Lucetta, of my fear:
A thousand oaths, an ocean of his tears,
And instances as infinite [3] of love,
Warrant me welcome to my Protheus.

Luc. All these are servants to deceitful men.

Jul. Base men, that use them to so base effect!
But truer stars did govern Protheus' birth:
His words are bonds, his oaths are oracles;
His love sincere, his thoughts immaculate;
His tears, pure messengers sent from his heart;
His heart as far from fraud, as heaven from earth.

Luc. Pray heaven, he prove so, when you come to him!

Jul. Now, as thou lov'st me, do him not that wrong,
To bear a hard opinion of his truth:
Only deserve my love, by loving him;
And presently go with me to my chamber,
To take a note of what I stand in need of,
To furnish me upon my longing journey [4].
All that is mine I leave at thy dispose,
My goods, my lands, my reputation;
Only, in lieu thereof, dispatch me hence.
Come, answer not, but to it presently;
I am impatient of my tarriance. [*Exeunt.*

ACT III. SCENE I.

Milan. *An Ante-room in the* Duke's *Palace.*

Enter Duke, Thurio, *and* Protheus.

Duke. Sir Thurio, give us leave, I pray, awhile;
We have some secrets to confer about.— [*Exit* Thurio.
Now, tell me, Protheus, what's your will with me?

---

[3] — as *infinite*] Old edit. *of* infinite. Johnson.
The emendation was made by the editor of the second folio.
                                                         Malone.

[4] — *my* longing *journey.*] D. Grey observes, that *longing* is a participle active, with a passive signification; for *longed*, wished or desired.
                                                         Steevens.

Pro.

Pro. My gracious lord, that which I would discover,
The law of friendship bids me to conceal:
But, when I call to mind your gracious favours
Done to me, undeserving as I am,
My duty pricks me on to utter that
Which else no worldly good should draw from me.
Know, worthy prince, Sir Valentine, my friend,
This night intends to steal away your daughter;
Myself am one made privy to the plot.
I know, you have determin'd to bestow her
On Thurio, whom your gentle daughter hates;
And should she thus be stolen away from you,
It would be much vexation to your age.
Thus, for my duty's sake, I rather chose
To cross my friend in his intended drift,
Than, by concealing it, heap on your head
A pack of sorrows, which would press you down,
Being unprevented, to your timeless grave.
  Duke. Protheus, I thank thee for thine honest care;
Which to requite, command me while I live.
This love of theirs myself have often seen,
Haply, when they have judg'd me fast asleep;
And oftentimes have purpos'd to forbid
Sir Valentine her company, and my court:
But, fearing lest my jealous aim [5] might err,
And so, unworthily, disgrace the man,
(A rashness that I ever yet have shunn'd,)
I gave him gentle looks; thereby to find
That which thyself hast now disclos'd to me.
And, that thou may'st perceive my fear of this,
Knowing that tender youth is soon suggested,
I nightly lodge her in an upper tower,
The key whereof myself have ever kept;
And thence she cannot be convey'd away.
  Pro. Know, noble lord, they have devis'd a mean
How he her chamber-window will ascend,
And with a corded ladder fetch her down;
For which the youthful lover now is gone,
And this way comes he with it presently;
Where, if it please you, you may intercept him.

  [5] *—jealous* aim] *Aim is guess* So, in *Romeo and Juliet*:
    "I *aim'd* so near when I suppos'd you lov'd." STEEVENS.

But,

But, good my lord, do it so cunningly,
That my discovery be not aimed at [6];
For love of you, not hate unto my friend,
Hath made me publisher of this pretence [7].

Duke. Upon mine honour, he shall never know
That I had any light from thee of this.

Pro. Adieu, my lord; Sir Valentine is coming. [*Exit.*

Enter VALENTINE.

Duke. Sir Valentine, whither away so fast?

Val. Please it your grace, there is a messenger
That stays to bear my letters to my friends,
And I am going to deliver them.

Duke. Be they of much import?

Val. The tenor of them doth but signify
My health, and happy being at your court.

Duke. Nay, then no matter; stay with me a while;
I am to break with thee of some affairs,
That touch me near, wherein thou must be secret.
'Tis not unknown to thee, that I have sought
To match my friend, Sir Thurio, to my daughter.

Val. I know it well, my lord; and, sure, the match
Were rich and honourable; besides, the gentleman
Is full of virtue, bounty, worth, and qualities
Beseeming such a wife as your fair daughter:
Cannot your grace win her to fancy him?

Duke. No, trust me; she is peevish, sullen, froward,
Proud, disobedient, stubborn, lacking duty;
Neither regarding that she is my child,
Nor fearing me as if I were her father:
And, may I say to thee, this pride of hers,
Upon advice, hath drawn my love from her;
And where [*] I thought the remnant of mine age
Should have been cherish'd by her child-like duty,
I now am full resolv'd to take a wife,
And turn her out to who will take her in:

---

[6] — *be not* aimed at;] 'Be not guess'd.' JOHNSON.

[7] — *of this pretence.*] *Pretence* is *design.* So, in *K. Lear:* " — to my affection to your honour, and no other *pretence* of danger." Again, in the same play: " — *pretence* and purpose of unkindness."
STEEVENS.

[*] *And* where—] *Where* for *whereas*. It is often so used by our old writers. MALONE.

Then

Then let her beauty be her wedding-dower;
For me and my possessions she esteems not.

Val. What would your grace have me to do in this?

Duke. There is a lady, Sir, in Milan, here [8],
Whom I affect; but she is nice, and coy,
And nought esteems my aged eloquence:
Now, therefore, would I have thee to my tutor,
(For long agone I have forgot to court;
Besides, the fashion of the time [9] is chang'd;)
How, and which way, I may bestow myself,
To be regarded in her sun-bright eye.

Val. Win her with gifts, if she respect not words;
Dumb jewels often, in their silent kind,
More than quick words, do move a woman's mind [1].

Duke. But she did scorn a present that I sent her.

Val. A woman sometime scorns what best contents her:
Send her another; never give her o'er;
For scorn at first makes after-love the more.
If she do frown, 'tis not in hate of you,
But rather to beget more love in you:
If she do chide, 'tis not to have you gone;
For why, the fools are mad, if left alone.
Take no repulse, whatever she doth say;
For, *get you gone,* she doth not mean, *away:*
Flatter, and praise, commend, extol their graces;
Though ne'er so black, say, they have angels' faces.
That man that hath a tongue, I say, is no man,
If with his tongue he cannot win a woman.

Duke. But she I mean, is promis'd by her friends

---

[8] —*sir, in* Milan, *here,*] It ought to be thus, instead of—*in* Verona, *here;* for the scene apparently is in Milan, as is clear from several passages in the first act, and in the beginning of the first scene of the fourth act. A like mistake has crept into the eighth scene of act ii. where Speed bids his fellow-servant Launce welcome to Padua. POPE.

[9] —*the fashion of the time*—] The modes of courtship, the acts by which men recommended themselves to ladies. JOHNSON.

[1] *Win her with gifts, if she respect not words;*
Dumb jewels often, in their silent kind,
More than quick words, do move a woman's mind.] An earlier writer than Shakspeare, speaking of women, has the same unfavourable (and, I hope, unfounded) sentiment:
" 'Tis wisdom to give much; a gift prevails,
" When deep persuasive oratory fails."
            Marlowe's *Hero and Leander.* MALONE.

VOL. III.   H   U to

Unto a youthful gentleman of worth;
And kept severely from resort of men,
That no man hath access by day to her.

Val. Why then I would resort to her by night.

Duke. Ay, but the doors be lock'd, and keys kept safe,
That no man hath recourse to her by night.

Val. What lets [2], but one may enter at her window?

Duke. Her chamber is aloft, far from the ground;
And built so shelving, that one cannot climb it
Without apparent hazard of his life.

Val. Why then, a ladder, quaintly made of cords,
To cast up, with a pair of anchoring hooks,
Would serve to scale another Hero's tower,
So bold Leander would adventure it.

Duke. Now, as thou art a gentleman of blood,
Advise me where I may have such a ladder.

Val. When would you use it? pray, Sir, tell me that.

Duke. This very night; for love is like a child,
That longs for every thing that he can come by.

Val. By seven o'clock I'll get you such a ladder.

Duke. But hark thee; I will go to her alone;
How shall I best convey the ladder thither?

Val. It will be light, my lord, that you may bear it
Under a cloak, that is of any length.

Duke. A cloak as long as thine will serve the turn?

Val. Ay, my good lord.

Duke. Then let me see thy cloak;
I'll get me one of such another length.

Val. Why, any cloak will serve the turn, my lord.

Duke. How shall I fashion me to wear a cloak?—
I pray thee, let me feel thy cloak upon me.—
What letter is this same? What's here?—*To Silvia?*
And here an engine fit for my proceeding!
I'll be so bold to break the seal for once. [*reads.*

My thoughts do harbour with my Silvia nightly;
  And slaves they are to me, that send them flying:
O, could their master come and go as lightly,
  Himself would lodge, where senseless they are lying.
My herald thoughts in thy pure bosom rest them [3];
  While I, their king, that thither them importune,
Do curse the grace that with such grace hath bless'd them,
  Because myself do want my servants' fortune:

I curse

---

[2] *What lets,*] i. e. what hinders. STEEVENS.

[3] *My*

I curse myself, for they are sent by me[4]*,*
That they should harbour where their lord should be.
What's here?
Silvia, this night I will enfranchise thee:
'Tis so; and here's the ladder for the purpose.—
Why, Phaëton, (for thou art Merops' son[5],)
Wilt thou aspire to guide the heavenly car,
And with thy daring folly burn the world?
Wilt thou reach stars, because they shine on thee?
Go, base intruder! over-weening slave!
Bestow thy fawning smiles on equal mates;
And think, my patience, more than thy desert,
Is privilege for thy departure hence:
Thank me for this, more than for all the favours,
Which, all too much, I have bestow'd on thee.
But if thou linger in my territories,
Longer than swiftest expedition
Will give thee time to leave our royal court,
By heaven, my wrath shall far exceed the love
I ever bore my daughter, or thyself.
Be gone, I will not hear thy vain excuse,
But, as thou lov'st thy life, make speed from hence.

                                       [*Exit* Duke.

Val. And why not death, rather than living torment?
To die, is to be banish'd from myself;
And Silvia is myself: banish'd from her,
Is self from self; a deadly banishment!
What light is light, if Silvia be not seen?
What joy is joy, if Silvia be not by?
Unless it be, to think that she is by,
And feed upon the shadow of perfection[6].

---

   [3] *My herald thoughts in thy pure bosom,* &c.] i. e. the thoughts contained in my letter. See p. 149, n. 9. MALONE.
   [4] — *for they are sent* —] *For* is the same as *for that, since.* JOHNSON.
   [5] — *Merops' son,*] Thou art Phaëton in thy rashness, but without his pretensions; thou art not the son of a divinity, but a *terræ filius*, a low-born wretch; Merops is thy true father, with whom Phaëton was falsely reproached. JOHNSON.
   This scrap of mythology Shakspeare might have found in the spurious play of *K. John*, 1591:
        " —— as sometime *Phaëton,*
      " Mistrusting silly *Merops* for his sire." STEEVENS.
   [6] *And feed upon the shadow of perfection.*]
    Animum pictura pascit inani. *Virg.* HENLEY.

Except I be by Silvia in the night,
There is no music in the nightingale;
Unless I look on Silvia in the day,
There is no day for me to look upon:
She is my essence; and I leave to be,
If I be not by her fair influence
Foster'd, illumin'd, cherish'd, kept alive.
I fly not death, to fly his deadly doom [7]:
Tarry I here, I but attend on death;
But, fly I hence, I fly away from life.

Enter PROTHEUS *and* LAUNCE.

Pro. Run, boy, run, run, and seek him out.
Launce. So-ho! so-ho!
Pro. What see'st thou?
Launce. Him we go to find: there's not a hair [8] on's head, but 'tis a Valentine.
Pro. Valentine?
Val. No.
Pro. Who then? his spirit?
Val. Neither.
Pro. What then?
Val. Nothing.
Launce. Can nothing speak? master, shall I strike?
Pro. Whom [9] would'st thou strike?
Launce. Nothing.
Pro. Villain, forbear.
Launce. Why, Sir, I'll strike nothing: I pray you—
Pro. Sirrah, I say, forbear: Friend Valentine, a word.
Val. My ears are stopp'd, and cannot hear good news,
So much of bad already hath possess'd them.
Pro. Then in dumb silence will I bury mine,
For they are harsh, untuneable, and bad.
Val. Is Silvia dead?
Pro. No, Valentine.

---

[7] *I fly not death, to fly his deadly doom:*] *To fly his doom,* used for *by flying,* or *in flying,* is a gallicism. The sense is, By avoiding the execution of his sentence I shall not escape death. If I stay here, I suffer myself to be destroyed; if I go away, I destroy myself. JOHNSON.

[8] *There's not a hair*—] Launce is still quibbling. He is now running down the *hare* that he started when he entered. MALONE.

[9] Whom—] Old Copy—*Who.* Corrected in the second folio.
MALONE.

Val.

Val. No Valentine, indeed, for facred Silvia!
Hath fhe forfworn me?
  Pro. No, Valentine.
  Val. No Valentine, if Silvia have forfworn me!—
What is your news?
  Launce. Sir, there's a proclamation that you are vanifh'd.
  Pro. That thou art banifh'd, O, that is the news,
From hence, from Silvia, and from me thy friend.
  Val. O, I have fed upon this woe already,
And now excefs of it will make me furfeit.
Doth Silvia know that I am banifhed?
  Pro. Ay, ay; and fhe hath offer'd to the doom,
(Which, unrevers'd, ftands in effectual force,)
A fea of melting pearl, which fome call tears:
Thofe at her father's churlifh feet fhe tender'd;
With them, upon her knees, her humble felf;
Wringing her hands, whofe whitenefs fo became them,
As if but now they waxed pale for woe:
But neither bended knees, pure hands held up,
Sad fighs, deep groans, nor filver-fhedding tears,
Could penetrate her uncompaffionate fire;
But Valentine, if he be ta'en, muft die.
Befides, her interceffion chafed him fo,
When fhe for thy repeal was fuppliant,
That to clofe prifon he commanded her,
With many bitter threats of 'biding there.
  Val. No more; unlefs the next word, that thou fpeak'ft,
Have fome malignant power upon my life:
If fo, I pray thee, breathe it in mine ear,
As ending anthem of my endlefs dolour.
  Pro. Ceafe to lament for that thou canft not help,
And ftudy help for that which thou lament'ft.
Time is the nurfe and breeder of all good.
Here if thou ftay, thou canft not fee thy love;
Befides, thy ftaying will abridge thy life.
Hope is a lover's ftaff; walk hence with that,
And manage it againft defpairing thoughts.
Thy letters may be here, though thou art hence;
Which, being writ to me, fhall be deliver'd
Even in the milk-white bofom of thy love [9].

The

---

[9] *Even in the* milk-white bofom of thy love.] So, in *Hamlet*:
" Thefe *to her excellent white bofom*, &c.

The time now serves not to expostulate:
Come, I'll convey thee through the city-gate;
And, ere I part with thee, confer at large
Of all that may concern thy love-affairs:
As thou lov'st Silvia, though not for thyself,
Regard thy danger, and along with me.

Val. I pray thee, Launce, an if thou seest my boy,
Bid him make haste, and meet me at the north gate.

Pro. Go, Sirrah, find him out. Come, Valentine.

Val. O my dear Silvia! hapless Valentine!

[*Exeunt* VALENTINE *and* PROTHEUS.

Launce. I am but a fool, look you; and yet I have the wit to think, my master is a kind of a knave: but that's all one, if he be but one knave [1]. He lives not now, that knows me to be in love: yet I am in love; but a team of horse shall not pluck [2] that from me; nor who 'tis I love, and

---

Trifling as the remark may appear, before the meaning of this *address of letters to the bosom of a mistress* can be understood, it should be known that women anciently had a pocket in the fore part of their stays, in which they not only carried lover-letters and love-tokens, but even their money and materials for needle-work. In many parts of England the rustic damsels still observe the same practice; and a very old lady informs me that she remembers when it was the fashion to wear very prominent stays, it was no less the custom for stratagem or gallantry to drop its literary favours within the front of them.

See Lord Surrey's Sonnets, 1557:

"My song, thou shalt attain to find the pleasant place,
"Where she doth live, by whom I live; may chance to have the grace,
"When she hath read, and seen the grief wherein I serve,
"*Between her breasts she shall thee put, there shall she thee reserve.*"
MALONE.

[1] — *but that's all one, if he be but one knave.*] I know not whether in Shakspeare's language, *one knave* may not signify a knave on only one occasion, a *single knave*. We still use a *double* villain for a villain beyond the common rate of guilt. JOHNSON.

I agree with Dr. Johnson, and will support his interpretation with indisputable authority. In the old play of *Damon and Pythias*, Arisippus declares of *Carisophus*, "you lose money by him if you sell him for *one knave*, for he serves for *twayne*." This phraseology is often met with: *Arragon* says, in the *Merchant of Venice*:

"With *one fool's* head I came to woo,
"But I go away with *two*."

And *Donne* begins one of his sonnets:

"I am *two fools*, I know,
"For *loving*, and for *saying so*, &c. FARMER.

[2] — *but a team of horse shall not pluck*—] I see how Valentine suffers for telling his love-secrets, therefore I will keep mine close. JOHNSON.

Perhaps

and yet 'tis a woman: but what woman, I will not tell myself; and yet 'tis a milk-maid: yet 'tis not a maid, for she hath had gossips [3]: yet 'tis a maid, for she is her master's maid, and serves for wages. She hath more qualities than a water-spaniel,—which is much in a bare Christian [4]. Here is the cat-log [*pulling out a paper.*] of her conditions [5]. Imprimis, *She can fetch and carry:* Why, a horse can do no more: nay, a horse cannot fetch, but only carry; therefore, is she better than a jade. Item, *She can milk;* look you, a sweet virtue in a maid with clean hands.

Enter SPEED.

Speed. How now, Signior Launce? what news with your mastership?

Launce. With my master's ship [6]? why, it is at sea.

Speed. Well, your old vice still; mistake the word: What news then in your paper?

Launce. The blackest news that ever thou heard'st.

Speed. Why, man, how black?

Launce. Why, as black as ink.

Speed. Let me read them.

Launce. Fie on thee, jolt-head; thou canst not read.

Speed. Thou liest; I can.

Launce. I will try thee: Tell me this: Who begot thee?

Speed. Marry, the son of my grandfather.

Launce. O illiterate loiterer! it was the son of thy grandmother [7]: this proves, that thou canst not read.

Speed.

Perhaps Launce was not intended to shew so much sense; but here indulges himself in talking contradictory nonsense. STEEVENS.

[3] *—for she hath had gossips:*] *Gossips* not only signify those who answer for a child in baptism, but the tattling women who attend lyings-in. The quibble between these is evident. STEEVENS.

[4] *— a bare Christian.*] *Launce* is quibbling on. *Bare* has two senses; *mere* and *naked.* In *Coriolanus* it is used in the first:

"'Tis but a *bare* petition of the state"

Launce uses it in both, and opposes the *naked* female to the water-spaniel *cover'd with hairs of remarkable thickness.* STEEVENS.

[5] *— conditions.*] i. e qualities. The old copy has *condition.* Corrected by Mr. Rowe. MALONE.

[6] *— with my master's ship?*] The old copy reads—*mastership.* The emendation was made by Mr. Theobald. MALONE.

[7] *— the son of thy grandmother:*] It is undoubtedly true that the mother only knows the legitimacy of the child. I suppose *Launce* infers,

Speed. Come, fool, come: try me in thy paper.

Launce. There; and saint Nicholas be thy speed [8]!

Speed. Imprimis, *She can milk.*

Launce. Ay, that she can.

Speed. Item, *She brews good ale.*

Launce. And therefore comes the proverb—Blessing of your heart, you brew good ale.

Speed. Item, *She can sew.*

Launce. That's as much as to say, Can she so?

Speed. Item, *She can knit.*

Launce. What need a man care for a stock with a wench, when she can knit him a stock [9]?

Speed. Item, *She can wash and scour.*

Launce. A special virtue; for then she need not be wash'd and scour'd.

Speed. Item, *She can spin.*

Launce. Then may I set the world on wheels, when she can spin for her living.

Speed. Item, *She hath many nameless virtues.*

Launce. That's as much as to say, bastard virtues; that, indeed, know not their fathers, and therefore have no names.

Speed. Here follow her vices.

Launce. Close at the heels of her virtues.

Speed. Item, *She is not to be kiss'd fasting* [1], *in respect of her breath.*

Launce. Well, that fault may be mended with a breakfast: Read on.

fers, that if he could read, he must have read this well-known observation. STEEVENS.

[8] *— saint Nicholas be thy speed!*] St. Nicholas presided over scholars, who were therefore called *St. Nicholas's clerks*. Hence, by a quibble between Nicholas and Old Nick, highwaymen, in *The First Part of Henry the Fourth*, are called *Nicholas's clerks*. WARBURTON.

That this saint presided over young scholars may be gathered from Knight's *Life of Dean Colet*, p. 362; for by the statutes of Paul's school there inserted, the children are required to attend divine service at the cathedral on his anniversary. The reason I take to be, that the legend of this saint makes him to have been a bishop, while he was a boy.

SIR J. HAWKINS.

[9] *— knit him a stock?*] i. e. a *stocking*. So, in *Twelfth Night*:

"*—it does indifferent well in a flame-colour'd stock*." STEEVENS.

[1] *— she is not to be kiss'd fasting,*] The old copy reads,—*she is not to be fasting*, &c. The necessary word, *kiss'd*, was first added by Mr. Rowe. STEEVENS.

Speed.

Speed. Item, *She hath a sweet mouth* [2].
Launce. That makes amends for her sour breath.
Speed. Item, *She doth talk in her sleep.*
Launce. It's no matter for that, so she sleep not in her talk.
Speed. Item, *She is slow in words.*
Launce. O villainy, that set this down among her vices! To be slow in words, is a woman's only virtue: I pray thee, out with't; and place it for her chief virtue.
Speed. Item, *She is proud.*
Launce. Out with that too; it was Eve's legacy, and cannot be ta'en from her.
Speed. Item, *She hath no teeth.*
Launce. I care not for that neither, because I love crusts.
Speed. Item, *She is curst.*
Launce. Well; the best is, she hath no teeth to bite.
Speed. Item, *She will often praise her liquor* [3].
Launce. If her liquor be good, she shall: if she will not, I will; for good things should be praised.
Speed. Item, *She is too liberal* [4].
Launce. Of her tongue she cannot; for that's writ down she is slow of: of her purse she shall not; for that I'll keep

---

[2] —*sweet mouth.*] This I take to be the same with what is now vulgarly called a *sweet tooth*, a luxurious desire of dainties and sweetmeats.
JOHNSON.

How a *luxurious desire of dainties* can make amends for *offensive breath*, I know not: I rather believe that by a *sweet mouth* is meant that she *sings sweetly*. In *Twelfth Night* we have heard of a *sweet breast* as the recommendation of a singer. It may however mean a *liquorish* mouth, in a wanton sense. So, in *Measure for Measure*:

"Their saucy *sweetness*, that do coin heaven's image, &c."
STEEVENS.

Mr. Steevens asks, how a desire for dainties can make amends for an offensive breath. It certainly can not; but he forgets that Launce replies to the *words* of Speed, not to his meaning. The quibble is preserved, and the *sweet* mouth makes equally amends for the sour breath, whatever the real signification of the former phrase may be.

A *sweet mouth* may possibly imply a disposition to wantonness, as well as a love of dainties; but it cannot in this place mean that she sings sweetly, for that would be a real perfection, and he is enumerating her vices. MASON.

[3] —*praise her liquor.*] That is, shew how well she likes it by drinking often. JOHNSON.

[4] —*too liberal.*] *Liberal*, is licentious and gross in language. So, in *Othello*: "Is he not a most profane and *liberal* counsellor?"
JOHNSON.

shut: now of another thing she may; and that I cannot help. Well, proceed.

Speed. Item, *She hath more hair than wit, and more faults than hairs, and more wealth than faults.*

Launce. Stop there; I'll have her: she was mine, and not mine, twice or thrice in that last article: Rehearse that once more.

Speed. Item, *She hath more hair than wit* [5],—

Launce. More hair than wit,—it may be; I'll prove it: The cover of the salt hides the salt, and therefore it is more than the salt: the hair, that covers the wit, is more than the wit; for the greater hides the less. What's next?

Speed. — *And more faults than hairs,*—

Launce. That's monstrous: O, that that were out!

Speed. — *And more wealth than faults.*

Launce. Why, that word makes the faults gracious [6]: Well, I'll have her: And if it be a match, as nothing is impossible—

Speed. What then?

Launce. Why, then will I tell thee,—that thy master stays for thee at the north gate.

Speed. For me?

Launce. For thee? ay; who art thou? he hath staid for a better man than thee.

Speed. And must I go to him?

Launce. Thou must run to him, for thou hast staid so long, that going will scarce serve the turn.

Speed. Why did'st not tell me sooner? 'pox of your love-letters! [*Exit.*

Launce. Now will he be swing'd for reading my letter; an unmannerly slave, that will thrust himself into secrets! —I'll after, to rejoice in the boy's correction. [*Exit.*

SCENE II.

The same. A Room in the Duke's Palace.

Enter DUKE *and* THURIO; PROTHEUS *behind.*

Duke. Sir Thurio, fear not, but that she will love you, Now Valentine is banish'd from her sight.

Thu.

---

[5] — *She hath more hair than wit,*—] An old English proverb. See Ray's Collection: " Bush natural, more hair than wit." STEEVENS.

[6] — *gracious:*

Thu. Since his exile she hath despis'd me most,
Forsworn my company, and rail'd at me,
That I am desperate of obtaining her.

Duke. This weak impress of love is as a figure
Trenched in ice [7]; which with an hour's heat
Dissolves to water, and doth lose his form.
A little time will melt her frozen thoughts,
And worthless Valentine shall be forgot.—
How now, Sir Protheus? Is your countryman,
According to our proclamation, gone?

Pro. Gone, my good lord.

Duke. My daughter takes his going grievously [*].

Pro. A little time, my lord, will kill that grief.

Duke. So I believe; but Thurio thinks not so.—
Protheus, the good conceit I hold of thee,
(For thou hast shewn some sign of good desert,)
Makes me the better to confer with thee.

Pro. Longer than I prove loyal to your grace,
Let me not live to look upon your grace.

Duke. Thou know'st, how willingly I would effect
The match between Sir Thurio and my daughter.

Pro. I do, my lord.

Duke. And also, I think, thou art not ignorant
How she opposes her against my will.

Pro. She did, my lord, when Valentine was here.

Duke. Ay, and perversely she persévers so.
What might we do to make the girl forget
The love of Valentine, and love Sir Thurio?

Pro. The best way is, to slander Valentine
With falshood, cowardice, and poor descent;
Three things that women highly hold in hate.

Duke. Ay, but she'll think, that it is spoke in hate.

---

[6] —*gracious:*] In old language, means *graceful.* So, in *K. John:*
   "There was not such a *gracious* creature born." STEEVENS.
   Mr. Steevens's interpretation of the word *gracious* has been controverted, but it is right. We have the same sentiment in *The Merry Wives of Windsor:*
   "O, what a world of vile ill-favour'd *faults*
   "Look *handsome* in *three hundred* pounds a year!" MALONE.

[7] Trenched *in ice;*] Cut, carved in ice, *Trencher,* to cut, Fr. JOHNS.

[*] —*grievously.*] So some copies of the first folio; others have, *heavily.* The word therefore must have been corrected, while the sheet was working off at the press. The word *Ay,* p. 154, l. 6, was infected in some copies in the same manner. MALONE.

Pro. Ay, if his enemy deliver it:
Therefore it must, with circumstance [8], be spoken
By one, whom she esteemeth as his friend.
  Duke. Then you must undertake to slander him.
  Pro. And that, my lord, I shall be loth to do:
'Tis an ill office for a gentleman;
Especially, against his very friend [9].
  Duke. Where your good word cannot advantage him,
Your slander never can endamage him;
Therefore the office is indifferent,
Being entreated to it by your friend.
  Pro. You have prevail'd, my lord: if I can do it,
By aught that I can speak in his dispraise,
She shall not long continue love to him.
But say, this weed her love from Valentine,
It follows not that she will love Sir Thurio.
  Thu. Therefore as you unwind her love [1] from him,
Lest it should ravel, and be good to none,
You must provide to bottom it on me:
Which must be done, by praising me as much
As you in worth dispraise Sir Valentine.
  Duke. And, Protheus, we dare trust you in this kind;
Because we know, on Valentine's report,
You are already love's firm votary,
And cannot soon revolt and change your mind.
Upon this warrant shall you have access,
Where you with Silvia may confer at large;
For she is lumpish, heavy, melancholy,
And, for your friend's sake, will be glad of you;
Where you may temper her [2], by your persuasion,
To hate young Valentine, and love my friend.
  Pro. As much as I can do, I will effect: —

---

[8] — *with circumstance.*] With the addition of such incidental particulars as may induce belief. JOHNSON.

[9] — *his very friend.*] *Very* is *immediate*. So, in *Macbeth*:
"And the *very* points they blow." STEEVENS.

[1] — *as you unwind her love*—] As you wind off her love from him, make me the *bottom* on which you wind it. The housewife's term for a ball of thread wound upon a central body, is a *bottom of thread*.
JOHNSON.

[2] — *you may temper her*—] Mould her, like wax, to whatever shape you please. So, in *King Henry IV.* P. ii: "I have him already *tempering* between my finger and my thumb; and shortly will I seal with him." MALONE.

But

But you, Sir Thurio, are not sharp enough;
You must lay lime ³, to tangle her desires,
By wailful sonnets, whose composed rhimes
Should be full fraught with serviceable vows.

Duke. Ay, Much is the force of heaven-bred poesy.

Pro. Say, that upon the altar of her beauty
You sacrifice your tears, your sighs, your heart:
Write, till your ink be dry; and with your tears
Moist it again; and frame some feeling line,
That may discover such integrity ⁴:—
For Orpheus' lute was strung with poets' sinews;
Whose golden touch could soften steel and stones,
Make tygers tame, and huge leviathans
Forsake unsounded deeps to dance on sands.
After your dire-lamenting elegies,
Visit by night your lady's chamber-window
With some sweet concert ⁵: to their instruments
Tune a deploring dump ⁶; the night's dead silence
Will well become such sweet-complaining grievance.
This, or else nothing, will inherit her ⁷.

Duke. This discipline shews thou hast been in love.

Thu. And thy advice this night I'll put in practice:
Therefore, sweet Protheus, my direction-giver,

---

³ — *lime*] That is *birdlime.* JOHNSON.

⁴ — *such integrity:*—] I suspect that a line following this has been lost; the import of which perhaps was

As her obdurate heart may penetrate. MALONE.

⁵ — *with some sweet* concert:] The old copy has *consort*, which I once thought might have meant in our author's time a band or company of musicians. So, in *Romeo and Juliet:*

"*Tyb.* Mercutio, thou *consort'st* with Romeo.

"*Mer. Consort!* what, dost thou make us *minstrels?*"
The subsequent words, "*To their instruments*—," seem to favour this interpretation; but other instances, that I have since met with, in books of our author's age, have convinced me that *consort* was only the old spelling of *concert*, and I have accordingly printed the latter word in the text. The epithet *sweet*, annexed to it, seems better adapted to the music itself than to the band. *Consort*, when accented on the first syllable, (as here) had, I believe, the former meaning; when on the second, it signified a company. So, in the next scene:

"What say'st thou? Wilt thou be of our *consort?*" MALONE.

⁶ *Tune a deploring* dump;] A *dump* was the ancient term for a *mournful elegy.* STEEVENS.

⁷ — *will inherit her.*] To *inherit*, is by our author, sometimes used, as in this instance, for *to obtain possession* of, without any idea of acquiring *by inheritance.* STEEVENS.

Let us into the city prefently
To fort⁸ fome gentlemen well fkill'd in mufic.
I have a fonnet, that will ferve the turn,
To give the onfet to thy good advice.

Duke. About it, gentlemen.

Pro. We'll wait upon your grace, 'till after fupper;
And afterward determine our proceedings.

Duke. Even now about it; I will pardon you⁹.

[*Exeunt.*

ACT IV. SCENE I.

A Foreſt near Mantua.

Enter certain Out-laws.

1 *Out.* Fellows, ſtand faſt; I ſee a paſſenger.

2 *Out.* If there be ten, ſhrink not, but down with 'em.

Enter VALENTINE *and* SPEED.

3 *Out.* Stand, Sir, and throw us that you have about you;
If not, we'll make you ſit, and rifle you.

Speed. Sir, we are undone! theſe are the villains
That all the travellers do fear ſo much.

Val. My friends,—

1 *Out.* That's not ſo, Sir; we are your enemies.

2 *Out.* Peace; we'll hear him.

3 *Out.* Ay, by my beard, will we;
For he's a proper man¹.

Val. Then know, that I have little wealth to loſe;

---

⁸ *To fort—*] i. e. to chooſe out. So, in *K. Richard III:*
"Yet I will *fort* a pitchy hour for thee." STEEVENS.

⁹ —*I will pardon you.*] I will excuſe you from waiting. JOHNSON.

¹ —*a proper man.*] i. e. a *well-looking* man; he has the appearance
of a gentleman. So, afterwards:
"And partly, ſeeing you are *beautified*
"With goodly ſhape."—
Again, in another play, "thou waſt the *propereſt* man in Italy."
MALONE.

A man

A man I am, cross'd with adversity;
My riches are these poor habiliments,
Of which if you should here disfurnish me,
You take the sum and substance that I have.

2 Out. Whither travel you?
Val. To Verona.
1 Out. Whence came you?
Val. From Milan.
3 Out. Have you long sojourn'd there?
Val. Some sixteen months; and longer might have staid,
If crooked fortune had not thwarted me.
2 Out. What, were you banish'd thence?
Val. I was.
2 Out. For what offence?
Val. For that which now torments me to rehearse:
I kill'd a man, whose death I much repent;
But yet I slew him manfully in fight,
Without false vantage, or base treachery.
1 Out. Why ne'er repent it, if it were done so:
But were you banish'd for so small a fault?
Val. I was, and held me glad of such a doom.
1 Out. Have you the tongues?
Val. My youthful travel therein made me happy;
Or else I often had been miserable.
3 Out. By the bare scalp of Robin Hood's fat friar [2],
This fellow were a king for our wild faction.
1 Out. We'll have him: Sirs, a word.
Speed. Master, be one of them;
It is an honourable kind of thievery.
Val. Peace, villain!
2 Out. Tell us this; Have you any thing to take to?
Val. Nothing, but my fortune.

---

[2] — *Robin Hood's fat friar,*] *Robin Hood* was captain of a band of robbers, and was much inclined to rob churchmen. JOHNSON.

By Robin Hood's *fat friar,* I believe, Shakspeare means *Friar Tuck*, who was confessor and companion to this noted outlaw. STEEVENS.

Dr. Johnson seems to have misunderstood this passage. The speaker does not swear by the scalp of some churchman who had been plundered, but by the shaven crown of Robin Hood's chaplain.—" We will live and die together, (says a personage in Peele's *Edward I.* 1593,) like Robin Hood, little John, *friar Tuck*, and Maide Marian."
MALONE.

3 Out.

3 *Out.* Know then, that some of us are gentlemen,
Such as the fury of ungovern'd youth
Thrust from the company of awful men [3]:
Myself was from Verona banished,
For practising to steal away a lady,
An heir, and near ally'd unto the duke [4].

2 *Out.* And I from Mantua, for a gentleman,
Who, in my mood [5], I stabb'd unto the heart.

1 *Out.* And I, for such like petty crimes as these.
But to the purpose,—(for we cite our faults,
That they may hold excus'd our lawless lives,)
And, partly, seeing you are beautify'd
With goodly shape; and by your own report
A linguist; and a man of such perfection,
As we do in our quality [6] much want:—

2 *Out.* Indeed, because you are a banish'd man,
Therefore, above the rest, we parley to you:
Are you content to be our general?
To make a virtue of necessity,
And live, as we do, in this wilderness?

3 *Out.* What say'st thou? wilt thou be of our consort?
Say, ay, and be the captain of us all:
We'll do thee homage, and be rul'd by thee,
Love thee as our commander, and our king.

---

[3] *— awful men:*] Reverend, worshipful, such as magistrates, and other principal members of civil communities. JOHNSON.

Awful is used by Shakspeare, in another place, in the sense of *lawful*. Second part of *Henry IV*. Act iv. sc. ii.

" We come within our *awful* banks again." TYRWHITT.

So, in *K. Henry V.* 1600:

" —— creatures that by *awe* ordain
" An act of order to a peopled kingdom." MALONE.

I think we should read *lawful* in opposition to *lawless* men. In judicial proceedings the word has this sense. SIR J. HAWKINS.

I believe we should read *lawful* men; i. e. legales homines. So, in the *Newe Boke of Justices*, 1560 :—" commaundinge him to the same to make an inquest and pannel of *lawful* men of his countie." For this remark I am indebted to Dr. Farmer. STEEVENS.

[4] *An heir, and near ally'd unto the duke.*] *Heir* in our author's time (as it sometimes is now) was applied to females, as well as males. The old copy reads—*and neece*. The change, which is very slight, (*neer* being formerly spelt *neere*) was made by Mr. Theobald. It likewise reads —*And heir.* The correction was made in the third folio. MALONE.

[5] *Who, in my mood,*] *Mood* is anger or resentment. MALONE.

[6] *— in our* quality—] i. e. in our profession. So, in the *Tempest:*
" —— talk
" Ariel, and all his *quality*." See p. 17. n. 3. MALONE.

1 *Out.*

1 Out. But if thou scorn our courtesy, thou diest.
2 Out. Thou shalt not live to brag what we have offer'd.
Val. I take your offer, and will live with you;
Provided, that you do no outrages [7]
On silly women, or poor passengers.
3 Out. No, we detest such vile base practices.
Come, go with us, we'll bring thee to our crews,
And shew thee all the treasure we have got;
Which, with ourselves, all rest at thy dispose. [*Exeunt.*

SCENE II.

Milan. *Court of the Palace.*

Enter PROTHEUS.

Pro. Already have I been false to Valentine,
And now I must be as unjust to Thurio.
Under the colour of commending him,
I have access my own love to prefer;
But Silvia is too fair, too true, too holy,
To be corrupted with my worthless gifts.
When I protest true loyalty to her,
She twits me with my falshood to my friend;
When to her beauty I commend my vows,
She bids me think, how I have been forsworn
In breaking faith with Julia whom I lov'd:
And, notwithstanding all her sudden quips [8],
The least whereof would quell a lover's hope,
Yet, spaniel-like, the more she spurns my love,
The more it grows, and fawneth on her still.
But here comes Thurio: now must we to her window,
And give some evening music to her ear.

Enter THURIO, *and Musicians.*

Thu. How now, Sir Protheus? are you crept before us?
Pro. Ay, gentle Thurio; for, you know, that love
Will creep in service where it cannot go.

---

[7] —— *no outrages*
On silly women, or poor passengers.] This was one of the rules of Robin Hood's government. STEEVENS.

[8] —— *sudden quips,*] That is, hasty passionate reproaches and scoffs. So Macbeth is in a kindred sense said to be *sudden*; that is, irascible and impetuous. JOHNSON.

Thu.

Thu. Ay, but, I hope, Sir, that you love not here.
Pro. Sir, but I do; or else I would be hence.
Thu. Whom? Silvia?
Pro. Ay, Silvia,—for your sake.
Thu. I thank you for your own. Now, gentlemen, Let's tune, and to it lustily a while.

Enter Host, *at a distance; and* Julia *in boy's cloaths.*

Host. Now, my young guest! methinks you're allycholly; I pray you, why is it?
Jul. Marry, mine host, because I cannot be merry.
Host. Come, we'll have you merry: I'll bring you where you shall hear music, and see the gentleman that you ask'd for.
Jul. But shall I hear him speak?
Host. Ay, that you shall.
Jul. That will be music. [*Music plays.*
Host. Hark! hark!
Jul. Is he among these?
Host. Ay: but peace, let's hear 'em.

SONG.

Who is Silvia? what is she,
  That all our swains commend her?
Holy, fair, and wise is she;
  The heavens such grace did lend her,
That she might admired be.

Is she kind, as she is fair?
  For beauty lives with kindness [9].
Love doth to her eyes repair,
  To help him of his blindness;
And, being help'd, inhabits there.

Then to Silvia let us sing,
  That Silvia is excelling;
She excels each mortal thing,
  Upon the dull earth dwelling:
To her let us garlands bring.

Host. How now? are you sadder than you were before? How do you, man? the music likes you not.

---

[9] — *beauty lives with kindness:*] Beauty without kindness *dies* unenjoyed, and undelighting. Johnson.

Jul. You miſtake; the muſician likes me not.
Hoſt. Why, my pretty youth?
Jul. He plays falſe, father.
Hoſt. How? out of tune on the ſtrings?
Jul. Not ſo; but yet ſo falſe, that he grieves my very heart-ſtrings.
Hoſt. You have a quick ear.
Jul. Ay, I would I were deaf! it makes me have a ſlow heart.
Hoſt. I perceive, you delight not in muſic.
Jul. Not a whit, when it jars ſo.
Hoſt. Hark, what fine change is in the muſic!
Jul. Ay; that change is the ſpite.
Hoſt. You would have them always play but one thing?
Jul. I would always have one play but one thing. But, Hoſt, doth this Sir Protheus, that we talk on, often reſort unto this gentlewoman?
Hoſt. I tell you what Launce, his man, told me, he loved her out of all nick [1].
Jul. Where is Launce?
Hoſt. Gone to ſeek his dog; which, to-morrow, by his maſter's command, he muſt carry for a preſent to his lady.
Jul. Peace! ſtand aſide; the company parts.
Pro. Sir Thurio, fear not you; I will ſo plead,
That you ſhall ſay, my cunning drift excels.
Thu. Where meet we?
Pro. At Saint Gregory's well.
Thu. Farewell.   [*Exeunt* Thurio *and Muſicians.*

SILVIA *appears above, at her window.*

Pro. Madam, good even to your ladyſhip.
Sil. I thank you for your muſic, gentlemen:
Who is that, that ſpake?
Pro. One, lady, if you knew his pure heart's truth,
You'd quickly learn to know him by his voice.
Sil. Sir Protheus, as I take it.
Pro. Sir Protheus, gentle lady, and your ſervant.
Sil. What is your will?
Pro. That I may compaſs yours.

---

[1] — *out of all nick.*] Beyond all reckoning or count. Reckonings are kept upon nicked or notched ſticks or tallies. WARBURTON.

As it is an inn-keeper who employs the alluſion, it is much in character. STEEVENS.

Sil. 'You have your wish; my will is even this [2],—
That presently you hie you home to bed.
Thou subtle, perjur'd, false, disloyal man!
Think'st thou, I am so shallow, so conceitless,
To be seduced by thy flattery,
That hast deceiv'd so many with thy vows?
Return, return, and make thy love amends.
For me,—by this pale queen of night I swear,
I am so far from granting thy request,
That I despise thee for thy wrongful suit;
And by and by intend to chide myself,
Even for this time I spend in talking to thee.

Pro. I grant, sweet love, that I did love a lady;
But she is dead.

Jul. 'Twere false, if I should speak it;
For, I am sure, she is not buried. [*Aside.*

Sil. Say, that she be; yet Valentine, thy friend,
Survives; to whom, thyself art witness,
I am betroth'd; And art thou not asham'd
To wrong him with thy importunacy?

Pro. I likewise hear, that Valentine is dead.

Sil. And so, suppose, am I; for in his grave [3],
Assure thyself, my love is buried.

Pro. Sweet lady, let me rake it from the earth.

Sil. Go to thy lady's grave, and call her's thence;
Or, at the least, in her's sepulcher thine.

Jul. He heard not that. [*Aside.*

Pro. Madam, if your heart be so obdurate,
Vouchsafe me yet your picture for my love,
The picture that is hanging in your chamber;
To that I'll speak, to that I'll sigh and weep:
For, since the substance of your perfect self
Is else devoted, I am but a shadow;
And to your shadow will I make true love.

Jul. If 'twere a substance, you would, sure, deceive it,
And make it but a shadow, as I am. [*Aside.*

Sil. I am very loath to be your idol, Sir;
But, since your falshood shall become you well [4]

To

---

[2] *You have your wish; my will is even this,—*] The word *will* is here ambiguous. He wishes to *gain* her *will*: she tells him, if he wants her *will*, he has it. JOHNSON.

[3] *— in his grave,*] The old copy has—*her* grave. The emendation was made by the editor of the second folio. MALONE.

[4] *But,*

To worship shadows, and adore false shapes,
Send to me in the morning, and I'll send it:
And so, good rest.

Pro. As wretches have o'er night,
That wait for execution in the morn.

[*Exeunt* PROTHEUS; *and* SILVIA, *from above.*

Jul. Host, will you go?
Host. By my hallidom, I was fast asleep.
Jul. Pray you, where lies Sir Protheus?
Host. Marry, at my house: Trust me, I think, 'tis almost day.
Jul. Not so; but it hath been the longest night
That e'er I watch'd, and the most heaviest. [*Exeunt.*

SCENE III.

The same.

Enter EGLAMOUR.

Egl. This is the hour that Madam Silvia
Entreated me to call, and know her mind;
There's some great matter she'd employ me in.—
Madam, madam!

SILVIA *appears above, at her window.*

Sil. Who calls?

---

⁴ *But, since your falshood shall become you well*] I once had a better opinion of an alteration proposed by Dr. Johnson [But since *you're false, it* shall, &c] than I have at present. I now believe the text is right, and that our author means, however licentious the expression,—But, since your falshood well becomes, or is well suited to, the worshipping of shadows, and the adoring of false shapes, send to me in the morning for my picture, &c. Or, in other words, But, since the worshipping of shadows and the adoring of false shapes shall well become *you, false as you are,* send, &c. *To worship shadows,* &c. I consider as the objective case, as well as *you.* There are other instances in these plays of a double accusative depending on the same verb. I have therefore followed the punctuation of the old copy, and not placed a comma after *falshood,* as in the modern editions. *Since* is, I think, here an adverb, not a preposition. MALONE.

There is no occasion for any alteration, if we only suppose that *it* is understood here, as in several other places.

But, since your falshood, shall become you well
To worship shadows and adore false shapes,—

i. e. But, since your falshood, *it* shall become you well, &c. Or indeed, in this place, *To worship shadows,* &c. may be considered as the nominative case to *shall become.* TYRWHITT.

Egl.

Egl. Your servant, and your friend;
One that attends your ladyship's command.
　Sil. Sir Eglamour, a thousand times good morrow.
　Egl. As many, worthy lady, to yourself.
According to your ladyship's impose [5],
I am thus early come, to know what service
It is your pleasure to command me in.
　Sil. O Eglamour, thou art a gentleman,
(Think not, I flatter, for, I swear, I do not,)
Valiant, wise, remorseful [6], well accomplish'd.
Thou art not ignorant, what dear good will
I bear unto the banish'd Valentine;
Nor how my father would enforce me marry
Vain Thurio, whom my very soul abhorr'd.
Thyself hast lov'd; and I have heard thee say,
No grief did ever come so near thy heart,
As when thy lady and thy true love died,
Upon whose grave thou vow'dst pure chastity [7]:
Sir Eglamour, I would to Valentine,
To Mantua, where, I hear, he makes abode;
And, for the ways are dangerous to pass,
I do desire thy worthy company,
Upon whose faith and honour I repose.
Urge not my father's anger, Eglamour,
But think upon my grief, a lady's grief;
And on the justice of my flying hence,
To keep me from a most unholy match,
Which heaven and fortune still reward with plagues.
I do desire thee, even from a heart

---

[5] — *your ladyship's* impose,] *Impose* is *injunction, command.* A task set at college, in consequence of a fault, is still called an *imposition.*
　　　　　　　　　　　　　　　　　　　　　STEEVENS.

[6] *Remorseful* is pitiful. STEEVENS.

[7] *Upon whose grave thou vow'dst pure chastity:*] It was common in former ages for widowers and widows to make vows of chastity in honour of their deceased wives or husbands. In Dugdale's *Antiquities of Warwickshire*, page 1013, there is the form of a commission by the bishop of the diocese for taking a vow of chastity made by a widow. It seems that, besides observing the vow, the widow was, for life, to wear a veil, and a mourning habit. The same distinction we may suppose to have been made in respect of male votarists; and therefore this circumstance might inform the players how Sir Eglamour should be drest; and will account for Silvia's having chosen him as a person in whom she could confide without injury to her own character. STEEVENS.

As full of forrows as the fea of fands,
To bear me company, and go with me:
If not, to hide what I have faid to thee,
That I may venture to depart alone.

Egl. Madam, I pity much your grievances [8];
Which fince I know they virtuoufly are plac'd,
I give confent to go along with you;
Recking as little [9] what betideth me,
As much I wifh all good befortune you.
When will you go?

Sil. This evening coming.

Egl. Where fhall I meet you?

Sil. At friar Patrick's cell,
Where I intend holy confeffion.

Egl. I will not fail your ladyfhip:
Good morrow, gentle lady.

Sil. Good morrow, kind Sir Eglamour. [*Exeunt.*

SCENE IV.

The fame.

Enter LAUNCE, *with his dog.*

When a man's fervant fhall play the cur with him, look you, it goes hard: one that I brought up of a puppy; one that I faved from drowning, when three or four of his blind brothers and fifters went to it! I have taught him—even as one would fay precifely, Thus I would teach a dog. I was fent to deliver him, as a prefent to Miftrefs Silvia, from my mafter; and I came no fooner into the dining-chamber, but he fteps me to her trencher [*], and fteals her capon's leg. O, 'tis a foul thing, when a cur cannot keep himfelf [1] in all companies! I would have, as one fhould fay, one that takes upon him to be a dog [2] indeed, to be, as it were, a dog at all things. If I had not had more wit than he, to take a fault upon me that he did, I think verily he had been hang'd for't; fure as I live, he had fuffer'd for't: you fhall judge.

[8] —— *grievances;*] Sorrows, forrowful affections. JOHNSON.
[9] Recking *as little* ——] To *reck* is to care for. STEEVENS.
[*] —— *to her* trencher,] See p. 55. n. 3. MALONE.
[1] —— *keep himfelf*] i. e. reftrain himfelf. STEEVENS.
[2] —— *to be a dog* ——] I believe we fhould read, *I would have*, &c. *one that takes upon him to be a dog*, to be a dog *indeed, to be*, &c. JOHNSON.

He thrufts me himfelf into the company of three or four gentlemen-like dogs, under the duke's table: he had not been there (blefs the mark) a piffing while [3], but all the chamber fmelt him. *Out with the dog,* fays one; *What cur is that?* fays another; *Whip him out,* fays the third; *Hang him up,* fays the duke: I, having been acquainted with the fmell before, knew it was Crab; and goes me to the fellow that whips the dogs [4]: *Friend,* quoth I, *you mean to whip the dog? Ay marry, do I,* quoth he. *You do him the more wrong,* quoth I; *'twas I did the thing you wot of.* He makes me no more ado, but whips me out of the chamber. How many mafters would do this for their fervant [5]? Nay, I'll be fworn, I have fat in the ftocks for puddings he hath ftolen, otherwife he had been executed: I have ftood on the pillory for geefe he hath kill'd, otherwife he had fuffer'd for't: thou think'ft not of this now!—Nay, I remember the trick you ferved me, when I took my leave of Madam Silvia [6]; did not I bid thee ftill mark me, and do as I do? When didft thou fee me heave up my leg, and make water againft a gentlewoman's farthingale? Didft thou ever fee me do fuch a trick?

Enter PROTHEUS *and* JULIA.

Pro. Sebaftian is thy name? I like thee well,
And will employ thee in fome fervice prefently.

Jul. In what you pleafe;—I will do what I can.

Pro. I hope thou wilt.—How, now, you whorefon peafant?
Where have you been thefe two days loitering?

Launce. Marry, Sir, I carry'd miftrefs Silvia the dog you bade me.

Pro. And what fays fhe to my little jewel?

[3] *— a piffing while,*] It appears from Ray's Collection, that this expreffion is proverbial. STEEVENS.

[4] *— the fellow that whips the dogs:*] This appears to have been part of the office of an *ufher of the table.* STEEVENS.

[5] *— their fervant?*] The old copy reads—*his* fervant? STEEVENS. Corrected by Mr. Pope. MALONE.

[6] *Madam* Silvia;] Dr. Warburton, without any neceffity I think, reads—Julia; " alluding to the leave his mafter and he took when they left Verona." But it appears from a former fcene, (as Mr. Heath has obferved,) that Launce was not prefent when Protheus and Julia parted. Launce on the other hand has juft taken leave of, i. e. parted from, (for that is all that is meant) Madam Silvia. MALONE.

Launce,

Launce. Marry, she says, your dog was a cur; and tells you, currish thanks is good enough for such a present.

Pro. But she receiv'd my dog?

Launce. No, indeed, did she not: here have I brought him back again.

Pro. What, didst thou offer her this from me?

Launce. Ay, Sir; the other squirrel [7] was stolen from me by the hangman's boys in the market-place: and then I offer'd her mine own; who is a dog as big as ten of yours, and therefore the gift the greater.

Pro. Go, get thee hence, and find my dog again,
Or ne'er return again into my sight.
Away, I say; Stay'st thou to vex me here?
A slave, that, still an end [8], turns me to shame. [*Ex.* LAU.
Sebastian, I have entertained thee,
Partly, that I have need of such a youth,
That can with some discretion do my business,
For 'tis no trusting to yon foolish lowt;
But, chiefly, for thy face, and thy behaviour;
Which (if my augury deceive me not,)
Witness good bringing up, fortune, and truth:
Therefore know thou [9], for this I entertain thee.
Go presently, and take this ring with thee,
Deliver it to Madam Silvia:
She lov'd me well, deliver'd it to me [1].

Jul. It seems, you lov'd her not, to leave her token [2]:
She's dead, belike.

Pro. Not so, I think, she lives.

Jul. Alas!

Pro. Why dost thou cry, alas?

Jul. I cannot choose but pity her.

Pro. Wherefore should'st thou pity her?

---

[7] — *the other* squirrel, &c.] Sir T. Hanmer reads—the other, *Squirrel*, &c. and consequently makes *Squirrel* the proper name of the beast. Perhaps Launce only speaks of it as a diminutive animal, more resembling a *squirrel* in size, than a dog. STEEVENS.

The subsequent words—" who is a dog *as big as ten of yours*," shew that Mr. Steevens's interpretation is the true one. MALONE.

[8] — *an end.*] i. e. *in the end*, at the conclusion of every business he undertakes. STEEVENS.

[9] — *know* thou,] The old copy has—*thee*. The emendation was made by the editor of the second folio. MALONE.

[1] *She lov'd me well, deliver'd it to me.*] i. e. She, *who* delivered it to me, lov'd me well. MALONE.

VOL. III.   I   *Jul.*

Jul. Because, methinks, that she lov'd you as well
As you do love your lady Silvia:
She dreams on him, that has forgot her love;
You dote on her, that cares not for your love.
'Tis pity, love should be so contrary;
And thinking on it makes me cry, alas!

Pro. Well, give her that ring, and therewithal
This letter;—that's her chamber.—Tell my lady,
I claim the promise for her heavenly picture.
Your message done, hie home unto my chamber,
Where thou shalt find me sad and solitary.
[*Exit* PROTHEUS.

Jul. How many women would do such a message?
Alas, poor Protheus! thou hast entertain'd
A fox, to be the shepherd of thy lambs:
Alas, poor fool! why do I pity him
That with his very heart despiseth me?
Because he loves her, he despiseth me;
Because I love him, I must pity him.
This ring I gave him, when he parted from me,
To bind him to remember my good will:
And now am I (unhappy messenger)
To plead for that, which I would not obtain;
To carry that, which I would have refus'd [3];
To praise his faith, which I would have disprais'd.
I am my master's true confirmed love;
But cannot be true servant to my master,
Unless I prove false traitor to myself.

---

[2] *It seems, you lov'd her not, to leave her token:*] To *leave* seems to be used here for *to part with*.
So, in *The Merchant of Venice:*
"I dare be sworn for him, he would not *leave* it,
"Or pluck it from his finger for the wealth
"That the world masters."
It is used with equal licence in a former scene, for to *cease*. "I leave to be, &c."—In the first copy *not* is inadvertently repeated by the carelessness of the printer:
It seems you lov'd her not, *not* leave her token.
The emendation was made in the second folio. Dr. Johnson would read:
It seems you loved her not, *nor love* her token. MALONE.

[3] *To carry that, which I would have refus'd;* &c.] The sense is, To go and present that which I wish to be not accepted, to praise him whom I wish to be dispraised. JOHNSON.

Yet

Yet will I woo for him; but yet so coldly,
As, heaven it knows, I would not have him speed.

Enter SILVIA, *attended.*

Gentlewoman, good day! I pray you, be my mean
To bring me where to speak with Madam Silvia.

   Sil. What would you with her, if that I be she?

   Jul. If you be she, I do entreat your patience
To hear me speak the message I am sent on.

   Sil. From whom?

   Jul. From my master, Sir Protheus, Madam.

   Sil. O,—he sends you for a picture?

   Jul. Ay, madam.

   Sil. Ursula, bring my picture there.   [*Picture brought.*
Go, give your master this: tell him from me,
One Julia, that his changing thoughts forget,
Would better fit his chamber, than this shadow.

   Jul. Madam, please you peruse this letter.—
Pardon me, Madam; I have unadvis'd
Deliver'd you a paper that I should not;
This is the letter to your ladyship.

   Sil. I pray thee, let me look on that again.

   Jul. It may not be; good madam, pardon me.

   Sil. There, hold.
I will not look upon your master's lines:
I know, they are stuff'd with protestations,
And full of new-found oaths; which he will break,
As easily as I do tear this paper.

   Jul. Madam, he sends your ladyship this ring.

   Sil. The more shame for him that he sends it me;
For, I have heard him say a thousand times,
His Julia gave it him at his departure:
Though his false finger have profan'd the ring,
Mine shall not do his Julia so much wrong.

   Jul. She thanks you.

   Sil. What say'st thou?

   Jul. I thank you, Madam, that you tender her:
Poor gentlewoman! my master wrongs her much.

   Sil. Dost thou know her?

   Jul. Almost as well as I do know myself:
To think upon her woes, I do protest,
That I have wept an hundred several times.

   Sil. Belike, she thinks, that Protheus hath forsook her.

Jul. I think she doth; and that's her cause of sorrow.

Sil. Is she not passing fair?

Jul. She hath been fairer, Madam, than she is:
When she did think my master lov'd her well,
She, in my judgment, was as fair as you;
But since she did neglect her looking-glass,
And threw her sun-expelling mask away,
The air hath starv'd the roses in her cheeks,
And pinch'd the lily-tincture of her face,
That now she is become as black as I [4].

Sil. How tall was she?

Jul. About my stature: for, at pentecost,
When all our pageants of delight were play'd,
Our youth got me to play the woman's part,
And I was trimm'd in madam Julia's gown;
Which served me as fit, by all men's judgment,
As if the garment had been made for me:
Therefore, I know she is about my height.
And, at that time I made her weep a-good [5],
For I did play a lamentable part:
Madam, 'twas Ariadne, passioning [6]
For Theseus' perjury, and unjust flight;
Which I so lively acted with my tears,
That my poor mistress, moved therewithal,
Wept bitterly; and, would I might be dead,
If I in thought felt not her very sorrow!

Sil. She is beholden to thee, gentle youth!—
Alas, poor lady! desolate and left!—
I weep myself, to think upon thy words.
Here, youth, there is my purse; I give thee this

---

[4] And pinch'd *the lily-tincture of her face,*
That now she is become as black as I.] The colour of a part pinch'd, is livid, as it is commonly termed, black and blue. The weather may therefore be justly said to *pinch,* when it produces the same visible effect. I believe this is the reason why the cold is said to *pinch.* JOHNSON.
Cleopatra says of herself——" Think on me,
" That am with Phœbus' amorous *pinches* black." STEEVENS.

[5] — *weep* a-good;] i. e. in good earnest. *Tout de bon.* Fr.
STEEVENS.

[6] — *'twas Ariadne, passioning*—] On her being deserted by Theseus in the night, and left on the Island of Naxos. MALONE.
To *passion* is used as a verb by writers contemporary with Shakspeare.
STEEVENS.

For thy sweet mistress' sake, because thou lov'st her.
Farewell. [*Exit* SILVIA.

Jul. And she shall thank you for't, if e'er you know her.—
A virtuous gentlewoman, mild, and beautiful.
I hope, my master's suit will be but cold,
Since she respects my mistress' love so much [7].
Alas, how love can trifle with itself!
Here is her picture: Let me see; I think,
If I had such a tire, this face of mine
Were full as lovely as is this of hers:
And yet the painter flatter'd her a little,
Unless I flatter with myself too much.
Her hair is auburn, mine is perfect yellow:
If that be all the difference in his love,
I'll get me such a colour'd periwig [8].
Her eyes are grey as glass [9]; and so are mine:
Ay, but her forehead's low [1], and mine's as high.
What should it be, that he respects in her,
But I can make respective [2] in myself,
If this fond love were not a blinded god?
Come, shadow, come, and take this shadow up,
For 'tis thy rival. O thou senseless form,
Thou shalt be worshipp'd, kiss'd, lov'd, and ador'd;

---

[7] *— my mistress' love so much.*] She had in her preceding speech called Julia *her friend*; but it is odd enough that she should there-fore call herself, when she is alone. Sir T. Hanmer read—"*his mistress*;" but without necessity. Our author knew that his audience considered the disguised Julia in the present scene as a page to Protheus, and this, I believe, and the love of antithesis, produced the expression. MALONE.

[8] *I'll get me such a colour'd periwig.*] It should be remembered, that false hair was worn by the ladies, long before *wigs* were in fashion. These false coverings, however, were called *periwigs*. STEEVENS.

See *Much Ado about Nothing*, Act ii. sc. iii.—" and her hair shall be of what colour it please God."—and the *Merchant of Venice*, Act. iii. sc. ii.

" So are those crisped snaky golden locks, &c." MALONE.

[9] *Her eyes are grey as glass;*] So Chaucer, in the character of his Prioress:

" Ful semely hire wimple y-pinched was;
" Hire nose tretis; hire *eyen grey as glas.*" THEOBALD.

[1] *— her forehead's low,*] A high forehead was in our author's time accounted a feature eminently beautiful. So, in *The History of Guy of Warwick,* " Felice his lady" is said to have " *the same high forehead as Venus.*" JOHNSON.

[2] *— respective—*] i. e. *respectful,* or *respectable.* STEEVENS.

And, were there senſe in his idolatry,
My ſubſtance ſhould be ſtatue in thy ſtead [3].
I'll uſe thee kindly for thy miſtreſs' ſake,
That us'd me ſo; or elſe, by Jove I vow,
I ſhould have ſcratch'd out your unſeeing eyes,
To make my maſter out of love with thee. [*Exit.*

ACT V. SCENE I.

The ſame. An Abbey.

Enter EGLAMOUR.

Egl. The ſun begins to gild the weſtern ſky;
And now it is about the very hour
That Silvia, at friar Patrick's cell, ſhould meet me.
She will not fail; for lovers break not hours,
Unleſs it be to come before their time;
So much they ſpur their expedition.

Enter SILVIA.

See, where ſhe comes: Lady, a happy evening!
    Sil. Amen, amen! go on, good Eglamour,
Out at the poſtern by the abbey-wall;
I fear, I am attended by ſome ſpies.

---

[3] *My ſubſtance ſhould be* ſtatue *in thy ſtead*] It would be eaſy to read with no more roughneſs than is to be found in many lines of Shakſpeare:
———— ſhould be *a* ſtatue in thy ſtead.
The ſenſe, as Mr. Edwards obſerves, is, " He ſhould have my ſubſtance as a *ſtatue*, inſtead of thee [the picture], who art a ſenſeleſs form." This word, however, is uſed without the article *a* in Maſſinger's *Great Duke of Florence*, and in Lord Surrey's tranſlation of the fourth Æneid. STEEVENS.

It appears from hence, and a paſſage in Maſſinger, that the word *ſtatue* was formerly uſed to expreſs a portrait. Julia is here addreſſing herſelf to a picture; and in *The City Madam* the young ladies are ſuppoſed to take leave of the *ſtatues* of their lovers, as they ſtile them, though Sir John, at the beginning of the ſcene, calls them *pictures*, and deſcribes them afterwards as nothing but ſuperficies, colours, and no ſubſtance. MASON.

Egl.

Egl. Fear not: the forest is not three leagues off;
If we recover that, we are sure enough [1].   [*Exeunt.*

SCENE II.

The same. A Room in the Duke's *Palace.*

Enter Thurio, Protheus, *and* Julia.

Thu. Sir Protheus, what says Silvia to my suit?
Pro. O, Sir, I find her milder than she was;
And yet she takes exceptions at your person.
Thu. What, that my leg is too long?
Pro. No; that it is too little.
Thu. I'll wear a boot, to make it somewhat rounder.
Pro. But love will not be spurr'd to what it loaths.
Thu. What says she to my face?
Pro. She says, it is a fair one.
Thu. Nay, then the wanton lies; my face is black.
Pro. But pearls are fair; and the old saying is,
Black men are pearls in beauteous ladies' eyes [2].
Jul. 'Tis true [3], such pearls as put out ladies' eyes;
For I had rather wink than look on them.   [*Aside.*
Thu. How likes she my discourse?
Pro. Ill, when you talk of war.
Thu. But well, when I discourse of love, and peace?
Jul. But better, indeed, when you hold your peace.
    [*Aside.*
Thu. What says she to my valour?
Pro. O, Sir, she makes no doubt of that.
Jul. She needs not, when she knows it cowardice.
    [*Aside.*
Thu. What says she to my birth?
Pro. That you are well deriv'd.
Jul. True; from a gentleman to a fool.   [*Aside.*
Thu. Considers she my possessions?
Pro. O, ay; and pities them.
Thu. Wherefore?

---

[1] — *sure enough.*] *Sure* is *safe, out of danger.* Johnson.

[2] *Black men are pearls,* &c.] " A black man is a jewel in a fair woman's eye,"—is one of Ray's proverbial sentences. Malone.

[3] Jul. *'Tis true,* &c.] This speech, which certainly belongs to Julia, is given in the old copy to Thurio. Mr. Rowe restored it to its proper owner. Steevens.

Jul. That such an ass should owe them. [*Aside.*
Pro. That they are out by lease [4].
Jul. Here comes the duke.

Enter Duke.

Duke. How now, Sir Protheus? how now, Thurio?
Which of you saw Sir Eglamour [*], of late?
Thu. Not I.
Pro. Nor I.
Duke. Saw you my daughter?
Pro. Neither.
Duke. Why, then she's fled unto that peasant Valentine;
And Eglamour is in her company.
'Tis true; for friar Laurence met them both,
As he in penance wander'd through the forest:
Him he knew well, and guess'd that it was she;
But, being mask'd, he was not sure of it:
Besides, she did intend confession
At Patrick's cell this even; and there she was not:
These likelihoods confirm her flight from hence.
Therefore, I pray you, stand not to discourse,
But mount you presently; and meet with me
Upon the rising of the mountain-foot
That leads toward Mantua, whither they are fled:
Dispatch, sweet gentlemen, and follow me. [*Exit.*
Thu. Why, this it is to be a peevish girl,
That flies her fortune when it follows her:
I'll after; more to be reveng'd on Eglamour,
Than for the love of reckless Silvia. [*Exit.*
Pro. And I will follow, more for Silvia's love,
Than hate of Eglamour that goes with her. [*Exit.*
Jul. And I will follow, more to cross that love,
Than hate for Silvia, that is gone for love. [*Exit.*

[4] *That they are out by lease.*] I suppose he means, because Thurio's folly has let them on disadvantageous terms. STEEVENS.
She pities Sir Thurio's possessions, because they are let to others, and are not in his own dear hands. Such appears to me to be the meaning. MASON.

[*] — *Sir Eglamour* —] Sir, which is not in the old copy, was inserted by the editor of the second folio. MALONE.

SCENE

SCENE III.

Frontiers of Mantua. *The Forest.*

Enter SILVIA *and* OUT-LAWS.

1 *Out.* Come, come;
Be patient, we must bring you to our captain.
   Sil. A thousand more mischances than this one
Have learn'd me how to brook this patiently.
   2 *Out.* Come, bring her away.
   1 *Out.* Where is the gentleman that was with her?
   3 *Out.* Being nimble-footed, he hath out-run us,
But Moyses, and Valerius, follow him.
Go thou with her to the west end of the wood,
There is our captain: we'll follow him that's fled;
The thicket is beset, he cannot 'scape.
   1 *Out.* Come, I must bring you to our captain's cave:
Fear not; he bears an honourable mind,
And will not use a woman lawlessly.
   Sil. O Valentine, this I endure for thee!   [*Exeunt.*

SCENE IV.

Another part of the Forest.

Enter VALENTINE.

Val. How use doth breed a habit in a man!
This shadowy desert, unfrequented woods,
I better brook than flourishing peopled towns:
Here can I sit alone, unseen of any,
And, to the nightingale's complaining notes,
Tune my distresses, and record my woes [5].
O thou that dost inhabit in my breast,
Leave not the mansion so long tenantless;
Lest, growing ruinous, the building fall,
And leave no memory of what it was [6]!

                                    Repair

---

[5] — record *my woes.*] To *record* anciently signified to *sing.* Sir John Hawkins informs me, that to *record* is a term still used by bird-fanciers, to express the first essays of a bird in singing. STEEVENS.

[6] *O thou, that dost inhabit in my breast,*
   Leave not the mansion so long tenantless;

Repair me with thy presence, Silvia;
Thou gentle nymph, cherish thy forlorn swain! —
What halloing, and what stir, is this to-day?
These are my mates, that make their wills their law,
Have some unhappy passenger in chace:
They love me well; yet I have much to do,
To keep them from uncivil outrages.
Withdraw thee, Valentine; who's this comes here?
[*Steps aside.*

Enter PROTHEUS, SILVIA, *and* JULIA.

Pro. Madam, this service I have done for you,
(Though you respect not aught your servant doth,)
To hazard life, and rescue you from him,
That would have forc'd your honour and your love.
Vouchsafe me, for my meed⁷, but one fair look;
A smaller boon than this I cannot beg,
And less than this, I am sure, you cannot give.
Val. How like a dream is this, I see, and hear!
Love, lend me patience to forbear a while. [*Aside.*
Sil. O miserable, unhappy that I am!
Pro. Unhappy were you, Madam, ere I came;
But, by my coming, I have made you happy.
Sil. By thy approach thou mak'st me most unhappy.
Jul. And me, when he approacheth to your presence.
[*Aside.*

Sil. Had I been seized by a hungry lion,
I would have been a breakfast to the beast,
Rather than have false Protheus rescue me.
O, heaven be judge, how I love Valentine,
Whose life's as tender to me as my soul;
And full as much (for more there cannot be,)
I do detest false perjur'd Protheus:
Therefore be gone, solicit me no more.
Pro. What dangerous action, stood it next to death,
Would I not undergo for one calm look?
O, 'tis the curse in love, and still approv'd⁸,
When women cannot love, where they're belov'd.
Sil.

*Left, growing ruinous, the building fall,
And leave no memory of what it was!* } It is hardly possible to point
out four lines in any of the plays of Shakspeare, more remarkable for
ease and elegance. STEEVENS.

⁷ — *my meed,*] i. e. reward. STEEVENS.

Sil. When Protheus cannot love, where he's belov'd.
Read over Julia's heart, thy first best love,
For whose dear sake thou didst then rend thy faith
Into a thousand oaths; and all those oaths
Descended into perjury, to love me.
Thou hast no faith left now, unless thou had'st two,
And that's far worse than none; better have none
Than plural faith, which is too much by one:
Thou counterfeit to thy true friend!

Pro. In love,
Who respects friend?

Sil. All men but Protheus.

Pro. Nay, if the gentle spirit of moving words
Can no way change you to a milder form,
I'll woo you like a soldier, at arms' end;
And love you 'gainst the nature of love, force you.

Sil. O heaven!

Pro. I'll force thee yield to my desire.

Val. Ruffian, let go that rude uncivil touch;
Thou friend of an ill fashion!

Pro. Valentine!

Val. Thou common friend, that's without faith or love [9];
(For such is a friend now,) treacherous man!
Thou hast beguil'd my hopes; nought but mine eye
Could have persuaded me: Now I dare not say,
I have one friend alive; thou would'st disprove me.
Who should be trusted, when one's own right hand [1]
Is perjur'd to the bosom? Protheus,
I am sorry, I must never trust thee more,
But count the world a stranger for thy sake.
The private wound is deepest: O time most accurst [2]!
'Mongst all foes, that a friend should be the worst!

[8] *— and still* approv'd,] *Approv'd is felt, experienced.* MALONE.

[9] *— that's without faith or love;*] *That's is perhaps here used, not for who is, but for id est, that is to say.* MALONE.

[1] *Who shall be trusted, when one's* own right hand] The old copy has not *own*; which was introduced into the text by Sir T. Hanmer. The second folio, to complete the metre, reads:
    Who shall be trusted *now*, when one's right hand—.
The addition, like all those made in that copy, appears to have been merely arbitrary; and the modern word is, in my opinion, more likely to have been the author's than the other. MALONE.

Pro.

Pro. My shame and guilt confounds me.—
Forgive me, Valentine: if hearty sorrow
Be a sufficient ransom for offence,
I tender it here; I do as truly suffer,
As e'er I did commit.

Val. Then I am paid;
And once again I do receive thee honest:—
Who by repentance is not satisfy'd,
Is nor of heaven, nor earth; for these are pleas'd;
By penitence the Eternal's wrath's appeas'd:—
And, that my love may appear plain and free,
All, that was mine in Silvia, I give thee [3].

Jul. O me unhappy! [*faints.*
Pro. Look to the boy.
Val. Why, boy! why wag! how now? what is the matter?
Pro. Look up; speak.

[2] *The private wound, is deepest, O time most accurst!*] *Deepest, highest* and other similar words, were sometimes used by the poets of Shakspeare's age as monosyllables. See p. 76 n. 3.
So, in our poet's 133d Sonnet:
"But slave to slavery my *sweetest* friend *most* be." MALONE.

[3] *All, that was mine in Silvia, I give thee.*] It is, I think, very odd, to give up his mistress thus at once, without any reason alledged. But our author probably followed the stories just as he found them in his novels as well as histories. POPE.

This passage either hath been much sophisticated, or is one great proof that the main parts of this play did not proceed from Shakspeare; for it is impossible he could make Valentine act and speak so much out of character, or give to Silvia so unnatural a behaviour, as to take no notice of this strange concession, if it had been made. HANMER.

Valentine, from seeing Silvia in the company of Protheus, might conceive she had escaped with him, from her father's court, for the purposes of love, though she could not foresee the violence which his villainy might offer, after he had seduced her under the pretence of an honest passion. If Valentine, however, be supposed to hear all that passed between them in this scene, I am afraid I have only to subscribe to the opinion of my predecessors. STEEVENS.

And, that my love, &c.] Transfer these two lines to the end of Thurio's speech in page 182, and all is right. Why then should Julia faint? It is only an artifice, seeing Silvia given up to Valentine, to discover herself to Protheus, by a pretended mistake of the rings. One great fault of this play is the hastening too abruptly, and without due preparation, to the denouement, which shews that, if it be Shakspeare's, (which I cannot doubt) it was one of his very early performances. BLACKSTONE.

Jul. O good Sir, my master charg'd me
To deliver a ring to Madam Silvia;
Which, out of my neglect, was never done.
   Pro. Where is that ring, boy?
   Jul. Here 'tis: this is it.   [*gives a ring.*
   Pro. How! let me see:
Why this is the ring I gave to Julia.
   Jul. O, cry your mercy, Sir, I have mistook;
This is the ring you sent to Silvia.   [*shews another ring.*
   Pro. But, how cam'st thou by this ring? at my depart
I gave this unto Julia.
   Jul. And Julia herself did give it me:
And Julia herself hath brought it hither.
   Pro. How! Julia!
   Jul. Behold her that gave aim to all thy oaths,
And entertain'd them deeply in her heart:
How oft hast thou with perjury cleft the root [4]?
O Protheus, let this habit make thee blush!
Be thou asham'd, that I have took upon me
Such an immodest raiment; if shame live
In a disguise of love [5]:
It is the lesser blot, modesty finds,
Women to change their shapes, than men their minds.
   Pro. Than men their minds! 'tis true: O heaven! were man
But constant, he were perfect: that one error
Fills him with faults; makes him run through all the sins:
Inconstancy falls off, ere it begins:
What is in Silvia's face, but I may spy
More fresh in Julia's with a constant eye?
   Val. Come, come, a hand from either:
Let me be blest to make this happy close;
'Twere pity two such friends should be long foes.
   Pro. Bear witness, heaven,
I have my wish for ever.
   Jul. And I mine.

      Enter OUT-LAWS, *with* DUKE *and* THURIO.

   Out. A prize, a prize, a prize!
   Val. Forbear, forbear, I say; it is my lord the duke.

---

[4] *How oft hast thou with perjury cleft the root?*] i. e. of her heart.
                                                           MALONE.

[5] — *if shame live, &c.*] That is, *if it be any shame to wear a disguise for the purposes of love.* JOHNSON.

Your grace is welcome to a man disgrac'd,
Banish'd Valentine?

Duke. Sir Valentine!

Thu. Yonder is Silvia; and Silvia's mine.

Val. Thurio, give back, or else embrace thy death;
Come not within the measure of my wrath [6]:
Do not name Silvia thine; if once again,
Milan shall not behold thee [7]. Here she stands,
Take but possession of her with a touch;—
I dare thee but to breathe upon my love.

Thu. Sir Valentine, I care not for her, I;
I hold him but a fool, that will endanger
His body for a girl that loves him not:
I claim her not, and therefore she is thine.

Duke. The more degenerate and base art thou,
To make such means for her as thou hast done,
And leave her on such slight conditions.—
Now, by the honour of my ancestry,
I do applaud thy spirit, Valentine,
And think thee worthy of an empress' love.
Know then, I here forget all former griefs [8],
Cancel all grudge, repeal thee home again.—
Plead a new state in thy unrival'd merit,
To which I thus subscribe—Sir Valentine,
Thou art a gentleman, and well deriv'd;
Take thou thy Silvia, for thou hast deserv'd her.

Val. I thank your grace; the gift hath made me happy.
I now beseech you, for your daughter's sake,
To grant one boon that I shall ask of you.

Duke. I grant it, for thine own, whate'er it be.

Val. These banish'd men, that I have kept withal,
Are men endued with worthy qualities;
Forgive them what they have committed here,

---

[6] — *the measure of my wrath:*] The length of my sword, the reach of my anger. JOHNSON.

[7] *Milan shall not behold thee.*] The old copy reads—*Verona* shall not hold thee. The correction was made by Mr. Theobald, who observes, that Thurio was a *Milanese*, and therefore the threat must be, " *Milan,* i. e. thy country, shall never see thee again; thou shalt not live to go back thither."—This emendation having been adopted by all the subsequent editors, I have not displaced it; yet, I suspect, the mistake was our author's own. MALONE.

[8] — *all former* griefs,] *Griefs* in old language frequently signified *grievances, wrongs.* MALONE.

And

And let them be recall'd from their exile:
They are reformed, civil, full of good,
And fit for great employment, worthy lord.

Duke. Thou hast prevail'd: I pardon them, and thee;
Dispose of them, as thou know'st their deserts.
Come, let us go; we will include all jars ⁹
With triumphs, mirth, and rare solemnity.

Val. And, as we walk along, I dare be bold
With our discourse to make your grace to smile:
What think you of this page, my lord?

Duke. I think the boy hath grace in him; he blushes.

Val. I warrant you, my lord; more grace than boy.

Duke. What mean you by that saying?

Val. Please you, I'll tell you as we pass along,
That you will wonder, what hath fortuned.—
Come, Protheus; 'tis your penance, but to hear
The story of your loves discovered:
That done, our day of marriage shall be yours;
One feast, one house, one mutual happiness ¹.   [*Exeunt.*

—— include *all jars*—] To *include* is to *shut up*. So, in *Macbeth:*
"———and *shut up*
" In measureless content." STEEVENS.

In this play there is a strange mixture of knowledge and ignorance, of care and negligence. The versification is often excellent, the allusions are learned and just; but the author conveys his heroes by sea from one inland town to another in the same country; he places the emperor at Milan, and sends his young men to attend him, but never mentions him more; he makes Protheus, after an interview with Silvia, say he has only seen her picture *; and, if we may credit the old copies, he has, by mistaking places, left his scenery inextricable. The reason of all this confusion seems to be, that he took his story from a novel, which he sometimes followed, and sometimes forsook, sometimes remembered, and sometimes forgot.

That this play is rightly attributed to Shakspeare, I have little doubt. If it be taken from him, to whom shall it be given? This question may be asked of all the disputed plays, except *Titus Andronicus*; and it will be found more credible, that Shakspeare might sometimes sink below his highest flights, than that any other should rise up to his lowest.
                                                                JOHNSON.

* This is a slight mistake of this most judicious critic, founded on a misapprehension of a passage in Act. II. See p. 136. *M*a*ne.*

MERRY

MERRY WIVES OF WINDSOR.

PERSONS REPRESENTED.

Sir John Falstaff.
Fenton.
Shallow, *a country Justice.*
Slender, *cousin to* Shallow.
Mr. Ford, }
Mr. Page, } *two gentlemen dwelling at* Windsor.
William Page, *a boy, son to* Mr. Page.
Sir Hugh Evans, *a Welch parson.*
Dr. Caius, *a French physician.*
Host of the Garter Inn.
Bardolph, }
Pistol, } *followers of* Falstaff.
Nym, }
Robin, *page to* Falstaff.
Simple, *servant to* Slender.
Rugby, *servant to* Dr. Caius.

Mrs. Ford.
Mrs. Page.
Mrs. Anne Page, *her daughter, in love with* Fenton.
Mrs. Quickly, *servant to* Dr. Caius.

Servants to Page, Ford, &c.

SCENE, Windsor; *and the parts adjacent.*

MERRY WIVES OF WINDSOR.[1]

ACT I. SCENE I.

Windsor. *Before* Page's *House.*

Enter Justice SHALLOW, SLENDER, *and Sir* HUGH EVANS.

Shal. Sir Hugh,[2] persuade me not; I will make a Star-chamber matter of it[3]: if he were twenty Sir John Falstaffs, he shall not abuse Robert Shallow, Esquire.

Slen.

A few of the incidents in this comedy might have been taken from some old translation of *Il Pecorone* by Giovanni Florentino. I have lately met with the same story in a very contemptible performance, intitled, *The fortunate, the deceived, and the unfortunate Lovers.* Of this book, as I am told, there are several impressions; but that in which I read it, was published in 1632, quarto. A something similar story occurs in *Piacevoli Notti di Straparola.* Nott. 4ª. Fav. 4ª.

This comedy was first entered at Stationers' Hall, Jan. 18, 1601, by John Busby. STEEVENS.

This play should be read between *K. Henry IV.* and *K. Henry V.*
JOHNSON.

A passage in the first sketch of the *Merry Wives of Windsor* shews, I think, that it ought rather to be read between *the First* and *the Second Part of King Henry IV.* in the latter of which young Henry becomes king. In the last act, Falstaff says:

" Herne the hunter, quoth you? am I a ghost?
" 'Sblood, the fairies hath made a ghost of me.
" What, hunting at this time of night
" I'le lay my life the mad *prince of Wales*
" Is stealing his father's deare."

And in this play, as it now appears, Mr. Page discountenances the addresses of Fenton to his daughter, because " he keeps company with the wild *prince,* and with Poins."

The

Slen. In the county of Gloster, justice of peace, and *coram.*

Shal.

The *Fishwife's Tale of Brainford* in WESTWARD FOR SMELTS, a book which Shakspeare appears to have read, (having borrowed from it part of the fable of *Cymbeline*,) probably led him to lay the scene of Falstaff's love-adventures at *Winsor*. It begins thus: "In *Winsor* not long agoe dwelt a sumpterman, who had to wife a very faire but wanton creature, over whom, not without cause, he was something jealous; yet had he never any proof of her inconstancy."

The reader who is curious in such matters, may find the story of the *Lovers of Pisa*, mentioned by Dr. Farmer in the following note, at the end of this play. MALONE.

The adventures of *Falstaff* in this play seem to have been taken from the story of the *Lovers of Pisa*, in an old piece, called "*Tarleton's Newes out of Purgatorie*." A late editor pretended to much knowledge of this fort; and I am sorry that it proved to be only pretension. In the first edition of the imperfect play, quarto, 1602, Sir Hugh Evans is called on the title-page, the *Welsh Knight*; and yet there are some persons who still affect to believe, that all our author's plays were originally published by *himself*. FARMER.

Queen Elizabeth was so well pleased with the admirable character of Falstaff in *The Two Parts of Henry IV.* that, as Mr. Rowe informs us, she commanded Shakspeare to continue it for one play more, and to shew him in love. To this command we owe *The Merry Wives of Winsor*; which, Mr. Gildon says, (*Remarks* on Shakspeare's plays, 8vo. 1710,) he was very well assured our author finished in a fortnight. But this must be meant only of the first imperfect sketch of this comedy. An old quarto edition which I have seen, printed in 1602, says, in the title page,—*as it hath been divers times acted before her majesty, and elsewhere*. This which we have here, was altered and improved by the author almost in every speech. POPE. THEOBALD.

Mr. Gildon has likewise told us, "that our author's house at Stratford bordered on the Church-yard, and that he wrote the scene of the Ghost in *Hamlet* there." But neither for this, nor the assertion that the play before us was written in a fortnight, does he quote any authority. The latter circumstance was first mentioned by Mr. Dennis. "This comedy," says he, in his Epistle Dedicatory to the *Comical Gallant*, (an alteration of the present play,) 1702, "was written at her [Queen Elizabeth's] command, and by her direction, and she was so eager to see it acted, that she commanded it to be finished in *fourteen days*; and was afterwards, as tradition tells us, very well pleased at the representation." The information, it is probable, came originally from Dryden, who from his intimacy with Sir William Davenant had an opportunity of learning many particulars concerning our author.

At what period Shakspeare new-modelled the *Merry Wives of Windsor* is unknown. I believe it was enlarged in 1603. See some conjectures on the subject in the *Attempt to ascertain the order of his plays*, ante. MALONE.

Shal. Ay, cousin Slender, and *Cust-alorum* ⁴.
Slen. Ay, and *ratolorum* too; and a gentleman born,
master

It is not generally known, that the first edition of *the Merry Wives of Windsor*, in its present state, is in the valuable folio, printed 1623, from whence the quarto of the same play, dated 1630, was evidently copied. The two earlier quartos, 1602, and 1619, only exhibit this comedy as it was originally written, and are so far curious, as they contain Shakspeare's first conceptions in forming a drama, which is the most complete specimen of his comic powers. T. WARTON.

² Sir *Hugh*,] *Sir* is the designation of a Bachelor of Arts in the Universities of Cambridge and Dublin; but is there always annexed to the surname;—Sir Evans, &c. In consequence, however, of this, all the inferior Clergy in England were distinguished by this title affixed to their Christian name for many centuries. Hence our author's *Sir Hugh* in the present play,—Sir Topaz in *Twelfth Night*, Sir Oliver in *As you like it*, &c. So lately as in the time of King William and Queen Mary, (as Sir John Hawkins has observed,) in a deposition in the Exchequer in a case of tithes, the witness, speaking of the Curate, stiles him *Sir Gyles*. MALONE.

Sir seems to have been a title formerly appropriated to such of the inferior clergy as were only *Readers* of the service, and not admitted to be preachers, and therefore were held in the lowest estimation; as appears from a remarkable passage in Machell's MS. *Collections for the history of Westmoreland and Cumberland*, in six volumes, folio, preserved in the Dean and Chapter's library at Carlisle. The reverend Thomas Machell, author of the Collections, lived temp. Car. II. Speaking of the little chapel of Martindale in the mountains of Westmoreland and Cumberland, the writer says, " There is little remarkable in or about it, but a neat chapel-yard, which by the peculiar care of the old Reader, Sir Richard*, is kept clean, and as neat as a bowling-green."—

* Richard Berket, Reader, Æt. 74. MS. note.

" Within the limits of myne own memory all *Readers* in chapels were called Sirs†, and of old have been writ so; whence, I suppose, such of the laity as received the noble order of knighthood being called Sirs too, for distinction sake had *Knight* writ after them; which had been superfluous, if the title of *Sir* had been peculiar to them. But now this *Sir Richard* is the only *Knight Templar* (if I may so call him) that retains the old style, which in other places is much laid aside, and grown out of use." PERCY.

³ — *a Star-chamber matter of it:*] See p. 191,—" The Council shall hear it; it is a riot;" and the note there. MALONE.

⁴ — *Cust-alorum.*] This is, I suppose, intended for a corruption of *Custos Rotulorum*. The mistake was hardly designed by the author, who, though he gives Shallow folly enough, makes him rather pedantic than illiterate. If we read:

Shal. *Ay, cousin Slender, and* Custos Rotulorum.

It

† In the margin is a MS. note seemingly in the hand-writing of Bp. Nicholson, who gave these volumes to the library.
" Since I can remember there was not a *reader* in any chapel but was called *Sir*."

master parson; who writes himself *armigero;* in any bill, warrant, quittance, or obligation, *armigero.*

Shal. Ay, that I do; and have done⁵ any time these three hundred years.

Slen. All his successors, gone before him, have done't; and all his ancestors, that come after him, may: they may give the dozen white luces in their coat.

Shal. It is an old coat.

Evans. The dozen white louses do become an old coat well;⁎ it agrees well, passant: it is a familiar beast to man, and signifies—love.

Shal. The luce is the fresh fish; the salt fish is an old coat⁶.

Slen.

It follows naturally:

Slen. Ay, and Ratolorum *too.* JOHNSON.

I think, with Dr. Johnson, that this blunder could scarcely be intended. *Shallow,* we know, had been bred to the law at *Clement's Inn.*—But I would rather read *custos* only; then *Slender* adds naturally, " Ay, and *rotulorum* too." He had heard the words *custos rotulorum,* and supposes them to mean different offices. FARMER.

Perhaps Shakspeare might have intended to ridicule the abbreviations sometimes used in writs and other legal instruments, with which his Justice might have been acquainted. In the old copy the word is printed *Cust-alorum,* as it is now exhibited in the text. If, however, this was intended, it should be *Cust-ulorum;* and, it must be owned, abbreviation by cutting off the beginning of a word is not authorized by any precedent, except what we may suppose to have existed in Shallow's imagination. MALONE.

⁵ *— and have done—*] i. e. all the Shallows *have done.* Shakspeare has many expressions equally licentious.⁎ MALONE.

⁎ *The dozen white louses do become an old coat well.*] A similar play of words is found in the ballad said to be made by Shakspeare on Sir Thomas Lucy. See vol. i. The arms of the Lucy family are three *luces* hariant; but I am informed that one of the shields in Charlecote church has *twelve luces* depicted on it. MALONE.

⁶ *The luce is the fresh fish; the salt fish is an old coat.*] Our author here alludes to the arms of Sir Thomas Lucy, who is said to have prosecuted him in the younger part of his life for a misdemesnor, and who is supposed to be pointed at under the character of Justice Shallow. The text however, by some carelessness of the printer or transcriber, has been so corrupted, that the passage, as it stands at present, seems inexplicable. Dr. Farmer's regulation appears to me highly probable; and in further support of it, it may be observed, that some other speeches, beside those he has mentioned, are misplaced in a subsequent part of this scene, as exhibited in the first folio. See p. 193. Mr. Smith's note is not, I think, worth insertion. MALONE.

I am not satisfied with any thing that has been offered on this difficult passage. All that Mr. Smith tells us, is a mere *gratis dictum.*

cannot

OF WINDSOR. 191

Slen. I may quarter, coz.

Shal. You may, by marrying.

Evans. It is marring, indeed, if he quarter it.

Shal. Not a whit.

Evans. Yes, py'r-lady; if he has a quarter of your coat, there is but three skirts for yourself, in my simple conjectures: but that is all one: If Sir John Falstaff have committed disparagements unto you, I am of the church, and will be glad to do my benevolence, to make atonements and compromises between you.

Shal. The Council shall hear it; it is a riot [7].

Evans. It is not meet the Council hear a riot; there is no fear of Got in a riot: the Council, look you, shall de-

---

cannot find that *salt fish* were ever really borne in heraldry. I fancy the latter part of the speech should be given to Sir *Hugh*, who is at cross purposes with the *Justice*. *Shallow* had said just before, the coat is an old one, and now, that it is the luce, the fresh fish.—No, replies the parson, it cannot be *old* and *fresh* too;—" the *salt fish* is an *old coat*." I give this with rather the more confidence, as a similar mistake has happened a little lower in the scene.—" *Slice*, I say!" cries out Corporal *Nym*, " *Pauca, pauca: Slice*, that's my humour." There can be no doubt, but *pauca, pauca*, should be spoken by *Evans*.

Again, a little before this, the copies give us:

Slender. You'll not confess, you'll not confess.

Shallow. That he will not—'tis your fault, 'tis your fault:—'tis a good dog.

Surely it should be thus:

Shallow. You'll not confess, you'll not confess.

Slender. That he will not.

Shallow. 'Tis your fault, 'tis your fault, &c.   FARMER.

This fugitive scrap of Latin, *pauca*, &c. is used in several old pieces, by characters who have no more of literature about them than *Nym*: In *Every Man in his Humour* it is called the *benchers phrase*.

The *luce* is a pike or jack. In Ferne's *Blazon of Gentry*, 1586, quarto, the arms of the Lucy family are represented as an instance, that " signs of the coat should something agree with the name. It is the coat of Geffray Lord Lucy. He did bear gules, three *lucies* hariant, argent."   STEEVENS.

[7] *The Council shall hear it; it is a riot.*] By the *Council* is only meant the court of star-chamber, composed chiefly of the king's council sitting in *Camera stellata*, which took cognizance of atrocious riots. In the old quarto, " the council shall know it," follows immediately after " I'll make a star-chamber matter of it."   BLACKSTONE.

So, in Sir John Harrington's *Epigrams*, 1618:

" No marvel, men of such a sumptuous dyet

" Were brought into the *Star-chamber* for a *ryot*."   MALONE.

See Stat. 13. Henry IV. c. 7.   GREY.

fire

fire to hear the fear of Got, and not to hear a riot; take your vizaments in that ⁸.

Shal. Ha! o' my life, if I were young again, the fword fhould end it.

Evans. It is petter that friends is the fword, and end it: and there is alfo another device in my prain, which, peradventure, prings goot difcretions with it: There is Anne Page, which is daughter to Mafter George Page ⁹, which is pretty virginity.

Slen. Miftrefs Anne Page? She has brown hair, and fpeaks fmall like a woman ¹.

Evans. It is that fery perfon for all the 'orld, as juft as you will defire; and feven hundred pounds of monies, and gold, and filver, is her grandfire, upon his death's-bed, (Got deliver to a joyful refurrections!) give, when fhe is able to overtake feventeen years old: it were a goot motion, if we leave our pribbles and prabbles, and defire a marriage between Mafter Abraham, and Miftrefs Anne Page.

Shal. Did her grandfire leave her feven hundred pounds ² ?

Evans.

---

⁸ *— your* vizaments *in that.*] i. e. *Advifement;* now an obfolete word.
STEEVENS.

⁹ *— Mafter* George Page,] The old copy has—*Thomas* Page. The emendation is Mr. Theobald's. MALONE.

¹ *—fpeaks fmall like a woman.*] Dr. Warburton has found more pleafantry here than I believe was intended. *Small* was, I think, not ufed, as he fuppofes, in an ambiguous fenfe, for " *little*, as well as *low*," but fimply for *weak, flender, feminine;* and the only pleafantry of the paffage feems to be, that poor Slender fhould characterife his miftrefs by a general quality belonging to her whole fex. In *A Midfummer Night's Dream,* Quince tells Flute, who objects to playing a woman's part, " You fhall play it in a mafk, and you may fpeak as *fmall* as you will." MALONE.

² Shal. *Did her grandfire leave her feven hundred pound?—I knew the young gentlewoman;* &c.] Thefe two fpeeches are by miftake given to Slender in the firft folio, the only authentic copy of this play. From the foregoing words it appears that *Shallow* is the perfon here addreffed; and on a marriage being propofed for his kinfman, he very naturally inquires concerning the lady's fortune. Slender fhould feem not to know what they are talking about; (except that he juft hears the name of Anne Page, and breaks out into a foolifh elogium on her;) for in p. 200, Shallow fays to him—" Coz, there is, as it were, a tender, a kind of tender, made a far off by Sir Hugh here; do you underftand me?" to which Slender replies—" if it be fo," &c. The tender, therefore, we fee, had been made to Shallow, and not to Slender; the former of which names fhould be prefixed to the two fpeeches before us.

Evans. Ay, and her father is make her a petter penny.

Shal. I know the young gentlewoman; she has good gifts.

Evans. Seven hundred pounds, and possibilities, is good gifts.

Shal. Well, let us see honest master Page: Is Falstaff there?

Evans. Shall I tell you a lie? I do despise a liar, as I do despise one that is false; or, as I despise one that is not true. The knight, Sir John, is there; and, I beseech you, be ruled by your well-willers. I will peat the door [*knocks.*] for master Page. What, hoa! Got pless your house here!

Enter PAGE.

Page. Who's there?

Evans. Here is Got's plessing, and your friend, and Justice Shallow: and here young Master Slender; that, peradventures, shall tell you another tale, if matters grow to your likings.

Page. I am glad to see your worships well: I thank you for my venison, Master Shallow.

Shal. Master Page, I am glad to see you: Much good do it your good heart! I wish'd your venison better; it was ill kill'd:—How doth good Mistress Page?—and I thank you always with my heart, la; with my heart.

Page. Sir, I thank you.

Shal. Sir, I thank you; by yea and no, I do.

Page. I am glad to see you, good Master Slender.

Slen. How does your fallow greyhound, Sir? I heard say, he was out-run on Cotsale [3].

Page.

In this play, as exhibited in the first folio, many of the speeches are given to characters to whom they do not belong. Printers, to save trouble, keep the names of the speakers in each scene ready composed, and are very liable to mistakes, when two names begin (as in the present instance,) with the same letter, and are nearly of the same length.—The present regulation was suggested by Mr. Capell. MALONE.

[3] *How does your fallow greyhound, Sir? I heard say, he was out-run on Cotsale.*] He means *Cotswold*, in *Gloucestershire*. In the beginning of the reign of James the First, by permission of the king, one Dover, a public-spirited attorney of Barton on the Heath, in Warwickshire, instituted on the hills of *Cotswold* an annual celebration of games, consisting of rural sports and exercises. These he constantly conducted in person, well mounted, and accoutred in a suit of his majesty's old cloaths; and they were frequented above forty years by the nobility and gentry for sixty miles round, till the grand rebellion abolished every libe-

VOL. III.   K   ral

Page. It could not be judg'd, Sir.
Slen. You'll not confess, you'll not confess.
Shal. That he will not;—'tis your fault, 'tis your fault⁴:—'Tis a good dog.
Page. A cur, Sir.
Shal. Sir, he's a good dog, and a fair dog: Can there be more said? he is good, and fair.—Is Sir John Falstaff here?
Page. Sir, he is within; and I would I could do a good office between you.
Evans. It is spoke as a Christian ought to speak.
Shal. He hath wrong'd me, Master Page.
Page. Sir, he doth in some sort confess it.
Shal. If it be confess'd, it is not redress'd; is not that so, Master Page? He hath wrong'd me;—indeed, he hath;—at a word, he hath;—believe me;—Robert Shallow, Esquire, saith, he is wrong'd.
Page. Here comes Sir John.

Enter Sir JOHN FALSTAFF, BARDOLPH, NYM, *and* PISTOL.

Fal. Now, Master Shallow; you'll complain of me to the king?
Shal. Knight, you have beaten my men, kill'd my deer, and broke open my lodge⁵.

---

ral establishment. I have seen a very scarce book, entitled, *Annalia Dubrensia*. *Upon the yearly celebration of Mr. Robert Dover's Olympic games upon Cotswold hills, &c. Lond.* 1636, quarto. There are recommendatory verses prefixed, written by Drayton, Jonson, Randolph, and many others, the most eminent wits of the times. The games, as appears by a curious frontispiece, were chiefly, wrestling, leaping, pitching the bar, handling the pike, dancing of women, various kinds of hunting, and particularly coursing the hare with greyhounds. T. WARTON.

The Cotswold hills in Gloucestershire are a large tract of downs, famous for their fine turf, and therefore excellent for coursing. I believe there is no village of that name. BLACKSTONE.

⁴ — *'tis your fault, 'tis your fault:*] Of these words, which are addressed to Page, the sense is not very clear. Perhaps Shallow means to say, that it is a known failing of Page's not to confess that his dog has been out-run. Or, the meaning may be,—*'tis your misfortune that he was out-run on Cotswold; be is, however, a good dog.* So perhaps the word is used afterwards by Ford, speaking of his jealousy:

" 'Tis my *fault*, master Page; I suffer for it." MALONE.

⁵ — *and broke open my lodge.*] This probably alludes to some real incident, at that time well known. JOHNSON.

So probably Falstaff's answer. FARMER.

Fal.

Fal. But not kiss'd your keeper's daughter?

Shal. Tut, a pin! this shall be answer'd.

Fal. I will answer it straight;—I have done all this:—That is now answer'd.

Shal. The Council shall know this.

Fal. 'Twere better for you, if 'twere known in counsel [6]: you'll be laugh'd at.

Evans. Pauca verba, Sir John; good worts.

Fal. Good worts! good cabbage [7].—Slender, I broke your head; What matter have you against me?

Slen. Marry, Sir, I have matter in my head against you; and against your coney-catching rascals [8], Bardolph, Nym, and Pistol. They carried me to the tavern, and made me drunk, and afterward pick'd my pocket [9].

Bar. You Banbury cheese [1]!

---

[6] *'Twere better for you, if 'twere known in counsel:*] Falstaff quibbles between *council* and *counsel*. The latter signifies *secrecy*. So, in *Hamlet:* "The players cannot keep *counsel*, they'll tell all."

Falstaff's meaning seems to be—'twere better for you if it were known only in *secrecy*, i. e. among your friends. A more public complaint would subject you to ridicule.

Thus, in Chaucer's prologue to the *Squieres Tale*, v. 10305, late edit:
"But wete ye what? in *consil* be it kyde,
"Me reweth sore I am unto hire teyde." STEEVENS.

The spelling of the old quarto, (*counsel*) as well as the general purport of the passage, fully confirms Mr. Steevens's interpretation—"*Shal.* Well, the *Counsel* shall know it. *Fal.* 'Twere better for you 'twere known in *counsel*. You'll be laugh'd at."

In an office-book of Sir Heneage Finch, Treasurer of the Chambers to Queen Elizabeth, (a MS. in the British Museum,) I observe that whenever the Privy *Council* is mentioned, the word is always spelt *Counsel*; so that the equivoque was less strained then than it appears now.

"Mum is *Counsell*, viz. *silence*," is among Howel's Proverbial Sentences. See his Dict. folio, 1660. MALONE.

[7] *Good worts! good cabbage:*] *Worts* was the ancient name of all the cabbage kind. STEEVENS.

[8] *—coney-catching rascals,*] A *coney-catcher* was, in the time of Elizabeth, a common name for a cheat or sharper. Green, one of the first among us who made a trade of writing pamphlets, published *A Detection of the Frauds and Tricks of Coney-catchers and Couzeners.* JOHNSON.

[9] *They carried me, &c.*] These words, which are necessary to introduce what Falstaff says afterwards, ("Pistol, did you pick Master Slender's purse?") I have restored from the early quarto. Of this circumstance, as the play is exhibited in the folio, Sir John could have no knowledge. MALONE.

[1] *You Banbury cheese!*] This is said in allusion to the thin carcase of Slender. STEEVENS.

K 2   *Slen.*

Slen. Ay, it is no matter.
Pist. How now, Mephostophilus[2]?
Slen. Ay, it is no matter.
Nym. Slice, I say! *pauca, pauca*[3]; slice! that's my humour.
Slen. Where's Simple, my man?—can you tell, cousin?
Evans. Peace: I pray you! Now let us understand: There is three umpires in this matter, as I understand: that is—Master Page, *fidelicet*, Master Page; and there is myself, *fidelicet*, myself; and the three party is, lastly and finally, mine host of the Garter.
Page. We three, to hear it, and end it between them.
Evans. Fery goot: I will make a prief of it in my note-book; and we will afterwards 'ork upon the cause, with as great discreetly as we can.
Fal. Pistol,—
Pist. He hears with ears.
Evans. The tevil and his tam! what phrase is this, *He hears with ear?* Why, it is affectations.
Fal. Pistol, did you pick Master Slender's purse?
Slen. Ay, by these gloves, did he, (or I would I might never come in mine own great chamber again else,) of seven groats in mill-sixpences[4], and two Edward shovel-boards[5], that

---

[2] *How now, Mephostophilus?*] This is the name of a spirit or familiar, in the old story book of *Sir John Faustus*, or *John Faust*: to whom our author afterwards alludes. It was a cant phrase of abuse. T. WARTON.

[3] *Slice, I say; pauca, pauca!*] Dr. Farmer (see a former note, p. 191, n. 6.) would transfer the Latin words to Evans. But the old copy, I think, is right. Pistol, in *K. Henry V.* uses the same language:

"— I will hold the *quondam* Quickly
"For the only she; and *pauca*, there's enough."

In the same scene Nym twice uses the word *sliça*. MALONE.

[4] —*mill-sixpences,*] It appears from a passage in Sir W. Davenant's *News from Plimouth*, that these mill'd sixpences were used by way of counters to cast up money:

"—— A few mill'd-sixpences, with which
"My purser casts accompt." STEEVENS.

[5] — *Edward Shovel-boards,*] He means the broad *shillings* of one of our kings, as appears from comparing these words with the corresponding passage in the old quarto: "Ay by this handkerchief did he;—two faire shovel-board *shillings*, besides seven groats in mill sixpences."

See also Vol. v. "Quoit him down, Bardolph, like a shove-groat shilling."

How twenty-eight pence could be lost in mill-*sixpences*, Slender, however, has not explained to us. MALONE.

Edward Shovel-boards are the broad shillings of Edward VI. Taylor the water poet, makes him complain:

"—— the

that cost me two shilling and two pence a-piece of Yead Miller, by these gloves.

Fal. Is this true, Pistol?

Evans. No; it is false, if it is a pick-purse.

Pist. Ha, thou mountain-foreigner!—Sir John, and master mine,

I combat challenge of this latten bilboe [6]:

> "———— the unthrift every day
> "With my face downwards do at *shove-board* play;
> "That had I had a beard, you may suppose,
> "They had worne it off, as they have done my nose."

And in a note he tells us: "Edw. shillings for the most part are used at *shove-board*." FARMER.

Dr Farmer's note, and the authority he quotes, might, I think, pass uncensured, unless better proofs could be produced in opposition to them. They have, however, been objected to; and we are positively told that Master Slender's "Edward Shovel-boards have *undoubtedly* been *broad shillings of Edward the Third*." I believe the broad shillings of that monarch were never before heard of, as he *undoubtedly* did not coin any shillings whatever. The following extract, for the notice of which I am indebted to Dr. Farmer, will probably shew the species of coin mentioned in the text. "I must here take notice before I entirely quit the subject of these last-mentioned shillings [of Edward VI.] that I have also seen some other pieces of good silver, greatly resembling the same, and of the same date, 1547, that have been so much thicker as to weigh about *half an ounce*, together with some others that have weighed an ounce." Folken's *Table of English silver coins*, p. 32. The former of these were probably what cost Master Slender two shillings and two-pence a-piece. As to the point of chronology (to use the objector's own words on another occasion) *it is not worth consideration*. REED.

That Shakspeare should here (as in all his other plays) have attributed the customs and manners of his own age to a preceding century, without any regard to chronology, cannot be a matter of surprise to any reader who is conversant with his compositions; nor is it to be wondered at, that the present *unfounded* objection should have been made by one, whose arguments in general, like those of our author's Gratiano, "are two grains of wheat hid in two bushels of chaff; you shall seek all day ere you find them, and, when you have them, they are not worth the search"

MALONE.

[6] *I combat challenge of this latten bilboe:*] Pistol, seeing Slender such a slim, puny wight, would intimate, that he is as thin as a plate of that compound metal, which is called *latten:* and which was, as we are told, the old *orichalc.* THEOBALD.

Latten is a mixed metal, made of copper and calamine. MALONE.

The sarcasm intended is, that Slender had neither courage nor strength, as a latten sword hath neither edge nor substance. HEATH.

I believe Theobald has given the true sense of *latten*, though he is wrong in supposing, that the allusion is to Slender's *thinness*. It is rather to his *softness* or *weakness*. TYRWHITT.

Word of denial in thy labras here [7];
Word of denial: froth and scum, thou liest.

Slen. By these gloves, then 'twas he.

Nym. Be advis'd, Sir, and pass good humours: I will say, *marry trap* [8], with you, if you run the nuthook's humour [9] on me; that is the very note of it.

Slen. By this hat, then he in the red face had it: for though I cannot remember what I did when you made me drunk, yet I am not altogether an ass.

Fal. What say you, Scarlet and John [1]?

Bard. Why, Sir, for my part, I say, the gentleman had drunk himself out of his five sentences.

Evans. It is his five senses: fye, what the ignorance is!

Bard. And being fap [2], Sir, was, as they say, cashier'd; and so conclusions pass'd the careires [3].

Slen.

---

[7] — *in thy labras here!* I suppose it should rather be read:
    Word of denial in my labras hear;
that is, *hear* the word of denial in *my lips. Thou ly'st.* JOHNSON.

We often talk of giving the lie in a man's *teeth*, or in his *throat.* Pistol chooses to throw the word of denial in the *lips* of his adversary, and is supposed to point to them as he speaks. STEEVENS.

There are few words in the old copies more frequently misprinted than the word *bear.* "*Thy lips,*" however, is certainly right, as appears from the old quarto: "I do retort the lie even in *thy gorge, thy gorge, thy gorge.*" MALONE.

[8] — *marry trap.*] When a man was caught in his own stratagem, I suppose the exclamation of insult was *marry, trap!* JOHNSON.

[9] — *nuthook's humour —*] *If you run the nuthook's humour on me,* is in plain English, *If you say I am a thief.* Enough is said on the subject of *looking mechanics out of windows,* in a note on *K. Henry IV.* STEEVENS.

[1] *Scarlet and John?*] The names of two of Robin Hood's companions; but the humour consists in the allusion to Bardolph's *red face;* concerning which, see *Henry IV.* Part ii. WARBURTON.

[2] *And being* fap,—] I know not the exact meaning of this cant word, neither have I met with it in any of our old dramatic pieces, which have often proved the best comments on Shakspeare's vulgarisms.—Dr. Farmer, indeed, observes, that to *fib* is to be *beat;* so that *fap* may mean being *beaten,* and *cashier'd,* turned *out of company.* STEEVENS.

The word *fap* is probably made from *sappa,* a drunken fellow, or a good for nothing fellow, whose virtues are all exhaled. Slender in his answer seems to understand that Bardolph had made use of a Latin word. S. W.

[3] — *careires.*] I believe this strange word is nothing but the French *carriere;* and the expression means, that *the common bounds of good behaviour were overpassed.* JOHNSON.

Cariere is a term of the *manege.* It is, I believe, properly the ring or circle wherein managed horses move. Bardolph means to say,

"and

Slen. Ay, you spake in Latin then too; but 'tis no matter; I'll ne'er be drunk whilst I live again, but in honest civil, godly company, for this trick: if I be drunk, I'll be drunk with those that have the fear of God, and not with drunken knaves.

Evans. So Got 'udge me, that is a virtuous mind.

Fal. You hear all these matters deny'd, gentlemen; you hear it.

Enter Mistress ANNE PAGE *with wine;* Mistress FORD *and* Mistress PAGE *following.*

Page. Nay, daughter, carry the wine in; we'll drink within. [*Exit* ANNE PAGE.

Slen. O heaven! this is Mistress Anne Page.

Page. How now, Mistress Ford?

Fal. Mistress Ford, by my troth, you are very well met: by your leave, good mistress. [*kissing her.*

Page. Wife, bid these gentlemen welcome:—Come, we have a hot venison pasty to dinner; come, gentlemen, I hope we shall drink down all unkindness.

[*Exeunt all but* SHAL. SLENDER, *and* EVANS.

Slen. I had rather than forty shillings, I had my book of Songs and Sonnets here [4]:—

Enter SIMPLE.

How now, Simple; where have you been; I must wait on myself, must I? You have not *The Book of Riddles* [5] about you, have you?

Sim.

" and so in the *end* he reel'd about with a circuitous motion, like a horse, *passing a carier.*" To *pass a carier* was the technical term. So in Nashe's *Have wi.b you to Saffron Walden,* &c. 1596: " — her hottest fury may be resembled to the *passing* of a brave *cariere* by a Pegasus."

Again, in Harrington's *Ariosto,* 1591, (the quotation is Mr. Steevens's):

" To stop, to start, to pass carier, to bound."

We find the term again used in *K. Henry V.* in the same manner as in the passage before us: " —— The king is a good king, but — he *passes* some humours and *carieres.*" MALONE.

[4] — *my book of* Songs and Sonnets *here.*] It cannot be supposed that poor Slender was himself a poet. He probably means the Poems of Lord Surrey and others, which were very popular in the age of Queen Elizabeth. They were printed in 1567, with this title: " *Songes and Sonnettes,* written by the right honorable Lord Henry Howard, late Earl of Surrey, and others."

Sim. Book of Riddles! why, did you not lend it to Alice Shortcake upon Allhallowmas last, a fortnight afore Michaelmas [6]?

Shal. Come, coz; come, coz; we stay for you. A word with you, coz: marry, this, coz: There is, as 'twere, a tender, a kind of tender, made afar off by Sir Hugh here;—Do you understand me?

Slen. Ay, Sir, you shall find me reasonable; if it be so, I shall do that that is reason.

Shal. Nay, but understand me.

Slen. So I do, Sir.

Evans. Give ear to his motions, Master Slender: I will description the matter to you, if you be capacity of it.

Slen. Nay, I will do as my cousin Shallow says; I pray you, pardon me; he's a justice of peace in his country, simple though I stand here.

Evans. But that is not the question; the question is concerning your marriage.

Shal. Ay, there's the point, Sir.

Evans. Marry, is it; the very point of it; to Mistress Anne Page.

Slen. Why, if it be so, I will marry her, upon any reasonable demands.

Evans. But can you affection the 'oman? Let us command to know that of your mouth, or of your lips; for divers philosophers hold, that the lips is parcel of the mouth [7];—Therefore, precisely, can you carry your goodwill to the maid?

Shal. Cousin Abraham Slender, can you love her?

Slen. I hope, Sir—I will do, as it shall become one that would do reason.

Slender laments that he has not this fashionable book about him, supposing it might have assisted him in paying his addresses to Anne Page. MALONE.

[5] *You have not* The Book of Riddles—] This appears to have been a popular book, and is enumerated with others in *The English Courtier and Country Gentleman*, Bl. l. quarto, 1586. Sig. H. 4. REED.

[6] — *upon Allhallowmas last, a fortnight afore Michaelmas?*] Allhallowmas being almost five weeks *after* Michaelmas, Mr. Theobald reads *Martlemas*; but Shakspeare (as Dr. Johnson has observed) probably intended a blunder. MALONE.

[7] — *the lips is* parcel *of the mouth;*] Parcel in our author's time signified *part*. It is yet used by lawyers in that sense. Mr. Reed, I find, has made the same observation. MALONE.

Evans.

Evans. Nay, Got's lords and his ladies, you must speak possitable, if you can carry her your desires towards her.

Shal. That you must: Will you, upon good dowry, marry her?

Slen. I will do a greater thing than that, upon your request, cousin, in any reason.

Shal. Nay, conceive me, conecive me, sweet coz; what I do, is to pleasure you, coz: Can you love the maid?

Slen. I will marry her, Sir, at your request; but if there be no great love in the beginning, yet heaven may decrease it upon better acquaintance, when we are marry'd, and have more occasion to know one another: I hope, upon familiarity will grow more contempt [a]: but if you say, *marry her*, I will marry her, that I am freely dissolved, and dissolutely.

Evans. It is a fery discretion answer; save, the faul' is in the 'ort dissolutely: the 'ort is, according to our meaning, resolute;—his meaning is good.

Shal. Ay, I think my cousin meant well.

Slen. Ay, or else I would I might be hang'd, la.

Re-enter Anne Page.

Shal. Here comes fair Mistress Anne:—Would I were young, for your sake, Mistress Anne!

Anne. The dinner is on the table; my father desires your worship's company.

Shal. I will wait on him, fair Mistress Anne.

Evans. Od's plessed will? I will not be absence at the grace. [*Exeunt* SHALLOW *and Sir H.* EVANS.

Anne. Will't please your worship to come in, Sir?

Slen. No, I thank you, forsooth, heartily; I am very well.

Anne. The dinner attends you, Sir. [b]

Slen. I am not a-hungry, I thank you, forsooth:—Go,

---

[a] *I hope, upon familiarity will grow more* contempt:] The old copy reads—*content.* The emendation is Mr. Theobald's. MALONE.

Theobald's conjecture may be supported by the same intentional blunder in *Love's Labour's Lost*:

"Sir, the contempts thereof are as touching me." STEEVENS.

[b] *The dinner attends you*, Sir.

Slen. —*Go, Sirrah, for all you are my men, go, wait upon my cousin Shallow.*] This passage shews that it was formerly the custom in England, as it is now in France, for persons to be attended at dinner by their own servants, wherever they dined. MASON.

Sirrah, for all you are my man, go, wait upon my cousin Shallow: [*Exit* SIMPLE.] A justice of peace sometime may be beholden to his friend for a man:—I keep but three men and a boy yet, till my mother be dead: But what though? yet I live like a poor gentleman born.

Anne. I may not go in without your worship: they will not sit, till you come.

Slen. I' faith, I'll eat nothing; I thank you as much as though I did.

Anne. I pray you, Sir, walk in.

Slen. I had rather walk here, I thank you: I bruis'd my skin the other day with playing at sword and dagger with a master of fence [9], three veneys for a dish of stew'd prunes [1]; and, by my troth, I cannot abide the smell of hot meat since. Why do your dogs bark so? be there bears i' the town?

Anne. I think, there are, Sir; I heard them talk'd of.

Slen. I love the sport well; but I shall as soon quarrel at it, as any man in England:—You are afraid, if you see the bear loose, are you not?

Anne. Ay, indeed, Sir.

Slen. That's meat and drink to me now: I have seen Sackerson loose [2], twenty times; and have taken him by the chain:

---

[9] — *a master of fence,*] *Master of defence,* on this occasion, does not simply mean a professor of the art of fencing, but a person who had taken his *master's degree* in it. I learn from one of the Sloanian MSS. (now in the British Museum, N° 2530. XXVI D.) which seems to be the fragment of a register formerly belonging to some of our schools where the "Noble Science of Defence" was taught from the year 1568 to 1583, that in this Art there were three degrees, viz. a *Master's*, a *Provost's*, and a *Scholar's*. For each of these a prize was play'd, as exercises are kept in Universities for similar purposes.

STEEVENS.

[1] — *three veneys for a dish of stew'd prunes;*] i. e. three *venues*, French. Three different set to's, *bouts*, a technical term. So, in our author's *Love's Labour's Lost:*

"— a quick *venew* of wit." STEEVENS.

Mr. Steevens's interpretation is not accurate. Slender means to say, that the wager for which he played was a dish of stew'd prunes, which was to be paid by him who received three *hits*. See Bullokar's *English Expositor*, 8vo. 1616: "*Venie*. A touch in the body at playing with weapons." See also Florio's Italian Dictionary, 1598. "*Toccо.* A touch or feeling. Also a *venie* at fence; a hit." MALONE.

[2] — *I have seen* Sackerson *Loose,*] *Sackerson,* or *Sacarson,* was the name of a bear that was exhibited in our author's time at Paris-Garden

chain [3]: but, I warrant you, the women have so cry'd and shriek'd at it, that it pass'd [4]:—but women, indeed, cannot abide 'em; they are very ill-favour'd rough things.

Re-enter PAGE.

Page. Come, gentle Master Slender, come; we stay for you.
Slen. I'll eat nothing, I thank you, Sir.
Page. By cock and pye [5], you shall not choose, Sir: come, come.
Slen. Nay, pray you, lead the way.
Page. Come on, Sir.
Slen. Mistress Anne, yourself shall go first.
Anne. Not I, Sir; pray you, keep on.
Slen. Truly, I will not go first; truly, la: I will not do you that wrong.
Anne. I pray you, Sir.
Slen. I'll rather be unmannerly, than troublesome: you do yourself wrong, indeed, la. [*Exeunt.*

SCENE II.

The same.

Enter Sir HUGH EVANS *and* SIMPLE.

Evans. Go your ways, and ask of Doctor Caius' house, which is the way: and there dwells one Mistress Quickly,

den in Southwark. See an old collection of *Epigrams* [by Sir John Davies] printed at Middleburg (without date, but in or before 1598):
" Publius, a student of the common law,
" To Paris-garden doth himself withdraw;—
" Leaving old Ployden, Dyer, and Broke, alone,
" To see old *Harry Hunkes* and *Sacarson.*"
Sacarson probably had his name from his keeper. So, in the *Puritan,* a comedy, 1607: " How many dogs do you think I had upon me?——Almost as many as *George Stone,* the liar; three at once."
MALONE.

[3] *— and have taken him by the chain:*] You dare as well take a *bear by the tooth—* is one of Ray's Proverbial Sentences. MALONE.

[4] *— that it pass'd.*] It pass'd, or *this passes,* was a way of speaking customary heretofore, to signify the *excess,* or extraordinary degree of any thing. The sentence completed would be, *This passes all expression,* or perhaps, *This passes all things.* We still use *passing* well, *passing* strange. WARBURTON.

[5] *By cock and pye,*] See a note on Act V. sc. i. K. *Henry IV.* P. ii. STEEVENS.

which

which is in the manner of his nurse, or his dry nurse, or his cook, or his laundry, his washer, and his wringer.

Simp. Well, Sir.

Evans. Nay, it is petter yet:—give her this letter; for it is a 'oman that altogether's acquaintance [6] with Mistress Anne Page; and the letter is, to desire and require her to solicit your master's desires to Mistress Anne Page: I pray you, be gone; I will make an end of my dinner; there's pippins and cheese to come. [*Exeunt.*

SCENE III.

A Room in the Garter Inn.

Enter FALSTAFF, HOST, BARDOLPH, NYM, PISTOL, *and* ROBIN.

Fal. Mine host of the Garter,—

Host. What says my bully-rook [7]? Speak scholarly, and wisely.

Fal. Truly, mine host, I must turn away some of my followers.

Host. Discard, bully Hercules; cashier: let them wag; trot, trot.

Fal. I sit at ten pounds a week.

Host. Thou'rt an emperor, Cæsar, Keisar [8], and Pheezar. I will entertain Bardolph; he shall draw, he shall tap: said I well *, bully Hector?

Fal.

---

[6] — *that* altogether's *acquaintance*] The old copy has—*altogethers* acquaintance. The emendation was made by Mr. Tyrwhitt. MALONE.

[7] — *my bully-rook?*] The latter part of this compound title is taken from the *rooks* at the game of chess. STEEVENS.

[8] — Keisar,] The preface to Stowe's Chronicle observes, that the Germans use the K for C, pronouncing *Keysar* for *Cæsar*, their general word for an emperor. TOLLET.

Shakspeare might have remembered in Spenser's *Tears of the Muses:*
" Which was the care of *Kesars* and of *kings*."

Pheesar was a made word from *pheese.* " I'll pheese you," says Sly to the Hostess in the *Taming of the Shrew.* MALONE.

* — *said I well—?*] Mr. Tyrwhitt observes, that a similar phrase is given to the *host* in the *Pardoneres Prologue*, CANT. TALES, v. 12246, edit. 1775; and supposes from this, and other circumstances of general resemblance, that Shakspeare, when he drew his *host of the Garter*, had
not

Fal. Do so, good mine host.

Host. I have spoke; let him follow: Let me see thee froth, and lime⁹: I am at a word; follow.   [*Exit* HOST.

Fal. Bardolph, follow him; a tapster is a good trade: An old cloak makes a new jerkin; a withered servingman, a fresh tapster¹: Go; adieu.

Bard. It is a life that I have desired: I will thrive.
[*Exit* BARDOLPH.

Pist. O base Gongarian wight? wilt thou the spigot wield²?

Nym. He was gotten in drink: Is not the humour conceited? His mind is not heroic, and there's the humour of it³.

Fal. I am glad, I am so acquit of this tinderbox; his thefts were too open: his filching was like an unskilful singer, he kept not time.

---

not forgotten his Chaucer. But the passage (as he remarked to Mr. Steevens) not being in any of the ancient printed editions, I imagine this phrase must have reached our author in some other way; for I suspect he did not devote much time to the perusal of old Mss.
MALONE.

⁹ —*and* lime:] Thus the quarto. The folio has—*and live.*
MALONE.

The reading of the old quarto of 1602 and 1619, *Let me see thee froth, and* lime, I take to be the true one. The Host calls for an immediate specimen of Bardolph's abilities as a tapster; and *frothing* beer and *liming* sack were tricks practised in the time of Shakspeare. The first was done by putting soap into the bottom of the tankard when they drew the beer; the other, by mixing *lime* with the sack (i. e. sherry) to make it sparkle in the glass. Falstaff himself complains of *limed* sack.
STEEVENS.

¹ —*a wither'd servingman, a fresh tapster*:] This is not improbably a parody on the old proverb—" A broken apothecary, a new doctor." See Ray's Proverbs, 3d edit. p. 2. STEEVENS.

² *O base Gongarian wight!* &c.] This is a parody on a line taken from one of the old bombast plays, beginning:
" O base Gongarian, wilt thou the distaff wield?"
I had marked the passage down, but forgot to note the play.—The folio reads *Hungarian*, which is likewise a cant term. In the *Merry Devil of Edmonton*, 1626, the merry Host says, " I have Knights and Colonels in my house, and must tend the *Hungarians.*" STEEVENS.

The word is *Gongarian* in the first edition, and should be continued, the better to fix the allusion. FARMER.

³ —*humour of it.*] This speech is partly taken from the corrected copy, and partly from the slight sketch in 1602. I mention it, that those who do not find it in either of the common old editions, may not suspect it to be spurious. STEEVENS.

Nym.

Nym. The good humour is, to steal at a minute's rest [4].

Pist. Convey, the wise it call: Steal! foh; a fico for the phrase!

Fal. Well, Sirs, I am almost out at heels.

Pist. Why then, let kibes ensue.

Fal. There is no remedy; I must coney-catch, I must shift.

Pist. Young ravens must have food [5].

Fal. Which of you know Ford of this town?

Pist. I ken the wight; he is of substance good.

Fal. My honest lads, I will tell you what I am about.

Pist. Two yards, and more.

Fal. No quips now, Pistol: Indeed I am in the waist two yards about: but I am now about no waste [6]; I am about thrift. Briefly, I do mean to make love to Ford's wife; I spy entertainment in her; she discourses, she carves [7], she gives the leer of invitation: I can construe the action of her familiar style; and the hardest voice of her behaviour, to be English'd rightly, is *I am Sir John Falstaff's.*

Pist. He hath study'd her well, and translated her well [8]; out of honesty into English.

Nym.

---

[4] *The good humour is, to steal at a minute's rest.*] 'Tis true, (says Nym) Bardolph did not keep time; did not steal at the critical and exact season, when he would probably be least observed. The true method is, to steal just at the instant when watchfulness is off its guard, and *reposes* but for a *moment.*—Mr. Langton would read—*minim's rest*, which certainly corresponds more exactly with the preceding speech; but Shakspeare scarcely ever pursues his metaphors far. MALONE.

[5] *Young ravens must have food.*] An adage. See Ray's *Proverbs.*
STEEVENS.

[6] —*about no waste*;] I find the same play on words in Heywood's *Epigrams*, 1562:

"Where am I least, husband? quoth he, in the *waist*;
"Which cometh of this, thou art vengeance strait lac'd.
"Where am I biggest, wife? in the *waste*, quoth she,
"For all is waste in you, as far as I see." STEEVENS.

[7] —*she carves,*] It should be remembered, that anciently the young of both sexes were instructed in *carving*, as a necessary accomplishment. In 1508, Wynkyn de Worde published "A Boke of Kervinge." So in *Love's Labour's Lost*, Biron says of Boyet, the French courtier, "He can *carve* too, and lisp." STEEVENS.

[8] *He hath studied her well, and translated her well*;] The first folio has—*will* in both places. *Well* is the reading of the early quarto.
MALONE.

Translation is not used in its common acceptation, but means to *explain*, as one language is explained by another. So, in *Hamlet*:

Nym. The anchor is deep [9]. Will that humour pass?

Fal. Now, the report goes, she has all the rule of her husband's purse; she hath legions of angels.

Pist. As many devils entertain [1]; and, *To her, boy,* say I.

Nym. The humour rises; it is good: humour me the angels.

Fal. I have writ me here a letter to her: and here another to Page's wife; who even now gave me good eyes too, examined my parts with most judicious eyliads [2]: sometimes the beam of her view gilded my foot, sometimes my portly belly [3].

Pist. Then did the sun on dung-hill shine [4].

Nym. I thank thee for that humour [5].

Fal.

---

[9] *The anchor is deep:*] Dr. *Johnson* very acutely proposes "the au*thor* is deep." He reads with the first copy, "he hath study'd her well;" and from this equivocal word, *Nym* catches the idea of *deepness*. But it is almost impossible to ascertain the diction of this whimsical character; and I meet with a phrase in *Fenner's Comptor's Commonwealth*, 1617, which perhaps may support the old reading: "Master *Decker's Bellman of London* hath set forth the vices of the time so lively, that it is impossible the *anchor* of any other man's braine could sound the sea of a more deepe and dreadful mischeefe." FARMER.

Nym, I believe, only means to say, the scheme for debauching Ford's wife is deep;—well laid. There is a similar corruption in the folio copy of *K. Lear.* In the quarto, 1608, signat. B, we find——"since what I *well* intend," instead of "since what I *will* intend," &c. which the folio exhibits. MALONE.

"The anchor is deep," may mean his hopes are well founded. In the year 1558, a ballad intituled, "Hold the *ancer* fast," is entered on the books of the Stationers' Company. STEEVENS.

[1] *As many devils entertain;*] i. e. do you retain in your *service* as many devils as she has angels.

So, in the *Two Gentlemen of Verona*:

"Sweet lady, *entertain* him for your *servant*."

This is the reading of the folio. MALONE.

The old quarto reads—As many devils attend her. STEEVENS.

[2] — *eyliads:*] This word is differently spelt in all the copies. I suppose we should write *œillades*, French. STEEVENS.

[3] — *sometimes the beam of her view gilded my foot, sometimes my portly belly.*] So, in our author's 20th Sonnet;

"An eye more bright than there's, less false in rolling,

"*Gilding* the object whereupon it gazeth." MALONE.

[4] *Then did the sun on dung-hill shine.*] So, in Lilly's *Euphues*, 1581:

"The sun shineth upon the dunghill." T. H. W.

[5] — *that humour.*] What distinguishes the language of Nym from that of the other attendants on Falstaff, is the constant repetition of

Fal. O, she did so course o'er my exteriors with such a greedy intention [6], that the appetite of her eye did seem to scorch me up like a burning-glass! Here's another letter to her: she bears the purse too; she is a region in Guiana, all gold and bounty [7]. I will be cheater to them both, and they shall be exchequers to me [8]; they shall be my East and West Indies, and I will trade to them both. Go, bear thou this letter to Mistress Page; and thou this to Mistress Ford: we will thrive, lads, we will thrive.

Pist. Shall I Sir Pandarus of Troy become,
And by my side wear steel? then, Lucifer take all!

Nym. I will run no base humour: here, take the humour letter; I will keep the 'haviour of reputation.

Fal. Hold, Sirrah, [*to* Rob.] bear you these letters tightly [9];
Sail like my pinnace [1] to these golden shores.—
Rogues, hence, avaunt! vanish like hail-stones, go;
Trudge, plod, away, o' the hoof; seek shelter, pack!
Falstaff will learn the humour of this age,
French thrift, you rogues; myself, and skirted page.

[*Exeunt* FALSTAFF *and* ROBIN.

Pist.

this phrase. In the time of Shakspeare such an affectation seems to have been sufficient to mark a character. In *Sir Giles Goosecap*, a play of which I have no earlier edition than that of 1606, the same peculiarity is mentioned in the hero of the piece: "——his only reason for every thing is, that *we are all mortal*; then hath he another pretty phrase too, and that is, he will *tickle the vanity* of every thing."

STEEVENS.

[6] — *intention*,] i. e. eagerness of desire. STEEVENS.
So in Hinde's *Eliosto Libidinoso*, 1606: "—— for princes are great marks, upon whom many eyes are *intended*." i. e. earnestly bent.

MALONE.

[7] — *she is a region in Guiana, all gold and bounty.*] After Sir Walter Raleigh's return from Guiana in 1596, a very few years before this play was written, very pompous accounts were published of the wealth of South America, and extraordinary hopes entertained about its produce. MALONE.

[8] *I will be cheater to them both, and they shall be exchequers to me;*] The same joke is intended here, as in *The Second Part of Henry the Fourth*, Act ii: "— I will bar no honest man my house, nor no cheater."—By which is meant *Escheatour*, an officer in the Exchequer, in no good repute with the common people. WARBURTON.

[9] — *tightly*;] i. e. cleverly, adroitly. So, in *Antony and Cleopatra*, Antony putting on his armour, says,

"—— my queen's a squire
"More *tight* at this, than thou." MALONE.

[1] — *my pinnace*] A small vessel with a square stern, having sails and oars, and carrying three masts; chiefly used (says Rolt, in his
Dictionary

Pist. Let vultures gripe thy guts[2]! for gourd, and fullam holds,
And high and low beguile the rich and poor[3]:
Tester I'll have in pouch, when thou shalt lack,
Base Phrygian Turk!

Nym. I have operations in my head[4], which be humours of revenge.

Pist. Wilt thou revenge?

Nym. By welkin, and her star!

Pist. With wit, or steel?

Nym. With both the humours, I:
I will discuss the humour of this love to Page[5].

Pist. And I to Ford shall eke unfold,
How Falstaff, varlet vile,
His dove will prove, his gold will hold,
And his soft couch defile.

Nym. My humour shall not cool: I will incense Page[6]

Dictionary of Commerce,) as a *scout* for intelligence, and for landing of men It likewise signifies (as Mr. Steevens has observed) a man of war's boat. MALONE.

[2] *Let vultures gripe thy guts!*] This hemistich is a burlesque on a passage in *Tamburlaine*, or *The Scythian Shepherd*, 1591, of which play a more particular account is given in one of the notes to *Henry IV*. P. ii. Act II. sc. iv. STEEVENS.

I suppose the following is the passage intended to be ridiculed:
"——and now doth ghastly death
"With greedy tallents (talons) *gripe* my bleeding heart,
"And like a harper [harpy] tyers on my life."

Again, ibid:
"*Griping* our *bowels* with retorted thoughts." MALONE.

[3] ——*for gourd, and fullam holds*,
And high and low beguile the rich and poor:] Cant terms for false dice.—*Gourds* were probably dice in which a secret cavity had been made; *fullams*, those which had been loaded with a small bit of lead. *High men* and *low men*, which were likewise cant terms, explain themselves. *High* numbers on the dice, at hazard, are from five to twelve, inclusive; *low*, from aces to four. MALONE.

[4] —*in my head*,] These words, which are omitted in the folio, were recovered by Mr. Pope from the early quarto. MALONE.

[5] *I will discuss the humour of this love to* Page.] The folio reads—to Ford; and in the next line—and I to *Page*, &c. But the reverse of this (as Mr. Steevens has observed) happens in Act ii. where Nym makes the discovery to Page, and Pistol to Ford. I have therefore corrected the text from the old quarto, where Nym declares he will make the discovery to Page; and Pistol says, " And I to *Ford* will likewise tell—." MALONE.

[6] *I will* incense *Page*—] To incense in Shakspeare's age meant to *instigate*. See Minsheu's Dictionary, 1617, in v. MALONE.

to deal with poison; I will possess him with yellowness[6], for the revolt of mien[7] is dangerous: that is my true humour.

Pist. Thou art the Mars of malecontents: I second thee; troop on. [*Exeunt.*

SCENE IV.

A Room in Dr. CAIUS's *House.*
Enter Mrs. QUICKLY, SIMPLE, *and* RUGBY.

Quick. What; John Rugby!—I pray thee, go to the casement, and see if you can see my master, Master Doctor Caius, coming: if he do, i'faith, and find any body in the house, here will be an old abusing of God's patience, and the king's English.

Rug. I'll go watch. [*Exit* RUGBY.

Quick. Go; and we'll have a posset for't soon at night, in faith, at the latter end of a sea-coal fire[8]. An honest, willing, kind fellow, as ever servant shall come in house withal; and, I warrant you, no tell-tale, nor no breed-bate[9]: his worst fault is, that he is given to prayer; he is something peevish[1] that way: but nobody but has his fault;—but let that pass. Peter Simple, you say your name is?

Sim. Ay, for fault of a better.

Quick. And Master Slender's your master?

Sim. Ay, forsooth.

Quick. Does he not wear a great round beard, like a glover's paring knife[*]?

Sim.

[6] — *yellowness.*] *Yellowness* is jealousy. JOHNSON.

[7] — *the revolt of mien*—] Is change of countenance; one of the effects he has been just ascribing to jealousy. STEEVENS.

Nym means, I think, to say, *t at kind of change in the complexion, which is caused by jealousy, renders the person possessed by such a passion dangerous*; consequently Ford will be likely to revenge himself on Falstaff, and I shall be gratified. I believe our author wrote—*that* revolt, &c. though I have not disturbed the text. y^e and y^t in the MSS. of his time were easily confounded. MALONE.

[8] — *at the latter end of a sea-coal fire.*] That is, when my master is in bed. JOHNSON.

[9] — *no breed*-bate:] *Bate* is an obsolete word, signifying strife, contention. STEEVENS.

[1] — *peevish*—] *Peevish* is foolish. So in *Cymbeline*, Act ii:
"— he's strange and *peevish.*" STEEVENS:
I believe, this is one of dame Quickly's blunders, and that she means *precise.* MALONE.

[*] — *a great*

Sim. No, forsooth: he hath but a little wee face [2], with a little yellow beard; a Cain-colour'd beard [3].

Quick. A softly-sprighted man, is he not?

Sim. Ay, forsooth: but he is as tall a man of his hands [4], as any is between this and his head; he hath fought with a warrener.

Quick. How say you?—O, I should remember him; Does he not hold up his head, as it were? and strut in his gait?

Sim. Yes, indeed, does he.

Quick. Well, heaven send Anne Page no worse fortune! Tell Master Parson Evans, I will do what I can for your master: Anne is a good girl, and I wish—

[1] *— a great round beard, &c.*] See a note on *K. Henry V.* Act iii. sc. vi: " And what a beard of the general's cut, &c." MALONE.

[2] *— a little wee face.*] *Wee*, in the northern dialect, signifies very little. COLLINS.

On the authority of the quarto, 1619, we might be led to read— *whey face:* " — somewhat of a weakly man, and has, as it were, a *whey* coloured beard." Macbeth calls one of the messengers *whey*-face. STEEVENS.

[3] *— a Cain-colour'd beard.*] Cain and Judas, in the tapestries and pictures of old, were represented with *yellow* beards. THEOBALD.

In an age, when but a small part of the nation could read, ideas were frequently borrowed from representations in painting or tapestry. A *cane*-colour'd beard however, (the reading of the quarto,) might signify a beard of the colour of *cane*, i. e. a sickly yellow; for *straw* coloured beards are mentioned in the *Midsummer Night's Dream.* STEEVENS.

The words of the quarto—a *whey*-colour'd beard, strongly favour this reading; for *whey* and *cane* are nearly of the same colour. MALONE.

[4] *— as tall a man of his hands,*] Perhaps this is an allusion to the jocky measure, *so many hands high,* used by grooms when speaking of horses. *Tall*, in our author's time, signified not only height of stature, but stoutness of body. The ambiguity of the phrase seems intended. PERCY.

Whatever may be the origin of this phrase, it is very ancient, being used by Gower. De Confessione Amantis, lib. v. fol. 118. b.

" A worthie knight was *of his borde,*
" There was none such in all the londe." STEEVENS.

Dr. Percy's account of the origin of this phrase can hardly be just; for " *a proper* man of his hands" was likewise a phrase of our author's age; and that cannot allude to the measure of horses.

" A tall man of his hands" sometimes meant quick-handed, active; and as Slender is here commending his master for his gymnastic abilities, perhaps the phrase is here used in that sense. See Florio's Italian Dictionary, 1598, in v. " *Manesco.* Nimble or quick-handed; a tall man of his hands." MALONE.

Re-enter RUGBY.

Rug. Out, alas! here comes my master.

Quick. We shall all be sheat [5]: Run in here, good young man; go into this closet. [*Shuts* Simple *in the closet.*] He will not stay long.—What, John Rugby! John, what, John, I say!—Go, John, go enquire for my master; I doubt, he be not well, that he comes not home:—*and down, down, adown-a* [6], &c. [*Sings.*

Enter Doctor CAIUS [7].

Caius. Vat is you sing? I do not like dese toys; Pray you, go and vetch me in my closet *un boitier verd* [8]; a box, a green-a box; Do intend vat I speak? a green-a box.

Quick. Ay, forsooth, I'll fetch it you. I am glad he went not in himself: if he had found the young man, he would have been horn-mad. [*Aside.*

Caius. Fe, fe, fe, fe! ma foi, il fait fort chaud. Je m'en vais à la Cour,—la grande affaire.

Quick. Is it this, Sir?

Caius. Ouy; mette le au mon pocket; Depeche, quickly:—Vere is dat knave Rugby?

[5] — *we shall all be sheat;*] i. e. scolded, roughly treated.
STEEVENS.

[6] — *and down, down, adown-a*, &c] To deceive her master, she sings as if at her work. SIR J. HAWKINS.
This appears to have been the burden of some song then well known. In *Every Woman in her Humour*, 1609, sign. E. 1. one of the characters says, " Hey, good boyes i'faith; now a threemans song, or the old *downe adowne*; well, things must be as they may; &c." REED.

[7] *Enter Doctor* Caius.] Dr. John Caius was a celebrated physician in the time of Queen Elizabeth, and founder of Caius college, in Cambridge. He was born in 1510, and died in 1567: He is said to have written a great part of Grafton's Chronicle. MALONE.
It has been thought strange, that our author should take the name of *Caius* for his Frenchman in this comedy; but Shakspeare was little acquainted with literary history; and without doubt, from his unusual name, supposed him to have been a foreign quack. Add to this, that the doctor was handed down as a kind of Rosicrucian: Mr. Ames had in MS. one of the " *secret Writings of Dr. Caius.*" FARMER.
This character of Dr. Caius might have been drawn from the life; as in *Jacke of Dover's Quest of Enquirie*, 1604, (perhaps a republication) a story called the *Foole of Windsor* begins thus: " Upon a time there was in *Windsor* a certaine simple *outlandishe doctor* of *physicke*, belonging to the deane, &c." STEEVENS.

[8] — *un boitier verd;*] *Boitier* in French signifies a case of surgeons instruments. GREY.
I believe it rather means a *box of salve*, or case to hold *simples*, for which Caius professes to seek. STEEVENS.

Quick.

Quick. What, John Rugby! John!

Rug. Here, Sir.

Caius. You are John Rugby, and you are Jack Rugby: Come, take-a your rapier, and come after my heel to de court.

Rug. 'Tis ready, Sir, here in the porch.

Caius. By my trot, I tarry too long:——Od's me! *Qu'ai j'oublié?* dere is some simples in my closet, dat I vill not for the varld I shall leave behind.

Quick. Ah me! he'll find the young man there, and be mad.

Caius. O *diable, dialle!* vat is in my closet?—Villainy! *laron!* [*pulling* Simple *out.*] Rugby, my rapier.

Quick. Good master, be content.

Caius. Verefore shall I be content-a?

Quick. The young man is an honest man.

Caius. Vat shall de honest man do in my closet? dere is no honest man dat shall come in my closet.

Quick. I beseech you, be not so flegmatic; hear the truth of it. He came of an errand to me from Parson Hugh.

Caius. Vell.

Sim. Ay, forsooth, to desire her to——

Quick. Peace, I pray you.

Caius. Peace-a your tongue :—Speak-a your tale.

Sim. To desire this honest gentlewoman, your maid, to speak a good word to Mistress Anne Page for my master in the way of marriage.

Quick. This is all, indeed, la; but I'll ne'er put my finger in the fire, and need not.

Caius. Sir Hugh send-a you?—Rugby, *baillez* me some paper: Tarry you a little-a while. [*writes.*

Quick. I am glad he is so quiet: if he had been thoroughly moved, you should have heard him so loud, and so melancholy;—But notwithstanding, man, I'll do your master what good I can: and the very yea and the no is, the French Doctor, my master—I may call him my master, look you, for I keep his house; and I wash, wring, brew, bake, scour, dress meat and drink [9], make the beds, and do all myself—

Sim.

---

[9] — *dress meat and drink,*] Dr. Warburton thought the word *drink* ought to be expunged; but by *drink* Dame Quickly might have intended

Sim. 'Tis a great charge, to come under one body's hand.

Quick. Are you avis'd o' that? you shall find it a great charge: and to be up early, and down late;—but notwithstanding, (to tell you in your ear; I would have no words of it;) my master himself is in love with mistress Anne Page: but notwithstanding that—I know Anne's mind—that's neither here nor there.

Caius. You jack'nape; give-a dis letter to Sir Hugh; by gar, it is a shallenge: I vill cut his throat in de park; and I vill teach a scurvy jack-a-nape priest to meddle or make:—you may be gone; it is not good you tarry here: by gar, I vill cut all his two stones; by gar, he shall not have a stone to trow at his dog. [*Exit* SIMPLE.

Quick. Alas, he speaks but for his friend.

Caius. It is no matter-a for dat:—do not you tell-a me dat I shall have Anne Page for myself?—by gar, I vill kill de Jack priest [*]; and I have appointed mine host of *de Jarterre* to measure our weapon:—by gar I vill myself have Anne Page.

Quick. Sir, the maid loves you, and all shall be well: we must give folks leave to prate: What, the good-jer [1]!

Caius. Rugby, come to the court vit me;—By gar, if I have not Anne Page, I shall turn your head out of my door:—Follow my heels, Rugby. [*Exeunt* CAIUS *and* RUGBY.

Quick. You shall have Ann fool's-head [2] of your own. No, I know Anne's mind for that: never a woman in

---

ed potage and soup, of which her master may be supposed to have been as fond as the rest of his countrymen. MALONE.

[*] *de Jack priest;*] *Jack* in our author's time was a term of contempt: So, saucy *Jack*, &c. See K. *Henry IV.* P. i. Act iii. sc. iii. "The prince is a *Jack*, a sneak-cup;" and *Much ado about Nothing*, Act. i. sc. i. "— do you play the flouting *Jack?*" MALONE.

[1] *What, the good jer!*] Mrs. Quickly scarcely ever pronounces a hard word rightly. *Good-jer* and *Good-year* were in our author's time common corruptions of *goujeres*; i. e. *morbus Gallicus*; and in the books of that age the word is as often written one way as the other.
MALONE.

[2] *You shall have Ann fool's-head*—] Mrs. Quickly, I believe, intends a quibble between *ann*, sounded broad, and *one*, which was formerly sometimes pronounced *on*, or with nearly the same sound. In the Scottish dialect *one* is written, and I suppose pronounced, *ane*.—In 1603, was published " *Ane* verie excellent and delectable Treatise, intituled *Philotus*," &c. MALONE.

Windsor knows more of Anne's mind than I do; nor can do more than I do with her, I thank heaven.

Fent. [*within.*] Who's within there, ho?

Quick. Who's there, I trow? Come near the house, I pray you.

Enter FENTON.

Fen. How now, good woman; how dost thou?

Quick. The better that it pleases your good worship to ask.

Fent. What news? how does pretty Mistress Anne?

Quick. In truth, Sir, and she is pretty, and honest, and gentle; and one that is your friend, I can tell you that by the way, I praise heaven for it.

Fent. Shall I do any good, thinkest thou? Shall I not lose my suit?

Quick. Troth, Sir, all is in hands above: but notwithstanding, Master Fenton, I'll be sworn on a book, she loves you:—Have not your worship a wart above your eye?

Fent. Yes, marry, have I; what of that?

Quick. Well, thereby hangs a tale;—good faith, it is such another Nan;—but, I detest [3], an honest maid as ever broke bread:—We had an hour's talk of that wart;—I shall shall never laugh but in that maid's company!—But, indeed, she is given too much to allicholly and musing: But, for you —Well, go to.

Fent. Well, I shall see her to-day: Hold, there's money for thee; let me have thy voice in my behalf: if thou seest her before me, commend me—

Quick. Will I? i'faith, that we will:—and I will tell your worship more of the wart, the next time we have confidence; and of other wooers.

Fent. Well, farewell; I am in great haste now. [*Exit.*

Quick. Farewell to your worship—Truly, an honest gentleman; but Anne loves him not; for I know Anne's mind as well as another does:—Out upon't, what have I forgot? [*Exit.*

3 — *but I detest,*] She means—*I protest.* MALONE.

ACT

ACT II. SCENE I.

Before PAGE's *House.*
Enter Mistress PAGE, *with a letter.*

Mrs. Page. What, have I 'scaped love-letters in the holy-day time of my beauty, and am I now a subject for them? Let me see: [*reads.*

Ask me no reason why I love you; for though love use reason for his precisian, he admits him not for his counsellor[1]: *You are not young, no more am I; go to then, there's sympathy: you are merry, so am I; Ha! ha! then there's more sympathy: you love sack, and so do I: Would you desire better sympathy? Let it suffice thee, Mistress Page, (at the least, if the love of a soldier can suffice,) that I love thee. I will not say, pity me, 'tis not a soldier-like phrase; but I say, love me. By me,*

> *Thine own true knight*
> *By day or night*[2],
> *Or any kind of light,*
> *With all his might,*
> *For thee to fight,*   John Falstaff.

---

[1] *— though love use reason for his* precisian, *he admits him not for his counsellor:*] By *precisian,* is meant one who pretends to a more than ordinary degree of virtue and sanctity. On which account they gave this name to the puritans of that time. WARBURTON.

Of this word I do not see any meaning that is very apposite to the present intention. Perhaps Falstaff said, *Though love use reason for his physician, he admits him not for his counsellor.* This will be plain sense. Ask not the *reason* of my love; the business of *reason* is not to assist love, but to *cure* it. There may however be this meaning in the present reading. *Though love,* when he would submit to regulation, may *use reason as his precisian,* or director in nice cases, yet when he is only eager to attain his end, he takes not reason for *his counsellor.* JOHNSON.

Dr. Johnson wishes to read *physician;* and this conjecture becomes almost a certainty from a line in our author's 147th sonnet:

"My reason the *physician* to my love, &c." FARMER.

[2] *Thine own true knight,*

By day or night.] This expression, which is ludicrously employed by Falstaff, anciently meant, *at all times.*

So, in the third book of Gower, *de Confessione Amantis:*

"The son cleped was Machayre,
"The daughter eke Canace hight,
"By daie bothe and eke by night."

Loud and still was another phrase of the same meaning. STEEVENS.

What

What a Herod of Jewry is this?—O wicked, wicked world! one that is well-nigh worn to pieces with age, to show himself a young gallant! What an unweigh'd behaviour [3] hath this Flemish drunkard pick'd (with the devil's name) out of my conversation, that he dares in this manner assay me? Why, he hath not been thrice in my company!—What should I say to him?—I was then frugal of my mirth:—heaven forgive me!—Why I'll exhibit a bill in the parliament for the putting down of fat men [4]. How shall I be revenged on him? for revenged I will be, as sure as his guts are made of puddings.

Enter Mistress FORD.

Mrs. Ford. Mistress Page! trust me, I was going to your house.

Mrs. Page. And, trust me, I was coming to you. You look very ill.

Mrs. Ford. Nay, I'll ne'er believe that; I have to show to the contrary.

Mrs. Page. 'Faith, but you do, in my mind.

Mrs. Ford. Well, I do then; yet, I say, I could show

[3] *What an unweigh'd behaviour—*] It has been suggested to me that we should read—*one*. STEEVENS.

[4] —*for the* putting down *of* fat men.] The word *fat*, which seems to have been inadvertently omitted in the folio, was restored by Mr. Theobald from the quarto, where the corresponding speech runs thus "Well, I shall trust *fat* men the worse, while I live, for his sake. O God; that I knew how to be revenged of him!"—Dr. Johnson, however, thinks that the insertion is unnecessary, as " Mrs. Page might naturally enough, in the first heat of her anger, rail at the sex for the fault of one." But the authority of the original sketch in quarto, and Mrs. Page's frequent mention of the size of her lover in the play as it now stands, in my opinion fully warrant the correction that has been made. Our author well knew that bills are brought into parliament for some purpose that at least appears *practicable*. Mrs. Page therefore in her passion might exhibit a bill for the putting down or destroying men of a particular description; but Shakspeare would never have made her threaten to introduce a bill to effect an *impossibility*; viz. the extermination of the whole species.

There is no error more frequent at the press than the omission of words. In a sheet of this work now before me, there was an *out*, (as it is termed in the printing-house,) that is, a passage omitted, of no less than ten lines. In every sheet some words are at first omitted.

The expression, *putting down*, is a common phrase of our municipal law. MALONE.

VOL. III. L you

you to the contrary: O, Mistress Page, give me some counsel!

Mrs. Page. What's the matter, woman?

Mrs. Ford. O woman, if it were not for one trifling respect, I could come to such honour!

Mrs. Page. Hang the trifle, woman; take the honour: What is it?—dispense with trifles;—what is it?

Mrs. Ford. If I would but go to hell for an eternal moment, or so, I could be knighted.

Mrs. Page. What?—thou liest!—Sir Alice Ford!—These knights will hack; and so thou should'st not alter the article of thy gentry [5].

Mrs. Ford. We burn day-light [6]:—here, read, read;—perceive how I might be knighted.—I shall think the

---

[5] *What?—thou liest! Sir Alice Ford!—These knights will hack; and so thou shouldst not alter the article of thy gentry.*] It is not impossible that Shakspeare meant by—*these knights will hack*—these knights will soon become *hackney'd* characters.—So many knights were made about the time this play was amplified (for the passage is neither in the copy 1602, nor 1619,) that such a stroke of satire might not have been unjustly thrown in. STEEVENS.

These knights will *hack*, (that is, become cheap and vulgar,) and therefore she advises her friend not to sully her gentry by becoming one. The whole of this discourse about knighthood is added since the first edition of this play (in 1602;) and therefore I suspect this is an oblique reflection on the prodigality of James I. in bestowing these honours.
BLACKSTONE.

Sir W. Blackstone supposes that the order of Baronets (created in 1611) was likewise alluded to. I have omitted that part of his note, because it appears to me highly probable that our author amplified the play before us at an earlier period. See *An Attempt to ascertain the order of Shakspeare's plays*, ante, Article, *Merry Wives of Windsor*.

Between the time of King James's arrival at Berwick in April 1603, and the 2d of May, he made two hundred and thirty-seven knights; and in the July following between three and four hundred. It is probable that the play before us was enlarged in that or the subsequent year, when this stroke of satire must have been highly relished by the audience.

By " these knights will hack" may have been meant.—These unworthy knights of the present day will be degraded by having their spurs *hack'd off*; the punishment (as Dr. Johnson has observed) of a recreant or undeserving knight. MALONE.

[6] *We burn day-light*;] i. e. we are wasting time in idle talk, when we ought to read the letter; resembling those, who waste candles by burning them in the day-time. So, in *Romeo and Juliet* (the quotation is Mr. Steevens's):

" We waste our lights in vain, like lamps by day." MALONE.

worse

worse of fat men, as long as I have an eye to make difference of men's liking: And yet he would not swear; prais'd women's modesty: and gave such orderly and well-behaved reproof to all uncomeliness, that I would have sworn his disposition would have gone to the truth of his words: but they do no more adhere, and keep place together, than the hundredth psalm to the tune of *Green Sleeves*[7]. What tempest, I trow, threw this whale, with so many tuns of oil in his belly, ashore at Windsor? How shall I be revenged on him? I think, the best way were to entertain him with hope, till the wicked fire of lust have melted him in his own grease.— Did you ever hear the like?

Mrs. Page. Letter for letter; but that the name of Page and Ford differs!—To thy great comfort in this mystery of ill opinions, here's the twin-brother of thy letter: but let thine inherit first; for, I protest, mine never shall. I warrant, he hath a thousand of these letters, writ with blank space for different names, (sure more,) and these are of the second edition: He will print them out of doubt; for he cares not what he puts into the press[8], when he would put us two. I had rather be a giantess, and lie under mount Pelion. Well, I will find you twenty lascivious turtles, ere one chaste man.

Mrs. Ford. Why, this is the very same; the very hand, the very words: What doth he think of us?

Mrs. Page. Nay, I know not: It makes me almost ready to wrangle with mine own honesty. I'll entertain myself like one that I am not acquainted withal; for, sure, unless he know some strain in me[9], that I know not myself, he would never have boarded me in this fury.

[7] —*Green Sleeves.*] A popular old ballad, that had appeared about twenty years before this play was written. MALONE.

From a passage in the *Loyal Subject*, by B. and Fletcher, it should seem that this old ballad was a wanton ditty. STEEVENS.

[8] —*press.*] *Press* is used ambiguously, for a *press* to print, and a *press* to squeeze. JOHNSON.

[9] —*some strain in me,*] Thus the old copies. The modern editors read, "some *stain* in me," but, I think, unnecessarily. A similar expression occurs in *The Winter's Tale*:

"With what encounter so uncurrent have I
"Strain'd, to appear thus?"

And again, in *Timon*:

"———— a noble nature
"May catch a *wrench*." STEEVENS.

Mrs. Ford. Boarding, call you it; I'll be sure to keep him above deck.

Mrs. Page. So will I; if he come under my hatches, I'll never to sea again. Let's be revenged on him: let's appoint him a meeting; give him a show of comfort in his suit; and lead him on with a fine-baited delay, till he hath pawn'd his horses to mine Host of the Garter.

Mrs. Ford. Nay, I will consent to act any villainy against him, that may not sully the chariness of our honesty[1]. O, that my husband saw this letter[2]! It would give eternal food to his jealousy.

Mrs. Page. Why, look, where he comes; and my good man too: he's as far from jealousy, as I am from giving him cause; and that, I hope, is an unmeasurable distance.

Mrs. Ford. You are the happier woman.

Mrs. Page. Let's consult together against this greasy knight: Come hither. [*They retire.*

Enter FORD, PISTOL, PAGE, *and* NYM.

Ford. Well, I hope, it be not so.

Pist. Hope is a curtail dog[3] in some affairs:
Sir John affects thy wife.

Ford. Why, Sir, my wife is not young.

Pist. He wooes both high and low, both rich and poor[*],
Both young and old, one with another, Ford;
He loves thy gally-mawfry[4]; Ford, perpend[5].

Ford.

---

[1] — *the chariness of our honesty.*] i. e. the *caution* which ought to attend on it. STEEVENS.

[2] *O, that my husband saw this letter!*] Surely Mrs. Ford does not wish to excite the jealousy, of which she complains. I think we should read —O, *if* my husband, &c. and thus the copy, 1619:

"Oh, lord, *if* my husband should see the letter! i'faith, this would even give edge to his jealousie." STEEVENS.

[3] — *curtail-dog*—] That is, a dog of small value;—what we now call a *cur*. MALONE.

[*] — *both high and low, both rich and poor,*] See Psalm 49. v. 2. GREY.

[4] — *gally-mawfry;* i. e. a medley. So, in the *Winter's Tale*:

"They have a dance, which the wenches say is a *gallimawfry* of gambols." Thus, in *A Woman never vex'd*, 1632:

"Let us show ourselves gallants or *galli-mawfries.*"

STEEVENS.

The first folio has—*the* gallymaufry. *Thy* was introduced by the editor of the second. *The* gallymawfry may be right: He loves a medley; all sorts of women, high and low, &c. Ford's reply, "Love my wife!"

Ford. Love my wife?

Pist. With liver burning hot: Prevent, or go thou,
Like Sir Actæon he, with Ring-wood at thy heels:—
O, odious is the name!

Ford. What name, Sir?

Pist. The horn, I say: Farewel.
Take heed; have open eye; for thieves do foot by night:
Take heed, ere summer comes, or cuckoo-birds do sing.—
Away, Sir Corporal Nym.—
Believe it, Page; he speaks sense [6].   [*Exit* PISTOL.

Ford. I will be patient; I will find out this.

Nym. And this is true; [*to* Page.] I like not the humour of lying. He hath wrong'd me in some humours: I should have borne the humour'd letter to her; but I have a sword, and it shall bite upon my necessity [7]. He loves

wife!" may refer to what Pistol had said before: " Sir John affects thy wife." *Thy gallymawfry* sounds however more like Pistol's language than the other; and therefore I have followed the modern editors in preferring it. MALONE.

[5] *Ford, perpend.*] This is perhaps a ridicule on a passage in the old comedy of *Cambyses*:

" My sapient words, I say, *perpend.*"

Again: " My queen, *perpend* what I pronounce."
Shakspeare has put the same word into the mouth of Polonius.
STEEVENS.

Pistol again uses it in *K. Henry V.*; so does the Clown in *Twelfth Night*: I do not believe therefore that any ridicule was here aimed at Preston, the author of Cambyses. MALONE.

[6] *Believe it, Page; he speaks* sense.] Dr. Johnson thought that the preceding word, " *Nym*," was only a designation of the speaker, and that these words belonged to him. Mr. Steevens's note shews that he was mistaken. Dr. Farmer would read—Believe it Page, he speaks; i. e. Page, believes what he says. MALONE.

Ford and Pistol, Page and Nym, enter in pairs, each pair in separate conversation; and while Pistol is informing Ford of Falstaff's design upon his wife, Nym is, during that time, talking *aside* to Page, and giving information of the like plot against *him*.—When Pistol has finished, he calls out to Nym to come *away*; but seeing that he and Page are still in close debate, he goes off alone, first assuring Page, he may depend on the truth of Nym's story. *Believe it, Page.* Nym then proceeds to tell the remainder of his tale out aloud. *And this is true,* &c. STEEVENS.

[7] *I have a sword, and it shall bite upon my necessity.*] Nym, to gain credit, says, that he is above the mean office of carrying love-letters; he has nobler means of living; *he has a sword, and upon his necessity,* that is, *when his need drives him to unlawful expedients,* his sword *shall bite.* JOHNSON.

your wife; there's the short and the long. My name is Corporal Nym; I speak, and I avouch. 'Tis true:—my name is Nym, and Falstaff loves your wife.—Adieu! I love not the humour of bread and cheese; and there's the humour of it. Adieu. [*Exit* NYM.

Page. The humour of it[8], quoth 'a! here's a fellow frights humour out of its wits.

Ford. I will seek out Falstaff.

Page. I never heard such a drawling, affecting rogue.

Ford. If I do find it, well.

Page. I will not believe such a Cataian[9], though the priest o' the town commended him for a true man.

Ford.

---

[8] *The humour of it,*] The following epigrams, taken from an old collection without date, but apparently printed before the year 1600, will best account for Nym's frequent repetition of the word *humour*. Epig. 27.

<blockquote>
Afke HUMOR: what a feather he doth weare,
It is his *humour* (by the Lord) he'll sweare;
Or what he doth with such a horse-taile locke,
Or why upon a whore he spends his stocke,—
He hath a *humour* doth determine so:
Why in the slop-throte fashion he doth goe,
With scarfe about his necke, hat without band,—
It is his *humour*. Sweet Sir, understand,
What cause his purse is so extreame distrest
That oftentimes is scarcely penny-blest;
Only a *humour*. If you question why
His tongue is ne'er unfurnish'd with a lye,—
It is his *humour* too he doth protest:
Or why with serjeants he is so opprest,
That like to ghosts they haunt him ev'rie day;
A rascal *humour* doth not love to pay.
Object why bootes and spurres are still in season,
His *humour* answers, *humour* is his reason.
If you perceive his wits in wetting shrunke,
It cometh of a *humour* to be drunke.
When you behold his lockes pale, thin, and poore,
The occasion is, his *humour* and a whoor,
And every thing that he doth undertake:
It is a veine, for senceless *humour's* sake. STEEVENS.
</blockquote>

[9] *I will not believe such a* Cataian,] A *Cataian* (from *Cataia* or *Cathay*, the ancient name of China) seems to have been a cant term of reproach in our author's time, denoting a *sharper*. Mr. Theobald thinks it meant a *boaster*; Dr. Warburton a liar, "from those who told incredible wonders of this new-discovered empire:" Dr. Johnson's explanation is —" This fellow hath such an odd appearance, is so unlike a man civilized and taught the duties of life, that I cannot credit him on any testimony of his veracity.—To be a foreigner (he adds) was always in England,

Ford. 'Twas a good sensible fellow [2]: Well.
Page. How now, Meg?
Mrs. Page. Whither go you, George?—Hark you.
Mrs. Ford. How now, sweet Frank? why art thou melancholy?
Ford. I melancholy! I am not melancholy.—Get you home, go.
Mrs. Ford. 'Faith, thou hast some crotchets in thy head now.—Will you go, Mistress Page?
Mrs. Page. Have with you.—You'll come to dinner, George?—Look, who comes yonder: she shall be our messenger to this paltry knight. [*Aside to Mrs. Ford.*

Enter Mistress QUICKLY.

Mrs. Ford. Trust me, I thought on her: she'll fit it.
Mrs. Page. You are come to see my daughter Anne?
Quick. Ay, forsooth: And, I pray, how does good Mistress Anne?
Mrs. Page. Go in with us, and see; we have an hour's talk with you.

[*Exeunt Mrs. Page, Mrs. Ford, and Mrs. Quickly.*
Page. How now, Master Ford?
Ford. You heard what this knave told me; did you not?
Page. Yes; And you heard what the other told me?
Ford. Do you think there is truth in them?
Page. Hang 'em, slaves! I do not think the knight would offer it: but these that accuse him in his intent towards our wives, are a yoke of his discarded men; very rogues, now they be out of service [3].

England, and I suppose every where else, a reason of dislike."—Mr. Steevens, with more probability, supposes it to mean a thief; "the Chinese, (anciently called Cataians) being said to be the most dexterous of all the nimble-fingered tribe." On the Stationers' books was entered in 1579, by Thomas Dawson, a book entitled, "*Of Cataia and the region of Sina, and of the* MARVAILOUS WONDERS *that have been seen in these parts.* MALONE.

[2] *'Twas a good sensible fellow:*] This, and the two preceding speeches of Ford, are spoken to himself, and have no connection with the sentiments of Page, who is likewise making his comment on what had passed, without attention to Ford. STEEVENS.

[3] *Very rogues, now they be out of service.*] A *rogue* is a wanderer, or *vagabond*, and, in its consequential signification, a *cheat*. JOHNSON.

L 4   *Ford.*

Ford. Were they his men?

Page. Marry, were they.

Ford. I like it never the better for that. Does he lie at the Garter?

Page. Ay, marry, does he. If he should intend this voyage toward my wife, I would turn her loose to him; and what he gets more of her than sharp words, let it lie on my head.

Ford. I do not misdoubt my wife; but I would be loth to turn them together: A man may be too confident: I would have nothing lie on my head [4]: I cannot be thus satisfied.

Page. Look, where my ranting host of the Garter comes: there is either liquor in his pate, or money in his purse, when he looks so merrily.—How, now, mine host?

Enter HOST *and* SHALLOW.

Host. How, now, bully-rook? thou'rt a gentleman: cavalero-justice, I say.

Shal. I follow, mine host, I follow.—Good even, and twenty, good Master Page! Master Page, will you go with us? we have sport in hand.

Host. Tell him, cavalero-justice; tell him, bully-rook?

Shal. Sir, there is a fray to be fought, between Sir Hugh the Welch priest, and Caius the French doctor.

Ford. Good mine host o' the Garter, a word with you.

Host. What say'st thou, bully-rook? [*They go aside.*

Shal. Will you [*to Page*] go with us to behold it? My merry host hath had the measuring of their weapons; and, I think, hath appointed them contrary places: for, believe me, I hear, the parson is no jester. Hark, I will tell you what our sport shall be.

Host. Hast thou no suit against my knight, my guest-cavalier?

Ford. None, I protest: but I'll give you a pottle of burnt sack to give me recourse to him, and tell him, my name is Brook [5]; only for a jest.

Host. My hand, bully: thou shalt have egress and regress; said I well? and thy name shall be Brook: It is a merry knight.—Will you go an-heirs [6]?

Shal.

---

[4] *I would have nothing lie on my head:*] Here seems to be an allusion to Shakspeare's favourite topic, the cuckold's horns.   MALONE.

[5] *— and tell him, my name is* Brook;] The folio reads—*Broom.* The true name was recovered from the quarto by Mr. Theobald.   MALONE.

[6] *Wil*

Shal. Have with you, mine host.

Page. I have heard, the Frenchman hath good skill in his rapier [7].

Shal. Tut, Sir, I could have told you more: In these times you stand on distance, your passes, stoccados, and I

---

[6] *Will you go an-heirs?*] There can be no doubt that this passage is corrupt. Perhaps we should read—Will you go *and hear us?* So, in the next page—" I had rather *bear them* scold than fight." MALONE.

The merry Host has already saluted them separately by titles of distinction; he therefore probably now addresses them collectively by a general one—*Will you go on,* heroes? or, as probably—*Will you go on,* hearts? He calls Dr. Caius *Heart of Elder*; and adds, in a subsequent scene of this play, *Farewell, my hearts.* STEEVENS.

[7] —*in his rapier.*] In the old quarto here follow these words:

Shal. I tell you what, Master Page; I believe the doctor is no jester; he'll lay it one [on]; for though we be justices and doctors and churchmen, yet we are the sons of women, Master Page.

Page. True, Master Shallow.

Shal. It will be found so, Master Page.

Page. Master Shallow, you yourself have been a great fighter, though now a man of peace.

Part of this dialogue is found afterwards in the third scene of the present act; but it seems more proper here, to introduce what Shallow says of the prowess of his youth. MALONE.

[8] —*my long sword,*] Before the introduction of rapiers, the swords in use were of an enormous length, and sometimes raised with both hands. Shallow, with an old man's vanity, censures the innovation by which lighter weapons were introduced, tells what he could once have done with his *long sword,* and ridicules the terms and rules of the rapier. JOHNSON.

Dr. Johnson's explanation of the *long sword* is certainly right; for the early quarto reads—my *two-hand* sword; so that they appear to have been synonymous.

Carleton, in his *Thankful Remembrance of God's Mercy,* 1625, speaking of the treachery of one Rowland York, in betraying the town of Deventer to the Spaniards in 1587, says; " he was a Londoner, famous among the *Cutters* in his time, for bringing in a new kind of fight —to run the point of a *rapier* into a man's body. This manner of fight he brought *first* into *England,* with great admiration of his audaciousness: when in England before that time, the use was, with little bucklers, and with *broad swords,* to strike, and not to thrust; and it was accounted unmanly to strike under the girdle."

The Continuator of Stowe's Annals, p. 1024, edit. 1631, supposes the rapier to have been introduced somewhat sooner, viz. about the 20th year of the reign of Queen Elizabeth, [1578] at which time, he says, Sword and Bucklers began to be disused. Shakspeare has here been guilty of a great anachronism in making Shallow ridicule the terms of the rapier in the time of Harry IV. an hundred and seventy years before it was used in England. MALONE.

L 5 know

know not what: 'tis the heart, Master Page; 'tis here, 'tis here. I have seen the time, with my long sword [8], I would have made you four tall fellows [9] skip like rats.

Host. Here, boys, here, here! shall we wag?

Page. Have with you:—I had rather hear them scold than fight.   [*Exeunt* HOST, SHALLOW, *and* PAGE.

Ford. Though Page be a secure fool, and stands so firmly on his wife's frailty [1], yet I cannot put off my opinion so easily: She was in his company at Page's house; and, what they made there [2], I know not. - Well, I will look further into't: and I have a disguise to sound Falstaff: If I find her honest, I lose not my labour; if she be otherwise, 'tis labour well bestow'd.   [*Exit.*

SCENE II.

A Room in the Garter Inn.

Enter FALSTAFF *and* PISTOL.

Fal. I will not lend thee a penny.

Pist. Why, then the world's mine oyster [3], which I with sword will open.—I will retort the sum in equipage [4].

Fal.

---

[9] — *tall fellows*—] A *tall fellow*, in the time of our author, meant a stout, bold, or courageous person. The elder quarto reads—*tall fencers.* STEEVENS.

[1] — *and stands so firmly on his wife's frailty,*] i. e. has such perfect confidence in his unchaste wife. *His wife's frailty* is the same as—his frail wife. So, in *Antony and Cleopatra*, we meet with *death and honour*, for *an honourable death.* MALONE.

To *stand on any thing*, signifies *to insist on it.* Ford supposes Page to insist on that virtue as steady, which he supposes to be without foundation. STEEVENS.

[2] — *and what they made there,*] An obsolete phrase signifying—what they *did* there. MALONE.

[3] — *the world's mine oyster,* &c.] Dr. Grey supposes Shakspeare to allude to an old proverb, "The mayor of Northampton opens *oysters* with his dagger," i. e. to keep them at a sufficient distance from his nose, that town being fourscore miles from the sea. STEEVENS.

[4] — *I will retort the sum in equipage.*] This is added from the old quarto of 1619, and means, I will pay you again in stolen goods. WARBURTON.

I rather believe he means, that he will pay him by waiting on him for nothing. That *equipage* ever meant *stolen goods*, I am yet to learn. STEEVENS.

Dr.

Fal. Not a penny. I have been content, Sir, you should lay my countenance to pawn: I have grated upon my good friends for three reprieves for you and your coach-fellow, Nym [5]; or else you had look'd through the grate, like a geminy of baboons. I am damn'd in hell, for swearing to gentlemen my friends, you were good soldiers, and tall fellows [6]: and when Mistress Bridget lost the handle of her fan [7], I took't upon mine honour, thou hadst it not.

Pist. Didst not thou share? hadst thou not fifteen pence?

Fal. Reason, you rogue, reason: Think'st thou, I'll endanger my soul *gratis*? At a word, hang no more about me, I am no gibbet for you:—go.—A short knife and a throng [8];—to your manor of Pickt-hatch [9], go.—You'll not bear a letter for me, you rogue!—you stand upon your honour!—Why, thou unconfinable baseness, it is as much as I can do, to keep the terms of my honour precise. I, I, I myself sometimes, leaving the fear of heaven on the left hand, and hiding mine honour in my necessity, am fain to shuffle,

to

Dr. Warburton may be right; for I find *equipage* was one of the cant words of the time. In *Davies' Papers Complaint*, (a poem which has erroneously been ascribed to *Donne*) we have several of them: " Embellish, blandishment, and *equipage*." Which words, he tells us in the margin, *savour of witless affectation*. FARMER.

Dr. Warburton's interpretation is, I think, right. *Equipage* indeed does not *per se* signify *stolen* goods, but such goods as Pistol promises to return, we may fairly suppose, would be *stolen*. *Equipage*, which, as Dr. Farmer observes, had been but newly introduced into our language, is defined by Bullokar in his *English Expositor*, 8vo. 1616, " Furniture, or provision for horsemanship, especially in triumphs or tournaments." Hence the modern use of this word. MALONE.

[5] *— your coach-fellow, Nym;*] i. e. he, who *draws* along with you; who is joined with you in all your knavery. So before, Page, speaking of Nym and Pistol, calls them a " *yoke* of Falstaff's discarded men." The word (as Mr. Steevens has observed) is used by Chapman in his Translation of the Iliad. MALONE.

[6] *— and tall fellows:*] See p. 226, n. 9; and p. 211, n. 4.

MALONE.

[7] *— lost the handle of her fan,*] 't should be remembered, that *fans* in our author's time, were more costly than they are at present, as well as of a different construction. They consisted of ostrich feathers, (or others of equal length and flexibility,) which were stuck into handles. The richer sort of these were composed of gold, silver, or ivory of curious workmanship. In the frontispiece to a play, called *Englishmen for my Money; or A pleasant Comedy of a Woman will have her Will*, 1616, is a portrait of a lady with one of these fans, which, after all, may prove the best commentary on the passage. The three other specimens are taken from the *Habiti Antichi et Moderni di tutto il Mondo*, published at

Venice,

228   MERRY WIVES

to hedge, and to lurch; and yet you, rogue, will enſconce your rags⁸, your cat-a-moutain looks, your red-lattice phraſes,

Venice, 1598, from the drawings of *Titian*, and *Ceſare Vecelli*, his brother. This faſhion was perhaps imported from Italy, together with many others, in the reign of King Henry VIII. if not in that of King Richard II.

Steevens.

It appears from *Marſton's Satires*, that the ſum of 40l. was ſometimes given for a fan in the time of Queen Elizabeth. Malone.

In the Sidney papers, publiſhed by *Collins*, a fan is preſented to Queen Elizabeth for a new year's gift, the handle of which was ſtudded with diamonds. T. Warton.

⁸ *A ſhort knife and a* throng:] So Lear: " — when cut-purſes come not to *throngs*." Warburton.

Mr. Dennis reads—*thong*; which has been followed, I think, improperly, by ſome of the modern editors.

Sir Thomas Overbury's *Characters*, 1616, furniſh us with a confirmation of the reading of the old copies: " The eye of this wolf is as quick in his head as a *cutpurſe* in a *throng*." Malone.

⁹ —*Pickt-hatch*,] *Pickt-hatch* was in *Turnbull-ſtreet*.

" —— Your whore doth live
" In Pict-hatch, Turnbull-ſtreet."
                        Amends for Ladies, a comedy by N. Field, 1639.

The derivation of the word may perhaps be diſcovered from the following paſſage in *Cupid's Whirligig*: " Set ſome *picks* upon your *hatch*, and

phrases ², and your bold-beating oaths, under the shelter of your honour! You will not do it, you?

Pist. I do relent: What would'st thou more of man?

Enter ROBIN.

Rob. Sir, here's a woman would speak with you.
Fal. Let her approach.

Enter Mistress QUICKLY.

Quick. Give your worship good-morrow.
Fal. Good-morrow, good wife.
Quick. Not so, an't please your worship.
Fal. Good maid, then.
Quick. I'll be sworn; as my mother was, the first hour I was born.
Fal. I do believe the swearer: What with me?
Quick. Shall I vouchsafe your worship a word or two?

and I pray, profess to keep a bawdy-house." Perhaps the unseasonable and obstreperous irruptions of the gallants of that age might render such a precaution necessary. STEEVENS.

This was a cant name of some part of the town noted for bawdy-houses. Sir T. Hanmer says, that this was "a noted harbour for thieves and pickpockets," who certainly were proper companions for a man of Pistol's profession. But Falstaff here more immediately means to ridicule another of his friend's vices; and there is some humour in calling Pistol's favourite brothel, his manor of *Pickt-hatch*. T. WARTON.

¹ — *ensconce* your rags, &c.] A *sconce* is a petty fortification. To *ensconce*, therefore, is to protect as with a fort. The word occurs again in *K. Henry IV.* Part i. STEEVENS.

² — red-lattice *phrases*,] Your ale-house conversation. JOHNSON.

Red-lattice at the doors and windows were formerly the external denotements of an ale-house. Hence the present *chequers*. Perhaps the reader will express some surprize, when he is told that shops, with the sign of the *chequers*, were common among the Romans. See a view of the left-hand street of Pompeii, (No. 9) presented by Sir William Hamilton (together with several others, equally curious,) to the *Antiquary Society.* STEEVENS.

The following passage in Braithwaite's *Strapado for the Divell*, 1615, confirms Mr. Steevens's observation.—" To the true discoverer of secrets, Monsieur *Bacchus*—Master gunner of the *pottle-pot* ordnance—prime-founder of *red lattices*, &c."

In *King Henry IV.* P. ii. Falstaff's page, speaking of Bardolph, says, " he called me even now, my Lord, through a *red lattice*, and I could see no part of his face from the window." MALONE.

Fal.

Fal. Two thousand, fair woman; and I'll vouchsafe thee the hearing.

Quick. There is one Mistress Ford, Sir;—I pray, come a little nearer this ways:—I myself dwell with Master Doctor Caius.

Fal. Well, on: Mistress Ford, you say,—

Quick. Your worship says very true: I pray your worship, come a little nearer this ways.

Fal. I warrant thee, nobody hears;—mine own people, mine own people.

Quick. Are they so? Heaven bless them, and make them his servants!

Fal. Well: Mistress Ford;—what of her?

Quick. Why, Sir, she's a good creature. Lord, lord! your worship's a wanton: Well, heaven forgive you, and all of us, I pray!

Fal. Mistress Ford;—come, Mistress Ford—

Quick. Marry, this is the short and the long of it; you have brought her into such a canaries[3], as 'tis wonderful. The best courtier of them all, when the court lay at Windsor[4], could never have brought her to such a canary. Yet there has been knights, and lords, and gentlemen, with their coaches; I warrant you, coach after coach, letter after letter, gift after gift; smelling so sweetly, (all musk,) and so rustling, I warrant you, in silk and gold; and in such alligant terms; and in such wine and sugar of the best, and the fairest, that would have won any woman's heart; and, I warrant you, they could never get an eye-wink of her.—I had myself twenty angels given me this morning: but I defy all angels, (in any such sort, as they say,) but in the way of honesty:—and, I warrant you, they could never get her so much as sip on a cup with the proudest of them all: and yet there has been earls, nay, which is more, pensioners[5]; but, I warrant you, all is one with her.

Fal.

---

[3] —*canaries*,] This is the name of a brisk light dance, and is therefore properly enough used in low language for any hurry or perturbation. JOHNSON.

It is highly probable, however, that *canaries* is only a mistake of Mrs. Quickly's for *quandaries*: and yet the Clown, in *As you like it*, says, "we that are true lovers run into strange capers." STEEVENS.

[4] —*lay at Winsfor*,] i. e. resided there. MALONE.

[5] —*earls, nay, which is more*, pensioners;] i. e. Gentlemen of the band of Pensioners.—"In the month of December," [1539,] says Stowe, Annals,

Fal. But what says she to me? be brief, my good she Mercury.

Quick. Marry, she hath receiv'd your letter; for the which she thanks you a thousand times: and she gives you to notify, that her husband will be absence from his house between ten and eleven.

Fal. Ten and eleven.

Quick. Ay, forsooth; and then you may come and see the picture, she says, that you wot of [6];—Master Ford, her husband, will be from home. Alas! the sweet woman leads an ill life with him; he's a very jealousy man; she leads a very frampold [7] life with him, good heart.

Fal. Ten and eleven: woman, commend me to her; I will not fail her.

Quick. Why you say well: But I have another messenger to your worship: Mistress Page hath her hearty commendations to you too;—and let me tell you in your ear, she's as fartuous a civil modest wife, and one (I tell you) that will not miss you morning or evening prayer, as any is in Windsor, whoe'er be the other: and she bade me tell your worship, that her husband is seldom from home; but, she hopes, there will come a time. I never knew a woman so dote upon a man; surely, I think you have charms, la; yes, in truth.

Fal.

Annals, p. 973, edit. 1605, " were appointed to waite on the king's person fifty Gentlemen, called *Pensioners*, or *Speares*, like as they were in the first yeare of the king; unto whom was assigned the summe of fiftie pounds, yerely, for the maintenance of themselves, and everie man two horses, or one horse and a gelding of service." Their dress was remarkably splendid, and therefore likely to attract the notice of Mrs. Quickly. Hence, in *A Midsummer Night's Dream*, our author has selected from all the tribes of flowers the *golden-coated* cowslips to be *pensioners* to the Fairy Queen:

" The cowslips tall her *pensioners* be,
" In their gold coats spots you see; &c." MALONE.

—*earls, nay, which is more,* pensioners;] This may be illustrated by a passage in Gervase Holles's *Life of the First Earl of Clare.* Biog. Brit. Art. HOLLES. " I have heard the Earl of Clare say, that when he was *pensioner* to the queen, he did not know a worse man of the whole band than himself; and that all the world knew he had then an inheritance of 4000l. a year." TYRWHITT.

[6] —*you wot of*;] To *wot* is to know. Obsolete. STEEVENS.

[7] —*frampold*—] This word I have never seen elsewhere, except in Dr. Hacket's *Life of Archbishop Williams,* where a *frampul* man signifies a peevish troublesome fellow. JOHNSON.

Ray,

Fal. Not I, I assure thee; setting the attraction of my good parts aside, I have no other charms.

Quick. Blessing on your heart for't!

Fal. But, I pray thee, tell me this; has Ford's wife, and Page's wife, acquainted each other how they love me?

Quick. That were a jest, indeed;—they have not so little grace, I hope:—that were a trick, indeed! But Mistress Page would desire you to send her your little page, of all loves [8]; her husband has a marvellous infection to the little page: and, truly, Master Page is an honest man. Never a wife in Windsor leads a better life than she does; do what she will, say what she will, take all, pay all, go to bed when she list, rise when she list, all is as she will; and, truly, she deserves it; for if there be a kind woman in Windsor, she is one. You must send her your page; no remedy.

Fal. Why, I will.

Quick. Nay, but do so then: and, look you, he may come and go between you both; and, in any case, have a nay-word [9], that you may know one another's mind, and the boy never need to understand any thing; for 'tis not good that children should know any wickedness: old folks, you know, have discretion, as they say, and know the world.

Fal. Fare thee well: commend me to them both: there's my purse; I am yet thy debtor.—Boy, go along with this woman.—This news distracts me!

[*Exeunt* QUICKLY *and* ROBIN.

Pist. This punk is one of Cupid's carriers [1]:—

Clap

Ray, among his *South* and *East* country words, says, that *frampald*, or *frampard*, signifies *fretful, peevish, cross, froward*. As *froward* (he adds) comes from *frow*, so may *frampard*. STEEVENS.

[8] *— to send her your little page, of all loves:*] *Of all loves*, is an adjuration only, and signifies no more, than if she had said, desires you to send him by *all means*. It is used in Decker's *Honest Whore*, Part i. 1635,—" conjuring his wife, *of all loves*, to prepare cheer fitting," &c. Again, in Holinshed's Chronicle, p. 1164. STEEVENS.

[9] *— A nay-word,*] i. e. a *watch-word*. So, in a subsequent scene: " We have a *nay-word* to know one another, &c." STEEVENS.

[1] *This punk is one of Cupid's carriers:*] Dr. Warburton's emendation, " This *pink*, &c." is plausible. A *pink* is a vessel whose form may be supposed to bear some resemblance to that of Mrs Quickly the bends and ribs compatting so that its sides bulge out very much, by which means it is enabled to carry greater burdens. They are often used (according to Chambers) as *flote-ships*. But there is no need of alteration. It is always dangerous to meddle with Pistol's language.

The

Clap on more sails; pursue, up with your fights [2];
Give fire; she is my prize, or ocean whelm them all!

[*Exit* PISTOL.

Fal. Say'st thou so, old Jack? go thy ways; I'll make more of thy old body than I have done. Will they yet look after thee? Wilt thou, after the expence of so much money, be now a gainer? Good body, I thank thee: Let them say, 'tis grosly done; so it be fairly done, no matter.

Enter BARDOLPH.

Bard. Sir John, there's one Master Brook below would fain speak with you, and be acquainted with you; and hath sent your worship a morning's draught of sack [*].

Fal. Brook, is his name?

Bard. Ay, Sir.

Fal. Call him in; [*Exit* BARDOLPH.] Such Brooks are welcome to me, that o'erflow such liquor. Ah! ha! Mistress Ford and Mistress Page, have I encompass'd you? go to; *via* [3]!

The allusion to the marine is sufficiently preserved by the word *carrier*, which is technical. *This punk is one of those vessels which Cupid employs in the carrying trade. Clap on more sails,* &c. MALONE.

[2] —*up with your* fights;] *Fights*, are *cloaths* hung round the ship to conceal the men from the enemy; and *close-fights* are *bulk-heads*, or any other shelter that the fabric of a ship affords. JOHNSON.

[*] —*one Master Brook below would fain speak with you, and be acquainted with you, and hath* sent your worship a morning's draught of sack.] It seems to have been a common custom at taverns, in our author's time, to send presents of wine from one room to another, either as a memorial of friendship, or (as in the present instance) by way of introduction to acquaintance. Of the existence of this practice the following anecdote of Ben Jonson and the ingenious Bishop Corbet furnishes a proof. " Ben Jonson was at a tavern, and in comes Bishop Corbet (but not so then) into the next room. Ben Jonson calls for a quart of *raw* wine, and gives it to the tapster. " Sirrah (says he) carry this to the gentleman in the next chamber, and tell him, I sacrifice my service to him." The fellow did, and in those words. Friend, says Dr. Corbet, I thank him for his love; but 'pr'ythee tell him from me that he is mistaken; for *sacrifices* are always *burnt.*" *Merry Passages and Jeasts*, Mss. Harl. 6395. MALONE.

[3] —*go to; via*!] This cant phrase of exultation is common in the old plays. STEEVENS.

Markham uses this word as one of the vocal helps necessary for reviving a horse's spirits in galloping large rings, when he grows slothful. Hence this cant phrase (perhaps from the Italian, *via*) may be used on other occasions to quicken or pluck up courage. TOLLET.

Re-enter

Re-enter BARDOLPH, *with* FORD *disguised.*

Ford. Bless you, Sir.

Fal. And you, Sir: Would you speak with me?

Ford. I make bold, to press with so little preparation upon you.

Fal. You're welcome: What's your will? Give us leave, drawer. [*Exit* BARDOLPH.

Ford. Sir, I am a gentleman that have spent much; my name is Brook.

Fal. Good Master Brook, I desire more acquaintance of you.

Ford. Good Sir John, I sue for yours: not to charge you [4]; for I must let you understand, I think myself in better plight for a lender than you are: the which hath something embolden'd me to this unseason'd intrusion; for they say, if money go before, all ways do lie open.

Fal. Money is a good soldier, Sir, and will on.

Ford. Troth, and I have a bag of money here troubles me: if you will help to bear it, Sir John, take all, or half, for easing me of the carriage.

Fal. Sir, I know not how I may deserve to be your porter.

Ford. I will tell you, Sir, if you will give me the hearing.

Fal. Speak, good Master Brook; I shall be glad to be your servant.

Ford. Sir, I hear you are a scholar—I will be brief with you;—and you have been a man long known to me, though I had never so good means, as desire, to make myself acquainted with you. I shall discover a thing to you, wherein I must very much lay open mine own imperfection: but, good Sir John, as you have one eye upon my follies, as you hear them unfolded, turn another into the register of your own; that I may pass with a reproof the easier, sith [5] you yourself know, how easy it is to be such an offender.

Fal. Very well, Sir; proceed.

Ford. There is a gentlewoman in this town, her husband's name is Ford.

Fal. Well, Sir.

---

[4] *— not to charge you;*] That is, not with a purpose of putting you to expence, or *being burthensome.* JOHNSON.

[5] *—sith*] i. e. Since. STEEVENS.

Ford.

Ford. I have long loved her, and, I proteſt to you, beſtow'd much on her; follow'd her with a doting obſervance, engroſs'd opportunities to meet her; fee'd every ſlight occaſion, that could but niggardly give me ſight of her; not only bought many preſents to give her, but have given largely to many, to know what ſhe would have given: briefly, I have purſued her, as love hath purſued me; which hath been, on the wing of all occaſions. But whatſoever I have merited, either in my mind, or in my means, meed [6], I am ſure, I have received none; unleſs experience be a jewel: that I have purchaſed at an infinite rate; and that hath taught me to ſay this:

Love like a ſhadow flies, when ſubſtance love purſues;
Purſuing that that flies, and flying what purſues. *

Fal. Have you receiv'd no promiſe of ſatisfaction at her hands?
Ford. Never.
Fal. Have you importuned her to ſuch a purpoſe?
Ford. Never.
Fal. Of what quality was your love then?
Ford. Like a fair houſe, built upon another man's ground; ſo that I have loſt my edifice, by miſtaking the place where I erected it.
Fal. To what purpoſe have you unfolded this to me?
Ford. When I have told you that, I have told you all. Some ſay, that, though ſhe appear honeſt to me, yet, in other places, ſhe enlargeth her mirth ſo far, that there is ſhrewd conſtruction made of her. Now, Sir, John, here is the heart of my purpoſe: You are a gentleman of excellent

---

[6] — *meed,*] i. e. reward. STEEVENS.
* *Love like a ſhadow flies,* &c.] Theſe lines have much the air of a quotation, but I know not whether they belong to any contemporary writer. In Florio's *Second Fruites*, 1591, I find the following verſes:
"Di donne e, et ſempre ſu natura,
"Odiar chi l'ama, e chi non l'ama cura."
Again:
"—————— Sono ſimili a crocodilli
"Chi per prender l'huomo, piangono, e preſo la devorano,
"Chi le fugge ſequono, e chi le ſeque fuggono."
Thus tranſlated by Florio,
"—————— they are like crocodiles,
"They weep to winne, and wonne they cauſe to die,
"*Follow men flying, and men following fly.*" MALONE.

breeding,

breeding, admirable difcourfe, of great admittance [7], authentic in your place and perfon, generally allow'd [8] for your many war-like, court-like, and learned preparations.

Fal. O, Sir!

Ford. Believe it, for you know it:—There is money; fpend it, fpend it; fpend more; fpend all I have; only give me fo much of your time in exchange of it, as to lay an amiable fiege [9] to the honefty of this Ford's wife: ufe your art of wooing, win her to confent to you; if any man may, you may as foon as any.

Fal. Would it apply well to the vehemence of your affection, that I fhould win what you would enjoy? Methinks, you prefcribe to yourfelf very prepofteroufly.

Ford. O, underftand my drift! fhe dwells fo fecurely on the excellency of her honour, that the folly of my foul dares not prefent itfelf; fhe is too bright to be look'd againft [1]. Now, could I come to her with any detection in my hand, my defires had inftance and argument [2] to commend themfelves; I could drive her then from the ward of her purity [3], her reputation, her marriage-vow, and a thoufand other her defences, which now are too ftrongly embattled againft me: What fay you to't, Sir John?

Fal. Mafter Brook, I will firft make bold with your money; next, give me your hand; and laft, as I am a gentleman, you fhall, if you will, enjoy Ford's wife.

---

[7] — *of great admittance,*] i. e. admitted into all, or the greateft companies. STEEVENS.

[8] — *generally allowed*—] *Allowed* is *approved.* So, in *K. Lear:*
"——— if your fweet fway
"*Allow* obedience, &c." STEEVENS.

[9] *to lay an* amiable *fiege*—] i. e. a fiege of love. So, in *Romeo and Juliet:*
"——— the *fiege* of *loving* terms." MALONE.

[1] — *fhe is too bright to be look'd againft.*]
Nimium lubricus afpici. Hor. MALONE.

[2] —*inftance and argument* —] *Inftance* is *example.* JOHNSON.

[3] *the ward of her purity,*—] i. e. the *defence* of it. STEEVENS.
Mr. Steevens is, I think, miftaken. What Ford means to fay is, that if he could once detect her in a crime, he fhould then be able to drive her from thofe defences with which fhe would otherwife ward off his addreffes; fuch as her *purity*, her reputation, her marriage-vow, &c.

So, in *The Winter's Tale:*
"——— Tell him, you're fure,
"All in Bohemia's well;—Say this to him,
"He's beat from his beft *ward.*" MASON.

Ford.

Ford. O good Sir!

Fal. Master Brook, I say you shall.

Ford. Want no money, Sir John, you shall want none.

Fal. Want no Mistress Ford, Master Brook, you shall want none. I shall be with her (I may tell you) by her own appointment; even as you came in to me, her assistant, or go-between, parted from me: I say, I shall be with her between ten and eleven; for at that time the jealous rascally knave, her husband, will be forth. Come you to me at night; you shall know how I speed.

Ford. I am blest in your acquaintance. Do you know Ford, Sir?

Fal. Hang him, poor cuckoldly knave! I know him not:—yet I wrong him, to call him poor; they say, the jealous wittoly knave hath masses of money; for the which his wife seems to me well-favour'd. I will use her as the key of the cuckoldly rogue's coffer; and there's my harvest-home.

Ford. I would you knew Ford, Sir; that you might avoid him, if you saw him:

Fal. Hang him, mechanical salt-butter rogue! I will stare him out of his wits; I will awe him with my cudgel: it shall hang like a meteor o'er the cuckold's horns: Master Brook, thou shalt know, I will predominate over the peasant, and thou shalt lie with his wife.—Come to me soon at night:—Ford's a knave, and I will aggravate his stile [4]; thou, Master Brook, shalt know him for a knave and cuckold: —come to me soon at night. [*Exit.*

Ford. What a damn'd Epicurean rascal is this!—My heart is ready to crack with impatience.—Who says, this is improvident jealousy? My wife hath sent to him, the hour is fix'd, the match is made: Would any man have thought this? See the hell of having a false woman! my bed shall be abused, my coffers ransack'd, my reputation gnawn at; and I shall not only receive this villainous wrong, but stand under the adoption of abominable terms, and by him that does me this wrong. Terms! names! Amaimon sounds well; Lucifer, well; Barbason [5] well; yet they are devils' additions,

the

---

[4] — *and I will aggravate his* stile:] *Stile* is a phrase from the herald's office. Falstaff means, that *he will add more titles to those he already enjoys.* STEEVENS.

[5] — *Amaimon—Barbason—*] The reader who is curious to know any particulars concerning these dæmons, may find them in Reginald

Scott's

the names of fiends: but cuckold! wittol-cuckold [*]! the devil himself hath not such a name. Page is an ass, a secure ass; he will trust his wife, he will not be jealous: I will rather trust a Fleming with my butter, Parson Hugh the Welchman with my cheese, an Irishman with my aqua-vitæ bottle [6], or a thief to walk my ambling gelding, than my wife with herself: then she plots, then she ruminates, then she devises: and what they think in their hearts they may effect; they will break their hearts but they will effect. Heaven be praised for my jealousy! Eleven o'clock [7] the hour; I will prevent this, detect my wife, be revenged on Falstaff, and laugh at Page: I will about it; better three hours too soon, than a minute too late. Fie, fie, fie! cuckold! cuckold! cuckold? [*Exit.*]

SCENE III.

Windsor Park.

Enter CAIUS *and* RUGBY.

Caius. Jack Rugby!
Rug. Sir.
Caius. Vat is de clock, Jack?

Scott's *Inventarie of the Names, Shapes, Powers, Government, and Effects of Devils and Spirits,* &c. p. 377, &c. From hence it appears that *Amaimon* was *king of the East,* and *Barbatos* a great *countie or earle.*
STEEVENS.

[*] —*wittol-cuckold!*] One who knows his wife's falsehood, and is contented with it;—from *witan,* Sax. to know. MALONE.

[6] — *an Irishman with my aqua-vitæ* bottle,] Heywood, in his *Challenge for Beauty,* 1636, mentions the love of *aqua-vitæ* as characteristic of the *Irish:*
  "The Briton he metheglin quaffs,
  "The Irish aqua-vitæ."
The Irish *aqua-vitæ*, I believe, was not brandy, but *usquebaugh,* for which Ireland has been long celebrated. MALONE.

Dericke, in *The Image of Irelande,* 1581, Sign. F 2, mentions *Ufbearde,* and in a note explains it to mean *aqua vitæ.* REED.

[7] *Eleven o'clock*—] Ford should rather have said *ten o'clock:* the time was between ten and eleven: and his impatient suspicion was not likely to stay beyond the time. JOHNSON.

It is necessary for the business of the piece that Falstaff should be at Ford's house before his return. Hence our author makes him name the later hour. See p. 248:—"The clock gives me my cue;—there *I shall find Falstaff.*" When he says above, " I shall prevent *this,*" he means, not the meeting, but his wife's effecting her purpose. MALONE.

Rug.

Rug. 'Tis paſt the hour, Sir, that Sir Hugh promiſed to meet.

Caius. By gar, he has ſave his ſoul, dat he is no come; he has pray his pible vell, dat he is no come: by gar, Jack Rugby, he is dead already, if he be come.

Rug. He is wiſe, Sir; he knew, your worſhip would kill him, if he came.

Caius. By gar, de herring is no dead, ſo as I vill kill him. Take your rapier, Jack; I vill tell you how I vill kill him.

Rug. Alas, Sir, I cannot fence.

Caius. Villainy, take your rapier.

Rug. Forbear; here's company.

Enter HOST, SHALLOW, SLENDER, *and* PAGE.

Hoſt. 'Bleſs thee, bully doctor.

Shal. 'Save you, Maſter Doctor Caius.

Page. Now, good maſter doctor!

Slen. Give you good-morrow, Sir.

Caius. Vat be all you, one, two, tree, four, come for?

Hoſt. To ſee thee fight, to ſee thee foin [8], to ſee thee traverſe, to ſee thee here, to ſee thee there; to ſee thee paſs thy punto, thy ſtock [9], thy reverſe, thy diſtance, thy montant. Is he dead, my Ethiopian? Is he dead, my Franciſco [*]? ha, bully! What ſays my Æſculapius? my Galen? my heart of elder [1]? ha! is he dead, bully Stale [2]? is he dead?

Caius. By gar, he is de coward Jack prieſt of the vorld; he is not ſhew his face.

Hoſt. Thou art a Caſtilian [3] king, Urinal! Hector of Greece, my boy!

Caius.

---

[8] — *to ſee thee* foin,] To *foin*, I believe, was the ancient term for making a thruſt in fencing, or tilting. STEEVENS.

[9] — *thy* ſtock,] *Stock* is a corruption of *ſtocata*, Ital. from which language the technical terms that follow are likewiſe adopted. STEEVENS.

[*] *my* Franciſco?] He means, my Frenchman. The quarto reads— my *Françoyes*. MALONE.

[1] — *my heart of elder?*] It ſhould be remember'd, to make this joke reliſh, that the *elder* tree has *no heart*. I ſuppoſe this expreſſion was made uſe of in oppoſition to the common one, *heart of oak*. STEEVENS.

[2] — bully *Stale?*] The reaſon why Caius is called bully *Stale*, and afterwards *Urinal*, muſt be ſufficiently obvious to every reader. STEEVENS.

[3] — *Caſtilian*

Caius. I pray you, bear vitnèfs that me have ſtay fix or ſeven, two, tree hours for him, and he is no come.

Shal. He is the wiſer man, maſter doctor: he is a curer of ſouls, and you a curer of bodies; if you ſhould fight, you go againſt the hair [4] of your profeſſions: is it not true, Maſter Page?

Page. Maſter Shallow, you have yourſelf been a great fighter, though now a man of peace.

Shal. Bodykins, Maſter Page, though I now be old, and of the peace, if I ſee a ſword out, my finger itches to make one: though we are juſtices, and doctors, and churchmen, Maſter Page, we have ſome ſalt of our youth in us; we are the ſons of women, Maſter Page.

Page. 'Tis true, Maſter Shallow.

Shal. It will be found ſo, Maſter Page. Maſter Doctor Caius, I am come to fetch you home. I am ſworn of the peace: you have ſhew'd yourſelf a wiſe phyſician, and Sir Hugh hath ſhewn himſelf a wiſe and patient churchman: you muſt go with me, Maſter Doctor.

Hoſt. Pardon, gueſt juſtice:—A word, Monſieur Mockwater [5].

Caius.

---

[3] — *Caſtilian*—] *Caſtilian* and *Ethiopian*, like *Cataian*, appear in our author's time to have been cant terms. I have met with them in more than one of the old comedies. I ſuppoſe *Caſtilian* was the cant term for *Spaniards* in general. STEEVENS.

I believe this was a popular ſlur upon the Spaniards, who were held in great *contempt* after the buſineſs of the *Armada*. Thus we have a *Treatiſe Paraenetical, wherein is ſhewed the right way to reſiſt the* Caſtilian *king:* and a ſonnet, prefixed to Lea's *Anſwer to the Untruths publiſhed in Spain, in glorie of their ſuppoſed Victory atchieved againſt our Engliſh Navie,* begins: "Thou fond *Caſtilian king!*"—and ſo in other places. FARMER.

Dr. Farmer, I believe, is right. The hoſt, who, availing himſelf of the poor Doctor's ignorance of Engliſh phraſeology, applies to him all kinds of opprobrious terms, here means to call him *a coward.* So, in *The Three Lords of London,* 1590:

"My lordes, what means theſe gallants to performe?
"Come theſe Caſtilian cowards but to brave?
"Do all theſe mountains move, to breed a mouſe?"

There may, however, be alſo an alluſion to his profeſſion, as a *water-caſter.*

I know not whether we ſhould not rather point—Thou art a Caſtilian, king-wrinal! &c.

In *K. Henry VIII.* Wolſey is called count-cardinal. MALONE.

[4] — againſt the *hair,* &c.] This phraſe is proverbial, and is taken from ſtroking the *hair* of animals a contrary way to that in which it grows.—We now ſay againſt the *grain.* STEEVENS.

[5] *A word,*

Caius. Mock-vater! vat is dat?

Host. Mock-water, in our English tongue, is valour, bully.

Caius. By gar, then I have as much mock-vater as de Englishman:—Scurvy jack-dog-priest! by gar, me vill cut his ears.

Host. He will clapper-claw thee tightly, bully.

Caius. Clapper-de-claw! vat is dat?

Host. That is, he will make thee amends.

Caius. By gar, me do look, he shall clapper-de-claw me; for, by gar, me vill have it.

Host. And I will provoke him to't, or let him wag.

Caius. Me tank you for dat.

Host. And moreover, bully,—But first, master guest, and Master Page, and eke cavalero Slender, go you through the town to Frogmore. [*Aside to them.*

Page. Sir Hugh is there, is he?

Host. He is there: see what humour he is in; and I will bring the doctor about by the fields: will it do well?

Shal. We will do it.

Page, Shal. and *Slen.* Adieu, good master doctor.

[*Exeunt* PAGE, SHALLOW, *and* SLENDER.

---

5 *A word, Monsieur* Mock-water.] The second of these words was recovered from the early quarto by Mr. Theobald. Some years ago I suspected that *mock-water*, which appears to me to afford no meaning, was corrupt, and that the author wrote—*Make*-water. I have since observed that the words *mock* and *make* are often confounded in the old copies, and have therefore now more confidence in my conjecture. It is observable that the host, availing himself of the Doctor's ignorance of English, annexes to the terms that he uses a sense directly opposite to their real import Thus, the poor Frenchman is made to believe, that "he will *clapper-claw* thee tightly," signifies, "he will make thee *amends*." Again, when he proposes to be his *friend*, he tells him, "for this I will be thy *adversary* toward Anne Page." So also, instead of "heart of *oak*," he calls him "heart of *elder*." In the same way, he informs him that *Make-water* means "*valour*."—In the old play called *the Life and Death of Lord Cromwell*, 1602, a female of this name is mentioned.

Dr. Farmer, however, observes to me, that *Make-water* may be the true reading, that term being used in some counties; signifying the oozing of a muck or dung-hill. MALONE.

The host means, I believe, to reflect on the inspection of urine, which made a considerable part of practical physic in that time; yet I do not well see the meaning of *mock-water*. JOHNSON.

To *mock*, in *Antony and Cleopatra*, undoubtedly signifies to *play with*. Shakspeare may therefore chuse to represent Caius as one to whom a *urinal* was a play-thing. STEEVENS.

VOL. III.   M   *Caius.*

Caius. By gar, me vill kill de prieſt; for he ſpeak for a jack-an-ape to Anne Page.

Hoſt. Let him die: but, firſt *, ſheath thy impatience; throw cold water on thy choler: go about the fields with me through Frogmore; I will bring thee where Miſtreſs Anne Page is, at a farm-houſe a feaſting; and thou ſhalt woo her: cry'd game⁶, ſaid I well?

Caius. By gar, me tank you for dat: by gar, I love you; and I ſhall procure-a you de good gueſt, de earl, de knight, de lords, de gentlemen, my patients.

Hoſt. For the which, I will be thy adverſary toward Anne Page; ſaid I well?

Caius. By gar, 'tis good; vell ſaid.

Hoſt. Let us wag then.

Caius. Come at my heels, Jack Rugby.   [*Exeunt.*

ACT III. SCENE I.

A field near Frogmore.

Enter Sir HUGH EVANS *and* SIMPLE.

Evans. I pray you now, good Maſter Slender's ſerving-man, and friend Simple by your name, which way have you looked for Maſter Caius, that calls himſelf *Doctor of Phyſic?*

Simple. Marry, Sir, the city-ward¹, the park-ward, every

---

* — *but, firſt,*] Theſe words were recovered from the old quarto by Mr. Theobald. MALONE.

⁶ — *cry'd game,*] We yet ſay, in colloquial language, that ſuch a one is — *game,* — or *game to the back.* Cry'd *game,* might mean, in thoſe days, — a *profeſs'd buck,* one who was as well known by the report of his gallantry, as he could have been by *proclamation.* Thus, in *Troilus and Creſſida:*

"On whoſe bright creſt, fame, with her loud'ſt O-yes,
"Cries, this is he."

Again: "Thou art proclaim'd a fool, I think."

Again, in *King Lear:* "— A proclaim'd prize." STEEVENS.

¹ — *the city-ward,*] i.e. towards London. So, in *K. Henry VI. P. i.*

"— you may perceive,

"Their powers are marching unto Paris-ward."

The

every way; old Windsor way, and every way but the town way.

Evans. I moft fehemently defire you, you will alfo look that way.

Simple. I will, Sir.

Evans. 'Plefs my foul! how full of cholers I am, and trempling of mind!—I shall be glad, if he have deceived me:—how melancholies I am!—I will knog his urinals about his knave's collard, when I have good opportunities for the ork:—'plefs my foul!

> *To fhallow rivers* [2], *to whofe falls*   [*fings.*
> *Melodious birds fing madrigals;*
> *There will we make our peds of rofes,*
> *And a thoufand fragrant pofies.*
> *To fhallow—*

'Mercy on me! I have a great difpofitions to cry.

> *Melodious birds fing madrigals;—*
> *When as I fat in Pabylon* [3],—
> *And a thoufand vagram pofies.*
> *To fhallow—*

Simple. Yonder he is coming, this way, Sir Hugh.

Evans. He's welcome:—

> *To fhallow rivers, to whofe falls—*

Heaven profper the right!—What weapons is he?

                                             Simple.

The firft folio has—*pitty*-ward, which in the fecond folio was corrupt-ed into —pitty-*wary*. The emendation was fuggefted by Mr. Steevens, who likewife propofes *petty*-ward. MALONE.

[2] *To fhallow rivers,* &c.] Thefe lines are part of an old fong written by Chriftopher Marlowe, which was firft publifhed imperfectly in 1599, and afterwards entire in a Collection of Verfes entitled *England's Helicon,* printed in 1600; beginning thus: " Come live with me, and be my love, &c." Evans in his panic mif-recites the lines, which in the original run thus:

> " There will we fit upon the rocks,
> " And fee the shepherds feed their flocks,
> " By fhallow rivers, to whofe falls
> " Melodious birds fing madrigals:
> " There will *I* make *thee* beds of rofes
> " *With* a thoufand fragrant pofies, &c."

In the modern editions the verfes fung by Sir Hugh have been cor-rected, I think, improperly. His mif-recitals were certainly intended. —He *fings* on the prefent occafion, to fhew that he is not afraid. So Bottom, in *A Midfummer Night's Dream:* " I will walk up and down here, and I will *fing,* that they shall hear, I am *not afraid.*" MALONE.

Simple. No weapons, Sir: There comes my master, Master Shallow, and another gentleman from Frogmore, over the stile, this way.

Evans. Pray you, give me my gown; or else keep it in your arms.

The musical notes to which this song was set, have been recovered by Sir John Hawkins from a MS. of Shakspeare's time. Not thinking them of much value, I omitted to insert them, but in compliance with the wishes of a musical friend I shall here give them a place.

Come live with me, and be my love, and we will all the pleasures prove, that hills and val-lies, dale and field, and all the crag-gy moun-tains yield.

Sir J. HAWKINS.

---

3 *When as I sat in Babylon,*—] This line is from the old version of the 137th Psalm:

"When we did sit in Babylon,
"The rivers round about,
"Then, in remembrance of Sion,
"The tears for grief burst out."

The word *rivers* in the second line may be supposed to have been brought to Sir Hugh's thoughts by the line of Mr. Marlowe's madrigal that he has just repeated; and in his fright he blends the sacred and prophane song together. The old quarto has—" There lived a man *in Babylon*," which was the first line of an old song mentioned in *Twelfth Night:*—but the other line is more in character. MALONE.

Enter

Enter PAGE, SHALLOW, *and* SLENDER.

Shal. How now, Master Parson? Good-morrow, good Sir Hugh. Keep a gamester from the dice, and a good student from his book, and it is wonderful.

Slen. Ah sweet Anne Page!

Page. Save you, good Sir Hugh!

Evans. 'Pless you from his mercy sake, all of you!

Shal. What! the sword and the word! do you study them both, Master Parson?

Page. And youthful still, in your doublet and hose, this raw rheumatic day?

Evans. There is reasons and causes for it.

Page. We are come to you, to do a good office, Master Parson.

Evans. Fery well: What is it?

Page. Yonder is a most reverend gentleman, who, belike, having received wrong by some person, is at most odds with his own gravity and patience, that ever you saw.

Shal. I have lived fourscore years, and upward; I never heard a man of his place, gravity, and learning, so wide of his own respect.

Evans. What is he?

Page. I think you know him; Master Doctor Caius, the renowned French physician.

Evans. Got's will, and his passion of my heart! I had as lief you would tell me of a mess of porridge.

Page. Why?

Evans. He has no more knowledge in Hibocrates and Galen—and he is a knave besides; a cowardly knave, as you would desires to be acquainted withal.

Page. I warrant you, he's the man should fight with him.

Slen. O, sweet Anne Page!

Enter HOST, CAIUS, *and* RUGBY.

Shal. It appears so, by his weapons:—Keep them asunder;—here comes Doctor Caius.

Page. Nay, good Master Parson, keep in your weapon.

Shal. So do you, good Master Doctor.

Host. Disarm them, and let them question; let them keep their limbs whole, and hack our English.

Cais.

Caius. I pray you, let-a me speak a word vit your ear. Verefore vill you not meet-a me?

Evans. Pray you, use your patience: In good time.

Caius. By gar, you are de coward, de Jack dog, John ape.

Evans. Pray you, let us not be laughing-stogs to other men's humours; I desire you in friendship, and I will one way or other make you amends:—I will knog your urinals about your knave's cogs-comb, for missing your meetings and appointments [4].

Caius. Diable!—Jack Rugby,—mine *Hoſt de Jarterre*, have I not stay for him, to kill him? have I not, at de place I did appoint?

Evans. As I am a Christians soul, now, look you, this is the place appointed; I'll be judgment by mine host of the Garter.

Hoſt. Peace, I say, Guallia and Gaul [5], French and Welch; soul-curer and body-curer.

Caius. Ay, dat is very good! excellent!

Hoſt. Peace, I say; hear mine host of the Garter. Am I politic? am I subtle? am I a Machiavel? Shall I lose my doctor? no; he gives me the potions, and the motions.— Shall I lose my parson? my priest? my Sir Hugh? no; he gives me the pro-verbs and the no-verbs.—Give me thy hand, terrestial; so:—Give me thy hand, celestial; so.— Boys of art, I have deceived you both; I have directed you to wrong places: your hearts are mighty, your skins are whole, and let burnt sack be the issue.—Come, lay their swords to pawn:—Follow me, lad of peace; follow, follow, follow.

Shal. Trust me, a mad host:—Follow, gentlemen, follow.

Slen. O, sweet Anne Page!

[*Exeunt* SHALLOW, SLENDER, PAGE, *and* HOST.

Caius. Ha! do I perceive dat? have you make-a de sot of us [6]? ha, ha!

---

[4] — *for missing your meetings and appointments*] These words, which are not in the folio, were recovered from the quarto by Mr. Pope. MALONE.

[5] Guallia *and* Gaul,] The folio reads—*Gallia* and Gaul; but the reading of the old quarto [Gawle and *Gawlia*] justifies the emendation now made, which was suggested by Dr. Farmer. *Guallia* is *Wallia.* MALONE.

Thus, in *K. Henry VI. P. ii. Gualtier* for *Walter.* STEEVENS.

[6] *make-a de sot of us?*] *Sot* in French signifies *a fool.* MALONE.

Evans. This is well; he has made us his vlouting-stog.—I desire you, that we may be friends; and let us knog our prains together, to be revenge on this same scall, scurvy [7], cogging companion, the host of the Garter.

Caius. By gar, vit all my heart; he promise to bring me vere is Anne Page: by gar, he deceive me too.

Evans. Well, I will smite his noddles;—Pray you follow. [*Exeunt.*

SCENE II.

The Street in Windsor.

Enter Mistress PAGE *and* ROBIN.

Mrs. Page. Nay, keep your way, little gallant; you were wont to be a follower, but now you are a leader: Whether had you rather lead mine eyes, or eye your master's heels?

Robin. I had rather, forsooth, go before you like a man, than follow him like a dwarf.

Mrs. Page. O, you are a flattering boy; now, I see, you'll be a courtier.

Enter FORD.

Ford. Well met, Mistress Page: Whither go you?

Mrs. Page. Truly, Sir, to see your wife; is she at home?

Ford. Ay; and as idle as she may hang together, for want of company: I think, if your husbands were dead, you two would marry.

Mrs. Page. Be sure of that—two other husbands.

Ford. Where had you this pretty weather-cock?

Mrs. Page. I cannot tell what the dickens his name is, my husband had him of: What do you call your knight's name, sirrah?

Rob. Sir John Falstaff.

Ford. Sir John Falstaff!

Mrs. Page. He, he; I can never hit on's name.—There is such a league between my good man and he!—Is your wife at home, indeed?

---

[7] — *scall, scurvy,*] *Scall* was an old word of reproach, as *scab* was afterwards. Chaucer imprecates on his *forivener:*

"Under thy longe lockes mayest thou have the *scalle.*" JOHNSON.
See Leviticus, 13th Ch.—v. 30, 31, and seqq. WHALLEY.

Ford.

Ford. Indeed, she is.

Mrs. Page. By your leave, Sir;—I am sick, till I see her. [*Exeunt Mrs* PAGE *and* ROBIN.

Ford. Has Page any brains? hath he any eyes? hath he any thinking? Sure they sleep; he hath no use of them. Why, this boy will carry a letter twenty miles, as easy as a cannon will shoot point-blank twelve score. He pieces-out his wife's inclination; he gives her folly motion, and advantage: and now she's going to my wife, and Falstaff's boy with her. A man may hear this shower sing in the wind!—and Falstaff's boy with her!—Good plots!—they are laid; and our revolted wives share damnation together.—Well; I will take him, then torture my wife, pluck the borrow'd veil of modesty from the so seeming Mistress Page⁸, divulge Page himself for a secure and wilful Actæon; and to these violent proceedings all my neighbours shall cry aim⁹. —[*Clock strikes.*] The clock gives me my cue, and my assurance bids me search; there I shall find Falstaff: I shall be rather praised for this, than mock'd; for it is as positive as the earth is firm*, that Falstaff is there: I will go.

Enter PAGE, SHALLOW, SLENDER, HOST, *Sir* HUGH EVANS, CAIUS, *and* RUGBY.

Shal. Page, &c. Well met, Master Ford'.

Ford. Trust me, a good knot: I have good cheer at home; and, I pray you, all go with me.

Shal. I must excuse myself, Master Ford.

Slen. And so must I, Sir; we have appointed to dine with Mistress Anne, and I would not break with her for more money than I'll speak of.

Shal. We have linger'd ¹ about a match between Anne

---

⁸ — *so seeming* Mistress Page,] *seeming* is *specious.* So, in *K. Lear:*
" If aught within that little *seeming* substance—.' STEEVENS.

⁹ — shall *cry aim.*] i. e. shall *encourage.* So, in Fenton's *Tragical Discourses,* 1567:—" standing rather in his window to—*cry aime,* than helping any-waye to part the fraye."

The phrase is taken from archery. It seems to have been the office of the *aim-crier,* to give notice to the *Archer* when he was within a proper distance of his mark, or in a direct line with it; and to point out why he failed to strike it. So, in the *Spanish Gipsie,* a com. 1653: —" great bobbers have shot at me;—but I myself *gave aim* thus:— wide four bows; short three and a half, &c." STEEVENS.

* — *as the earth is firm,*] So, in *Macbeth:*
" ———— Thou sure and *firm-set earth*—." MALONE.

¹ *We*

Page and my cousin Slender, and this day we shall have our answer.

Slen. I hope, I have your good will, father Page.

Page. You have, master Slender; I stand wholly for you:—but my wife, master doctor, is for you altogether.

Caius. Ay, by gar; and de maid is love-a me; my nursh-a Quickly tell me so mush.

Host. What say you to young Master Fenton? he capers, he dances, he has eyes of youth, he writes verses, he speaks holy-day [2], he smells April and May [3]: he will carry't, he will carry't; 'tis in his buttons [4]; he will carry't.

[1] *We have linger'd—*] They have not linger'd very long. The match was proposed by Sir Hugh but the day before. JOHNSON.

Shallow represents the affair as having been *long in hand*, that he may better excuse himself and *Slender* from accepting *Ford*'s invitation on the day when it was to be concluded. STEEVENS.

Perhaps we should read—*linguer'd*, or *languer'd*, which may have been a provincial word for *talked*, from *lingua*, Lat. or *langue*, Fr. "Let thy tongue *langer* with arguments of state," occurs in *Twelfth Night*; but it must be owned, there is reason to suspect that it is an error of the press.—*Un languard* in French is a prattler; and *languayer* signifies to talk. *Linguist* and *linguacious* are both English terms, and in Blount's *Glossography* we meet with the substantive *Luguer*. MALONE.

[2] — *he writes verses, he speaks holyday,*] i. e. in an high-flown, fustian style. It was called *a holy-day style*, from the old custom of acting their farces of the *mysteries* and *moralities*, which were turgid and bombast, on holy-days. So, in *Much Ado about Nothing*: "I cannot woo in *festival terms.*" And again, in *The Merchant of Venice*:

"Thou spend'st such *high-day* wit in praising him."

WARBURTON.

I suspect that Dr. Warburton's supposition that this phrase is derived from the season of acting the old mysteries, is but an *holy-day* hypothesis; and have preserved his note only for the sake of the passages he quotes. Fenton is not represented as a talker of bombast.

He speaks holyday, I believe, means only, his language is more *curious* and *neatly chosen* than that used by ordinary men. MALONE.

— *he speaks holyday,*] So, in *K. Henry IV.* P. i.

"With many *holiday* and *lady terms.*" STEEVENS.

[3] — *he smells April and May.*] This was the phraseology of the time; not "he smells *of* April," &c. So, in *Measure for Measure:*—"he would mouth with a beggar of fifty, though she *smelt brown bread and garlick.*" MALONE.

[4] — *'tis in his buttons;*] Alluding to an ancient custom among the country fellows, of trying whether they should succeed with their mistresses, by carrying the *bachelor's buttons* (a plant of the *Lychnis* kind, whose flowers resemble a coat button in form) in their pockets. And they judged of their good or bad success, by their growing, or their not growing there. SMITH.

Page. Not by my consent, I promise you. The gentleman is of no having[5]: he kept company with the wild prince and Poins; he is of too high a region, he knows too much. No, he shall not knit a knot in his fortunes with the finger of my substance: if he take her, let him take her simply; the wealth I have waits on my consent, and my consent goes not that way.

Ford. I beseech you, heartily, some of you go home with me to dinner: besides your cheer, you shall have sport; I will shew you a monster.——Master doctor, you shall go;—so shall you, Master Page;—and you, Sir Hugh.

Shal. Well, fare you well;—we shall have the freer wooing at Master Page's. [*Exeunt* SHAL. *and* SLEND.

Caius. Go home, John Rugby; I come anon.
[*Exit* RUGBY.

Host. Farewell, my hearts: I will to my honest knight Falstaff, and drink canary with him. [*Exit* HOST.

Ford. [*Aside.*] I think, I shall drink in pipe-wine first with him; I'll make him dance[6]. Will you go, gentles?

All. Have with you, to see this monster. [*Exeunt.*

SCENE III.

A Room in Ford's *House.*

Enter Mrs. FORD, *and Mrs.* PAGE.

Mrs. Ford. What, John! what, Robert!
Mrs. Page. Quickly, quickly: Is the buck-basket—
Mrs. Ford. I warrant:—What, Robin, I say.

---

[5] —*of no having:*] *Having* is the same as *estate* or *fortune*. JOHNS. So, in *Macbeth:*
    "Of noble *having*, and of royal hope." STEEVENS.

[6] *I shall drink* in pipe *wine first with him; I'll make him dance*] *Pipe* is known to be a vessel of wine, now containing two hogsheads. *Pipe* wine is therefore wine, not from the *bottle*, but the pipe; and the jest consists in the ambiguity of the word, which signifies both a cask of wine, and a musical instrument. JOHNSON.

Canary, as Mr. Tyrwhitt has observed, is the name of a dance as well as of a wine. The phrase—" to drink *in* pipe wine" always seemed to me a very strange one, till I met with the following passage in King James's first speech to his parliament, in 1604; by which it appears that "to drink *in*" was the phraseology of the time: "— who either, being old, have retained their first drunken *in* liquor," &c.

MALONE.

Enter

Enter SERVANTS *with a Basket.*

Mrs. Page. Come, come, come.
Mrs. Ford. Here, set it down.
Mrs. Page. Give your men the charge; we must be brief.
Mrs. Ford. Marry, as I told you before, John, and Robert, be ready here hard-by in the brew-house; and when I suddenly call you, come forth, and (without any pause, or staggering,) take this basket on your shoulders: that done, trudge with it in all haste, and carry it among the whitsters in Datchet mead, and there empty it in the muddy ditch, close by the Thames' side.
Mrs. Page. You will do it?
Mrs. Ford. I have told them over and over; they lack no direction: Be gone, and come when you are call'd.
[*Exeunt* Servants.
Mrs. Page. Here comes little Robin.

Enter ROBIN.

Mrs. Ford. How now, my eyas-musket[7]? what news with you?
Rob. My master Sir John is come in at your back-door, Mistress Ford: and requests your company.
Mrs. Page. You little Jack-a-lent[8], have you been true to us?
Rob. Ay, I'll be sworn: My master knows not of your being here; and hath threaten'd to put me into everlasting liberty, if I tell you of it; for, he swears, he'll turn me away.
Mrs. Page. Thou'rt a good boy; this secrecy of thine shall be a tailor to thee, and shall make thee a new doublet and hose—I'll go hide me.
Mrs. Ford. Do so:—Go tell thy master, I am alone.—Mistress Page, remember you your cue. [*Exit* Robin.

---

[7] — *my eyas-musket?*] *Eyas* is a young unsledg'd hawk; I suppose from the Italian *Niafo*, which originally signified any young bird taken from the nest unfledg'd, afterwards a young hawk. *Musket* signifies a sparrow hawk, or the smallest species of hawks. WARBURTON.

Eyas-musket is the same as *infant Lilliputian.* STEEVENS.

[8] — *Jack-a-lent,*] A *Jack o' lent* was a puppet thrown at in Lent, like throw-cocks. STEEVENS.

Mrs. Page. I warrant thee; if I do not act it, hiss me.

[*Exit Mrs.* PAGE.

Mrs. Ford. Go to then; we'll use this unwholesome humidity, this gross watry pumpion; we'll teach him to know turtles from jays [9].

Enter FALSTAFF.

Fal. Have I caught thee, *my heavenly jewel* [1]? Why, now let me die, for I have lived long enough [2]; this is the period of my ambition: O this blessed hour!

Mrs. Ford. O sweet Sir John!

Fal. Mistress Ford, I cannot cog, I cannot prate, Mistress Ford. Now shall I sin in my wish: I would thy husband were dead; I'll speak it before the best lord, I would make thee my lady.

Mrs. Ford. I your lady, Sir John! alas, I should be a pitiful lady.

Fal. Let the court of France shew me such another; I see how thine eye would emulate the diamond: Thou hast the right arched bent [3] of the brow, that becomes the ship-tire [4], the tire-valiant [5], or any tire of Venetian admittance [6].

Mrs.

---

[9] —*from jays.*] So, in *Cymbeline*:

"———— some *jay* of Italy,
"Whose mother was her painting, &c." STEEVENS.

[1] *Have I caught my heavenly jewel?*] Is the first line of the second song in Sidney's *Astrophel and Stella.* TOLLET.

[2] *Why, now let me die; for I have lived long enough;*] This sentiment, which is of sacred origin, is here indecently introduced. It appears again, with somewhat less of profaneness, in the *Winter's Tale*, Act iv. and in *Othello*, Act ii. STEEVENS.

[3] —*arched bent*—] Thus the quartos 1602, and 1619. The folio reads—*arched beauty*. STEEVENS.

The reading of the quarto is supported by a passage in *Antony and Cleopatra:*

"Eternity was in our lips and eyes,
"Bliss in our *brows-bent*." MALONE.

[4] —*that becomes the ship-tire,*] The *ship-tire* was an open head-dress, with a kind of scarf depending from behind. Its name of *ship-tire* was, I presume, from its giving the wearer some resemblance of a ship (as Shakspeare says) *in all her tri*—: with all her pennants out, and flags and streamers flying. WARBURTON.

In the fifth Act Fenton mentions that his mistress is to meet him,

"With ribbons pendant flaring 'bout her head."

This probably was what is here called the *ship-tire*. MALONE.

[5] —*the tire* valiant,] I would read *tire* volant. Stubbs, who describes most minutely every article of female dress, has mentioned none

Mrs. Ford. A plain kerchief, Sir John: my brows become nothing else; nor that well neither.

Fal. Thou art a traitor⁷ to say so: thou would'ſt make an abſolute courtier; and the firm fixture of thy foot would give an excellent motion to thy gait, in a ſemi-circled farthingale. I ſee what thou wert, if fortune thy foe were not⁸; nature is thy friend⁹:—Come, thou canſt not hide it.

of theſe terms, but ſpeaks of vails depending from the top of the head, and flying behind in looſe folds. The word *volant* was in uſe before the age of Shakſpeare.—Tire *vellet,* which is the reading of the old quarto, may be printed, as Mr. Tollet obſerves, by miſtake, for tire-*velvet.* We know that *velvet hoods* were worn in the age of Shakſpeare. STEEVENS.

Among the preſents ſent by the Queen of Spain to the Queen of England, in April 1605, was a *velvet* cap with gold buttons. Catharine's cap in *the Taming of the Shrew* is likewiſe of velvet. Tire-*volant,* however, I believe, with Mr. Steevens, was the poet's word. " Their heads (ſays Naſhe in 1594) with their *top and top-gallant* lawne baby caps, and ſnow-reſembled ſilver curlings, they make a plain puppet-ſtage of. Their breaſts they embuſke up on hie, and their round roſeate buds they immodeſtly lay forth, to ſhew, at their hands there is fruit to be hoped." *Chriſt's Tears over Jeruſalem,* 4to 1594.
MALONE.

⁶ — *of Venetian admittance.*] i. e. of a faſhion received from Venice. So, in *Weſtward Hoe,* 1606, by Decker and Webſter: " —— now ſhe's in that *Italian head-tire* you ſent her." Dr. Farmer propoſes to read—*of Venetian remittance.* STEEVENS.

In how much requeſt the Venetian tyre formerly was held, appears from Burton's *Anatomy of Melancholy,* 1624: " — let her have the Spaniſh gate, [gait] the *Venetian* tire, Italian complements and endowments." MALONE.

⁷ — *a traitor* —] i. e. to thy own merit. STEEVENS.
The folio reads—thou art a *tyrant,* &c. but the reading of the quarto appears to me far better. MALONE.

⁸ — *fortune thy foe* —] " was the beginning of an old ballad, in which were enumerated all the misfortunes that fell upon mankind, through the caprice of fortune." See note on *the Cuſtom of the Country,* Act i. ſc. i. by Mr. Theobald. REED.

The firſt ſtanza of this popular ballad was as follows:

" Fortune, my foe, why doſt thou frown on me?
" And will my fortune never better be?
" Wilt thou, I ſay, for ever breed my pain,
" And wilt thou not reſtore my joys again?"

In the *Gentleman's Magazine* for Auguſt 1780, p. 371, it is obſerved, that " the tune was the ſame as *Death and the Lady;* and that the lamentations of criminals have been generally ſung to this tune for two hundred years paſt." MALONE.

⁹ — *nature is thy friend:*] *Is,* which is not in the old copy, was introduced by Mr. Pope. MALONE.

Mrs. Ford. Believe me, there's no such thing in me.

Fal. What made me love thee? let that persuade thee, there's something extraordinary in thee. Come, I cannot cog, and say, thou art this and that, like a many of these lisping haw-thorn buds, that come like women in men's apparel, and smell like Bucklers-bury [1] in simple-time; I cannot: but I love thee;[*] none but thee; and thou deservest it.

Mrs. Ford. Do not betray me, Sir; I fear, you love Mistress Page.

Fal. Thou might'st as well say, I love to walk by the Counter-gate; which is as hateful to me as the reek of a lime-kiln.

Mrs. Ford. Well, heaven knows, how I love you; and you shall one day find it.

Fal. Keep in that mind; I'll deserve it.

Mrs. Ford. Nay, I must tell you, so you do; or else I could not be in that mind.

Rob. [*within.*] Mistress Ford, mistress Ford! here's Mistress Page at the door, sweating, and blowing, and looking wildly, and would needs speak with you presently.

Fal. She shall not see me; I will ensconce me behind the arras.

Mrs. Ford. Pray you, do so; she's a very tattling woman.— [FALSTAFF *hides himself.*

Enter Mrs. PAGE, *and* ROBIN.

What's the matter? how now?

Mrs. Page. O, Mistress Ford, what have you done?— You're shamed, you are overthrown, you are undone for ever.

Mrs. Ford. What's the matter, good Mistress Page?

Mrs. Page. O well-a-day, Mistress Ford! having an honest man to your husband, to give him such cause of suspicion!

---

[1] —like *Bucklers-bury*, &c.] *Bucklers-bury*, in the time of Shakspeare, was chiefly inhabited by druggists, who sold all kind of herbs, green as well as dry. STEEVENS.

[*] *I cannot cog, and say thou art this,* &c.] So in *Wily Beguil'd*, 1606:
　"I cannot play the dissembler,
　"And woo my love with courting ambages,
　"Like one whose love hangs on his smooth tongue's end;
　"But in a word I tell the sum of my desires,
　"I love fair Lelia." MALONE.

Mrs. Ford. What cause of suspicion?

Mrs. Page. What cause of suspicion? Out upon you! how am I mistook in you?

Mrs. Ford. Why, alas! what's the matter?

Mrs. Page. Your husband's coming hither, woman, with all the officers in Windsor, to search for a gentleman, that, he says, is here now in the house, by your consent, to take an ill advantage of his absence: You are undone.

Mrs. Ford. Speak louder.[a] [*Aside.*]—'Tis not so, I hope.

Mrs. Page. Pray heaven it be not so, that you have such a man here; but 'tis most certain your husband's coming with half Windsor at his heels, to search for such a one. I come before to tell you: If you know yourself clear, why I am glad of it: but if you have a friend here, convey, convey him out. Be not amazed; call all your senses to you; defend your reputation, or bid farewell to your good life for ever.

Mrs. Ford. What shall I do?—There is a gentleman, my dear friend; and I fear not mine own shame, so much as his peril: I had rather than a thousand pound, he were out of the house.

Mrs. Page. For shame, never stand *you had rather*, and *you had rather;* your husband's here at hand, bethink you of some conveyance: in the house you cannot hide him.— O, how have you deceived me!—Look, here is a basket; if he be of any reasonable stature, he may creep in here; and throw foul linen upon him, as if it were going to bucking: Or, it is whiting-time, send him by your two men to Datchet mead.

Mrs. Ford. He's too big to go in there: What shall I do?

Re-enter FALSTAFF.

Fal. Let me see't, let me see't! O let me see't! I'll in, I'll in;—follow your friend's counsel;—I'll in.

Mrs. Page. What! Sir John Falstaff! Are these your letters, knight?

[a] *Speak louder.*] i. e. that Falstaff who is retired may hear. This passage is only found in the two elder quartos. STEEVENS.

Fal.

Fal. I love thee, and none but thee[3]; help me away: let me creep in here; I'll never——

[*He goes into the basket; they cover him with foul linen.*]

Mrs. Page. Help to cover your master, boy: Call your men, Mistress Ford:—You dissembling knight!

Mrs. Ford. What, John, Robert, John! [*Exit Robin. Re-enter Servants.*] Go take up these clothes here, quickly; Where's the cowl-staff?* look, how you drumble[4]: carry them to the laundress in Datchet mead[5]; quickly, come.

Enter FORD, PAGE, CAIUS, *and Sir* HUGH EVANS.

Ford. Pray you, come near: if I suspect without cause, why then make sport at me, then let me be your jest; I deserve it.—How now? whither bear you this?

Serv. To the laundress, forsooth.

Mrs. Ford. Why, what have you to do whither they bear it? You were best meddle with buck-washing.

Ford. Buck? I would I could wash myself of the buck! Buck, buck, buck? Ay, buck; I warrant you, buck, and of the season too; it shall appear[6]. [*Exeunt Servants, with*

---

[3] —*and none but thee;*] These words, which are characteristic, and spoken to Mrs Page aside, I have restored from the early quarto. He had used the same words before to Mrs. Ford. MALONE.

* The *cowl-staff* is a staff used for carrying a large tub or basket with two handles. In Essex the word *cowl* is yet used for a tub. MALONE.

[4] —*how you drumble;*] The reverend Mr. Lambe, the editor of the ancient metrical history of the *Battle of Flodden*, observes, that —*look, how you drumble,* means—*how confused you are*; and that in the North, *drumbled ale* is *muddy disturbed ale.* STEEVENS.

A *drumble*-drone in the western dialect signifies a *drone*, or *drumble*-bee. Mrs. Page therefore may mean—How lazy and stupid you are! be more alert. MALONE.

To *drumble,* in Devonshire, signifies to mutter in a sullen and inarticulate voice. HENLEY.

[5] —*carry them to the laundress in Datchet mead;*] Mr. Dennis objects, with some degree of reason, to the probability of the circumstance of Falstaff's being carried to Datchet mead, and thrown into the Thames. "It is not likely (he observes) that Falstaff would suffer himself to be carried in the basket as far as Datchet mead, which is half a mile from Windsor, and it is plain that they could not carry him, if he made any resistance." MALONE.

[6] —*it shall appear.*] Ford seems to allude to the cuckold's horns. So afterwards: "—*and so butts himself on the forehead, crying, peer out, peer out.*" *Of the season* is a phrase of the forest. MALONE.

So,

with the basket.] Gentlemen, I have dream'd to-night; I'll tell you my dream. Here, here, here be my keys; ascend my chambers, search, seek, find out: I'll warrant, we'll unkennel the fox: Let me stop this way first: So, now uncape [7].

Page. Good Master Ford, be contented: you wrong yourself too much.

Ford. True, Master Page. Up, gentlemen; you shall see sport anon: follow me, gentlemen. [*Exit.*

Evans. This is a fery fantastical humours, and jealousies.

Caius. By gar, 'tis no de fashion of France: it is not jealous in France.

Page. Nay, follow him, gentlemen; see the issue of his search. [*Exeunt* EVANS, PAGE, *and* CAIUS.

Mrs. Page. Is there not a double excellency in this?

Mrs. Ford. I know not which pleases me better, that my husband is deceived, or Sir John.

Mrs. Page. What a taking was he in, when your husband ask'd who was in the basket!

Mrs. Ford. I am half afraid, he will have need of washing; so throwing him into the water will do him a benefit.

Mrs. Page. Hang him, dishonest rascal! I would, all of the same strain were in the same distress.

Mrs. Ford. I think, my husband hath some special suspicion of Falstaff's being here; for I never saw him so gross in his jealousy till now.

Mrs. Page. I will lay a plot to try that: And we will yet have more tricks with Falstaff: his dissolute disease will scarce obey this medicine.

Mrs. Ford. Shall we send that foolish carrion [8], Mis-

So, in a letter written by Queen Catharine in 1526. Howard's Collection, Vol. I. p. 212: "We will and command you, that ye delyver, or cause to be delyvered unto our trusty and well-beloved John Creasse — one buck *of season*." "The season of the bynd or doe (says Manwood) doth begin at Holyrood-day, and lasteth till Candelmas." *Forest Laws*, 1598. MALONE.

[7] *So, now uncape.*] The allusion is to the stopping every hole at which a fox could enter, before they *uncape* or turn him out of the bag in which he was brought. I suppose every one has heard of a *bag-fox*.
STEEVENS.

[8] — *that* foolish *carrion*,] The old copy has—*foolishion* carrion. The correction was made by the editor of the second folio. MALONE.

tress Quickly, to him, and excuse his throwing into the water; and give him another hope, to betray him to another punishment?

Mrs. Page. We'll do it; let him be sent for to-morrow eight o'clock, to have amends.

Re-enter FORD, PAGE, CAIUS, *and Sir* HUGH EVANS.

Ford. I cannot find him: may be the knave bragg'd of that he could not compass.

Mrs. Page. Heard you that?

Mrs. Ford. Ay, ay, peace [9]:—You use me well, Master Ford, do you?

Ford. Ay, I do so.

Mrs. Ford. Heaven make you better than your thoughts!

Ford. Amen.

Mrs. Page. You do yourself mighty wrong, Master Ford.

Ford. Ay, ay; I must bear it.

Evans. If there be any pody in the house, and in the chambers, and in the coffers, and in the presses, heaven forgive my sins at the day of judgment!

Caius. By gar, nor I too; dere is no bodies.

Page. Fye, fye, Master Ford! are you not ashamed? What spirit, what devil, suggests this imagination? I would not have your distemper in this kind, for the wealth of Windsor Castle.

Ford. 'Tis my fault, Master Page: I suffer for it.

Evans. You suffer for a pad conscience: your wife is as honest a 'omans, as I will desires among five thousand, and five hundred too.

Caius. By gar, I see 'tis an honest woman.

Ford. Well;—I promised you a dinner: Come, come, walk in the park: I pray you, pardon me; I will hereafter make known to you, why I have done this.—Come, wife;—come, Mistress Page; I pray you pardon me; pray heartily, pardon me.

Page. Let's go in, gentlemen; but, trust me, we'll mock him. I do invite you to-morrow morning to my house to

---

[9] *Ay, ay, peace:*] These words were recovered from the early quarto by Mr. Theobald. But in his and the other modern editions, *I,* the old spelling of the affirmative particle, has inadvertently been retained.
MALONE.

breakfast;

breakfast; after, we'll a birding together; I have a fine hawk for the bush: Shall it be so?

Ford. Any thing.

Evans. If there is one, I shall make two in the company.

Caius. If there be one or two, I shall make-a de turd.

Evans. In your teeth [1]: for shame.

Ford. Pray you go, Master Page.

Evans. I pray you now, remembrance to-morrow on the lousy knave, mine host.

Caius. Dat is good; by gar, vit all my heart.

Evans. A lousy knave; to have his gibes, and his mockeries. [*Exeunt.*

SCENE IV.

A Room in Page's House.

Enter FENTON *and Mistress* ANNE PAGE.

Fent. I see, I cannot get thy father's love;
Therefore, no more turn me to him, sweet Nan.

Anne. Alas! how then?

Fent. Why, thou must be thyself.
He doth object, I am too great of birth;
And that, my state being gall'd with my expence,
I seek to heal it only by his wealth:
Besides these, other bars he lays before me,—
My riots past, my wild societies;
And tells me, 'tis a thing impossible
I should love thee, but as a property.

Anne. May be, he tells you true.

Fent. No, heaven so speed me in my time to come!
Albeit, I will confess, thy father's wealth [2]

---

[1] *In your teeth:*] This dirty restoration was made by Mr. Theobald. Evans's application of the doctor's words is not in the folio. STEEVENS.

[2] — *father's wealth*] Some light may be given to those who shall endeavour to calculate the increase of English wealth, by observing, that Latymer, in the time of Edward VI. mentions it as a proof of his father's prosperity, *That though but a yeoman, he gave his daughters five pounds each for her portion.* At the latter end of Elizabeth, seven hundred pounds were such a temptation to courtship, as made all other motives suspected. Congreve makes twelve thousand pounds more than a counterbalance to the affectation of Belinda. No poet would now fly his favourite character at less than fifty thousand. JOHNSON.

Was.

Was the firſt motive that I woo'd thee, Anne:
Yet, wooing thee, I found thee of more value
Than ſtamps in gold, or ſums in ſealed bags;
And 'tis the very riches of thyſelf
That now I aim at.

Anne. Gentle Maſter Fenton,
Yet ſeek my father's love; ſtill ſeek it, Sir;
If opportunity and humbleſt ſuit
Cannot attain it, why then—Hark you hither.

[*They converſe apart.*

Enter SHALLOW, SLENDER, *and Mrs.* QUICKLY.

Shal. Break their talk, Miſtreſs Quickly; my kinſman
ſhall ſpeak for himſelf.

Slen. I'll make a ſhaft or a bolt on't [3]: 'ſlid, 'tis but
venturing.

Shal. Be not diſmay'd.

Slen. No, ſhe ſhall not diſmay me: I care not for that—
but that I am afeard.

Quick. Hark ye; Maſter Slender would ſpeak a word
with you.

Anne. I come to him.—This is my father's choice.
O, what a world of vile ill-favour'd faults
Looks handſome in three hundred pounds a year! [*Aſide.*

Quick. And how does good Maſter Fenton? Pray you, a
word with you.

Shal. She's coming; to her, coz. O boy, thou hadſt a
father!

Slen. I had a father, Miſtreſs Anne;—my uncle can
tell you good jeſts of him:—Pray you, uncle, tell Miſtreſs
Anne the jeſt, how my father ſtole two geeſe out of a pen,
good uncle.

Shal. Miſtreſs Anne, my couſin loves you.

Slen. Ay, that I do; as well as I love any woman in
Gloceſterſhire.

Shal. He will maintain you like a gentlewoman.

Slen. Ay, that I will, come cut and long-tail [4], under the
degree of a 'ſquire.

Shal.

---

[3] *I'll make a ſhift or a bolt on't:*] This is enumerated by Ray, amongſt
others, in his Collection of proverbial phraſes. REED.
  The *ſhaft* was ſuch an arrow as ſkilful archers employed. The *bolt*
in this proverb means, I think, the *fool's* bolt. MALONE.

[4] —*come*

Shal. He will make you a hundred and fifty pounds jointure.

Anne. Good Master Shallow, let him woo for himself.

Shal. Marry, I thank you for it; I thank you for that good comfort. She calls you, coz: I'll leave you.

Anne. Now, Master Slender.

Slen. Now, good Mistress Anne.

Anne. What is your will?

Slen. My will? od's heartlings, that's a pretty jest, indeed! I ne'er made my will yet, I thank heaven; I am not such a sickly creature, I give heaven praise.

Anne. I mean, master Slender, what would you with me?

Slen. Truly, for mine own part, I would little or nothing with you: Your father, and my uncle, have made motions: if it be my luck, so; if not, happy man be his dole [5]! They can tell you how things go, better than I can: You may ask your father; here he comes.

Enter PAGE *and Mistress* PAGE.

Page. Now, Master Slender:—Love him, daughter Anne.—

Why, how now! what does Master Fenton here?
You wrong me, Sir, thus still to haunt my house.
I told you, Sir, my daughter is dispos'd of.

Fent. Nay, Master Page, be not impatient.

Mrs. Page. Good Master Fenton, come not to my child.

Page. She is no match for you.

Fent. Sir, will you hear me?

Page. No, good Master Fenton.

---

4 — *come cut and long tail,*—] i. e. let who will come as a suitor, of *whatever degree* he may be, under the degree of a squire. The phrase of *cut and long tail* had its origin from the practice of sometimes cutting the tails of dogs and horses, and leaving others in their natural state; so that (as Mr. Reed has observed) under the description of *cut and long tail* the whole species of those animals is included. *Cut*, in consequence of this practice, was in our author's time a common name of a horse, as both *cut* and *curtail* were designations of a dog, of whose tail a part had been cut off. MALONE.

So, in *The First Part of the Eighth Liberal Science, &c. by Ulpian Fulwel,* 1576:—" yea, even their very *dogs*, Rug, Rig, and Rible, yea, *cut and long-tails,* they shall be welcome." STEEVENS.

5 — *happy man be his dole!*] A proverbial expression. See Ray's Collection, p. 116. edit. 1737. STEEVENS.

Come,

Come, Master Shallow; come, son Slender; in:—
Knowing my mind, you wrong me, Master Fenton.

[*Exeunt* PAGE, SHALLOW, *and* SLENDER.

Quick. Speak to Mistress Page.

Fent. Good Mistress Page, for that I love your daughter
In such a righteous fashion as I do,
Perforce, against all checks, rebukes, and manners,
I must advance the colours of my love,
And not retire: Let me have your good will.

Anne. Good mother, do not marry me to yond' fool.

Mrs. Page. I mean it not; I seek you a better husband.

Quick. That's my master, Master Doctor.

Anne. Alas, I had rather be set quick i' the earth,
And bowl'd to death with turnips [6].

Mrs. Page. Come, trouble not yourself: Good Master Fenton,
I will not be your friend, nor enemy:
My daughter will I question how she loves you,
And as I find her, so am I affected;
'Till then, farewell, Sir:—She must needs go in;
Her father will be angry.

Fent. Farewell, gentle mistress; farewell, Nan [7].

[*Exeunt Mrs.* PAGE *and* ANNE.

Quick. This is my doing now;—Nay, said I, will you cast away your child on a fool, and a physician [8]? Look on, Master Fenton:—this is my doing.

Fent.

---

[6] *Anne. Alas, I had rather be set quick i' the earth, And bowl'd to death with turnips.*] This is a common proverb in the southern counties. I find almost the same expression in Ben Jonson's *Bartholomew Fair*: "Would I had been set in the ground, all but the head of me, and had my brains bowl'd at." COLLINS.

[7] *Farewell, gentle mistress; farewell, Nan.*] *Mistress* is here used as a trisyllable. MALONE.

[8] —*fool, and a physician?*] I should read *fool* or a *physician*, meaning Slender and Caius. JOHNSON.

Sir Tho. Hanmer reads according to Dr. Johnson's conjecture. This may be right.—Or my dame Quickly may allude to the proverb, a man of *forty* is either a *fool* or a *physician*; but she asserts her master to be both. FARMER.

I believe the old copy is right, and that Mrs Quickly means to insinuate that she had addressed *at the same time* both Mr. and Mrs. Page on the subject of their daughter's marriage, one of whom favoured Slender, and the other Caius. "—on a fool *or* a physician," would be more accurate, but not so sufficiently suitable to dame Quickly, *refer re singula singulis*. Thus: " You two are going to throw away your
daughter

Fent. I thank thee; and I pray thee, once to-night [9] Give my sweet Nan this ring: There's for thy pains. [*Exit.*

Quick. Now heaven send thee good fortune! A kind heart he hath: a woman would run through fire and water for such a kind heart. But yet, I would my master had Mistress Anne; or I would Master Slender had her; or, in sooth, I would Master Fenton had her: I will do what I can for them all three; for so I have promised, and I'll be as good as my word; but speciously [1] for Master Fenton. Well, I must of another errand to Sir John Falstaff from my two mistresses; What a beast am I to slack it? [*Exit.*

SCENE V.

A Room in the Garter Inn.

Enter FALSTAFF *and* BARDOLPH.

Fal. Bardolph, I say—

Bard. Here, Sir.

Fal. Go fetch me a quart of sack; put a toast in't. [*Exit* BARD.] Have I lived to be carried in a basket, like a barrow of butcher's offal; and to be thrown into the Thames? Well; if I be served such another trick, I'll have my brains ta'en out, and butter'd, and give them to a dog for a new year's gift. The rogues slighted me into the river with as little remorse as they would have drown'd a bitch's blind puppies [2], fifteen i' the litter: and you may know by

daughter on a fool and a physician; you, Sir, on the former, and you, Madam, on the latter." MALONE.

Mr. Dennis, of irascible memory, who altered this play, and brought it on the stage, in the year 1702, under the title of *The Comical Gallant*, (when, thanks to the alterer, it was fairly damn'd,) has introduced the proverb at which Mrs. Quickly's allusion appears to be pointed.
STEEVENS.

[9] *—once to night—*] i. e. *sometime* to-night. So, in a letter from the sixth Earl of Northumberland; (quoted in the notes on the Household book of the fifth earl of that name:) " *—notwithstanding I trust to be able once* to set up a chapell of myne owne." STEEVENS.

—speciously—] She means to say *specially*. STEEVENS.

[2] *—a bitch's blind puppies,*] The old copy reads—a *bind bitch's* puppies. The emendation was made by Mr. Theobald. MALONE.

The transposition may be justified from the following passage in the *Two Gentlemen of Verona*: " —one that I saved from drowning, when three or four of his *blind* brothers and sisters went to it." STEEVENS.

my

my size, that I have a kind of alacrity in sinking; if the bottom were as deep as hell, I should down. I had been drown'd, but that the shore was shelvy and shallow; a death that I abhor; for the water swells a man; and what a thing should I have been, when I had been swell'd! I should have been a mountain of mummy.

Re-enter BARDOLPH, *with the wine.*

Bar. Here's Mistress Quickly, Sir, to speak with you.

Fal. Come, let me pour in some sack to the Thames water; for my belly's as cold, as if I had swallow'd snow-balls for pills to cool the reins. Call her in.

Bard. Come in, woman.

Enter Mrs. QUICKLY.

Quick. By your leave; I cry you mercy: Give your worship good morrow.

Fal. Take away these chalices: Go brew me a pottle of sack finely.

Bard. With eggs, Sir?

Fal. Simple of itself; I'll no pullet-sperm in my brewage. [*Exit* BARD.] How now?

Quick. Marry, Sir, I come to your worship from Mistress Ford.

Fal. Mistress Ford! I have had ford enough: I was thrown into the ford; I have my belly full of ford.

Quick. Alas the day! good heart, that was not her fault: she does so take on with her men; they mistook their erection.

Fal. So did I mine, to build upon a foolish woman's promise.

Quick. Well, she laments, Sir, for it, that it would yern your heart to see it. Her husband goes this morning a birding; she desires you once more to come to her between eight and nine: I must carry her word quickly: she'll make you amends, I warrant you.

Fal. Well, I will visit her: Tell her so; and bid her think, what a man is: let her consider his frailty, and then judge of my merit.

Quick. I will tell her.

Fal. Do so. Between nine and ten, say'st thou?

Quick. Eight and nine, Sir.

Fal. Well, be gone: I will not miss her.

Quick.

Quick. Peace be with you, Sir! [*Exit.*
Fal. I marvel, I hear not of Master Brook; he sent me word to stay within: I like his money well. O, here he comes.

Enter FORD.

Ford. Bless you, Sir!
Fal. Now, Master Brook? you come to know what hath pass'd between me and Ford's wife?
Ford. That, indeed, Sir John, is my business.
Fal. Master Brook, I will not lie to you; I was at her house the hour she appointed me.
Ford. And how sped you, Sir *?
Fal. Very ill-favour'dly, Master Brook.
Ford. How, Sir? Did she change her determination?
Fal. No, Master Brook: but the peaking cornuto her husband, Master Brook, dwelling in a continual 'larum of jealousy, comes me in the instant of our encounter, after we had embraced, kiss'd, protested, and, as it were, spoke the prologue of our comedy; and at his heels a rabble of his companions, thither provoked and instigated by his distemper, and forsooth, to search his house for his wife's love.
Ford. What, while you were there?
Fal. While I was there.
Ford. And did he search for you, and could not find you?
Fal. You shall hear. As good luck would have it, comes in one Mistress Page; gives intelligence of Ford's approach; and, by her invention, and Ford's wife's distraction, they convey'd me into a buck-basket.
Ford. A buck-basket!
Fal. By the Lord, a buck-basket: ramm'd me in with foul shirts and smocks, socks, foul stockings, greasy napkins; that, Master Brook, there was the rankest compound of villainous smell, that ever offended nostril.
Ford. And how long lay you there?
Fal. Nay, you shall hear, Master Brook, what I have suffer'd to bring this woman to evil for your good. Being thus cramm'd in the basket, a couple of Ford's knaves, his hinds, were call'd forth by their mistress, to carry me in the name of foul cloaths to Datchet lane: they took me on their

* — how *sped you, Sir?*] The word *how* I have restored from the old quarto. MALONE.

shoulders; met the jealous knave their master in the door; who ask'd them once or twice, what they had in their basket *: I quaked for fear, lest the lunatic knave would have search'd it; but fate, ordaining he should be a cuckold, held his hand. Well; on went he for a search, and away went I for foul cloaths. But mark the sequel, Master Brook: I suffer'd the pangs of three several deaths³: first, an intolerable fright, to be detected with⁴ a jealous rotten bell-wether: next, to be compass'd, like a good bilbo⁵, in the circumference of a peck †, hilt to point, heel to head: and then, to be stopp'd in, like a strong distillation, with stinking cloaths that fretted in their own grease: think of that—a man of my kidney⁶,—think of that; that am as subject to heat, as butter; a man of continual dissolution and thaw; it was a miracle, to 'scape suffocation. And in the height of this bath, when I was more than half stew'd in grease, like a Dutch dish, to be thrown into the Thames, and cool'd, glowing hot, in that surge, like a horse-shoe; think of that —hissing hot—think of that, Master Brook.

Ford. In good sadness, Sir, I am sorry that for my sake you have suffer'd all this. My suit then is desperate; you'll undertake her no more?

Fal. Master Brook, I will be thrown into Ætna, as I have been into Thames, ere I will leave her thus. Her husband is this morning gone a birding: I have received from

---

* — *what they had in their basket:*] So, in p. 256: " What a taking was he in, when your husband ask'd who was in the basket!" But Ford had asked no such question. See p. 257. Our author seems seldom to have revised his plays. MALONE.

³ — *several deaths:*] Thus the folio and the most correct of the quartos. The first quarto reads—*egregious* deaths. STEEVENS.

⁴ — *detected* with—] Thus the old copies. *With* was sometimes used for *of*. So, a little after:

" I rather will suspect the sun *with* cold "

Detected *of* a jealous, &c. would have been the common grammar of the times. The modern editors read *by*. STEEVENS.

⁵ — *bilbo,*] A *bilbo* is a Spanish blade, of which the excellence is flexibleness and elasticity. JOHNSON.

—*bilbo,* from *Bilboa,* a city of Biscay, where the best blades are made. STEEVENS.

† — *of a peck,*] Thus the folio. The old quarto reads—*of a pack;* and perhaps rightly. Pedlar's packs are sometimes of such a size as to admit of Falstaff's description; but who but a Lilliputian could be " compassed in a *peck?*" MALONE.

⁶ — *kidney;*] Kidney in this phrase now signifies *kind* or *qualities,* but Falstaff means, *a man whose kidnies are as fat as mine.* JOHNSON.

her

her another embassy of meeting; 'twixt eight and nine is the hour, Master Brook.

Ford. 'Tis past eight already, Sir.

Fal. Is it? I will then address me [7] to my appointment. Come to me at your convenient leisure, and you shall know how I speed; and the conclusion shall be crown'd with your enjoying her: Adieu. You shall have her, Master Brook; Master Brook, you shall cuckold Ford. [*Exit.*

Ford. Humph! ha! is this a vision? is this a dream? do I sleep? Master Ford, awake; awake, Master Ford; there's a hole made in your best coat, Master Ford. This 'tis to be married! this 'tis to have linen, and buck-baskets! —Well, I will proclaim myself what I am: I will now take the lecher; he is at my house: he cannot 'scape me; 'tis impossible he should; he cannot creep into a half-penny purse, nor into a pepper-box: but, lest the devil that guides him should aid him, I will search impossible places. Though what I am I cannot avoid, yet to be what I would not, shall not make me tame: if I have horns to make one mad, let the proverb go with me, I'll be horn-mad [8]. [*Exit.*

ACT IV. SCENE I.

The Street.

Enter *Mrs.* PAGE, *Mrs.* QUICKLY, *and* WILLIAM.

Mrs. Page. Is he at Master Ford's already, think'st thou?

Quick. Sure, he is by this; or will be presently: but truly,

---

[7] — *address me—*] i. e. make myself ready. So, in *K. Henry V:* "To-morrow for our march we are *address'd*." STEEVENS.

[8] — *I'll be horn-mad.*] There is no image which our author appears so fond of, as that of cuckolds' horns. Scarcely a light character is introduced that does not endeavour to produce merriment by some allusion to horned husbands. As he wrote his plays for the stage rather than the press, he perhaps reviewed them seldom, and did not observe this repetition; or finding the jest, however frequent, still successful, did not think correction necessary. JOHNSON.

truly, he is very courageous mad, about his throwing into the water. Mistress Ford desires you to come suddenly.

Mrs. Page. I'll be with her by and by; I'll but bring my young man here to school: Look, where his master comes; 'tis a playing-day, I see.

Enter Sir HUGH EVANS.

How now, Sir Hugh? no school to-day?

Evans. No; Master Slender is let the boys leave to play.

Quick. Blessing of his heart!

Mrs. Page. Sir Hugh, my husband says, my son profits nothing in the world at his book; I pray you, ask him some questions in his accidence.

Evans. Come hither, William; hold up your head; come.

Mrs. Page. Come on, Sirrah; hold up your head; answer your master, be not afraid.

Evans. William, how many numbers is in nouns?

Will. Two.

Quick. Truly I thought there had been one number more; because they say, od's nouns.

Evans. Peace your tatlings. What is *fair*, William?

Will. Pulcher.

Quick. Poulcats! there are fairer things than poulcats, sure.

Evans. You are a very simplicity 'oman; I pray you, peace. What is *Lapis*, William?

Will. A stone.

Evans. And what is a stone, William?

Will. A pebble.

Evans. No, it is *Lapis*; I pray you, remember in your prain.

Will. Lapis.

Evans. That is a good William. What is he, William, that does lend articles?

Will. Articles are borrow'd of the pronoun; and be thus declined, *Singulariter, nominativo, hic, hæc, hoc.*

---

[1] This is a very trifling scene, of no use to the plot, and I shou'd think of no great delight to the audience; but Shakspeare best knew what would please. JOHNSON.

We may suppose this scene to have been a very entertaining one to the audience for which it was written. Many of the old plays exhibit pedants instructing their scholars. STEEVENS.

Evans.

Evans. .*Nominative*, big, bag, hog;—pray you, mark: *genitivo*, *hujus*: Well, what is your *accusative case*?

Will. *Accusativo*, hinc.

Evans. I pray you, have your remembrance, child; *Accusativo*, hing, hang, hog.

Quick. Hang hog is Latin for bacon, I warrant you.

Evans. Leave your prabbles, 'oman. What is the focative case, William?

Will. O—*vocativo*, O.

Evans. Remember, William; focative is, *caret*.

Quick. And that's a good root.

Evans. 'Oman, forbear.

Mrs. Page. Peace.

Evans. What is your *genitive case plural*, William?

Will. *Genitive case?*

Evans. Ay.

Will. Genitive,—horum, harum, horum [2].

Quick. 'Vengeance of *Jenny's* case? fie on her!—never name her, child, if she be a whore.

Evans. For shame, 'oman.

Quick. You do ill to teach the child such words: he teaches him to hick and to hack [3], which they'll do fast enough of themselves; and to call, horum:—fie upon you!

Evans. 'Oman, art thou lunatics? hast thou no understandings for thy cases, and the numbers of the genders? Thou art a foolish Christian creatures, as I would desires.

Mrs. Page. Pr'ythee, hold thy peace.

Evans. Shew me now, William, some declensions of your pronouns.

Will. Forsooth, I have forgot.

Evans. It is *ki*, *kæ*, *cod*; if you forget your *kies*, your *kæs* [4], and your *cods*, you must be preeches [5]. Go your ways, and play, go.

Mrs.

---

[2] *—borum, barum, borum.*] Taylor, the water-poet, has borrowed this jest, such as it is, in his character of a strumpet:

"And come to *borum, barum, whorum*, then
"She proves a great proficient among men." STEEVENS.

[3] *—to hick and to hack,*] Sir William Blackstone thought that this, "in Dame Quickly's language, signifies to *stammer* or *hesitate*, as boys do in saying their lessons;" but Mr. Steevens, with more probability, supposes it signifies, in her language—*to do mischief.* MALONE.

[4] *—your kies, your kæs,* &c.] All this ribaldry is likewise found in Taylor, the water-poet. See fol. edit. p. 106. STEEVENS.

N 3   [5] *you*

Mrs. Page. He is a better scholar, than I thought he was.

Evans. He is a good sprag [6] memory. Farewell, Mistress Page.

Mrs. Page. Adieu, good Sir Hugh. Get you home, boy.—Come, we stay too long. [*Exeunt.*

SCENE II.

A Room in FORD'S *House.*

Enter FALSTAFF *and Mrs.* FORD.

Fal. Mistress Ford, your sorrow hath eaten up my sufferance: I see, you are obsequious in your love, and I profess requital to a hair's breadth; not only, Mistress Ford, in the simple office of love, but in all the accoutrement, complement, and ceremony of it. But are you sure of your husband now?

Mrs. Ford. He's a birding, sweet Sir John.

Mrs. Page. [*within.*] What hoa, gossip Ford! what hoa!

Mrs. Ford. Step into the chamber, Sir John. [*Exit* FALSTAFF.

Enter Mistress PAGE.

Mrs. Page. How now, sweetheart? who's at home besides yourself?

Mrs. Ford. Why, none but mine own people.

Mrs. Page. Indeed?

Mrs. Ford. No, certainly:—Speak louder. [*Aside.*

Mrs. Page. Truly, I am so glad you have nobody here.

Mrs. Ford. Why?

Mrs. Page. Why, woman, your husband is in his old lunes [7] again: he so takes on [8] yonder with my husband; so

---

[5] *you must be preeches.*] Sir Hugh means to say—you must be breech'd: i. e. flogg'd. To *breech* is to *fog*. So, in the *Taming of the Shrew*:

"I am no *breeching* scholar in the schools." STEEVENS.

[6] —*sprag*—] I am told that this word is still used by the common people in the neighbourhood of Bath, where it signifies *ready, alert, sprightly*, and is pronounced as if it was written—*sprack*. STEEVENS.

A *sprack* lad or wench, says Ray, is *apt to learn, ingenious.* REED.

[7] —*lunes*—] i. e. lunacy, frenzy. See a note on the *Winter's Tale,* Act ii. sc. ii. The folio reads *lines,* instead of *lunes.* The elder quartos—his old *vaine* again. STEEVENS.

The correction was made by Mr. Theobald. MALONE.

rails

rails against all married mankind; so curses all Eve's daughters, of what complexion soever; and so buffets himself on the forehead, crying, *Peer-out, peer-out* [9]! that any madness, I ever yet beheld, seem'd but tameness, civility, and patience, to this his distemper he is in now: I am glad the fat knight is not here.

Mrs. Ford. Why, does he talk of him?

Mrs. Page. Of none but him; and swears, he was carried out, the last time he search'd for him, in a basket: protests to my husband, he is now here; and hath drawn him and the rest of their company from their sport, to make another experiment of his suspicion: but I am glad the knight is not here; now he shall see his own foolery.

Mrs. Ford. How near is he, Mistress Page?

Mrs. Page. Hard by; at street end; he will be here anon.

Mrs. Ford. I am undone!—the knight is here.

Mrs. Page. Why, then you are utterly shamed, and he's but a dead man. What a woman are you?—Away with him, away with him; better shame than murther.

Mrs. Ford. Which way should he go? how should I bestow him? Shall I put him into the basket again?

Enter FALSTAFF.

Fal. No, I'll come no more i' the basket: May I not go out, ere he come?

Mrs. Page. Alas, three of Master Ford's brothers watch the door with pistols, that none shall issue out; otherwise you might slip away ere he came. But what make you here [1]?

Fal. What shall I do?—I'll creep up into the chimney.

---

[8] *—he so takes on—*] *To take on,* which is now used for *to grieve,* seems to be used by our author for *to rage.* JOHNSON.

It is used by Nash in *Pierce Pennilesi his Supplication to the Devil,* 1592, in the same sense: " Some will *take on* like a madman, if they see a pig come to table." MALONE.

[9] *—peer-out,*] That is, *appear horns.* Shakspeare is at his old lunes. JOHNSON.

Shakspeare here refers to the practice of children, when they call on a snail to push forth his horns:

Peer out, peer out, peer out of your hole,
" Or else I'll beat you black as a coal. HENLEY.

[1] *But what make you here?*] i. e. What do you here? MALONE.

Mrs. Ford. There they always use to discharge their birding-pieces: Creep into the kiln-hole *.

Fal. Where is it?

Mrs. Ford. He will seek there on my word. Neither press, coffer, chest, trunk, well, vault, but he hath an abstract² for the remembrance of such places, and goes to them by his note: There is no hiding you in the house.

Fal. I'll go out then.

Mrs. Page. If you go † out in your own semblance, you die, Sir John. Unless you go out disguis'd—

Mrs. Ford. How might we disguise him?

Mrs. Page. Alas the day, I know not. There is no woman's gown big enough for him; otherwise, he might put on a hat, a muffler, and a kerchief, and so escape.

Fal. Good hearts, devise something: any extremity, rather than a mischief.

Mrs. Ford. My maid's aunt, the fat woman of Brentford, has a gown above.

Mrs. Page. On my word, it will serve him; she's as big as he is; and there's her thrum'd hat, and her muffler too³: Run up, Sir John.

Mrs. Ford. Go, go, sweet Sir John; Mistress Page, and I, will look some linen for your head.

Mrs. Page. Quick, quick; we'll come dress you straight: put on the gown the while. [*Exit* FALSTAFF.

Mrs. Ford. I would, my husband would meet him in this shape: he cannot abide the old woman of Brentford; he

---

* *Creep into the kiln-hole.*] I suspect, these words belong to Mrs. Page. See Mrs. Ford's next speech. That, however, may be a second thought; a correction of her former proposal: but the other supposition is more probable. MALONE.

² — *an abstract*] i. e. a short note or description. So, in *Hamlet*: —" the abstract and brief chronicle of the times." MALONE.

† *Mrs. Page. If you go, &c.*] In the first folio, by the mistake of the compositor, the name of Mrs. Ford is prefixed to this speech and the next. For the correction now made the present editor is answerable. The editor of the second folio put the two speeches together, and gave them both to Mrs. Ford. The threat of danger from *without* ascertains the first to belong to Mrs. Page. See her speech on Falstaff's re-entrance. MALONE.

³ — *her thrumb'd hat and her muffler too;*] The *thrum* is the end of a weaver's warp, and we may suppose, was used for the purpose of making coarse hats. A *muffler* was some part of dress that covered the face. STEEVENS.

A *thrumb'd* hat was made of very coarse woollen cloth. See Minsheu's Dict. 1617, in v. *Thrumb'd is, formed of thrums.* MALONE.

swears,

swears, she's a witch; forbade her my house, and hath threaten'd to beat her.

Mrs. Page. Heaven guide him to thy husband's cudgel; and the devil guide his cudgel afterwards!

Mrs. Ford. But is my husband coming?

Mrs. Page. Ay, in good sadness, is he; and talks of the basket too, howsoever he hath had intelligence.

Mrs. Ford. We'll try that; for I'll appoint my men to carry the basket again, to meet him at the door with it, as they did last time.

Mrs. Page. Nay, but he'll be here presently: let's go dress him like the witch of Brentford.

Mrs. Ford. I'll first direct my men, what they shall do with the basket. Go up, I'll bring linen for him straight. [*Exit.*

Mrs. Page. Hang him, dishonest varlet! we cannot misuse him enough [4].
We'll leave a proof, by that which we will do,
Wives may be merry, and yet honest too:
We do not act, that often jest and laugh;
'Tis old but true, *Still swine eat all the draugh* [5]. [*Exit.*

Re-enter Mrs. FORD, *with two Servants.*

Mrs. Ford. Go, Sirs, take the basket again on your shoulders; your master is hard at door; if he bid you set it down, obey him: quickly, dispatch. [*Exit.*

1st. Serv. Come, come, take it up.

2d. Serv. Pray heaven, it be not full of knight [6] again.

1st. Serv. I hope not; I had as lief bear so much lead.

Enter FORD, PAGE, SHALLOW, CAIUS, *and Sir* HUGH EVANS.

Ford. Ay, but if it prove true, Master Page, have you any way then to unfool me again?—Set down the basket, villain:—Somebody call my wife:—You youth in a basket,

---

[4] — *misuse him enough.*] *Him* which was accidentally omitted in the first folio, was inserted by the editor of the second. MALONE.

[5] *Still swine,* &c.] This is a proverbial sentence. See Ray's Collection. MALONE.

[6] — *of knight*] Thus the only authentic copy, the first folio. The editor of the second reads—of *the* knight; I think, unnecessarily. We have just had—" hard *at door.*" MALONE.

come out here?¹!—O, you panderly rascals! there's a knot, a gang⁸, a pack, a conspiracy, against me: Now shall the devil be shamed. What! wife, I say! come, come forth; behold what honest clothes you send forth to bleaching.

Page. Why, this passes⁹! Master Ford, you are not to go loose any longer; you must be pinion'd.

Evans. Why, this is lunatics! this is mad as a mad dog!

Shal. Indeed, Master Ford, this is not well; indeed.

Enter Mrs. FORD.

Ford. So say I too, Sir.—Come hither, Mistress Ford; Mistress Ford, the honest woman, the modest wife, the virtuous creature, that hath the jealous fool to her husband!—I suspect without cause, mistress, do I?

Mrs. Ford. Heaven be my witness, you do, if you suspect me in any dishonesty.

Ford. Well said, brazen-face; hold it out.—Come forth, Sirrah.   [*Pulls the clothes out of the basket.*

Page. This passes.

Mrs. Ford. Are you not ashamed? let the clothes alone.

Ford. I shall find you anon.

Evans. 'Tis unreasonable! Will you take up your wife's clothes? Come away.

Ford. Empty the basket, I say.

Mrs. Ford. Why, man, why—

Ford. Master Page, as I am a man, there was one convey'd out of my house yesterday in this basket; Why may not he be there again? In my house I am sure he is: my in-

---

⁷ You *youth in a basket* come out here!] This reading I have adopted from the early quarto. The folio has only—" Youth in a basket!"
                                         MALONE.

—⁸ *a gang,*] Old Copy—*gin.* Corrected by Mr. Rowe. *Ging*, however, as I have restored the text, was the word intended by the poet, and was anciently used for *gang.* So in Ben Jonson's *New Inn*, 1631:

"The secret is, I would not willingly
"See or be seen to any of this *ging*,
"Especially the lady."

Again, in *The Alchemist*, 1610:

"— Sure he has got
"Some bawdy picture to call all this *ging*;
"The friar and the boy, or the near motion," &c.
                                         MALONE.

⁹ —*this passes!*] See p. 225, not. 4. MALONE.

telligence

telligence is true; my jealousy is reasonable: Pluck me out all the linen.

Mrs. Ford. If you find a man there, he shall die a flea's death.

Page. Here's no man.

Shal. By my fidelity, this is not well, Master Ford; this wrongs you [1].

Evans. Master Ford, you must pray, and not follow the imaginations of your own heart: this is jealousies.

Ford. Well, he's not here I seek for.

Page. No, nor no where else but in your brain.

Ford. Help to search my house this one time: if I find not what I seek, shew no colour for my extremity, let me for ever be your table-sport; let them say of me, As jealous as Ford, that search'd a hollow walnut for his wife's leman [2]. Satisfy me once more; once more search with me.

Mrs. Ford. What hoa, Mistress Page! come you, and the old woman down; my husband will come into the chamber.

Ford. Old woman! What old woman's that?

Mrs. Ford. Why, it is my maid's aunt of Brentford.

Ford. A witch, a quean, an old cozening quean! Have I not forbid her my house? She comes of errands, does she? We are simple men; we do not know what's brought to pass under the profession of fortune-telling. She works by charms [3], by spells, by the figure, and such daubery [4] as this is; beyond

---

[1] —*this wrongs you.*] This is below your character, unworthy of your understanding, injurious to your honour. So, in *The Taming of the Shrew*, Bianca, being ill treated by her rugged sister, says,
 " You *wrong* me much, indeed you *wrong* yourself."
JOHNSON.

[2] — his wife's *leman*] *Leman*, i. e. *lover*, is derived from *leef*, Dutch, *beloved*, and *man*. STEEVENS.

[3] *She works by charms, &c.*] Concerning some *old woman of Brentford*, there are several ballads. *Julian of Brentford's last Will and Testament* was entered on the Stationers' books in March, 1599. STEEVENS.

This without doubt was the person here alluded to; for in the early quarto Mrs. Ford says—" my maid's aunt, *Gillian* of *Brentford*, hath a gown above." So also, in *Westward Hoe*, a com. 1607: " I doubt that old hag, *Gillian of Brainford*, has bewitch'd me." MALONE.

[4] — such *daubery*—] *Dauberies* are *disguises*. So, in *K. Lear*, Edgar says, " I cannot *daub* it farther." STEEVENS.

Perhaps rather—such *gross falsehood*, and *imposition*. In our author's time a *dauber* and a *plasterer* were synonymous. See Minshew's DICT. in v. " To lay it on with a *trowel*," was a phrase of that time, applied

yond our element: we know nothing.—Come down, you witch, you hag you; come down, I say.

Mrs. Ford. Nay, good, sweet husband;—good gentlemen, let him not strike the old woman [5].

Enter FALSTAFF *in women's clothes, led by Mrs.* PAGE.

Mrs. Page. Come, mother Prat, come, give me your hand.

Ford. I'll *prat* her:—Out of my door, you witch!—[*beats him.*] You rag [6], you baggage, you polecat, you ronyon [7]! out! out! I'll conjure you, I'll fortune-tell you.

[*Exit* FALSTAFF.

Mrs. Page. Are you not ashamed? I think you have kill'd the poor woman.

Mrs. Ford. Nay, he will do it:—'Tis a goodly credit for you.

Ford. Hang her, witch!

Evans. By yea and no, I think, the 'oman is a witch indeed: I like not when a 'oman has a great peard; I spy a great peard under his muffler [8].

Ford. Will you follow, gentlemen? I beseech you follow; see but the issue of my jealousy: if I cry out thus upon no trail [9], never trust me when I open again.

Page.

to one who uttered a gross lie. Or it may signify superficial, external appearances. So, in another play:

"So smooth he daub'd his vice with shew of virtue." MALONE.

[5] — *let him not strike the old woman.*] *Not*, which was inadvertently omitted in the first folio, was supplied by the second. MALONE.

[6] — *you rag.*] This opprobrious term is again used in *Timon of Athens:* "—thy father, that poor rag—." Mr. Rowe unnecessarily dismissed this word, and introduced *bag* in its place. MALONE.

[7] — *ronyon!*] *Ronyon*, applied to a woman, means, as far as can be traced, much the same with *scall* or *scab* spoken of a man. JOHNSON.

From *Rogneux,* Fr. So, in *Macbeth:*

"Aroint thee, witch, the rump-fed ronyon cries." STEEVENS.

[8] *I spy a great peard under his muffler.*] One of the marks of a supposed witch was a beard. See *Macbeth.* STEEVENS.

Should we not read—under *her* muffler? MALONE.

As the second stratagem, by which Falstaff escapes, is much the grosser of the two, I wish it had been practised first. It is very unlikely that Ford, having been so deceived before, and knowing that he had been deceived, would suffer him to escape in so slight a disguise.

JOHNSON.

[9] — *cry out thus upon no trail,*] The expression is taken from the hunters. *Trail* is the scent left by the passage of the game. *To cry out,* is to *open* or *bark.* JOHNSON.

So,

Page. Let's obey his humour a little further: Come, gentlemen. [*Exeunt* PAGE, FORD, SHAL. *and* EVANS.

Mrs. Page. Trust me, he beat him most pitifully.

Mrs. Ford. Nay, by the mass that he did not; he beat him most unpitifully, methought.

Mrs. Page. I'll have the cudgel hallow'd, and hung o'er the altar; it hath done meritorious service.

Mrs. Ford. What think you? May we, with the warrant of woman-hood, and the witness of a good conscience, pursue him with any further revenge?

Mrs. Page. The spirit of wantonness is, sure, scared out of him; if the devil have him not in fee-simple, with fine and recovery, he will never, I think, in the way of waste, attempt us again [1].

Mrs. Ford. Shall we tell our husbands how we have served him?

Mrs. Page. Yes, by all means; if it be but to scrape the figures out of your husband's brains. If they can find in their hearts, the poor unvirtuous fat knight shall be any further afflicted, we two will still be the ministers.

Mrs. Ford. I'll warrant, they'll have him publicly shamed: and, methinks, there would be no period [2] to the jest, should he not be publicly shamed.

Mrs. Page. Come, to the forge with it then, shape it: I would not have things cool. [*Exeunt.*

SCENE III.

A Room in the Garter Inn.

Enter HOST *and* BARDOLPH.

Bard. Sir, the Germans desire to have three of your horses: the duke himself will be to-morrow at court, and they are going to meet him.

So, in *Hamlet:*
"How chearfully on the false *trail* they cry!
"Oh! this is counter, ye false Danish *dogs!*" STEEVENS.

[1] — *in the way of waste, attempt us again.*] i. e. he will not make further attempts to ruin us, by corrupting our virtue, and destroying our reputation. STEEVENS.

[2] — *no period* —] Shakspeare seems by *no period*, to mean, *no proper catastrophe.* STEEVENS.

Our author often uses *period,* for *end* or *conclusion.* So, in *King Richard III:*
"O, let me make the *period to* my curse. MALONE.

Host.

Host. What duke should that be, comes so secretly? I hear not of him in the court: Let me speak with the gentlemen; they speak English?

Bard. Ay, Sir; I'll call them to you[3].

Host. They shall have my horses; but I'll make them pay, I'll sauce them: they have had my houses a week at command; I have turn'd away my other guests: they must come off[4]; I'll sauce them: Come. [*Exeunt.*

SCENE IV.

A Room in Ford's *House.*

Enter Page, Ford, *Mrs.* Page, *Mrs.* Ford, *and Sir* Hugh Evans.

Evans. 'Tis one of the best discretions of a 'oman as ever I did look upon.

Page. And did he send you both these letters at an instant?

Mrs. Page. Within a quarter of an hour.

Ford. Pardon me, wife: Henceforth do what thou wilt; I rather will suspect the sun with cold[5], Than thee with wantonness: now doth thy honour stand, In him that was of late an heretic, As firm as faith.

Page. 'Tis well, 'tis well; no more. Be not as extreme in submission, As in offence; But let our plot go forward: let our wives Yet once again, to make us public sport,

---

[3] — *I'll call them to you.*] Old Copy—I'll call *him*. Corrected in the third folio. MALONE.

[4] — *they must come off;*] *To come off,* is, *to pay.* In this sense it is used by Decker, Heywood, Middleton, Massinger, and other comic writers. STEEVENS.

In John Heywood's play of *the Four P's*, the pedlar says,

"—— if you be willing to buy,

"Lay down money; *come off* quickly." FARMER

The phrase is used by Chaucer, *Friar's Tale,* 338, edit. Urry.
TYRWHITT.

[5] — *with cold,*] The old copy reads—*gold.* The emendation is Mr. Rowe's. So, in *Wyts-card for Smelts,* a pamphlet which Shakspeare certainly had read: "I answere in the behalfe of one, who is as free from disloyaltie, as is the sunne from darkness, or the fire from COLD." A husband is speaking of his wife. MALONE.

Appoint

Appoint a meeting with this old fat fellow,
Where we may take him, and difgrace him for it.

Ford. There is no better way than that they fpoke of.

Page. How! to fend him word they'll meet him in the park at midnight! Fie, fie; he'll never come.

Evans. You fay, he has been thrown in the rivers; and has been grievoufly peaten, as an old 'oman: methinks, there fhould be terrors in him, that he fhould not come; methinks, his flefh is punifh'd, he fhall have no defires.

Page. So think I too,

Mrs. Ford. Devife but how you'll ufe him when he comes,
And let us two devife to bring him thither.

Mrs. Page. There is an old tale goes, that Herne the hunter,
Sometimes a keeper here in Windfor foreft,
Doth all the winter time, at ftill midnight,
Walk round about an oak, with great ragg'd horns;
And there he blafts the tree, and takes the cattle [6];
And makes milch-kine yield blood, and fhakes a chain
In a moft hideous and dreadful manner:
You have heard of fuch a fpirit; and well you know,
The fuperftitious idle-headed eld [7]
Receiv'd, and did deliver to our age,
This tale of Herne the hunter for a truth.

Page. Why, yet there want not many, that do fear
In deep of night to walk by this Herne's oak:
But what of this?

Mrs. Ford. Marry, this is our device;
That Falftaff at that oak fhould meet with us,
Difguis'd like Herne, with huge horns on his head [8].

Page.

---

[6] *—and takes the cattle;*] To *take*, in Shakfpeare, fignifies to feize or ftrike with a difeafe, to blaft. So, in *Lear:*

"—— Strike her young bones,
"Ye *taking* airs, with lamenefs. JOHNSON.

[7] *—idle-headed eld*] *Eld* feems to be ufed here, for what our poet calls in *Macbeth—the olden time.* It is employed in *Meafure for Meafure,* to exprefs *age* and *decrepitude:*

"—— doth beg the alms
"Of palfied *eld.*" STEEVENS.

I rather imagine it is ufed here for *old perfons.* MALONE.

[8] *Difguis'd like Herne, with huge horns on his head.*] This line, which is not in the folio, was properly reftored from the old quarto by Mr. Theobald. He at the fame time introduced another,—" We'll fend him

Page. Well, let it not be doubted but he'll come,
And in this shape: When you have brought him thither,
What shall be done with him? what is your plot?

Mrs. Page. That likewise have we thought upon, and thus:
Nan Page my daughter, and my little son,
And three or four more of their growth, we'll dress
Like urchins, ouphes⁹, and fairies, green and white,
With rounds of waxen tapers on their heads,
And rattles in their hands; upon a sudden,
As Falstaff, she, and I, are newly met,
Let them from forth a saw-pit rush at once
With some diffused song ¹; upon their sight,.
We two in great amazedness will fly:
Then let them all encircle him about,
And, fairy-like, to-pinch the unclean knight ²;
And ask him, why, that hour of fairy revel,
In their so sacred paths he dares to tread
In shape prophane.

Mrs. Ford. And till he tell the truth,.

him word to meet us in the field,"—which is clearly unnecessary, and indeed improper; for the word *field* relates to two preceding lines of the quarto, which have not been introduced:
"Now, for that Falstaff has been so deceiv'd,
"As that he dares not venture to the *house*,
"We'll send him word to meet us in the *field*." MALONE.

⁹ — *urchins, ouphes,*—] The primitive signification of *urchin* is a hedge-hog. Hence it comes to signify any thing little and dwarfish. *Ouph* is the Teutonic word for a *fairy* or *goblin*. STEEVENS.

¹ *With some diffused song;*] i. e. wild, irregular, discordant. That this was the meaning of the word, I have shewn in a note on another play by a passage from one of Greene's pamphlets, in which he calls a dress of which the different parts were made after the fashions of different countries, "a *diffused* attire." MALONE.

² *And, fairy-like, to-pinch the unclean knight;*] This use of *to* in composition with verbs, is very common in Gower and Chaucer, but must have been rather antiquated in the time of Shakspeare. See Gower, *De Confessione Amantis*, B. iv. fol. 7.
"All *to-tore* is myn araie."
And Chaucer, *Reeve's Tale*, 1169:
"———— mouth and nose *to-broke*." TYRWHITT.

This use of the preposition *to* was not entirely antiquated in our author's time. See Spenser, B iv. c. 7. B. v. c. 8. STEEVENS.

So Milton, in his Masque:
"Were all *to*-ruffled, and sometimes impair'd. MALONE.

Let the supposed fairies pinch him found [3],
And burn him with their tapers.

Mrs. Page. The truth being known,
We'll all present ourselves; dis-horn the spirit,
And mock him home to Windsor.

Ford. The children must
Be practis'd well to this, or they'll ne'er do't.

Evans. I will teach the children their behaviours; and I will be like a jack-an-apes also, to burn the knight with my taber.

Ford. That will be excellent. I'll go and buy them vizards.

Mrs. Page. My Nan shall be the queen of all the fairies, Finely attired in a robe of white.

Page. That silk will I go buy;—and in that time [4] Shall Master Slender steal my Nan away,   [*Aside.*
And marry her at Eton.—Go, send to Falstaff straight.

Ford. Nay, I'll to him again in name of Brook:
He'll tell me all his purpose: Sure he'll come.

Mrs. Page. Fear not you that: Go get us properties [5]
And tricking for our fairies [6].

Evans. Let us about it: It is admirable pleasures, and fery honest knaveries.
         [*Exeunt* PAGE, FORD, *and* EVANS.

Mrs. Page. Go, Mistress Ford,
Send Quickly to Sir John, to know his mind.
         [*Exit Mrs.* FORD.
I'll to the doctor; he hath my good will,
And none but he, to marry with Nan Page.
That Slender, though well landed, is an ideot;
And he my husband best of all affects:
The doctor is well money'd, and his friends
Potent at court; he, none but he, shall have her,
Though twenty thousand worthier come to crave her.
         [*Exit.*

---

[3] — *pinch him* found,] i. e. *soundly.* The adjective used as an adverb. STEEVENS.

[4] — *and, in* that time] *That time* relates to the time of the mask with which Falstaff was to be entertained. WARBURTON.

[5] — *properties*—] *Properties* are little incidental necessaries to a theatre, exclusive of scenes and dresses. STEEVENS.

[6] — tricking *for our fairies.*] To *trick,* is to dress out. STEEVENS.

SCENE

SCENE V.

A Room in the Garter Inn.

Enter HOST *and* SIMPLE.

Host. What would'ſt thou have, boor? what, thick-ſkin[7]? ſpeak, breathe, diſcuſs; brief, ſhort, quick, ſnap.

Simple. Marry, Sir, I come to ſpeak with Sir John Falſtaff from Maſter Slender.

Host. There's his chamber, his houſe, his caſtle, his ſtanding-bed, and truckle-bed[8]; 'tis painted about with the ſtory of the prodigal, freſh and new: Go, knock and call; he'll ſpeak like an *Anthropophaginian*[9] unto thee: Knock, I ſay.

Simp. There's an old woman, a fat woman gone up into his chamber; I'll be ſo bold as ſtay, Sir, till ſhe come down: I come to ſpeak with her, indeed.

Host. Ha! a fat woman! the Knight may be robb'd: I'll call.—Bully Knight! Bully Sir John! ſpeak from thy lungs military: Art thou there? it is thine hoſt, thine Epheſian[*], calls.

Fal. [*above.*] How now, mine hoſt?

Host. Here's a Bohemian-Tartar[1] tarries the coming down of thy fat woman: Let her deſcend, bully, Let her deſcend; my chambers are honourable: Fie! privacy? fie!

Enter

---

[7] — *what, thick-ſkin?*] I meet with this term of abuſe in Warner's *Albions England*, 1602, book vi. chap. 30:

"That he ſo foul a *thick-ſkin* ſhould ſo fair a lady catch."
STEEVENS.

[8] — *ſtanding-bed, and truckle-bed;*] The uſual furniture of chambers in that time was a ſtanding-bed, under which was a *trockel*, *truckle*, or *running-bed*. In the ſtanding-bed lay the maſter, and in the truckle-bed the ſervant. So, in Hall's *Account of a ſervile tutor:*

"He lieth in the *truckle-bed*,
"While his young maſter lieth o'er his head." JOHNSON.

[9] — *Anthropophaginian.*—] i. e. a cannibal. See *Othello*, Act i. ſc. iii. It is here uſed as a ſounding word to aſtoniſh *Simple*. STEEVENS.

[*] — *thine* Epheſian,] This was a cant term of the time. So, in K. *Henry IV.* P. ii. Act. ii. ſc. ii. "*P. Henry.* What company? *Page. Epheſians*, my lord, of the old church." See the note there. MALONE.

[1] — *Bohemian-Tartar*—] The French call a *Bohemian* what we call a *Gypſy*; but I believe the Hoſt means nothing more than, by a wild appellation, to inſinuate that Simple makes a ſtrange appearance.
JOHNSON.

In

Enter FALSTAFF.

Fal. There was, mine hoft, an old fat woman even now with me; but fhe's gone.

Simp. Pray you, Sir, was't not the wife woman of Brentford² ?

Fal. Ay, marry was it, muffel-fhell³; What would you with her?

Simp. My mafter, Sir, my Mafter Slender, fent to her, feeing her go thorough the ftreets, to know, Sir, whether one Nym, Sir, that beguiled him of a chain, had the chain, or no.

Fal. I fpake with the old woman about it.

Simp. And what fays fhe, I pray, Sir?

Fal. Marry, fhe fays, that the very fame man, that beguiled Mafter Slender of his chain, cozen'd him of it.

Simp. I would, I could have fpoken with the woman herfelf; I had other things to have fpoken with her too, from him.

Fal. What are they? let us know.

Hoft. Ay, come; quick.

Simp. I may not conceal them, Sir *.

Hoft. Conceal them, or thou dieft.

Simp. Why, Sir, they were nothing but about Miftrefs Anne Page; to know, if it were my mafter's fortune to have her, or no.

Fal. 'Tis, 'tis his fortune.

Simp. What, Sir?

Fal. To have her,—or no: Go; fay, the woman told me fo.

<hr/>

In Germany, there were feveral companies of vagabonds, &c. called *Tartars* and *Zigens*. " Thefe are the fame in my opinion," fays Mezeray, " as thofe the French call *Bohemians*, and the Englifh Gypfies." Bulteel's *Tranflation of Mezeray's Hift. of France*, ad an. 1417.
TOLLET.

² — *the wife woman of Brentford?*] In our author's time female dealers in palmiftry and fortune-telling were ufually denominated *wife women*. So the perfon from whom Heywood's play of *The Wife Woman of Hogfdon*, 1638, takes its title, is employed in anfwering many fuch queftions as are the object of Simple's enquiry. REED.

³ — *muffel-fhell;*] He calls poor Simple *muffel-fhell*, becaufe he ftands with his mouth open. JOHNSON.

* Simp. *I may*, &c.] In the old copy this fpeech is given to Falftaff. Corrected by Mr. Rowe. I mention this error, becaufe it juftifies other fimilar corrections that have been made. MALONE.

Simp.

Simp. May I be so bold to say so, Sir?

Fal. Ay, Sir Tike; who more bold⁴?

Simp. I thank your worship: I shall make my master glad with these tidings. [*Exit* SIMPLE.

Host. Thou art clerkly⁵, thou art clerkly, Sir John: Was there a wise woman with thee?

Fal. Ay, that there was, mine Host; one, that hath taught me more wit than ever I learn'd before in my life: and I paid nothing for it neither, but was paid⁶ for my learning.

Enter BARDOLPH.

Bard. Out, alas, Sir! cozenage! meer cozenage!

Host. Where be my horses? speak well of them, varletto.

Bard. Run away with the cozeners: for so soon as I came beyond Eton, they threw me off, from behind one of them, in a slough of mire; and set spurs, and away, like three German devils, three Doctor Faustus's⁷.

Host. They are gone but to meet the duke, villain: do not say, they be fled; Germans are honest men.

Enter Sir HUGH EVANS.

Evans. Where is mine host?

Host. What is the matter, Sir?

Evans. Have a care of your entertainments: there is a friend of mine come to town, tells me, there is three couzin germans, that has cozen'd all the hosts of Readings, of Maidenhead, of Colebrook, of horses and money. I tell you for good will, look you: you are wise, and full of gibes and vlouting-stogs; and 'tis not convenient you should be cozen'd: Fare you well. [*Exit.*

---

⁴ *Ay, Sir Tike; who more bold?*] The folio reads—Ay, Sir, *like*, &c. The emendation, which is supported by the old quarto, (where we find Ay, *Tike*, &c.) was suggested by Dr. Farmer. MALONE.

⁵ — *clerkly*,—] i. e. scholar-like STEEVENS.

⁶ *I paid nothing for it neither, but was paid*—] He alludes to the beating which he had just received. The same play on words occurs in *Cymbeline*, Act v. " — sorry you have *paid* too much, and sorry that you are *paid* too much." STEEVENS.

To *pay* in our author's time often signified to *beat*. So, in *K. Henry IV.* P. i. " — seven of the eleven I *paid*." MALONE.

⁷ — three German devils, three *Doctor Faustus's*.] *John Faust*, commonly called *Doctor Faustus*, was a German. STEEVENS.

Enter

Enter CAIUS.

Caius. Vere is mine *Hoſt de Jarterre?*

Hoſt. Here, Maſter Doctor, in perplexity, and doubtful dilemma.

Caius. I cannot tell vat is dat: But it is tell-a me, dat you make grand preparation for a duke *de Jarmany:* by my trot, dere is no duke, dat the court is know to come: I tell you for good vill: adieu. [*Exit.*

Hoſt. Hue and cry, villain, go:—aſſiſt me, Knight; I am undone:—fly, run, hue and cry, villain! I am undone!

[*Exeunt* HOST *and* BARDOLPH.

Fal. I would, all the world might be cozen'd; for I have been cozen'd, and beaten too. If it ſhould come to the ear of the court, how I have been transform'd, and how my transformation hath been waſh'd and cudgel'd, they would melt me out of my fat, drop by drop, and liquor fiſhermen's boots with me; I warrant, they would whip me with their fine wits, till I were as creſt-fall'n as a dry'd pear. —I never proſper'd ſince I foreſwore myſelf at *Primero* [8]. Well, if my wind were but long enough to ſay my prayers [9], I would repent.—

[8] — *at* Primero.] A game at cards. JOHNSON.

Primero was in Shakſpeare's time the faſhionable game. In the Earl of Northumberland's letters about the powder plot, Joſc. Percy was playing at *Primero* on a Sunday, when his uncle the conſpirator called on him at Eſſex Houſe. This game is again mentioned in our author's *Henry VIII.* PERCY.

" *Frimero* and *Primaviſta,* two games of cardes. *Primum et primum viſum,* that is, firſt, and firſt ſcene, becauſe he that can ſhew ſuch an order of cardes, wins the game." See Minſheu's DICT. 1647.—In the *Sydney Papers,* is the following account of an altercation that happened between our poet's generous patron, and one Willoughby, at this game: " The quarrel of my Lord Southampton to Ambroſe Willoughby grew upon this: That he, with Sir Walter Rawley and Mr. Parker, being at *Primero* in the preſence-chamber, the queen was gone to bed; and he being there, as ſquire of the body, deſired them to give over. Soon after he ſpoke to them againe, that if they would not leave, he would call in the guard to pull down the bord; which Sir Walter Rawley ſeeing, put up his money, and went his wayes; but my Lord Southampton took exceptions at hym, and told hym, he would remember yᵗ: and ſo finding hym between the Tennis-court wall and the garden, ſtrooke him; and Willoughby pull'd of ſome of his lockes." This happened in the beginning of 1598. MALONE.

[9] — *to ſay my prayers,*] Theſe words were reſtored from the early quarto by Mr. Pope. They were probably omitted in the folio on account of the Stat 3. Jac. I. ch. 21. MALONE.

Enter

Enter Mistress QUICKLY.

Now! whence come you?

Quick. From the two parties, forsooth.

Fal. The devil take one party, and his dam the other, and so they shall be both bestow'd! I have suffer'd more for their sakes, more than the villainous inconstancy of man's disposition is able to bear.

Quick. And have not they suffer'd? Yes, I warrant; speciously one of them; Mistress Ford, good heart, is beaten black and blue, that you cannot see a white spot about her.

Fal. What tell'st thou me of black and blue? I was beaten myself into all the colours of the rainbow; and I was like to be apprehended for the witch of Brentford; but that my admirable dexterity of wit, my counterfeiting the action of an old woman[1], deliver'd me, the knave constable had set me i'the stocks, i'the common stocks, for a witch.

Quick. Sir, let me speak with you in your chamber: you shall hear how things go; and I warrant, to your content. Here is a letter will say somewhat. Good hearts, what ado here is to bring you together! Sure, one of you does not serve heaven well[2], that you are so cross'd.

Fal. Come up into my chamber. [*Exeunt.*

SCENE VI.

Another Room in the Garter Inn.

Enter FENTON *and* HOST.

Host. Master Fenton, talk not to me; my mind is heavy, I will give over all.

---

[1] — *action of an old woman,*] Mr. Theobald reads *wold*-woman, i. e. frantic, crazy; but the reading of the old copy is fully supported by what Falstaff says afterwards to Ford: " I went to her, Master Brook, as you see, like a poor old man; but I came from her, Master Brook, like a poor old woman. MALONE.

Falstaff by counterfeiting such weakness and infirmity, as would naturally be pitied in an old woman, averted the punishment to which he would otherwise have been subjected, on the suspicion that he was a witch. STEEVENS.

[2] *Sure, one of you does not serve heaven well,* &c.] The great fault of this play is the frequency of expressions so profane, that no necessity of preserving character can justify them. There are laws of higher authority than those of criticism. JOHNSON.

Fent.

OF WINDSOR.   287

Fent. Yet hear me speak: Assist me in my purpose,
And, as I am a gentleman, I'll give thee
A hundred pound in gold, more than your loss.

Host. I will hear you Master Fenton; and I will, at the least, keep your counsel.

Fent. From time to time I have acquainted you
With the dear love I bear to fair Anne Page;
Who, mutually, hath answered my affection
(So far forth as herself might be her chooser,)
Even to my wish: I have a letter from her
Of such contents as you will wonder at;
The mirth whereof² so larded with my matter,
That neither, singly, can be manifested,
Without the shew of both;—wherein fat Falstaff³
Hath a great scene: the image of the jest⁴

[*Shewing the letter.*

I'll shew you here at large. Hark, good mine host:
To-night at Herne's oak, just 'twixt twelve and one,
Must my sweet Nan present the fairy queen;
The purpose why, is here⁵; in which disguise,
While other jests are something rank on foot⁶,

---

² *The mirth whereof—*] Thus the old copy. Mr Pope and all the subsequent editors read—The mirth *whereof's* so larded, &c. but the old reading is the true one, and the phraseology that of Shakspeare's age: *Whereof* (as I suspected when my original note was written) was formerly used as we now use *thereof*; " — the mirth *thereof* being so larded," &c. So, in *Mount Tabor, or Private Exercises of a Penitent Sinner*, 8vo. 1639: " In the mean time [they] closely conveyed under the cloaths wherewithal he was covered, a visard, like a swine's snout, upon his face, with three-wire chains fastened thereunto, the other end *whereof being* holden severally by those three ladies; who fall to singing again," &c. MALONE.

³ —————— *wherein fat Falstaff,* &c.
Hath a great scene:] The first folio reads:
Without the shew of both : fat Falstaff, &c.
I have supplied the word that was probably omitted at the press, from the early quarto, where, in the corresponding place, we find—
Wherein fat Falstaff hath a mighty scare [scene].
The editor of the second folio, to supply the metre, arbitrarily reads,
Without the shew of both:—fat Sir John Falstaff—. MALONE.

⁴ — *the image of the jest*] Image is *representation*. So, in K. *Richard III*:
" And liv'd by looking on his *images*." STEEVENS.
These words allude to a custom still in use, of hanging out painted representations of shows. HENLEY.

⁵ — *is here;*] i. e. in the letter. STEEVENS.

⁶ *While other jests are something rank on foot,*] i. e. while they are hotly pursuing other merriment of their own. STEEVENS.

Her

Her father hath commanded her to slip
Away with Slender, and with him at Eton
Immediately to marry: she hath consented:
Now, Sir,
Her mother, even strong against that match [7],
And firm for Doctor Caius, hath appointed
That he shall likewise shuffle her away,
While other sports are tasking of their minds [8],
And at the deanery, where a priest attends,
Straight marry her: to this her mother's plot
She, seemingly obedient, likewise hath
Made promise to the doctor:—Now, thus it rests:
Her father means she shall be all in white;
And in that habit, when Slender sees his time
To take her by the hand, and bid her go,
She shall go with him:—her mother hath intended,
The better to denote [9] her to the doctor,
(For they must all be mask'd and vizarded,)
That, quaint in green [1], she shall be loose enrobed,

With

---

[7] — *even strong against that match*,] *Even* strong, is *as strong, with a similar degree of strength.* So, in *Hamlet,* " *even* Christian" is *fellow* Christian. STEEVENS.

[8] — *tasking of their minds,*] So, in another play of our author:
" ——— some things of weight,
" That *task* our thoughts concerning us and France."
STEEVENS.

[9] — *to denote*—] In the Mss. of our author's age *n* and *u* were formed so very much alike, that they are scarcely distinguishable. Hence it was, that in the old copies of these plays one of these letters is frequently put for the other. From the cause assigned, or from an accidental inversion of the letter *n* at the press, the first folio in the present instance reads—*deuote,* *u* being constantly employed in that copy instead of *v.* The same mistake has happened in several other places. Thus, in *Much ado about Nothing,* 1623, we find, " he is *turu'd* orthographer," instead of *turn'd.* Again, in *Othello*:—" to the contemplation, mark, and *deuotement* of her parts," instead of *denotement.* Again, in *King John*: 'This *expeditious* charge, instead of *expedition's.* Again, ibid: *invulnerable* for *invulnerable.* Again, in *Hamlet,* 1605, we meet with this very word put by an error of the press for *denote:*
" Together with all forms, modes, shapes of grief,
" That can *deuote* me truly."
The present emendation, which was suggested by Mr. Steevens, is fully supported by a subsequent passage quoted by him:—" the white will *decipher* her well enough." MALONE.

[1] — *quaint in green,*] may mean fantastically drest in green. So, in Milton's *Masque at Ludlow Castle*:
" ——— left the place,
" And this *quaint* habit, breed astonishment."

With ribbands pendant, flaring 'bout her head;
And when the doctor fpies his vantage ripe,
To pinch her by the hand, and, on that token,
The maid hath given confent to go with him.

Hoſt. Which means ſhe to deceive; father or mother?

Fent. Both, my good Hoſt, to go along with me:
And here it reſts—that you'll procure the vicar
To ſtay for me at church, 'twixt twelve and one,
And, in the lawful name of marrying,
To give our hearts united ceremony.

Hoſt. Well, huſband your device; I'll to the vicar:
Bring you the maid, you ſhall not lack a prieſt.

Fent. So ſhall I evermore be bound to thee;
Beſides, I'll make a preſent recompence. [*Exeunt.*

ACT V. SCENE I.

A Room in the Garter Inn.

Enter FALSTAFF *and Mrs.* QUICKLY.

Fal. Pr'ythee, no more prattling;—go.—I'll hold:—
This is the third time; I hope, good luck lies in odd numbers. Away, go; they ſay, there is divinity in odd numbers, either in nativity, chance, or death.—Away.

Quick. I'll provide you a chain; and I'll do what I can to get you a pair of horns.

Fal. Away, I ſay; time wears: hold up your head, and mince [1]. [*Exit Mrs.* QUICKLY.

Enter FORD.

How now, Maſter Brook? Maſter Brook, the matter will

In the *Two Gentlemen of Verona,* Act iii. ſc. i. *quaintly* is uſed for *ingeniouſly:*
"——— a ladder *quaintly* made of cords." STEEVENS.
In Daniel's SONNETS, 1594, it is uſed for *fantaſtic:*
"Prayers prevail not with a *quaint* diſdain." MALONE.

[1] *— hold up your head, and mince.*] To *mince* is to walk with affected delicacy. So, in the *Merchant of Venice:*
"——— turn two *mincing* ſteps
"Into a manly ſtride." STEEVENS.

be known to-night, or never. Be you in the Park about midnight, at Herne's oak, and you shall see wonders.

Ford. Went you not to her yesterday, Sir, as you told me you had appointed?

Fal. I went to her, Master Brook, as you see, like a poor old man: but I came from her, Master Brook, like a poor old woman. That same knave, Ford her husband, hath the finest mad devil of jealousy in him, Master Brook, that ever govern'd frenzy. I will tell you.—He beat me grievously in the shape of a woman; for in the shape of man, Master Brook, I fear not Goliah with a weaver's beam; because I know also, life is a shuttle. I am in haste; go along with me; I'll tell you all, Master Brook. Since I pluck'd geese, play'd truant, and whipp'd top, I knew not what 'twas to be beaten, till lately. Follow me: I'll tell you strange things of this knave Ford; on whom to-night I will be revenged, and I will deliver his wife into your hand. —Follow: Strange things in hand, Master Brook! follow.

[*Exeunt.*

SCENE II.

Windsor Park.

Enter PAGE, SHALLOW, *and* SLENDER.

Page. Come, come; we'll couch i' the castle-ditch, till we see the light of our fairies.—Remember, son Slender, my daughter[2].

Slen. Ay, forsooth; I have spoke with her, and we have a nay-word[3], how to know one another. I come to her in white, and cry, *mum;* she cries, *budget;* and by that we know one another.

Shal. That's good too; But what needs either your *mum,* or her *budget?* the white will decipher her well enough.— It hath struck ten o'clock.

Page. The night is dark; light and spirits will become it well. Heaven prosper our sport! No man means evil but

[2] — *my* daughter.] The word *daughter* was inadvertently omitted in the first folio. The emendation was made by the editor of the second. MALONE.

[3] — a *nay-word,*—] i. e. a watch-word. Mrs. Quickly has already used it in this sense. STEEVENS.

the

the devil [4], and we shall know him by his horns.—Let's away; follow me. *[Exeunt.*

SCENE III.

The Street in Windsor.

Enter Mistress PAGE, *Mrs.* FORD, *and Dr.* CAIUS.

Mrs. Page. Master Doctor, my daughter is in green: when you see your time, take her by the hand, away with her to the deanery, and dispatch it quickly: Go before into the park; we two must go together.

Caius. I know vat I have to do; Adieu.

Mrs. Page. Fare you well, Sir. [*Exit* CAIUS] My husband will not rejoice so much at the abuse of Falstaff, as he will chafe at the doctor's marrying my daughter; but 'tis no matter; better a little chiding, than a great deal of heart-break.

Mrs. Ford. Where is Nan now, and her troop of fairies? and the Welch devil, Hugh [5]?

Mrs. Page. They are all couch'd in a pit hard by Herne's oak [6], with obscured lights; which, at the very instant of Falstaff's and our meeting, they will at once display to the night.

Mrs. Ford. That cannot choose but amaze him.

Mrs. Page. If he be not amazed, he will be mock'd; if he be amazed, he will every way be mock'd.

Mrs. Ford. We'll betray him finely.

Mrs. Page. Against such lewdsters, and their lechery, Those that betray them do no treachery.

[4] *No man means evil but the devil,*] In the ancient interludes and moralities, the beings of supreme power, excellence, or depravity, are occasionally styled *men.* So, in *Much Ado about Nothing,* Dogberry says, "God's a good *man.*" Again, in *Jeronimo, or the First Part of the Spanish Tragedy,* 1605:
"You're the last *man* I thought on, save the *devil.*" STEEVENS.

[5] *— and the Welch devil,* Hugh?] So afterwards: "Well said, fairy Hugh." The old copy reads—*and the Welch devil Herne.* Theobald saw the error, and substituted *Evans.* MALONE.
I suppose only the letter H. was set down in the MS; and therefore, instead of *Hugh* (which seems to be the true reading,) the editors substituted *Herne.* STEEVENS.

[6] *— in a pit hard by Herne's oak,*] An *oak,* which may be that alluded to by Shakspeare is still standing close to a *pit* in Windsor Forest. It is yet shewn as the *oak of Herne.* STEEVENS.

Mrs. Ford. The hour draws on; To the oak, to the oak! [*Exeunt.*

SCENE IV.

Windsor Park.

Enter Sir HUGH EVANS, *and Fairies.*

Evans. Trib, trib, fairies; come; and remember your parts: be pold, I pray you; follow me into the pit; and when I give the watch-'ords, do as I pid you; Come, come; trib, trib. [*Exeunt.*

SCENE V.

Another Part of the Park.

Enter FALSTAFF *disguis'd, with a buck's head on.*

Fal. The Windsor bell hath struck twelve; the minute draws on: Now, the hot-blooded gods assist me!—Remember, Jove, thou wast a bull for thy Europa; love set on thy horns.—O powerful love! that, in some respects, makes a beast a man; in some other, a man a beast.—You were also, Jupiter, a swan, for the love of Leda;—O omnipotent love! how near the god drew to the complexion of a goose?—A fault done first in the form of a beast;—O Jove, a beastly fault! and then another fault in the semblance of a fowl; think on't, Jove; a foul fault.—When gods have hot backs, what shall poor men do [7]? For me, I am here a Windsor stag; and the fattest, I think, i' the forest: Send me a cool rut-time, Jove, or who can blame me to piss my tallow [8]?—Who comes here? my doe?

Enter

---

[7] *When gods have hot backs, what shall poor men do?*] Shakspeare had perhaps in his thoughts the argument which Cherea employed in a similar situation. TER. *Eun.* Act iii. sc. v:

"———————— Quia consimilem luserat
" Jam olim ille ludum, impendio magis animus gaudebat mihi
" Deum sese in hominem convertisse, atque per alienas tegulas
" Venisse clanculum per impluvium, fucum factum mulieri.
" At quem deum? qui templa cœli summa sonitu concutit.
" *Ego homuncio hoc non facerem?* Ego vero illud ita feci, ac lubens."

A translation of Terence was published in 1598. The same thought is found in Lily's *Euphues*, 1580: " I think in those days love was well ratified on earth, when lust was so full authorized by the gods in heaven." MALONE.

[8] *Send*

Enter Mistress FORD, *and Mistress* PAGE.

Mrs. Ford. Sir John? art thou there, my deer? my male deer?

Fal. My doe with the black scut?—Let the sky rain potatoes; let it thunder to the tune of *Green Sleeves;* hail kissing-comfits, and snow eringoes; let there come a tempest of provocation⁹, I will shelter me here.

[*embracing her.*

Mrs. Ford. Mistress Page is come with me, sweet-heart.

Fal. Divide me like a bribe-buck¹, each a haunch: I will keep my sides to myself, my shoulders for the fellow of this walk², and my horns I bequeath your husbands. Am I a woodman³? ha! Speak I like Herne the hunter? Why, now

---

⁸ *Send me a cool rut-time, Jove; or who can blame me to* piss *my tallow?*] This, I find, is technical. In Tuberville's *Boke of Hunting,* 1575: "During the time of their rut, the harts live with small sustenance.—The red mushroome helpeth well to make them *pisse their greace,* they are then in so vehement heate, &c." FARMER.

In Ray's *Collection of Proverbs,* the phrase is yet further explained: "*He has piss'd his tallow.* This is spoken of bucks who grow lean after rutting-time, and may be applied to men." STEEVENS.

⁹ *Let the sky rain* potatoes;—*hail* kissing-comfits, *and snow* eringoes; *let there come a tempest of provocation,*—] Potatoes, when they were first introduced into England, were supposed to be strong provocatives. See Mr. Collins's note on a passage in *Troilus and Cressida,* Act v. sc. ii. *Kissing-comfits* were sugar plums, perfumed to make the breath sweet.

Holinshed informs us, that in the year 1583, for the entertainment of Prince Alasco was performed "a verie statelie tragedie named *Dido,* wherein the Queen's hauket (with Æneas' narration of the destruction of Troie,) was livelie described in a marchpaine patterne,— *the tempest wherein it hailed small confetti, rained rose-water, and snew an artificial kind of snow,* all strange, marvellous, and abundant." On this circumstance very probably Shakspeare was thinking, when he put the words quoted above into the mouth of Falstaff. STEEVENS.

¹ —*like a* brib'd buck,] Thus all the old copies, mistakingly: it must be *bribe-buck;* i.e. a buck sent for a bribe. THEOBALD.

² —*my shoulders to the fellow of this* walk,] A *walk* is that district in a forest, to which the jurisdiction of a particular keeper extends. So, in Lodge's *Rosalynde,* 1592. "Tell me, forester, under whom maintainest thou thy *walke?*" MALONE.

To the keeper the *shoulders* and *humbles* belong as a perquisite. GREY.

So in Holinshed, 1586, vol. i. p. 202. "The keeper by a custom—hath the skin, head, *umbles,* chine, and *shoulders.*" STEEVENS.

³ *Am I a* woodman?] A *woodman* in its original signification meant an archer; but in our author's time it was sometimes used in a wanton

now is Cupid a child of conscience; he makes restitution.—
As I am a true spirit, welcome! [*Noise within.*

   Mrs. Page. Alas! what noise?
   Mrs. Ford. Heaven forgive our sins!
   Fal. What shall this be?
   Mrs. Ford. } Away, away.   [*They run off.*
   Mrs. Page.

   Fal. I think the devil will not have me damn'd, lest the oil that is in me should set hell on fire; he would never else cross me thus.

Enter Sir HUGH EVANS, *like a satyr;* Mrs. QUICKLY, *and* PISTOL; ANNA PAGE, *as the Fairy Queen, attended by her brother and others, dressed like fairies, with waxen tapers on their heads* [4].

   Quick. Fairies, black, grey, green, and white,
You moon-shine revellers, and shades of night,
You orphan-heirs of fixed destiny [5],
                                                  Attend

---

sense. So Lucio says of the Duke, in *Measure for Measure*, "He's a better woodman than thou tak'st him for." It seems in the passage before us to have both senses. MALONE.

[4] This stage-direction I have formed on that of the old quarto, corrected by such circumstances as the poet introduced when he new-modeled his play. In the folio there is no direction whatsoever. Mrs. Quickly and Pistol seem to have been but ill suited to the delivery of the speeches here attributed to them; nor are either of those personages named by Ford in a former scene, where the intended plot against Falstaff is mentioned. It is highly probable, (as a modern editor has observed,) that the performer who had represented Pistol, was afterwards, from necessity, employed among the fairies; and that his name thus crept into the copies. He here represents *Puck*, a part which in the old quarto is given to Sir Hugh. The introduction of Mrs Quickly, however, cannot be accounted for in the same manner; for in the first sketch in quarto, she is particularly described as *the Queen of the Fairies*, a part which our author afterwards allotted to ANNE PAGE. MALONE.

[5] *You orphan-heirs of fixed destiny.*] Dr. Warburton corrects *orphan*, to *ouphen*; and not without plausibility, as the word *ouphes* occurs both before and afterwards. But, I fancy, in acquiescence to the vulgar doctrine, the address in this line is to a part of the troop, as mortals by birth, but adopted by the fairies: *orphans* in respect of their real parents, and now only dependent on *destiny* herself. A few lines from Spenser B. iii. C. 3. st. 26. edit. 1590, will sufficiently illustrate this passage:

    "The man whom *heavens* have ordaynd to bee
    "The spouse of *Britomart*, is *Arthegall*.
    "He wonneth in the land of *Fayeree*,
  —   "Yet is no *Fary* borne, ne sib at all
                                               "To

Attend your office, and your quality *.—)
Crier Hobgoblin, make the fairy o-yes.

Pist. Elves, list your names; silence, you airy toys⁶,
Cricket, to Windsor chimneys shalt thou leap:
Where fires thou find'st unrak'd, and hearths unswept,
There pinch the maids as blue as bilberry⁷:
Our radiant queen hates sluts, and sluttery.

Fal. They are fairies; he, that speaks to them, shall die:
I'll wink and couch; No man their works must eye.

[*Lies down upon his face.*

Evans. Where's *Pede?* Go you, and where you find a maid,
That ere she sleep, has thrice her prayers said,
Raise up the organs of her fantasy,
Sleep she as sound as careless infancy;
But those, as sleep, and think not on their sins,
Pinch them, arms, legs, backs, shoulders, sides and shins⁸.

Quick.

"To elfes, but sprong of seed terrestriall,
"And whilome by false *Fairies* stolen away,
"Whiles yet in infant cradle he did crall, &c." FARMER.

Dr. Warburton objects to their being *heirs* to Destiny, who was still in being. But Shakspeare, I believe, uses *heirs*, with his usual laxity, for *children*. So, to *inherit* is used in the sense of to *possess.* MALONE.

* —*and your quality.*] See p. 17, n. 3. and p. 160, n. 6.
MALONE.

⁶ *Crier Hobgoblin, make the fairy o-yes.*
Elves, list your names; silence, you airy toys.] These two lines were certainly intended to rhime together, as the preceding and subsequent couplets do: and accordingly, in the old editions, the final words of each line are printed, *oyes* and *toyes*. This therefore is a striking instance of the inconvenience which has arisen from modernizing the orthography of Shakspeare. TYRWHITT.

⁷ —*as bilberry:*] The *bilberry* is the *whortleberry*. Fairies were always supposed to have a strong aversion to sluttery. Thus, in the old song of *Robin Good Fellow.* See Dr. Percy's *Reliques*, &c. Vol. III:
"When house or hearth doth sluttish lye,
"I pinch the maidens black and blue, &c." STEEVENS.

⁸ —*Go you, and where you find a maid,*
That, ere she sleep, hath thrice her prayers said,
Raise up the organs of her fantasy,
Sleep she as sound as careless infancy;
But those, as sleep, and think not on their sins,
Pinch them, arms, legs, backs, shoulders, sides, and shins.] i. e. Go you, and wherever you find a maid asleep, that hath thrice prayed to the deity, though, in consequence of her innocence, she sleep as soundly as an infant, elevate her fancy, and amuse her tranquil mind with some delightful vision; but those whom you find asleep, without having previously thought on their sins, and prayed to heaven for forgive-

Quick. About, about;
Search Windsor castle, elves, within and out:
Strew good luck, ouphes, on every sacred room [*];
That it may stand till the perpetual doom,
In state as wholesome [9], as in state 'tis fit;
Worthy the owner, and the owner it.
The several chairs of order look you scour
With juice of balm, and every precious flower [1]:
Each fair instalment coat, and several crest,
With loyal blazon, evermore be blest!
And nightly, meadow-fairies, look, you sing,
Like to the Garter's compass, in a ring:
The expressure that it bears, green let it be,
More fertile-fresh than all the field to see;
And, *Honi Soit Qui Mal y Pense*, write,
In emerald tufts, flowers purple, blue, and white;
Like saphire, pearl, and rich embroidery,
Buckled below fair knight-hood's bending knee:
Fairies use flowers for their charactery [2].
Away; disperse: But, till 'tis one o'clock,
Our dance of custom, round about the oak
Of Herne the hunter, let us not forget.

ness, pinch, &c. It should be remembered, that those persons who sleep very soundly, seldom dream. Hence the injunction " to raise up the organs of her fantasy," " Sleep she, &c." i. e. *though she sleep as sound,* &c.

The fantasies with which the mind of the virtuous maiden is to be amused, are the reverse of those with which Oberon disturbs Titania in *A Midsummer-Night's Dream*:

"There sleeps Titania;—
"With the juice of this I'll streak her eyes,
"And make her full of *hateful fantasies*." MALONE.

Dr. Warburton, who appears to me to have totally misunderstood this passage, reads—*Rein up,* &c. in which he has been followed, in my opinion too hastily, by the subsequent editors. MALONE.

[*] *— on every sacred room;*] See Chaucer's *Cant. Tales,* v. 3482. edit. Tyrwhitt. "On foure halves of the hous aboute," &c.
MALONE.

[9] *— as wholsome,*] *Wholsome* here signifies *integer.* He wishes the castle may stand in its present state of perfection. WARBURTON.

[1] *The several chairs of order look you scour*
With juice of balm, &c.] It was an article of our ancient luxury, to rub tables, &c. with aromatic herbs. Pliny informs us, that the Romans did the same, to drive away evil spirits. STEEVENS.

[2] *— for their* charactery.] For the matter with which they make letters. JOHNSON.

Evans.

Evans. Pray you, lock hand in hand; yourselves in order set:
And twenty glow-worms shall our lanthorns be,
To guide our measure round about the tree.
But, stay; I smell a man of middle earth [3].

Fal. Heavens defend me from that Welch fairy! lest he transform me to a piece of cheese!

Pist. Vile worm, thou wast o'er-look'd even in thy birth [4].

Quick. With trial-fire touch me his finger-end:
If he be chaste, the flame will back descend,
And turn him to no pain [*]; but if he start,
It is the flesh of a corrupted heart.

Pist. A trial, come.

---

[3] —*of middle earth.*] Spirits are supposed to inhabit the ethereal regions, and fairies to dwell under ground; men therefore are in a middle station. JOHNSON.

So, in the ancient metrical romance of *Syr Guy of Warwick*, bl. l. no date:

"Thou mayest them flea with dint of sfwearde,
"And win the fayrest mayde *of middle erde.*"

Again, in Gower, *De Confessione Amantis*, fol. 26:

"Adam, for pride, lost his price
"In *myddell erth.*" STEEVENS.

Middle earth, says the Glossarist to Gawin Douglas's Translation of Virgil, is only *this* earth, ab A. S. myddan eard, *mundus.* MALONE.

[4] Vile *worm, thou wast o'er-look'd even in thy birth.*] The old copy reads—*vild.* That *vild*, which so often occurs in these plays, was not an error of the press, but the old spelling and the pronunciation of the time, appears from these lines of Heywood, in his *Pleasant Dialogues and Dramas*, 1637:

"EARTH. What goddess, or how styl'd?
"AGE. Age am I call'd.
"EARTH. Hence, false virago *vild!*"

However, as the spelling of the original copy of our author's plays has not been adhered to in the modern editions, there is no reason why this in particular should be preserved. In a passage in the *Tempest*, I have inadvertently retained the old spelling of this word. MALONE.

[*] *And* turn *him to no pain:*] This appears to have been the common phraseology of our author's time. So again, in *The Tempest:*

"—— O, my heart bleeds,
"To think of the *teen* that I have *turn'd you to.*"

Again in *K. Henry VI. P.* iii.

"Edward, what satisfaction canst thou make,
"For bearing arms, for stirring up my subjects,
"And all the trouble thou hast *turn'd me to?*"

Of this line there is no trace in the original play, on which the Third Part of *K. Henry VI* was formed. MALONE.

Evans. Come, will this wood take fire?

[*They burn him with their tapers.*

Fal. Oh, oh, oh!

Quick. Corrupt, corrupt, and tainted in desire!
About him, fairies; sing a scornful rhime:
And, as you trip, still pinch him to your time.

SONG.   *Fie on sinful phantasy!*
   Fie on lust and luxury [5] *!*
   Lust is but a bloody fire [6]*,*
   Kindled with unchaste desire,
   Fed in heart; whose flames aspire,
   As thoughts do blow them, higher and higher.
   Pinch him, fairies, mutually;
   Pinch him for his villainy;
   Pinch him, and burn him, and turn him about,
   Till candles, and star-light, and moon-shine be out.

During this song, the fairies pinch Falstaff [7]. *Doctor* Caius *comes one way, and steals away a fairy in green;* Slender *another way, and takes off a fairy in white; and* Fenton *comes and steals away Mrs.* Anne Page. *A noise of hunting is made within. All the fairies run away.* Falstaff *pulls off his buck's head, and rises.*

Enter PAGE, FORD, *Mrs.* PAGE, *and Mrs.* FORD. *They lay hold on him.*

Page. Nay; do not fly: I think, we have watch'd you now;
Will none but Herne the hunter serve your turn?

---

[5] — and luxury!] Luxury *is here used for* incontinence. So, in K. Lear: "To't luxury, pell-mell, for I lack soldiers." STEEVENS.

[6] Lust is but a bloody fire,] A bloody fire, *means a fire in the blood.* In *K. Henry IV.* P. ii. Act iv. the same expression occurs:
 "Led on by bloody youth," &c.
i. e. sanguine youth. STEEVENS.
 So also, in *the Tempest:*
  " — the strongest oaths are straw
  " To the fire i' the blood." MALONE.
In Sonnets by H. C. [Henry Constable.] 1594, we find the same image:
  " Lust is a fire, that for an hour or twaine
  " Giveth a scorching blaze, and then he dies;
  " Love a continual furnace doth maintaine," &c. MALONE.

[7] — *the* fairies pinch *Falstaff.*] So, in Lilly's *Endymion,* 1591. "The fairies dance, and with a song pinch him." STEEVENS.

Mrs.

Mrs. Page. I pray you, come; hold up the jest no higher:—
Now, good Sir John, how like you Windsor wives?
See you these, husband? do not these fair yokes
Become the forest better than the town [8]?

Ford. Now, Sir, who's a cuckold now?—Master Brook, Falstaff's a knave, a cuckoldly knave; here are his horns, Master Brook: And, Master Brook, he hath enjoyed nothing of Ford's but his buck-basket, his cudgel, and twenty pounds of money; which must be paid to Master Brook [9]; his horses are arrested for it, Master Brook.

Mrs. Ford. Sir John, we have had ill luck; we could never meet. I will never take you for my love again, but I will always count you my deer.

Fal. I do begin to perceive, that I am made an ass.

Ford. Ay, and an ox too; both the proofs are extant.

Fal. And these are not fairies? I was three or four times in the thought, they were not fairies: and yet the guiltiness of my mind, the sudden surprize of my powers, drove the grossness of the foppery into a receiv'd belief, in despight of the teeth of all rhime and reason, that they were fairies. See now, how wit may be made a Jack-a-lent [1], when 'tis upon ill employment!

Evans. Sir John Falstaff, serve Got, and leave your desires, and fairies will not pinse you.

Ford. Well said, fairy Hugh.

Evans. And leave your jealousies too, I pray you.

Ford. I will never mistrust my wife again, till thou art able to woo her in good English.

---

[8] *See you these, husband? do not these fair yokes*
Become the forest better than the town?] Mrs. Page's meaning is this. Seeing the horns (the types of cuckoldom) in Falstaff's hand, she asks her husband, whether these yokes are not more proper in the *forest* than in the *town*; i. e. than in his own family. THEOBALD.

The editor of the second folio changed *yokes* to—*oaks*. MALONE.

[9] —*to Master Brook;*] We ought rather to read with the old quarto, —" which must be paid to Master Ford;" for as Ford, to mortify Falstaff, addresses him throughout this speech by the name of *Brook,* the defending himself by the same name creates a confusion. A modern editor plausibly enough reads—" which must be paid *to,* Master Brook;" but the first sketch shews that *to* is right; for the sentence, as it stands in the quarto, will not admit *too.* MALONE.

[1] —*how wit may be made a* Jack-a-lent,] See p. 251, n. 8. MALONE.

Fal.

Fal. Have I lay'd my brain in the sun, and dried it, that it wants matter to prevent so gross o'er-reaching as this? Am I ridden with a Welch goat too? Shall I have a coxcomb of frize [2]? 'tis time I were choak'd with a piece of toasted cheese.

Evans. Seese is not good to give putter; your pelly is all putter.

Fal. Seese and putter! Have I lived to stand at the taunt of one that makes fritters of English? This is enough to be the decay of lust and late-walking, through the realm.

Mrs. Page. Why, Sir John, do you think, though we would have thrust virtue out of our hearts by the head and shoulders, and have given ourselves without scruple to hell, that ever the devil could have made you our delight?

Ford. What, a hodge-pudding? a bag of flax?

Mrs. Page. A puff'd man?

Page. Old, cold, wither'd, and of intolerable entrails?

Ford. And one that is as slanderous as Satan?

Page. And as poor as Job?

Ford. And as wicked as his wife?

Evans. And given to fornications, and to taverns, and sack, and wine, and metheglins, and to drinkings, and swearings, and starings, pribbles and prabbles?

Fal. Well, I am your theme; you have the start of me; I am dejected; I am not able to answer the Welch flannel [3]; ignorance itself is a plummet o'er me [4]: use me as you will.

---

[2] — *a coxcomb of frize?*] i. e. a fool's cap made out of Welch materials. Wales was famous for this cloth. STEEVENS.

[3] — *the Welch* flannel;] The very word is derived from a *Welch* one, so that it is almost unnecessary to add that *flannel* was originally the manufacture of Wales. STEEVENS.

It probably might make part of Sir Hugh's dress. EDWARDS.

[4] *Ignorance itself is a plummet o'er me:*] The meaning may be, I am so enfeebled, that *ignorance itself* weighs me down and oppresses me.
JOHNSON.

Perhaps Falstaff's meaning may be this: "Ignorance itself is a plummet o'er me: i. e. *above me;*" ignorance itself is not so low as I am, by the length of a *plummet-line.* TYRWHITT.

Dr. Johnson, for *plummet*, proposes to read *plume*; Dr. Farmer suggests—*planet.* The latter conjecture (says Mr. Steevens) derives some import from a passage in *K. Henry VI.* where Queen Margaret says, that Suffolk's face

"———— rul'd like a wand'ring *planet* over me."

I am satisfied with the old reading. MALONE.

Ford.

Ford. Marry, Sir, we'll bring you to Windsor, to one Master Brook, that you have cozen'd of money, to whom you should have been a pandar: over and above that you have suffered, I think, to repay that money will be a biting affliction.

Mrs. Ford. Nay, husband [3], let that go to make amends: Forgive that sum, and so we'll all be friends.

Ford. Well, here's my hand: all's forgiven at last.

Page. Yet be cheerful, Knight: thou shalt eat a posset to-night at my house; where I will desire thee to laugh at my wife [6], that now laughs at thee: Tell her, Master Slender hath married her daughter.

Mrs. Page. Doctors doubt that; if Anne Page be my daughter, she is, by this, Doctor Caius' wife. [*Aside.*

Enter SLENDER.

Slen. Whoo, ho! ho! father Page!

Page. Son! how now? how now, son? have you dispatch'd?

Slen. Dispatch'd! I'll make the best in Gloucestershire know on't; would I were hang'd, la, else.

Page. Of what, son?

Slen. I came yonder at Eton to marry Mistress Anne Page, and she's a great lubberly boy: If it had not been i'th e church, I would have swinged him, or he should have swinged me. If I did not think it had been Anne Page, would I might never stir, and 'tis a post-master's boy.

Page. Upon my life then you took the wrong.

Slen. What need you tell me that? I think so, when I took a boy for a girl: If I had been married to him, for all he was in woman's apparel, I would not have had him.

Page. Why, this is your own folly; Did not I tell you, how you should know my daughter by her garments?

---

[5] *Mrs. Ford. Nay, husband,* &c.] This and the following little speech I have inserted from the old quartos. The retrenchment, I presume, was by the players. Sir John Falstaff is sufficiently punished, in being disappointed and exposed. The expectation of his being prosecuted for the twenty pounds, gives the conclusion too tragical a turn. Besides, it is *poetical justice* that Ford should sustain this loss, as a fine for his unreasonable jealousy. THEOBALD.

[6] — *laugh at my wife,*] The two plots are excellently connected, and the transition very artfully made in this speech. JOHNSON.

Slen.

Slen. I went to her in white [7], and cry'd *mum*, and she cry'd *budget*, as Anne and I had appointed; and yet it was not Anne, but a post-master's boy.

Evans. Jeshu! Master Slender, cannot you see but marry boys [8]?

Page. O, I am vex'd at heart: What shall I do?

Mrs. Page. Good George, be not angry: I knew of your purpose; turn'd my daughter into green; and, indeed, she is now with the Doctor at the deanery, and there married.

Enter CAIUS.

Caius. Vere is Mistress Page? By gar, I am cozened; I ha' married *un garçon*, a boy; *un paisan*, by gar, a boy; it is not Anne Page: by gar, I am cozened.

Mrs. Page. Why, did you take her in green?

Caius. Ay, by gar, and 'tis a boy: be gar, I'll raise all Windsor. [*Exit* CAIUS.

Ford. This is strange! Who hath got the right Anne?

Page. My heart misgives me: Here comes Master Fenton.

Enter FENTON *and* ANNE PAGE.

How now, Master Fenton?

Anne. Pardon, good father! good my mother, pardon!

Page. Now, Mistress? how chance you went not with Master Slender?

Mrs. Page. Why went you not with Master Doctor, maid?

Fent. You do amaze her: Hear the truth of it.
You would have married her most shamefully,
Where there was no proportion held in love.
The truth is, She and I, long since contracted,
Are now so sure, that nothing can dissolve us.
The offence is holy, that she hath committed:
And this deceit loses the name of craft,

---

[7] — *in white,*] The old copy, by the inadvertence of either the author or transcriber, reads—*in green*; and in the two subsequent speeches of Mrs. Page, instead of *green* we find *white*. The corrections, which are fully justified by what has preceded, (see p. 288,) were made by Mr. Pope. MALONE.

[8] — *marry boys?*] This and the next speech are likewise restorations from the old quarto. STEEVENS.

Of disobedience, or unduteous title;
Since therein she doth evitate and shun
A thousand irreligious cursed hours,
Which forced marriage would have brought upon her.

Ford. Stand not amaz'd: here is no remedy:—
In love, the heavens themselves do guide the state;
Money buys lands, and wives are sold by fate.

Fal. I am glad, though you have ta'en a special stand to strike at me, that your arrow hath glanced.

Page. Well, what remedy⁹? Fenton, heaven give thee joy!
What cannot be eschew'd, must be embrac'd.

Fal. When night-dogs run, all sorts of deer are chas'd¹.

Evans. I will dance and eat plums at your wedding².

Mrs. Page. Well, I will muse no further:—Master Fenton,
Heaven give you many, many merry days!—
Good husband, let us every one go home,
And laugh this sport o'er by a country fire;
Sir John and all.

Ford. Let it be so:—Sir John,
To Master Brook, you yet shall hold your word;
For he, to-night, shall lie with Mistress Ford³. [*Exeunt.*

---

⁹ *Page. Well, what remedy?*—] In the first sketch of this play, which, as Mr. Pope observes, is much inferior to the latter performance, the only sentiment of which I regret the omission, occurs at this critical time. When Fenton brings in his wife, there is this dialogue:

Mrs. Ford. *Come, Mistress Page, I must be bold with you,*
'Tis pity to part love that is so true.
Mrs. Page. [Aside.] *Although that I have mis'd in my intent,*
Yet I am glad my husband's match is cross'd.
—*Here Fenton, take her* —
Evans. *Come, Master Page, you must needs agree.*
Ford. *I' faith, Sir, come, you see your wife is pleas'd.*
Page. *I cannot tell, and yet my heart is eas'd;*
And yet it doth me good the doctor miss'd.
Come hither, Fenton, and come hither, daughter. JOHNSON.

¹ —*all sorts of deer are chas'd.*] Young and old, does as well as bucks. He alludes to Fenton's having just *run down* Anne Page.
MALONE.

² *I will dance, &c.*] This speech was restored from the first quarto by Mr. Pope; but inserted improperly before that of Falstaff, which seems to have been intended to rhime with the preceding line. MALONE.

³ Of this play there is a tradition preserved by Mr. Rowe, that it was written at the command of Queen Elizabeth, who was so delighted with the character of Falstaff, that she wished it to be diffused through more plays; but suspecting that it might pall by continued uniformity, directed
the

the poet to diversify his manner, by shewing him in love. No task is harder than that of writing to the ideas of another. Shakspeare knew what the queen, if the story be true, seems not to have known, that by any real passion of tenderness, the selfish craft, the careless jollity, and the lazy luxury of Falstaff must have suffered so much abatement, that little of his former cast would have remained. Falstaff could not love, but by ceasing to be Falstaff. He could only counterfeit love, and his professions could be prompted, not by the hope of pleasure, but of money. Thus the poet approached as near as he could to the work enjoined him; yet having perhaps in the former plays completed his own idea, seems not to have been able to give Falstaff all his former power of entertainment.

This comedy is remarkable for the variety and number of the personages, who exhibit more characters appropriated and discriminated, than perhaps can be found in any other play.

Whether Shakspeare was the first that produced upon the English stage the effect of language distorted and depraved by provincial or foreign pronunciation, I cannot certainly decide [*]. This mode of forming ridiculous characters can confer praise only on him, who originally discovered it, for it requires not much of either wit or judgment; its success must be derived almost wholly from the player, but its power in a skilful mouth, even he that despises it, is unable to resist.

The conduct of this drama is deficient; the action begins and ends often before the conclusion, and the different parts might change places without inconvenience; but its general power, that power by which all works of genius shall finally be tried, is such, that perhaps it never yet had reader or spectator, who did not think it too soon at an end.

JOHNSON.

The story of *The two Lovers of Pisa*, from which (as Dr. Farmer has observed) Falstaff's adventures in this play seem to have been taken, is thus related in *Tarleton's Newes out of Purgatorie*, bl. let. no date. [Entered in the Stationer's Books, June 16, 1590.]

"In Pisa, a famous cittie of Italye, there liued a gentleman of good linage and landes, feared as well for his wealth, as honoured for his vertue; but indeed well thought on for both; yet the better for his riches. This gentleman had one onelye daughter called Margaret, who for her beauty was liked of all, and desired of many; but neither might their sutes, nor her owne preuaile about her fathers resolution, who was determyned not to marrye her, but to such a man as should be able in abundance to maintain the excellency of her beauty. Diuers yourg gentlemen proffered large feoffments, but in vaine; a maide shee must bee still; till at last an olde doctor in the towne, that professed phisicke, became a sutor to her; who was a welcome man to her father, in that he was one of the welthiest men in all Pisa. A tall strippling he was, and a proper youth, his age about fourscore; his head as white as milke, wherein for offence sake there was left neuer a tooth; but it is no matter; what he

[*] In the *Three Ladies of London*, 1584, is the character of an *Italian* merchant, very strongly marked by foreign pronunciation. Dr. Dodypoll, in the comedy which bears his name, is, like Caius, a French physician. This piece appeared at least a year before the *Merry Wives of Windsor*. The hero of it speaks such another jargon as the anxia-venith of Sir Hugh, and like him is cheated of his mistress. In several other pieces, more ancient than the earliest of Shakspeare's, provincial characters are introduced. STEEVENS.

wanted

wanted in person he had in the purse; which the poore gentlewoman little regarded, wishing rather to tie herselfe to one that might fit her content, though they liued meanely, then to him with all the wealth in Italye. But shee was yong and forcſt to follow her fathers direction, who vpon large couenants was content his daughter ſhould marry with the doctor, and whether ſhe like him or no, the match was made up, and in ſhort time ſhe was married. The poore wench was bound to the ſtake, and had not onely an old impotent man, but one that was ſo iealous, as none might enter into his houſe without ſuſpicion, nor ſhe doo any thing without blame: the leaſt glance, the ſmalleſt countenance, any ſmile, was a manifeſt inſtance to him, that ſhee thought of others better than himſelfe; thus he himſelfe liued in a hell, and tormented his wife in as ill perplexitie. At laſt it chaunced, that a young gentleman of the citie comming by her houſe, and ſeeing her looke out at her window, noting her rare and excellent proportion, fell in loue with her, and that ſo extreamelye, as his paſſions had no means till her fauour might mittigate his heartſicke diſcontent. The young man that was ignorant in amorous matters, and had neuer beene vſed to courte anye gentlewoman, thought to reueale his paſſions to ſome one freend, that might giue him counſaile for the winning of her loue; and thinking experience was the ſureſt maiſter, on a daye ſeeing the olde doctor walking in the churche, (that was Margarets huſband,) little knowing who he was, he thought this the fitteſt man to whom he might diſcouer his paſſions, for that hee was olde and knewe much, and was a phiſition that with his drugges might helpe him forward in his purpoſes: ſo that ſeeing the old man walke ſolitary, he ioinde vnto him, and after a curteous ſalute, tolde him he was to impart a matter of great import vnto him; wherein if hee would not onely be ſecrete, but indeuour to pleaſure him, his pains ſhould bee euery way to the full conſidered. You muſt imagine, gentleman, quoth Mutio, for ſo was the doctors name, that men of our profeſſion are no blabs, but hold their ſecrets in their hearts' bottome; and therefore reueale what you pleaſe, it ſhall not onely be concealed, but cured; if either my art or counſaile may do it. Upon this Lionello, (ſo was the young gentleman called) told and diſcourſt vnto him from point to point how he was falne in loue with a gentlewoman that was married to one of his profeſſion; diſcouered her dwelling and the houſe; and for that he was vnacquainted with the woman, and a man little experienced in loue matters, he required his fauour to further him with his aduiſe. Mutio at this motion was ſtung to the hart, knowing it was his wife hee was fallen in loue withal: yet ſo conceale the matter, and to experience his wiue's chaſtity, and that if ſhe plaide falſe, he might be reuengde on them both, he diſſembled the matter, and anſwered, that he knewe the woman very well, and commended her highly; but ſaide, ſhe had a churle to her huſband, and therefore he thought ſhe would bee the more tractable: trie her man, quoth hee; fainte hart neuer woonne fair lady; and if ſhee will not be brought to the bent of your bowe, I will prouide ſuch a potion as ſhall diſpatch all to your owne content; and to giue you further inſtructions for opportunitie, knowe that her huſband is foorth euery afternoone from three till ſixe. Thus farre I haue aduiſed you, becauſe I pitty your paſſions as my ſelfe being once a louer: but now I charge thee, reueale it to none whomſoeuer, leaſt it doo diſparage my credit, to meddle in amorous matters. The young gentleman not onely promised all carefull secrecy, but gaue him harty thanks for his good counsell, promising to meete him there the next day, and tell him what newes. Then hee left the old man, who was almost mad for feare his wife any way should play false. He saw by experience, braue men came to besiege the castle, and seeing it was in a womans custodie, and had so weake a gouernor as himselfe, he doubted it would in time be deliuered up: which feare made him almost franticke, yet he driude of the time in great torment, till he might heare from his riual. Lionello, he hastes him home, and sutes him in his brauerye, and goes downe towards the house of Mutio, where he sees her at her windowe, whom he courted with a passionate looke, with such an humble salute, as shee might perceiue how the gentleman was affectionate. Margaretta looking earnestlye upon him, and noting the perfection of his proportion, accounted him in her eye the flower of all Pisa; thinkte her selfe fortunate if she might haue him for her freend, to supply those defaultes that she found in Mutio. Sundry times that afternoone he past by her window, and he cast not vp more louing lookes, then he receiued gratious fauours: which did so incourage him, that the next daye betweene three and sixe hee went to her house, and knocking at the doore, desired to speake with the mistris of the house, who hearing by her maids description what he was, commaunded him to come in, where she intertained him with all curtesie.

" The youth that neuer before had giuen the attempt to couet a ladye, began his exordium with a blushe; and yet went forward so well, that hee discourst vnto her howe hee loued her, and that if it might please her so to accept of his seruice, as of a freende euer vowde in all duetye to bee at her commaunde, the care of her honour should bee deerer to him then his life, and hee would be ready to prise her discontent with his bloud at all times.

" The gentlewoman was a little coye, but before they part they concluded that the next day at foure of the clock hee should come thither and eate a pound of cherries, which was resolued on with a succado des labres; and so with a loath to depart they tooke their leaues. Lionello, as joyful a man as might be, hyed him to the church to meete his olde doctor, where hee found him in his olde walke. What newes, syr, quoth Mutio? How haue you sped? Even as I can wishe, quoth Lionello; for I haue been with my mistresse, and haue found her so tractable, that I hope to make the olde peasant her husband looke broadheaded by a paire of brow-antlers. How deepe this strooke into Mutios hart, let them imagine that can conjecture what iclousie is; insomuch that the olde doctor askte, when should be the time: marry, quoth Lionello, to morrow at foure of the clock in the afternoone; and then Maister Doctor, quoth hee, will I dub the olde squire knight of the forked order.

" Thus they past on in chat, till it grew late; and then Lyonello went home to his lodging, and Mutio to his house, couering all his sorrowes with a merrye countenance, with full resolution to reuenge them both the next day with extremetie. He past the night as patiently as he could, and the next day after dinner away hee went, watching when it should bee four of the clocke. At the houre iustly came Lyonello, and was intertained with all curtesie: but scarse had they
kist,

kist, ere the maide cried out to her mistresse that her maister was at the doore; for he hasted, knowing that a horne was but a little while in grafting. Margaret at this alarum was amazed, and yet for a shifte chopt Lyonello into a great driefatte full of feathers, and sat her downe close to her woorke: by that came Mutio in blowing; and as though hee came to looke somewhat in haste, called for the keyes of his chambers, and looked in euerye place, searching so narrowlye in euerye corner of the house, that he left not the very priuie vnsearcht. Seeing he could not finde him, hee saide nothing, but saying himself not well at ease, stayde at home, so that poore Lionello was faine to staye in the drifatte till the olde churle was in bed with his wife: and then the maide let him out at a backe doore, who went home with a flea in his eare to his lodging.

"Well, the next daye he went againe to meete his doctor, wheme hee found in his woonted walke. What news, quoth Mutio? How haue you sped*? A poxe of the olde slaue, quoth Lionello, I was no sooner in, and had giuen my mistresse one kisse, but the ielous asse was at the door; the maide spied him, and, cryed, *her maister*: so that the poore gentlewoman for verye shifte, was faine to put me in a drifatte of feathers that stoode in an olde chamber, and there I was faine to tarrie while he was in bed and asleepe, and then the maide let me out, and I departed.

"But it is no matter; 'twas but a chaunce; and I hope to crye quittance with him ere it be long. As how, quoth Mutio? Marry thus, quoth Lionello: she sent me woord by her maide this daye, that upon Thursday next the old churle suppeth with a patient of his a mile out of Pisa, and then I feare not but to quitte him for all. It is well, quoth Mutio; fortune bee your freende. I thank you, quoth Lionello; and so after a little more prattle they departed.

"To be shorte, Thursday came; and about fiue of the clocke foorth goes Mutio, no further than a freendes house of his, from whence hee might deserye who went into his house. Straight hee sawe Lionello enter in; and after goes hee, insomuche that hee was scarselye sitten downe, before the mayde cryed out againe, *my maister comes*. The good wife that before had prouided for afterclaps, had found out a priuie place between two seelings of a plauncher, and there she thrust Lionello; and her husband came sweting. What news, quoth shee, driues you home again so soone, husband? Marrye, sweete wife, (quoth he) a fearfull dreame that I had this night, which came to my remembrance; & that was this: Methought there was a villeine that came secretly into my house with a naked poinard in his hand, and hid himselfe; but I could not finde the place: with that mine nose bled, and I came backe; and by the grace of God I will seeke eury corner in the house for the quiet of my minde. Marry, I pray you doo, husband, queth she. With that he lockt in all the doors, and began to search euery chamber, euery hole, euery chest, euery tub, the very well; he stabd euery fetherbed through, and made hauocke, like a mad man, which made him thinke all was in vaine, and hee began to blame his eies that thought they saw that which they did not. Upon this he reste halfe lunaticke, and all night he was very wakefull; that towards the morning he fell into a dead sleepe, and then was Lionello conueighed away.

* See *The Merry Wives of Windsor*, p. 265.

" In

"In the morning when Mutio wakened, hee thought how by no meanes hee should be able to take Lyonello tardy: yet he laid in his head a most dangerous plot, and that was this. Wife, quoth he, I must the next Monday ride to Vycensa to visit an olde patient of mine; till my returne, which will be some ten dayes, I will haue thee stay at our little graunge house in the countrey. Marry very well content, husband, quoth she; with that he kist her, and was verye pleasant, as though he had suspected nothing, and away hee flinges to the church, where hee meetes Lionello. What Sir, quoth he, what newes? Is your mistresse yours in possession? No, a plague of the old slaue, quoth he; I think he is either a witch, or els woorkes by magick; for I can no sooner enter in the doors, but he is at my backe, and so he was againe yester-night; for I was not warm in my seat before the maide cried, *my maister comes;* and then was the poore soule faine to conuiegh me between two seelings of a chamber in a fit place for the purpose: wher I laught hartely to myself, to see how he sought every corner, ransackt euery tub, and stabd euery featherbed,—but in vaine; I was safe enough till the morning, and then when he was fast asleepe, I lept out. Fortune frowns on you, quoth Mutio; Ay, but I hope, quoth Lionello, this is the last time, and now shee will begin to smile; for on Monday next he rides to Vicensa, and his wife lyes at a grange house a little of the towne, and there in his absence I will reuenge all forepassed misfortunes. God send it be so, quoth Mutio; and took leaue. These two louers longed for Monday, and at last it came. Early in the morning Mutio horst himselfe, and his wife, his maide, and a man, and no more, and away he rides to his grange house; where after he had brok his fast he took his leaue, and away towards Vicensa. He rode not far ere by a falle way he returned into a thicket, and there with a company of cuntry peasants lay in an ambuscade to take the young gentleman. In the afternoon comes Lionello gallopping; and assoon as he came within sight of the house, he sent back his horse by his boy, & went easily afoot, & there at the very entry was entertained by Margaret, who led him vp ye staires, and conuaid him into her bedchamber, saying he was welcome into so mean a cottage; but quoth she, now I hope fortune shall not enuy the purity of our loues. Alas, alas, mistris, (cried the maid,) heer is my maister, and 100 men with him, with bils and staues. We are betraid, quoth Lionel, and I am but a dead man. Feare not, quoth she, but follow me; and straight she carried him downe into a lowe parlor, where stoode an old rotten chest full of writinges. She put him into that, and couered him with old papers and euidences, and went to the gate to meete her husband. Why Signior Mutio, what means this hurly burly, quoth she? Vile & shamelesse strumpet as thou art, thou shalt know by and by, quoth he. Where is thy loue? All we haue watcht him, & seen him enter in: now quoth he, shal neither thy tub of feathers nor thy seeling serue, for perish he shall with fire, or els fall into my hands. Doo thy worst, jealous foole, quoth she; I ask thee no sauour. With that in a rage he beset the house round, and then set fire on it. Oh! in what a perplexitie was poore Lionello, that was shut in a chest, and the fire about his eares? And how was Margaret passionat, that knew her louer in such danger? Yet she made light of the matter, and as one in a rage called her maid to her and said; Come on, wench; seeing thy maister mad
with

with ielousie hath set the house and al my liuing on fire, I will be reuenged vpon him; help me heer to lift this old chest where all his writings and deeds are; let that burne first; and assoon as I see that on fire I will walk towards my freends: for the old foole wil be beggard, and I will refuse him. Mutio that knew al his obligations and statutes lay there, puld her back, and bad two of his men carry the chest into the feeld, and see it were safe; himself standing by and seeing his house burned downe, sticke and stone. Then quieted in his minde he went home with his wife, and began to flatter her, thinking assuredly y^t he had burnd her paramour; causing his chest to be carried in a cart to his house at Pisa. Margaret impatient went to her mothers, and complained to her and to her brethren of the iealousie of her husband; who maintained her it be true, and desired but a daies respite to proue it. Wel, hee was bidden to supper the next night at her mothers, she thinking to make her daughter and him freends againe. In the meane time he to his woonted walk in the church, & there *præter expectationem* he found Lionello walking. Wondring at this, he straight enquires, what news? What newes, Maister Doctor, quoth he, and he fell in a great laughing; in faith yesterday I scapt a scowring; for, syrrah, I went to the grange house, where I was appointed to come, and I was no sooner gotten vp the chamber, but the magicall villeine her husband beset the house with bils and staues, and that he might be sure no seeling nor corner should shrowde me, he set the house on fire, and so burnt it to the ground. Why, quoth Mutio, and how did you escape? Alas, quoth he, wel fare a womans wit! She conueighed me into an old chest ful of writings, which she knew her husband durst not burne; and so was I saued and brought to Pisa, and yesternight by her maide let home to my lodging. This, quoth he, is the pleasantest iest that euer I heard; and vpon this I haue a sute to you. I am this night bidden foorth to supper; you shall be my guest; onelye I will craue so much fauour, as after supper for a pleasant sporte to make relation what successe you haue had in your loues. For that I will not sticke, quoth he; and so he carried Lionello to his mother-in-lawes house with him, and discoured to his wines brethren who he was, and how at supper he would disclose the whole matter; for quoth he, he knowes not that I am Margarets husband. At this all the brethren bad him welcome, & so did the mother too; and Margaret she was kept out of sight. Supper-time being come, they fell to their victals, & Lionello was carrowst vnto by Mutio, who was very pleasant, to draw him to a merry humour, that he might to the ful discourse the effect & fortunes of his loue. Supper being ended, Mutio requested him to tel to the gentlemen what had hapned between him & his mistresse. Lionello with a smiling countenance began to describe his mistresse, the house and street where she dwelt, how he fell in loue with her, and how he vsed the counsell of this doctor, who in all his affaires was his secretarye. Margaret heard all this with a great feare; & when he came at the last point she caused a cup of wine to be giuen him by one of her sisters wherein was a ring that he had giuen Margaret. As he had told how he escapt burning, and was ready to confirm all for a troth, the gentlewoman drunke to him; who taking the cup, and seeing the ring, hauing a quick wit and a reaching head, spide the fetch, and perceiued that all this while this was his louers husband, to whome hee had reuealed these escapes. At this drinking ye wine, and swallowing

the

the ring into his mouth, he went forward: Gentlemen, quoth he, how like you of my loues and my fortunes? Wel, quoth the gentlemen; I pray you is it true? As true, quoth he, as if I would be so simple as to reueal what I did to Margarets husband; for know you, gentlemen, that I knew this Mutio to be her husband whom I notified to be my louer; and for y^t he was generally known through Pisa to be a iealous fool, therefore with these tales I brought him into this paradice, which indeed are follies of mine owne braine; for trust me, by the faith of a gentleman, I neuer spake to the woman, was neuer in her companye, neither doo I know her if I see her. At this they all fell in a laughing at Mutio, who was ashamde that Lionello had so scoft him; but all was well, —they were made friends; but the iest went so to his hart, that he shortly after died, and Lionello enjoyed the ladye; and for that they two were the death of the old man, now are they plagued in purgatory, and he whips them with nettles."

It is observable that in the foregoing novel (which, I believe Shakspeare had read,) there is no trace of the buck-hasket.—In the first tale of *The Fortunate, the Deceived, and Unfortunate Lovers*, (of which I have an edition printed in 1684, but the novels it contains had probably appeared in English in our author's time,) a young student of Bologna is taught by an old doctor how to make love; and his first essay is practised on his instructor's wife. The jealous husband having tracked his pupil to his house, enters unexpectedly, fully persuaded that he should detect the lady and her lover together; but the gallant is protected from his fury by being concealed *under a heap of linen half-dried*; and afterwards informs him, (not knowing that his tutor was likewise his mistress's husband,) what a lucky escape he had. It is therefore, I think, highly probable that Shakspeare had read both stories. MALONE

MEASURE

MEASURE FOR MEASURE.

PERSONS REPRESENTED.

Vincentio, *duke of* Vienna.
Angelo, *lord deputy in the duke's absence.*
Escalus, *an ancient lord, joined with* Angelo *in the deputation.*
Claudio, *a young gentleman.*
Lucio, *a fantastic.*
Two other like gentlemen.
Varrius*, *a gentleman, servant to the duke.*
Provost.
Thomas, } *two friars.*
Peter,
A justice.
Elbow, *a simple constable.*
Froth, *a foolish gentleman.*
Clown, *servant to Mrs.* Overdone.
Abhorson, *an executioner.*
Barnardine, *a dissolute prisoner.*

Isabella, *sister to* Claudio.
Mariana, *betrothed to* Angelo.
Juliet, *beloved by* Claudio.
Francisca, *a nun.*
Mistress Overdone, *a bawd.*

Lords, gentlemen, guards, officers, and other attendants.

SCENE, Vienna.

* Varrius might be omitted, for he is only once spoken to, and says nothing. JOHNSON.

MEASURE FOR MEASURE[1].

ACT I. SCENE I.

A Room in the Duke's Palace.

Enter DUKE, ESCALUS, Lords *and* Attendants.

Duke. Escalus—
Escal. My Lord.
Duke. Of government the properties to unfold,
Would seem in me to affect speech and discourse;

Since

---

[1] The story is taken from Cinthio's *Novels*, Decad. 8. Novel 5.
POPE.

We are sent to Cinthio for the plot of *Measure for Measure*, and Shakspeare's judgment hath been attacked for some deviations from him in the conduct of it, when probably all he knew of the matter was from Madam *Isabella*, in the *Heptameron* of Whetstone, Lond. 4to. 1582.— She reports, in the fourth dayes Exercise, the rare Historie of *Promos and Cassandra*. A marginal note informs us, that *Whetstone* was the auther of the *Comedie* on that subject; which likewise had probably fallen into the hands of Shakspeare. FARMER.

There is perhaps not one of Shakspeare's plays more darkened than this by the peculiarities of its author, and the unskilfulness of its editors, by distortions of phrase, or negligence of transcription. JOHNSON.

Shakspeare took the fable of this play from the *Promos and Cassandra* of G. Whetstone, published in 1578. See Theobald's note at the end.

A hint, like a seed, is more or less prolific, according to the qualities of the soil on which it is thrown. This story, which in the hands of Whetstone produced little more than barren insipidity, under the culture of Shakspeare became fertile of entertainment. The curious reader will find that the old play of *Promos and Cassandra* exhibits an almost complete embryo of *Measure for Measure*; yet the hints on which it is formed are so slight, that it is nearly as impossible to detect them, as it is to point out in the acorn the future ramifications of the oak.

Since I am put to know [2], that your own science
Exceeds, in that, the lists [3] of all advice
My strength can give you: Then no more remains,
But that to your sufficiency ** as your worth is able,
And let them work [4]. The nature of our people,

Our

The reader will find the argument of G. Whetstone's *Promos and Cassandra*, at the end of this play. It is too bulky to be inserted here. See likewise the piece itself among *Six old Plays on which Shakspeare founded*, &c. published by S. Leacroft, Charing-cross. STEEVENS

Measure for Measure was, I believe, written in 1603. See an *Attempt to ascertain the order of Shakspeare's plays*, ante. MALONE

[2] *Since I am put to know,*—] *I am put to know* may mean, *I am obliged to acknowledge.* So, in *King Henry VI*. Part II. sc. i:
"—— had I first been *put to* speak my mind." STEEVENS.

[3] —*lists*] Bounds, limits. JOHNSON.

[4] ——— *Then no more remains,*
*But that to your sufficiency ** as your worth is able,*
And let them work.] I have not the smallest doubt that the compositor's eye glanced from the middle of the second of these lines to that under it in the MS and that by this means two half lines have been omitted. The very same error may be found in *Macbeth*, edit. 1632:
"——— which, being taught, return,
"To plague *the ingredients of our poison'd chalice*
"To our own lips."
instead of
"———which, being taught, return,
"To plague the *inventor. This even-handed justice*
"*Commends the* ingredients of our poison'd chalice," &c.

Again, in *Much ado about Nothing*, edit. 1623. p. 103:
"And I will break with her. Was't not to this end, &c."
instead of
"And I will break with her, *and with her father,*
"*And thou shalt have her*. Was't not to this end, &c."

Again, in *Romeo and Juliet*, folio, 1623:
"And hither shall he come, and that very night
"Shall Romeo," &c.
instead of
"And hither shall he come, *and be and I*
"*Will watch thy waking,* and that very night
"Shall Romeo," &c.

Mr. Theobald would supply the defect thus:
But that to your sufficiency *you add*
Due diligence, as your worth is able, &c.

Sir T. Hanmer reads:
But that to your sufficiency *you join*
A will to serve us, as your worth is able, &c.

The following passage, in *K. Henry IV*. P. i. which is constructed in a manner somewhat similar to the present when corrected, appears to me to strengthen the supposition that two half lines have been lost;

"Send

Our city's institutions, and the terms
For common justice⁵, you are as pregnant in⁶,
As art and practice hath enriched any
That we remember: There is our commission,
From which we would not have you warp.—Call hither,
I say, bid come before us Angelo.—[*Exit an attendant.*
What figure of us think you he will bear?
For you must know, we have with special soul⁷
Elected him our absence to supply;
Lent him our terror, drest him with our love;
And given his deputation all the organs
Of our own power: What think you of it?

Escal. If any in Vienna be of worth
To undergo such ample grace and honour,
It is Lord Angelo.

Enter ANGELO.

Duke. Look where he comes.
Ang. Always obedient to your Grace's will,
I come to know your pleasure.

" Send *danger* from the east unto the west,
" So *honour* cross it from the north to south,
" And let them grapple."

Sufficiency is skill in government; ability to execute his office. *And let them work*, a figurative expression; *Let them ferment*. MALONE.

Some words seem to have been lost here, the sense of which, perhaps, may be thus supplied:

———— *then no more remains,*
But that to your sufficiency you put
A zeal as willing as your worth is able, &c. TYRWHITT.

⁵ ———— *and the terms*
For common justice,] *Terms* means the technical language of the courts. An old book called *Les Termes de la Ley*, (written in Henry the Eighth's time) was in Shakspeare's days, and is now, the accidence of young students in the law. BLACKSTONE.

⁶ — *as pregnant in,*] *Pregnant* is ready, knowing. JOHNSON.

⁷ — *with special soul*] By the words *with special soul elected him*, I believe, the poet meant no more than *that he was the immediate choice of his heart*. So, in the *Tempest:*

———— " for several virtues
" Have I lik'd several women, never any
" With so full soul, but some defect," &c. STEEVENS.

Again, in *Troilus and Cressida:*

———— " never did young man fancy
" With so eternal and so fix'd a soul." MASON.

This seems to be only a translation of the usual formal words inserted in all royal grants: ——— " *de gratia nostra speciali, et ex mero motu*—." MALONE.

To one that can my part in him advertise⁷;
Hold therefore, Angelo⁸;
In our remove, be thou at full ourself;
Mortality and mercy in Vienna
Live in thy tongue and heart: Old Escalus,
Though first in question⁹, is thy secondary:
Take thy commission.

Ang. Now, good my Lord,
Let there be some more test made of my metal,
Before so noble and so great a figure
Be stamp'd upon it.

Duke. No more evasion:
We have with a leaven'd and prepar'd choice¹
Proceeded to you; therefore take your honours.
Our haste from hence is of so quick condition,
That it prefers itself, and leaves unquestion'd
Matters of needful value. We shall write to you,

---

⁷ ——— *I do bend my speech*
To one that can my part in him advertise;] I believe the meaning is,—I am talking to one who is himself already sufficiently conversant with the nature and duties of my office;—of that office, which I have now delegated to him.
So, in *Timon of Athens:*
"It is our *part*, and promise to the Athenians,
"To speak with Timon."

⁸ *Hold therefore, Angelo:*] That is, continue to be Angelo; hold as thou art. JOHNSON.
I believe that—*Hold therefore Angelo,* are the words which the duke utters on tendering his commission to him. He concludes with—*Take thy commission.* STEEVENS.
If a full point be put after *therefore,* the duke may be understood to speak of himself. *Hold therefore,* i. e. Let me therefore hold, or stop. And the sense of the whole passage may be this. The duke, who has begun an exhortation to Angelo, checks himself thus, "But I am speaking *to one, that can in him* [in, or by himself] apprehend *my part* [all that I have to say]: I will therefore say no more [on that subject]." He then merely signifies to Angelo his appointment.
TYRWHITT.

⁹ —*first in question,*] That is, first called for; first appointed.
JOHNSON.

¹ *We have with a leaven'd and prepared choice*] *Leaven'd choice* is one of Shakspeare's harsh metaphors. His train of ideas seems to be *leavened.* When bread is *leavened* it is left to ferment: a *leavened* choice is therefore a choice not hasty, but considerate, not declared as soon as it fell into the imagination, but suffered to work long in the mind.
JOHNSON

As time and our concernings shall importune,
How it goes with us; and do look to know
What doth befall you here. So, fare you well:
To the hopeful execution do I leave you
Of your commissions.

Ang. Yet, give leave, my Lord,
That we may bring you something on the way [2].

Duke. My haste may not admit it;
Nor need you, on mine honour, have to do
With any scruple: your scope [3] is as mine own;
So to inforce, or qualify the laws,
As to your soul seems good. Give me your hand;
I'll privily away: I love the people,
But do not like to stage me to their eyes;
Though it do well, I do not relish well
Their loud applause, and *aves* vehement;
Nor do I think the man of safe discretion,
That does affect it. Once more, fare you well.

Ang. The heavens give safety to your purposes!
Escal. Lead forth, and bring you back in happiness!
Duke. I thank you: Fare you well. [*Exit.*
Escal. I shall desire you, Sir, to give me leave
To have free speech with you; and it concerns me
To look into the bottom of my place:
A power I have; but of what strength and nature
I am not yet instructed.

Ang. 'Tis so with me:—Let us withdraw together,
And we may soon our satisfaction have
Touching that point.

Escal. I'll wait upon your honour. [*Exeunt.*

SCENE II.

A Street.

Enter LUCIO, *and two* GENTLEMEN.

Lucio. If the Duke, with the other dukes, come not to composition with the king of Hungary, why then all the dukes fall upon the king.

---

[2] — *bring you something on the way.*] i. e. accompany you. The same mode of expression is to be found in almost every writer of the times.
REED.

[3] *your scope* —] That is, your amplitude of power. JOHNSON.

1st. Gent.

1st. Gent. Heaven grant us its peace, but not the king of Hungary's!

2d. Gent. Amen.

Lucio. Thou concludeſt like the ſanctimonious pirate, that went to ſea with the ten commandments, but ſcraped one out of the table.

2d. Gent. Thou ſhalt not ſteal?

Lucio. Ay, that he razed.

1st. Gent. Why, 'twas a commandment to command the captain and all the reſt from their functions; they put forth to ſteal: There's not a ſoldier of us all, that, in the thankſ-giving before meat, doth reliſh the petition well that prays for peace.

2d. Gent. I never heard any ſoldier diſlike it.

Lucio. I believe thee; for, I think, thou never waſt where grace was ſaid.

2d. Gent. No? a dozen times at leaſt.

1st. Gent. What? in metre⁴?

Lucio. In any proportion, or in any language.

1st. Gent. I think, or in any religion.

Lucio. Ay! why not? Grace is grace, deſpight of all controverſy⁵: As for example; Thou thyſelf art a wicked villain, deſpight of all grace.

1st. Gent. Well, there went but a pair of ſheers between us⁶.

Lucio. I grant; as there may between the liſt and the velvet: Thou art the liſt.

1st. Gent. And thou the velvet: thou art good velvet; thou art a three-pil'd piece, I warrant thee: I had as lief be a liſt of an Engliſh kerſey, as be pil'd, as thou art pil'd, for a French velvet⁷. Do I ſpeak feelingly now?

Lucio.

---

⁴ *— in metre?*] In the primers, there are metrical graces, ſuch as, I ſuppoſe, were uſed in Shakſpeare's time. JOHNSON.

⁵ *Grace is grace, deſpight of all controverſy:*] The queſtion is, whether the ſecond gentleman has ever heard grace. The firſt gentleman limits the queſtion to *grace in metre.* Lucio enlarges it to *grace in any* form *or language.* The firſt gentleman, to go beyond him, ſays, *or in any religion,* which Lucio allows, becauſe the nature of things is unalterable; grace is as immutably grace, as his merry antagoniſt is a *wicked villain.* Difference in religion cannot make a *grace* not to be *grace,* a *prayer* not to be *holy;* as nothing can make a *villain* not to be a *villain.* This ſeems to be the meaning, ſuch as it is. JOHNSON.

⁶ *— there went but a pair of ſheers between us.*] We are both of the ſame piece. JOHNSON.

⁷ *—pil'd,*

Lucio. I think thou dost; and, indeed, with most painful feeling of thy speech: I will, out of thine own confession, learn to begin thy health; but, whilst I live, forget to drink after thee.

1st. Gent. I think, I have done myself wrong; have I not?

2d. Gent. Yes, that thou hast; whether thou art tainted or free.

1st. Gent. Behold, behold, where Madam Mitigation comes [8]! I have purchased as many diseases under her roof, as come to—

2d. Gent. To what, I pray?

1st. Gent. Judge.

2d. Gent. To three thousand dollars a year [9].

1st. Gent. Ay, and more.

Lucio. A French crown more [1].

1st. Gent. Thou art always figuring diseases in me: but thou art full of error; I am sound.

Lucio. Nay, not as one would say, healthy; but so sound, as things that are hollow: thy bones are hollow; impiety has made a feast of thee.

Enter BAWD.

1st. Gent. How now? Which of your hips has the most profound sciatica?

[7] — *pill'd, as thou art pil'd, for a French velvet*] The jest about the pile of a French velvet alludes to the loss of hair in the French disease, a very frequent topic of our author's jocularity. Lucio finding that the gentleman understands the distemper so well, and mentions it so feelingly, promises to remember to drink his health, but to forget *to drink after him.* It was the opinion of Shakspeare's time, that the cup of an infected person was contagious. JOHNSON.

The jest lies between the similar sound of the words *pill'd* and *pil'd*. This I have elsewhere explained, under a passage in *Henry VIII*: "*Pill'd* priest thou liest." STEEVENS.

[8] *Behold, behold, where Madam Mitigation comes!*] In the old copy this speech, and the next but one, are attributed to Lucio. The present regulation was suggested by Mr. Pope. What Lucio says afterwards, "*A French* crown more," proves that it is right. He would not utter a sarcasm against himself. MALONE.

[9] *To three thousand dollars a year.*] A quibble intended between *dollars* and *dolours*. HANMER.

The same jest occurred before in the *Tempest.* JOHNSON.

[1] *A French crown more.*] Lucio means here not the piece of money so called, but that *venereal* scab, which among the surgeons is styled *corona Veneris.* THEOBALD.

Bawd.

Bawd. Well, well; there's one yonder arrested, and carry'd to prison, was worth five thousand of you all.

1st. Gent. Who's that, I pr'ythee?

Bawd. Marry, Sir, that's Claudio, Signior Claudio.

1st. Gent. Claudio to prison! 'tis not so.

Bawd. Nay, but I know, 'tis so: I saw him arrested; saw him carry'd away; and, which is more, within these three days his head's to be chopp'd off.

Lucio. But, after all this fooling, I would not have it so: Art thou sure of this?

Bawd. I am too sure of it: and it is for getting Madam Julietta with child.

Lucio. Believe me, this may be: he promised to meet me two hours since; and he was ever precise in promise-keeping.

2d. Gent. Besides, you know, it draws something near to the speech we had to such a purpose.

1st. Gent. But most of all agreeing with the proclamation.

Lucio. Away; let's go learn the truth of it.

[*Exeunt* LUCIO *and* GENTLEMEN.

Bawd. Thus, what with the war, what with the sweat [2], what with the gallows, and what with poverty, I am custom-shrunk. How now? what's the news with you?

Enter CLOWN [3].

Clown. Yonder man is carry'd to prison.

Bawd. Well; what has he done?

---

[2] —*what with the sweat,*] This may allude to the *sweating sickness,* of which the memory was very fresh in the time of Shakspeare; but more probably to the method of cure then used for the diseases contracted in brothels. JOHNSON.

[3] *Enter Clown.*] As this is the first clown who makes his appearance in the plays of our author, it may not be amiss, from a passage in *Tarlton's News out of Purgatory,* to point out one of the ancient dresses appropriated to the character; "— I have one attired in russet, with a " button'd cap on his head, a bag by his side, and a strong bat in his " hand; so artificially attired for a clown, as I began to call Tarlton's " woonted shape to remembrance." STEEVENS.

Such perhaps was the dress of the Clown in *All's Well that ends Well* and *Twelfth Night;* Touchstone in *As you like it,* &c. The present clown however (as an anonymous writer has observed) is only the tapster of a brothel, and probably was not so apparelled. MALONE.

Clown. A woman [4].

Bawd. But what's his offence?

Clown. Groping for trouts in a peculiar river [5].

Bawd. What, is there a maid with child by him?

Clown. No; but there's a woman with maid by him:—You have not heard of the proclamation, have you?

Bawd. What proclamation, man?

Clown. All houses in the suburbs [6] of Vienna must be pluck'd down.

Bawd. And what shall become of those in the city?

Clown. They shall stand for seed: they had gone down too, but that a wife burgher put in for them.

Bawd. But shall all our houses of resort in the suburbs be pull'd down [7]?

Clown. To the ground, Mistress.

Bawd. Why, here's a change, indeed, in the commonwealth! What shall become of me?

---

[4] — *What has he done?*

Clown. A woman.] The ancient meaning of the verb to *do* (though now obsolete) may be guess'd at from the following passage:

"*Chiron.* Thou hast undone our mother.

"*Aaron.* Villain, I've *done* thy mother." *Titus Andronicus*.

Again, in Ovid's *Elegies*, translated by Marlowe, printed at Middlebourg, no date;

"The strumpet with the stranger will not *do*,

"Before the room is clear, and door put to."

Hence the name of Over-*done*, which Shakspeare has appropriated to his bawd. COLLINS.

[5] — *in a peculiar river.*] i. e. a river belonging to an individual; not public property. MALONE.

[6] *All houses in the suburbs—*] This is surely too general an expression, unless we suppose that *all* the houses in the suburbs were bawdy-houses. It appears too, from what the bawd says below, "*But shall all our houses of resort* in the suburbs be pulled down?" that the clown had been particular in his description of the houses which were to be pulled down. I am therefore inclined to believe that we should read here, *all bawdy-houses*, or *all houses of resort* in the suburbs. TYRWHITT.

[7] *But shall all our houses of resort in the suburbs be pull'd down?*] This will be understood from the Scotch law of *James*'s time, concerning *huires* (whores); "that commoun women be put at the *utmost endes of townes*, queire least perril of fire is." Hence *Ursula* the pig-woman, in *Bartholomew-Fair*: "I, I, gamesters, meek a plain, plump, soft wench of the suburbs, do!" FARMER.

See Martial, where *summaeniana*, and *suburbana* are applied to prostitutes. STEEVENS.

The licenced houses of resort at *Vienna* are at this time all in the suburbs, under the permission of the Committee of Chastity. S. W.

Clown. Come; fear not you: good counsellors lack no clients: though you change your place, you need not change your trade; I'll be your tapster still. Courage; there will be pity taken on you; you that have worn your eyes almost out in the service, you will be considered.

Bawd. What's to do here, Thomas Tapster? Let's withdraw.

Clown. Here comes Signior Claudio, led by the Provost to prison: and there's Madam Juliet. [*Exeunt.*

SCENE III.

The same.

Enter PROVOST, CLAUDIO, JULIET, *and* OFFICERS; LUCIO, *and two* GENTLEMEN.

Claud. Fellow, why dost thou shew me thus to the world?
Bear me to prison, where I am committed.

Prov. I do it not in evil disposition,
But from Lord Angelo by special charge.

Claud. Thus can the demi-god, authority,
Make us pay down for our offence by weight.—
The words of heaven;—on whom it will, it will;
On whom it will not, so; yet still 'tis just⁸.

Lucio.

---

⁸ *Thus can the demi-god, authority,*
Make us pay down for our offence by weight.—
The words of heaven;—on whom it will, it will;
On whom it will not, so; yet still 'tis just.] The demi-god, Authority, makes us pay the full penalty of our offence, and its decrees are as little to be questioned as the words of heaven, which pronounces its pleasure thus:—I punish and remit punishment according to my own uncontroulable will; and yet who can say, what dost thou?—*Make us pay down for our offence by weight,* is a fine expression to signify paying the full penalty. The metaphor is taken from paying money by *weight,* which is always exact; not so by *tale,* on account of the practice of diminishing the species. WARBURTON.

I suspect that a line is lost. JOHNSON.

It may be read, *the* sword *of heaven.*

Thus can the demi-god, Authority,
Make us pay down for our offence, by weight;—
The sword *of heaven;—on whom,* &c.

Authority is then poetically called *the sword of heaven,* which will spare or punish, as it is commanded. The alteration is slight, being made only by taking a single letter from the end of the word, and placing it at the beginning.

This

Lucio. Why, how now, Claudio? whence comes this restraint?

Claud. From too much liberty, my Lucio, liberty:
As surfeit is the father of much fast,
So every scope by the immoderate use
Turns to restraint: Our natures do pursue
(Like rats that ravin [9] down their proper bane,)
A thirsty evil; and when we drink, we die.

Lucio. If I could speak so wisely under an arrest, I would send for certain of my creditors: And yet, to say the truth, I had as lief have the foppery of freedom, as the morality [1] of imprisonment.——What's thy offence, Claudio?

Claud. What, but to speak of would offend again.

Lucio. What is it? murder?

Claud. No.

Lucio. Lechery?

Claud. Call it so.

Prov. Away, Sir; you must go.

Claud. One word, good friend:—Lucio, a word with you. [*Takes him aside.*

This very ingenious and elegant emendation was suggested to me by the Rev. Dr. Roberts, of Eaton; and it may be countenanced by the following passage in the *Cobler's Prophecy*, 1594;

"—In brief they are *the swords of heaven* to punish."

Sir W. Davenant, who incorporated this play of Shakspeare with *Much ado about Nothing*, and formed out of them a Tragi-comedy called *The Law against Lovers*, omits the two last lines of this speech; I suppose, on account of their seeming obscurity. STEEVENS.

The very ingenious emendation proposed by Dr. Roberts is yet more strongly supported by another passage in the play before us, where this phrase occurs [Act iii. sc. last];

"He who the *sword of heaven* will bear,
"Should be as holy as severe;"

yet I believe the old copy is right. MALONE.

Notwithstanding Dr. Roberts's ingenious conjecture, the text is certainly right. *Authority* being absolute in Angelo, is finely stiled by Claudio, *the demigod*. To his uncontroulable power, the poet applies a passage from St. Paul to the Romans, ch. ix. v. 15, 18, which he properly stiles, *the words of heaven:* for his faith to Moses, I will have mercy on whom I will have mercy, &c. And again, Therefore hath he mercy on whom he will have mercy, &c. HENLEY.

[9] *Like rats that* ravin, &c.] To *ravin* was formerly used for eagerly or voraciously devouring any thing. REED.

Ravin is an ancient word for *prey*. STEEVENS.

[1] —*as the* morality—] The old copy has *mortality*. It was corrected by Sir William Davenant. MALONE.

Lucio.

Lucio. A hundred, if they'll do you any good.—
Is lechery so look'd after?

Claud. Thus stands it with me:—Upon a true contract,
I got possession of Julietta's bed [2];
You know the lady; she is fast my wife,
Save that we do the denunciation lack
Of outward order: this we came not to,
Only for propagation of a dower [3]
Remaining in the coffer of her friends;
From whom we thought it meet to hide our love,
Till time had made them for us. But it chances,
The stealth of our most mutual entertainment,
With character too gross, is writ on Juliet.

Lucio. With child, perhaps?

Claud. Unhappily, even so.
And the new deputy now for the duke—
Whether it be the fault and glimpse of newness [4];
Or whether that the body politic be
A horse whereon the governor doth ride,
Who, newly in the seat, that it may know
He can command, let's it straight feel the spur:
Whether the tyranny be in his place,
Or in his eminence that fills it up,
I stagger in:—But this new governor
Awakes me all the enrolled penalties,

[2] *I got possession of Julietta's bed,* &c.] This speech is surely too indelicate to be spoken concerning Juliet, before her face, for she appears to be brought in with the rest, though she has nothing to say. The Clown points her out as they enter; and yet from Claudio's telling Lucio, *that he knows the lady,* &c. one would think she was not meant to have made her personal appearance on the scene. STEEVENS.

Claudio may be supposed to speak to Lucio apart. MALONE.

[3] *Only for* propagation *of a dower*—] The meaning of the speaker is sufficiently clear, yet this term appears a very strange one. Sir William Davenant seems also to have thought so; for he reads

"Only for the *assurance of a dowry*."

Perhaps we should read— *ade for* prorogation—. MALONE.

[4] *Whether it be the* fault and glimpse *of newness;*] Fault, I apprehend, does not refer to any enormous act done by the deputy, (as Dr. Johnson seems to have thought) but to *newness*. The *fault and glimpse* is the same as *the faulty glimpse*. And the meaning seems to be—*Whether it be the* fault *of* newness, *a fault arising from the mind being dazzled by a novel authority, of which the new governor has yet had only a glimpse—has yet taken only a hasty survey; or whether,* &c. Shakspeare has many similar expressions. MALONE.

Which

Which have, like unscour'd armour⁵, hung by the wall,
So long, that nineteen zodiacs have gone round,
And none of them been worn; and, for a name,
Now puts the drowsy and neglected act
Freshly on me⁶:—'tis, surely, for a name.

Lucio. I warrant, it is: and thy head stands so tickle⁷ on thy shoulders, that a milk-maid, if she be in love, may sigh it off. Send after the duke, and appeal to him.

Claud. I have done so, but he is not to be found.
I pr'ythee, Lucio, do me this kind service:
This day my sister should the cloister enter,
And there receive her approbation⁸:
Acquaint her with the danger of my state;
Implore her, in my voice, that she make friends
To the strict deputy; bid herself assay him;
I have great hope in that: for in her youth
There is a prone and speechless dialect⁹,

Such

---

⁵ — *like unscour'd armour,*] So, in *Troilus and Cressida:*
"Like rusty mail in monumental mockery." STEEVENS.

⁶ ——— But this new governor
Awakes *me all the* enrolled penalties,
Which have, like unscour'd armour, hung by the wall,
So long ———
Now puts the drowsy and neglected act.
Freshly on me:] Lord Stafford, in the conclusion of his Defence in the House of Lords, had, perhaps, these lines in his thoughts:
" It is now full two hundred and forty years since any man was touched for this alledged crime, to this height, before myself.—Let us rest contented with that which our fathers have left us; and not *awake* those *sleeping* lions, to our own destruction, by raking up *a few musty records, that have lain so many ages by the walls,* quite *forgotten* and *neglected.*" MALONE.

⁷ —*so tickle*] i. e. ticklish. This word is frequently used by our old dramatic authors. STEEVENS.

⁸ — *her approbation:*] i. e. enter on her *probation*, or *noviciate.* So again, in this play:
" I, in *probation* of a sisterhood"—.
Again, in *The Merry Devil of Edmonton,* 1608:
" Madam, for a twelvemonth's *approbation*,
" We mean to make the trial of our child." MALONE.

⁹ — *prone and speechless dialect,*] *Prone,* I believe, is used here for prompt, significant, expressive (though speechless), as in our author's *Rape of Lucrece* it means *ardent, head-strong,* rushing forward to its object:
" O that *prone* lust should stain so pure a bed!"
Again, in *Cymbeline:* " Unless a man would marry a gallows, and beget young gibbets, I never saw any one so *prone.*" MALONE.

Prone,

Such as moves men; beside, she hath prosperous art,
When she will play with reason and discourse,
And well she can persuade.

Lucio. I pray, she may: as well for the encouragement of the like, which else would stand under grievous imposition [1]; as for the enjoying of thy life, who I would be sorry should be thus foolishly lost at a game of tick-tack [2]. I'll to her.

Claud. I thank you, good friend Lucio.

Lucio. Within two hours—

Claud. Come, officer, away. [*Exeunt.*

SCENE IV.

A Monastery.

Enter DUKE, *and Friar* THOMAS.

Duke. No; holy father; throw away that thought;
Believe not that the dribbling dart of love
Can pierce a cómplete bosom [3]: why I desire thee
To give me secret harbour, hath a purpose
More grave and wrinkled than the aims and ends
Of burning youth.

Prone, perhaps, may stand for *humble,* as *a prone posture* is *a posture of supplication.* So, in the *Opportunity,* by Shirley, 1640:
"You have *prostrate* language."
The same thought occurs in the *Winter's Tale:*
"The silence often of pure innocence
"Persuades, when speaking fails."
Sir *W. D'Avenant,* in his alteration of the play, changes *prone* to *sweet.* I mention some of his variations, to shew that what appear difficulties to us were difficulties to him, who, living nearer the time of Shakspeare, might be supposed to have understood his language more intimately. STEEVENS.

[1] *—under grievous imposition;*] I once thought it should be *inquisition;* but the present reading is probably right. *The crime would be under grievous penalties imposed.* JOHNSON.

[2] *—lost at a game of* tick-tack.] *Tick-tack* is a game at tables. "Jouer au *tric-trac*" is used in French, in a wanton sense. MALONE. The same phrase, in Lucio's wanton sense, occurs in *Lusty Iuventus.*
STEEVENS.

[3] *Believe not that the dribbling dart of love Can pierce a complete bosom:*] Think not that a breast *completely armed* can be pierced by the dart of love, that comes *fluttering without force.* JOHNSON.

Fri.

Fri. T. May your grace speak of it?

Duke. My holy Sir, none better knows than you
How I have ever lov'd the life remov'd [4];
And held in idle price to haunt assemblies,
Where youth, and cost, and witless bravery [5] keeps.
I have deliver'd to Lord Angelo
(A man of stricture [6], and firm abstinence)
My absolute power and place here in Vienna,
And he supposes me travell'd to Poland;
For so I have strew'd it in the common ear,
And so it is receiv'd: Now, pious Sir,
You will demand of me, why I do this?

Fri. T. Gladly, my Lord.

Duke. We have strict statutes, and most biting laws,
(The needful bits and curbs to head-strong steeds,)
Which for these fourteen years we have let sleep [7];

Even

---

[4] —*the life* remov'd;] i. e. a life of retirement, a life removed from the bustle of the world. STEEVENS.

So, in *Hamlet*: "It waits you to a more *removed* ground." MALONE.

[5] —and *witless* bravery—] *Bravery* in old language often means, *splendour of dress*. And was supplied by the second folio. MALONE.

[6] *A man of* stricture,] *Stricture* for *strictness*. JOHNSON.

[7] *We have strict statutes, and most biting laws,*
    (The needful bits and curbs to head-strong steeds,)
    Which for these fourteen years we have let sleep;] The old copy reads —head-strong *weeds*, and—let *slip*. Both the emendations were made by Mr. Theobald. The latter may derive support (as he has observed) from a subsequent line in this play:

"The law hath not been dead, though it hath *slept*."

So, also, from a passage in *Hamlet*:

" ———— How stand I then,
" That have a father kill'd, a mother stain'd,
" Excitements of my reason and my blood,
" And *let all sleep?*"

If *slip* be the true reading, (which, however, I do not believe,) the sense may be—which for these fourteen years we have suffered to *pass unnoticed, unobserved*; for so the same phrase is used in *Twelfth Night*: "Let him *let this matter slip*, and I'll give him my horse, grey Capilet."

Mr. Theobald altered *fourteen* to *nineteen*, to make the Duke's account correspond with a speech of Claudio's in a former scene, but without necessity. Claudio would naturally represent the period during which the law had not been put in practice, greater than it really was. MALONE.

Theobald's correction is misplaced. If any correction is really necessary,

Even like an o'er-grown lion in a cave,
That goes not out to prey: Now, as fond fathers
Having bound up the threat'ning twigs of birch,
Only to stick it in their children's sight,
For terror, not to use; in time the rod
Becomes more mock'd, than fear'd⁸: so our decrees,
Dead to infliction, to themselves are dead;
And liberty plucks justice by the nose;
The baby beats the nurse, and quite athwart
Goes all decorum.

   Fri. T. It rested in your grace
To unloose this tied-up justice, when you pleas'd:
And it in you more dreadful would have seem'd,
Than in Lord Angelo.

   Duke. I do fear, too dreadful:
Sith⁹ 'twas my fault to give the people scope,
'Twould be my tyranny to strike, and gall them,
For what I bid them do: For we bid this be done,
When evil deeds have their permissive pass,
And not the punishment. Therefore, indeed, my father,
I have on Angelo impos'd the office;
Who may, in the ambush of my name, strike home,
And yet my nature never in the fight,
To do it slander¹: And to behold his sway,
I will, as 'twere a brother of your order,
Visit both prince and people: therefore, I pr'ythee,
Supply me with the habit, and instruct me
How I may formally in person bear me²

                                         Like

---

cessary, it should have been made where Claudio, in a foregoing line, says *nineteen* years. I am disposed to take the Duke's words.
                                                                            WHALLEY.

  ⁸ *Becomes more mock'd, than fear'd:*] *Becomes* was added by Mr. Pope, to restore sense to the passage, some such word having been left out. STEEVENS.

  ⁹ *Sith*—] i. e. since. STEEVENS.

  ¹ *To do it slander:*] The original copy reads—To do *in* slander. The emendation was Sir Thomas Hanmer's. In the preceding line the first folio appears to have—*fight;* which seems to be countenanced by the words *ambush* and *strike. Sight* was introduced by Mr. Pope.
                                                                            MALONE.

 Hanmer's emendation is supported by a passage in *Henry IV.* P. i:
    " *Do me no slander,* Douglass, I dare fight " STEEVENS.

  ² — *in person bear me*] *Me,* which seems to have been accidentally omitted in the old copy, was inserted by Mr. Steevens. MALONE.

                                                                                 So

Like a true friar. More reasons for this action,
At our more leisure shall I render you;
Only, this one:—Lord Angelo is precise;
Stands at a guard [3] with envy; scarce confesses
That his blood flows, or that his appetite
Is more to bread than stone: Hence shall we see,
If power change purpose, what our seemers be. [*Exeunt.*

SCENE V.

A Nunnery.

Enter ISABELLA *and* FRANCISCA.

Isab. And have you nuns no farther privileges?
Fran. Are not these large enough?
Isab. Yes, truly: I speak not as desiring more;
But rather wishing a more strict restraint
Upon the sister-hood, the votarists of Saint Clare.
Lucio. [*within.*] Ho! Peace be in this place!
Isab. Who's that which calls?
Fran. It is a man's voice: Gentle Isabella,
Turn you the key, and know his business of him;
You may, I may not; you are yet unsworn:
When you have vow'd, you must not speak with men,
But in the presence of the prioress:
Then, if you speak, you must not shew your face;
Or, if you shew your face, you must not speak.
He calls again; I pray you, answer him. [*Exit* FRAN.

Isab. Peace and prosperity! Who is't that calls?

Enter LUCIO.

Lucio. Hail, virgin, if you be; as those cheek-roses
Proclaim you are no less! Can you so stead me,
As bring me to the sight of Isabella,
A novice of this place, and the fair sister
To her unhappy brother Claudio?
Isab. Why her unhappy brother? let me ask;
The rather, for I now must make you know
I am that Isabella, and his sister.

So, in the *Tempest:*
"———— some good instruction give,
"How I may *bear me* here." STEEVENS.
[3] *Stands at a guard*—] Stands on terms of defiance. JOHNSON.

Lucio.

Lucio. Gentle and fair, your brother kindly greets you:
Not to be weary with you, he's in prison.
  Isab. Woe me! For what?
  Lucio. For that, which, if myself might be his judge [4],
He should receive his punishment in thanks:
He hath got his friend with child.
  Isab. Sir, mock me not:—your story [5].
  Lucio. 'Tis true:—I would not [6].—Though 'tis my familiar sin
With maids to seem the lapwing [7], and to jest,
Tongue far from heart [8],—play with all virgins so,

   I hold

---

[4] *For that, which, if myself might be his judge,*] Perhaps these words were transposed at the press. The sense seems to require—That, for which, &c. MALONE.

[5] *Sir, make me not your story.*] Thus the old copy. I have no doubt that we ought to read (as I have printed,) Sir, mock me not:—your story.

So, in *Macbeth:*

  "Thou com'st to use thy tongue:—*thy story* quickly."

In *King Lear* we have—"Pray, do not *mock* me."
I beseech you, Sir, (says Isabel) do not play upon my fears; reserve this idle talk for some other occasion;—proceed at once to your tale. Lucio's subsequent words, [" 'Tis true,"— i. e. you are right; I thank you for reminding me;] which, as the text has been hitherto printed, had no meaning, are then pertinent and clear. Mr Pope was so sensible of the impossibility of reconciling them to what preceded in the old copy, that he fairly omitted them.
What Isabella says afterwards, fully supports this emendation:

  "You do blaspheme the good, in *mocking* me."

I have observed that almost every passage in our author, in which there is either a broken speech, or a sudden transition without a connecting particle, has been corrupted by the carelessness of either the transcriber or compositor. See a note on *Love's Labour's Lost,* Act ii. sc. i:

  " A man of—sovereign, peerless, he's esteem'd."

And another on *Coriolanus,* Act. i. scene iv:

  " You shames of Rome! you herd of—— Boils and plagues
  " Plaister you o'er!" MALONE.

[6] *I would not.*] i. e. Be assured, I would not mock you. So afterwards: " Do not believe it;" i. e. Do not suppose that I would mock you. MALONE.

[7] *With maids to seem the lapwing,*] The lapwings fly with seeming fright and anxiety far from their nests, to deceive those who seek their young. HANMER.

See Ray's Proverbs; "The *lapwing* cries, *tongue far from heart.*" The farther she is from her nest, where her heart is with her young ones, she is the louder, or perhaps all tongue. SMITH.

See *the Comedy of Errors,* Act iv. sc. iii. GREY.

[8] *Though 'tis my familiar sin*

   With,

I hold you as a thing ensky'd, and sainted;
By your renouncement, an immortal spirit;
And to be talk'd with in sincerity,
As with a saint.

Isab. You do blaspheme the good, in mocking me.

Lucio. Do not believe it. Fewness and truth [9], 'tis thus:
Your brother and his lover have embrac'd [1]:
As those that feed grow full; as blossoming time,
That from the seedness the bare fallow brings
To teeming foyson, even so her plenteous womb
Expresseth his full tilth and husbandry [2].

Isab.

[*With maids to seem the lapwing, and to jest,*
Tongue far from heart—play with all virgins so, &c.] This passage has been pointed in the modern editions thus:

  " 'Tis true;—I would not (though 'tis my familiar sin
  " With maids to seem the lapwing, and to jest,
  " Tongue far from heart) play with all virgins so;
  " I hold you, &c.

According to this punctuation, Lucio is made to deliver a sentiment directly opposite to that which the author intended. *Though 'tis my common practice to jest with and to deceive all virgins, I would not so play with all virgins.*

The sense, as the text is now regulated, appears to me clear and easy. 'Tis very true, (says he) *I ought indeed, as you say, to proceed at once to my fury. Be assured, I would not mock you. Though it is my familiar practice to jest with maidens, and, like the lapwing, to deceive them by my insincere prattle, though, I say, it is my ordinary and habitual practice* to sport in this manner with all virgins, *yet I should never think of treating you so;* for I consider you, in consequence of your having renounced the world, as an immortal spirit, as one to whom I ought to speak with as much sincerity as if I were addressing a saint. MALONE.

[9] *Fewness and truth,*] i. e. in *few words*, and those true ones. *In few*, is many times thus used by Shakspeare. STEEVENS.

[1] *Your brother and his lover*—] i. e. his mistress; *lover*, in our author's time, being applied to the female as well as the male sex. Thus, one of his poems, containing the lamentation of a deserted maiden, is entitled " *A Lover's* Complaint."

So, in Tarleton's *Newes out of Purgatory*, bl. l. no date; " — he spide the fetch, and perceived that all this while this was his *lover's* husband, to whom he had revealed these escapes." MALONE.

[2] ——— *as blossoming time,*
   That from the seedness the bare fallow brings
   To teeming foyson; so her plenteous womb
   Expresseth his full tilth and husbandry.] This sentence, as Dr. Johnson has observed, is apparently ungrammatical. I suspect two half lines have been lost. Perhaps however an imperfect sentence was intended, of which there are many instances in these plays;—or, *as* might have been used in the sense of *like*. *Teeming foyson* is abundant plenty. *Tilth* is *tillage*.

So

Isab. Some one with child by him?—My cousin Juliet?
Lucio. Is she your cousin?
Isab. Adoptedly; as school-maids change their names,
By vain though apt affection.
Lucio. She it is.
Isab. O let him marry her!
Lucio. This is the point.
The duke is very strangely gone from hence;
Bore many gentlemen, myself being one,
In hand, and hope of action³: but we do learn
By those that know the very nerves of state,
His givings out were of an infinite distance
From his true-meant design. Upon his place,
And with full line⁴ of his authority,
Governs Lord Angelo; a man, whose blood
Is very snow-broth; one who never feels
The wanton stings and motions of the sense;
But doth rebate and blunt his natural edge
With profits of the mind, study and fast.
He (to give fear to use⁵ and liberty,
Which have, for long, run by the hideous law,
As mice by lions,) hath pick'd out an act,
Under whose heavy sense your brother's life
Falls into forfeit: he arrests him on it;
And follows close the rigour of the statute,
To make him an example: all hope is gone,
Unless you have the grace⁶ by your fair prayer
To soften Angelo: and that's my pith
Of business⁷ 'twixt you and your poor brother.

So, in our author's 3d Sonnet;
"For who is she so fair, whose unear'd *womb*
"Disdains the *tillage* of my husbandry?" MALONE.

³ *Bore many gentlemen,———*
In hand and hope of action:] To *bear in hand* is a common phrase for *to keep in expectation and dependance;* but we should read,
——— with *hope of action.* JOHNSON.

⁴ *And with full line———*] With full extent, with the whole length.
JOHNSON.

⁵ ——— *to give fear to use———*] To intimidate *use,* that is, practices long countenanced by *custom.* JOHNSON.

⁶ *Unless you have the grace———*] That is, the acceptableness, the power of gaining favour. So, when she makes her suit, the Provost says:
Heaven give thee moving graces! JOHNSON.

⁷ ——— *my pith*
Of business———] The inmost part, the main of my message. JOHNSON.

Isab

Isab. Doth he so seek his life?
Lucio. Has censur'd him [8]
Already; and, as I hear, the provost hath
A warrant for his execution.
Isab. Alas! what poor ability's in me
To do him good?
Lucio. Assay the power you have.
Isab. My power! Alas! I doubt—
Lucio. Our doubts are traitors,
And make us lose the good we oft might win,
By fearing to attempt: Go to Lord Angelo,
And let him learn to know, when maidens sue,
Men give like gods; but when they weep and kneel,
All their petitions are as freely theirs [9]
As they themselves would owe them [1].
Isab. I'll see what I can do.
Lucio. But, speedily.
Isab. I will about it straight;
No longer staying but to give the mother [2]
Notice of my affair. I humbly thank you:
Commend me to my brother: soon at night
I'll send him certain word of my success.
Lucio. I take my leave of you.
Isab. Good Sir, adieu. [*Exeunt.*

[8] *Has censur'd him*——] We should read, I think, He *has censured him*, &c. In the Mss. of our author's time, and frequently in the printed copy of these plays, *he has*, when intended to be contracted, is written —*h'as*. Hence, probably the mistake here.
So, in *Othello*, 4to. 1622:
"And it is thought abroad, that 'twixt my sheets
"H'as done my office."
Again, in *All's Well that Ends Well,* p. 247, folio 1623, we find *H'as* twice, for *He has*. See also *Twelfth Night*, p. 258, edit. 1623: "*h'as* been told so," for "*he has* been told so."
MALONE.

— censur'd *him*——] i. e. sentenced him. So, in *Othello*:
"—— to you, lord governor,
"Remains the *censure* of this hellish villain." STEEVENS.

[9] *All their petitions are as freely theirs*] All their requests are as freely granted to them, are granted in as full and beneficial a manner, as they themselves could wish. The editor of the second folio arbitrarily reads—*as truly theirs*; which has been followed in all the subsequent copies. MALONE.

[1] — *would owe them.*] To *owe* signifies in this place, as in many other, to possess, to have. STEEVENS.

[2] — *the mother*] The abbess, or prioress. JOHNSON.

ACT II. SCENE I.

A Hall in ANGELO's *House.*

Enter ANGELO, ESCALUS, *a* JUSTICE, PROVOST [2], *Officers, and other Attendants.*

Ang. We must not make a scare-crow of the law,
Setting it up to fear the birds of prey [3],
And let it keep one shape, till custom make it
Their perch, and not their terror.
  Escal. Ay, but yet
Let us be keen, and rather cut a little,
Than fall, and bruise to death [4]: Alas! this gentleman,
Whom I would save, had a most noble father.
Let but your honour know [5],
(Whom I believe to be most strait in virtue,)
That, in the working of your own affections,
Had time coher'd with place, or place with wishing,
Or that the resolute acting of your blood [6]
Could have attain'd the effect of your own purpose,
Whether you had not sometime in your life

---

[2] *Provost,*] A provost is generally the executioner of an army,
STEEVENS.

" A Provost martial" Minsheu explains " Prevost des Mareschaux:
" Præfectus *rerum capitalium*, prætor rerum capitalium." REED.

A prison for military offenders is at this day, in some places, called
the *Prevôt*. MALONE.

[3] —*to fear the birds of prey,*] To *fear* is to *affright*, to *terrify*.
STEEVENS.

[4] *Than fall, and bruise to death:*] i. e. fall *the axe;*—or rather, let the
criminal fall, &c. MALONE.

Shakspeare has used the same verb active in *the Comedy of Errors*, and
As you Like it. STEEVENS.

[5] *Let but your honour know,*] To *know* is here to *examine*, to take cognisance. So, in *A Midsummer Night's Dream*:

  " Therefore, fair Hermia, question your desires;
  " Know of your truth, examine well your blood." JOHNSON.

[6] —*of your blood,*] Old copy—*our* blood. Corrected by Mr Rowe.
The sense undoubtedly requires, " — which now you can use him *for*,"
but the text certainly appears as the poet left it. I have elsewhere shewn
that he frequently uses these elliptical expressions. MALONE.

Err'd

Err'd in this point which now you censure him[7],
And pull'd the law upon you.

Ang. 'Tis one thing to be tempted, Escalus,
Another thing to fall. I not deny,
The jury, passing on the prisoner's life,
May, in the sworn twelve, have a thief or two
Guiltier than him they try: What's open made
To justice, that justice seizes. What know the laws,
That thieves do pass on thieves[8]? 'Tis very pregnant[9]
The jewel that we find, we stoop and take it,
Because we see it; but what we do not see,
We tread upon, and never think of it.
You may not so extenuate his offence,
For I have had such faults[1], but rather tell me,
When I that censure him do so offend,
Let mine own judgment pattern out my death,
And nothing come in partial Sir, he must die.

Escal. Be it as your wisdom will.

Ang. Where is the Provost?

Prov. Here, if it like your honour.

Ang. See that Claudio
Be executed by nine to-morrow morning:
Bring him his confessor, let him be prepar'd;
For that's the utmost of his pilgrimage. [*Exit* PROVOST.

Escal. Well, heaven forgive him! and forgive us all!
Some rise by sin, and some by virtue fall[2]:

Some

---

[7] — *which now you censure him.*] Some word seems to be wanting to make this line sense. Perhaps, we should read—which now you censure him *for.* STEEVENS.

[8] ——— *What know the laws, That thieves do pass on thieves?*] How can the administrator of the laws take cognizance of what I have just mentioned? How can they know, whether the jurymen who *decide* on the life or death of thieves be themselves as criminal as those whom they try? *To pass on* is a forensick term. So in the well-known provision of MAGNA CHARTA;—" nec *super eum ibimus,* nec *super eum mittemus,* nisi per legale judicium parium suorum, vel per legem terræ." MALONE.

[9] *'Tis very pregnant,*] 'Tis *plain* that we must act with bad as with good; we punish the faults, as we take the advantages, that lie in our way, and what we do not see we cannot note. JOHNSON.

[1] *For I have had such faults,*] That is, *because, by reason that* I have had such faults. JOHNSON.

[2] *Some rise &c.*] This line is in the first folio printed in Italics, as a quotation. All the folios read in the next line;

Some run from brakes of ice, and answer none. JOHNSON.

A brake

Some run from brakes of vice, and answer none;
And some condemned for a fault alone.

Enter ELBOW, FROTH, CLOWN, *Officers, &c.*

Elb. Come, bring them away: if these be good people in a common-weal, that do nothing but use their abuses in common houses, I know no law: bring them away.

Ang. How now, Sir! What's your name? and what's the matter?

Elb. If it please your honour, I am the poor duke's constable, and my name is Elbow; I do lean upon justice, Sir, and do bring in here before your good honour two notorious benefactors.

Ang. Benefactors? Well; what benefactors are they?—Are they not malefactors?

Elb. If it please your honour, I know not well what they are: but precise villains they are, that I am sure of; and void of all profanation in the world, that good Christians ought to have.

Escal. This comes off well [3]; here's a wise officer.

A *brake* anciently meant not only a *sharp bit*, a *snaffle*, but also the engine with which farriers confined the legs of such unruly horses, as would not otherwise submit themselves to be shod, or to have a cruel operation performed on them. This in some places is still called a smith's *brake*. I likewise find from Holinshed, p. 670, that the *brake* was an engine of torture. It was called the Duke of Exeter's daughter. See Blackstone's COMMENT. IV. 320, 321.

If Shakspeare alluded here to this engine, the sense of this passage will be: *Some run more than once from engines of punishment, and answer no interrogatories; while some are condemned to suffer for a single trespass.*

A yet plainer meaning may be deduced from the same words. A *brake* meant a bush. By *brakes of vice*, therefore, may be meant a collection, a number, a *thicket* of vices.

Mr. Tollet is of opinion that, by *brakes of vice*, Shakspeare means only the *thorny paths of vice*. STEEVENS.

I am not satisfied with either the old or present reading of this very difficult passage; yet have nothing better to propose. The modern reading, *vice*, was introduced by Mr. Rowe. In *K. Hen. VIII.* we have

" 'Tis but the fate of place, and the rough *brake*
" That *virtue* must go through." MALONE.

[3] *This comes off well;*] This is nimbly spoken; this is volubly uttered. JOHNSON.

The same phrase is employed in *Timon of Athens*, and elsewhere; but in the present instance it is used ironically. The meaning of it, when seriously applied to speech, is—This is well delivered, this story is well told. STEEVENS.

Ang. Go to: What quality are they of? Elbow is your name? Why dost thou not speak, Elbow⁴?

Clown. He cannot, Sir; he's out at elbow.

Ang. What are you, Sir?

Elb. He, Sir? a tapster, Sir; parcel-bawd⁵; one that serves a bad woman; whose house, Sir, was, as they say, pluck'd down in the suburbs; and now she professes a hot-house⁶, which, I think, is a very ill house too.

Escal. How know you that?

Elb. My wife, Sir, whom I detest⁷ before heaven and your honour—

Escal. How! thy wife?

Elb. Ay, Sir; whom, I thank heaven, is an honest woman;—

Escal. Dost thou detest her therefore?

Elb. I say, Sir, I will detest myself also, as well as she, that this house, if it be not a bawd's house, it is pity of her life, for it is a naughty house.

Escal. How dost thou know that, constable?

Elb. Marry, Sir, by my wife; who, if she had been a woman cardinally given, might have been accused in fornication, adultery, and all uncleanness there.

Escal. By the woman's means?

Elb. Ay, Sir, by Mistress Overdone's means⁸: but as she spit in his face, so she defy'd him.

Clown. Sir, if it please your honour, this is not so.

⁴ *Why dost thou not speak,* Elbow?] Says Angelo to the constable.—" He cannot, Sir, quoth the *Clown,* he's *out at elbow.*" I knew not whether this quibble be generally observed; he is *out* at the word *Elbow,* and out at the *elbow* of his coat. The *Constable,* in his account of Master Froth and the Clown, has a stroke at the *puritans,* who were very zealous against the stage about this time. " Precise villains they are, that " I am sure of; and void of all profanation in the world, that good " Christians ought to have." FARMER.

⁵ —*a tapster, Sir; parcel-bawd;*] This we should now express by saying, *he is half-tapster, half-bawd.* JOHNSON.
Thus in *K. Henry IV:* "a *parcel* gilt goblet." STEEVENS.

⁶ —*she professes a hot-house;*] A *hot-house* is an English name for a *bagnio.* JOHNSON.

⁷ —*whom I detest—*] He means—*protest.* MALONE.

⁸ *Ay, Sir, by Mistress Overdone's means;*] Here seems to have been some mention made of Froth, who was to be accused, and some words therefore may have been lost, unless the irregularity of the narrative may be better imputed to the ignorance of the constable. JOHNSON.

Elb.

Elb. Prove it before these varlets here, thou honourable man, prove it.

Escal. Do you hear how he misplaces? [*To Angelo.*

Clown. Sir, she came in great with child; and longing (saving your honour's reverence,) for stew'd prunes⁹; Sir, we had but two in the house, which at that very distant time ¹ stood, as it were, in a fruit-dish, a dish of some three-pence; your honours have seen such dishes; they are not China dishes, but very good dishes.

Escal. Go to, go to; no matter for the dish, Sir.

Clown. No, indeed, Sir, not of a pin; you are therein in the right: but to the point: as I say, this Mistress Elbow, being, as I say, with child, and being great belly'd, and longing, as I said, for prunes; and having but two in the dish, as I said, Master Froth here, this very man, having eaten the rest, as I said, and, as I say, paying for them very honestly; for, as you know, Master Froth, I could not give you three-pence again:

Froth. No, indeed.

Clown. Very well: you being then, if you be remember'd, cracking the stones of the foresaid prunes;

Froth. Ay, so I did, indeed.

Clown. Why, very well: I telling you then, if you be remember'd, that such a one, and such a one, were paid cure of the thing you wot of, unless they kept very good diet, as I told you;

Froth. All this is true.

Clown. Why, very well then,

Escal. Come, you are a tedious fool: to the purpose.—What was done to Elbow's wife, that he hath cause to complain of? Come me to what was done to her.

Clown. Sir, your honour cannot come to that yet.

Escal. No, Sir, nor I mean it not.

Clown. Sir, but you shall come to it, by your honour's leave: And, I beseech you, look into Master Froth here, Sir; a man of fourscore pound a year; whose father dy'd at Hallomas:—Was't not at Hallowmas, Master Froth?

Froth. All-hallond eve.

---

⁹ *—stew'd prunes;*] Stewed prunes were to be found in every brothel. See a note on the 3d scene of the 3d act of the First Part of *King Henry IV.* In the old copy *prunes* are spelt, according to vulgar pronunciation, *prewyns.* STEEVENS.

¹ *—at that very distant time—*] He means *instant.* MALONE.

Clown. Why, very well; I hope here be truths: He, Sir, sitting, as I say, in a lower chair,[2] Sir;—'twas in *The Bunch of Grapes,* where, indeed, you have a delight to sit, Have you not?

Froth. I have so; because it is an open room, and good for winter.

Clown. Why, very well then;—I hope here be truths.

Ang. This will last out a night in Russia,
When nights are longest there: I'll take my leave,
And leave you to the hearing of the cause;
Hoping, you'll find good cause to whip them all.

Escal. I think no less: Good morrow to your lordship.

[*Exit* ANGELO.

Now, Sir, come on: What was done to Elbow's wife, once more?

Clown. Once, Sir? there was nothing done to her once.

Elb. I' beseech you, Sir, ask him what this man did to my wife.

Clown. I beseech your honour, ask me.

Escal. Well, Sir; What did this gentleman to her?

Clown. I beseech you, Sir, look in this gentleman's face:—Good Master Froth, look upon his honour; 'tis for a good purpose: Doth your honour mark his face?

Escal. Ay, Sir, very well.

Clown. Nay, I beseech you mark it well.

Escal. Well, I do so.

Clown. Doth your honour see any harm in his face?

Escal. Why, no.

Clown. I'll be supposed[3] upon a book, his face is the worst thing about him: Good then; if his face be the worst thing about him, how could Master Froth do the constable's wife any harm? I would know that of your honour?

Escal. He's in the right: Constable, what say you to it?

Elb. First, an it like you, the house is a respected house; next, this is a respected fellow; and his mistress is a respected woman.

[2] *— in a lower* chair,] One of the editors, plausibly enough, proposes to read—in a lower *chamber*, which derives some support from the subsequent words—" *where,* indeed, you have a delight to sit." But the old reading is intelligible, and therefore should not be changed. A *lower* chair is a chair lower than *ordinary.* MALONE.

[3] *I'll be* supposed—] He means *deposed.* MALONE.

Clown. By this hand, Sir, his wife is a more respected person than any of us all.

Elb. Varlet, thou liest; thou liest, wicked varlet: the time is yet to come, that she was ever respected with man, woman, or child.

Clown. Sir, she was respected with him before he marry'd with her.

Escal. Which is the wiser here? Justice, or Iniquity [4]?—Is this true?

Elb. O thou caitiff! O thou varlet! O thou wicked Hannibal [5]! I respected with her, before I was marry'd to her? If ever I was respected with her, or she with me, let not your worship think me the poor duke's officer:—Prove this, thou wicked Hannibal, or I'll have mine action of battery on thee.

Escal. If he took you a box of the ear, you might have your action of slander too.

Elb. Marry, I thank your good worship for it: What is't your worship's pleasure I shall do with this wicked caitiff?

Escal. Truly, officer, because he hath some offences in him, that thou wouldst discover if thou couldst, let him continue in his courses, till thou know'st what they are.

Elb. Marry, I thank your worship for it:—Thou seest, thou wicked varlet now, what's come upon thee; thou art to continue now, thou varlet; thou art to continue.

Escal. Where were you born, friend? [*To Froth.*
Froth. Here in Vienna, Sir.
Escal. Are you of fourscore pounds a year?
Froth. Yes, and't please you, Sir?
Escal. So.—What trade are you of, Sir? [*To the Clown*
Clown. A tapster; a poor widow's tapster.
Escal. Your mistress's name?
Clown. Mistress Overdone.
Escal. Hath she had any more than one husband?
Clown. Nine, Sir; Overdone by the last.

---

[4] *Justice, or Iniquity?*] Elbow, the officer of justice, or Pompey, the instrument of vice? MALONE.

Justice and *Iniquity* were, I suppose, two personages well known to the audience by their frequent appearance in the old moralities. The words, therefore, at that time produced a combination of ideas, which they have now lost. JOHNSON.

[5] — *Hannibal,*] Mistaken by the constable for *Cannibal.* JOHNSON.

Escal. Nine—Come hither to me, Master Froth. Master Froth, I would not have you acquainted with tapsters; they will draw you [6], Master Froth, and you will hang them: Get you gone, and let me hear no more of you.

Froth. I thank your worship: For mine own part, I never come into any room in a taphouse, but I am drawn in.

Escal. Well; no more of it, Master Froth: farewell. Come you hither to me, master tapster; what's your name, master tapster?

Clown. Pompey.

Escal. What else?

Clown. Bum, Sir.

Escal. Troth, and your bum is the greatest thing about you; so that, in the beastliest sense, you are Pompey the great. Pompey, you are partly a bawd, Pompey, howsoever you colour it in being a tapster: Are you not? Come, tell me true; it shall be the better for you.

Clown. Truly, Sir, I am a poor fellow that would live.

Escal. How would you live, Pompey? by being a bawd? What do you think of the trade, Pompey? is it a lawful trade?

Clown. If the law will allow it, Sir.

Escal. But the law will not allow it, Pompey; nor it shall not be allowed in Vienna.

Clown. Does your worship mean to geld and spay all the youth of the city?

Escal. No, Pompey.

Clown. Truly, Sir, in my poor opinion, they will to't then: If your worship will take order for the drabs and the knaves, you need not to fear the bawds.

Escal. There are pretty orders beginning, I can tell you: it is but heading and hanging.

Clown. If you head and hang all that offend that way but for ten year together, you'll be glad to give out a commission

---

[6] —*they will draw you,*] *Draw* has here a cluster of senses. As it refers to the tapster, it signifies *to drain, to empty*; as it is related to *hang*, it means *to be conveyed to execution on a hurdle*. In Froth's answer, it is the same as *to bring along by some motive or power.* JOHNSON.

[7] —*greatest thing about you;*] This fashion, of which, perhaps, some remains were to be found in the age of Shakspeare, seems to have prevailed originally in that of Chaucer, who, in the *Persones Tale* speaks of it thus: " Some of hem shewen the bosse and shape, &c. in the wrappping of hir hosen, and *eke the buttokkes of hem behinde*, &c." Greene, in one of his pieces, mentions the *great bumme of Paris*.

STEEVENS.

for

for more heads. If this law hold in Vienna ten year, I'll rent the fairest house in it, after three pence a bay[8]: If you live to see this come to pass, say, Pompey told you so.

Escal. Thank you, good Pompey: and, in requital of your prophecy, hark you,—I advise you, let me not find you before me again upon any complaint whatsoever, no, not for dwelling where you do; if I do, Pompey, I shall beat you to your tent, and prove a shrewd Cæsar to you; in plain dealing, Pompey, I shall have you whipt: so for this time, Pompey, fare you well.

Clown. I thank your worship for your good counsel; but I shall follow it, as the flesh and fortune shall better determine.

Whip me? No, no; let carman whip his jade;
The valiant heart's not whipt out of his trade. [*Exit.*

Escal. Come hither to me, Master Elbow, come hither, master constable. How long have you been in this place of constable?

Elb. Seven year and a half, Sir.

Escal. I thought, by your readiness[9] in the office, you had continued in it some time: You say, seven years together?

Elb. And a half, Sir.

Escal. Alas! it hath been great pains to you! They do you wrong to put you so oft upon't: Are there not men in your ward sufficient to serve it?

Elb. Faith, Sir, few of any wit in such matters: as they are chosen, they are glad to choose me for them; I do it for some piece of money, and go through with all.

Escal. Look you, bring me in the names of six or seven, the most sufficient of your parish.

Elb. To your worship's house, Sir?

Escal. To my house: Fare you well.—What's o'clock, think you?

Just. Eleven, Sir.

---

[8] *I'll rent the fairest house in it, after three pence* a bay:] A bay of building is, in many parts of England, a common term, of which the best conception that I could ever attain, is, that it is the space between the main beams of the roof; so that a barn crossed twice with beams is a barn of three *bays*. JOHNSON.

[9] — *by your readiness*—] Old Copy—*the* readiness. Corrected by Mr. Pope. In the MSs. of our author's age, y^e and y^r (for so they were frequently written) were easily confounded. MALONE.

Escal. I pray you home to dinner with me.
Just. I humbly thank you.
Escal. It grieves me for the death of Claudio;
But there's no remedy.
Just. Lord Angelo is severe.
Escal. It is but needful:
Mercy is not itself, that oft looks so;
Pardon is still the nurse of second woe:
But yet,—Poor Claudio!—There's no remedy.
Come, Sir. [*Exeunt.*

SCENE II.

Another Room in the same.

Enter PROVOST, *and a* SERVANT.

Serv. He's hearing of a cause; he will come straight:
I'll tell him of you.
Prov. Pray you, do. [*Exit* Servant.] I'll know
His pleasure; may be, he will relent: Alas,
He hath but as offended in a dream!
All sects, all ages smack of this vice; and he
To die for it!—

Enter ANGELO.

Ang. Now, what's the matter, Provost?
Prov. Is it your will Claudio shall die to-morrow?
Ang. Did I not tell thee, yea? hadst thou not order?
Why dost thou ask again?
Prov. Lest I might be too rash:
Under your good correction, I have seen,
When after execution, judgment hath
Repented o'er his doom.
Ang. Go to; let that be mine:
Do you your office, or give up your place,
And you shall well be spared.
Prov. I crave your honour's pardon.—
What shall be done, Sir, with the groaning Juliet?
She's very near her hour.
Ang. Dispose of her
To some more fitter place; and that with speed.

Re-enter SERVANT.

Serv. Here is the sister of the man condemn'd,
Desires access to you.

Ang.

Ang. Hath he a sister?
Prov. Ay, my good Lord; a very virtuous maid,
And to be shortly of a sister-hood,
If not already.
Ang. Well, let her be admitted. [*Exit* Servant.
See you the fornicatress be remov'd;
Let her have needful, but not lavish, means;
There shall be order for it.

Enter LUCIO *and* ISABELLA.

Prov. Save your honour! * [*offering to retire.*
Ang. Stay a little while ¹.—[*to Isab.*] You are welcome:
What's your will?
Isab. I am a woeful suitor to your honour.
Please but your honour hear me.
Ang. Well; what's your suit?
Isab. There is a vice, that most I do abhor,
And most desire should meet the blow of justice;
For which I would not plead, but that I must;
For which I must not plead, but that I am
At war, 'twixt will, and will not ².
Ang. Well; the matter?
Isab. I have a brother is condemn'd to die:
I do beseech you, let it be his fault,
And not my brother ³.

---

* *Save your honour.*] *Your honour*, which is so often repeated in this scene, was in our author's time the usual mode of address to a lord. It had become antiquated after the Restoration; for Sir William D'Avenant, in his alteration of this play, has substituted *your excellence* in the room of it. MALONE.

¹ *Stay a little while.*] It is not clear why the provost is bidden to stay, nor when he goes out. JOHNSON.

Stay a little while is said by Angelo, in answer to the words " *Save your honour;*" which denoted the Provost's intention to *depart*. Isabella uses the same words to Angelo, when she *goes out*, near the conclusion of this scene. So also, when she offers to retire, on finding her suit ineffectual: " Heaven keep your honour!" MALONE.

² *For which I must not plead, but that I am*
At war, 'twixt will, and will not.] i. e. for which I must not plead, but that there is a conflict in my breast betwixt my affection for my brother, which induces me to plead for him, and my regard to virtue, which forbids me to intercede for one guilty of such a crime; and I find the former more powerful than the latter. MALONE.

³ ——— *let it be his fault,*
And not my brother.] i. e. let his fault be condemned, or extirpated; but let not my brother himself suffer. MALONE.

Prov. Heaven give thee moving graces!

Ang. Condemn the fault, and not the actor of it!
Why, every fault's condemn'd, ere it be done:
Mine were the very cypher of a function,
To fine the faults[4], whose fine stands in record,
And let go by the actor.

Isab. O just, but severe law!
I had a brother then.—Heaven keep your honour!
[*retiring.*

Lucio. Give't not o'er so: to him again, intreat him;
Kneel down before him, hang upon his gown;
You are too cold: if you should need a pin,
You could not with more tame a tongue desire it:
To him, I say.

Isab. Must he needs die?

Ang. Maiden, no remedy.

Isab. Yes; I do think that you might pardon him,
And neither heaven, nor man, grieve at the mercy.

Ang. I will not do't.

Isab. But can you, if you would?

Ang. Look, what I will not, that I cannot do.

Isab. But might you do't, and do the world no wrong,
If so your heart were touch'd with that remorse[5]
As mine is to him?

Ang. He's sentenc'd; 'tis too late.

Lucio. You are too cold. [*To Isab.*

Isab. Too late? why, no; I, that do speak a word,
May call it back again[6]: Well believe this[7],
No ceremony that to great ones 'longs,
Not the king's crown, nor the deputed sword,
The marshal's truncheon, nor the judge's robe,
Become them with one half so good a grace,
As mercy does. If he had been as you,
And you as he, you would have slipt like him;
But he, like you, would not have been so stern.

---

[4] *To fine the faults—*] To fine means, I think, to pronounce the *fine* or sentence of the law, appointed for certain crimes. Mr. Theobald, without necessity, reads *find*. The repetition is much in our author's manner. MALONE.

[5] — with that *remorse*,] Remorse in this place, as in many others, is pity. See *Othello*, Act. iii. STEEVENS.

[6] *May call it back again:*] The word *back* was inserted by the editor of the second folio, for the sake of the metre. MALONE.

[7] Well *believe this,*] Be thoroughly assured of this. THEOBALD.

Ang.

Ang. Pray you, be gone.

Isab. I would to heaven I had your potency,
And you were Isabel! should it then be thus?
No; I would tell what 'twere to be a judge,
And what a prisoner.

Lucio. Ay, touch him: there's the vein.   [*Aside.*

Ang. Your brother is a forfeit of the law,
And you but waste your words.

Isab. Alas! alas!
Why, all the souls that were [8], were forfeit once;
And he that might the vantage best have took,
Found out the remedy: How would you be,
If he, which is the top of judgment, should
But judge you as you are? O, think on that;
And mercy then will breathe within your lips,
Like man new made.[9]

Ang. Be you content, fair maid:
It is the law, not I, condemns your brother:
Were he my kinsman, brother, or my son,
It should be thus with him;—he must die to-morrow.

Isab. To-morrow? O, that's sudden! Spare him, spare him.
He's not prepar'd for death! Even for our kitchens
We kill the fowl of season; shall we serve heaven
With less respect than we do minister
To our gross selves? Good, good my lord, bethink you:
Who is it that hath died for this offence?
There's many have committed it.

Lucio. Ay, well said.

Ang. The law hath not been dead, though it hath slept:[*]
Those many had not dared to do that evil,
If the first man that did the edict infringe[1],

---

[8] —*all the souls that were,*] This is false divinity. We should read, *are*. WARBURTON.

[] *And mercy then will breathe within your lips, Like man new made.*] You will then appear as tender-hearted and merciful as the first man was in his days of innocence, immediately after his creation. MALONE.

I rather think the meaning is, *You will change the severity of your present character. In familiar speech, You will be quite another man.* JOHNSON.

[*] *The law hath not been dead, though it hath slept.*] So, in *The Spanish Tragedy*, 1605:
"Nor dies revenge, although he sleep awhile." MALONE.

[1] *If the first man, &c.*] The word *was* hath been supplied by the modern editors. I would rather read, *If he, the first, &c.* TYRWHITT.
Man was introduced by Mr. Pope. MALONE.

Had answer'd for his deed: now, 'tis awake;
Takes note of what is done; and, like a prophet,
Looks in a glass², that shews what future evils,
(Either now, or by remissness new-conceiv'd,
And so in progress to be hatch'd and born,)
Are now to have no successive degrees,
But where they live, to end³.

Isab. Yet, shew some pity.

Ang. I shew it most of all, when I shew justice;
For then I pity those I do not know⁴,
Which a dismiss'd offence would after gall;
And do him right, that, answering one foul wrong,
Lives not to act another. Be satisfied;
Your brother dies to-morrow; be content.

Isab. So you must be the first, that gives this sentence;
And he that suffers: O, it is excellent

To

---

² —— *and, like a prophet,*
Looks in a glass—] See *Macbeth*, Act iv. sc. i. STEEVENS.

This alludes to the fopperies of the *beril*, much used at that time by cheats and fortune-tellers to predict by. WARBURTON.

The *beril*, which is a kind of crystal, hath a weak tincture of red in it. Among other tricks of astrologers, the discovering of past or future events was supposed to be the consequence of looking into it. See Aubrey's *Miscellanies*, p. 165, edit. 1721. REED.

³ *But*, where *they live, to end.*] The old copy reads—But, here they live, to end. Sir Thomas Hanmer substituted *ere* for *here*; but *where* was, I am persuaded the author's word.

So, in *Coriolanus*, Act v. sc. v.
" —— but *there to end,*
" WHERE he was to begin, and give away
" The benefit of our levies." &c.

Again, in *Julius Cæsar*:
" And WHERE *I did begin, there shall I end.*" MALONE.

The prophecy is not, that future evils should end, *ere*, or before, they are born; or, in other words, that there should be no more evil in the world (as Sir T. Hanmer by his alteration seems to have understood it); but, that they should *end* WHERE they *began*, i. e. with the criminal; who being punished for his first offence, could not proceed by *successive degrees*, in wickedness, nor excite others, by his impunity, to vice. So, in the next speech:

" And do him right, that, answering *one* foul wrong,
" Lives not to act *another.*"

It is more likely that a letter should have been omitted at the press, than that one should have been added.

The same mistake has happened in *the Merchant of Venice*, Folio, 1623, p. 175, col. 2:—' ha, ha, *here* in Genoa."—instead of—" *where?* in Genoa?" MALONE.

⁴ *I shew it most of all, when I shew justice.*
For then I pity those I do not know.] This was one of Hale's memorials.

To have a giant's strength; but it is tyrannous,
To use it like a giant.

Lucio. That's well said.

Isab. Could great men thunder
As Jove himself does, Jove would ne'er be quiet,
For every pelting⁵, petty officer,
Would use his heaven for thunder; nothing but thunder.—
Merciful heaven!
Thou rather, with thy sharp and sulphurous bolt,
Split'st the unwedgeable and gnarled oak⁶,
Than the soft myrtle;—But man, proud man⁷!
Drest in a little brief authority;
Most ignorant of what he's most assur'd,
His glassy essence,—like an angry ape,
Plays such fantastic tricks before high heaven,
As make the angels weep⁸; who, with our spleens,
Would all themselves laugh mortal⁹.

Lucio. O, to him, to him, wench: he will relent;
He's coming; I perceive't.

rials. *When I find myself swayed to mercy, let me remember, that there is a mercy likewise due to the country.* JOHNSON.

⁵ —*pelting*—] i. e. paltry. STEEVENS.

So, in *The Two Noble Kinsmen*, 1634:

"Thou bring'st such *pelting* scurvy news continually,
"Thou art not worthy life." MALONE.

⁶ —*gnarled oak*,] *Gnarre* is the old English word for a *knot in wood.*
STEEVENS.

So, in *Antonio's Revenge*, 1602:

"Till by degrees the rough and *gnarly* trunk
"Be riv'd in sunder."

⁷ *Than the soft myrtle;—But man, proud man!*] The defective metre of this line shews that some word was accidentally omitted at the press; probably some additional epithet to *man*; perhaps *weak*;—"but man, *weak*, proud man—." The editor of the second folio, to supply the defect, reads—*O but man*, &c. which, like almost all the other emendations of that copy, is the worst and the most improbable that could have been chosen. MALONE.

⁸ *As make the angels weep*;] The notion of angels weeping for the sins of men is rabbinical.—*Ob peccatum flentes angelos inducunt Hebræorum magistri.*—Grotius ad S. Lucam. THEOBALD.

⁹ —*who, with our spleens,*

Would all themselves laugh mortal.] i. e. who, if they were endued with the organs of man—with our spleens, would laugh themselves out of immortality; or, as we say in common life, laugh themselves dead. THEOBALD.

The ancients thought that immoderate laughter was caused by the bigness of the spleen. WARBURTON.

Prov.

Prov. Pray heaven she win him!

Isab. We cannot weigh our brother with ourself [1]:
Great men may jest with saints; 'tis wit in them;
But, in the less, foul profanation.

Lucio. Thou'rt in the right, girl; more o' that.

Isab. That in the captain's but a choleric word,
Which in the soldier is flat blasphemy.

Lucio. Art avis'd o' that? more on't.

Ang. Why do you put these sayings upon me?

Isab. Because authority, though it err like others,
Hath yet a kind of medicine in itself,
That skins the vice o' the top: Go to your bosom;
Knock there; and ask your heart, what it doth know
That's like my brother's fault: if it confess
A natural guiltiness, such as is his,
Let it not sound a thought upon your tongue
Against my brother's life.

Ang. She speaks, and 'tis
Such sense, that my sense breeds with it [2].—Fare you well.

---

[1] *We cannot weigh our brother with ourself:*] We mortals, proud and foolish, *cannot* prevail on our passions to *weigh* or compare *our brother*, a being of like nature and like frailty, *with ourself.* We have different names and different judgments for the same faults committed by persons of different condition. JOHNSON.

The reading of the old copy, *ourself,* which Dr. Warburton changed to *yourself,* is supported by a passage in the fifth act:
"————If he had so offended,
"He would have *weigh'd* thy *brother* by *himself,*
"And not have cut him off." MALONE.

[2] — *that my sense breeds with it.*] That is, new thoughts are stirring in my mind, new conceptions are *hatched* in my imagination. So we say to *brood* over thought. JOHNSON.

Sir W. Davenant's alteration favours the sense of the old reading [*breeds*, which Mr. Pope changed to *bleeds*]:
"————She speaks such sense
"As with my reason breeds such images
"As she has excellently form'd. STEEVENS.

I rather think the meaning is—She delivers her sentiments with such propriety, force, and elegance, that my *sensual desires* are inflamed by what she says. *Sense* has been already used in this play with the same signification:
"————one who never feels
"The wanton stings and motions of the *sense.*"
The word *breeds* is used in the same sense in *The Tempest:*
"Fair encounter
"Of two most rare affections! Heavens rain grace
"On that which *breeds* between them." MALONE.

Isab.

Isab. Gentle my lord, turn back.
Ang. I will bethink me:—Come again to-morrow.
Isab. Hark, how I'll bribe you: Good, my lord, turn back.
Ang. How! bribe me?
Isab. Ay, with such gifts, that heaven shall share with you.
Lucio. You had marr'd all else.
Isab. Not with fond shekels [3] of the tested gold [4],
Or stones, whose rates [5] are either rich, or poor,
As fancy values them; but with true prayers,
That shall be up at heaven, and enter there,
Ere sun-rise; prayers from preserved souls [6],
From fasting maids, whose minds are dedicate
To nothing temporal.
Ang. Well: come to me to-morrow.
Lucio. Go to; 'tis well; away. [*Aside* to *Isab.*
Isab. Heaven keep your honour safe!
Ang. Amen:
For I am that way going to temptation,
Where prayers cross [7]. [*Aside.*
Isab.

---

[3] — *fond shekels*] *Fond* means very frequently in our author *foolish*. It signifies in this place *valued or prized by folly*. STEEVENS.

[4] — *tested gold*,] cuppelled, brought to the *test*, refined. JOHNSON.
The cuppel is called by the refiners a *test*. Vide Harris's Lex. Tech. Voce CUPPELL. Sir J. HAWKINS.

[5] *whose rates*—] The old copy has—*rate*. This necessary emendation was made by Mr. Malone. MALONE.

[6] — *preserved souls*,] i. e. preserved from the corruption of the world. The metaphor is taken from fruits preserved in sugar. WARBURTON.

[7] *Amen:*
For I am that way going to temptation,
Where prayers cross.] Which way Angelo is going to temptation, we begin to perceive; but how *prayers cross* that way, or cross each other, at that way, more than any other, I do not understand.
Isabella prays that his *honour* may be safe, meaning only to give him his title; his imagination is caught by the word *honour:* he feels that his honour is in danger, and therefore, I believe, answers thus:
I am that way going to temptation,
Which your prayers cross.
That is, I am tempted to lose that honour of which thou implorest the preservation. The temptation under which I labour is that which thou hast unknowingly *thwarted* with thy prayer. He uses the same mode of language a few lines lower. Isabella, parting, says: *Save your honour* Angelo catches the word—*Save it! from what?*
From thee; even from thy virtue! JOHNSON.
The best method of illustrating this passage will be to quote a similar one from the *Merchant of Venice*, Act iii. sc. i.
" *Sal.*

Isab. At what hour to-morrow
Shall I attend your lordship?

Ang. At any time 'fore noon.

Isab. Save your honour!

[*Exeunt* LUCIO, ISABELLA, *and* PROVOST.

Ang. From thee; even from thy virtue!—
What's this? what's this? Is this her fault, or mine?
The tempter, or the tempted, who sins most? Ha!
Not she; nor doth she tempt: but it is I,
That lying by the violet, in the sun⁸,
Do, as the carrion does, not as the flower,
Corrupt with virtuous season. Can it be,
That modesty may more betray our sense
Than woman's lightness⁹? Having waste ground enough,
Shall we desire to raze the sanctuary,

"*Sal.* I would it might prove the end of his losses!
"*Sola.* Let me say *Amen* betimes, *lest the devil cross thy prayer.*"
For the same reason Angelo seems to say *Amen* to Isabella's prayer; but, to make the expression clear, we should read perhaps—*Where prayers are crossed.* TYRWHITT.

I believe, the meaning is—May Heaven grant your prayer! May my honour be preserved! for I find I am going into that way or road of temptation, where prayers *only* can *thwart* the temptation, and prevent it from overcoming me.

To *cross* is used in the same sense in *Timon of Athens:* "This devil knew not what he did, when he made man politick; he *crossed* himself by it." Again, in the play before us: "I may make my case as Claudio's, to *cross* this in the least."

Or, perhaps, the speaker means,—I am going into the road of temptation, into which we daily pray that we may not be led. Our Lord's prayer may have been here in Shakspeare's thoughts. MALONE.

⁸ —————— *it is I,*
That lying by the violet, in the sun, &c.] I am not corrupted by her, but by my own heart, which excites foul desires under the same benign influences that exalt her purity, as the carrion grows putrid by those beams which increase the fragrance of the violet. JOHNSON.

⁹ —————— *Can it be*
That modesty may more betray our sense
Than woman's lightness?] So, in *Promos and Cassandra,* 1578:
" I do protest her modest wordes hath wrought in me a maze,
" Though she be faire, she is not deckt with garish shewes for gaze.
" Hir bewtie lures, her lookes cut off fond suits with chast disdain.
" O God, I feele a sodaine change, that doth my freedome chayne.
" What didst thou say? fie, *Promos,* fie, &c." STEEVENS.

Sense has in this passage the same signification as in that above "—*that my sense breeds with it.*" MALONE.

And

And pitch our evils there [1]? O, fie, fie, fie!
What dost thou? or what art thou, Angelo?
Dost thou desire her foully, for those things
That make her good? O, let her brother live:
Thieves for their robbery have authority,
When judges steal themselves. What? do I love her,
That I desire to hear her speak again,
And feast upon her eyes? What is't I dream on?
O cunning enemy, that, to catch a saint,
With saints dost bait thy hook! Most dangerous
Is that temptation, that doth goad us on
To sin in loving virtue: never could the strumpet,
With all her double vigour, art, and nature,
Once stir my temper; but this virtuous maid
Subdues me quite:—Ever, till now,
When men were fond, I smil'd, and wonder'd how [2].

SCENE III.

A Room in a Prison.

Enter DUKE, *habited like a Friar, and* PROVOST.

Duke. Hail to you, Provost! so I think, you are.
Prov. I am the Provost: What's your will, good friar?
Duke. Bound by my charity, and my bless'd order,

---

[1] *And pitch our evils there?*] So, in *K. Henry VIII*:
"Nor build their *evils* on the graves of great men."
Neither of these passages appear to contain a very elegant allusion. *Evils*, in the present instance, undoubtedly stands for *forices*. Dr. Farmer assures me he has seen the word used in this sense by our ancient writers; and it appears from Harrington's *Metamorphosis of Ajax*, &c. that the privies were originally so contrived, even in royal palaces, as to deserve the title of *evils* or nuisances. STEEVENS.

No language could more forcibly express the aggravated profligacy of Angelo's passion, which the purity of Isabella served but the more to inflame.—The desecration of edifices devoted to religion, by converting them to the most abject purposes of nature, was an eastern method of expressing contempt. See 2 Kings, x. 27. HENLEY.

One of Sir John Berkenhead's queries confirms the foregoing observation:

"Whether, ever since the House of Commons has been locked up, the speakers chair has not been a *close-stool?*

"Whether it is not seasonable to stop the nose of my *evil?* Two CENTURIES OF PAUL's CHURCH-YARD, 8vo. no date. MALONE.

[2] *I smil'd, and wonder'd how.*] As a day must now intervene between this conference of Isabella with Angelo, and the next, the act might more properly end here; and here, in my opinion, it was ended by the poet. JOHNSON.

I come

I come to visit the afflicted spirits
Here in the prison*: do me the common right
To let me see them; and to make me know
The nature of their crimes, that I may minister
To them accordingly.

Prov. I would do more than that, if more were needful.

Enter JULIET.

Look, here comes one; a gentlewoman of mine,
Who falling in the flames of her own youth³,
Hath blister'd her report: She is with child;
And he that got it, sentenc'd: a young man
More fit to do another such offence,
Than die for this.

Duke. When must he die?

---

* *I come to visit the afflicted spirits*
Here in the prison.] This is a Scriptural expression very suitable to the grave character which the Duke assumes: "—by which also he went and preached unto *the spirits in prison*." 1 Pet. iii. 19.
WHALLEY.

³ *Who falling in the* flames *of her own youth,*
Hath blister'd *her report:*] The old copy has—*flawes*. The correction was made by Dr. Warburton. In support of this emendation, it should be remembered, that *flawes* (for so it was anciently spelled) and *flames* differ only by a letter that is very frequently mistaken at the press. The same mistake is found in *Macbeth*, Act ii. sc. i. edit. 1623:
"— my steps, which they *may walk*,"—instead of—*which way*.
Again, in this play of *Measure for Measure*, Act v. sc. i. edit. 1623:
—" give *we* your hand;" instead of *me*.—In a former scene of the play before us we meet with—" *burning* youth."
Again, in *All's Well that Ends Well*:
"————— Yet, in his idle *fire*,
" To buy his will, it would not seem too dear."
To fall IN, (not *into*) was the language of the time. So in *Cymbeline*:
"————— Almost spent with hunger,
" I am fallen *in* offence." MALONE.
Sir W. Davenant reads *flames*, instead of *flaws*, in his *Law against Lovers*, a play almost literally taken from *Measure for Measure*, and *Much Ado about Nothing*. FARMER.
Shakspeare has *flaming youth* in *Hamlet*, and Greene, in his *Never too Late*, 1616, says—" he measured the *flames of youth* by his own dead cinders." *Blister'd her report*, is *disfigured her fame*. *Blister* seems to have reference to the *flames* mentioned in the preceding line. A similar use of this word occurs in *Hamlet*:
"————— takes the rose
" From the fair forehead of an innocent love,
" And sets a *blister* there." STEEVENS.

Prov.

Prov. As I do think, to-morrow.—
I have provided for you; stay a while [*To Juliet.*
And you shall be conducted.

Duke. Repent you, fair one, of the sin you carry?

Juliet. I do; and bear the shame most patiently.

Duke. I'll teach you how you shall arraign your conscience,
And try your penitence, if it be sound,
Or hollowly put on.

Juliet. I'll gladly learn.

Duke. Love you the man that wrong'd you?

Juliet. Yes, as I love the woman that wrong'd him.

Duke. So then, it seems, your most offenceful act
Was mutually committed?

Juliet. Mutually.

Duke. Then was your sin of heavier kind than his.

Juliet. I do confess it, and repent it, father.

Duke. 'Tis meet so, daughter: But lest you do repent [4],
As that the sin hath brought you to this shame—
Which sorrow is always toward ourselves, not heaven;
Shewing, we would not spare heaven [5], as we love it,
But as we stand in fear—

Juliet. I do repent me, as it is an evil;
And take the shame with joy.

Duke. There rest [6].
Your partner, as I hear, must die to-morrow,
And I am going with instruction to him;
Grace go with you! *Benedicite.*   [*Exit.*

Juliet. Must die to-morrow! O injurious love [7],

---

[4] *But lest you do repent,*] is only a kind of negative imperative—*Ne te pœniteat,*—and means, repent not on this account. STEEVENS.

I think that a line at least is wanting after the first of the Duke's speech. It would be presumptuous to attempt to replace the words; but the sense, I am persuaded, is easily recoverable out of Juliet's answer. I suppose his advice, in substance, to have been nearly this: Take care, *lest you repent* [not so much of your fault, as it is an evil,] *as that the sin hath brought you to this shame.* Accordingly, Juliet's answer is explicit to this point:

"I do repent me, as it is an evil,
"And take the shame with joy." TYRWHITT.

[5] *Shewing, we would not spare heaven,*] i. e. spare to *offend* heaven. MALONE.

[6] *There rest.*] Keep yourself in this temper. JOHNSON.

[7] *O injurious love,*] O love, that is injurious in expediting Claudio's death, and that respites me a life, which is a burthen to me worse than death! TOLLET.

That

That respites me a life, whose very comfort
Is still a dying horror!
   Prov. 'Tis pity of him.   [*Exeunt.*

SCENE IV.

A Room in ANGELO'S *House.*

Enter ANGELO.

   Ang. When I would pray and think, I think and pray
To several subjects: heaven hath my empty words;
Whilst my invention [8], hearing not my tongue,
Anchors on Isabel [9]: Heaven in my mouth [1],
As if I did but only chew his name;
And in my heart, the strong and swelling evil
Of my conception: The state, whereon I studied,
Is like a good thing, being often read,
Grown fear'd and tedious [2]; yea, my gravity,
Wherein (let no man hear me) I take pride,
Could I, with boot [3], change for an idle plume,
Which the air beats for vain. O place! O form [4]!
                                                        How

---

[8] *Whilst my invention,*] By *invention*, I believe the poet means *imagination*. STEEVENS.
   So in our author's 103d sonnet:
         " —————— a face,
         " That overgoes my blunt *invention* quite."
Again, in *K. Henry V*:
         " O for a muse of fire, that would ascend
         " The brightest heaven of *invention!*" MALONE.
[9] *Anchors on Isabel.*] We meet with the same singular expression in *Antony and Cleopatra*:
         " There would he *anchor* his aspect, and die
         " With looking on his life." MALONE.
[1] *Heaven in my mouth,*] i.e. Heaven *being* in my mouth. MALONE.
[2] *Grown fear'd and tedious;*] What we go to with reluctance may be said to be *fear'd*. JOHNSON.
[3] *—with boot,*] *Boot* is profit, advantage, gain. STEEVENS.
[4] *—change for an idle plume,*
   Which the air beats for vain. O place! O form! &c.] There is, I believe, no instance in Shakspeare, or any other author, of "*for vain*" being used for "*in vain.*" Besides; has the air or wind *less* effect on a feather than on twenty other things? or rather, is not the reverse of this the truth? An *idle plume* assuredly is not that "ever-fixed mark," of which our author speaks elsewhere, "that looks on tempests, and is never shaken." The old copy has *vaine*, in which way a *vane* or weather-cock was formerly spelt. [See *Minsheu's* DICT. 1617, *in verb.*—
                                                        So

How often doſt thou with thy caſe [5], thy habit,
Wrench awe from fools, and tie the wiſer ſouls
To thy falſe ſeeming [6]? Blood, thou ſtill art blood [7]:
Let's write good angel on the devil's horn [8],
'Tis not the devil's creſt.

Enter

So alſo, in *Love Labour's Loſt*, Act iv. ſc. i. edit. 1623: "What *vaine?* what weathercock?"] I would therefore read—*vane*.—I would exchange my gravity, ſays Angelo, for an idle feather, which being driven along by the wind, ſerves, to the ſpectator, for a *vane* or weathercock. So, in *The Winter's Tale:*
  "I am a *feather* for each *wind* that blows."
And in the *Merchant of Venice* we meet with a kindred thought:
  ———"I ſhould be ſtill
  "Plucking the *graſs*, *to know where ſits the wind.*"
The omiſſion of the article is certainly awkward, but not without example. Thus, in *K. Lear*:
  "Hot queſtriſts after him met him *at gate*."
Again, in *Coriolanus*: "Go, ſee him out *at gates*."
Again, in *Titus Andronicus*: "Aſcend, fair queen, *Pantheon*."
Again, in the *Winter's Tale*: "'Pray heartily, he be *at palace!*"
Again, in *Cymbeline*: "Nor tent, to *bottom*, that."
The author, however, might have written—
  ——— an idle plume,
  Which the air beats for vane o' the place.—O form,
  How often doſt *thou*—&c.
The pronoun *thou*, referring to only *one* antecedent, appears to me ſtrongly to ſupport ſuch a regulation. MALONE.

[5] —*caſe*,] For outſide; garb; external ſhew. JOHNSON.

[6] *Wrench awe from fools, and tie the wiſer ſouls*
To thy falſe ſeeming?] Here Shakſpeare judiciouſly diſtinguiſhes the different operations of high place upon different minds. Fools are frighted, and wiſe men are allured. Thoſe who cannot judge but by the eye, are eaſily awed by ſplendour; thoſe who conſider men as well as conditions, are eaſily perſuaded to love the appearance of virtue dignified with power. JOHNSON.

[7] —*Blood, thou ſtill art blood*;] The old copy reads—Blood, thou art blood. Mr. Pope, to ſupply the ſyllable wanting to complete the metre, reads—blood, thou art *but* blood! But the word now introduced appears to me to agree better with the context, and therefore more likely to have been the author's.—*Blood* is uſed here, as in other places, for *temperament of body*. MALONE.

[8] *Let's write good angel on the devil's* horn,
'Tis not the devil's creſt.] i. e. let the moſt wicked thing have but a virtuous pretence, and it ſhall paſs for innocent. WARBURTON.

It ſhould be remembered that the devil is uſually repreſented with *horns* and cloven feet.—Dr. Johnſon would read—'Tis *yet* the devil's creſt. He acknowledges, however, that the paſſage may be underſtood, according to Dr. Warburton's explanation. "O place, how doſt thou impoſe upon the world by falſe appearances! ſo much, that if we *write*
  good

Enter SERVANT.

How now, who's there?

Serv. One Isabel, a sister, desires access to you.

Ang. Teach her the way. [*Exit Serv.*] O heavens!
Why does my blood thus muster to my heart [9];
Making both it unable for itself,
And dispossessing all my other parts
Of necessary fitness?
So play the foolish throngs with one that swoons;
Come all to help him, and so stop the air
By which he should revive: and even so
The general, subject to a well-wish'd king [1],

Quit

good angel on the devil's horn, 'tis not taken any longer to be the *devil's* *crest*. In this sense, *Blood thou art*, &c. is an interjected exclamation." —The old copy appears to me to require no alteration.

MALONE.

[9] *—to my heart;*] Of this speech there is no other trace in *Promos* *and Cassandra* than the following:

"Both hope and dreade at once my harte doth touch." STEEVENS.

[1] *The general, subject to a well-wish'd king,*] General was, in our author's time, a word for *people*, so that the *general* is the *people*, or multitude, *subject* to a king. So, in *Hamlet*: "The play pleased not the *million:* 'twas caviare to the *general.*" JOHNSON.

The use of this phrase, "*the general,*" for the people, continued so late as to the time of Lord Clarendon:—" as rather to be consented to, than that *the general* should suffer." Hist. B. V. p. 530. 8vo. MALONE.

Twice in *Hamlet* our author uses *subject* for *subjects:*

"So nightly toils the *subject* of the land." Act i. sc. i.

Again, Act i. sc. ii:

"The lists and full proportions all are made

"Out of his *subject.*" STEEVENS.

So the Duke had before (Act i. scene ii.) expressed his dislike of popular applause;

"I'll privily away. I love the people,

"But do not like to stage me to their eyes.

"Though it do well, I do not relish well

"Their loud applause and *aves* vehement;

"Nor do I think the man of safe discretion,

"That does affect it."

I cannot help thinking that Shakspeare, in these two passages, intended to flatter that unkingly weakness of James the First, which made him so impatient of the crowds that flocked to see him, especially upon his first coming, that, as some of our historians say, he restrained them by a proclamation. Sir Symonds D'Ewes, in his Memoirs of his own Life, (a MS. in the British Museum,) has a remarkable passage with regard to this humour of James. After taking notice, that the king going to
parlia-

Quit their own part, and in obsequious fondness
Crowd to his presence, where their untaught love
Must needs appear offence.

Enter ISABELLA.

How now, fair maid?
   Isab. I am come to know your pleasure.
   Ang. That you might know it, would much better please me,
Than to demand what 'tis. Your brother cannot live.
   Isab. Even so?—Heaven keep your honour! [*retiring.*—
   Ang. Yet may he live a while; and, it may be,
As long as you, or I: Yet he must die.
   Isab. Under your sentence?
   Ang. Yea.
   Isab. When, I beseech you? that in his reprieve,
Longer, or shorter, he may be so fitted,
That his soul sicken not.
   Ang. Ha! Fie, these filthy vices! It were as good
To pardon him, that hath from nature stolen
A man already made [2], as to remit
Their sawcy sweetness, that do coin heaven's image
In stamps that are forbid [3]: 'tis all as easy
Falsely to take [4] away a life true made,

---

parliament, on the 30th of January, 1620-1, " spake lovingly to the people, and said, God bless ye, God bless ye;" he adds these words, " contrary to his former hasty and passionate custom, which often, in his sudden distemper, would bid a pox or a plague on such as flocked to see him." TYRWHITT.

  [2] —————— *that hath from nature stolen*
   A man already made,] i. e. that hath killed a man. MALONE.
  [3] *Their sawcy sweetness, that do coin* heaven's image
   In stamps that are forbid;] We meet with nearly the same words in *King Edward III.* a tragedy, 1596, certainly prior to this play;
   " —————— And will your sacred self
   " Commit high treason 'gainst the *king of heaven,*
   " 'To *stamp* his *image* in *forbidden metal?*"
These lines are spoken by the Countess of Salisbury, whose chastity (like Isabel's) was assailed by her sovereign.
   Their sawcy sweetness Dr. Warburton interprets, *their sawcy indulgence of the appetite.* Perhaps it means nearly the same as what is afterwards called *sweet uncleanness.* MALONE.
  [4] *Falsely to take*—] F*alsely* is the same with *dishonestly, illegally*: so *false,* in the next lines, is *illegal, illegitimate.* JOHNSON.

As to put mettle in restrained means,
To make a false one⁵.

Isab. 'Tis set down so in heaven, but not in earth⁶.

Ang. Say you so? then I shall poze you quickly.
Which had you rather, That the most just law
Now took your brother's life; or, to redeem him⁷,
Give up your body to such sweet uncleanness,
As she that he hath stain'd?

---

⁵ *As to put* mettle *in restrained means,*
To make a false one.] Mettle, the reading of the old copy, which was changed to *metal* by Mr. Theobald, (who has been followed by the subsequent editors,) is supported not only by the general purport of the passage, (in which our author having already illustrated the sentiment he has attributed to Angelo by an allusion to coining, would not give the same image a second time,) but by a similar expression in *Timon:*

"——— thy father, that poor rag,
"Must be thy subject; who in spite *put stuff*
"To some she-beggar, and compounded thee,
"Poor rogue hereditary."

Again, in the *Winter's Tale:*

"As rank as any flax wench, that *puts* to,
"Before her troth-plight."

The controverted word is found again in the same sense in *Macbeth:*

"———thy undaunted *mettle* should compose
"Nothing but males."

Again, in *K. Richard II:*

"——— that bed, that womb,
"That *mettle*, that self-mould that fashion'd thee,
"Made him a man."

Again, in *Timon of Athens:*

"——— Common mother, thou,
"Whose womb unmeasurable, and infinite breast,
"Teems and feeds all; whose self-same *mettle*,
"Whereof thy proud child, arrogant man, is puff'd,
"Engenders the black toad," &c.

Means is here used for *medium*, or *object*, and the sense of the whole is this: 'Tis as easy *wickedly to deprive a man born in wedlock of life, as to have unlawful commerce with a maid, in order to give life to an illegitimate child.* The thought is simply, that murder is as easy as fornication; and the inference which Angelo would draw, is, that it is as improper to pardon the latter as the former. The words—*to make a false one*—evidently referring to *life,* shew that the preceding line is to be understood in a natural, and not in a metaphorical, sense. MALONE.

⁶ *'Tis set down so in heaven, but not in earth.*] What you have stated is undoubtedly the Divine law; murder and fornication are both forbid by the *canon of scripture;*—but on *earth* the latter offence is considered as less heinous than the former. MALONE.

⁷ —*or, to redeem him,*] The old copy has—*and to redeem him.*—The emendation was made by Sir William D'Avenant. MALONE.

Isab.

Isab. Sir, believe this,
I had rather give my body than my soul[8].
　Ang. I talk not of your soul; Our compell'd sins
Stand more for number than for accompt[9].
　Isab. How say you?
　Ang. Nay, I'll not warrant that; for I can speak
Against the thing I say. Answer to this;—
I, now the voice of the recorded law,
Pronounce a sentence on your brother's life:
Might there not be a charity in sin,
To save this brother's life?
　Isab. Please you to do't,
I'll take it as a peril to my soul,
It is no sin at all, but charity.
　Ang. Pleas'd you to do't, at peril of your soul[1],
Were equal poize of sin and charity.
　Isab. That I do beg his life, if it be sin,
Heaven, let me bear it! your granting of my suit,
If that be sin, I'll make it my morn prayer
To have it added to the faults of mine,
And nothing of your, answer[2].

[8] *I had rather give my body than my soul.*] Isabel, I believe, uses the words, "give my body," in a different sense from that in which they had been employed by Angelo. She means, I think, *I had rather die, than forfeit my eternal happiness by the prostitution of my person.* MALONE.

[9] ———— *Our compell'd sins
Stand more for number than for accompt.*] Actions to which we are compelled, however numerous, are not imputed to us by heaven as crimes. If you cannot save your brother but by the loss of your chastity, it is not a voluntary but compelled sin, for which you cannot be accountable. MALONE.

[1] *Pleas'd you to do't, at peril, &c.*] The reasoning is thus: Angelo asks whether there might not be a charity in sin to save this brother. Isabella answers, that if Angelo will save him, she will stake her soul that it were charity, not sin. Angelo replies, that if Isabella would save him at the hazard of her soul, it would be not indeed no sin, but a sin to which the charity would be equivalent. JOHNSON.

[2] *And nothing of your answer.*] This passage would be clear, I think, if it were pointed thus:

　　To have it added to the faults of mine,
　　And nothing of your, answer.

So that the substantive *answer* may be understood to be joined in construction with *mine* as well as *your.* The faults *of mine answer* are the faults *which I am to answer for.* TYRWHITT.

And nothing of your answer, means, *and make no part of those for which you shall be called to answer.* STEEVENS.

VOL. III.　　　R　　　　　　　　*Ang.*

Ang. Nay, but hear me:
Your sense pursues not mine: either you are ignorant,
Or seem so, craftily [3]; and that's not good.
  Isab. Let me be ignorant [4], and in nothing good,
But graciously to know I am no better.
  Ang. Thus wisdom wishes to appear most bright,
When it doth tax itself: as these black masks
Proclaim an enshield beauty [5] ten times louder

---

[3] *Or seem so,* craftily,] Old copy—*crafty.* Corrected by Sir William D'Avenant. MALONE.

[4] *Let me be ignorant,*] *Me* is wanting in the original copy. The emendation was made by the editor of the second folio. MALONE.

[5] *Proclaim an* enshield *beauty—*] An *enshield beauty* is *a shielded beauty, a beauty covered as with a shield.* STEEVENS.
  This should be written *en-shell'd,* or *in-shell'd,* as it is in *Coriolanus,* Act iv. sc. vi.

  " Thrusts forth his horns again into the world
  " That were in-shell'd when Marcius stood for Rome."

These *Masks* must mean, I think, the *Ladies of the audience;* however improperly a compliment to them is put into the mouth of Angelo. As Shakspeare would hardly have been guilty of such an indecorum to flatter a common audience, I think this passage affords ground for supposing that the play was written to be acted at court. Some strokes of particular flattery to the king I have already pointed out; and there are several other general reflections, in the character of the duke especially, which seem calculated for the royal ear. TYRWHITT.

I do not think so well of the conjecture in the latter part of this note, as I did some years ago; and therefore I should wish to withdraw it. Not that I am inclined to adopt the idea of the author of REMARKS, &c. p. 20. as I see no ground for supposing that Isabella *had any mask in her hand.* My notion at present is, that the phrase *these black masks* signifies nothing more than *black masks;* according to an old idiom of our language, by which the demonstrative pronoun is put for the prepositive article.— See the *Glossary to Chaucer,* Ed. 1775. v. *This, Thise.* Shakspeare seems to have used the same idiom, not only in the passage quoted by Mr. Steevens from *Romeo and Juliet,* but also in 1 *H. IV.* Act i. sc. iii.

———and, but for *these* vile guns,
He would himself have been a soldier.

With respect to the former part of this note, though the *Remarker* has told us, that " *en-shield* is CERTAINLY put by contraction for *en-shielded,* I have no objection to leaving my conjecture in its place, till some authority is produced for such an usage of *enshield* or *enshielded.*
TYRWHITT.

Sir *W. D'Avenant* reads—*as a black mask;* but I am afraid Mr. Tyrwhitt is too well supported in his first supposition, by a passage at the beginning of *Romeo and Juliet:*

" *These* happy *masks* that kiss fair ladies' brows,
" Being *black,* put us in mind they hide the fair." STEEVENS.

Than

Than beauty could display'd.—But mark me;
To be received plain, I'll speak more gross:
Your brother is to die.

  Isab. So.

  Ang. And his offence is so, as it appears
Accountant to the law upon that pain [6].

  Isab. True.

  Ang. Admit no other way to save his life,
(As I subscribe not that [7], nor any other,
But in the loss of question [8],) that you, his sister,
Finding yourself desir'd of such a person,
Whose credit with the judge, or own great place,
Could fetch your brother from the manacles
Of the all-binding law [9]; and that there were
No earthly mean to save him, but that either
You must lay down the treasures of your body
To this suppos'd, or else to let him suffer [1];
What would you do?

---

[6] *—upon that pain.*] *Pain* is here for *penalty, punishment.* JOHNSON.

[7] (*As I* subscribe *not that,*] To *subscribe* means, *to agree to.*
                                            STEEVENS.

So, in Marlowe's *Lust's Dominion,* 1657:
  "*Subscribe* to his desires."
Milton uses the word in the same sense.

[8] *But in the loss of question.*—] This expression I believe means, *but in idle supposition,* or *conversation that tends to nothing,* which may, therefore, in our author's language, be call'd *the loss of question.*

Thus, in *Coriolanus,* Act iii. sc. i:
  "The which shall turn you to no other harm,
  "Than so much *loss of time.*"

Question, in Shakspeare, often bears this meaning. So, in his *Rape of Lucrece:*
  "And after supper long he *questioned*
  "With modest Lucrece, &c." STEEVENS.

Question is used here, as in many other places, for *conversation.*
                                            MALONE.

[9] *Of the all-binding law.*—] The old copy has—*all-building.* The emendation is Mr. Theobald's. MALONE.

[1] *—or else to let him suffer.*] Sir Thomas Hanmer reads more grammatically—"or else *to* let him suffer." But our author is frequently inaccurate in the construction of his sentences. I have therefore adhered to the old copy: *You must be under the necessity* (to let, &c.) must be understood.

So, in Holinshed's *Hist. of Scotland,* p. 150: "—asleep they were so fast, that a man might have rendered the chamber over them, sooner than to have awaked them out of their drunken sleep."
                                            MALONE.

Isab. As much for my poor brother, as myself;
That is, Were I under the terms of death,
The impression of keen whips I'd wear as rubies,
And strip myself to death, as to a bed
That longing I have been sick for, ere I'd yield
My body up to shame.

Ang. Then must your brother die.

Isab. And 'twere the cheaper way:
Better it were, a brother died at once²,
Than that a sister, by redeeming him,
Should die for ever.

Ang. Were not you then as cruel as the sentence
That you have slander'd so?

Isab. Ignomy in ransom³, and free pardon,
Are of two houses: lawful mercy
Is nothing kin to foul redemption.

Ang. You seem'd of late to make the law a tyrant;
And rather prov'd the sliding of your brother
A merriment than a vice.

Isab. O, pardon me, my lord; it oft falls out,
To have what we would have, we speak not what we mean:
I something do excuse the thing I hate,
For his advantage that I dearly love.

Ang. We are all frail.

Isab. Else let my brother die,
If not a feodary, but only he⁴,

O we,

---

² —*a brother died at once,*] Perhaps we should read—*for once.* JOHNSON.

³ *Ignomy in ransom,*] *Ignomy* was in our author's time used for *ignominy*. So again, in *K. Henry IV.* Part i.

"Thy *ignomy* sleep with thee in thy grave—"

Sir W. D'Avenant's alteration of these lines may prove a reasonably good comment on them:

Ignoble ransom no proportion bears
To pardon freely given. MALONE.

⁴ *If not a feodary, but only he,* &c.] Shakspeare has the same allusion in *Cymbeline:*

"—— senseless bauble,
"Art thou a *feodary* for this act?"

The old copy reads—*thy weakness.* STEEVENS.

I have shewn, in a note on *Cymbeline*, that *feodary* was used by Shakspeare in the sense of an *associate*, and such undoubtedly is its signification here.

After having ascertained the true meaning of this word, I must own, that the remaining part of the passage before us is extremely difficult.

I would,

MEASURE FOR MEASURE. 365

Owe [5], and succeed by weakness.

Ang. Nay, women are frail too.

Isab. Ay, as the glasses where they view themselves;
Which are as easy broke as they make forms.
Women!—Help heaven! men their creation mar
In profiting by them [6]. Nay, call us ten times frail;
For we are soft as our complexions are,
And credulous to false prints [7].

Ang. I think it well:
And from this testimony of your own sex,
(Since, I suppose, we are made to be no stronger
Than faults may shake our frames,) let me be bold;—
I do arrest your words; Be that you are,
That is, a woman; if you be more, you're none;
If you be one, (as you are well express'd
By all external warrants,) shew it now,
By putting on the destin'd livery.

Isab. I have no tongue but one: gentle my lord,
Let me intreat you, speak the former language [8].

Ang.

I would, however, restore the original reading *thy*, and the meaning should seem to be this. "We are all frail," says Angelo. "Yes," replies Isabella; if he has not one associate in his crime, if no other person own and follow the same criminal courses which you are now pursuing, let my brother suffer death.

I think it, however, extremely probable that something is omitted. It is observable that the line—"Owe and succeed thy weakness," does not, together with the subsequent line,—"Nay, women are frail too,"—make a perfect verse; from which it may be conjectured that the compositor's eye glanced from the word *succeed* to *weakness* in a subsequent hemistich, and that by this oversight the passage is become unintelligible. MALONE.

[5] *Owe,*—] To owe is, in this place, to *own*, to *hold*, to have possession. JOHNSON.

[6] *In profiting by them.*] In imitating them, in taking them for examples. JOHNSON.

I rather think the meaning is —in *taking advantage* of their weakness. A French sense: *se profiter.* MALONE.

[7] *For we are soft as our complexions are,*
And credulous to false prints.] So, in *Twelfth Night*:
"How easy is it for the proper false
"In women's waxen hearts to set their forms!
"Alas! our frailty is the cause, not we;
"For, such as we are made of, such we be." MALONE.

And credulous to false prints. i. e. we take any impression.
WARBURTON.

R 3 [8] —*speak*

Ang. Plainly conceive, I love you.
Isab. My brother did love Juliet:
And you tell me, that he shall die for it.
Ang. He shall not, Isabel, if you give me love.
Isab. I know, your virtue hath a licence in't [9],
Which seems a little fouler than it is [1],
To pluck on others.
Ang. Believe me, on mine honour,
My words express my purpose.
Isab. Ha! little honour to be much believ'd,
And most pernicious purpose!—Seeming, seeming [2]!—
I will proclaim thee, Angelo; look for't:
Sign me a present pardon for my brother,
Or, with an out-stretch'd throat, I'll tell the world
Aloud, what man thou art.
Ang. Who will believe thee, Isabel?
My unsoil'd name, the austereness of my life,
My vouch against [3] you, and my place i' the state,
Will so your accusation over-weigh,
That you shall stifle in your own report,
And smell of calumny [4]. I have begun;
And now I give my sensual race the rein [*]:
Fit thy consent to my sharp appetite;

---

[8] —*Speak the former language.*] Isabella answers to his circumlocutory courtship, that she has not *her tongue.* She does not understand this new phrase, and desires him to talk his *former language,* that is, to talk as he talked before. JOHNSON.

[9] *I know your virtue hath a licence in't,*] Alluding to the licences given by ministers to their spies, to go into all suspected companies, and join in the language of malecontents. WARBURTON.

[1] *Which seems a little fouler, &c.*] So, in *Promos and Cassandra:*
"*Cas.* Renowned lord, you use this speech (I hope) your thrall to trye;
"If otherwise, my brother's life so deare I will not bye.
"*Pro.* Fair dame, my outward looks my inward thoughts bewray;
"If you mistrust, to search my harte, would God you had a kaye."
STEEVENS.

[2] *Seeming, seeming!*—] Hypocrisy, hypocrisy; counterfeit virtue.
JOHNSON.

[3] *My vouch against*] means no more than denial. JOHNSON.

[4] *That you shall stifle in your own report,*
And smell of calumny.] A metaphor from a lamp or candle extinguished in its own grease. STEEVENS.

[*] *And now I give my sensual race the rein:*] And now I give my senses the rein, in the race they are now running. HEATH.

Lay

Lay by all nicety, and prolixious blushes [5],
That banish what they sue for; redeem thy brother
By yielding up thy body to my will;
Or else he must not only die the death [6],
But thy unkindness shall his death draw out
To lingering sufferance: answer me to-morrow,
Or, by the affection that now guides me most,
I'll prove a tyrant to him: As for you,
Say what you can, my false o'erweighs your true [7].   [*Exit.*

Isab. To whom should I complain? Did I tell this,
Who would believe me? O perilous mouths,
That bear in them one and the self-same tongue,
Either of condemnation or approof!
Bidding the law make court'sy to their will;
Hooking both right and wrong to the appetite,
To follow, as it draws! I'll to my brother:
Though he hath fallen by prompture [8] of the blood,
Yet hath he in him such a mind of honour [9],
That had he twenty heads to tender down
On twenty bloody blocks, he'd yield them up,
Before his sister should her body stoop
To such abhorr'd pollution.
Then Isabel, live chaste, and brother, die:
More than our brother is our chastity.

---

[5] *—and* prolixious *blushes,*] That maiden modesty, which is *slow* in yielding to the wishes of a lover. MALONE.

The word *prolixious* is not peculiar to Shakspeare. It is used by Drayton, and by Nashe. STEEVENS.

[6] *—die the death,*] This seems to be a solemn phrase for death inflicted by law. JOHNSON.

It is a phrase taken from scripture, as is observed in a note on the *Midsummer Night's Dream.* STEEVENS.

The phrase is *a good phrase,* as Shallow says, but I do not conceive it to be either of *legal* or *scriptural* origin. Chaucer uses it frequently.— See Cant. Tales, ver. 607.

"They were adradde of him, as of *the deth.*" ver 1222.

"*The deth* he feleth thurgh his herte smite." It seems to have been originally a mistaken translation of the French *La Mort.* TYRWHITT.

[7] *—my* false *o'erweighs your* true.] *False* and *true* are here used as substantives. My *falsehood* will outweigh your *truth.* So, in our author's 113th Sonnet:

"My most true mind thus maketh mine *untrue.*" MALONE.

[8] *—prompture*] Suggestion, temptation, instigation. JOHNSON.

[9] *—such a mind of honour,*] This, in Shakspeare's language, may mean, *such an honourable mind,* as he uses elsewhere, *mind of love,* for *loving mind.* STEEVENS.

I'll tell him yet of Angelo's requeſt,
And fit his mind to death, for his ſoul's reſt.   [*Exit.*

ACT III. SCENE I.

A Room in the Priſon.

Enter DUKE, CLAUDIO, *and* PROVOST.

Duke. So, then you hope of pardon from Lord Angelo?
Claud. The miſerable have no other medicine,
But only hope:
I have hope to live, and am prepar'd to die.
Duke. Be abſolute for death [1]; either death, or life,
Shall thereby be the ſweeter. Reaſon thus with life—
If I do loſe thee, I do loſe a thing,
That none but fools would keep [2]: a breath thou art,
(Servile to all the ſkiey influences,)
That doſt this habitation, where thou keep'ſt [3],

                                             Hourly

---

[1] *Be abſolute for death;*] Be determined to die, without any hope of life. Horace,——
" *The hour which exceeds expectation will be welcome.*" JOHNSON.

[2] *That none but fools would keep;*] The meaning is, that *none but fools would wiſh to keep life;* or, *none but fools would keep* it, if choice were allowed. JOHNSON.

Keep in this place, I believe, may not ſignify *preſerve*, but *care for*. " No longer for to liven I ne *kepe*," ſays Æneas, in *Chaucer's* Dido Queen of Carthage; and elſewhere, " That I *kepe* not rehearſed be:" i. e. which I *care not* to have rehearſed.

Again, in the *Knightes Tale*, late edit. ver. 2240:
" I *kepe* nought of armes for to yelpe." STEEVENS.

Mr. Steevens's explanation is confirmed by a paſſage in *the Dcheſs of Malfy*, by Webſter, (1623) an author who has frequently imitated Shakſpeare, and who perhaps followed him in the preſent inſtance:
" Of what is't *fools* make ſuch vain *keeping?*
" Sin their conception, their birth weeping;
" Their *life* a general miſt of error;
" Their death a hideous ſtorm of terror."
See the Gloſſary to Mr. Tyrwhitt's edit. of the *Canterbury's Tales* of Chaucer. v. *kepe.* MALONE.

[3] *That doſt this habitation, where thou keep'ſt.*] The editors have changed *doſt to do*, without neceſſity or authority. The conſtruction is
not

Hourly afflict: merely, thou art death's fool;
For him thou labour'st by thy flight to shun,
And yet run'st toward him still⁴: Thou art not noble;
For all the accommodations that thou bear'st,
Are nurs'd by baseness⁵: Thou art by no means valiant;
For thou dost fear the soft and tender fork
Of a poor worm⁶: Thy best of rest is sleep⁷.

And not, "the skiey influences that do," but, "a breath thou art, that dost" &c. If " Servile to all the skiey influences" be inclosed in a parenthesis, all the difficulty will vanish. PORSON.

⁴ ——— *merely, thou art death's fool:*
For him thou labour'st by thy flight to shun,
And yet run'st toward him still.] In those old farces called *Moralities*, the *fool* of the piece, in order to shew the inevitable approaches of death, is made to employ all his stratagems to avoid him; which, as the matter is ordered, bring the *fool* at every turn into his very jaws. So that the representations of these scenes would afford a great deal of good *mirth* and *morals* mixed together. WARBURTON.

It is observed by the editor of *the Sad Shepherd*, 8vo. 1783, p. 154, that the initial letter of Stowe's *Survey* contains a representation of a struggle between *Death* and the *Fool*; the figures of which were most probably copied from those characters, as formerly exhibited on the stage. REED.

⁵ *Are nurs'd by baseness:*] Dr. Warburton is undoubtedly mistaken in supposing that by *baseness* is meant *self-love*, here assigned as the motive of all human actions. Shakspeare only meant to observe, that a minute analysis of life at once destroys that splendour which dazzles the imagination. Whatever grandeur can display, or luxury enjoy, is procured by *baseness*, by offices of which the mind shrinks from the contemplation. All the delicacies of the table may be traced back to the shambles and the dunghill, all magnificence of building was hewn from the quarry, and all the pomp of ornament dug from among the damps and darkness of the mine. JOHNSON.

This is a thought which Shakspeare delights to express. So, in *Antony and Cleopatra:*

" ———our dungy earth alike
" Feeds man as beast."

Again:

" Which sleeps, and never palates more the *dung*,
" *The beggar's nurse, and Cæsar's.*" STEEVENS.

⁶ ——— *the soft and tender fork*
Of a poor worm.] *Worm* is put for any creeping thing or serpent. Shakspeare supposes falsely, but according to the vulgar notion, that a serpent wounds with his tongue, and that his tongue is *forked*. He confounds reality and fiction; a serpent's tongue is *soft*, but not *forked* nor hurtful. If it could hurt, it could not be *soft*. In the *Midsummer Night's Dream* he has the same notion:

" ——— *With doubler tongue*
" *Than thine, O serpent, never adder stung.*" JOHNSON.

And that thou oft provok'st [3]; yet grosly fear'st
Thy death, which is no more: Thou art not thyself [9];
For thou exist'st on many a thousand grains
That issue out of dust: Happy thou art not:
For what thou hast not, still thou striv'st to get;
And what thou hast, forget'st: Thou art not certain;
For thy complexion shifts to strange effects [1],
After the moon: If thou art rich, thou art poor;
For, like an ass, whose back with ingots bows,
Thou bear'st thy heavy riches but a journey,
And death unloads thee: Friend hast thou none;
For thine own bowels, which do call thee sire,
The mere effusion of thy proper loins,
Do curse the gout, serpigo [2], and the rheum,
For ending thee no sooner: Thou hast nor youth, nor age;
But, as it were, an after-dinner's sleep,
Dreaming on both [3]: for all thy blessed youth [4]

Becomes

Shakspeare might have caught this idea from old tapestries or paintings in which the tongues of serpents and dragons always appear barbed like the point of an arrow. STEEVENS.

[7] *Thy best of rest is sleep*, &c.] Evidently from the following passage of Cicero: "Habes *somnum imaginem mortis, eamque quotidie induis, & dubitas quin sensus in morte nullus sit cum in ejus simulacro videas esse nullum sensum.*" But the Epicurean insinuation is, with great judgment, omitted in the imitation. WARBURTON.

Here Dr. Warburton might have found a sentiment worthy of his animadversion. I cannot without indignation find Shakspeare saying that *death is only sleep*, lengthening out his exhortation by a sentence which, in the friar is impious, in the reasoner is foolish, and in the poet trite and vulgar. JOHNSON.

This was an oversight in Shakspeare; for in the second scene of the fourth act, the Provost speaks of the desperate Barnardine, as one who regards death only as a *drunken sleep*. STEEVENS.

I apprehend Shakspeare means to say no more, than that the passage from this life to another is as easy as sleep; a position in which there is surely neither folly nor impiety. MALONE.

[8] — *thou oft provok'st*;] i. e. solicitest, procurest. MALONE.

[9] *Thou art not thyself*:] Thou art perpetually repaired and renovated by external assistance; thou subsistest upon foreign matter, and hast no power of producing or continuing thy own being. JOHNSON.

[1] — *strange effects*] For *effects* read *affects*; that is *affections, passions* of mind, or disorders of body variously *affected*. So, in *Othello*: " The *young affects*." JOHNSON.

[2] —*serpigo*.] The *serpigo* is a kind of tetter. STEEVENS.

[3] — *Thou hast nor youth, nor age;
But, as it were, an after-dinner's sleep,
Dreaming on both*;] This is exquisitely imagined. When we are young, we busy ourselves in forming schemes for succeeding time, and

Becomes as aged, and doth beg the alms
Of palsied eld [5]; and when thou art old, and rich,
Thou hast neither heat, affection, limb, nor beauty [6],
To make thy riches pleasant. What's yet in this,
That bears the name of life? Yet in this life
Lie hid more thousand deaths [7]: yet death we fear,
That makes these odds all even.
 Claud. I humbly thank you.

                To

miss the gratifications that are before us; when we are old, we amuse the languor of age with the recollection of youthful pleasures or performances; so that our life, of which no part is filled with the business of the present time, resembles our dreams after dinner, when the events of the morning are mingled with the designs of the evening. JOHNSON.

 4 —— *for all thy blessed youth*
  Becomes as aged, and doth beg the alms
  Of palsied eld; and when thou art old and rich,
  Thou hast neither heat, &c.] Shakspeare declares that man hath *neither youth nor age;* for in *youth,* which is the *happiest* time, or which might be the happiest, he commonly wants means to obtain what he could enjoy; he is dependent on *palsied eld; must beg alms* from the coffers of hoary avarice; and being very niggardly supplied, *becomes as aged,* looks, like an old man, on happiness which is beyond his reach. And, when *he is old and rich,* when he has wealth enough for the purchase of all that formerly excited his desires, he has no longer the powers of enjoyment;

 ——*has neither heat, affection, limb, nor beauty,*
  To make his riches pleasant. JOHNSON.

 The sentiment contained in these lines, which Dr. Johnson has explained with his usual precision, occurs again in the forged letter that Edmund delivers to his father, as written by Edgar; *King Lear*, Act i. sc. ii.: "This policy, and reverence of age, makes the world bitter to the best of our times; keeps our fortunes from us till our oldness cannot relish them.."—Dr. Johnson would read *of good youth;* but the words above, printed in Italicks, support, I think, the reading of the old copy—"*blessed* youth," and shew that any emendation is unnecessary.
                MALONE.

 5 *Of palsied eld;*] *Eld* is generally used for *old age, decrepitude.* It is here put for *old people, persons worn out with years.* STEEVENS.

 So, in Marston's *Dutch Courtezan*, 1605:
  "Let colder *eld* their strong objections move."
 Again, in our author's *Merry Wives of Windsor*:
  "The superstitious idle-headed *eld*"
 Gower uses it for age as opposed to youth:
  "His *eld* had turn'd to youth."
        De Confessione Amantis, lib. v. fol. 106.

 6 *Thou hast neither heat, affection, limb, nor beauty,*] By "heat" and "affection" the poet meant to express *appetite,* and by "limb," and "beauty," *strength.* EDWARDS.

 7 —— *more thousand deaths:*] The meaning is not only *a thousand deaths,* but *a thousand deaths* besides what have been mentioned. JOHNSON.

To sue to live, I find, I seek to die;
And, seeking death, find life: Let it come on.

Enter ISABELLA.

Isab. What, ho! Peace here; grace and good company!
Prov. Who's there? come in: the wish deserves a welcome.
Duke. Dear Sir, ere long I'll visit you again.
Claud. Most holy Sir, I thank you.
Isab. My business is a word or two with Claudio
Prov. And very welcome. Look, signior, here's your sister.
Duke. Provost, a word with you.
Prov. As many as you please.
Duke. Bring me to hear them speak³, where I may be
Conceal'd.   [*Exeunt* DUKE *and* PROVOST.
Claud. Now, sister, what's the comfort?
Isab. Why,
As all comforts are; most good, most good, in deed⁹:
Lord Angelo, having affairs to heaven,
Intends you for his swift embassador,
Where you shall be an everlasting leiger:
Therefore your best appointment ¹ make with speed;
To-morrow you set on.
                                    Claud.

---

⁸ *Bring me to hear them speak, where I may be*] The old copy read:
Bring them to hear me speak, &c.
The emendation was suggested by Mr. Steevens. The editor of the second folio, after the word *Conceal'd*, has added,—" Yet hear them." But the alterations made in that copy do not deserve the smallest credit. There are undoubted proofs that they were merely arbitrary; and in general they are also extremely injudicious.   MALONE.

⁹ *As all comforts are; most good, most good, in deed:*] If this reading be right, Isabella must mean that she brings something better than *words* of comfort, she brings an assurance of *deeds*. This is harsh and constrained, but I know not what better to offer.   JOHNSON.

I believe *in deed*, as explained by Dr. Johnson, is the true reading. So in *Macbeth*:
    " We're yet but young *in deed*."   STEEVENS.
I would point the lines thus:
    Claud. Now, sister, what's the comfort?
    Isab. Why, as all comforts are, most good. Indeed Lord Angelo, &c.
Indeed is the same as *in truth*, or *truly*, the common beginning of speeches in Shakspeare's age. See Charles the First's Trial. The king and Bradshaw seldom say any thing without this preface: " Truly, Sir——."   BLACKSTONE.

¹ —— *an everlasting leiger:*

Claud. Is there no remedy?

Isab. None, but such remedy, as, to save a head,
To cleave a heart in twain.

Claud. But is there any?

Isab. Yes, brother, you may live;
There is a devilish mercy in the judge,
If you'll implore it, that will free your life,
But fetter you till death.

Claud. Perpetual durance?

Isab. Ay, just, perpetual durance; a restraint,
Though all the world's vastidity ² you had,
To a determin'd scope ³.

Claud. But in what nature?

Isab. In such a one as (you consenting to't)
Would bark your honour from that trunk you bear,
And leave you naked.

Claud. Let me know the point.

Isab. O, I do fear thee, Claudio; and I quake,
Lest thou a feverous life should'st entertain,
And six or seven winters more respect
Than a perpetual honour. Dar'st thou die?
The sense of death is most in apprehension;
And the poor beetle ⁴, that we tread upon,
In corporal sufferance finds a pang as great
As when a giant dies.

Claud.

Therefore your best appointment—] *Leiger* is the same with resident. *Appointment*; preparation; act of fitting, or state of being fitted for any thing. So in old books, we have a knight well *appointed*; that is, well armed and mounted, or fitted at all points. JOHNSON

The word *appointment*, on this occasion, should seem to comprehend confession, communion, and absolution. "Let him (says *Escalus*) be furnished with divines, and have all charitable preparation." The king in *Hamlet*, who was cut off prematurely, and without such preparation, is said to be *disappointed*. *Appointment*, however, may be more simply explained by the following passage in *The Antipodes*, 1638:

"———— your lo. ging
"Is decently *appointed*." i.e. prepared, furnished. STEEVENS.

² Though *all the world's vastidity—*] The old copy has—*Through*. Corrected by Mr. Pope. MALONE.

³ —*a restraint,—*
To a determin'd scope.] A confinement of your mind to one painful idea; to ignominy, of which the remembrance can neither be suppressed nor escaped. JOHNSON.

⁴ *The poor beetle,* &c.] The reasoning is, *that death is no more than every being must suffer, though the dread of it is peculiar to man;* or perhaps, *that we are inconsistent with ourselves, when we so much dread that which*

Claud. Why give you me this shame?
Think you I can a resolution fetch
From flowery tenderness? If I must die,
I will encounter darkness as a bride,
And hug it in mine arms [5].
　　Isab. There spake my brother; there my father's grave
Did utter forth a voice! Yes, thou must die:
Thou art too noble to conserve a life
In base appliances. This outward-sainted deputy,—
Whose settled visage and deliberate word
Nips youth i' the head, and follies doth emmew [6],
As faulcon doth the fowl [7],—is yet a devil;
His filth within being cast [8], he would appear
A pond as deep as hell.
　　Claud. The princely Angelo [9]?
　　Isab. O, 'tis the cunning livery of hell,
The damned'st body to invest and cover
In princely guards! Dost thou think, Claudio,
If I would yield him my virginity,
Thou might'st be freed?
　　Claud. O heavens! it cannot be.

Isab.

which we carelessly inflict on other creatures, that feel the pain as acutely as we. JOHNSON.

　　[5] ——— *If I must die,*
　　　I will encounter darkness as a bride,
　　　And hug it in mine arms.] So, in *Antony and Cleopatra*:
　　　　　" ——— I will be
　　　" *A bridegroom* in my *death*; and run into 't,
　　　" As to a lover's bed." MALONE.

[6] —*follies doth* emmew,] Forces follies to lie in cover, without daring to show themselves. JOHNSON.

[7] *As faulcon doth the fowl,*] In whose presence the follies of youth are afraid to show themselves, as the fowl is afraid to flutter while the falcon hovers over it. So, in *K. Henry VI.* P. iii:
　　" ——— not he that loves him best,
　　" The proudest he that holds up Lancaster,
　　" Dares stir a wing, if Warwick shakes his bells."
To *emmew* is a term in falconry. STEEVENS.

[8] —*being cast*,] To *cast* a pond is to empty it of mud. JOHNSON.

[9] *The* princely *Angelo?*
　—princely *guards!*] The first folio has, in both places, *prenzie*, from which the other folios made *princely*, and every editor may make what he can. JOHNSON.

Princely guards mean no more than the ornaments of royalty, which Angelo is supposed to assume during the absence of the duke. STEEV.

A guard,

Isab. Yes, he would give it thee, from this rank offence [1],
So to offend him still: This night's the time
That I should do what I abhor to name,
Or else thou diest to-morrow.
  Claud. Thou shalt not do't.
  Isab. O, were it but my life,
I'd throw it down for your deliverance
As frankly as a pin [2].
  Claud. Thanks, dear Isabel.
  Isab. Be ready, Claudio, for your death to-morrow.
  Claud. Yes.—Has he affections in him,
That thus can make him bite the law by the nose,
When he would force it? Sure it is no sin;
Or of the deadly seven it is the least [3].
  Isab. Which is the least?
  Claud. If it were damnable [4], he, being so wise,

  A *guard*, in old language, meant a welt or border of a garment; "because (says Minsheu) it *gards* and keeps the garment from tearing." These borders were sometimes of lace. So, in the *M. of Venice:*
    "—Give him a livery
    "More *guarded* than his fellows." MALONE.

  [1] —*from this rank offence,*] I believe means, *from the time* of my committing this offence, you might persist in sinning with safety. The advantages you would derive from my having such a secret of his in my keeping would ensure you from further harm on account of the same fault, however frequently repeated. STEEVENS.

  [2] —*as a pin!* So, in *Hamlet:*
    "I do not set my life at a *pin's* fee." STEEVENS.

  [3] Has he affections &c.] *Is he actuated by passions that impel him to transgress the law, at the very moment that he is enforcing it against others?* [I find, he is.] Surely then, since this is so general a propensity, since the judge is as criminal as he whom he condemns, *it is no sin,* or at least a *venial* one. So, in the next Act:
    "—A deflower'd maid,
    "And by an eminent body that *enforc'd*
    "The law against it."
Force is again used for *enforce* in *K. Henry VIII:*
    "If you will now unite in your complaints,
    "And *force* them with a constancy."
Again, in *Coriolanus:*
    "Why *force* you this?" MALONE.

  [4] *If it were damnable,* &c.] Shakspeare shews his knowledge of human nature in the conduct of Claudio. When Isabella first tells him of Angelo's proposal, he answers, with honest indignation, agreeably to his settled principles, *Thou shalt not do't.* But the love of life being permitted to operate, soon furnishes him with sophistical arguments; he believes it cannot be very dangerous to the soul, since Angelo, who is so wise, will venture it. JOHNSON.

Why

Why, would he for the momentary trick
Be perdurably fin'd⁵?—O Ifabel!
   Ifab. What fays my brother?
   Claud. Death is a fearful thing.
   Ifab. And fhamed life a hateful.
   Claud. Ay, but to die, and go we know not where;
To lie in cold obftruction, and to rot;
This fenfible warm motion⁶ to become
A kneaded clod; and the delighted fpirit⁷
To bathe in fiery floods, or to refide
In thrilling regions of thick-ribbed ice;
To be imprifon'd in the viewlefs winds,
And blown with reftlefs violence round about
The pendant world: or to be worfe than worft
Of thofe, that lawlefs and incertain thoughts⁸
Imagine howling!—'tis too horrible!
The wearieft and moft loathed worldly life,
That age, ach, penury⁹, and imprifonment
Can lay on nature, is a paradife
To what we fear of death¹.

                                                Ifab.

---

⁵ *Be perdurably fin'd?*] *Perdurably* is laftingly. STEEVENS.

⁶ *This fenfible warm motion.*—] *Motion* is an organized body. MALONE.

⁷ —*delighted fpirit*] i. e. the fpirit accuftomed here to eafe and delights. This was properly urged as an aggravation to the fharpnefs of the torments fpoken of. WARBURTON.

I think with Dr. Warburton, that by the *delighted* fpirit is meant, *the foul once accuftomed to delight*, which of courfe muft render the fufferings, afterwards defcribed, lefs tolerable. Thus our author calls youth, *bleffed*, in a former fcene, before he proceeds to fhew its wants and its inconveniencies. STEEVENS.

⁸ —*lawlefs and incertain* thoughts] Conjecture fent out to wander without any certain direction, and ranging through all poffibilities of pain. JOHNSON.

Old Copy—*thought.* Corrected by Mr. Theobald. MALONE.

⁹ —*penury*,] The old copy has—*perjury.* Corrected by the editor of the fecond folio. MALONE.

¹ *To what we fear of death.*] Moft certainly the idea of the " fpirit bathing in fiery floods," or of refiding " in thrilling regions of thickribbed ice," is not original to our poet; but I am not fure that they came from the Platonic hell of Virgil.—The monks alfo had their hot and their cold hell; " the fyrfte is fyre that ever brenneth, and never gyveth lighte," fays an old homily: " The feconde is paffing cold, that yf a greate hylle of fyre were caft therein, it fhould torne to yce." One of their legends, well remembered in the time of Shakfpeare, gives us a dialogue between a bifhop and a foul tormented in a piece of ice which was brought to cure a *brenning boute* in his feet.—Another tells us of the foul of a monk faftened to a rock, which the winds were to

                                                                   blow

Isab. Alas! alas!

Claud. Sweet sister, let me live:
What sin you do to save a brother's life,
Nature dispenses with the deed so far,
That it becomes a virtue.

Isab. O you beast!
O faithless coward! O dishonest wretch!
Wilt thou be made a man out of my vice?
Is't not a kind of incest [2], to take life
From thine own sister's shame? What should I think?
Heaven shield, my mother play'd my father fair!
For such a warped slip of wilderness [3]
Ne'er issued from his blood. Take my defiance [4]:
Die; perish! might but my bending down
Reprieve thee from thy fate, it should proceed:
I'll pray a thousand prayers for thy death,
No word to save thee.

Claud. Nay, hear me, Isabel.

---

blow about for a twelvemonth, and purge of its enormities. Indeed this doctrine was before now introduced into poetic fiction, as you may see in a poem, " where the lover declareth his pains to exceed far the pains of hell," among the many miscellaneous ones subjoined to the works of Surrey: of which you will soon have a beautiful edition from the able hand of my friend Dr. Percy. Nay, a very learned and inquisitive brother-antiquary hath observed to me, on the authority of Blefkenius, that this was the ancient opinion of the inhabitants of Iceland, who were certainly very little read either in the poet or the philosopher. FARMER.

Lazarus, in the *Shepherd's Calendar*, is represented to have seen these particular modes of punishment in the infernal regions:

" Secondly, I have seen in hell a flood frozen as ice, wherein the envious men and women were plunged unto the navel, and then suddainly came over them a right cold and great wind, that grieved and pained them right sore, &c. STEEVENS.

[2] *Is't not a kind of incest,*—] In Isabella's declamation there is something harsh, and something forced and far-fetched. But her indignation cannot be thought violent, when we consider her not only as a virgin, but as a nun. JOHNSON.

[3] —*a warped slip of wilderness*] *Wilderness* is here used for *wildness*, the state of being disorderly.

So, in *Old Fortunatus*, 1600:

" But I in *wilderness* totter'd out my youth."

The word, in this sense, is now obsolete, though employed by Milton:

" The paths, and bowers, doubt not, but our joint hands
" Will keep from *wilderness* with ease." STEEVENS.

[4] —*take my defiance:*] *Defiance* is refusal. So, in *Romeo and Juliet:*
" I do *defy* thy commiseration." STEEVENS.

Isab.

Isab. O fie, fie, fie!
Thy sin's not accidental, but a trade⁵:
Mercy to thee would prove itself a bawd:
'Tis best that thou diest quickly. [*going.*
 Claud. O hear me, Isabella.

Re-enter DUKE.

Duke. Vouchsafe a word, young sister, but one word.
 Isab. What is your will?
 Duke. Might you dispense with your leisure, I would by and by have some speech with you: the satisfaction I would require is likewise your own benefit.
 Isab. I have no superfluous leisure; my stay must be stolen out of other affairs; but I will attend you a while.
 Duke. [*to Claudio aside.*] Son, I have over-heard what hath past between you and your sister. Angelo had never the purpose to corrupt her; only he hath made an assay of her virtue, to practise his judgment with the disposition of natures: she, having the truth of honour in her, hath made him that gracious denial, which he is most glad to receive: I am confessor to Angelo, and I know this to be true: therefore prepare yourself to death: Do not satisfy your resolution with hopes that are fallible⁶? to-morrow you must die; go to your knees, and make ready.
 Claud. Let me ask my sister pardon. I am so out of love with life, that I will sue to be rid of it.
 Duke. Hold you there⁷: Farewell. [*Exit* CLAUDIO.

Re-enter PROVOST.

Provost, a word with you.
 Prov. What's your will, father?
 Duke. That now you are come, you will be gone: Leave me a while with the maid; my mind promises with my habit, no loss shall touch her by my company.

---

⁵ —*but a trade :*] A custom; a practice; an established habit. So we say of a man much addicted to any thing, *he makes a trade of it.*
 JOHNSON.

⁶ *Do not satisfy your resolution with hopes that are fallible:*] Do not rest with satisfaction on *hopes that are fallible.* STEEVENS.
 Perhaps the meaning is, Do not satisfy or content yourself with that kind of resolution, which acquires strength from a latent hope that it will not be put to the test; a hope, that in your case, if you rely upon it, will deceive you. MALONE.

⁷ *Hold you there:*] Continue in that resolution. JOHNSON.

Prov.

Prov. In good time [8].   [*Exit* Provost.

Duke. The hand that hath made you fair, hath made you good: the goodness, that is cheap in beauty, makes beauty brief in goodness; but grace, being the soul of your complexion, should keep the body of it ever fair.— The assault, that Angelo hath made to you, fortune hath convey'd to my understanding; and, but that frailty hath examples for his falling, I should wonder at Angelo: How would you do to content this substitute, and to save your brother?

Isab. I am now going to resolve him: I had rather my brother die by the law, than my son should be unlawfully born. But oh, how much is the good Duke deceived in Angelo! If ever he return, and I can speak to him, I will open my lips in vain, or discover his government.

Duke. That shall not be much amiss: Yet, as the matter now stands, he will avoid your accusation; he made trial of you only. Therefore fasten your ear on my advisings; to the love I have in doing good, a remedy presents itself. I do make myself believe, that you may most uprighteously do a poor wronged lady a merited benefit; redeem your brother from the angry law; do no stain to your own gracious person; and much please the absent Duke, if, peradventure, he shall ever return to have hearing of this business.

Isab. Let me hear you speak farther: I have spirit to do any thing that appears not foul in the truth of my spirit.

Duke. Virtue is bold, and goodness never fearful. Have you not heard speak of Mariana the sister of Frederick, the great soldier, who miscarried at sea?

Isab. I have heard of the Lady, and good words went with her name.

Duke. Her should this Angelo have marry'd; was affianced to her by oath [9], and the nuptial appointed: between which time of the contract, and limit of the solemnity [*], her

---

[8] *In good time.*] i. e. *à la bonne heure*, so be it, very well.
                                                                    STEEVENS.
[9] —*by oath,*] *By* inserted by the editor of the second folio.
                                                                    MALONE.
[*] —*and limit of the solemnity,*] So, in *King John*:
  " Prescribes how long the virgin state shall last,—
  " Gives *limits* unto holy nuptial rites." i. e. appointed times.
                                                                    MALONE.

brother

brother Frederick was wreck'd at sea, having in that perish'd vessel the dowry of his sister. But mark, how heavily this befel to the poor gentlewoman: there she lost a noble and renowned brother, in his love toward her ever most kind and natural; with him the portion and sinew of her fortune, her marriage-dowry; with both, her combinate husband[1], this well-seeming Angelo.

Isab. Can this be so? Did Angelo so leave her?

Duke. Left her in her tears, and dry'd not one of them with his comfort; swallow'd his vows whole, pretending, in her, discoveries of dishonour: in few, bestow'd her on her own lamentation[2], which yet she wears for his sake: and he, a marble to her tears, is washed with them, but relents not.

Isab. What a merit were it in death, to take this poor maid from the world! What corruption in this life, that it will let this man live!—But how out of this can she avail?

Duke. It is a rupture that you may easily heal: and the cure of it not only saves your brother, but keeps you from dishonour in doing it.

Isab. Shew me how, good father.

Duke. This fore-named maid hath yet in her the continuance of her first affection; his unjust unkindness, that in all reason should have quenched her love, hath, like an impediment in the current, made it more violent and unruly.—Go you to Angelo; answer his requiring with a plausible obedience; agree with his demands to the point: only refer yourself to this advantage[3]—first, that your stay with him may not be long; that the time may have all shadow and silence in it; and the place answer to convenience; this being

---

[1] *—her* combinate *husband,*] Combinate is betrothed, settled by contract. STEEVENS.

[2] *—bestow'd* her on *her own lamentation,*] I once thought that we ought to read—bestow'd *on* her her own lamentation, but the old copy may be right; and any change, grounded on unusual phraseology, is dangerous. In *Much Ado about Nothing*, we find diction as uncommon:

" Impose *me* to what penance your invention
" Can lay upon my sin."

" Bestow'd her on her own lamentation," is, left her to her sorrows. MALONE.

[3] *—only refer yourself to this advantage,*] This is scarcely to be reconciled to any established mode of speech. We may read, *only reserve yourself to*, or *only reserve to yourself this advantage*. JOHNSON.

granted

granted in courſe, now follows all. We ſhall adviſe this wronged maid to ſtead up your appointment, go in your place; if the encounter acknowledge itſelf hereafter, it may compel him to her recompence: and here, by this, is your brother ſaved, your honour untainted, the poor Mariana advantaged, and the corrupt deputy ſcaled [4]. The maid will I frame, and make fit for his attempt. If you think well to carry this as you may, the doubleneſs of the benefit defends the deceit from reproof. What think you of it?

Iſab. The image of it gives me content already; and, I truſt, it will grow to a moſt proſperous perfection.

Duke. It lies much in your holding up. Haſte you ſpeedily to Angelo; if for this night he intreat you to his bed, give him promiſe of ſatisfaction. I will preſently to St. Luke's; there, at the moated grange [5] reſides this dejected Mariana: At that place call upon me; and diſpatch with Angelo, that it may be quickly.

Iſab. I thank you for this comfort: Fare you well, good father. [*Exeunt ſeverally.*

---

[4] —*the corrupt deputy* ſcaled.] To *ſcale*, as may be learn'd from a note to *Coriolanus*, Act i. ſc. i. moſt certainly means, to *diſorder*, to *diſconcert*, to *put to flight*. An army routed is called by Hollinſhed, an army *ſcaled*. The word ſometimes ſignifies to *diffuſe* or diſperſe; at others, as I ſuppoſe in the preſent inſtance, to *put into confuſion*.
STEEVENS.

[5] —*the moated* grange] A *grange* is a ſolitary farm-houſe. So, in *Othello*:
"——— this is Venice;
"My houſe is not a *grange*." STEEVENS.

A *grange*, in its original ſignification, meant the farm-houſe of a monaſtery (from *grana* gerendo,) from which it was always at ſome little diſtance. One of the monks was uſually appointed to inſpect the accounts of the farm. He was called the Prior of the Grange;—in barbarous Latin, *Grangiarius*. Being placed at a diſtance from the monaſtery, and not connected with any other buildings, Shakſpeare, with his wonted licence, uſes it, both here and in *Othello*, in the ſenſe of a *ſolitary* farm-houſe. MALONE.

I have ſince obſerved that the word was uſed in the ſame ſenſe by the contemporary writers. So, in Tarleton's *Newes out of Purgatory*, printed about the year 1590:—" Till my return I would have thee ſtay at our little *grange* houſe in the country."

Again, in Daniel's *Complaint of Roſamond*, 1594:
"Thus wrought to ſin, ſoon was I train'd from court
"To a ſolitary *grange*."

In Lincolnſhire they at this day call every lone-houſe that is unconnected with others, a *grange*. MALONE.

SCENE

SCENE II.

The Street before the Prison.

Enter DUKE *as a Friar; to him* ELBOW, CLOWN, *and Officers.*

Elb. Nay, if there be no remedy for it, but that you will needs buy and sell men and women like beasts, we shall have all the world drink brown and white bastard [6].

Duke. O heavens! what stuff is here?

Clown. 'Twas never merry world, since, of two usuries [7], the merriest was put down, and the worser allow'd by order of law a furr'd gown to keep him warm; and furr'd with fox and lamb-skins too [8], to signify, that craft, being richer than innocency, stands for the facing.

Elb. Come your way, Sir:—Bless you, good father friar.

Duke. And you, good brother father [9]: What offence hath this man made you, Sir?

Elb. Marry, Sir, he hath offended the law; and, Sir, we take him to be a thief too, Sir; for we have found upon him, Sir, a strange pick-lock, which we have sent to the deputy.

Duke. Fie, Sirrah; a bawd, a wicked bawd!
The evil that thou causest to be done,

---

[6] *bastard.*] A kind of sweet wine, then much in vogue, from the Italian, *bastardo*. WARBURTON.

See a note on *Hen. IV.* P. i. Act ii. sc. iv. STEEVENS.

Bastard was raisin-wine. See Minsheu's Dictionary, in v. and Cole's Latin Dictionary, 1679. MALONE.

[7] —*face of two usuries*, &c.] *Usury* may be used by an easy licence for the *professors of usury*. JOHNSON.

[8] *And furr'd with fox and lamb-skins too*, &c.] Fox-skins and lamb-skins were both used as facings to cloth in Shakspeare's time. See the Statute of Apparel, 24 Henry VIII. c. xiii. Hence *fox-furr'd slave* is used as an opprobrious epithet in *Wily Beguiled*, 1606, and in other old comedies. See also *Characterism*, or *Lenton's Leisures*, &c. 1631:—
" An *usurer is an old fox*, clad in *lamb-skin*, who hath pray'd [prey'd] so long abroad," &c. MALONE.

[9] *And you, good brother father;*] In return to Elbow's blundering address of *good father friar*, i. e. *good father brother*, the duke humorously calls him, in his own style, *good brother father*. This would appear still clearer in French. *Dieu vous benisse, mon pere frere.—Et vous aussi, mon frere pere.* There is no doubt that our *friar* is a corruption of the French *frere*. TYRWHITT.

That

That is thy means to live: Do thou but think
What 'tis to cram a maw, or clothe a back,
From such a filthy vice: say to thyself,—
From their abominable and beastly touches
I drink, I eat, array myself, and live [9].
Canst thou believe thy living is a life,
So stinkingly depending? Go, mend, go, mend.

Clown. Indeed, it does stink in some sort, Sir; but yet, Sir, I would prove—

Duke. Nay, if the devil have given thee proofs for sin, Thou wilt prove his. Take him to prison, officer; Correction and instruction must both work, Ere this rude beast will profit.

Elb. He must before the deputy, Sir; he has given him warning: the deputy cannot abide a whore-master: if he be a whore-monger, and comes before him, he were as good go a mile on his errand.

Duke. That we were all, as some would seem to be, From our faults, as faults from seeming, free [1]!

---

[9] *—I eat,* array *myself, and live.*] The old copy reads—I eat *away* myself.——The emendation was made by Mr. Bishop. MALONE.

[1] *From our faults, as faults from* seeming, *free!*] I read,

Free from all faults, or faults from seeming free;

that men were really good, or that their faults were known: that men were free from faults, *or* faults from *hypocrisy.* So Isabella calls Angelo's hypocrisy, *seeming, seeming.* JOHNSON.

I think we should read with Hanmer:

Free from *all* faults, as *from faults* seeming free.

i. e. I *wish we were all as good as we appear to be;* a sentiment very naturally prompted by his reflection on the behaviour of Angelo. Hanmer has only transposed a word to produce a convenient sense.

STEEVENS.

The original copy has not *Free* at the beginning of the line. It was added unnecessarily by the editor of the second folio, who did not perceive that *our,* like many words of the same kind, was used by Shakspeare as a dissyllable. The reading—from *all* faults, which all the modern editors have adopted, (I think, improperly,) was first introduced in the fourth folio. Dr. Johnson's conjectural reading, *or,* appears to me very probable. The compositor might have caught the word *as* from the preceding line. If *as* be right, Dr. Warburton's interpretation is perhaps the true one. Would we were all as free from faults, as faults are free from, or destitute of, *soundness,* or *seeming.* This line is rendered harsh and obscure by the word *free,* being dragged from its proper place for the sake of the rhyme. MALONE.

Enter LUCIO.

Elb. His neck will come to your waist, a cord, Sir [2].

Clown. I spy comfort; I cry, bail: Here's a gentleman, and a friend of mine.

Lucio. How now, noble Pompey? What, at the heels of Cæsar? Art thou led in triumph? What, is there none of Pigmalion's images, newly made woman [3], to be had now, for putting the hand in the pocket and extracting it clutch'd? What reply? Ha? What say'st thou to this tune, matter, and method? Is't not drown'd i' the last rain [4]? Ha?—

---

[2] *His neck will come to your waist, a cord, Sir.*] That is, his neck will be tied, like your waist, with a rope. The friars of the Franciscan order, perhaps of all others, wear a hempen cord for a girdle. Thus Buchanan:

"*Fœcundemant suis,*
"*Variatus terga funibus.*" JOHNSON.

[3] —*Pigmalion's images, newly made woman,*] By *Pigmalion's images newly made woman,* I believe, Shakspeare meant no more than—Have you no women now to recommend to your customers, as fresh and untouched as *Pigmalion's* statue was, at the moment when it became flesh and blood? The passage may, however, contain some allusion to a pamphlet printed in 1598, called—*The Metamorphosis of Pigmalion's Images, and certain Satires.* STEEVENS.

If *Marston's Metamorphosis of Pigmalion's Image* be alluded to, I believe it must be in the *argument.*—" The maide (by the power of Venus) was metamorphosed into a living woman." FARMER.

Perhaps the meaning is,—Is there no courtezan, who being *newly made woman,* i. e. *lately debauched,* still retains the appearance of chastity, and looks as cold as a statue, to be had, &c.

The following passage in *Blunt Master Constable,* a comedy, by Middleton, 1602, seems to authorize this interpretation:

"*Laz.* Are all these women?
"*Imp.* No, no, they are half men, and half women.
"*Laz.* You apprehend too fast. I mean by women, wives; for wives are no maids, nor are maids women."

Mulier in Latin had precisely the same meaning. MALONE.

[4] *What say'st thou to this tune, matter, and method? Is't not drown'd i' the last rain?*] It is a common phrase used in low raillery of a man crest-fallen and dejected, that *he looks like a drown'd puppy.* Lucio, therefore, asks him, whether he was *drown'd in the last rain,* and therefore cannot speak. JOHNSON.

He rather asks him whether his *answer* was not drowned in the last rain, for Pompey returns *no answer* to any of his questions: Or, perhaps, he means to compare Pompey's miserable appearance to a *drown'd mouse.* So, in *K. Henry VI.* P. i. sc. ii:

"Or piteous they will look, like *drowned mice.* STEEVENS

What

What fay'ft thou, trot⁵? Is the world as it was, man? Which is the way⁶? Is it fad, and few words? Or how? The trick of it?

Duke. Still thus, and thus! still worse!

Lucio. How doth my dear morsel, thy mistress? Procures she still? Ha?

Clown. Troth, Sir, she hath eaten up all her beef, and she is herself in the tub⁷.

Lucio. Why, 'tis good; it is the right of it; it must be so: Ever your fresh whore, and your powder'd bawd: An unshunn'd consequence; it must be so: Art going to prison, Pompey?

Clown. Yes, faith, Sir.

Lucio. Why 'tis not amiss, Pompey: Farewell: Go; say, I sent thee thither. For debt, Pompey? Or how?⁸?

Elb. For being a bawd, for being a bawd.

Lucio. Well, then imprison him: If imprisonment be the due of a bawd, why, 'tis his right: Bawd is he, doubtless, and of antiquity too; bawd-born. Farewell, good Pompey: Commend me to the prison, Pompey: You will turn good husband now, Pompey? you will keep the house⁹.

Clown. I hope, Sir, your good worship will be my bail.

Lucio. No, indeed, will I not, Pompey; it is not the wear¹. I will pray, Pompey, to increase your bondage: if you take it not patiently, why, your mettle is the more:— Adieu, truſty Pompey.—Bleſs you, Friar.

Duke. And you.

Lucio. Does Bridget paint ſtill, Pompey? Ha?

Elb. Come your ways, Sir; come.

---

⁵ *What ſay'ſt thou, trot?*] *Trot,* or, as it is now often pronounced, honeſt *trout,* is a familiar addreſs to a man among the provincial vulgar. JOHNSON.

⁶ *Which is the way?*] *What is the mode now?* JOHNSON.

⁷ *—in the tub.*] The method of cure for venereal complaints is groſsly called the *powdering tub.* JOHNSON.

It was ſo called from the method of cure. See the notes on the *tub-faſt* and the *diet,* in *Timon,* Act iv. STEEVENS.

⁸ *—Go; ſay, I ſent thee thither. For debt, Pompey? Or how?*] Lucio firſt offers him the uſe of his name to hide the ſeeming ignominy of his caſe; and then very naturally deſires to be informed of the true reaſon why he was ordered into confinement. STEEVENS.

⁹ *You will turn good* huſband *now, Pompey; you will keep the houſe.*] Alluding to the etymology of the word *huſband.* MALONE.

¹ *—it is not the wear.*] i. e. it is not the faſhion. STEEVENS.

Clown. You will not bail me then, Sir?

Lucio. Then, Pompey, nor now².—What news abroad, friar? What news?

Elb. Come your ways, Sir, come.

Lucio. Go—to kennel, Pompey, go³:

[*Exeunt* ELBOW, CLOWN, *and Officers.*

What news, Friar, of the duke?

Duke. I know none: Can you tell me of any?

Lucio. Some say, he is with the Emperor of Russia; other some, he is in Rome: But where is he, think you?

Duke. I know not where: But wheresoever, I wish him well.

Lucio. It was a mad fantastical trick of him, to steal from the state, and usurp the beggary he was never born to. Lord Angelo dukes it well in his absence; he puts transgression to't.

Duke. He does well in't.

Lucio. A little more lenity to lechery would do no harm in him: something too crabbed that way, Friar.

Duke. It is too general a vice⁴, and severity must cure it.

Lucio. Yes, in good sooth, the vice is of a great kinddred; it is well ally'd: But it is impossible to extirp it quite, Friar, till eating and drinking be put down. They say, this Angelo was not made by man and woman, after the downright way⁵ of creation: Is it true, think you?

Duke. How should he be made then?

Lucio. Some report, a sea-maid spawn'd him:—Some, that he was begot between two stock-fishes:—But it is certain, that when he makes water, his urine is congeal'd ice; that I know to be true: And he is a motion ungenerative, that's infallible⁶.

Duke.

---

² *Then Pompey, nor now.*] The meaning, I think, is, *I will neither bail thee* then, nor now. So again, in this play:

"*More nor less* to others paying." MALONE.

³ *Go—to kennel, Pompey,—go:*] It should be remembered, that *Pompey* is the common name of a dog, to which allusion is made in the mention of a *kennel*. JOHNSON.

⁴ *It is too general a vice,*] *Yes,* replies Lucio, *the vice is of great linndred; it is well ally'd,* &c. As much as to say, Yes, truly, it is general; for the greatest men have it as well as we little folks. A little lower he taxes the Duke personally with it. EDWARDS.

⁵ —*after the downright way—*] Old copy—*this* downright. Corrected by Mr. Pope. MALONE.

⁶ —*and*

Duke. You are pleasant, Sir; and speak apace.

Lucio. Why, what a ruthless thing is this in him, for the rebellion of a cod-piece, to take away the life of a man? Would the duke, that is absent, have done this? Ere he would have hang'd a man for the getting a hundred bastards, he would have paid for the nursing of a thousand: He had some feeling of the sport; he knew the service, and that instructed him to mercy.

Duke. I never heard the absent duke much detected for women [7]; he was not inclined that way.

Lucio. O, Sir, you are deceived.

Duke. 'Tis not possible.

Lucio. Who? not the duke? Yes, your beggar of fifty;—and his use was, to put a ducat in her clack-dish [8]; the duke had crochets in him: He would be drunk too; that let me inform you.

---

[6] *—and he is a motion ungenerative, that's infallible.*] In the former editions:—*And he is a motion generative; that's infallible.* This may be sense; and Lucio, perhaps, may mean, that though Angelo have the organs of generation, yet that he makes no more use of them, than if he were an inanimate puppet. But I rather think our author wrote, —*and he is a motion* ungenerative, because Lucio again in this very scene says,—*this ungenitured agent will unpeople the province with continency.*
THEOBALD.

A *motion generative* certainly means a *puppet of the masculine gender;* a thing that appears to have those powers of which it is not in reality possessed. STEEVENS.

[7] *—much detected for women;*] This appears so like the language of Dogberry, that at first I thought the passage corrupt, and wished to read *suspected.* But perhaps *detected* had anciently the same meaning. So, in an old collection of tales, entitled, *Wits, Fits, and Fancies,* 1595:—" An officer whose daughter was *detected* of dishonestie, and generally so reported—." That *detected* is there used for *suspected,* and not in the present sense of the word, appears, I think, from the words that follow— *and generally so reported,* which seems to relate not to a *known* but *suspected* fact. *Detected,* however, may mean *notoriously charged,* or *guilty.* So, in North's Translation of Plutarch:—" he only of all other kings in his time was most *detected* with this vice of lecacrie." Again, in Howe's Abridgment of Stowe's Chronicle, 1618, p. 563: " In the month of February, divers traiterous persons were apprehended, and *detected* of most wicked conspiracie against his majesty:—the 7th of September certaine of them wicked subjects were indicted," &c.
MALONE.

[8] *—clack-dish.*] The beggars, two or three centuries ago, used to proclaim their want by a wooden dish with a moveable cover, which they clacked, to shew that their vessel was empty. STEEVENS.

Duke. You do him wrong, surely.

Lucio. Sir, I was an inward of his [9]: A shy fellow was the duke [*]: and, I believe, I know the cause of his withdrawing.

Duke. What, I pr'ythee, might be the cause?

Lucio. No—pardon;— 'tis a secret must be lock'd within the teeth and the lips: but this I can let you understand—The greater file of the subject [1] held the duke to be wise.

Duke. Wise? why, no question but he was.

Lucio. A very superficial, ignorant, unweighing fellow.

Duke. Either this is envy in you, folly, or mistaking; the very stream of his life, and the business he hath helmed [2], must, upon a warranted need, give him a better proclamation. Let him be but testimonied in his own bringings forth, and he shall appear, to the envious, a scholar, a statesman, and a soldier: Therefore, you speak unskilfully; or, if your knowledge be more, it is much darken'd in your malice.

Lucio. Sir, I know him, and I love him.

Duke. Love talks with better knowledge, and knowledge with dearer love [3].

Lucio. Come, Sir, I know what I know.

Duke. I can hardly believe that, since you know not what you speak. But, if ever the duke return, (as our prayers are he may,) let me desire you to make your answer before him: If it be honest you have spoke, you have courage to maintain it: I am bound to call upon you; and, I pray you, your name?

Lucio. Sir, my name is Lucio; well known to the duke.

Duke. He shall know you better, Sir, if I may live to report you.

---

[9] *—an* inward *of his:*] *Inward* is intimate. STEEVENS.

[*] *—a shy fellow was the duke:*] The meaning of this term may be best explained by the following lines in the fifth act:
 " —the wicked'st caitiff on the ground,
 " May seem as shy, as grave, as just, as absolute," &c.
  MALONE.

[1] *The greater file of the subject*] The larger list, the greater number. JOHNSON.

So, in *Macbeth:* "— the valued *file.*" STEEVENS.

[2] *—the business he hath helmed,*] *The difficulties he hath steer'd through.* A metaphor from navigation. STEEVENS.

[3] *—with* dearer *love.*] Old copy—*dear.* Corrected by Sir T. Hanmer.
  MALONE.

Lucio.

Lucio. I fear you not.

Duke. —O, you hope the duke will return no more; or you imagine me too unhurtful an opposite [4]. But, indeed, I can do you little harm: you'll forswear this again.

Lucio. I'll be hang'd first: thou art deceived in me, Friar.—But no more of this: Canst thou tell, if Claudio die to-morrow, or no?

Duke. Why should he die, Sir?

Lucio. Why? for filling a bottle with a tun-dish. I would, the duke, we talk of, were return'd again: this ungenitur'd agent [5] will unpeople the province with continency; sparrows must not build in his house-eves, because they are lecherous. The duke yet would have dark deeds darkly answer'd; he wou'd never bring them to light: would he were return'd! Marry, this Claudio is condemn'd for untrussing. Farewell, good Friar; I pr'ythee, pray for me. The duke, I say to thee again, would eat mutton on Fridays [6]. He's now past it; yet, and I say to thee, he would mouth with a beggar, though she smelt brown bread and garlic [7]: say, that I said so. Farewell. [*Exit.*

Duke. No might nor greatness in mortality
Can censure 'scape; back-wounding calumny
The whitest virtue strikes: What king so strong,
Can tie the gall up in the slanderous tongue?
But who comes here?

---

[4] —*an opposite.*] In old language meant an *adversary.* MALONE.

[5] —*ungenitur'd agent*] This word seems to be form'd from *genitoirs*, a word which occurs in Holland's Pliny, tom. ii. p. 321, 560, 589, and comes from the French *genitoires*, the *genitals.* TOLLET.

[6] mutton *on Fridays.*] A wench was called a *laced mutton.*
THEOBALD.

So, in *Doctor Faustus*, 1604, Lechery says; "I am one that loves an inch of raw *mutton* better than an ell of *Friday* stockfish." STEEVENS.

Lucio's words have certainly been rightly explained. The phrase, however, had its origin in times of popery. "In Queen Marye's daies, (says an Abbot of Westminster in a debate in the House of Lords, in 1559,) your honours do know right well, how the people of this realm did live in an order, and would not run before the lawes, nor openly disobey the queenes highnesses procedings and proclamations;—there was no open *flesh-eatinge*, nor shambles-keeping in the lent, and *daies* prohibited." Strype's *Annals of the Reformation*, Vol. I. Append. p. 26.
MALONE.

See *the Two Gent. of Verona*, p. 109. n. 9. MALONE.

[7] —*though she* smelt brown bread and garlic;] This was the phraseology of our author's time. In the *Merry Wives of Windsor*, Master Fenton is said to "*smell April and May*," not, "to smell *of.*" &c.
MALONE.

Enter ESCALUS, PROVOST, BAWD, *and Officers.*

Escal. Go, away with her to prison.

Bawd. Good my Lord, be good to me; your honour is accounted a merciful man: good my lord.

Escal. Double and treble admonition, and still forfeit in the same kind? This would make mercy swear, and play the tyrant [8].

Prov. A bawd of eleven years continuance, may it please your honour.

Bawd. My Lord, this is one Lucio's information against me: Mistress Kate Keep-down was with child by him in the duke's time, he promised her marriage; his child is a year and a quarter old, come Philip and Jacob: I have kept it myself; and see how he goes about to abuse me.

Escal. That fellow is a fellow of much licence:—let him be called before us.—Away with her to prison: Go to; no more words. [*Exeunt Bawd and Officers.*] Provost, my brother Angelo will not be alter'd; Claudio must die to-morrow: let him be furnish'd with divines, and have all charitable preparation: if my brother wrought by my pity, it should not be so with him.

Prov. So please you, this friar hath been with him, and advised him for the entertainment of death.

Escal. Good'even, good Father.

Duke. Bliss and goodness on you!

Escal. Of whence are you?

Duke. Not of this country, though my chance is now
To use it for my time: I am a brother
Of gracious order, late come from the see [9],
In special business from his holiness.

Escal. What news abroad i' the world?

Duke. None, but that there is so great a fever on goodness, that the dissolution of it must cure it: novelty is only in

---

[8] —*mercy swear, and play the tyrant.*] I do not much like *mercy swear*, the old reading; or *mercy swerve*, Dr. Warburton's correction. I believe it should be—This would make mercy *severe*. FARMER.

There is surely no need of emendation. We say at present, such a thing *is enough to make a parson swear*, i. e. deviate from a proper respect to decency, and the sanctity of his character.

The idea of *swearing* agrees very well with that of a *tyrant* in our ancient mysteries. STEEVENS.

[9] —*from the see,*] The folio reads, *from the sea.* JOHNSON.

The emendation, which is undoubtedly right, was made by Mr. Theobald. In Hall's Chronicle, *sea* is often written for *see*. MALONE.

request;

request; and it is as dangerous to be aged in any kind of course, as it is virtuous to be constant in any undertaking. There is scarce truth enough alive, to make societies secure; but security enough, to make fellowships accurs'd *: much upon this riddle runs the wisdom of the world. This news is old enough, yet it is every day's news. I pray you, Sir, of what disposition was the duke?

Escal. One, that, above all other strifes, contended especially to know himself.

Duke. What pleasure was he given to?

Escal. Rather rejoicing to see another merry, than merry at any thing which profess'd to make him rejoice: a gentleman of all temperance. But leave we him to his events, with a prayer they may prove prosperous; and let me desire to know, how you find Claudio prepar'd? I am made to understand, that you have lent him visitation.

Duke. He professes to have received no sinister measure from his judge, but most willingly humbles himself to the determination of justice: yet had he framed to himself by the instruction of his frailty, many deceiving promises of life; which I, by my good leisure, have discredited to him, and now is he resolved¹ to die.

Escal. You have paid the heavens your function, and the prisoner the very debt of your calling. I have labour'd for the poor gentleman, to the extremest shore of my modesty; but my brother justice have I found so severe, that he hath forced me to tell him, he is indeed— justice².

Duke. If his own life answer the straitness of his proceeding, it shall become him well; wherein if he chance to fail, he hath sentenced himself.

Escal. I am going to visit the prisoner: fare you well.

Duke. Peace be with you! [*Exeunt* ESCAL. *and* PROV.

---

* *There is scarce truth enough alive to make societies secure; but security enough to make fellowships accurs'd*] The speaker here alludes to those legal securities into which "fellowship" leads men to enter for each other. So, in *K. Henry IV.* P. ii. "He would not take his bond and yours; he liked not the *security.*" Falstaff in the same scene, plays, like the Duke, on the same word; "I had as lief they should put ratsbane in my mouth, as offer to stop it with *security.* I look'd, he should have sent me two and twenty yards of sattin—and he sent me *security.* Well, he may sleep in *security,*" &c. MALONE.

¹ — *resolved*] i. e. satisfied. REED.
² — *be is indeed—justice.*] Summum jus, summa injuria. STEEVENS.

He, who the sword of heaven will bear,
Should be as holy as severe;
Pattern in himself to know,
Grace to stand, and virtue go [3];
More or less to others paying,
Than by self-offences weighing.
Shame to him, whose cruel striking
Kills for faults of his own liking!
Twice treble shame on Angelo,
To weed my vice, and let his grow [4]!
O, what may man within him hide,
Though angel on the outward side [5]!
How may likeness, made in crimes,
Mocking, practise on the times,
To draw with idle spiders' strings
Most pond'rous and substantial things [6]!

Craft

[3] *Pattern in himself to know,*
Grace to stand, and virtue go;] This passage is very obscure, nor can be cleared without a more licentious paraphrase than any reader may be willing to allow. *He that bears the sword of heaven should be not less holy than severe; should be able to discover in himself a pattern of such grace as can avoid temptation, together with such virtue as dares venture abroad into the world without danger of seduction.* STEEVENS.

"*Pattern in himself to know,*" is, to experience in his own bosom an original principle of action, which, instead of being borrowed or copied from others, might serve as a *pattern* to them. Our author, in *the Winter's Tale*, has again used the same kind of imagery:

"By the *pattern* of mine own thoughts I cut out
The purity of his."

In *the Comedy of Errors* he uses an expression equally hardy and licentious—"And will have no *attorney* but *myself*;"—which is an absolute catachresis; an attorney importing precisely a person appointed to act for another.

In *Every Woman in her Humour*, 1609, we find the same expression:

"—— he hath but shown
"A *pattern in himself*, what thou shalt find
"In others." MALONE.

[4] *To weed my vice, and let his grow!*] *My*, does not, I apprehend, relate to the duke in particular, who had not been guilty of any vice, but to any indefinite person.—The meaning seems to be—*To destroy by extirpation* (as it is expressed in another place) a fault that I have committed, and to suffer his own vices to grow to a rank and luxuriant height.— The speaker, for the sake of argument, puts himself in the case of an offending person. MALONE.

[5] *Though angel on the outward side!*] Here we see what induced our author to give the outward-sainted deputy the name of Angelo. MALONE.

[6] *How may likeness, made in crimes,*
Mocking practise on the times,

To

Craft against vice I must apply:
With Angelo to-night shall lie
His old betrothed, but despis'd;
So disguise shall, by the disguis'd⁷,
Pay with falshood false exacting,
And perform an old contracting. [*Exit.*

*To draw with idle spider's strings
Most pond'rous and substantial things!*] The old copy reads—*Making practise*, &c. which renders the passage ungrammatical, and unintelligible. For the emendation now made the present editor is answerable. A line in *Macbeth* may add some support to it:

"Away, and *mock the time* with fairest show."

There is no one more convinced of the general propriety of adhering to old readings. I have strenuously followed the course which was pointed out and successfully pursued by Dr. Farmer and Mr. Steevens, that of elucidating and supporting our author's genuine text by illustrations drawn from the writings of his contemporaries. But in some cases alteration is a matter not of choice, but necessity; and surely the present is one of them. Dr. Warburton, to obtain some sense, omitted the word *To* in the third line; in which he was followed by all the subsequent editors. But omission, in my apprehension, is, of all the modes of emendation, the most exceptionable.—In the passage before us, it is clear from the context, that some *verb* must have stood in either the first or second of these lines. Some years ago I conjectured that, instead of *made*, we ought to read *wade*, which was used in our author's time in the sense of *to proceed*. But having since had occasion to observe how often the words *mock* and *make* have been confounded in these plays, I am now persuaded that the single error in the present passage is, the word *Making* having been printed instead of *Mocking*, a word of which our author has made very frequent use, and which exactly suits the context. In this very play we have had *make* instead of *mock*. [See p. 331.] In the hand-writing of that time the small *e* was merely a straight line; so that if it happened to be subjoined and written very close to an *o*, the two letters might easily be taken for an *a*. Hence I suppose it was, that these words have been so often confounded.—The awkwardness of the expression—"*Making* practice," of which I have met with no example, may be likewise urged in support of this emendation.

Likeness is here used for *specious* or *seeming* virtue. So, before: "O seeming, seeming!" The sense then of the passage is—How may persons assuming the *likeness* or semblance of virtue, *while they are in fact guilty of the grossest crimes, impose with this* counterfeit *sanctity upon the world, in order to draw to themselves by the flimsiest pretensions the most solid advantages*; i. e. pleasure, honour, reputation, &c.!

In *Much Ado about Nothing* we have a similar thought:

"O, what authority and show of truth
"Can cunning sin cover itself withall!" MALONE.

⁷ *So disguise shall, by the disguis'd*,] So *disguise* shall, by means of a person *disguised*, return an *injurious demand* with a *counterfeit person*.

JOHNSON.

ACT IV. SCENE I.

A Room in MARIANA's *House.*

Enter MARIANA, *and a Boy who sings.*

SONG.   Take, oh, take those lips away [1],
           That so sweetly were forsworn;
         And those eyes, the break of day,
           Lights that do mislead the morn:
         But my kisses bring again,
                   bring again,
         Seals of love, but seal'd in vain,
                   seal'd in vain.

Mari. Break off thy song, and haste thee quick away;
Here comes a man of comfort, whose advice
Hath often still'd my brawling discontent.—   [*Exit* Boy.

Enter DUKE.

I cry you mercy, Sir; and well could wish,
You had not found me here so musical:

[1] *Take, oh, take,*] This is part of a little song of Shakspeare's own writing, consisting of two stanzas, and so extremely sweet, that the reader won't be displeased to have the other.

   Hide, oh, hide those hills of snow,
     Which thy frozen bosom bears,
   On whose tops the pinks that grow,
     Are of those that April wears.
   But first set my poor heart free,
   Bound in those icy chains by thee.   WARBURTON.

This song is entire in Beaumont's *Bloody Brother.* The latter stanza is omitted by Mariana, as not suiting a female character. THEOBALD.

This song is found entire in Shakspeare's Poems, printed in 1640; but that is a book of no authority: Yet I believe that both these stanzas were written by our author. MALONE.

Our poet has introduced one of the same thoughts in his 142d sonnet:
   "————not from those lips of thine
   " That have prophan'd their scarlet ornaments,
   " And seal'd false bonds of love, as oft as mine."   STEEVENS.
Again, in his *Venus and Adonis:*
   " Pure lips, sweet seals in my soft lips imprinted,
   " What bargains may I make, still to be sealing?"   MALONE.

It occurs also in the old black letter translation of *Amadis of Gaule,* quarto, p. 171:—" rather with *kisses* (which are counted the *seals of love*) they chose to confirm their unanimitie, than otherwise to offend a resolved patience." REED.

Let

Let me excuse me, and believe me so—
My mirth is much displeas'd, but pleas'd my woe².

Duke. 'Tis good: though music oft hath such a charm,
To make bad, good, and good provoke to harm.
I pray you, tell me, hath any body enquired for me here to-day? much upon this time have I promised here to meet.

Mari. You have not been inquired after: I have sat here all day.

Enter ISABELLA.

Duke. I do constantly ³ believe you:—The time is come, even now. I shall crave your forbearance a little; may be, I will call upon you anon for some advantage to yourself.

Mari. I am always bound to you. [*Exit.*

Duke. Very well met, and welcome.
What is the news from this good deputy?

Isab. He hath a garden circummur'd with brick⁴,
Whose western side is with a vineyard back'd;
And to that vineyard is a planched gate⁵,
That makes his opening with this bigger key:
This other doth command a little door,
Which from the vineyard to the garden leads:
There have I made my promise to call on him,
Upon the heavy middle of the night⁶.

Duke. But shall you on your knowledge find this way?

Isab. I have ta'en a due and wary note upon't;
With whispering and most guilty diligence,

---

² *My mirth is much displeas'd, but pleas'd my woe.*] Though the music sooth'd my sorrows, it had no tendency to produce light merriment.
JOHNSON.

³ —*constantly*—] Certainly, without fluctuation of mind. JOHNSON.

⁴ —*circummur'd with brick.*] Circummur'd, wall'd round. JOHNSON.
"He caused the doors to be mured and cased up"
Painter's Palace of Pleasure.

⁵ — *a planched gate.*] i. e. a gate made of boards. *Planche*, Fr.
So, in Sir Arthur Gorge's translation of Lucan, 1614:
"Yet with his hoofes doth beat and rent
"The planched floore, the barres, and chaines." STEEVENS.

⁶ *There have I*, &c.] In the old copy the lines stand thus:
There have I made my promise upon the
Heavy middle of the night, to call upon him. STEEVENS.
The present regulation was made by Mr. Steevens. MALONE.

In

In action all of precept[7], he did shew me
The way twice o'er.

Duke. Are there no other tokens
Between you 'greed, concerning her observance?

Isab. No, none, but only a repair i' the dark;
And that I have possess'd him[8], my most stay
Can be but brief: for I have made him know
I have a servant comes with me along,
That stays upon me[9]; whose persuasion is,
I come about my brother.

Duke. 'Tis well borne up.
I have not yet made known to Mariana
A word of this:—What, ho! within! come forth!

Re-enter MARIANA.

I pray you, be acquainted with this maid;
She comes to do you good.

Isab. I do desire the like.

Duke. Do you persuade yourself that I respect you?

Mari. Good Friar, I know you do; and have found it.

Duke. Take then this your companion by the hand,
Who hath a story ready for your ear:
I shall attend your leisure; but make haste;
The vaporous night approaches.

Mari. Will't please you walk aside?

[*Exeunt* MARI. *and* ISAB.

Duke. O place and greatness, millions of false eyes[1]
Are struck upon thee! * volumes of report

---

[7] *In action all of precept,*] i. e. shewing the several turnings of the way with his hand: which action contained so many precepts, being given for my direction. WARBURTON.

· I rather think we should read, *In precept all of action,* that is, *in direction given not by words, but by mute signs.* JOHNSON.

[8] —*I have poss:fs'd him,*] I have made him clearly and strongly comprehend. JOHNSON.

[9] *That stays upon me:*] So, in *Macbeth*:
"Worthy Macbeth, we *stay upon* your leisure." STEEVENS.

[1] —*false eyes*] That is, Eyes insidious and traiterous. JOHNSON.

* *O place and greatness, millions of false eyes*
Are stuck upon thee!] So, in Chaucer's *Sompnour's Tale*,
late edit. v. 7633:
"There is full many an eye, and many an ere
"Awaiting on a lord," &c. STEEVENS.

Run

Run with these false and most contrarious quests [2]
Upon thy doings! thousand 'scapes of wit
Make thee the father of their idle dream,
And rank thee in their fancies!—Welcome! How agreed?

Re-enter MARIANA *and* ISABELLA.

Isab. She'll take the enterprize upon her, father,
If you advise it.
Duke. It is not my consent,
But my intreaty too.
Isab. Little have you to say,
When you depart from him, but, soft and low,
Remember now my brother.
Mari. Fear me not.
Duke. Nor, gentle daughter, fear you not at all:
He is your husband on a pre-contract:
To bring you thus together, 'tis no sin;
Sith that the justice of your title to him
Doth flourish the deceit [3]. Come, let us go;
Our corn's to reap, for yet our tithe's to sow [4]. [*Exeunt.*

SCENE II.

A Room in the Prison.

Enter PROVOST *and* CLOWN.

Prov. Come hither, sirrah: Can you cut off a man's head?

Clown.

---

[2] — *these false and most contrarious quests.*] Lying and contradictory messengers. ANONYMOUS.
So, in *Othello:*
" The senate has sent out three several *quests*." STEEVENS.
I incline to think that *quests* here means *inquisitions*, in which sense the word was used in Shakspeare's time. See Minsheu's Dict. in v. Cole in his Latin Dictionary, 1679, renders " *Aquest*" by " *examen, inquisitio.*"
MALONE.

[3] *Doth* flourish *the deceit.*] *Flourish* is *ornament in general.* So, in another play of Shakspeare:
" —empty trunks o'er *flourish'd* by the devil." STEEVENS.

[4] — *for yet our tithe's to sow.*] Mr. Theobald reads *tilth*, which Dr. Farmer observes is provincially used for *land till'd*, prepared for sowing; and Mr. Steevens has shewn, that to *sow tilth* was a phrase once in use. This conjecture appears to me extremely probable. It must however be confessed that our author has already used the word *tilth* in
this

Clown. If the man be a batchelor, Sir, I can: but if he be a marry'd man, he is his wife's head, and I can never cut off a woman's head.

Prov. Come, Sir, leave me your snatches, and yield me a direct answer. To-morrow morning are to die Claudio and Barnardine: here is in our prison a common executioner, who in his office lacks a helper: if you will take it on you to assist him, it shall redeem you from your gyves; if not, you shall have your full time of imprisonment, and your deliverance with an unpity'd whipping; for you have been a notorious bawd.

Clown. Sir, I have been an unlawful bawd, time out of mind; but yet I will be content to be a lawful hangman. I would be glad to receive some instruction from my fellow partner.

Prov. What ho, Abhorson! Where's Abhorson, there?

Enter ABHORSON.

Abhor. Do you call, Sir?

Prov. Sirrah, here's a fellow will help you to-morrow in your execution: If you think it meet, compound with him by the year, and let him abide here with you; if not, use him for the present, and dismiss him: He cannot plead his estimation with you; he hath been a bawd.

Abhor. A bawd, Sir? Fie upon him, he will discredit our mystery.

Prov. Go to, Sir; you weigh equally; a feather will turn the scale. [*Exit.*

Clown. Pray, Sir, by your good favour, (for, surely, Sir, a good favour⁵ you have, but that you have a hanging look,) do you call, Sir, your occupation a mystery?

Abhor. Ay, Sir; a mystery.

Clown. Painting, Sir, I have heard say, is a mystery; and your whores, Sir, being members of my occupation, using painting, do prove my occupation a mystery: but what mystery there should be in hanging, if I should be hang'd, I cannot imagine.

this play, in its common acceptation, for *tillage*; which would not suit here:
" —— so, her plenteous womb
" Expresseth his full *tilth* and husbandry." MALONE.
I believe *tythe* is right, and that the expression is proverbial, in which *tythe* is taken, by an easy metonymy, for *harvest*. JOHNSON.
⁵ —— *a good favour*] Favour is countenance. STEEVENS.

Abhor.

Abhor. Sir, it is a mystery.

Clown. Proof.

Abhor. Every true man's apparel fits your thief⁶: If it be too little for your thief, your true man thinks it big enough; if it be too big for your thief, your thief thinks it little enough: so every true man's apparel fits your thief.

Re-enter PROVOST.

Prov. Are you agreed?

Clown. Sir, I will serve him; for I do find, your hangman is a more penitent trade than your bawd; he doth oftner ask forgiveness⁷.

Prov.

---

⁶ *Every true man's apparel fits your thief,*] So, in *Promos and Cassandra,* 1578, the Hangman says:

"Here is nyne and twenty suits of apparell for my share."
STEEVENS.

A *true man*, in the language of our author's time, means an *honest man*, and was generally opposed to *thief*. Our jurymen are to this day called "good men and true." The following words—"If it be too little, &c." are given in the old copy to the *Clown*: the train of the argument shews decisively that they belong to Abhorson. The present arrangement, which is clearly right, was suggested by Mr. Theobald.
MALONE.

The sense of this speech is this: Every true man's apparel, which the thief robs him of, fits the thief; because, if it be too little for the thief, the true man thinks it big enough; i. e. a purchase too good for him. So that this fits the thief in the opinion of the true man. But if it be too big for the thief, yet the thief thinks it little enough; i. e. of value little enough. So that this fits the thief in his own opinion. The pleasantry of the joke consists in the equivocal sense of *big enough,* and *little enough.* WARBURTON.

There is still a further equivoque. The true man's *apparel*, which way soever it be taken, *fitting* the thief, the speaker considers him as a *fitter of apparel*, i. e. a tailor.

This, it must be acknowledged, on the first view, seems only to prove the *thief's* trade, not the *hangman's*, a mystery; which latter was the thing to be proved; but the argument is brought home to the hangman also, by the following state of it. "If (says Mr. Heath) Dr. Warburton had attended to the argument by which the bawd proves his own profession to be a mystery, he would not have been driven to the groundless supposition, 'that part of the dialogue had been lost or dropped.' The argument of the hangman is exactly similar to that of the bawd. As the latter puts in his claim to the whores, as members of his occupation, and, in virtue of their painting, would enroll his own fraternity in the mystery of painters; so the former equally lays claim to the thieves as members of his occupation, and in *their* right endeavours to rank his brethren, the hangmen, under the mystery of *fitters of apparel,* or tailors." MALONE.

7 — *ask*

MEASURE FOR MEASURE.

Prov. You, Sirrah, provide your block and your axe, to-morrow four o'clock.

Abhor. Come on, bawd; I will instruct thee in my trade; follow.

Clown. I do desire to learn, Sir; and, I hope, if you have occasion to use me for your own turn, you shall find me yare [8]: for truly Sir, for your kindness, I owe you a good turn [9].

Prov. Call hither Barnardine and Claudio:
[*Exeunt* CLOWN *and* ABHORSON.
The one has my pity; not a jot the other,
Being a murtherer, though he were my brother.

Enter CLAUDIO.

Look, here's the warrant, Claudio, for thy death:
'Tis now dead midnight, and by eight to-morrow
Thou must be made immortal. Where's Barnardine?

Claud. As fast lock'd up in sleep, as guiltless labour
When it lies starkly [1] in the traveller's bones:
He will not wake.

Prov. Who can do good on him?
Well, go, prepare yourself. But hark, what noise?
[*Knocking within.*
Heaven give your spirits comfort!—[*Exit* CLAUDIO.]
By and by:—
I hope it is some pardon or reprieve,
For the most gentle Claudio.—Welcome, father.

Enter DUKE.

Duke. The best and wholesomest spirits of the night
Envellop you, good Provost! Who call'd here of late?

Prov. None, since the curfew rung?

Duke. Not Isabel?

---

[7] — *ask forgiveness*] So, in *As You Like It*:
"——— The common executioner,
"Whose heart the accustom'd sight of death makes hard,
"Falls not the axe upon the humbled neck,
"But first *begs pardon*." STEEVENS.

[8] — *yare*:] i. e. handy. STEEVENS

[9] *a good turn*] i. e. a turn off the ladder. He quibbles on the phrase according to its common acceptation. FARMER.

[1] — *starkly*] Stiffly. These two lines afford a very pleasing image.
JOHNSON.

Prov.

Prov. No.
Duke. They will then [2], ere't be long.
Prov. What comfort is for Claudio?
Duke. There's some in hope.
Prov. It is a bitter deputy.
Duke. Not so; not so; his life is parallel'd
Even with the stroke [3] and line of his great justice;
He doth with holy abstinence subdue
That in himself, which he spurs on his power
To qualify [4] in others: were he meal'd [5]
With that which he corrects, then were he tyrannous;
But this being so [6], he's just.—Now are they come.—

[*Knocking within.* PROVOST *goes out.*]

This is a gentle Provost; Seldom, when
The steeled gaoler is the friend of men.—
How now? What noise? That spirit's possess'd with haste,
That wounds the unsisting postern [7] with these strokes.

[PROVOST *returns, speaking to one at the door.*]

Prov. There he must stay, until the officer
Arise to let him in; he is call'd up.
Duke. Have you no countermand for Claudio yet,
But he must die to-morrow?
Prov. None, Sir, none.
Duke. As near the dawning, Provost, as it is,
You shall hear more ere morning.
Prov. Happily,
You something know; yet, I believe, there comes
No countermand; no such example have we:

---

[2] *They will then,*] Perhaps *she* will then. Sir J. HAWKINS.
[3] *Even with the stroke*—] *Stroke* is here put for the *stroke* of a pen or a line. JOHNSON.
[4] —*To qualify*] To temper, to moderate; as we say, wine is *qualified* with water. JOHNSON.
[5] —*were he meal'd*] Were he sprinkled; were he defiled. A figure of the same kind our author uses in *Macbeth*:
  " *The blood-bolter'd Banquo.*" JOHNSON.
Mealed is mingled, compounded; from the French *mesler*.
 BLACKSTONE.
[6] *But this being so*—] The tenor of the argument seems to require—But this *not* being so———. Perhaps, however, the author meant only to say—But, his life being paralleled, &c. he's just. MALONE.
[7] *That wounds the unsisting postern*] *Unsisting* may signify "never at rest," always opening. BLACKSTONE.
Mr. Rowe reads—*unresisting*; Sir T. Hanmer—*unresting*. MALONE.

Besides,

Besides, upon the very siege of justice [8],
Lord Angelo hath to the public ear
Profess'd the contrary.

Enter a MESSENGER.

Duke. This is his lordship's man [9].

Prov. And here comes Claudio's pardon [1].

Mess. My lord hath sent you this note; and by me this further charge, that you swerve not from the smallest article of it, neither in time, matter, or other circumstance. Good morrow; for, as I take it, it is almost day.

Prov. I shall obey him. [*Exit* MESSENGER.

Duke. This is his pardon; purchas'd by such sin, [*Aside.*
For which the pardoner himself is in:
Hence hath offence his quick celerity,
When it is borne in high authority:
When vice makes mercy, mercy's so extended,
That for the fault's love, is the offender friended.—
Now, Sir, what news?

Prov. I told you: Lord Angelo, be-like, thinking me remiss in mine office, awakens me with this unwonted putting on: methinks, strangely; for he hath not used it before.

---

[8] — *siege of justice,*] i. e. *seat of justice. Siege,* Fr. STEEVENS.

[9] *This is his lordship's man.*] The old copy has *his lord's man.* Corrected by Mr. Pope. In the MS. plays of our author's time they often wrote *Lo.* for Lord, and *Lord.* for Lordship; and these contractions were sometimes improperly followed in the printed copies. MALONE.

[1] Enter a Messenger.
Duke. *This is his lordship's man.*
Prov. *And here comes Claudio's pardon.*] The Provost has just declared a fixed opinion that the execution will not be countermanded, and yet, upon the first appearance of the Messenger he immediately guesses that his errand is to bring Claudio's pardon. It is evident, I think, that the names of the speakers are misplaced. If we suppose the Provost to say;
This is his lordship's man,
it is very natural for the Duke to subjoin,
And here comes Claudio's pardon.
The Duke might believe, upon very reasonable grounds, that Angelo had now sent the pardon. It appears that he did so, from what he says to himself, while the Provost is reading the letter;
This is his pardon; purchas'd by such sin—— TYRWHITT.

When, immediately after the Duke had hinted his expectation of a pardon, the Provost sees the Messenger, he supposes the Duke to have *known something,* and changes his mind. Either reading may serve equally well. JOHNSON.

Duke.

Duke. Pray you, let's hear

Prov. [reads.] *Whatsoever you may hear to the contrary, let Claudio be executed by four of the clock; and, in the afternoon, Barnardine: for my better satisfaction, let me have Claudio's head sent me by five. Let this be duly perform'd; with a thought, that more depends on it than we must yet deliver. Thus fail not to do your office, as you will answer it at your peril.*
What say you to this, Sir?

Duke. What is that Barnardine, who is to be executed in the afternoon?

Prov. A Bohemian born; but here nursed up and bred: one that is a prisoner nine years old [2].

Duke. How came it, that the absent duke had not either deliver'd him to his liberty, or executed him? I have heard, it was ever his manner to do so.

Prov. His friends still wrought reprieves for him: And, indeed, his fact, till now in the government of lord Angelo, came not to an undoubtful proof.

Duke. Is it now apparent?

Prov. Most manifest, and not deny'd by himself.

Duke. Hath he borne himself penitently in prison? How seems he to be touch'd?

Prov. A man that apprehends death no more dreadfully, but as a drunken sleep; careless, reckless, and fearless of what's past, present, or to come; insensible of mortality, and desperately mortal [3].

Duke. He wants advice.

Prov. He will hear none: he hath evermore had the liberty of the prison; give him leave to escape hence, he would not: drunk many times a day, if not many days entirely drunk. We have very oft awaked him, as if to carry him to execution, and shew'd him a seeming warrant for it: it hath not moved him at all.

---

[2] *— one that is a prisoner nine years old.*] i. e. That has been confined these nine years. So, in *Hamlet:* "Ere we were two days old at sea, a pirate of very warlike preparation, &c." MALONE.

[3] *—desperately mortal.*] This expression is obscure. I am inclined to believe, that *desperately mortal* means *desperately mischievous.* Or *desperately mortal* may mean a man likely to die in a *desperate* state, without reflection or repentance. JOHNSON.
The word is often used by Shakspeare in the sense first affixed to it by Dr. Johnson, which I believe to be the true one. So, in *Othello:*
"And you, ye *mortal* engines," &c. MALONE.

Duke.

Duke. More of him anon. There is written in your brow, Provost, honesty and constancy: if I read it not truly, my ancient skill beguiles me; but in the boldness of my cunning, I will lay myself in hazard. Claudio, whom here you have warrant to execute, is no greater forfeit to the law than Angelo who hath sentenced him: To make you understand this in a manifested effect, I crave but four days respite; for the which you are to do me both a present and a dangerous courtesy.

Prov. Pray, Sir, in what?

Duke. In the delaying death.

Prov. Alack! how may I do it? Having the hour limited; and an express command, under penalty, to deliver his head in the view of Angelo; I may make my case as Claudio's, to cross this in the smallest.

Duke. By the vow of mine order, I warrant you, if my instructions may be your guide. Let this Barnardine be this morning executed, and his head borne to Angelo.

Prov. Angelo hath seen them both, and will discover the favour [4].

Duke. O, death's a great disguiser; and you may add to it. Shave the head, and tie the beard [5]; and say, it was the desire of the penitent to be so bared [6] before his death: You know the course is common [7]. If any thing fall to you upon

---

[4] —*the* favour.] See p. 398, n. 5. MALONE.

[5] —*and tie the beard*;] A beard tied would give a very new air to that face, which had never been seen but with the beard loose, long, and squalid JOHNSON.

Mr. Simpson proposed to read—*die* the beard; and Mr. Steevens has shewn, that it was the custom to *die* beards in our author's time. The text being intelligible, I have made no change, though the conjecture appears extremely probable. MALONE.

[6] —*to be so* bared—] These words relate to what has just preceded,—*shave the head.* The modern editions following the fourth folio, read—*to be so barb'd;* but the old copy is certainly right. So, in *All's well that ends well:* " I would the cutting of my garment would serve the turn, or the *baring* of my beard; and to say it was in stratagem." MALONE.

[7] *You know the course is common.*] P. Mathieu, in his *Heroyke Life and Death of Henry the Fourth of France,* says, that Ravilliac, in the midst of his tortures, lifted up his head, and shooke a spark of fire from his *beard.* " This unprofitable care, he adds, to save it, being noted, afforded matter to diverse to praise the *custome* in *Germany, Swisserland,* and divers other places, *to shave off,* and then to burn all the haire from all parts of the bodies of those who are convicted for any notorious crimes." Grimston's *Translation,* 4to. 1612, p. 181. REED.

this

this, more than thanks and good fortune, by the saint whom I profess, I will plead against it with my life.

Prov. Pardon me, good father; it is against my oath.

Duke. Were you sworn to the duke, or to the deputy?

Prov. To him, and to his substitutes.

Duke. You will think you have made no offence, if the duke avouch the justice of your dealing?

Prov. But what likelihood is in that?

Duke. Not a resemblance, but a certainty. Yet, since I see you fearful, that neither my coat, integrity, nor persuasion can with ease attempt you, I will go further than I meant, to pluck all fears out of you. Look you, Sir, here is the hand and seal of the duke: You know the character, I doubt not; and the signet is not strange to you.

Prov. I know them both.

Duke. The contents of this is the return of the duke; you shall anon over-read it at your pleasure; where you shall find, within these two days he will be here. This is a thing, that Angelo knows not: for he this very day receives letters of strange tenor; perchance of the duke's death; perchance, entering into some monastery; but, by chance, nothing of what is writ [8]. Look, the unfolding star calls up the shepherd: Put not yourself into amazement, how these things should be: all difficulties are but easy when they are known. Call your executioner, and off with Barnardine's head: I will give him a present shrift, and advise him for a better place. Yet you are amazed; but this shall absolutely resolve you. Come away; it is almost clear dawn.

[*Exeunt.*

SCENE III.

Another Room in the same.

Enter CLOWN.

Clown. I am as well acquainted here, as I was in our house of profession [9]: one would think, it were Mistress Overdone's own house, for here be many of her old custo-

---

[8] —*nothing of what is writ.*] We should read—*here writ;*—the Duke pointing to the letter in his hand. WARBURTON.

[9] *in our house of* profession:] i. e. in my late mistress's house, which was a *professed*, a notorious bawdy-house. MALONE.

mers.

mers. First, here's young Master Rash[1]; he's in for a commodity of brown paper and old ginger[2], ninescore and seventeen pounds; of which he made five marks, ready money: marry, then, ginger was not much in request, for the old women were all dead. Then is there here one Master Caper, at the suit of Master Three-pile the mercer, for some four suits of peach-colour'd sattin, which now peaches him a beggar. Then have we here young Dizy, and young Master Deep-vow, and Master Copper-spur, and Master Starve-lacky the rapier and dagger-man, and young Drop-heir that kill'd lusty Pudding, and Master Forthright[3] the tilter, and brave

[1] *First, here's young Master* Rash, &c.] All the names here mentioned are characteristical. *Rash* was a stuff formerly worn. *Sericum rasum.* See Minsheu's Dict. in v. *Rash,* and Florio's Italian Dict. 1598, in v. *rascia, rascetta.* MALONE.

This enumeration of the inhabitants of the prison affords a very striking view of the practices predominant in Shakspeare's age. Besides those whose follies are common to all times, we have four fighting men and a traveller. It is not unlikely that the originals of the pictures were then known. JOHNSON.

[2] —*a commodity of brown paper and old ginger,*] In our author's time it was a common practice of money-lenders to give the borrower a small sum of money, and some commodity of little value, which in the loan was estimated at perhaps ten times its value. The borrower gave a bond or other security, as if the whole had been advanced in money, and sold the commodity for whatever he could. Sometimes no money whatsoever was advanced; but the unfortunate borrower accepted of some goods of a trifling value, as equivalent to a large sum. The following passage in Greene's *Defence of Coney-catching,* 1592, (the quotation is Mr. Steevens's) fully illustrates that before us: "—o that if he borrow an hundred pounds, he shall have forty in silver, and threescore in wares, as lutestrings, hobby-horses, or *brown paper,* or cloath, &c."

The practices of the money-lenders of Shakspeare's time, are thus described by Nashe, in his pamphlet, entitled *Christ's Teares over Jerusalem,* 1594: "He [a usurer] fails acquainted with gentlemen, frequents ordinaries and dicing-houses dayly, where when some of them at play have lost all their money, he is very diligent at hand, on their chaines and bracelets, or jewels, to lend them *half the value.* Now this is the nature of young gentlemen, that where they have broke the ise, and borrowed once, they will come again the second time; and that these young foxes know as well as the beggar knows his dish. But at the second time of their coming, it is doubtful to say, whether they shall have money or no. The world growes hard, and we are all mortal; let him make him any assurance before a judge, and they shall have some hundred pounds *per consequence,* in *silks* and *velvets.* The third time if they come, they shall have *baser commodities.* The fourth time, *lutestrings* and GREY PAPER. MALONE.

[3] — *Master*

brave Master Shoe-tye the great traveller [4], and wild Half-can that stabb'd Pots, and, I think forty more; all great doers in our trade [5], and are now for the Lord's sake [6].

Enter

[3] —*Master* Forthright] The old copy reads *Forthlight*; but should not *Forthlight* be *Forthright*, alluding to the line in which the thrust is made? JOHNSON.

Shakspeare uses this word in the *Tempest*: " Through *forthrights* and meanders." Again, in *Troilus and Cressida*, Act iii. sc. iii :
" Or hedge aside from the direct *forthright*." STEEVENS.

I have no doubt that Dr. Johnson's correction is right. An anonymous writer defends the old reading, by supposing the allusion to be to the fencer's threat of making the *light* shine through his antagonist.— Had he produced any proof that such an expression was in use in our author's time, his observation might have some weight. It is probably a phrase of the present century. MALONE.

[4] —*and brave Master* Shoetye *the great traveller,*] At this time shoe-strings were generally worn. STEEVENS.

Brave, in old language, meant *fine, splendid in dress.* The finery which induced our author to give his traveller the name of *Shoe-tye*, was used on the stage in his time. " Would not this, Sir, (says Hamlet) and a forest of feathers—with two *Provencial roses* on my raz'd *shoes*, get me a fellowship in a cry of players, Sir?" MALONE.

[5] —*all great* doers *in our trade.*] The word *doers* is used here in a wanton sense. See Mr. Collins's note, Act i. sc. ii. MALONE.

[6] —*for the Lord's sake.*] i. e. to beg for the rest of their lives.
WARBURTON.

I rather think this expression intended to ridicule the puritans, whose turbulence and indecency often brought them to prison, and who considered themselves as suffering for religion.

It is not unlikely that men imprisoned for other crimes, might represent themselves to casual enquirers, as suffering for puritanism, and that this might be the common cant of the prison. In Donne's time, every prisoner was brought to jail by *sur.tish.p.* JOHNSON.

The phrase which Dr. Johnson has justly explained, is used in *A New Trick to cheat the Devil*, 1636: "—I held it, wife, a deed of charity, and did it *for the Lord's sake.*" STEEVENS.

I believe Dr. Warburton's explanation is right. It appears from a poem entitled, *Paper's Complaint*, printed among Davies's epigrams, (about the year 1611) that this was the language in which prisoners who were confined for debt, addressed passengers:

" Good gentle writers, *for the Lord's sake, for the Lord's sake,*
" Like *Ludgate prisoner*, lo, I, *begging*, make
" My mone."

The meaning, however, may be, to beg or *borrow* for the rest of their lives. A passage in *Much Ado about Nothing* may countenance this interpretation :—" He wears a key in his ear, and a lock hanging to it, and *borrows* money in *God's name*, the which he hath used so long, and never paid, that men grow hard-hearted, and will lend nothing *for God's sake.*"

Mr

Enter ABHORSON.

Abhor. Sirrah, bring Barnardine hither.

Clown. Master Barnardine! you must rise and be hang'd, Master Barnardine!

Abhor. What ho, Barnardine!

Barnar. [*within.*] A pox o' your throats! Who makes that noise there? What are you?

Clown. Your friends, Sir; the hangman: You must be so good, Sir, to rise and be put to death.

Barnar. [*within.*] Away, you rogue, away; I am sleepy.

Abhor. Tell him, he must awake, and that quickly too.

Clown. Pray, Master Barnardine, awake till you are executed, and sleep afterwards.

Abhor. Go in to him, and fetch him out.

Clown. He is coming, Sir, he is coming; I hear his straw rustle.

Enter BARNARDINE.

Abhor. Is the axe upon the block, Sirrah?

Clown. Very ready, Sir.

Barnar. How now, Abhorson? What's the news with you?

Abhor. Truly, Sir, I would desire you to clap into your prayers; for, look you, the warrant's come.

Barnar. You rogue, I have been drinking all night, I am not fitted for't.

Clown. O, the better, Sir; for he that drinks all night, and is hang'd betimes in the morning, may sleep the sounder all the next day.

Enter DUKE.

Abhor. Look you, Sir, here comes your ghostly father: Do we jest now, think you?

Duke. Sir, induced by my charity, and hearing how hastily you are to depart, I am come to advise you, comfort you, and pray with you.

Barnar. Friar, not I; I have been drinking hard all night, and I will have more time to prepare me, or they shall

Mr. Pope reads—*and are now in* for the Lord's sake. Perhaps unnecessarily. In *K. Henry IV.* P. i. Falstaff says,—" there's not three of my hundred and fifty left alive; and *they are for* the town's end—to beg during life." MALONE.

beat

beat out my brains with billets: I will not consent to die this day, that's certain.

Duke. O Sir, you must: and therefore, I beseech you, look forward on the journey you shall go.

Barnar. I swear, I will not die to-day for any man's persuasion.

Duke. But hear you—

Barnar. Not a word: if you have any thing to say to me, come to my ward; for thence will not I to-day. [*Exit.*

Enter PROVOST.

Duke. Unfit to live, or die: O gravel heart!—
After him, fellows; bring him to the block.

[*Exeunt* ABHORSON *and* CLOWN.

Prov. Now, Sir, how do you find the prisoner?

Duke. A creature unprepar'd, unmeet for death;
And, to transport him [7] in the mind he is,
Were damnable.

Prov. Here in the prison, father,
There died this morning of a cruel fever
One Ragozine, a most notorious pirate,
A man of Claudio's years; his beard, and head,
Just of his colour: What if we do omit
This reprobate, till he were well inclin'd;
And satisfy the deputy with the visage
Of Ragozine, more like to Claudio?

Duke. O, 'tis an accident that heaven provides!
Dispatch it presently; the hour draws on
Prefix'd by Angelo: See, this be done,
And sent according to command; whiles I
Persuade this rude wretch willingly to die.

Prov. This shall be done, good father, presently,
But Barnardine must die this afternoon:
And how shall we continue Claudio,
To save me from the danger that might come,
If he were known alive?

Duke. Let this be done;—Put them
In secret holds, both Barnardine and Claudio:
Ere twice the sun hath made his journal greeting
To yond generation [8], you shall find
Your safety manifested.

Prov.

---

[7] — *to transport him*] To remove him from one world to another. The French *trépas* affords a kindred sense. JOHNSON.

VOL. III. T *T.

Prov. I am your free dependant.
Duke. Quick, dispatch, and send the head to Angelo.
[*Exit Provost.*

Now will I write letters to Angelo—
The Provost, he shall bear them—whose contents
Shall witness to him, I am near at home;
And that, by great injunctions, I am bound
To enter publicly: him I'll desire
To meet me at the consecrated fount,
A league below the city; and from thence,
By cold gradation and weal-balanced form [9],
We shall proceed with Angelo.

Re-enter PROVOST.

Prov. Here is the head; I'll carry it myself.
Duke. Convenient is it: Make a swift return;
For I would commune with you of such things,
That want no ear but yours.
Prov. I'll make all speed. [*Exit.*
Isab. [*within.*] Peace, ho, be here!
Duke. The tongue of Isabel:—She's come to know,
If yet her brother's pardon be come hither:
But I will keep her ignorant of her good,
To make her heavenly comforts of despair,
When it is least expected [1].

Enter ISABELLA.

Isab. Ho, by your leave.
Duke. Good morning to you, fair and gracious daughter.
Isab. The better, given me by so holy a man.
Hath yet the deputy sent my brother's pardon?

[8] *To yond generation,*] Prisons are generally so constructed as not to admit the rays of the sun. Hence the Duke here speaks of its greeting only those *without* the doors of the jail, to which he must be supposed to point when he speaks these words. Sir T. Hanmer, I think without necessity, reads—To *the under* generation, which has been followed by subsequent editors.
Journal, in the preceding line, is *daily.* Journalier, Fr. MALONE.
[9] —weal balanced *form,*] Thus the old copy. Mr. Heath thinks that *well*-balanced is the true reading; and Hanmer was of the same opinion. STEEVENS.
[1] *When it is least expected.*] A better reason might have been given.—It was necessary to keep Isabella in ignorance, that she might with more keenness accuse the deputy. JOHNSON.

Duke.

Duke. He hath releas'd him, Isabel, from the world:
His head is off, and sent to Angelo.
  Isab. Nay, but it is not so.
  Duke. It is no other:
Shew your wisdom, daughter, in your close patience.
  Isab. O, I will to him, and pluck out his eyes.
  Duke. You shall not be admitted to his sight.
  Isab. Unhappy Claudio! Wretched Isabel!
Injurious world! Most damned Angelo!
  Duke. This nor hurts him, nor profits you a jot:
Forbear it therefore; give your cause to heaven.
Mark, what I say; which you shall find
By every syllable, a faithful verity:
The duke comes home to-morrow;—nay, dry your eyes;
One of our convent, and his confessor,
Gives me this instance: Already he hath carry'd
Notice to Escalus and Angelo;
Who do prepare to meet him at the gates,
There to give up their power. If you can, pace your wisdom
In that good path, that I would wish it go;
And you shall have your bosom [2] on this wretch,
Grace of the duke, revenges to your heart,
And general honour.
  Isab. I am directed by you.
  Duke. This letter then to friar Peter give;
'Tis that he sent me of the duke's return:
Say, by this token, I desire his company
At Mariana's house to-night. Her cause, and yours,
I'll perfect him withal; and he shall bring you
Before the duke; and to the head of Angelo
Accuse him home, and home. For my poor self,
I am combined by a sacred vow [3],
And shall be absent. Wend [4] you with this letter:
Command these fretting waters from your eyes
With a light heart; trust not my holy order,
If I pervert your course.—Who's here?

---

  [2] *—your bosom—*] Your wish; your heart's desire. JOHNSON.
  [3] *I am combined by a sacred vow,*] I once thought this should be confined, but Shakspeare uses combine for to *bind by a pact or agreement*; so he calls Angelo the *combinate* husband of Mariana. JOHNSON.
  [4] *Wend you—*] To *wend* is to *go*. STEEVENS.

MEASURE FOR MEASURE.

Enter LUCIO.

Lucio. Good even! Friar, where is the Provost?

Duke. Not within, Sir.

Lucio. O, pretty Isabella, I am pale at mine heart, to see thine eyes so red; thou must be patient: I am fain to dine and sup with water and bran; I dare not for my head fill my belly; one fruitful meal would set me to't: But they say the duke will be here to-morrow. By my troth, Isabel, I lov'd thy brother: if the old fantastical duke of dark corners⁵ had been at home, he had lived.

[*Exit* ISABELLA.

Duke. Sir, the duke is marvellous little beholden to your reports; but the best is, he lives not in them⁶.

Lucio. Friar, thou knowest not the duke so well as I do: he's a better woodman⁷ than thou takest him for.

Duke. Well, you'll answer this one day. Fare ye well.

Lucio. Nay, tarry, I'll go along with thee; I can tell thee pretty tales of the duke.

Duke. You have told me too many of him already, Sir, if they be true; if not true, none were enough.

Lucio. I was once before him for getting a wench with child.

Duke. Did you such a thing?

Lucio. Yes, marry, did I: but I was fain to forswear it; they would else have marry'd me to the rotten medlar.

Duke. Sir, your company is fairer than honest: Rest you well.

---

⁵ *if the old fantastical duke of dark* corners—] This duke who meets his mistresses in by-places. So, in *K. Henry VIII.*:

"There is nothing I have done yet, o' my conscience,
"Deserves a corner." MALONE.

Sir Thomas Hanmer reads, *the odd fantastical duke,* but *old* is a common word of aggravation in ludicrous language, as, *there was old revelling.* JOHNSON.

⁶ —*he lives not in them.*] i. e. his character depends not on them.
STEEVENS.

⁷ —*woodman,*] A *woodman* seems to have been an attendant or servant to the officer called *Forrester.* See *Manwood on the Forest Laws,* 4to. 1615, p. 46. It is here however used in a wanton sense, and was probably, in our author's time, generally so received. REED.

So, in the *Merry Wives of Windsor,* Falstaff says to his mistresses,—
"Am I a *woodman?* Ha!" STEEVENS.

Lucio. By my troth, I'll go with thee to the lane's end: If bawdy talk offend you, we'll have very little of it: Nay, Friar, I am a kind of burr, I shall stick. [*Exeunt.*

SCENE IV.

A Room in ANGELO'*s House.*

Enter ANGELO *and* ESCALUS.

Escal. Every letter he hath writ hath disvouch'd other.

Ang. In most uneven and distracted manner. His actions shew much to madness; pray heaven, his wisdom be not tainted! And why meet him at the gates, and re-deliver our authorities there?

Escal. I guess not.

Ang. And why should we proclaim it in an hour before his entering, that, if any crave redress of injustice, they should exhibit their petitions in the street?

Escal. He shews his reason for that: to have a dispatch of complaints; and to deliver us from devices hereafter, which shall then have no power to stand against us.

Ang. Well; I beseech you, let it be proclaim'd:
Betimes i' the morn [8], I'll call you at your house:
Give notice to such men of sort and suit [9],
As are to meet him.

Escal. I shall, Sir: fare you well. [*Exit.*

Ang. Good night.—
This deed unshapes me quite, makes me unpregnant [1],
And dull to all proceedings. A deflower'd maid!
And by an eminent body, that enforc'd
The law against it!—But that her tender shame
Will not proclaim against her maiden loss,
How might she tongue me? Yet reason dares her?—no [2]:

For

---

[8] —*let it be proclaim'd:*
  Betimes i' the morn, &c.] Perhaps it should be pointed thus:
  ——— *let it be proclaim'd*
  Betimes i' the morn: I'll call you at your house.
So above: *And why should we proclaim it in an hour before his entering*—?
  MALONE.

[9] —*sort and suit,*] Figure and rank. JOHNSON.

[1] —*makes me unpregnant,*] In the first scene the Duke says that *Escalus* is *pregnant,* i. e. ready in the forms of law. *Unpregnant* therefore, in the instance before us, is *unready, unprepared.*
  STEEVENS.

[2] —*Yet reason dares her? no!*] Yet does not reason *challenge* or in-

For my authority bears off a credent bulk,
That no particular scandal³ once can touch,
But it confounds the breather. He should have liv'd,
Save that his riotous youth, with dangerous sense,
Might, in the times to come, have ta'en revenge,
By so receiving a dishonour'd life,
With ransom of such shame. 'Would yet he had liv'd!
Alack, when once our grace we have forgot,
Nothing goes right; we would, and we would not⁴. [*Exit.*

SCENE V.

Fields without the Town.

Enter DUKE *in his own Habit, and Friar* PETER.

Duke. These letters⁵ at fit time deliver me.
[*Giving letters.*
The Provost knows our purpose, and our plot.

cite her to accuse me?—no, (answers the speaker) for my authority, &c. To *dare*, in this sense, is yet a school-phrase; Shakspeare probably learnt it there. He has again used the word with the same signification (as Mr. Steevens observes) in *K. Henry IV.* P. i.:

" Unless a brother should a brother *dare*
" To gentle exercise, &c."

Again, more appositely, in *K. Henry VI.* P. ii.:

" What dare not Warwick, if false Suffolk *dare him.*"
MALONE.

³ —*my authority bears off a credent bulk,*
That no particular scandal, &c.] *Credent* is *creditable, inferring credit, not questionable.* The old English writers often confound the active and passive adjectives. So Shakspeare, and Milton after him, use *inexpressive* for *inexpressible.*—*Particular* is *private,* a French sense. No scandal from any *private* mouth can reach a man in my authority.
JOHNSON.

The old copy reads—*bears of,* in which way *off* was formerly often spelt. *Bears off* Mr. Steevens interprets—*carries with it.* Perhaps Angelo means, that his authority will ward off or set aside the weightiest and most probable charge that can be brought against him. MALONE.

⁴ —*we would, and we would not.*] Here undoubtedly the act should end, and was ended by the poet; for here is properly a cessation of action, and a night intervenes, and the place is changed, between the passages of this scene, and those of the next. The next act beginning with the following scene, proceeds without any interruption of time or change of place. JOHNSON.

⁵ *These letters*—] Peter never delivers the letters, but tells his story without any credentials. The poet forgot the plot which he had formed. JOHNSON.

The

The matter being afoot, keep your inſtruction,
And hold you ever to our ſpecial drift;
Though ſometimes you do blench⁶ from this to that,
As cauſe doth miniſter. Go, call at Flavius' houſe,
And tell him, where I ſtay: give the like notice
To Valentius, Rowland, and to Craſſus,
And bid them bring the trumpets to the gate;
But ſend me Flavius firſt.

Fri. P. It ſhall be ſpeeded well.   [*Exit Friar.*

Enter VARRIUS.

Duke. I thank thee, Varrius; thou haſt made good
   haſte:
Come, we will walk: There's other of our friends
Will greet us here anon, my gentle Varrius.   [*Exeunt.*

SCENE VI.

Street near the City Gate.

Enter ISABELLA *and* MARIANA.

Iſab. To ſpeak ſo indirectly, I am loth;
I would ſay the truth; but to accuſe him ſo,
That is your part: yet I am advis'd to do it;
He ſays, to veil full purpoſe⁷.

Mari. Be rul'd by him.

Iſab. Beſides, he tells me, that, if peradventure
He ſpeak againſt me on the adverſe ſide,
I ſhould not think it ſtrange; for 'tis a phyſic,
That's bitter to ſweet end.

---

⁶ —*you do* blench—] To *blench* is to ſtart off, to fly off.
                                                                     STEEVENS.

⁷ *He ſays, to* veil full *purpoſe.*] To *vail full purpoſe*, may, with very little force on the words, mean, *to hide the whole extent of our deſign*, and therefore the reading may ſtand; yet I cannot but think Mr. Theobald's alteration [t' availful *purpoſe*] either lucky or ingenious.
                                                                       JOHNSON.

If Dr. Johnſon's explanation be right, (as I think it is,) the word ſhould be written—*veil*, as it is now printed in the text.

That *vail* was the old ſpelling of *veil*, appears from a line in *The Merchant of Venice*, folio 1623:

"Vailing an Indian beauty—"

for which in the modern editions *veiling* has been rightly ſubſtituted.
                                                                         MALONE.

Mari. I would, friar Peter—
Isab. O, peace; the friar is come.

Enter Friar PETER.[8]

Fri. P. Come, I have found you out a stand most fit,
Where you may have such vantage on the duke,
He shall not pass you: Twice have the trumpets sounded;
The generous[9] and gravest citizens
Have hent the gates[1], and very near upon
The duke is ent'ring; therefore hence, away. [*Exeunt.*

ACT V. SCENE I.

A public Place near the City Gate.

MARIANA (*veil'd*), ISABELLA, *and* PETER, *at a Distance. Enter at opposite Doors,* DUKE, VARRIUS, *Lords;* ANGELO, ESCALUS, LUCIO, PROVOST, *Officers, and Citizens.*

Duke. My very worthy cousin, fairly met:—
Our old and faithful friend, we are glad to see you.
Ang. and Escal. Happy return be to your royal grace!
Duke. Many and hearty thankings to you both.

---

[8] *Enter Friar* PETER.] This play has two friars, either of whom might singly have served. I should therefore imagine, that Friar Thomas, in the first act, might be changed, without any harm, to Friar Peter; for why should the Duke unnecessarily trust two in an affair which required only one. The name of Friar Thomas is never mentioned in the dialogue, and therefore seems arbitrarily placed at the head of the scene. JOHNSON.

[9] *The generous, &c.*] i. e. the *most noble*, &c. *Generous* is here used in its Latin sense. "Virgo *generosa* et nobilis." Cicero. Shakspeare uses it again in *Othello*:

"——— the *generous* islanders
"By you invited———." STEEVENS.

[1] *Have hent the gates,*] Have seized or taken possession of the gates. JOHNSON.

Hent, henten, hende, (says Junius, in his *Etymologicon,*) Chaucero est, capere, assequi, prehendere, arripere, ab A. S. hendan. MALONE.

We

We have made inquiry of you; and we hear
Such goodness of your justice, that our soul
Cannot but yield you forth to public thanks,
Fore-running more requital.

   Ang. You make my bonds still greater.

   Duke. O, your desert speaks loud; and I should wrong it,
To lock it in the wards of covert bosom,
When it deserves with characters of brass
A forted residence, 'gainst the tooth of time
And razure of oblivion: Give me your hand,
And let the subjects see, to make them know
That outward courtesies would fain proclaim
Favours that keep within.—Come, Escalus;
You must walk by us on our other hand;—
And good supporters are you.

   Peter *and* Isabella *come forward.*

   Fri. P. Now is your time; speak loud, and kneel before him.

   Isab. Justice, O royal Duke! Vail your regard [2]
Upon a wrong'd, I would fain have said, a maid!
O worthy prince, dishonour not your eye
By throwing it on any other object,
Till you have heard me in my true complaint,
And given me justice, justice, justice, justice!

   Duke. Relate your wrongs: In what? By whom? Be brief:
Here is lord Angelo sha'l give you justice;
Reveal yourself to him.

   Isab. O worthy Duke,
You bid me seek redemption of the devil:
Hear me yourself; for that which I must speak
Must either punish me, not being believ'd,
Or wring redress from you: hear me, O hear me; here.

   Ang. My Lord, her wits, I fear me, are not firm;
She hath been a suitor to me for her brother,
Cut off by course of justice.

---

  [2] *—Vail your regard.*] that is, withdraw your thoughts from higher things, let your notice descend upon a wronged woman. To *vail*, is to lower. Johnson.

  This is one of the few expressions which might have been borrowed from the old play of *Promos and Cassandra*, 1578:

    " —— vail thou thine ears." Steevens.

Isab. By course of justice!

Ang. And she will speak most bitterly, and strange.

Isab. Most strange, but yet most truly, will I speak;
That Angelo's forsworn; is it not strange?
That Angelo's a murtherer; is't not strange?
That Angelo is an adulterous thief,
An hypocrite, a virgin-violater;
Is it not strange, and strange?

Duke. Nay, it is ten times strange.

Isab. It is not truer he is Angelo,
Than this is all as true as it is strange;
Nay, it is ten times true; for truth is truth
To the end of reckoning*.

Duke. Away with her:—Poor soul,
She speaks this in the infirmity of sense.

Isab. O prince, I conjure thee, as thou believ'st
There is another comfort than this world,
That thou neglect me not, with that opinion
That I am touch'd with madness; make not impossible
That which but seems unlike; 'tis not impossible,
But one, the wicked'st caitiff on the ground,
May seem as shy, as grave, as just, as absolute³,
As Angelo; even so may Angelo,
In all his dressings⁴, characts⁵, titles, forms,
Be an arch-villain; believe it, royal prince,
If he be less, he's nothing; but he's more,
Had I more name for badness.

* ———*truth is truth*
To the end of reckoning.] That is, truth has no gradations; nothing which admits of increase can be so much what it is, as *truth is truth.*—There may be a *strange* thing, and a thing *more strange*; but if a proposition be *true*, there can be none *more true*. JOHNSON.

³ —*as shy, as grave, as just, as absolute,*] *As shy*; as reserved, as abstracted; *as just*; as nice, as exact; *as absolute*; as complete in all the round of duty. JOHNSON.

⁴ *In all his dressings,* &c.] In all his semblance of virtue, in all his habiliments of office. JOHNSON.

⁵ —*characts,*] i. e. characters. See Dugdale, *Orig. Jurid.* p. 81:—
" That he use, ne hide, no charme, ne *caracte*." TYRWHITT.

Charact signifies an inscription. The stat. 1 Edw. VI. c. 2. directed the seals of office of every bishop to have " certain *characts* under the king's arms, for the knowledge of the diocese." *Characters* are the letters in which an inscription is written. *Charactery* is the materials of which characters are composed.

" Fairies use flowers for their *charactery*." *Merry Wives of Windsor.*

Duke. By mine honesty,
If she be mad, (as I believe no other,)
Her madness hath the oddest frame of sense,
Such a dependency of thing on thing,
As e'er I heard in madness [6].
　Isab. Gracious Duke,
Harp not on that; nor do not banish reason
For inequality [7]; but let your reason serve
To make the truth appear, where it seems hid;
And hide the false, seems true [8].
　Duke. Many that are not mad,
Have, sure, more lack of reason.—What would you say?
　Isab. I am the sister of one Claudio,
Condemn'd upon the act of fornication
To lose his head; condemn'd by Angelo;
I, in probation of a sisterhood,
Was sent to by my brother: One Lucio
As then the messenger;—
　Lucio. That's I, an't like your Grace:
I came to her from Claudio, and desir'd her
To try her gracious fortune with Lord Angelo,
For her poor brother's pardon.
　Isab. That's he, indeed.
　Duke. You were not bid to speak.
　Lucio. No, my good Lord;
Nor wish'd to hold my peace.
　Duke. I wish you now then;
Pray you, take note of it: and when you have
A business for yourself, pray heaven, you then
Be perfect.

[6] *As e'er I heard in madness.*] I suspect Shakspeare wrote,
　　As ne'er I heard in madness. MALONE.

[7] ——*do not banish reason*
　　For inequality:] Let not the high quality of my adversary prejudice you against me. JOHNSON.
　I imagine, the meaning rather is—*Do not suppose I am mad, because I speak passionately and unequally.* MALONE.

[8] *And hide the false, seems true.*] And for ever *hide*, i. e. plunge into eternal darkness, the false one, i. e. Angelo, who now seems honest. Many other words would have expressed our poet's meaning better than *hide;* but he seems to have chosen it merely for the sake of opposition to the preceding line. Mr. Theobald unnecessarily reads—*Not* hide the false—which has been followed by the subsequent editors.
　　　　　　　　　　　　　MALONE.

　　　　　　　　　　　　　　Lucio.

Lucio. I warrant your honour.

Duke. The warrant's for yourself; take heed to it.

Isab. This gentleman told somewhat of my tale.

Lucio. Right.

Duke. It may be right; but you are in the wrong
To speak before your time.—Proceed.

Isab. I went
To this pernicious caitiff deputy.

Duke. That's somewhat madly spoken.

Isab. Pardon it;
The phrase is to the matter.

Duke. Mended again: the matter;—Proceed.

Isab. In brief—to set the needless process by,
How I persuaded, how I pray'd, and kneel'd,
How he refell'd me [9], and how I reply'd;
(For this was of much length,) the vile conclusion
I now begin with grief and shame to utter:
He would not, but by gift of my chaste body
To his concupiscible intemperate lust,
Release my brother; and, after much debatement,
My sisterly remorse [1] confutes mine honour,
And I did yield to him: But the next morn betimes,
His purpose surfeiting [2], he sends a warrant
For my poor brother's head.

Duke. This is most likely!

Isab. O, that it were as like, as it is true [3] !

Duke. By heaven, fond wretch [4], thou know'st not what
thou speak'st;
Or else thou art suborn'd against his honour,
In hateful practice [5]: First, his integrity
Stands without blemish:—next, it imports no reason,
That with such vehemency he should pursue
Faults proper to himself: if he had so offended,
He would have weigh'd thy brother by himself,

---

[9] *How he refell'd me,*] To *refel* is to refute. STEEVENS.

[1] *My sisterly remorse*—] i. e. pity. STEEVENS.

[2] *His purpose surfeiting,*] So, in *Othello*:
" —my hopes, not *surfeited* to death." STEEVENS.

[3] *O, that it were as like, as it is true!*] The meaning, I think, is: O, that it had as much of the *appearance*, as it has of the *reality*, of truth! MALONE.

[4] —*fond wretch.*] Fond wretch is *foolish* wretch. STEEVENS.

[5] *In hateful practice:*] Practice was used by the old writers for any unlawful or insidious stratagem. JOHNSON.

And

And not have cut him off: Some one hath set you on;
Confess the truth, and say by whose advice
Thou cam'st here to complain.

Isab. And is this all?
Then, oh, you blessed ministers above,
Keep me in patience; and, with ripen'd time,
Unfold the evil which is here wrapt up
In countenance [6]!—Heaven shield your grace from woe,
As I, thus wrong'd, hence unbelieved go!

Duke. I know, you'd fain be gone:—An officer!
To prison with her:—Shall we thus permit
A blasting and a scandalous breath to fall
On him so near us? This needs must be a practice [7].—
Who knew of your intent, and coming hither?

Isab. One that I would were here, Friar Lodowick.

Duke. A ghostly father, belike:—Who knows that Lodowick?

Lucio. My lord, I know him; 'tis a medling Friar;
I do not like the man: had he been lay, my Lord,
For certain words he spake against your grace
In your retirement, I had swing'd him soundly.

Duke. Words against me? This' a good Friar, belike!
And to set on this wretched woman here
Against our substitute!—Let this Friar be found.

Lucio. But yesternight, my Lord, she and that Friar
I saw them at the prison: a sawcy Friar,
A very scurvy fellow.

Friar P. Blessed be your royal grace!
I have stood by, my Lord, and I have heard
Your royal ear abus'd: First, hath this woman
Most wrongfully accus'd your substitute;
Who is as free from touch or soil with her,
As she from one ungot.

Duke. We did believe no less.
Know you that Friar Lodowick, that she speaks of?

Friar P. I know him for a man divine and holy;
Not scurvy, nor a temporary medler [8],

As

---

[6] *In countenance!*] i. e. in partial favour. WARBURTON.
Perhaps rather, in fair appearance, in the external sanctity of this outward-tainted Angelo. MALONE.

[7] — *practice*] *Practice*, in Shakspeare, very often means *shameful artifice*, unjustifiable stratagem. STEEVENS.

[8] — *nor a temporary medler*,] It is hard to know what is meant by a tem-

As he's reported by this gentleman;
And, on my trust, a man that never yet
Did, as he vouches, misreport your grace.

 Lucio. My Lord, most villainously; believe it.

 Friar P. Well, he in time may come to clear himself;
But at this instant he is sick, my Lord,
Of a strange fever: Upon his mere request [9],
(Being come to knowledge that there was complaint
Intended 'gainst lord Angelo,) came I hither,
To speak, as from his mouth, what he doth know
Is true, and false; and what he with his oath,
And all probation, will make up full clear,
Whensoever he's convented [1]. First, for this woman;
(To justify this worthy nobleman,
So vulgarly [2] and personally accus'd,)
Her shall you hear disproved to her eyes,
Till she herself confess it.

 Duke. Good Friar, let's hear it.

   ISABELLA *is carried off, guarded; and*
    MARIANA *comes forward.*

---

a temporary medler.] 'In its usual sense, as opposed to *perpetual*, it cannot be used here. It may stand for *temporal:* the sense will then be, *I know him for a holy man, one that meddles not with* secular *affairs.* It may mean *temporising: I know him to be a holy man, one who would not* temporise, *or take the opportunity of your absence to defame you.* JOHNSON.

A *temporary medler* means, I believe, one who seizes all such opportunities as the time affords, to meddle or interfere in the business of others.
                MALONE.

[9] — *his* mere *request,*] Solely, *entirely* upon his request. MALONE.

[1] *Whensoever he's* convented.] To *convent* and to *convene* are derived from the same Latin verb, and have exactly the same meaning. STEEV.

[2] *So* vulgarly—] Meaning either so *grosly*, with such *indecency* of invective, or by so *mean* and inadequate witnesses. JOHNSON.

Vulgarly, I believe, means *publicly*. The *vulgar are the common people*. Daniel uses *vulgarly* for *among the common people;*

  "——— and which pleases *vulgarly.*" STEEVENS.

Mr. Steevens's interpretation is certainly the true one. So, in *The Comedy of Errors*, Act iii. sc. i.

   "A vulgar comment will be made of it;
   "And that supposed by the *common rout—*
   "That may," &c.

Again, in *Twelfth Night*:

   "——— for 'tis a *vulgar* proof,
   "That very oft we pity enemies." MALONE.

                   Do

Do you not smile at this, lord Angelo?—
O heaven! the vanity of wretched fools!
Give us some seats. Come, cousin Angelo:
In this I'll be impartial³; be you judge
Of your own cause.—Is this the witness, friar?
First, let her shew her face⁴; and, after, speak.

  Mari. Pardon, my lord; I will not shew my face,
Until my husband bid me.

  Duke. What, are you marry'd?

  Mari. No, my lord.

  Duke. Are you a maid?

  Mari. No, my lord.

  Duke. A widow then?

  Mari. Neither, my lord.

  Duke. Why, you are nothing then:—neither maid, widow, nor wife *?

  Lucio. My Lord, she may be a punk; for many of them are neither maid, widow, nor wife.

  Duke. Silence that fellow: I would he had some cause
To prattle for himself.

  Lucio. Well, my Lord.

  Mari. My Lord, I do confess, I ne'er was marry'd;
And I confess, besides, I am no maid;
I have known my husband; yet my husband knows not,
That ever he knew me.

  Lucio. He was drunk then, my Lord; it can be no better.

  Duke. For the benefit of silence, 'would thou wert so too.

  Lucio. Well, my Lord.

---

³ *In this I'll be impartial;*] *Impartial* was sometimes used in the sense of *partial*. In the old play of *Swetnam the Woman-hater*, Atlanta cries out, when the judges decree against the women:

    " You are *impartial*, and we do appeal
    " From you to judges more indifferent." FARMER.

So, in Marston's *Antonio and Mellida*, 2d part, 1602:

    " —— There's not a beauty lives,
    " Hath that *impartial* predominance
    " O'er my affects, as your enchanting graces."

Again, in *Romeo and Juliet*, 1597:

    " Cruel, unjust, *impartial* destinies!"

Again: "—— this day, this unjust, *impartial* day."

In the language of our author's time *im* was frequently used as an augmentative or intensive particle. MALONE.

⁴ — *her face;*] The original copy reads—*your face*. The emendation was made by the editor of the second folio. MALONE.

* *Neither maid, widow, nor wife?*] This is a proverbial phrase to be found in Ray's Collection. STEEVENS.

Duke.

Duke. This is no witness for lord Angelo.
Mari. Now I come to't, my Lord:
She, that accuses him of fornication,
In self-same manner doth accuse my husband:
And charges him, my Lord, with such a time,
When I'll depose I had him in mine arms,
With all the effect of love.
   Ang. Charges she more than me?
   Mari. Not that I know.
   Duke. No? you say, your husband.
   Mari. Why, just, my Lord, and that is Angelo,
Who thinks, he knows, that he ne'er knew my body,
But knows, he thinks, that he knows Isabel's.
   Ang. This is a strange abuse [5]:—Let's see thy face.
   Mari. My husband bids me; now I will unmask.
                                        [*unveiling.*
This is that face, thou cruel Angelo,
Which, once thou swor'st, was worth the looking on:
This is the hand, which, with a vow'd contract,
Was fast belock'd in thine: this is the body,
That took away the match from Isabel,
And did supply thee at thy garden-house [6],
In her imagin'd person.
   Duke. Know you this woman?
   Lucio. Carnally, she says.
   Duke. Sirrah, no more.
   Lucio. Enough, my Lord.
   Ang. My Lord, I must confess, I know this woman;
And, five years since, there was some speech of marriage
Betwixt myself and her: which was broke off,
Partly, for that her promised proportions
Came short of composition [7]; but, in chief,

                                                             For

---

[5] *This is a strange abuse:*] *Abuse* stands in this place for *deception*, or *puzzle*. So, in *Macbeth*, "— *my strange and self* abuse," means *this strange deception of myself*. JOHNSON.

[6] *And did supply thee at thy* garden-house,] A *garden-house* in the time of our author was usually appropriated to purposes of intrigue. So, in SKIALETHIA, *or a shadow of truth, in certain Epigrams and Satyres*, 1598:
    " Who coming from The CURTAIN, sneaketh in
    " To some old *garden* noted *house for sin.*"
Again, in the *London Prodigal*, a com. 1605: " Sweet lady, if you have any friend, or *garden-house*, where you may employ a poor gentleman as your friend, I am yours to command in all secret service." MALONE.

[7] —— *her promised proportions*
                                                              Came

For that her reputation was disvalued
In levity: since which time, of five years,
I never spake with her, saw her, nor heard from her,
Upon my faith and honour.

   Mari. Noble prince,
As there comes light from heaven, and words from breath,
As there is sense in truth, and truth in virtue,
I am affianc'd this man's wife, as strongly
As words could make up vows: and, my good Lord,
But Tuesday night last gone, in his garden-house,
He knew me as a wife: As this is true,
Let me in safety raise me from my knees:
Or else for ever be confixed here,
A marble monument!

   Ang. I did but smile till now;
Now, good my Lord, give me the scope of justice:
My patience here is touch'd: I do perceive,
These poor informal women [8] are no more
But instruments of some more mightier member,
That sets them on: Let me have way, my Lord,
To find this practice out.

   Duke. Ay, with my heart;
And punish them unto your height of pleasure.—
Thou foolish Friar; and thou pernicious woman,
Compact with her that's gone! think'st thou, thy oaths,
Though they would swear down each particular saint,
Were testimonies against his worth and credit,
That's seal'd in approbation [9]?—You, lord Escalus,

                                               Sit

   Came short of composition;] Her fortune, which was promised proportionate to mine, fell short of the *composition,* that is, contract or bargain. JOHNSON.

   [8] *These poor informal women—*] *Informal* signifies *out of their senses.* In the *Comedy of Errors,* we meet with these lines:
      "———— I will not let him stir,
      "Till I have us'd the approv'd means I have,
      "With wholsome syrups, drugs, and holy prayers,
      "To make of him a *formal* man again."
Formal, in this passage, evidently signifies *in his senses.* The lines are spoken of Antipholis of Syracuse, who is behaving like a madman. Again, in *Antony and Cleopatra:*
      "Thou shouldst come like a fury crown'd with snakes,
      "Not like a *formal* man." STEEVENS.

   [9] *That's seal'd in approbation?*] When any thing subject to counterfeits is tried by the proper officers and approved, a stamp or *seal* is put
                                               upon

Sit with my cousin; lend him your kind pains
To find out this abuse, whence 'tis deriv'd.—
There is another Friar that set them on;
Let him be sent for.

Friar P. Would he were here, my Lord; for he, indeed,
Hath set the women on to this complaint:
Your Provost knows the place where he abides,
And he may fetch him.

Duke. Go, do it instantly.— [*Exit* PROVOST.
And you, my noble and well-warranted cousin,
Whom it concerns to hear this matter forth[1],
Do with your injuries as seems you best,
In any chastisement: I for a while
Will leave you; but stir not you, till you have well
Determined upon these slanderers.

Esca. My Lord, we'll do it throughly.——[*Exit* DUKE.
Signior Lucio, did not you say, you knew that friar Lodowick to be a dishonest person?

Lucio. *Cucullus non facit monachum:* honest in nothing,
but in his cloaths; and one that hath spoke most villainous
speeches of the duke.

Escal. We shall entreat you to abide here till he come,
and enforce them against him: we shall find this Friar a notable fellow.

Lucio. As any in Vienna, on my word.

Escal. Call that same Isabel here once again; [*to an Attendant.*] I would speak with her: pray you, my Lord,
give me leave to question; you shall see how I'll handle her.

Lucio. Not better than he, by her own report.

Escal. Say you?

Lucio. Marry, Sir, I think, if you handled her privately, she would sooner confess; perchance, publicly she'll be ashamed.

Re-enter Officers, with ISABELLA; *the* DUKE *in the Friar's habit, and* PROVOST.

Escal. I will go darkly to work with her.

---

upon it, as among us on plate, weights, and measures. So the duke
says, that Angelo's faith has been tried, *approved*, and *seal'd* in testimony
of that *approbation*, and, like other things so *sealed*, is no more to be called
in question. JOHNSON.

[1] *— to bear this matter forth.*] To bear it to the end; to search it to
the bottom. JOHNSON.

Lucio.

Lucio. That's the way; for women are light at midnight [2].

Escal. Come on, mistress; [*to* Isabella.] here's a gentlewoman denies all that you have said.

Lucio. My Lord, here comes the rascal I spoke of; here with the Provost.

Escal. In very good time:—speak not you to him, till we call upon you.

Lucio. Mum.

Escal. Come, Sir, did you set these women on to slander lord Angelo? they have confess'd you did.

Duke. 'Tis false.

Escal. How! know you where you are?

Duke. Respect to your great place! and let the devil [3] Be sometimes honour'd for his burning throne:—
Where is the duke? 'tis he should hear me speak.

Escal. The duke's in us; and we will hear you speak: Look, you speak justly.

Duke. Boldly, at least:—But, O, poor souls,
Come you to seek the lamb here of the fox?
Good night to your redress. Is the Duke gone?
Then is your cause gone too. The Duke's unjust,
Thus to retort your manifest appeal [4],
And put your trial in the villain's mouth,
Which here you come to accuse.

Lucio. This is the rascal; this is he I spoke of.

Escal. Why, thou unreverend and unhallow'd Friar!
Is't not enough, thou hast suborn'd these women
To accuse this worthy man; but, in foul mouth,
And in the witness of his proper ear,
To call him villain?
And then to glance from him to the Duke himself;
To tax him with injustice?—Take him hence;

---

[2] *— are light at midnight.*] This is one of the words on which Shakspeare chiefly delights to quibble. Thus, Portia in the *Mer. of Venice*: " Let me give *light*, but let me not be *light*." STEEVENS.

[3] *Respect to your great place! and let the devil,* &c.] I suspect that a line preceding this has been lost. MALONE.
Shakspeare was a reader of Philemon Holland's translation of Pliny; and in the 5th book and 8th chapter, might have met with this idea: " The Augylæ *do no worship* to any but to the *devils* beneath." STEEVENS.

[4] *— to retort your manifest appeal,*] To *refer back* to Angelo the cause in which you *appealed* from Angelo to the Duke. JOHNSON.

To the rack with him:—We'll touze you joint by joint,
But we will know this purpose⁵: What, unjust?
    Duke.   Be not so hot; the Duke
Dare no more stretch this finger of mine, than he
Dare rack his own; his subject am I not,
Nor here provincial⁶: My business in this state
Made me a looker-on here in Vienna,
Where I have seen corruption boil and bubble,
Till it o'er-run the stew: laws, for all faults;
But faults so countenanc'd, that the strong statutes
Stand like the forfeits in a barber's shop⁷,
As much in mock as mark.
                                                            Escal.

⁵ —this purpose:] The old copy has—*his* purpose. The emendation was made by Sir T. Hanmer. I believe the passage has been corrected in the wrong place; and would read:

—— We'll touze *him* joint by joint,
But we will know *his* purpose. MALONE.

⁶ *Nor here provincial:*] Nor here, *accountable*. The meaning seems to be, I am not one of his natural subjects, nor of any dependent province. JOHNSON.
The different orders of monks have a chief, who is called the General of the Order; and they have also superiors, subordinate to the general, in the several provinces through which the order may be dispersed. The Friar therefore means to say, that the Duke dare not touch a finger of his, for he could not punish him by his own authority, as he was not his subject; nor through that of the superior, as he was not of that province. MASON.

⁷ *Stands like the forfeits in a barber's shop,*] Barber's shops were, at all times, the resort of idle people:

 " Tonstrina erat quædam: bic sedebamus ferè
 " Plerumque eam operiri———"

which Donatus calls *apta sedes otiosis.* Formerly with us, the better sort of people went to the barber's shop to be trimmed; who then practised the under parts of surgery; so that he had occasion for numerous instruments, which lay there ready for use; and the idle people, with whom his shop was generally crowded, would be perpetually handling and misusing them. To remedy which, I suppose, there was placed up against the wall a table of forfeits, adapted to every offence of this kind; which, it is not likely, would long preserve its authority. WARBURTON.
This explanation may serve till a better is discovered. But whoever has seen the instruments of a chirurgeon, knows that they may very easily be kept out of improper hands in a very small box, or in his pocket.
                                                            JOHNSON.
It was formerly part of a *barber's* occupation to *pick* the *teeth* and *ears.*
                                                            STEEVENS.
The forfeits in a barber's shop were brought forward by Mr. Kenrick, with a parade worthy of the subject. FARMER.
It may be proper to add, that in a newspaper called *the Daily Magazine,*

Escal. Slander to the state! Away with him to prison.

Ang. What can you vouch against him, signior Lucio? Is this the man, that you did tell us of?

Lucio. 'Tis he, my Lord. Come hither, goodman bald-pate: Do you know me?

Duke. I remember you, Sir, by the sound of your voice: I met you at the prison, in the absence of the Duke.

Lucio. O, did you so? And do you remember what you said of the Duke?

Duke. Most notedly, Sir.

Lucio. Do you so, Sir? And was the Duke a flesh-monger, a fool, and a coward[8], as you then reported him to be?

Duke. You must, Sir, change persons with me, ere you make that my report: you, indeed, spoke so of him; and much more, much worse.

Lucio. O thou damnable fellow! Did not I pluck thee by the nose, for thy speeches?

Duke. I protest, I love the Duke, as I love myself.

Lucio. Hark! how the villain would close now, after his treasonable abuses.

Escal. Such a fellow is not to be talk'd withal:—Away with him to prison:—Where is the Provost?—Away with him to prison; lay bolts enough upon him: let him speak no more: Away with those giglots too[9], and with the other confederate companion.

[*The* PROVOST *lays hands on the* DUKE.

Duke. Stay, Sir; stay a while.

Ang. What! resists he? Help him, Lucio.

Lucio. Come, Sir; come, Sir; come, Sir: foh, sir; Why, you bald-pated, lying rascal! you must be hooded, must you? Show your knave's visage, with a pox to you! show

---

zine, or, *London Advertiser*, Oct. 15, 1773, which I am informed, was conducted by Mr Kenrick, he almost acknowledges, that the Verses exhibiting a catalogue of these forfeits, which he pretended to have met with at Malton or Thirsk, in Yorkshire, were a *forgery*. MALONE.

[8] *—and a coward,*] So, again afterwards:

"*You, sirrah, that know me for a fool, a coward,*"

"*One all of luxury—.*"

But Lucio had not, in the former conversation, mentioned *cowardice* among the faults of the Duke. Such failures of memory are incident to writers more diligent than this poet. JOHNSON.

[9] *—those giglots too,*] A *giglot* is a wanton wench. STEEVENS.

your

your sheep-biting face, and be hang'd an hour¹! Will't not off? [*Pulls off the Friar's hood, and discovers the* DUKE.

Duke. Thou art the first knave, that e'er made a Duke.—
First, Provost, let me bail these gentle three:
Sneak not away, Sir; [*to Lucio.*] for the Friar and you
Must have a word anon:—lay hold on him.

Lucio. This may prove worse than hanging.

Duke. What you have spoke, I pardon; sit you down.—
[*to Escalus.*
We'll borrow place of him:—Sir, by your leave: [*to Ang.*
Hast thou or word, or wit, or impudence,
That yet can do the office? If thou hast,
Rely upon it, till my tale be heard,
And hold no longer out.

Ang. O my dread Lord,
I should be guiltier than my guiltiness,
To think that I can be undiscernable,
When I perceive, your grace, like power divine,
Hath look'd upon my passes² : Then, good prince,
No longer session hold upon my shame,
But let my trial be mine own confession;
Immediate sentence then, and sequent death,
Is all the grace I beg.

Duke. Come hither, Mariana:—
Say, wast thou e'er contracted to this woman?

Ang. I was, my Lord.

Duke. Go take her hence, and marry her instantly,—
Do you the office, Friar; which consummate³,
Return him here again:—Go with him, Provost.
[*Exeunt* ANGELO, MARIANA, PETER, *and* PROVOST.

---

¹ *Slew your sheep-biting face, and be* hang'd *an hour* !] Dr. Johnson's alteration [an how?] is wrong. In the *Alchemist*, we meet with " a man that has been *strangled an hour*."—" What, Piper, ho: *be hang'd a-while*," is a line of an old madrigal. FARMER.

A similar expression is found in Ben Jonson's *Bartholomew Fair*, 1614: " Leave the bottle behind you, and be curs'd *a while*." MALONE. The poet evidently refers to the ancient mode of punishing by the *cellistrigium*, or the original pillory, made like that part of the pillory at present which receives the neck, only it was placed horizontally, so that the culprit hung suspended in it by his chin, and the back of his head. A distinct account of it may be found, if I mistake not, in Mr. Barrington's *Observations on the Statutes*. HENLEY.

² — *my* passes:] i. e. what has past in my administration. STEEV.

³ — *which consummate,*] i. e. which being consummated. MALONE.

F f 4 *cal.*

Escal. My Lord, I am more amaz'd at his dishonour,
Than at the strangeness of it.
   Duke. Come hither, Isabel:
Your Friar is now your prince: as I was then
Advertising, and holy [4] to your business,
Not changing heart with habit, I am still
Attorney'd at your service.
   Isab. O, give me pardon,
That I, your vassal, have employ'd and pain'd
Your unknown sovereignty.
   Duke. You are pardon'd, Isabel:
And now, dear maid, be you as free to us [5].
Your brother's death, I know, sits at your heart;
And you may marvel, why I obscur'd myself,
Labouring to save his life; and would not rather
Make rash remonstrance of my hidden power,
Than let him so be lost: O, most kind maid,
It was the swift celerity of his death,
Which I did think with slower foot came on,
That brain'd my purpose [6]: But peace be with him!
That life is better life, past fearing death,
Than that which lives to fear; make it your comfort,
So happy is your brother.

Re-enter ANGELO, MARIANA, PETER, *and* PROVOST.

   Isab. I do, my Lord.
   Duke. For this new-married man, approaching here,
Whose salt imagination yet hath wrong'd
Your well-defended honour, you must pardon
For Mariana's sake: but as he adjudg'd your brother,
(Being criminal, in double violation
Of sacred chastity, and of promise-breach [7],

---

[4] *Advertising, and holy—*] Attentive and faithful. JOHNSON.

[5] *— be you as free to us.*] Be as *generous* to us; pardon us as we have pardoned you. JOHNSON.

[6] *That brain'd my purpose:*] We now use in conversation a like phrase. *This it was that knocked my design on the head.* JOHNSON.

[7] *— and of promise-breach,*] Our author ought to have written—" in double violation of sacred chastity, and of *promise*,' instead of—promise-breach. Sir T. Hanmer reads—and *in* promise-breach; but change is certainly here improper, Shakspeare having many similar inaccuracies. *Double* indeed may refer to Angelo's conduct to Mariana and Isabel; yet still some difficulty will remain: for then he will be said to be " *criminal* [instead of *guilty*] *of* promise-breach." MALONE.

Thereon

Thereon dependant, for your brother's life,)
The very mercy of the law cries out
Most audible, even from his proper tongue [8],
An Angelo for Claudio, death for death.
Haste still pays haste, and leisure answers leisure;
Like doth quit like, and *Measure* still *for Measure* [9].
Then, Angelo, thy fault's thus manifested;
Which though thou would'st deny, denies thee vantage [1];
We do condemn thee to the very block
Where Claudio stoop'd to death, and with like haste;—
Away with him.

Mari. O, my most gracious Lord,
I hope you will not mock me with a husband!

Duke. It is your husband mock'd you with a husband;
Consenting to the safeguard of your honour,
I thought your marriage fit; else imputation,
For that he knew you, might reproach your life,
And choke your good to come: for his possessions,
Although by confiscation they are ours [2],
We do instate and widow you withal,
To buy you a better husband.

Mari. O, my dear lord,
I crave no other, nor no better man.

Duke. Never crave him; we are definitive.

Mari. Gentle my liege,— [*kneeling.*

Duke. You do but lose your labour;
Away with him to death.—Now, Sir, [*to* Lucio.] to you.

Mari. O, my good lord!—Sweet Isabel, take my part;

---

[8] *— even from his proper tongue,*] Even from Angelo's own tongue. So, above: "*—in the witness of his proper ear—*" &c. JOHNSON.

[9] So, in the Third Part of *K. Henry VI*:
 "*Measure for Measure* must be answered." STEEVENS.

Shakspeare might have remembered these lines in *A Warning for faire Women*, a tragedy, 1599 (but apparently written some years before):
 "The trial now remains, as shall conclude
 "*Measure for Measure*, and lost blood for blood." MALONE.

[1] *Which though thou would'st deny, denies thee vantage:*] The denial of which will avail thee nothing. So, in the *Winter's Tale:*
 "Which to deny, concerns more than avails." MALONE.

[2] *Although by confiscation they are ours,*] This reading was furnished by the editor of the second folio. The original copy has *confutation*, which may be right;—by his being confuted, or proved guilty of the fact which he had denied. This however being rather harsh, I have followed all the modern editors in adopting the emendation that has been made. MALONE.

Lend

Lend me your knees, and all my life to come
I'll lend you, all my life to do you service.

Duke. Against all sense you do importune her [3];
Should she kneel down, in mercy of this fact,
Her brother's ghost his paved bed would break,
And take her hence in horror.

Mari. Isabel,
Sweet Isabel, do yet but kneel by me;
Hold up your hands, say nothing, I'll speak all.
They say, best men are moulded out of faults;
And, for the most, become much more the better
For being a little bad: so may my husband.
O Isabel! will you not lend a knee!

Duke. He dies for Claudio's death.

Isab. Most bounteous Sir,   [*kneeling.*
Look, if it please you, on this man condemn'd,
As if my brother liv'd: I partly think,
A due sincerity govern'd his deeds,
Till he did look on me [4]; since it is so,
Let him not die: My brother had but justice,

---

[3] *Against all sense you do importune her:*] The meaning required is, against all reason and natural affection; Shakspeare, therefore, judiciously uses a single word that implies both; *sense* signifying both reason and affection. JOHNSON.

The same expression occurs in the *Tempest*, Act ii.
"You cram these words into my ears, against
"The stomach of my *sense.*" STEEVENS.

[4] *Till he did look on me;*] The duke has justly observed that Isabel is importuned against all sense to solicit for Angelo, yet here against all sense she solicits for him. Her argument is extraordinary.

A due sincerity govern'd his deeds,
Till he did look on me; since it is so,
Let him not die.

That Angelo had committed all the crimes charged against him, as far as he could commit them, is evident. The only *intent* which *his act did not overtake*, was the defilement of Isabel. Of this Angelo was only intentionally guilty.

Angelo's crimes were such, as must sufficiently justify punishment, whether its end be to secure the innocent from wrong, or to deter guilt by example; and I believe every reader feels some indignation when he finds him spared. From what extenuation of his crime, can Isabel, who yet supposes her brother dead, form any plea in his favour? Since *he was good 'till he looked on me, let him not die.* I am afraid our varlet poet intended to inculcate, that women think ill of nothing that raises the credit of their beauty. and are ready, however virtuous, to pardon any act which they think incited by their own charms. JOHNSON.

VOL. III.   U   I a

In that he did the thing for which he died;
For Angelo,
His act did not o'ertake his bad intent [5];
And must be bury'd but as an intent,
That perish'd by the way: thoughts are no subjects;
Intents but merely thoughts.

 Mari. Merely, my lord.

 Duke. Your suit's unprofitable; stand up, I say.—
I have bethought me of another fault;—
Provost, how came it, Claudio was beheaded
At an unusual hour?

 Prov. It was commanded so.

 Duke. Had you a special warrant for the deed?

 Prov. No, my good lord; it was by private message.

 Duke. For which I do discharge you of your office:
Give up your keys.

 Prov. Pardon me, noble Lord:
I thought it was a fault, but knew it not;
Yet did repent me, after more advice [6];
For testimony whereof, one in the prison,
That should by private order else have died,
I have reserv'd alive.

 Duke. What's he?

 Prov. His name is Barnardine.

 Duke. I would thou had'st done so by Claudio.—
Go, fetch him hither; let me look upon him. [*Exit* Prov.

 Escal. I am sorry, one so learned and so wise
As you, lord Angelo, have still appear'd,
Should slip so grosly, both in the heat of blood,
And lack of temper'd judgment afterward.

 Ang. I am sorry, that such sorrow I procure;
And so deep sticks it in my penitent heart,
That I crave death more willingly than mercy;
'Tis my deserving, and I do entreat it.

Re-enter PROVOST, BARNARDINE, CLAUDIO, *and*
JULIET.

 Duke. Which is that Barnardine?

 Prov. This, my Lord.

---

[5] *His act did not o'ertake his bad intent;*] So, in *Macbeth*:
 " The flighty purpose never is o'ertook,
 " Unless the *deed* go with it." STEEVENS.

[6] *— after more advice:*] i. e. after more consideration. STEEVENS.

Duke.

Duke. There was a friar told me of this man;—
Sirrah, thou art said to have a stubborn soul,
That apprehends no further than this world,
And squar'st thy life according; Thou'rt condemn'd;
But, for those earthly faults [7], I quit them all;
And pray thee, take this mercy to provide
For better times to come.—Friar, advise him;
I leave him to your hand.—What muffled fellow's that?

Prov. This is another prisoner, that I sav'd,
Who should have died when Claudio lost his head;
As like almost to Claudio, as himself. *[unmuffles* Claudio.

Duke. If he be like your brother, [*to* Isab.] for his sake
Is he pardon'd; And, for your lovely sake,
Give me your hand, and say you will be mine,
He is my brother too; but fitter time for that.
By this, lord Angelo perceives he's safe [8];
Methinks, I see a quick'ning in his eye;
Well, Angelo, your evil quits you well [9];
Look that you love your wife [1]; her worth, worth yours [2].—
I find an apt remission in myself;
And yet here's one in place I cannot pardon [3];—
You, sirrah, [*to* Lucio] that knew me for a fool, a coward,
One all of luxury [4], an ass, a mad-man;
Wherein have I so deserved of you,
That you extol me thus?

---

[7] —*for those earthly faults,*] Thy faults, so far as they are punishable on earth, so far as they are cognizable by temporal power, I forgive. JOHNSON.

[8] —*perceives he's safe;*] It is somewhat strange that Isabel is not made to express either gratitude, wonder, or joy, at the sight of her brother. JOHNSON.

[9] —*your evil quits you well:*] *Quits you,* recompenses, requites you. JOHNSON.

[1] *Look, that you love your wife;*] So, in *Promos,* &c.
"Be loving to good Cassandra, thy wife." STEEVENS.

[2] —*her worth, worth yours.*] That is, her value is equal to your value; the match is not unworthy of you. JOHNSON.

[3] —*here's one in place I cannot pardon;*] The duke only means to frighten *Lucio,* whose final sentence is to marry the woman whom he had wronged, on which all his other punishments are remitted. SEEV.

[4] *One all of* luxury,—] *Luxury,* in our author's time, signified *concupiscence.* MALONE.

U 2   *Lucio.*

Lucio. 'Faith, my Lord, I spoke it but according to the trick [5]; If you will hang me for it, you may, but I had rather it would please you, I might be whip'd.

Duke. Whip'd first, Sir, and hang'd after.—
Proclaim it, Provost, round about the city;
If any woman's wrong'd by this lewd fellow,
(As I have heard him swear himself, there's one
Whom he begot with child,) let her appear,
And he shall marry her; the nuptial finish'd,
Let him be whip'd and hang'd.

Lucio. I beseech your highness, do not marry me to a whore! Your highness said even now, I made you a duke; good my lord, do not recompence me, in making me a cuckold.

Duke. Upon my honour thou shalt marry her.
Thy slanders I forgive; and therewithal
Remit thy other forfeits [6].—Take him to prison;
And see our pleasure herein executed.

Lucio. Marrying a punk, my Lord, is pressing to death, whipping and hanging.

Duke. Sland'ring a prince deserves it.—
She, Claudio, that you wrong'd, look you restore.—
Joy to you, Mariana!—love her, Angelo;
I have confess'd her, and I know her virtue.—
Thanks, good friend Escalus, for thy much goodness [7];

There's

---

[5] *— according to the trick:*] To my custom, my habitual practice. JOHNSON.

According to the *trick*, is, according to the fashion of thoughtless youth. So, in *Love's Labour's Lost:* "—yet I have a *trick* of the old rage" Again, in a collection of epigrams, entitled *Wit's Bedlam*, printed about the year 1615,

"Carnus calls lechery a *trick* of youth;
"So he grows old; but this trick hurts his growth."

MALONE.

[6] *— thy other forfeits:*] Thy other punishments. JOHNSON.

To *forfeit*, anciently signified, *to commit a carnal offence.* STEEVENS.

So, in the 12th Pageant of the Coventry Collection of Mysteries, the Virgin Mary tells Joseph:

"I dede never *forfete* with man, I wys."

[7] *Thanks, good friend Escalus, for thy much goodness:*] I have always thought that there is great confusion in this concluding speech. If my criticism would not be censured as too licentious, I should regulate it thus:

Thanks, good friend Escalus, for thy much goodness.
Thanks, Provost, for thy care and secresy;
We shall employ thee in a worthier place.

Forgive

There's more behind, that is more gratulate [8].
Thanks, Provoſt, for thy care, and ſecreſy;
We ſhall employ thee in a worthier place;—
Forgive him, Angelo, that brought you home
The head of Ragozine for Claudio's;
The offence pardons itſelf.—Dear Iſabel,
I have a motion much imports your good;
Whereto if you'll a willing ear incline.
What's mine is yours, and what is yours is mine;—
So bring us to our palace; where we'll ſhow
What's yet behind, that's meet you all ſhould know [9].

[*Exeunt.*

Forgive him, Angelo, that brought you home
The head of Ragozine for Claudio's.
　Ang.　*The offence pardons itſelf.*
　Duke.　*There's more behind*
That is more gratulate. Dear Iſabel,
I have a motion, &c.　JOHNSON.

[8] — *that is more* gratulate.] i. e. *to be more rejoiced in;* meaning, I ſuppoſe, that there is another world, where he will find yet great reaſon to rejoice in conſequence of his upright miniſtry. *Eſcalus* is repreſented as an ancient nobleman, who, in conjunction with *Angelo*, had reached the higheſt office of the ſtate. He, therefore, could not be ſufficiently rewarded here; but is neceſſarily referred to a future and more exalted recompence.　STEEVENS.

　Mr. Maſon (whoſe book did not reach my hands till the firſt ſix of theſe plays had been printed) concurs with me in the explanation of this paſſage, and ſupports it by the Duke's words in the beginning of the fifth act:

"—————— and we hear
" Such goodneſs of your juſtice, that our ſoul
" Cannot but yield you forth to public *thanks*,
" *Fore-running more requital.*"

Heywood alſo, in his *Apology for Actors*, 1612, uſes to *gratulate*, in the ſenſe of to *reward*: " I could not chuſe but *gratulate* your honeſt endeavours with this remembrance."　MALONE.

I think the Duke means to ſay,—I thank thee, Eſcalus, for thy upright conduct during thy adminiſtration of government. At ſome future time I ſhall ſhew you ſome more ſubſtantial, more *gratulatory*, and acceptable marks of my approbation, than mere thanks.　MALONE.

[9] I cannot help taking notice with how much judgment Shakſpeare has given turns to this ſtory from what he found it in Cynthio Giraldi's novel. In the firſt place, the brother is there actually executed, and the governour ſends his head in a bravado to the ſiſter, after he had debauched her on promiſe of marriage; a circumſtance of too much horror and villainy for the ſtage. And, in the next place, the ſiſter afterwards is, to ſolder up her diſgrace, married to the governour, and begs his life of the emperour, though he had unjuſtly been the death of her brother. Both which abſurdities the poet has avoided by the epiſode

sode of Mariana, a creature purely of his own invention. The duke's remaining incognito at home to supervise the conduct of his deputy, is also entirely our authour's fiction.

This story was attempted for the scene before our author was fourteen years old, by one George Whetstone, in *Two Comical Discourses*, as they are called, containing the right excellent and famous history of Promos and Cassandra, printed with the black letter, 1578. The authour going that year with Sir Humphrey Gilbert to Norimbega, left them with his friends to publish. THEOBALD.

The novel of Cynthio Giraldi, from which Shakspeare is supposed to have borrowed this fable, may be read in *Shakspeare illustrated*, elegantly translated, with remarks which will assist the enquirer to discover how much absurdity Shakspeare has admitted or avoided.

I cannot but suspect that some other had new-modelled the novel of Cynthio, or written a story which in some particulars resembled it, and that Cynthio was not the author whom Shakspeare immediately followed. The emperor in Cynthio is named Maximine; the duke, in Shakspeare's enumeration of the persons of the drama, is called Vincentio. This appears a very slight remark; but since the duke has no name in the play, nor is ever mentioned but by his title, why should he be called Vincentio among the *persons*, but because the name was copied from the story, and placed superfluously at the head of the list by the mere habit of transcription? It is therefore likely that there was then a story of Vincentio duke of Vienna, different from that of Maximine emperor of the Romans.

Of this play the light or comic part is very natural and pleasing, but the grave scenes, if a few passages be excepted, have more labour than elegance. The plot is rather intricate than artful. The time of the action is indefinite; some time, we know not how much, must have elapsed between the recess of the duke and the imprisonment of Claudio; for he must have learned the story of Mariana in his disguise, or delegated his power to a man already known to be corrupted. The unities of action and place are sufficiently preserved. JOHNSON.

The duke probably had learnt the story of Mariana in some of his former retirements, 'having ever loved the life removed" (page 328): And he had a suspicion that Angelo was but a *seemer* (page 330), and therefore he stays to watch him. BLACKSTONE.

The Fable of Whetstone's *Promos and Cassandra*, 1578.

" The Argument of the whole *History*."

" In the cyttie of *Julio* (sometimes under the dominion of *Corvinus* kynge of *Hungarie*, and *Bohemia*,) there was a law, that what man so ever committed adultery should lose his head, and the woman offender should weare some disguised apparel, during her life, to make her infamously noted. This severe lawe, by the favour of some merciful magistrate, became little regarded, until the time of lord *Promos* authority; who convicting a young gentleman named *Andrugio* of incontinency, condemned both him and his minion to the execution of this statute. *Andrugio* had a very virtuous and beautiful gentlewoman to his sister, named *Cassandra: Cassandra*, to enlarge her brother's life, submitted an humble petition to the lord *Promos*: *Promos* regarding her good behaviours, and fantasying her great beawtie, was much delighted with the sweete

sweete order of her talke; and doyng good, that evil might come thereof, for a time he repryved her brother: but wicked man, tourning his liking into unlawfull lust, he set downe the spoile of her honour, raunsome for her brothers life: chaste *Cassandra*, abhorring both him and his sute, by no persuasion would yeald to this raunsome. But in fine, wonne with the importunitye of hir brother (pleading for life), upon these conditions she agreed to *Promos*. First, that he should pardon her brother, and after marry her. *Promos*, as fearelesf in promisse, as carelesse in performance, with solemne vowe sygned her conditions; but worse than any infydell, his will satisfyed, he performed neither the one nor the other: for to keepe his auctoritye unspotted with favour, and to prevent *Cassandra*'s clamors, he commaunded the gayler secretly, to present *Cassandra* with her brother's head. The gayler, (touched) with the outcryes of *Andrugio*, (abhorryng *Promos*' lewdenes) by the providence of God provided thus for his safety. He presented *Cassandra* with a felons head newlie executed; who knew it not, being mangled, from her brothers (who was set at libertie by the gayler). [She] was so agreeved at this trecherye, that, at the point to kyl her self, she spared that stroke, to be avenged of *Promos*: and devysing a way, she concluded, to make her fortunes knowne unto the kinge. She, executing this resolution, was so highly favoured of the king, that forthwith he hasted to do justice on *Promos*: whose judgment was, to marry *Cassandra*, to repaire her crased honour; which donne, for his hainous offence, he should lose his head. This maryage solemnnised, *Cassandra*, tyed in the greatest bondes of affection to her husband, became an earnest suter for his life: the kinge, tendring the general benefit of the commonweale before her special case, although he favoured her much, would not graunte her sute. *Andrugio* (disguised among the company) sorrowing the griefe of his sister, bewrayde his safety, and craved pardon. The kinge, to renowne the vertues of *Cassandra*, pardoned both him and *Promos*. The circumstances of this rare historye, in action livelye followeth."

Whetstone, however, has not afforded a very correct analysis of his play, which contains a mixture of comic scenes, between a Bawd, a Pimp, Felons, &c. together with some serious situations which are not described. STEEVENS.

One paragraph of the foregoing narrative being strangely confused in the old copy, by some carelesness of the printer, I have endeavoured to rectify it, by transposing a few words, and adding two others which are included within crotchets. MALONE.

END OF VOL. III.

www.ingramcontent.com/pod-product-compliance
Lightning Source LLC
Chambersburg PA
CBHW020533300426
44111CB00008B/646